Psychotherapeutic Interventions for Emotion Regulation

PSYCHOTHERAPEUTIC INTERVENTIONS FOR EMOTION REGULATION

EMDR and Bilateral Stimulation for Affect Management

John Omaha

W. W. NORTON & COMPANY
New York • London

For information about permission to reproduce
selections from this book, write to
Permissions, W. W. Norton & Company, Inc.,
500 Fifth Avenue, New York, NY 10110

Production Manager: Leeann Graham
Manufacturing by Haddon Craftsmen, Inc.

Library of Congress Cataloging-in-Publication Data (TK)

W. W. Norton & Company, Inc.,
500 Fifth Avenue, New York, N.Y. 10110
www.wwnorton.com

W. W. Norton & Company Ltd.,
Castle House, 75/76 Wells St., London W1T 3QT

3 5 7 9 0 8 6 4 2

Dedication

for
Reina
1966–2001

Table of Contents

· ·

APPENDICES

List of Figures
and Tables

. . . .

Acknowledgments

. . . .

Like all scientific works, this book builds on an accumulated body of knowledge and depends for its execution on the contributions of others besides myself. Several great minds have synthesized the overarching theories forming the foundation on which my work is built, and I am compelled to honor their work here. John Bowlby's attachment theory, Sylvan Tomkins's affect theory, Paul MacLean's limbic system hypothesis, Joseph LeDoux's synthesis of regulatory neurophysiology, and Allan Schore's theory unifying attachment, neurophysiology, and emotion regulation constitute the most significant, vitally essential pillars without which the present volume could not have been created. To these may be added the researches of innumerable investigators and authors whose work I have relied upon—and cited where directly applicable—to support and illustrate the concepts presented here.

I offer a special acknowledgement to Cindy Browning who "just noticed" for me the uniqueness and value of the affect skills I had created and who encouraged me to formulate the skills into a coherent presentation. Along the way I had brief, but helpful communications with Dante Cicchetti, Carroll Izard, Peter Lang, Carol Magai, Allan Schore, and Eric Youngstrom, and I thank them for their support.

I acknowledge the support, encouragement, and skill of my editor at W. W. Norton, Deborah Malmud, without whose prodding and guidance there would be no book. I express my deep appreciation to Tom Cloyd for his thorough reading of the manuscript and for his extensive and detailed critical comments.

I acknowledge the many clients who have allowed me to use material from their therapy sessions to illustrate points I make in the book. Their courageous therapeutic process provided the substance for my observations and guided my creative process as I formulated the skills presented here.

Ultimately, the responsibility for every word in this book is mine. I take responsibility or blame for the book's organization, its style, and for any errors of fact, misstatement, misrepresentation, or omission.

In a very real sense, this volume is my child. As a parent, I take pride in my offspring. Like any parent, I hope my progeny adds some measure to the expanding body of human knowledge and acumen and that it contributes some good to the world. Now it is time to separate from my creation and let it find its place in the world. I give it my blessings as I give it to you.

PSYCHOTHERAPEUTIC INTERVENTIONS FOR EMOTION REGULATION

Introduction

Toward an Affect Centered Therapy

The present work represents a new phase in a profound revolution in psychotherapy, in which affects take their rightful place of equality with cognitions, drives, and behavior among the modalities that must be interpreted by theory and embraced by therapy in understanding both normal and pathological personality development (Cicchetti, Ackerman, & Izard, 1995). The book synthesizes experimental and theoretical advances regarding the primacy of affect in both human psychological health and dysfunction. These advances are translated into practical clinical applications the clinician can immediately utilize. The clinical interventions presented here are solidly grounded in recent experimental advances in understanding the developmental neurobiology of affect (Schore, 1994). These skills and concepts lay the foundation for a new approach to treating psychopathology that begins with the affects.

The four chapters of Part I assemble current empirical and theoretical information into a coherent picture of how self structure emerges in the context of the infant–caregiver dyad as the child is socialized for affect regulation within the dyad. When the dyad functions optimally, the child learns good affect regulation skills and at the same time an adaptive, positively functioning self structure organizes itself. When the dyad is impaired for whatever reason, adequate affect regulation skills are not transmitted to a greater or lesser degree resulting in the emergence of a more or less maladaptive, impaired, and negatively functioning self structure. Research and theory presented in Part I are thematically united by the principle that affect regulation and self structure are intimately interrelated and arise conjointly. The first four chapters point toward the clinical skills presented in Part II, the psychotherapeutic interventions for affect regulation that are the focus of this book. Theory and research are presented to support the practice of these interventions, referred to collectively as affect management skills training (AMST). The seven

1

basic and several ancillary AMST interventions presented in Chapters 5 through 11 are designed to remediate deficits in affect regulation and conjunctively promote the emergence of a more adaptive, positively functioning self. The theoretical and empirical justifications of the first four chapters and the AMST clinical interventions transmitted in the next six chapters, lay the foundation for a new school of therapy, affect centered therapy (ACT). Chapter 12 presents some of the principles of ACT and illustrates how affect dysregulation and impaired self structure may present in certain disorders. Three authors who have also created therapies oriented toward affect are Fosha (2000), Greenberg (2001), and Johnson (2002).

AFFECT CENTERED THERAPY AND THE AFFECT MANAGEMENT SKILLS TRAINING PROTOCOL

Affect Centered Therapy is a psychotherapeutic orientation constituting a theory for the origin of the patient's problems and a treatment for those problems that is derived from its theoretical principles. The patient's current problems are believed to originate in impairments of affect and emotion regulation. Affect Management Skills Training is a protocol that remediates impairment of affect and emotion regulation. The protocol consists of seven fundamental skills and a number of ancillary skills. AMST constitutes the first phase of ACT. Theory, supported by clinical impressions, suggests that clients must be provided with the tools to recognize, tolerate, and regulate both comfortable and distressing affects and emotions *before* they can safely and productively proceed to the second phase of ACT in which the causes of the current problems are uncovered and resolved. The skills of AMST provide for containment of disturbing material, establishment of an internal image of safety, affect recognition, affect tolerance, detachment from affect, and affect regulation. There are seven fundamental skills.

Skill I, *containment*, addresses the fact that many clients come to therapy burdened with intrusive thoughts and memories that are assembled with painful emotions. Therefore, at the outset of therapy, a container is created to separate and enclose this disturbing material. The containment skill employs a client-generated image of a "container sufficient to hold every disturbing thing" so as to wall off memories of adverse experience and the distressing emotions associated with them. Moving this material into the container is facilitated by tactile alternating bilateral stimulation (TABS) which can be provided manually by tapping on the client's knees or by the battery powered TheraTapper™. With this material contained, the client receives immediate relief and can more easily learn the rest of the skill set. During Phase II of ACT, this material can be removed from containment for processing. For example, a bulimic patient's bingeing and purging behaviors and their antecedent causes would be among the "disturbing things" her unconscious would place in containment. After completing the AMST protocol in Phase I of therapy for her bulimia, the client would be assisted in removing "bulimia and everything associated with it" from her container as the initial step in uncovering and treating the causes of the disorder.

Skill II, *safe place*, develops an internal image of safety and security, elaborating it in visual, auditory, olfactory, and tactile perceptual modes. Many clients have never before developed such an internal image. The safe place image can be used to self-soothe in stressful daily life situations or in session when processing distressing material. AMST skill II extends Shapiro's (1995, 2001) use of sensations in her 8-step safe place exercise. Skill II explicitly focuses on four sensory modalities: sight, hearing, smell, and touch. Skill II also assembles the safe place image with cognitions of safety and the emotion safety, and it teaches the client to identify sensations accompanying the emotion of safety. In skill II and throughout the protocol, TABS facilitates effective, efficient skills acquisition. Both containment and safe place establish a foundation for the remainder of AMST, skills III to VII, which focus on recognizing, tolerating, and regulating specific affects.

Affect management consists of affect recognition, affect tolerance, and affect regulation. In setting up skills III to VII, the client selects a target affect, usually beginning with fear affect, that will be the protocol's first focus. A rating scale is introduced that allows the client to differentiate between high and low levels of fear and to avoid potentially overwhelming levels of fear arousal. She is asked to retrieve a memory of a time she felt fear at a low, manageable intensity. Of course, the client is in fact recalling fear emotion, but at its core is the fear affect she will be learning to recognize, tolerate, and regulate. Her remembered experience is named the target scene and functions as the focus for skills III to VII.

Skill III, *sensation-affect-identification*, transmits the ability to recognize an affect by the physical sensations the client experiences as he holds the image of the target scene. These physical sensations constitute the qualia for the affect. Once he has acquired skill III enabling him to recognize fear affect, he is in a position to learn how to tolerate it.

Skill IV, *sensation as signal*, links deployment of an image for affect tolerance to the appearance of the qualia for the target affect. Tolerance for fear affect is transmitted through the image of a grounding resource, which is client generated and may take many forms; for example, a grounding cord, grounding roots, magnetic boots, or other images enable the client to feel connected to the ground. The grounding resource assists the client in staying grounded and present while she experiences the target affect in the target scene. Skill IV, facilitated by TABS, links deployment of the grounding resource to the qualia accompanying fear affect so that its utilization becomes automatic.

Skill V, *grounded and present*, completes the affect tolerance component of AMST by linking the index affect as experienced in the target scene with the grounding resource image and with a cognition, "I can stay grounded and present while I am feeling fear." Again, TABS facilitates this assembly process. The affect tolerance skills transmitted by the grounding resource and skills IV and V provide the client with the tools to intervene in acting out behaviors such as bingeing or purging, substance abuse, and verbal or physical violence.

Skill VI, *noticing*, imparts to the client the ability to detach from images, memories, thoughts, and sensations that accompany the index affect in the target scene. Previously clients were identified with these affect-assembled modalities. Skill VI builds on skills III, IV, and V. When the client has deployed the skill IV grounding resource and has affirmed with skill V his ability to stay grounded and present while he experiences the affect target, he can then "just notice" the thoughts, memories, and affects assembled with the target affect. The noticing skill promotes disidentification from the remembered material; the skill allows the client to step outside her problem and observe it and thereby creates a larger context for the problem. The creation of a larger context expands the client's self structure.

Skill VII, *regulation*, provides images for regulating affects. There are two regulatory resources, one for down-regulating distressing affect and a separate one for up-regulating comfortable affects. Down-regulation is accomplished by the disposal resource; up-regulation is facilitated by the gauge resource. The image of a disposal resource, which may be a garbage chute, a sink disposal, or a bottomless pit, is created to facilitate the client's attenuation of distressing affect. With TABS facilitation the client learns to decrease a negative affect like fear. A companion image, the gauge resource is developed to help the client increase positive affects like interest and joy. Utilization of the regulatory images is facilitated by TABS.

AFFECT AND EMOTION

Affects are the genetically hard-wired, physiological building blocks from which feeling, emotion, and mood are constructed. A distinction must be drawn among them to establish a solid foundation from the outset. Because affect is the primordium, it will be introduced first. The human genome codes for a limited number of unique responses, affects, which are elicited by changes in environmental stimulus patterns and are discriminated from one another by physiological and behavioral criteria. The nine basic affects are excitement, joy, startle, fear, anger, anguish, shame, disgust, and dissmell (Nathanson, 1992). (*Dissmell* refers to the pattern of actions produced by a noxious odor. The pattern includes wrinkling the nose, raising the upper lip, and avoidant behavior.) The neurobiology of fear has been well researched, and based on these findings it appears that each affect has a unique neurophysiological expression that is genetically encoded. The nervous system transmits signals to various effector sites where affects are translated into physiological responses such as change in heart rate, alteration in smooth or striated muscle tension, or perspiration. Affects are universal, and although no person can truly know another's experience, it is in our shared affective life that we humans most closely approach commonality simply because we are all similarly hard-wired for the experience of affects.

An affect becomes a feeling when the organism becomes aware of the affect. The physiological signals generated by an affect are called *qualia*. The qualia accompanying an affect constitute the organism's experience of the affect. Thus, a person becomes aware of an affect when she notices the qualia of the affect, and at that moment the affect becomes a feeling. In common usage, people use the word *feeling* when referring to their emotions and affects, and they refer to their experience of affects through the associated qualia when they say, for example, "I *feel* angry," or "I *feel* sad."

Emotion manifests a higher level of complexity in the affective system, because emotion involves memory. Affects are experienced in particular situations, and the events and the affects assembled with them are stored in memory and retrieved again and again in new situations. Affects modified by experience become emotions. In emotion, affects are assembled with images, memories, cognitions, introjects, and other affects. Affects are often experienced in combinations, and these assemblages of affects also contribute to the more complex phenomenon of emotion. The basic building blocks, the affects, assemble into complex neural networks that grow more elaborate over time. Complexity does not always equate with order, however. In childhood, if affects are experienced too intensely, as, for example, during traumatic events, the system can be overwhelmed, and chaos rather than order results. Emotion is the complex experience of affect alloyed by memory, thought, and image. As Nathanson (1992) wrote, "affect is biology, emotion is biography" (p. 50).

Emotions are as diverse, nearly as numerous, and every bit as unique as the people who experience them. While there are only a small number of affects, the emotions number in the hundreds. Where affect is relatively straightforward, emotion is convoluted. Emotion is also idiosyncratic. Because emotion is amalgamated from affects modified by an individual's unique history, emotion experience entails far less mutuality than affective experience. For example, what any one client means by the word *relief* is unique to that person. For one individual, the emotion of relief may be assembled with childhood memories of termination of physical abuse; for another person, relief may be accompanied by images of slaking intense thirst with a cold glass of water.

Throughout the book, I have attempted to adhere to a consistent usage of the words *affect* and *emotion*. I will use the word *affect* when I am specifically referring to one of the limited number of discrete, hard-wired, genetically determined human biological responses. Use of the word *affect* will indicate that I intend to reduce an emotional phenomenon to its neurophysiological basis. I will use the word *emotion* in all other instances. Thus, when I mean to indicate the fully nuanced phenomenon in which affects are assembled with each other, with experience, with images, with memories, with other emotions, or with cognitions, then I will use the word *emotion*. When I am referring to a client's experience, I will use the word *emotion*, except when a client reports awareness of affect or emotion, and then the word *feeling* will be used.

Complication arises because the word for an affect is the same as the word for an emotion. The term *fear*, for example, applies to both the affect fear and the emotion fear. The same words are used to describe the basic affects as are used to describe the corresponding emotion. Fear affect becomes fear emotion when it is assembled with idiosyncratic experience, idiosyncratic images, and unique combinations of other affects and other emotions in the individual. For example, a particular client may fear the affect fear. She may go to extremes to avoid feeling fear, because it so rapidly compounds itself, cycling ever deeper into anxiety, and then panic. This avoidance may lead her to stay indoors, avoid people, and restrict her contact with the world. For her, fear affect is assembled with memories of times she felt fear, images of people who caused fear, cognitions such as "I am a fraidy-cat" or "If I go there I'll get scared." In this case fear affect has become fear emotion. For other clients, fear affect may be assembled with images of a school bully, a punitive parent, a snake, or with an image of not getting homework done on time. For still others, fear affect may be assembled with other affects. For example, in the daredevil, fear may assemble with excitement; in the spousal abuser it may assemble with shame and elicit anger. In each of these examples, fear affect has become fear emotion. Throughout the book, when I mean to describe a discrete affect such as the affect fear, and intend to distinguish it from the emotion of the same name, the words *fear affect* will be used; when the emotion, qua emotion, is discussed, this will be indicated by the words *fear emotion*. The same language will be used in other instances where an affect and an emotion share the same name. Thus, *sadness affect* and *sadness emotion* will discriminate the different usages.

The term *mood* refers to affective states or processes that consume the organism and alter normal patterns of responding, perceiving, and thinking over a more extended time frame. For example, the *Diagnostic and Statistical Manual* (American Psychiatric Association, 1994, DSM-IV) specifies a two-week period for a major depressive episode. While affects and emotions are focused on an immediate object or situation, moods are characterized by diffuseness and globality (Fridja, 1993). Moods lack the object orientation that is a distinctive feature of emotions. As Fridja wrote, "Moods are thus affective states without an object" (1993, p. 381). Whereas affects and emotions play out over a relatively brief time span, moods last longer—Lewis (2000) called them "extended affective states" (p. 46). Moods are pervasive, changing social, occupational, and relationship functioning. The person in a joyful mood will relate joyously to a variety of elements in the environment, while the person in an angry mood will respond with irritation to the same elements. Cognition and emotion interact in mood in a complex manner. For example, a depressed mood may originate from persistent beliefs about the self or others. A person in a depressed mood may hold unrealistic negative attributions toward the self. In an anxious mood, a person may feel the whole world is endangering the self. The emotion associations in mood may activate cognitive networks with the result that learning, judgment, and memory may be biased over time. Lewis (2000) notes that the stable mood state appears to be sustained in some way by affect and favors a self-sustaining feedback mechanism. ACT proposes that, at least in the case of depressed moods, the self-sustaining process may consist of an intrapsychic conflict between two affects; for example, anger and disgust.

Emotion derives from autobiography, and therefore it is what we experience. However, because affect derives from physiology and neurophysiology, affect is what we regulate. The client who comes for help controlling his "temper" is speaking of an emotion. For this client, anger affect has assembled with memories, images, thoughts, and sensations to form the emotion that he names temper. The term *temper* is a common usage. Clients and clinicians use the common language of emotion to communicate with each other. The client may call his temper an emotion or a feeling. Clients rarely reduce emotion words to their affective roots. Yet, after you have taught your client the AMST protocol you will learn from this book, and he has learned to "control his temper," what he will in fact be doing is regulating anger affect, which, like all affects, is generated neurophysiologically and expressed in physiological terms. AMST employs images, sensations, and cognitions to build regulatory skills in the client that enable him to attenuate or arouse affects. AMST uses the client's images and memories to deconstruct the client's emotion and tease out the underlying affect or affects. It is these underlying affects that are regulated. This book teaches *affect* management skills, not *emotion* management skills, because it is the affect at the core of the emotion that is being regulated. When the client has mastered the skills of affect management, he will be able to regulate his emotions because affects are the building blocks of emotions. This introduction to affect and emotion leads naturally to an overview of the book's subject, training in skills for affect management.

AFFECT MANAGEMENT SKILLS TRAINING

AMST is the first system to provide for direct regulation of affects at their inception. Affect expression originates with neural activity. AMST employs images to modify the neurophysiological process of affect expression. By intervening in affect expression at its neurophysiological origin through the use of regulatory imagery, AMST modifies the cascade of processes that begin with affective arousal. Chapter 1 explains how affective arousal motivates physiological change, cognition, and behavior. Neurophysiological activity is the primary process engendering physiological, cognitive, and behavioral processes, and AMST alters these derivative processes by altering arousal levels for the primary affective process. Other systems of emotion regulation, as we will see, have attempted to alter affective arousal by altering physiology, thought process, or behavior. These are derivative or secondary processes, and therefore I refer to these methods as indirect emotion regulation protocols. AMST provides for direct regulation of affects, because AMST employs images to alter the primary neurophysiological processes that generate the secondary processes of physiology, cognition, and behavior. In using images to repair affect dysregulation, AMST makes use of the same imagistic mechanisms by which affect regulation is acquired during childhood. Chapter 2 describes the development of affect regulation from birth through adolescence, demonstrating how representations of caregivers form in the context of the infant–caregiver dyad and become the basis for both affect arousal and affect attenuation in the child. The chapter emphasizes the conceptual identity between the normal process of affective socialization occurring in childhood in the context of the infant–caregiver dyad and the psychotherapeutic process occurring in adulthood in the context of the client–therapist dyad.

Other therapeutic systems provide indirect approaches to affect regulation. Some systems attempt to modify the primary affective process by altering a secondary process that may be a sensation, cognition, behavior, or some combination of these. Several therapies that target stress and anger attempt to change affective responding by changing the client's physiological state through deep breathing and progressive muscle tension and relaxation. Rational–emotive therapy (RET) attempts to alter dysfunctional affective responding by changing the client's cognitive structures, that is, his thoughts and beliefs. Cognitive–behavioral therapy (CBT) combines behavioral change strategies with cognitive change strategies to alter maladaptive affective responding. Another therapeutic school, family systems therapy, attempts to influence affect by manipulating the internal representations of developmentally important persons from the family of origin. Still other therapies make use of the therapeutic dyad as a change agent. Psychoanalysis, greatly simplified, believes that the client's distress—which we define as emotion dysregulation—can be resolved by analyzing and working through the transference. Person centered therapy teaches that the client's distress can be resolved by the supportive, attuned relationship with the therapist. These therapeutic schools appear to believe that affect dysregulation is a symptom of the client's maladjustment. In contradistinction, AMST and ACT believe the client's physiological, cognitive, and behavioral maladjustments are manifestations of affect dysregulation. According to ACT, the first step in helping the client to achieve a more positive functioning is to repair the deficits in affect regulation. AMST provides the client with skills to regulate affects adaptively.

AMST is a brief intervention that can be taught to every client at the beginning of therapy and then integrated into any clinician's practice. The protocol can provide immediate relief for the client's suffering, because it transmits affect regulation skills from the outset of therapy. It can quickly assist the client to more adaptive functioning in both the short and long term, because it is designed to remediate deficits in affect regulation. In my own practice, I teach the skill set to every client so as to establish a baseline of adaptive affect and emotion functioning. Clinicians reading this book will come from diverse theoretical backgrounds and should realize that the skills taught here are meant to enhance outcomes from their established method of practice. AMST can be integrated with family systems, cognitive–behavioral, rational–emotive, psychoanalytic, or person centered therapies. While the protocol can be used in conjunction with other therapeutic approaches, it does constitute the initial phase of ACT.

The affect management skill set is multidimensional and directive and also highly interactive. The AMST skills have been carefully crafted to assemble images, affects, sensations, and cognitions into unified constructs. Each of these dimensions is essential to assuring positive outcomes, and no modality can be separated out from the others. In this respect, AMST is a coordinated protocol. The clinician takes a directive stance as the coach who knows more about affects and their regulation than the client. The clinician has the responsibility to transmit skills to the client that were not transmitted in the client's childhood. Through teaching these skills, the clinician begins the process of repairing deficits in the client's self structure. The need for directiveness in the therapeutic dyad, which may be uncomfortable for some clinicians, derives from the theoretical basis of a psychotherapy focused on affect. In part the interactivity of AMST arises from its use of ideomotor signaling to bypass the client's cognitive defenses. The term *ideomotor signaling* refers to a technique for getting information from the unconscious mind. As used by AMST it consists of asking the client to raise her index finger when she has completed an affective task. Ideomotor signaling facilitates a more direct communication between the therapist and the client's unconscious. The interactivity of AMST also stems from its use of client self-report. The protocol adapts appraisal scales from eye movement desensitization and processing (EMDR; Shapiro, 2001), expands them, and adapts them to suit the protocol's goals. The two appraisal scales allow the clinician and client to assess client stress or discomfort and to assess client progress in attaining protocol goals.

AMST is unique in that it employs an affect to facilitate acquisition of affect management skills. The protocol uses alternating bilateral stimulation in the tactile mode to elicit surprise–startle affect at a subthreshold level, which is beneath the client's conscious awareness. Elicitation of surprise affect can be accomplished by tapping on the client's knees or hands, or it can be supplied by a battery powered device, the TheraTapper™*, that delivers a slight, tactile "buzzing" sensation to the palms of the hands. Tactile alternating bilateral stimulation (TABS) by means of tapping or use of the TheraTapper™ supplies an important element of the coordinated, multidimensional AMST protocol. Using an affect to promote effective, efficient skills acquisition is called *affect mediation*. Subthreshold startle affect mediates the skills acquisition in the AMST protocol.

EMDR

For readers unfamiliar with EMDR, the present section presents an overview of this powerful therapy. AMST originally emerged within the environment of EMDR as an adjunct to using EMDR in treatment of alcoholism, addictions, nicotine dependency, and eating disorders (Omaha, 1998, 1999, 2000). AMST utilizes some of the tools created by Shapiro (2001). EMDR is an active, multidimensional, coordinated, empirically validated psychological protocol for resolving the sequelae of traumatic events and for treating clinical disorders caused by trauma. EMDR employs side-to-side eye movements or forms of alternating bilateral stimulation as one component of its integrated protocol. The eye movements appear to be an active treatment component (Kavanagh, Freese, Andrade, & May, 2001; Lohr, Tolin, & Kleinknecht, 1996; Montgomery & Ayllon, 1994).

The EMDR procedure consists of eight phases (Shapiro, 2001). In phase one, a careful client history identifies the client's dysfunctional behaviors and symptoms that will be targeted in EMDR therapy, and a treatment plan is created. Client suitability is assessed during this phase: "A major criterion of the suitability of clients for EMDR is their ability to deal with the high levels of disturbance potentially precipitated by the processing of dysfunctional information" (Shapiro, 1995, p. 68). A primary thrust of AMST is to improve the client's ability to withstand high levels of emotional disturbance so that he can successfully engage his adverse and traumatic material and process it adaptively and effectively. AMST was created with the intention of improving client suitability for EMDR.

EMDR's second phase prepares clients for the therapy by explaining its theory and protocol. In the preparation phase, clients are also provided with relaxation and visualization techniques. In the third EMDR phase, assessment, clients are helped to identify and refine a distressing memory or event constituting the target for processing. A negative belief about the self associated with the target,

---

*TheraTappers (Patent No. 6,001,073) can be ordered from: DNMS Institute, LLC (http://www. theratapper.com, sales@theratapper.com, Phone: 1-210-561-7881, FAX: 1-210-561-7806) or John Omaha Enterprises, LLC (http://www.johnomahaenterprises.com, Phone: 1-530-899-7719).

an emotion assembled with the target, and physical sensations accompanying the target are all identified. A positive cognition about the self in relation to the target is also identified for later installation, once the distressing material has been processed. The level of distress caused by the material is assessed using a subjective scale.

Desensitization is the fourth phase of EMDR. The client is asked to hold in awareness the target image, the negative cognition, emotion, and physical sensations, and sets of eye movements are initiated. These sets continue until the level of disturbance associated with the target has decreased to neutrality or near it. Once the target has been adaptively processed and desensitized, the positive cognition is installed, replacing the previously held negative belief about the self. Installation of the positive cognition constitutes the fifth phase. The client holds the target image in mind and brings up the new, positive, self-referential belief, and with sets of eye movements, this belief is installed. "I am okay just the way I am" is an example of a positive belief that might be installed, replacing, for example, the negative belief "I am flawed."

In the sixth phase, the client is asked to scan his or her body for remaining tension, and any residual physiological distress is then targeted in additional sets of eye movements. Closure is the seventh phase of the EMDR treatment protocol. Instructions are given to help the client cognitively distance herself from the target material. The goal of this phase is to restore a state of emotional balance in the client by the end of the session. Reevaluation, the eight phase takes place at the beginning of the next session following a session of target processing. The client is asked to reassess the previous target to ascertain if treatment effects have persisted. Further processing is instituted as required.

Perkins and Rouanzoin (2002) have recently evaluated current views regarding EMDR while summarizing the extensive literature empirically supporting it. This therapy is an effective treatment for either civilian or combat-related PTSD. EMDR is a more rapid treatment than exposure therapy. A 15-month follow up study demonstrated that treatment gains persisted over that time period. Results with EMDR are not due to a placebo effect. EMDR differs from exposure therapy by using brief, interrupted periods of attention to traumatic memories followed by free association. Stickgold (2002) has proposed that EMDR operates by repetitively redirecting attention, thus creating a neurobiological state in which traumatic memories can be cortically integrated. Cortical integration is believed to reduce the strength of episodic, traumatic memories. Furthermore, EMDR-facilitated cortical integration is also proposed to decrease the amygdala-dependent negative affect associated with the traumatic memory.

USING AMST

This book is written for all clinicians working in the field of mental health including psychiatrists, psychologists, psychotherapists, marriage and family counselors, and social workers. Familiarity with or training in EMDR (Shapiro, 2001) is not a prerequisite for learning the skills taught here. The book teaches clinicians skills that can be effectively and efficiently transmitted to clients to help them immediately begin to move toward a happier, freer, less fear-driven, less shame-based life. These skills are simple. Once developed, they may operate in the client with conscious awareness, or unconsciously, or in a mixture. The skills persist. Positive changes in the client's traditional responses to emotion-laden experience accumulate, gaining momentum. Theory tells us that affect regulation is a central factor in the self-organization of a client's personality (Izard, Ackerman, Schoff, & Fine, 2000). The skills presented here begin the process of remediating the client's defects of affect regulation, and as a result, the client's personality begins to reorganize around a functional core of adaptive skills.

AMST is a recent development. I compiled the first version in November 2000. In February 2001, I presented the initial AMST workshop to a group of EMDR-trained clinicians in New York City, and in July that year I presented a workshop at EMDR International with Cindy Browning (Browning & Omaha, 2001). Since that time, many EMDR-trained clinicians have learned and used the AMST protocol.

Empirical support and empirical validation are the touchstones of modern psychotherapy. Clinical impressions for a new protocol are usually gathered before the protocol is subjected to rigorous empirical test. In this book you will read case reports from 17 clients who experienced AMST in their therapies. These clinical impressions provide support for the protocol. Many therapists have supplied their own clinical impressions of the effectiveness of AMST through the on-line discussion group I moderate for therapists who have taken an AMST workshop, and some of these will be cited in the book's narrative. The first empirical research on AMST is beginning to appear. AMST was a component of a therapy for eating disorders that also employed EMDR and showed promising outcomes in a single case design study (Omaha, 2000). Waltner-Toews (2002) has reported promising results in a small single case design pilot study with obsessive-compulsive disorder that used AMST in a group setting. Brown and Gilman (S. Brown, personal communication, February 17, 2003) showed that "AMST was an important component in providing positive outcomes" in a small multiple single case design study with dual diagnosis (PTSD and substance abuse) participants from a court ordered drug program in which AMST was used in conjunction with the EMDR standard protocol (Brown & Gilman, 2003). A major objective in writing this book is to stimulate further empirical outcome research on AMST.

ACT AND AMST

ACT is an overarching construct of which AMST constitutes the first phase. ACT is a complete therapy in that it proposes a theory for the origin of the patient's problems and provides a treatment for those problems derived from its theoretical principles. ACT is based on a developmental model that relates the patient's current difficulties to antecedent experiences. The emerging ACT therapy provides tools and techniques for identifying and then resolving the affect-laden experiences and internal affective conflicts believed to operate in many Axis I and II disorders. Other ACT interventions promote the emergence of more adaptive self structures in clients.

Three Principles of Affect Centered Therapy

Three principles guide the ACT approach to psychotherapy. The first principle of ACT asserts that affects are primary determinants of human behavior and cognition. Affective primacy originates from the developmental fact that the affects come on-line first and that behavior, thought, neurological structure, the self, and consciousness all emerge from and are structured by affective transactions between the organism and the environment, including, of course, the people in it. Behavior, cognition, and experience are viewed as secondary determinants because their influence depends on the affects with which they are assembled.

A second principle states that the self is structured during and by the process of affective socialization across a succession of milieus beginning with the infant–caregiver dyad, continuing with the family, and expanding to include school and society. The same principles of this developmental model apply to the emergence of an adaptive, positively functioning self as to the emergence of a maladaptive, negatively functioning self. Maladaptive, negatively functioning self structures are formed in response to and as a means of managing affects arising as a result of the vicissitudes, adversities, and traumas that are experienced across the developmental domains. ACT is grounded in theories advanced by Bowlby (1969), Schore (1994), and Sroufe (1996, 1997).

The third principle derives from these first two and structures and organizes the ACT approach to therapy itself. The principle asserts that in order to treat psychopathology, deficits in affect regulation must be remediated and then past experiences that have caused affect dysregulation must be uncovered and resolved. Affect dysregulation is believed to originate from one or both of two sources. The first source consists of failures to transmit skills for adaptive affect regulation, which is termed *childhood deficit experience*. The second source is adverse or traumatic childhood experience. A corollary to the third principle states that the maladaptive organization of self must be restructured, and ACT teaches a number of techniques for accomplishing this. ACT continues to develop new techniques for restructuring the self.

ACT therapy consists of two phases. In phase 1, the AMST skill set is transmitted to the client. When the client can recognize, tolerate, and regulate the range of emotions, therapy can proceed to the second phase in which he can uncover and resolve the adversities and traumas that have contributed to his emotion dysregulation and deficient self structure. In this second phase, therapeutic interventions facilitate the emergence of a more adaptive self structure. To reiterate, the AMST skill set conveyed in this book constitutes the essential first phase of ACT. While AMST can stand alone and provide benefit to the client in and of itself, and while it can also be incorporated into other therapeutic approaches, AMST is solidly embedded in the larger theoretical and therapeutic milieu of ACT. Just as, for example, a clinician can incorporate Gestalt techniques into a family systems approach to therapy, so too can a clinician adapt AMST techniques to the same family systems—or any other—approach to therapy.

AMST, ACT, EMDR, and Other Psychotherapies

AMST is compatible with all psychotherapeutic orientations. The skills and tools of the protocol can be integrated into psychoanalysis (e.g., Goldman & Milman, 1978), self psychology (Kohut & Wolf, 1978), rational–emotive therapy (Ellis & Dryden, 1987), cognitive therapy (Beck, 1976), dialectical behavioral therapy (Linehan, 1993), and family systems therapy (Bowen, 1978). Furthermore, ACT's affect orientation has the potential to complement the theory and practice and improve the outcomes of these other schools.

AMST can be integrated into the practice of EMDR (Shapiro, 2001). AMST is a protocol that teaches affect regulation, and because EMDR treats disorders characterized by affect dysregulation, the AMST skills can improve the effectiveness of EMDR therapy. AMST was originally created within the environment of EMDR and has now moved to a position of independence. The theoretical framework of ACT has the potential to provide an etiological and ontological foundation for EMDR. ACT incorporates some EMDR techniques into its expanding assemblage of therapeutic interventions. ACT, AMST, and EMDR all make use of alternating bilateral stimulation. ACT and AMST use *tactile* alternating bilateral stimulation supplied by a TheraTapper™, which delivers a gentle vibrating stimulus alternating from side to side through hand-held probes. EMDR employs side to side eye movements postulated to induce a dual attention stimulation condition (Shapiro, 2001). It must be emphasized that this book teaches AMST employing TABS. This book does *not* teach EMDR; only trainers or instructors approved by the EMDR International Association can legitimately teach EMDR.

ACT and EMDR are significantly different therapeutic orientations characterized by divergent points of view in four crucial areas. ACT has a fundamentally different conception of how a personality system moves from dysfunction towards adaptive, positive functioning. ACT has a significantly different view of the primacy of affect and emotion. ACT's theory of personality is different from the theory upon which EMDR is based. ACT and EMDR propose different theories to explain the effectiveness of bilateral stimulation, whether supplied by eye movements or TABS, in producing positive therapeutic outcomes.

How Healing Occurs

ACT and EMDR propose different hypotheses for the process by which a personality system moves from maladaptation to positive adaptation. EMDR is founded on Shapiro's hypothesis of an innate adaptive information processing system (AIPS) that is proposed to move automatically towards healing (Shapiro, 2001, 2002). Shapiro wrote that "inherent in all of us is a physiological information-processing system that integrates the perceptions of sensory input and the cognitive components of experience into an associated internal memory network to allow for ecological, healthful, balanced functioning" (2000, p. 9). According to Shapiro, the AIPS automatically moves toward healthy functioning. The EMDR model proposes that trauma prevents or blocks the automatic movement toward healing and that once trauma-induced blockage is removed, the AIPS again will automatically restore the system to adaptive functioning.

ACT proposes that movement in therapy from dysfunction toward positively adaptive functioning depends upon the quality of the therapeutic dyad and the internal representation the client forms of the therapist. Movement towards positive functioning also depends upon the nature of the client's internal representations of self and others and the relations among them. The therapeutic change process consists of transformations in the client's internal representations of developmentally important others as well as transformations of internal representations of self. For these transformations to occur, the client must be provided with an internal image of an important other person—usually the therapist is the model for this image—who is emotionally attuned, accepting, and sensitively responding. The image of the therapist functions as a template against which the client compares the internal images of persons who were developmentally important as well as self representations. A mismatch between images of therapist and images of self and others elicits affects that may include disgust, anger, sadness, shame, and fear. Healing occurs when arousal of disgust, anger, sadness, shame, and fear affects is attenuated as the therapist guides the client's personality system towards a resolution of representations of developmentally important others and a transformation of the self representation.

This process of change in the direction of positive functioning relies on the propensity of the central nervous system (CNS) for synthesis—the capacity to assimilate, accommodate, organize, and integrate its experiences from the beginning of life. The synthetic function is the innate (i.e., genetically determined) property of the CNS, as the object relations theorists recognized (Horner, 1984). Siegel (2002a) defined integration as the "functional coupling of distinct and differentiated elements into a coherent process or functional whole" (p. 100). Assimilation, accommodation, organization, and integration are the basic functions of the CNS constituting Shapiro's "physiological information-processing system that integrates the perceptions of sensory input and the cognitive components of experience into an associated internal memory network" (2002, p. 9). ACT postulates that EMDR's AIPS is in fact a construct that is acquired during the course of early socialization. This construct develops in the context of the dyads that are operative during childhood, in particular the dyads involving the infant and maternal caregiver and the infant and paternal caregiver. Whereas EMDR proposes that the AIPS moves toward healthy functioning, ACT posits that the system moves toward adaptive functioning, not necessarily healthy functioning. The nature of adaptive functioning is determined by the context structured by the currently operative dyads and by the nature and quality of the current internal representations the client possesses. During childhood, the client's synthetic function promoted the child's survival by facilitating adaptation within his or her developmental environment. When the early environment was deficient, the attachment was negatively impacted, and a distressed personality structure emerged, a situation made worse if the environment included adversity and trauma as well. A personality structured by deficit experience and adverse and traumatic experience, while it may have been adaptive in its developmental environment, will experience maladaptation in the social environments of adolescence and adulthood. The stress entailed by maladaptation or the consequences resulting from negative functioning will bring the individual to therapy.

In the context of a therapeutic dyad, the client's personality system will move toward adaptive functioning as it is defined in the dyad. In the therapeutic dyad, one partner is designated the *client*, and this partner is presumed to be less healthfully and less adaptively functioning than the therapist partner. The therapist is present to help, to guide, and to model healthful and adaptive functioning. The therapeutic dyad functions to remediate the impairments in the client's self structure that originated in the client's developmental dyad of childhood. The client forms an internal representation of the therapist. This representation serves as a template for the client's restructuring of his or her schemas. For the most part, therapists model healthful, adaptive functioning. For that reason, most clients experience a change in functioning toward adaptivity and health in the course of EMDR therapy. Shapiro (2001, 2002) ascribed to the putative self-healing mechanism of the AIPS the qualities that are actually inherent in the therapeutic dyad. Siegel (2002a) affirmed the ACT approach when he wrote:

> In general, psychotherapy can be seen as the basis for a form of attachment relationship, one in which the patient seeks proximity to (i.e., wants to have a physical and emotional closeness with) the therapist, has a safe haven (is soothed when upset), and achieves an internal working model of security (called a "secure base") derived from the patterns of communication between therapist and patient." (p. 106)

In the therapeutic dyad, the therapist models trust in her own perceptions, acceptance of the emotional states of the client, bonding, experience of joy and intimacy, achievement of a sense of greater purpose, commitment to service, and interpersonal connection, and the client incorporates these qualities because the therapist models them. Because the therapist embodies these qualities, the client is able to integrate them and as a result is able to "enter terrifying states and process information" from unresolved trauma (Siegel, 2002a, p. 107). As Siegel wrote, "This interpersonal communicative experience may cause these rigidly constrained or disorganized states, which are at the core of unresolved trauma, to be dramatically—and permanently—altered" (p. 107).

Viewpoint Toward Affects

ACT and EMDR are similar in one respect and fundamentally different in another in regard to affects. The similarity pertains to their shared viewpoint that trauma is determined by the unresolved affect bound with experience and stored physiologically. The difference arises from ACT's greater emphasis on the determining influence of early social context on affective responding across the life span.

ACT proposes that beginning from the first months of life the emerging human personality is both conditioned by and responding to the demands of its social context for affect regulation. The personality may be viewed as the means by which the organism regulates its affects within that social context. From ACT's viewpoint, the personality is primarily an assemblage of the organism's behavioral, structural, cognitive, sensational, and affective transactional schemas for managing affects and emotions. Attainment of higher human capacities like service to humanity and spirituality depend almost entirely upon the prior establishment of a well-organized, integrated, differentiated self system capable of functional affect regulation.

EMDR focuses upon the organism's traumatic experiences, while ACT focuses on the emergence of structure in the organism's self system. Shapiro (2002) wrote that "any of the ubiquitous experiences of childhood can qualify as a 'Small t' trauma" (pp. 14–15). From EMDR's perspective, childhood development appears to be the cumulative record of 'Small t' and 'Big T' traumas, all of which are assembled with unresolved affects. Apparently, according to EMDR, the lesser traumas to a lesser extent and the greater traumas to a greater extent overwhelm the AIPS and prevent its spontaneous restoration of the system to healthy functioning.

From ACT's perspective, the organism's early experiences in the developmental dyad set the basic personality structure and determine therefore what its subsequent responding will be. Whether an event arouses distressing levels of affect or not will depend upon the organism's attachment status and affective socialization. If the maternal caregiver is sensitive, appropriately responsive, soothing, and caring, the toddler will form an internal representation of her that embodies these qualities and then will rely on that representation for self-soothing in times of stress. For this child, the vicissitudes of life will be less likely to arouse distressing levels of affect because the child can self soothe. This child's early affective socialization engendered a resilient self structure. In contrast, an infant whose maternal caregiver is absent or neglectful, insensitive or unresponsive, will form an internal representation of the caregiver embodying her qualities. This child will lack a self structure that includes an internal locus of soothing, and as a result, many of life's vicissitudes will be distressing.

Because of its theoretical orientation toward affect, ACT is able to understand and directly and effectively intervene for the client's benefit in the area of self-worth. ACT proposes that negative self-reflective cognitions about the self— i.e., statements of impaired self-worth such as "I am flawed," "I am a failure," and "I am unworthy"—are driven by affects, in particular, disgust affect, directed at the self. A client's statement of self-directed negative attribution will have a history across that client's developmental time span, and will have originated in part in negative affects broadcast at the client in childhood by important attachment figures. Developmentally, the client's present negative self attributions may also have originated in negative affects elicited in the client in childhood by inappropriate experiences forced on the client. ACT has adopted and then expanded a central technique from EMDR called *cognitive interweave*. In cognitive interweave, the therapist deliberately elicits from the client useful information in the form of imagery, movement or verbalizations "that would have been expected to associate spontaneously in unimpeded processing" (Shapiro, 2002, p. 43). ACT, as has already been explained, does not support the notion of *spontaneous processing*. From the ACT perspective, processing is largely guided through therapist modeling or through the therapist's directives. ACT's intervention could be called an *affective interweave*, because the therapist directs the client to notice what affects are being broadcast at the client by a parent in the childhood scene being processed. ACT is different from EMDR, because ACT accords early affective socialization a position of primacy in determining how the self is structured and as a result how the organism responds to life's vicissitudes across the life span.

Theory of Personality

EMDR and ACT differ in the theory of personality upon which each one is based. EMDR defines personality in terms of experiences. Shapiro (2002) wrote that personality is "an accumulation of characteristic internal patterns and responses" that are believed to result from an interaction between genetic predisposition and experiences (p. 10). For EMDR, the accumulation of responses and patterns characterizing an adaptive personality is "considered to be engendered by adequately processed childhood experiences that have laid the groundwork for adaptive behaviors" (p. 10). The adequate processing of childhood experience lays the foundation for appropriate responding to current situations. Shapiro wrote further that dysfunctional processing of current distress is "engendered by inadequately processed [childhood] experiences that are activated by current conditions" (p. 10). Apparently for EMDR, the locus of adequate processing lies entirely within the organism and is manifested in the putative AIPS.

In contradistinction to EMDR, ACT stresses the central importance of structure—i.e., representations of self and others—in defining personality. The personality is more than the sum of its patterns and responses. According to ACT, experience in the developmental dyad during the early years determines how the brain structures itself, which in turn determines how the organism tolerates later experiences of adversity and trauma. ACT separates the experiences that determine personality into two categories, attachment, which refers to experiences from birth to three or four years of life, and childhood socioemotional history, which lasts through adolescence. Referring to early experience, Siegel (2002a) wrote:

> [T]he early years of life—during establishment of the basic brain circuits that mediate such processes as emotional and behavioral regulation, interpersonal relatedness, language, and memory—are the most crucial for people to receive the kinds of experiences that enable proper development to occur. (p. 88)

Separating attachment from subsequent history stresses the centrality of the developmental dyad in determining the basic structure of the personality. Personality is socially constructed, first within the context of the developmental infant–maternal caregiver dyad, then within the context of an expanding array of other dyads. The personality system that emerges out of this socialization process is primarily an affect regulating entity. If there were deficiencies in the caregiver's affective contribution to the dyad, the child's personality structure and hence its capability to manage affect will be conditioned by those deficiencies. If there was adversity or trauma in the dyad and subsequent socioemotional history, the individual's personality structure will be determined by the affects experienced and the organism's efforts to regulate them.

The quality of the socially-organized personality structure, emerging from interactions in the developmental dyad, determines how successfully the organism will resolve the vicissitudes of the subsequent developmental periods. ACT emphasizes the social construction of the organism's mechanisms for participating in pleasant experiences and processing stressful experiences, and thus ACT differs from EMDR's focus on whether childhood events were adaptively processed or not. ACT stresses the representations of self and others that are formed early in life and that determine current functioning. Personality is crafted from the internal working models, which are also called representations of self and other, that are formed beginning in the first months of life. These representations are assembled with affects, memories, sensations, and thoughts. These complex constructs determine the self's current functioning in present circumstances.

These considerations have important therapeutic consequences. ACT begins therapy with AMST which is structured to remediate the deficits in affect regulation from the client's childhood that have determined the client's personality structure and consequently his or her current maladaptation and negative functioning. Reflecting its focus on internal representations, AMST seeks to uncover affect regulating ego states. Affect regulating ego states are parts of the self that may have formed to protect the self system by dissociating sensations or affects out of awareness, or that manifest hypervigilant perspectives that protect the system by preventing it from trusting itself or the social context. In Phase II of ACT, where the causal antecedent experiences of current problems are uncovered, ACT focuses on child ego states, symptom-expressing ego states, introjected parents that function as ego states, and false self identities that are another form of ego state. ACT also facilitates maturation of the authentic self, a nascent ego state that is brought up to currency on the client's developmental time line. ACT's focus on ego states, their affect-managing functions, and the affective transactions among them, as well as its focus on the experiences that engendered the ego states distinguishes it from EMDR which focuses solely on experience.

The Mechanism of Action of Bilateral Stimulation

ACT and EMDR propose different theories to explain the effect of bilateral stimulation. EMDR proposes that the side to side eye movements or other forms of alternating bilateral stimulation induce a dual-attention stimulation that Shapiro believes directly affects cognitive processes. Shapiro (2002) offered several possible mechanisms for the eye movement effects. Shifts in cognitive content and attribution correlated with eye movements could be due to interference with working memory, elicitation of an orienting response, creation of a relaxation response, activation of rapid eye movement responses like those seen in dreaming, distraction, evocation of a reparative physiological state, or cognitive loading. In discussing the dual-attention stimulation that she believes explains EMDR's effectiveness, Shapiro (2002) wrote "there is a good possibility that the primary common denominator is the attentional element" (p. 28).

ACT and AMST propose a mechanism based in affect. The eye movements or other form of alternating bilateral stimulation are hypothesized to elicit surprise–startle affect, the effect of which is to "blank the mind" briefly. ACT proposes that the common denominator among forms of alternating bilateral stimulation is the affective element. Elicitation of surprise–startle is hypothesized to briefly interrupt ongoing energy flows along established neural pathways. From a biological perspective, surprise–startle functions to prepare the mind to deal with a suddenly appearing novel stimulus. In the context of AMST or ACT, tactile alternating bilateral stimulation (TABS) the usual mode of delivering alternating stimulation, is believed to interrupt established ways of thinking, feeling, sensing, and behaving, and thereby to allow new modes to emerge. Surprise–startle interrupts established connections between thoughts and allows new connections to form; it breaks up established connections between images and internal representations of self and other, and thereby allows new relationships to emerge. Very importantly, as AMST is being transmitted to the client, TABS facilitated surprise–startle breaks up old patterns of emotion responding and allows new, more adaptive patterns to organize.

THE CENTRALITY OF AFFECT AND EMOTION

Clinicians know that clients who come to the counseling office are often suffering because of difficulty in managing their emotions. Affect and its dysregulation cause most of the problems for people that bring them to therapy. No matter what the diagnosis, it is the problem of affect and the maladaptive defenses and self structures that have emerged to manage it that have impelled the client to seek professional help. The client may act out his or her emotions—a behavioral management script—with consequences for the client in the sphere of interpersonal relations. The client may regulate his emotions with a substance—alcohol, drugs, nicotine, food—with social, legal, medical, and career consequences. In other clients, a repressive emotion management self-structure may have emerged, and this client presents with depression. Still others may find their way to therapy because they are troubled by process addictions in areas of gambling, pornography, or sex. In these addictions the process of gambling or sex serves to facilitate emotion regulation. Finally, in some clients the maturation of the affect regulation process was derailed at such an early developmental stage that a disordered or severely fragmented personality emerged, as, for example, with clients suffering from borderline personality disorder, narcissistic personality disorder, or dissociative identity disorder. For each of these classes of clients, the skills taught in this book can provide immediate relief. Clients present with emotional distress, and by teaching them to manage the affects that are the building blocks of their emotions, the clinician can help them achieve improvements in mood, attitude, thinking, and functioning.

The Dialectic between Affect and Cognition

In part, the history of psychology over the past hundred years is the record of swings between thesis and antithesis in a grand dialectical disputation regarding the primacy of affect versus cognition. William James, Charles Darwin, and Sigmund

Freud (Damasio, 1999; LeDoux, 1996, for a summary) introduced the thesis that emotion is a central causal element in human behavior (Zajonc, 1984). Lazarus (1982) was the most cogent advocate for the antithesis to James, Darwin, and Freud, asserting that cognitive appraisal is the central construct in determining behavior. In the nature of the dialectic, thesis and antithesis are followed by synthesis. By 1984, Lazarus and Folkman were proposing that causality between emotion and cognition was "bidirectional" (1984, p. 274). Nearly a decade later, newly formulated theory (e.g., Izard, 1993) suggested both cognitive *and* noncognitive causation for emotion. That synthesis immediately became the polar opposite of yet another antithesis, one expounded by Freeman (2000) and Lewis (2000) among others, suggesting that cognitions and affects coemerge as affective–cognitive structures. Emotions—and the affects that are their building blocks—have cycled from being viewed as the cause of thought to being viewed as causing thought, to being viewed as coadjunctively arising together with thought.

Affects and emotions influence the substance of perceptions, the content of thought, and the type of actions undertaken. Affects motivate, and the affect a person is experiencing will determine what behaviors get motivated. How people appraise a situation and the decisions they make are swayed by affect and emotion. Even moral judgments—once believed to be the exclusive bastion of thought—turn out to be motivated in part by affect. Consciousness itself, humanity's most prized quality, arises from affective experience. Children learn affect regulation almost from birth, and the effects of adaptive and less than adaptive affect and emotion socialization have observable effects in several domains as early as preschool age. AMST teaches affect and emotion regulation, and when affects and emotions are adaptively regulated, perceptions, thoughts, appraisals, motivation, judgments, and consciousness itself can change in the direction of positive functioning.

Emotion and Perception

Affective state alters how people perceive others. A client feeling shame will see and hear the clinician differently from a client feeling anger. Emotion influences perception (Izard, 1991), and the neural pathways through which it does so are now known. LeDoux (1996) discussed the projections from the affect-processing amygdala to the cortical sensory areas and cortical sensory processing areas. Reciprocal connections between sensory receiving and processing areas of the brain provide a means by which the amygdala can exert affective influence on cortical areas that are processing the stimuli that have activated the amygdala. Knowing about these anatomical connections helps explain results from an early experiment on emotion influence of perception (Izard, 1991). Subjects were either treated discourteously and made angry by an experimenter, or they were made happy by friendly treatment. The happy subjects perceived significantly more happy faces in pictures of emotion expression shown them, while the hostile subjects saw more anger expressions. Social psychologists have demonstrated that affective state alters how people are perceived (Forgas, 1995). It influences attitudes, impacts language use and intergroup behavior, and affects stereotyping, survey research, and self-perception. Forgas's affect infusion model (1995) demonstrates how affectively loaded information "exerts an influence on and becomes incorporated into the judgmental process . . . eventually coloring the judgmental outcome" (p. 39).

Emotion and Thought

An angry person's thoughts will be different from those of a calm person. Normal human cognitive functioning is impacted by affect and emotion (Forgas, 1995; Lazarus, 1982). Lazarus (1982) believed that thought precedes affect, and he has defined affect in such a way that it is a cognitive function. He wrote: "Emotion results from an evaluative perception . . . between a person (or animal) and the environment" (p. 1023). In Lazarus's view, there is never a situation in which an affect or emotion precedes a cognition. Zajonc (1984) mounted an exhaustive criticism of Lazarus's position. Zajonc argued that the cognitive and affective systems are independent, that there are some situations in which affect is primary, and that for the most part the two systems operate interdependently. In the earliest stages of development, as we will discuss in more detail in Chapter 1, the affect system is sufficient for affective arousal, and as Zajonc notes in discussing the neonate, "no cognitive appraisal is necessary (or even possible)" (p. 119). Neuroanatomy supports a direct connection between perception and affect that is not subject to appraisal. All mammalian brains apparently have a direct link from the retina to the hypothalamus that provides for generation of an affective reaction on the basis of purely sensory input. Izard has synthesized these points of view into a proposal for four systems for affect and emotion activation, three of which provide for noncognitive information processing (Izard, 1993). In infancy affects are the primary motivators of behavior, and as cognition develops, the affective and cognitive systems become interdependent.

Emotion, Appraisal, and Judgment

How the adolescent client "sizes up" the therapy situation will be strongly affected by his or her affective state. Affect influences the cognitive process of appraisal (Forgas, 1995). Mood affects judgment about or appraisal of the self. Happy people make greater attributions to stable, internal causes for their successes, and sad people make fewer such attributions (Forgas, 1995). Punitive judgments about the self form a basis for depression in both adolescents and adults (Blumberg & Izard, 1985; Fridja, 1993). Blumberg and Izard (1985) showed that depressed children, like depressed adults, endorse sadness, and Forgas (1995) demonstrated that in normal adults, sadness influences the quality of judgments made by the self about the self. The interaction of cognition and affect clearly creates the preconditions for the downward spiral of depression.

Mood also conditions the judgments made by partners regarding a relationship conflict (Forgas, 1995). Sad partners attributed more globality, stability, and internality to causes of conflict than did happy partners. These attributions were far more pronounced when the conflict was serious than when it was simple.

Mood can influence decision making at several stages, because it appears the process of making a decision occurs in a hierarchically structured manner (Isen,

1993). Decision making is not a monolithic process. Isen suggests that command decisions or evaluations may precede actually addressing a problem, and these command decisions are subject to affect intrusion. Affect can enter into—intrude on—the command level decision and derail a decision even before the problem itself is considered. The importance of the task, its utility, control over the outcome, and hedonic consequences—all of which are influenced by affective considerations—may be evaluated before the task itself is addressed, or dismissed. Thus, a person in a depressed mood may fail to make a decision about going to a movie, for example, because his depressed affective state causes him to fail to consider the movie since "I won't enjoy it anyway."

Risk taking is a special form of appraisal and decision making. Positive-affect subjects endorsed greater willingness to take, risk on a purely hypothetical task, but when the proposition involved the possibility of real, meaningful loss, the positive-affect subjects were more risk-averse than the negative-affect subjects (Isen, 1993).

Emotion and Decision Making

What a client is feeling will determine what a client will decide. An angry spouse's decision about the marriage will be different from a fearful or a joyful spouse's decision. The influence of both positive and negative affect on decision making has been extensively investigated (Isen, 1993). Positive and negative affect have different influences on retrieval from memory. Positive affect can be experimentally induced by watching a few minutes of a comedy film or viewing cartoons. Experimentally induced positive affect has been demonstrated to improve retrieval of positively valenced material from memory. Negative affect is less effective or ineffective in cuing retrieval of negative material. Positive affect influences how material is organized in memory as well as the context for thought. In a positive affect state, subjects produce more associations to neutral material, they categorize more flexibly, they see more similarities between items, and they discriminate more differences between them as well. As a result of these effects, positive-state subjects perform better in an assessment of creativity. They also do better in a test of negotiation performance, and in a positive state, outcomes of negotiation are improved. The influence of positive affect is complex, depending upon variables of task importance, affective valence of subject material, and motive to maintain the positive state. Empirical research supports the commonplace advice to "wait until you calm down before you make a decision."

Damasio (1994) argued that thought itself, the basis of appraisal, decision making, judgment, and motivation, is inextricably interwoven with and dependent upon brain functions that include body awareness and emotion. Damasio speaks of a "body-minded brain" (pp. 223–244 ff). He argued that "somatic markers" (p. 173), the unpleasant gut feelings that arise when a bad logical outcome appears in mind during cognitive processing, improve the efficiency of the reasoning process. He hypothesized that the body is the frame of reference for mind and that "our very organism rather than some absolute external reality is used as the ground reference for the construction we make of the world around us" (p. xvi). This explains why the spouse dominated by anger affect may not be able to recognize that he is making a bad choice when he decides to leave the marriage. Alternatively, the spouse influenced by interest affect may be able to access the optimal level of shame affect that apparently helps people recognize when they are making a bad decision.

Emotion and Motivation

Affective state influences motivation, and different affects motivate different behavioral outcomes. The client experiencing excitement affect will be motivated to make different responses toward a behavioral modification plan than the client experiencing fear. Like decision making, motivation has been shown to be influenced by emotion in a complex fashion (Isen, 1993). Positive affect appears to motivate by promoting variety seeking, but only in situations that do not engender thoughts of negative outcomes. Positive affects—interest–excitement and enjoyment–joy—also appear to stimulate "intrinsic motivation," that is, interest in the task for its own qualities as opposed to "extrinsic motivation," a monetary reward. Positiveaffect subjects endorsed more "liking" for a task than did the controls, which also indicates intrinsic motivation. Fear, on the other hand, motivates escape, and anticipation of fear impels avoidance (Izard, 1993). Therefore, the therapist can improve clients' outcomes on their treatment plans by developing a state where excitement rather than fear is salient.

Emotion and Moral Judgment

The more personally involved one is in a judgment, the stronger is the influence of affect. Being personally involved in any judgment, even a moral judgment, equates with having feelings about the judgment, and the decisions people make about moral issues will be influenced by their emotions. Lawmakers, judges, police and military officers, citizens, therapists, and students are regularly required to make moral judgments. Is it right to cheat on a test? Should I report this person to child protective services? A vote or an opinion on abortion, the death penalty, war, or civil rights implies a moral judgment, and all such judgments have an affective component. A fascinating functional magnetic resonance imaging (fMRI) study has indicated that emotion is involved in formulating moral judgments, an area that rationalists have believed to be purely cognitive (Greene, Sommerville, Nystrom, Darley, & Cohen, 2001). Subjects in the study were administered a 60-item moral dilemma assessment. Items in the assessment were assigned to one of three conditions: moral-personal, moral-impersonal, and nonmoral. A moral-personal dilemma is one requiring close contact; for example, *pushing* one person to his death in front of a train in order to save the lives of five persons. This is contrasted with a moral-impersonal dilemma in which *throwing a switch* will cause the train to kill one person thereby saving the lives of five people. Philosophers studying these dilemmas were puzzled by studies showing that subjects would choose to throw a switch, but not push a person, to sacrifice one life in order to save five. The authors captured fMRI data while subjects completed the assessment. The results showed that when making moral-personal judgments, three areas of subjects' brains known to be associated with emotion processing were activated. These areas—medial frontal gyrus, posterior cingulate gyrus, and angular gyrus, bilateral—were not activated, or were significantly less activated, during the moral-impersonal and nonmoral conditions. In addition, areas associated with working memory, which were activated in the moral-impersonal and nonmoral conditions, were less active during the moral-personal condition. Subjects who concluded that it was "appropriate" to push one person to his death to save five took much longer to reach the decision than to resolve a moral-impersonal dilemma. The authors conclude, "the increased emotional responses generated by the moral-personal dilemmas have an influence on and are not merely incidental to moral judgment" (p. 2107).

Emotion and Consciousness

Damasio (1999) has argued forcefully that consciousness itself is a function of affect and emotion and the sensations generated in the body by affects. Using his observations of individuals with brain lesions, Damasio showed that consciousness, wakefulness, and low-level attention can be separated, but consciousness and emotion cannot be separated. He argued for a core consciousness that is a simple biological phenomenon, that is not exclusively human, and that does not depend upon working memory, conventional memory, reasoning, or language. Extended consciousness is built on this core consciousness and does require both conventional and working memory. This extended consciousness is a complex biological and cultural phenomenon with several levels of organization. It evolves across lifetimes and is language-dependent.

For Damasio, consciousness emerges when the organism becomes aware that its own state has been changed by an encounter with an object in the environment. Objects in the environment are represented by neural patterns in sensory cortices. By a similar process, the organism knows itself as an object represented inside its own brain. Feelings, the somatic sensations accompanying affects and emotions, inform the organism that its state has changed as a result of environmental encounters. Because the human organism holds a representation of itself in mind as an object, the organism is aware of changes in itself as signaled by the feelings accompanying affects and emotions. Self-awareness *is* this process. As Damasio (1999) wrote: "The apparent self emerges as the feeling of a feeling" (p. 31). As we will demonstrate in this book's second section, AMST incorporates Damasio's theoretical framework. AMST develops the client's awareness of sensations and emotions and thereby facilitates the building of self-structure and the elaboration of consciousness.

Emotion Regulation in Childhood

The effects on the child of the caregiver's style of affective socialization can be observed as early as preschool age. The term *affective socialization* refers to the processes taking place between the child and its caretakers and others through which the child comes to feel as it does. An expanding body of empirical research has demonstrated that emotion and its regulation are already playing a crucial role in the lives of preschool children. Chapter 2 will discuss the development of emotions from birth onward in greater detail. Our central thesis is that a preschooler's problems with affect regulation and with transitioning from family to peer society have their origins in infancy and early childhood. Furthermore, the problems that bring the client to the counseling office today may also be traced to that client's infancy and childhood. The review of the literature in Chapter 2 will support our conclusions that the adverse consequences of impaired affective socialization in the family of origin are observable in preschool social, academic, and psychological functioning and that these consequences may contribute to psychopathology in childhood, adolescence, and adulthood.

A DEVELOPMENTAL HYPOTHESIS

This book proposes that the individuals we see as clients in adulthood are people whose childhoods were characterized in part by failures of emotion learning and socialization. These individuals emerged from the family of infancy and early childhood with impairments in their ability to manage emotions. Emotion management entails emotion recognition (also known as *emotion knowledge*), emotion tolerance, and emotion regulation. Impairments of emotion knowledge, which can already be observed in preschool children, cluster into three categories (Izard, Fine, et al., 2001; Schultz, Izard, Ackerman, & Youngstrom, 2001). The first category is emotion recognition knowledge, the ability to accurately recognize emotions from their displays on another's face. Emotion recognition knowledge is assessed by presenting standardized pictures of facial displays of emotions and asking children to name them. Emotion recognition knowledge implies that the child can recognize emotions in himself as a precondition for recognizing them in another. The second category is emotion situation knowledge, the capacity to correctly name the emotion appropriate to a situation. The child subject is read a brief vignette—for example, a child is given a present—and asked to name the emotion the person would feel. The third aspect of emotion knowledge is emotion role taking: This means that the child can properly identify how a person in a vignette is actually feeling based on their facial and other expressions when that expression is discordant with what the culturally conditioned normative emotion might be in that situation. Children who grow up to become adults with psychopathologies are often people who have difficulties managing their emotions. These difficulties in adulthood arise in part because of problems with emotion socialization in childhood. Problems with emotion socialization can be identified by deficits in preschoolers' emotion recognition knowledge, emotion situation knowledge, and emotion role taking.

Healthy, adaptive emotion education and socialization should be the birthright of all children. Our clients, to a greater or lesser degree, did not receive the "good enough" emotion education and socialization that is every child's due. Things that should happen for every child did not happen for this child. Impairments of emotion learning and socialization contribute to our clients' affect dysregulation.

As a result of impairments in emotion management originating in the family of origin, these individuals experienced more difficulty in preschool peer relationships and developed less prosocial behaviors and more maladaptive psychological problems. One can begin to recognize the process by which the elements of a distressed personality emerge. I use the word *distressed* to refer to the personality characterized in part by impaired emotion management, because the word connotes being under great stress as well as being in a state of danger. The distressed person is in need of relief from the stress and suffering caused in part by his or her impairments of emotion regulation. Furthermore, affect dysregulation endangers the distressed person in social situations, at work, in relationships, and in relations with the law, because the distressed individual is at risk for the consequences of acting out, inappropriate emotion expression, conflict, and vicarious emotional expression through the abuse of legal or illicit substances.

Emergence of the Distressed Self Structure

An infant's experiences with her caregiver determine the primordial structure of her emerging self. That primordial structure then specifies the nature of her interactions with the environment in the next developmental stage, and in turn that interaction of previous conditioning with current experience directs the further structuring of her personality. The process by which experience and prior conditioning interact to produce further structure in the personality is called *self-organization*. This iterative process occurring over developmental stages results in successively more ordered, more determined personality structure. Principles of self-organization (Izard et al., 2000; Lewis, 2000) describe how early experience guides and directs the spontaneous emergence of more ordered, more determined personality structure. Affective socialization is one of the most potent, early forces acting to determine the structure of the emerging self or personality. Affective socialization in infancy and childhood is critical because it molds the most fundamental qualities of the personality and determines the nature of the developmental pathway upon which the child embarks. When early affective socialization is adequate, the emerging personality is more likely to become adaptive and positively functioning. When early affective socialization is impaired, the emerging self is more likely to develop maladaptively and to function in a less positive way.

The person who appears for therapy today is more likely to be a person who exited the family of infancy and early childhood with impaired emotion management skills. In the preschool social environment, those impairments of emotion management conditioned negative assessments by peers and teachers, entailed less competent academic performance, and predicted internalizing and externalizing behaviors. The accumulating difficulties in peer relationships, with teachers, with academic performance, and with aggressiveness or withdrawal, further determined a self that became increasingly organized around a core of affective–cognitive structures of failure or inadequacy. Affect dysregulation progressed from difficulty with recognizing and managing the core affects of anger, fear, joy, or sadness to difficulty recognizing and managing the more complex constructs of shame affect and disgust affect or the emotions of contempt and loneliness (Lonigan, Carey, & Finch, 1994).

An overarching principle of self-organization theory is that from birth onward at least through adolescence the self is in the process of continuously self-organizing. This self interacts with a social environment that responds positively or negatively to it (Denham, Zoller, & Couchoud, 1994; Schultz et al., 2001; Youngstrom, Izard, & Ackerman, 1999). A dynamic reciprocity exists. The consequences of positive or negative outcomes in each emotion-laden situation determine the structure across time and experience of the self that is organizing.

This book proposes that three factors combine to influence the emergence of personality. When all three are on balance positive, a positively functioning, well-adapted self emerges. When the balance tilts negatively, then a distressed personality is more likely to form. The first factor is genetics, which will be discussed in Chapter 1 when we learn how inheritance sets the thresholds for affects. The second factor is attachment, and refers to the quality of the relationship between infant and caregiver during the first three to four years of life. When there are failures of affect and emotion socialization in the family of origin during this early period, a developmental pathway is enjoined that can lead to emergence of an increasingly distressed self. Failures of affect and emotion socialization during attachment are termed *deficit experience*, and the effects of deficit experience will be discussed in depth in Chapter 2. The third factor is childhood socioemotional history and refers to the quality of life's vicissitudes in the period from 3 or 4 years through adolescence. When the quality is relatively benign, the developmental outcomes are positive. When there is adverse or traumatic experience during this period, negative outcomes are more probable. I will briefly discuss adverse and traumatic childhood experience in this Introduction and offer a lengthier presentation in Chapter 3.

Adversity: Compounding the Problem

Adverse childhood experience is a large collective grouping that subsumes the full range of stressful childhood events (Anda et al., 1999). Childhood physical and sexual abuse have traditionally been conceptualized as trauma (e.g., Briere & Runtz, 1993; Herman, 1992). In addition to these traumatic events, adverse childhood experiences include experiences of verbal abuse, a battered mother, parental separation or divorce, mental illness in the household, household substance abuse, and incarcerated household members. Adverse and traumatic childhood experiences are things that should never happen to any child and did happen to this child. These lists of acts or actions have traditionally defined traumatic experience, but in recent years theorists have begun to redefine trauma in terms of its effect on the victim. Shapiro (1995) has been a leader in this movement.

When a child is subjected to certain events—being verbally abused, witnessing spousal abuse, being sexually abused, being physically abused—the result is that the nervous system is imbalanced (Shapiro, 1995). Trauma is now defined as experience that imbalances or overwhelms the nervous system. Apparently adverse childhood experiences of all kinds induce imbalance. Shapiro wrote: "the information acquired at the time of the [traumatic] event, including images, sounds, affect, and physical sensations, is maintained neurologically in its disturbing state" (p. 30). When information acquired at the time of trauma is maintained in an excitatory state, it is referred to as "trauma coded" (Schwartz, Galperin, & Masters, 1995a).

In particular, the emotions experienced at the time of the traumatic event become trauma coded. Trauma coded emotions along with trauma coded sensations and thoughts are held in a state-specific, excitatory form in which they are more likely to be elicited subsequently in any situation sharing any valence with the original situation. Trauma coded emotions are unresolved. They may be elicited by internal or external stimuli. Trauma coded emotions are distressing because they recur and because they adversely affect current behavior. They may be assembled with images in the form of nightmares or flashbacks, or they may be elicited in current situations where they appear in an extreme form that is inappropriate to the present situation.

Adverse and traumatic childhood experiences contribute to the emergence of a distressed personality. Emergence of a distressed personality is one of the sequelae of adverse and traumatic childhood experience. A healthy attachment and "good enough" affect and emotion socialization can ameliorate the effects of adverse and traumatic childhood experience. Deficit experience, where present, can worsen the effects of adversity and trauma for the emerging self. The distressed personality of adolescence and adulthood can result from adverse or traumatic childhood experience, from deficit experience, or from a combination of the two.

A VOYAGE OF BOTH THEORY AND PRACTICE

In the course of this book, we will discover how the collectivity of the emotions and their properties and vicissitudes contribute along with other factors to formation of the personality or self, whether adaptive or distressed. The principal objective of this book is practical: the transmission of clinical skills that are immediately applicable. The goal is to transmit AMST skills with sufficient clarity and detail that clinicians can apply the protocol in their psychotherapeutic practice. Theory and research are presented to substantiate the skills and to broaden the reader's knowledge of affects, emotions, and their vicissitudes.

The book's journey is divided into two major sections. The first, comprising Chapters 1 through 4, provides the foundation for the very practical skills taught in the second section, Chapters 5 through 11. The final chapter offers the beginnings of an ACT, demonstrating how principles and techniques transmitted in earlier chapters can be integrated into the second phase of therapy. Chapter 1 describes the emotion system, and Chapter 2 lays out the development of emotion regulation from birth through adolescence. Chapter 3 teaches the causes of emotion dysregulation, and Chapter 4 demonstrates how emotion dysregulation presents in psychopathology. The argument constructed through out Part I is that acquisition of affect and emotion regulation skills is the first key to mental health, and failures of their regulation are central to many of the problems that distress people and bring them to our offices. A corollary of this argument is that acquisition of affect and emotion regulation skills will facilitate the deeper work of trauma resolution. Clinicians will come to understand how a client's working through, deconstruction of defenses, and personality reorganization are all facilitated by first teaching the client the skills to regulate his or her affects.

Part II of the book teaches practical, effective, efficient techniques for affect regulation. Teaching these skills is the principal objective of this book. The clinician will immediately be able to use the techniques and methods presented herein. These skills can form the basis of a brief therapy whose goal can be the immediate improvement of the client's emotion regulation status. The skills presented in Part II can usually be taught to the client in six one hour sessions. The skills may also form the basis of a longer term therapy designed to restructure the client's self system. AMST and ACT assert that learning emotion management remediates deficits in the client's early childhood experience and that acquisition of affect regulation skills is a necessary prerequisite for reorganization of the self toward a more adaptive, more positively functioning state.

Part I

EMOTION REGULATION IN HEALTH AND DISORDER

Chapter 1

Emotion Regulation: The Foundation of Self

Emotions are everywhere, motivating all human activity. They are a lot like the tectonic plates of the earth's crust: often they are deeply hidden, expressing themselves in complex surface features. Occasionally they explode to the surface like a volcano's violent eruption. We are so captivated by and immersed in the surface features, the art, poetry, politics, relationships, sex, sports, work, play, love, wars, and violence that we often fail to attend to the emotions at play in life's activities. Sroufe (1996) proposed that emotions are constructs that can be operationally defined by behaviors accompanying them. Some of these behaviors are facial expressions, some are motor behaviors, some vocal, and some autonomic. Notice your own facial expression, and motoric, vocal, and autonomic responses as you visualize for a moment the face of one of your children or someone else dear to you. Now visualize a police officer stopping your vehicle and notice again how your face, body, voice, and autonomic system respond. Now visualize the events of September 11, 2001, and again check your emotional response. For each visualization you may be aware of the shifting balance between the rational mind and the emotional mind (Goleman, 1995). Often, the rational mind is more prominent in awareness, providing as it does the act of comprehension. Just as powerful though, the emotional mind provides another way of knowing that is impulsive and powerful. The balance operates "with emotion feeding into and informing the operations of the rational mind, and the rational mind refining and sometimes vetoing the inputs of the emotions" (Goleman, 1995, p. 9). To experience how the balance can be destroyed, visualize for a moment someone threatening the child you imaged above.

Human interactions are conversations in which emotional and rational information are equally exchanged although for the most part people are far less aware of the emotive component. Like everyday interactions, the therapeutic encounter is both a rational and emotional conversation. The therapeutic conversation is fraught with emotions, and the vectors go from therapist to client as well as from client to clinician. Many clinicians will be familiar with the cassette of emotions Theodore Millon offers in presenting Ann, his first patient with a diagnosis of border line personality disorder (BPD), "she may exhibit conflicting emotions simultaneously toward others and herself, most notably love, rage, and guilt" (Millon, 1998, p. 13). Linehan (1993) discussed the affective vector from therapist toward the borderline client. The therapist can vacillate between "unchecked empathy, warmth, and friendliness" (p. 383) and rage when the client questions the therapist's competence or overwhelms the therapist with neediness. Therapists must regularly control their own emotions in the service of the client's best interests. A clinician may suppress disgust when listening to a bulimic patient's disclosures regarding vomiting, or anguish when a client uncovers childhood sexual abuse. Many therapists may not be aware of how the affect of interest functions in suppressing emotional reactions to client disclosures, or how the affect of enjoyment–joy motivates a return day after day to the therapeutic encounter.

THE HUMAN AFFECT SYSTEM

In order to comprehend the primacy of affects in human experience, in order to understand that affect regulation forms the foundation of healthy human adaptation, and that affect dysregulation is the basis of the clinical and personality disorders, we must begin by defining the affects. This chapter will specify how each affect is recognized and will establish a neurobiological basis for its expression. This information serves the book's practical goal of transmitting affect management skills training (AMST), because the affect-oriented therapist must become adept at navigating the territory of affects and emotions to best help the client.

The brain is the physiological platform that generates the affects, cognitions, sensations, memories, impulses, behaviors, and drives that together constitute human experience. These elements interact, reflecting the interconnectedness of the anatomical elements of the platform. Tomkins (1962, 1963, discussed in Nathanson, 1992) distinguished between affects, feelings, emotions, and moods. He taught that the affects are hard-wired in the brain. Affects are a limited number of genetically determined responses defined "within a complex perceptual-cognitive-physiological-behavioral reaction" (Sroufe, 1996, p. 37). Affects become feelings when we become aware of them, according to Tomkins. Affects develop into emotions as we accumulate experience and memories relating to them. The concept of an emotion also includes the affective responses we feel toward affects, as when one says, "I feel really ashamed that I got so angry." Tomkins identified nine fundamental affects: interest–excitement, enjoyment–joy, surprise–startle, fear–terror, distress–anguish, anger-rage, dissmell, disgust, and shame-humiliation. Izard (1991) has modified and expanded the basic set to include guilt, contempt, and shyness. As we will see, socialization of these fundamental affects, their tempering by experience, and their interactions with each other, with cognition, and with drives engenders an elaborate *emotionscape* consisting of hundreds of nuanced emotions. Our practical goal, driven by clinical concerns, is to develop a language we can use as a basis for the therapeutic skills and tools of AMST.

Evolution of the Physiological Platform of the Emotion System

To grasp the extraordinary power of affects and emotions in a client's psychopathology—for example, the anorexic's ability to starve herself to death or the spousal abuser's inability to control his violent behaviors—it helps to see the all too human client as having evolved from reptilian forebears. Evolution of the primate brain from its reptilian and protomammalian ancestors is intertwined with evolution of the affect system. MacLean (1990, 1993) described the evolution of the mammalian brain. He argued that as the human forebrain evolved and expanded from its ancestors, it retained many of the structures and features of those forebears. The central evolutionary fact is that as the three elements of the human brain—the reptilian brain, the limbic system, and the neomammalian brain—evolved from our reptilian ancestors, the emotion system evolved with it. The remnants of our reptilian ancestors' contribution to the human brain can be recognized in what MacLean termed the *R-complex*. Understanding the R-complex and its interrelations with the limbic system and forebrain can help conceptualize some of the problems clients bring to therapy.

The repetitive behaviors of obsessive–compulsive disorder (OCD) and the motor and vocal tics of Tourette's disorder, as well as many normal human behaviors like face rubbing, can be traced to patterns inherited from our reptilian ancestors. Understanding how the affect system interconnects with the R-complex will help us make sense of Waltner-Toews's (2002) promising study showing that AMST can help alleviate OCD symptoms. The R-complex apparently regulates the daily master routines and subroutines of our activity cycle. Also known as the striatal complex, the primarily dopaminergic R-complex resides at the core of what MacLean termed the triune brain (see Figure 1.1). The R-complex receives neural projections from both the limbic system and the neocortex. Based on extensive studies in lizards and monkeys and on analysis of human clinical conditions (Parkinson's disease, Huntington's chorea, and Sydenham's chorea), MacLean hypothesized that the R-complex generates what he called *protomentation*, a term that refers to repetitive behaviors like walking the same path day after day and to imitative behaviors like copying others. It also refers to our positive responses to representations such as faces, fetishes, the visual arts, and advertising. Displacement behavior, grooming, face rubbing, hand rubbing, and head scratching, for example, is apparently generated by the R-complex. The R-complex also generates the four types of nonverbal behaviors that MacLean called prosematic displays: signature, territorial, courtship, and submission. The signature display is an identifying behavior by which organisms announce their unique individuality. The lizards MacLean studied accomplish this with head bobs. Inner city gang members achieve the same goal with complex finger signal displays called "flashing signs." Human males' territorial display consists of widening the eyes and holding the arms away from the torso. Submission

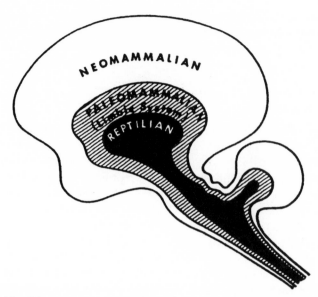

Figure 1.1. The Triune Brain. The diagram illustrates MacLean's hypothesis of the evolution of the human forebrain from its reptilian and early mammalian ancestors. The limbic system evolved as the early mammals (paleomammals) emerged from the reptiles. Adapted from P. MacLean (1990).

entails briefly ducking the head and closing the eyes. We are probably most familiar with the upward jerking of eyebrows as the person glances sideways that defines flirtation, a form of courtship behavior in many cultures.

From a clinical perspective, R-complex involvement is suggested in OCD, in which repetitive, displacement-type subroutine behaviors such as, hand washing develop and eventually interfere with master routines (e.g., going to work). The robust connections between the limbic system and the R-complex at least provide anatomical support for the belief that affect generated in the limbic system could be involved in generating the repetitive behaviors of OCD. The fact that AMST interventions could result in a significant reduction of OCD behaviors (Waltner-Toews, 2002) suggests, although it does not prove, that compulsive behaviors originating in the R-complex may function to regulate overwhelming affect, and that when the organism is provided with alternative means to regulate affect, the OCD behaviors disappear. The verbalizations of Tourette's syndrome demonstrate as well how a subroutine can interfere with the master routine of communication. MacLean also suggested that displacement behaviors such as face rubbing occur when electrical activity in the limbic system spills over into the R-complex. The clinician can notice these displacement behaviors as indicators of emotional activity. Through its connections to the limbic system and forebrain, the R-complex, a primitive part of the human brain that we inherit from our reptilian ancestors, plays a role in some of the disorders AMST can help treat.

The limbic system, where much of our primitive affect originates, evolved from reptilian precursors and with it came many of the behaviors we identify as uniquely human. As mammals evolved from reptiles, three new types of behaviors appeared: nursing and maternal care, audiovisual communication for maintaining contact between infant and mother, and play (MacLean, 1990). Nursing and maternal care and the behaviors for maintaining contact are central features of the attachment system (Bowlby, 1969), which will be discussed in detail in Chapter 2. Paralleling the evolutionary appearance of mammals with their unique new behaviors, the primitive, rudimentary cortex of our reptilian ancestors ballooned out to become the paleomammalian formation or limbic system (MacLean, 1990). In its earliest embodiment in primitive mammalian ancestors, based as it was on the sense of smell, this system, which was essentially reflexive, used smell to signal the body as to what to flee, what to attack, what to eat, what to mate with. Integrating data from anatomical studies, from neurophysiological experiments, and from clinical findings, MacLean created the limbic system hypothesis. Maternal caregiving behavior, attachment, and affect socialization are tightly interwoven components that affect formation of both adaptive and maladaptive self structures. We can better understand how AMST facilitates improved client functioning by developing a conception of the limbic system's evolution and its robust interconnectedness with all organ systems.

The limbic system functions as a central processing unit where inputs from the external environment, the internal somatic environment, and the forebrain are assembled in the early stage of creating impulses to behavior. Forming a ring around the brainstem, the limbic system comprises three nuclear divisions: the amygdala, septum, and thalamocingulate. The hippocampus, a prominent limbic cortical structure, interconnects to the amygdalar and septal nuclei (MacLean, 1993). The limbic system receives information from visceral systems concerned with maintenance and reproduction of the body itself. Inputs from somatic systems concerned with adjustment to the environment also reach the limbic system. The elements of the limbic system project to the hypothalamus, backward to the R-complex, and forward to the neocortex. Because they are thus reciprocally interconnected, the limbic system elements function as information hubs correlating immediate experience, sensation, perception, emotion, and memory. Limbic system elements provide information to the organism in the form of qualia, the "simple sensory qualities" of colors and tones (Damasio, 1999). Information about the internal environment is also transmitted as qualia, the sensory feelings. Elements of the limbic system amplify or decrease the intensity of feelings. Our sense of time and space is generated in the limbic system. The free-floating affective feelings that tell us what is real, true, and important arise in the limbic system, and the system is involved in our sense of personal identity. The limbic system and the emotion awareness it conveys provided a selective advantage to our protomammalian evolutionary progenitors.

LeDoux (1996) has highlighted the two central elements of MacLean's limbic system hypothesis. One was his emphasis on evolution as the key to understanding affects: As the paleomammalian cortex and then the neocortex evolved from the R-complex, the affect system evolved with it. The second central element of the limbic system hypothesis was the concept that feelings arise when information from the outside world is assembled with body sensations. In critically examining the limbic system concept, LeDoux has called attention to the fact that the limbic system includes areas, in particular the hippocampus, that are less involved in emotion and autonomic regulation than in cognition. According to LeDoux, "evidence that one limbic area is involved in some emotional process has often been generalized to validate the idea the limbic system as a whole is involved in emotion" (p 102). He continued, "there may not be one emotional system in the brain but many" (p. 103). Recent neurophysiological evidence demonstrating that fear is regulated in the amygdala while disgust is regulated in the insula supports the belief that there are multiple affective systems operating in the brain (Calder, Lawrence, & Young, 2001; Krolak-Salmon et al., 2003).

AMST is founded on a developmental and evolutionary concept of the affects, and it integrates the centrality of sensations to affect regulation that is implicit in the limbic hypothesis. Clinical application of AMST will be assisted by comprehending the plurality of the limbic system. The evolutionary construct can help in the counseling office too. It helps to know that some affective elements, such as fear and anger, are evolutionarily very old, coming to us from reptilian progenitors, while others, such as disgust, come from the first protomammalian forebears. Still others, such as shame and sadness, are even more recent, probably having evolved after mammals were well established. AMST manipulates cognitions as well as affects, sensations, and behaviors, and the protocol's approach to cognitions can best be understood when they are placed in the same evolutionary context as the affects. We turn our attention now to the evolution of the forebrain where cognitions are believed to originate.

The forebrain evolved from the limbic system, and that fact helps us comprehend how profoundly affect influences thought. Knowing that the forebrain evolved out of the limbic system will also clarify how a neocortical structure, the orbitofrontal cortex, came to have a central position in the regulation of affects. In MacLean's triune brain model, the forebrain is called the neomammalian formation. It consists of the neocortex and thalamic structures and constitutes the third component of the triune brain (MacLean, 1990). Connecting the visual, auditory, and somatic systems, the neomammalian formation is primarily oriented to the external world. It functions in problem solving, learning, memory for detail, language, and communication of subjective states. Because the cognitive brain (neocortex) evolved out of the affective brain (limbic system), the emotion system forms the basis of the cognition system. Emotions organize and motivate perception, thought, and action. They motivate and organize individual behavior and social behavior. New research has demonstrated that even moral decision making, a behavior we have cherished as being entirely cognitive, is driven by emotion (Greene et al., 2001) And, as we shall learn in Chapter 2, our very self-concept develops out of the process of acquisition of emotional regulation skills. With this brief background in evolutionary neurobiology, let us now look at the affects themselves and how they have evolved as the central nervous system itself evolved.

Evolution of the Affects

We can best comprehend the power of affects by realizing that they evolved from reflexes as the human brain evolved. Izard (1991) has developed the evolutionary theme, describing how affects have evolved out of the more primitive reflexes, instincts, and drives, paralleling the evolution of the human brain from its more primitive antecedents. Affect systems have been selected by evolutionary forces acting again and again in situations that have regularly recurred in the lives of individuals and populations over time (LeDoux, 1996).Reflexes are the paradigmatic behaviors of the brainstem. Direct stimulation of a receptor provides the necessary and sufficient motivation for a reflex. The eye blink and gag reflexes in humans are good examples, as is the withdrawal reflex from a painful stimulus. These are automatic actions. There is no appraisal process. In the evolutionary model, the eye blink reflex constitutes the evolutionary ancestor of the affect surprise–startle; the gag reflex is the forerunner of the affect disgust; the withdrawal reflex is the forerunner of the avoidance and fear affect. Instincts, characteristic of infrahuman species, are more complex than reflexes. Hormonal changes motivate the instincts, which appear as characteristic and stereotypical fixed action patterns. The behaviors known collectively as *attachment*, which we shall discuss in more detail in the next chapter, may be the closest humans come to instinctual behavior. As noted earlier, affects evolved from reflexes as the limbic system evolved from the reptilian brain. Affect regulation is transmitted from primary caregiver to infant in the context of the infant–caregiver dyad, which is driven by instinctual attachment behaviors. Grasping these central facts helps us understand the power of affects and the importance of AMST for regulating them.

Physiological drives such as the sex drive or hunger drive can assemble with affects to produce the characteristic behaviors of some clinical disorders. An organism's physiology provides constantly updated information about its basic survival needs. Drives are the behaviors motivated by these physiological needs. These include hunger, thirst, waste elimination, pain avoidance, and sex. Signals from internal receptors, such as the body's system for measuring blood oxygenation, signal the body's homeostatic status. Some of the drives are very important in regulating the newborn's behavior. Psychology has largely discarded Freud's drive theory which attempted to explain all human behavior in terms of sex drive and aggression drive (Nathauson, 1992). We will examine some instances where emotions have assembled with cognitions and drives in disordered states. For example, the hunger drive is apparently assembled with trauma coded emotions and cognitions in the eating disorders. The sex drive can be assembled with trauma coded emotions and cognitions in the paraphilias. When therapists understand how drives and affects can become associated in clinical disorders, they can readily see the importance of teaching the client new affect regulation skills with AMST and then desensitizing trauma coded affects with ACT.

Understanding affects in the context of an evolutionary model helps us grasp how affects manifest in personality disorders. The evolutionary point of view toward emotions teaches that the basic affects, the building blocks for the range of emotions, can be seen as developing from fundamental biological needs (Izard, 1991). Reviewing briefly the fundamental biological basis of the affects may help the clinician to develop a metaphorical sense about the functional significance of emotion for the clinically or personality disordered client. When a client is fearful, for example, his biology is telling him his survival is threatened. By way of illustration, the *DSM-IV* does not mention the affect fear in discussing BPD, nor did Millon in the quote cited above, yet the therapist can better understand his borderline client and her needs if he understands that "frantic efforts to avoid real or imagined abandonment"(APA, 1994, p. 654) describes the borderline client's behavior and is assembled with intense fear that her physical survival is threatened. Fear affect and instinctually driven attachment behavior intertwine in BPD, and understanding these chthonic origins can demystify BPD for the affect centered therapist.

Evolution of each of the basic affects was conditioned by survival needs. From the evolutionary viewpoint, fear is the affect of protection, a response to pain or threat that ensures survival whether through immobilization or flight. Anger affect defends personal, physical integrity by destroying blocks to survival needs. Disgust affect has evolved from the need to reject toxic substances (e.g., rotten meat). Incorporation, the adaptive behavior of taking in food and water, is the biological basis of acceptance, which is a component of the affect of yearning for merger that I propose later in this chapter. Responses associated with sex, the biological behavior of reproduction, are the basis for joy affect. Deprivation, the biological basis of distress–anguish affect, reflects the loss of a pleasurable object, and in particular this may derive from separation from the attachment figure. The surprise–startle affect is based on the orienting response, the biological behavior of reacting to new objects in the environment. Exploration, a biological behavior that leads to new sources of food and new habitats, is the basis of interest–excitement, the fundamental affect in curiosity. Shame, contempt, and guilt, relative late comers to the emotionscape, regulate destructive aggression and maintain social cohesion, necessary factors in the survival of a social creature like the human.

Descartes and the Enlightenment biased us toward cognition and the belief that humans have escaped our animal origins on the wings of thought. In fact, we humans are fundamentally emoting beings who think. As Nathanson (1992) stated, "[affect] is a form of thinking—the action thinking of the old brain" (p. 60). The concept of an affect system entirely distinct from the cognition, behavior, and motivation systems is no longer tenable in light of recent neurophysiological research. Forgas (1995) discussed the history of the separation of experience into discrete dimensions of cognition and affect. Lazarus (1982) exemplified the position that cognition is the primary process in all experience, while Zajonc (1984) and Izard (1993) presented the opposing view that affect precedes and is distinct from cognition. The current synthesis, as exemplified by Freeman (2000), suggests that limbic and neocortical areas in each brain hemisphere, contributing affect, sensation, and cognition, enter into "a cooperative state" (p. 230) leading to intentional action. Neurodynamics has replaced the out-dated billiard ball analogy for generating behavior and awareness. Understanding affects and cognitions from an evolutionary perspective highlights the importance of adaptive affect regulation for the emergence of the positively functioning self. This understanding also emphasizes the crucial necessity for remediating deficiencies in affect regulation with AMST as a component of treating psychopathology from an affect centered perspective.

Features of the Emotion System

We have seen how affects evolved in parallel with the evolution of the brain itself. Let us now examine some of the general properties of affects in preparation for looking at key affects individually. Learning the general properties of affects will position clinican readers to make best use of AMST for the client's benefit.

Affects Motivate and Arouse: Affects fundamentally facilitate either approach or avoidance. Lang (1995) described affects and emotions as action dispositions comprised of functional behaviors, evaluative and expressive language, and physiological events mediated by the somatic and autonomic nervous system. For Lang (1995), the affects "reflect central activation and preparation for action" (p. 373). He divided affects into two systems: the appetitive system of approach, which is consummatory, sexual, and nurturant and the aversive system of avoidance or escape, which is protective, withdrawing, and defensive. Each affect in the two affect systems, according to Lang, can be distributed along two dimensions, valence and activation. Affective valence is primary and bipolar, distributed between positivity (the appetitive pole) and negativity (the aversive, unpleasant pole). The second dimension is activation or system arousal, which affects the physiological and neural components of either or both of the valence dimensions. Lang and his laboratory have developed a standard set of 360 affect- and emotion-eliciting pictures. Study participants view the picture set and are then rated for affective valence and arousal. Significantly, subjects' facial muscle activity, pulse rate, and skin conductance covary with the parameters of affective valence and arousal. Lang's work supports the central position AMST accords to sensations.

Autonomic Mediation: The autonomic nervous system mediates an organism's affective experience. Each of the fundamental emotions has its own unique signature of brain, heart, pulmonary, striated muscle, smooth muscle, and skin responses (Izard, 1991), reflecting the fact that each emotion has its unique signature pattern of autonomic nervous system activation. These responses in turn manifest the fact that limbic, cortical, and R-complex structures all project to the autonomic nervous system whose two branches, parasympathetic and sympathetic, in turn dually innervate all organs, glands, and smooth muscles save the piloerectors. Afferent sensory fibers carry information about the body's autonomic and motoric response status back to the central nervous system thus producing the qualia, the feelings of an emotion. This feedback from the neuromuscular-expressive system and from the neural, motor, and somatic systems produces conscious awareness of the emotion, telling us what emotion we are experiencing.

The felt quality of an affect is unique (Nathanson, 1992) and stable over life (Izard, 1991). Clinically, as we will learn in Part II of the book, the AMST develops the client's awareness of these sensations and teaches him to cognize the related affects.

Amplification: Affects function to amplify the highly specific stimulus pattern that sets each affect in motion (Nathanson, 1992). The affects operate in association with the reticular activating system, an auxiliary system in the brainstem that amplifies or attenuates levels of neural system activation (Izard, 1991). As Nathanson wrote, "Whatever is important to us is made so by affect. Affect is the engine that drives us" (p. 59).

Facial Display: Each affect manifests in a unique facial display. Izard (1991) studied the outward expression of emotion. His laboratory demonstrated that each of the fundamental affects has its own action pattern in the eyes, mouth, and forehead regions of the face. These outward signs communicate to others what we are feeling. They are a vital component of the dialectic between therapist and patient. The clinician will have little difficulty in recognizing intense emotional expression, because it reveals itself in compelling actions and responses that take over large portions of the body's response system (Izard, 1991). However, mild and moderate emotion is often manifest in physiological responses that may be below the level of conscious awareness. As we shall learn, the AMST is designed in part to raise these less compelling signals to awareness.

Thresholds: Each affect apparently has its own threshold, which appears to be genetically determined. The threshold can be low, in which case the individual is exquisitely sensitive to that affect, or it can be high, in which case the person has difficulty experiencing that affect. Research may have uncovered the genetic basis of thresholds for distress–anguish affect (Zubieta et al., 2003). Using techniques from molecular biology and neurophysiology, the research demonstrated that subjects who were sensitive to pain had two copies (LL) of a gene coding a low activity form of an enzyme that degrades dopamine. Participants with a high threshold for pain had two copies (HH) of a high activity form of the enzyme. Pain, which was induced by injecting saline into the jaw muscle, elicited the affect distress–anguish. The LL genotype conferred a low threshold for distress–anguish affect, and the HH genotype conferred a high threshold. We will learn how distress affect is elicited by sustained, greater than optimal stimulation. Too much perceptual stimulation and too much separation (loss) trigger distress. These results help clarify how the same experience of loss can provoke anguish in one client and stoic acceptance in another. The results also help us understand that clients with whom we use AMST have different genetic makeups and that genetic variability may explain some differences in emotion responding.

Affective Priming: A fearful client will be more susceptible to a startle response than a happy client. The emotions prime other responses according to Lang's motivational priming hypothesis (1995). Images, memories, cognitions, and impulses to behavior that are linked in the brain to the motivational system that is currently engaged will have a higher probability of access at a stronger potential output strength. Material that is not linked to the engaged motivational system will be less likely to appear or will appear at a lower activity level. Lang (1995) has demonstrated how the unconditioned exteroceptive reflex of startle ("startle reflex") is affected by the emotion priming state of the organism. Using the eye blink component of the startle reflex, Lang demonstrated that aversive stimuli (i.e., negatively valenced pictures), augment the startle reflex, while appetitive stimuli, such as pleasant pictures, inhibit the startle reflex. Comparative neuroanatomical studies between rat and human suggest that the amygdala plays a key role in motivational priming of defensive reflexes. AMST is based in part on the concept of affective priming. The preparation for skills III to VII affectively primes the client by asking her to visualize a time she felt anger, for example. Affectively priming the client for anger at a low level of arousal opens a neural network that includes images, cognitions, and memories. The affect oriented clinician will consciously employ affective priming for the client's benefit throughout the therapy.

Affects Motivate Cognitions: An angry client will think angry thoughts, and a sad client will think sad ones. Affects assemble with cognitions in the brain to form affective–cognitive structures in which image, thought, symbol, and affect are linked in a unit (Izard, 1991) Lewis (2000) called the unit an *emotional interpretation*; Freeman (2000) called the same unit an *intentional state*. These become organized into a unit because they are frequently associated. Neurophysiological research has uncovered a fundamental property of neurons called long term potentiation (LTP) that explains how affective–cognitive structures might form as the brain learns and memories are constructed (LeDoux, 1996). Affect provides the element of motivation in the affective–cognitive structure, which is the basis for an impulse to behavior, something Izard (1991) called a *specific action tendency*. Linkage of all three elements is termed an *affective–cognitive–behavioral structure*. AMST clinicians realize that affects provide the principle motivations for thoughts and behaviors.

Self-Organization of Affective Experience: Recall for a moment a client who has gotten in touch with an experience of loss and notice how his episode of sadness developed. As he retrieved an image of the loss, his flow of words may have been interrupted, and this may have been followed by a brief behavioral stilling. Then a flush appeared briefly on his cheeks and the corners of his mouth turned down. His eyes filmed. Then suddenly tears formed, followed by sobs, as sadness affect overtook him completely. The sad client's experience of sadness has organized itself within the client, gaining momentum as it recruits more and more systems. The most current understanding employs principles of self-organization theory to describe the development of an affective experience (Mascolo, Harkins, & Harakal, 2000). The component systems approach describes affective experiences arising from a series of partially distinct systems that includes appraisal, the affect producing systems encompassing all the autonomic and central nervous systems that generate feeling tone, and finally the voluntary and involuntary overt action systems.

Every therapist has had the clincial experience of watching a client's grief emerge, beginning perhaps with a memory to which a thought was added. The rapidly emerging experience gathers up sadness affect, brings autonomic responses on board, and soon the client is weeping, manifesting the emotional experience in overt behavior. Knowing how emotion experiences organize themselves, the affect oriented therapist can transmit skills to help the client intervene in the experience at its inception and thereby transmit mastery to the client.

Affects Influence Perceptions: Emotions and affects influence what we see and hear, and perceptions can be changed by the affect being experienced by the perceiver (Izard, 1991). Izard and coworkers induced anger in one experimental cohort and happiness in another, then presented the same set of pictures of emotion expressions to both groups. The angry cohort saw more anger expressions, while the happy cohort saw more happy expressions. An angry client will perceive the clinician in a different way from an interested or a shame-based client. An affect oriented clinician can help a client more accurately perceive his environments by teaching him AMST skills to regulate his affects.

Dissociation: Clients are often unaware of affects that have been evoked for them and are having an effect in their lives. This is because affects and emotions can be dissociated out of awareness. Braun (1988a) conceptualized mental health as the congruent, parallel functioning of four experiential elements, behavior, affect, sensation, and knowledge (BASK) on a time continuum. Dissociation is "the separation of an idea or thought process from the mainstream of consciousness" (p. 5). He explained that dissociation can occur in one or more of the BASK levels, and gave hypnotically induced anesthesia as an example of dissociating sensation and affect out of awareness. Herman (1992) discussed how overwhelming emotion can be removed from consciousness, which she defined as constriction. One of the sequelae of trauma, constriction is an "alteration of consciousness" (p. 42) characterized by numbing, "a state of detached calm in which terror, rage, and pain dissolve" (p. 42). Dissociation of affect occurs across a range of psychopathologies; it is not confined to the so-called dissociative disorders. Depressed people are often angry and unaware of it. Eating disordered clients often dissociate disgust, shame, and anger affects out of awareness. AMST provides the clinician with skills she can use to teach her client to bring formerly dissociated affects to awareness, where the client can learn to manage them.

Reality Testing: The affects ground consciousness in the body through the qualia, the physiological signals accompanying each affect, and this grounding provides the basis for reality testing. Affects and emotions are essential for the development of the ego function of reality testing (Rapaport, 1953, cited in Izard, 1991; Spitz [1965] and Jacobsen [1964] cited in Blanck & Blanck [1994]). Anna Freud (1992) defined reality testing as the ego function that allows the child to distinguish between sensations arising from outside the body and those arising inside. As the child develops, reality testing provides discriminations between fantasy, dream, wish, or imagination on the one hand and actuality on the other. For example, reality testing gives the infant the ability to distinguish between the wish for food and its actual manifestation. Later, with the help of the memory function, reality testing enables discrimination between self and object, and it is promoted by verbalizing first the content of the outer world and then the content of the inner world. Negative affect is essential to the development of reality testing, because both pleasure and unpleasure must be experienced before the function of judgment can crystallize. Clients with poorly developed reality testing abilities often have impairments in affect recognition, tolerance, and recognition. The borderline client, for example, may have difficulty distinguishing between the fantasy of being abandoned and actual abandonment. AMST is a protocol that can help these individuals, because it teaches the client to orient to the body and its physiological signals, thereby promoting reality testing.

Affects are Modular: Phobias demonstrate the property of affects to assemble with almost any image. A live tarantula may evoke interest in Bud, and terror in Babs who may not even want to look at pictures of spiders or hear them mentioned in conversation. The affects have the quality of abstractness, meaning that there is no inherent association between an affect and the eliciting stimulus (Nathanson, 1992). For example, the affect fear can be associated with a percept, a cognition, another affect, a memory, or an image. For some the image of a snake elicits fear and for others it elicits interest–excitement. Many clients learned to fear their emotions in childhood. For example, fear of anger appears to be a clinical finding in some depression. In these clients, anger expression was not allowed or was punished in childhood, and anger was dissociated out of awareness. This client cannot mobilize healthy aggression (assertiveness) in the service of the self. Depression may result from the constant expenditure of energy over time to keep anger out of awareness. As we will learn, the AMST can help this client connect with the sensations and then the qualia of anger.

Because affects are modular, any affect can be assembled with any other system's output. Nathanson (1992) called this property *generality*. Affect is independent of context. Affect can be assembled with drives, such as sex, hunger, or elimination. It can be assembled with other affects, with any thought, with any image, with any memory. One client may feel intense excitement assembled with the sex drive, while another may feel intense disgust. The client with posttraumatic stress disorder (PTSD) who has a sexual abuse history may experience fear affect assembled with the sex drive, while the client with dissociative identity disorder (DID) may experience startle affect assembled with the sex drive. Affects can even be sequestered in a portion of the body. My work with binge eating disorder (Omaha, 2000) and anorexia nervosa (Omaha, 2002, unpublished data) suggests that in these cases, disgust affect was assembled with the client's body fat (see Chapter 4).

Many clinicians have undoubtedly had clients say "I hate myself," or "I am furious with myself," or "I feel ashamed of myself." In each of these instances, an affect has assembled with the self-representation. Just as affects can assemble with representations of others, so they can assemble with the internal image of the self. When a client sitting in your office says, "I'm sad about my mom," you are observing the assembly of distress–anguish affect with the client's internal image of her mother. Clients may also assemble sadness with their self-image, which can result in such statements as, "I am pitiful." At the core of these statements lies an image of the self, thoughts, and memories of loss, and sadness affect assembled with the construct. A subsequent section will define the concept of self (see p. 48–52).

Elicitation: Affects and the stimuli that elicit them are tightly coupled. Each affect is elicited by a different stimulus pattern. Affects are analogues of the eliciting stimuli (Nathanson, 1992). The profile and time course of each affect matches the profile and time course of the eliciting stimulus. Nathanson offered the startle response as an example. Startle is a brief response to a brief stimulus, and thus the time course of startle matches the stimulus profile for startle. The stimulus that elicits anguish, for example, the loss of an attachment figure, is a prolonged stimulus—the loss persists over time—and the affective response is similarly prolonged.

Internal and Social Affective Process: When Stan is angry, his jaw muscles tense and his lips compress. If he is self-aware, these signals will tell him he's feeling angry. Just like Stan, the people around Stan perceive these same cues and give him a wide berth because, whether they are consciously aware of it or not, these cues tell them Stan is angry. Considered as information, affects give status reports to the self and to others. As they are expressed through the body's organ systems, affects continually provide information to the self through these feedback loops (Nathanson, 1992). Izard (1991) called this the internal process of affect, something he distinguishes from the social process of affect. In the social process, affect provides information to others about one's own state, and furthermore one person's emotion expression produces behavior in another person. In this manner, affects form the basis of socialization. The social process of affect lies at the core of marriage, childcare, and the social contract.

Affective Exchanges: From birth onwards, in every social situation, we humans are constantly engaged in affective exchanges. Infants broadcast affects at parents that signal their physiological status. A baby may broadcast distress when he's hungry or wet, or he may broadcast enjoyment when he's dry and fed. These same types of affective exchanges occur across the lifespan. Nathanson (1992) called the person displaying an affect a *broadcaster*. One who observes the broadcaster is called a *resonator* because if he chooses to, the resonator can experience the broadcaster's affect by mimicking the facial changes observed in the other and by recalling previous experiences of the broadcast affect. Mimicking the facial expression and recalling past experiences of the broadcast affect serve to autostimulate that affect, and since affects can be autostimulated, the resonator will experience the broadcast affect. Broadcasting, resonating, and autostimulating constitute a triad at the core of all affective exchanges. When infants broadcast affects, parents resonate and autostimulate, and so this triad forms the basis of good parenting. Affective exchanges can have adverse consequences, as, for example, when an alcoholic broadcasts anger and his codependent wife resonates with it and through autostimulation experiences anger that is not hers. Broadcast, resonance, and autostimulation form the basis of projection, projective identification, transference, and countertransference. It is through affective exchanges that we develop the function of empathy. Socialization of affect, Nathanson explains, teaches us to regulate our own affects and to regulate affects broadcast by others. Often individuals are socialized out of awareness of their own affective experience, and sometimes they may have no defenses or their defenses are permeable in terms of affect broadcast by another. The AMST boundary skill can remediate poor defenses against another's broadcast emotion. The social process of affect is a critical element in psychotherapy. For example,when the therapist shows acceptance, the client is able to accept the previously unacceptable.

Development of Affective Expression: Infants lack the ability to modulate levels of affective expression. As the self develops over time, a greater range of behavioral responses to an affect or emotion emerges (Lewis, 1993a). One developmental model hypothesizes that the newborn has one bipolar affective state at birth. One pole is negative or distressed; the other is positive or satiated. Emotion states are believed to differentiate out of this primitive state through maturation, socialization, and cognitive development. An alternative model suggests that some emotion states are preprogrammed, present at birth in an already developed form. The affects emerge at different stages on the developmental time-line. Four affects, shame, contempt, guilt, and shyness, require development of a self-concept in order to be experienced, and so these appear later. Development produces the ability to express fundamental emotional motivations through more organized and more complex behaviors. Faced with a fearful situation, the fundamental response is always avoidance, but the avoidant behavior is different across developmental time. In childhood, one may literally run away from a fearful situation, while the same individual in adulthood may "talk his way out" of a situation. The affect oriented clinician will recognize when a client's affect expression is unmodulated and infantile, just as he will recognize when another client demonstrates mature affect management skills. The clinician will tailor his treatment plan according to the client's affect regulation capability. The AMST may be regarded as remediating developmental deficits, because it teaches the client more organized and more complex behavioral responses to affects.

Blending: The primary affects are capable of intermingling. When elicited in nonexperimental situations, emotions often emerge in blends. Experimental situations tend to elicit the index emotion of interest to the experimenter (Stearns, 1993). Plutchik developed a theory for emotion blending from his list of eight primary affects that he arrayed on a wheel (see LeDoux, 1996 for a discussion). The secondary emotions arise from dyads blended from neighbors on the affect wheel. According to Plutchik, love is compounded from joy and acceptance, curiosity from surprise and acceptance, and modesty from fear and acceptance. Clinician readers will often have heard clients use the word *hate*. Many believe this emotion lies solely on the anger-rage continuum, but this is not entirely true.

Plutchik's theory suggests hate is compounded of anger affect and disgust affect. His theory helps us understand that the power of hatred arises from its assembly of anger with the primitive affect disgust. How many times have you heard a client say, "I hate myself!"? What exactly is going on when a client says that one part of of his being, the *I*, feels hatred for another part of his being, the *self* of *myself*? The question demands that *self* be defined.

AFFECT AND SELF

Just as we can hold an image of another person in mind, for example, a spouse, child, lover, partner, parent, team mate, or sibling, so too do we hold images of ourselves in mind. This internal representation of one's own body, its history, sensations, thoughts, memories, and affects and emotions *is* the self. Complicating the concept of self though is the fact that there are several selves, not just one, so the self is more properly thought of as a system of selves, rather than a single, unique entity. The normal self actually constitutes *several* collections of images of itself as well as memories, thoughts, and patterns of behavior relating to each collection that a human organism holds in mind. There are several collections or groupings, because there is not one self, there are several. The self is an ensemble of performers, it is not a soloist. Each of these images or self representations is assembled with affects and emotions. Usually one of the part selves comprising the self system is more dominant in the normal individual, and this part is what Watkins and Watkins (1997) termed the *core ego*.

> The core ego contains a number of behavioral and experiential items that are
> more or less constant in the normal individual, and which present to the individual
> and to the world a fairly consistent determination of the way he and others perceive
> his self. (p. 26)

The parts of the self system have relations with each other and emotional responses for each other. It is because humans are constituted of more or less distinct parts that a client can say, "I hate myself." The very construction of the statement implies that there is one part hating and another part judged to be hateful. Just as we humans engage in affective transactions with other humans, we also conduct *intrapsychic* affective transactions between parts of the self system. Intrapsychic affective transactions appear to play a role in depression and other psychopathologies, and a major thrust of AMST is to help the client identify the affects, while a thrust of affect centered therapy (ACT) is to help the client resolve the conflicts.

Watkins and Watkins's concept of core ego appears to correspond to what Damasio has termed the *autobiographical self* (1999), an entity built out of the individual's history that is stored in autobiographical memory. This self is the cumulative record of interactions between organism and environment and includes a record of physical experience, emotional experience, and behavioral acts. Interactions between organism and environment induce change in the organism—Damasio called these *second-order changes*—and these changes also contribute to the autobiographical self. Associated with the autobiographical self is a form of consciousness that Damasio referred to as *extended consciousness*. Extended consciousness, which is multilayered and elaborate, provides the organism with a unique identity that is oriented to personal historical time. Like the autobiographical self, extended consciousness evolves over the life span. According to Damasio, extended consciousness depends upon and derives from affects and emotions and the sensations accompanying them. Consciousness and affect are inseparable. Because the autobiographical self depends upon extended consciousness, and since extended consciousness cannot be separated from affect, it follows that the self is inseparable from affect. This point is central to AMST and ACT. Throughout the book a recurring theme states that AMST builds self and consciousness. AMST and ACT may be thought of as change agents that contribute to refashioning the autobiographical self. The self in the moment is reconfigured from moment to moment as the self interacts with a succession of objects in the environment. Autobiographical memory provides the stable framework of facts and experiences that orients and positions and embeds the self as it interacts with objects in the environment from moment to moment. The therapist is an important object in the environment, and interactions between therapist and client-self result in changes in the autobiographical self. AMST and ACT optimize those interactions with the result that therapeutic outcomes are positive.

Damasio referred to a single autobiographical self, but it is much more the case, especially in psychopathology, that the self is a collective of part selves. Watkins and Watkins (1997) termed these part selves *ego states*. Drawing from observations of the relationship among consciousness, intention, and behavior in waking, dream, and hypnotic states, these authors observed, "persons are multiplicities, not unities" (p. 9). Clusters of cognitions, sensations, memories, and emotions form within the overall structure that is here termed the *self system*, and these clusters constitute the ego states. The word *personality* is equivalent to *self system*, as I am using the term, but *personality* is so heavily freighted with extraneous associations that its use would complicate this presentation. The self system, then, is an assemblage of ego states, and at any one time, usually one of the ego states is dominant and is the one currently held in awareness. Watkins and Watkins (1997) referred to this as the "self in the now" (p. 5), and termed it the *executive ego state*. These authors wrote that an ego state is "*an organized system of behavior and experience whose elements are bound together by some common principle, and which is separated from other such states by a boundary that is more or less permeable*" (p. 25). Affective and emotional experience constitutes one of the elements bound together in an ego state, and this fact elevates the ego state concept to central importance for AMST and ACT. Substance abuse disorder illustrates the ego state concept. During periods when a substance abuser is not actively using, a nonabusing ego state is executive. At these times, the substance abuser may work, exercise, engage in family life, go to church, and socialize. When the substance abusing ego state becomes executive, the abuser buys drugs and uses them, avoids the family, and neglects his work, social life, church, and exercise. Like substance abuse disorder, bulimia is characterized by an alteration between situations where a binge ego state is executive, a purge ego state is executive, or a normally functioning ego state is executive. In bipolar disorder, a manic ego state alternates with a depressed ego state. In each of these disorders, executive control of the system shifts between different ego states. It will be useful to take a moment and examine what happens when executive control shifts from one part of the self system to another.

When the alcoholic steps up to the bar and orders a cocktail, he is experiencing himself as a drinker. His "drinking ego state" has become executive. There may be considerable delusional cognitions about his ability to manage his drinking assembled with this ego state, but the point for our purposes now is just to notice that he *feels* like a person who drinks. He may have just come from an AA meeting, and his drinking constitutes a relapse, which makes the ancillary point that at the moment of taking a drink, he does *not* feel like a person who doesn't drink; that is, his sober ego state is no longer executive. Watkins and Watkins (1997) discussed this shift of executive function in terms of Federn's concept of cathexis (1952). Cathexis is the psychological energy that activates psychological process. An internal representation, such as, an ego state, can be suffused with ego cathexis, and then that representation is experienced as being the self. When the ego state is not assembled with ego cathexis, it is experienced as not being a part of the self; it is experienced as an object. (In fairness, Federn believed that cathexis had two forms, object cathexis and ego cathexis; I have simplified his concept to one energy, that of ego cathexis, which is either assembled with a representation in which case it feels like self, or it is not, in which case the representation is experienced as an object.) As Watkins and Watkins wrote: "self is an energy, not a content, an energy that has only one characteristic, *the feeling of selfness*" (pp. 14–15). Thus, when the alcoholic enters a cocktail lounge, his drinking ego state is becoming executive and he *feels* like a man who drinks. Assembled with this ego state is the delusional belief that he is also a man who can "hold his liquor." The extent to which his sober ego state has become an object may be observed in his language, as when he says, "Yeah, sometimes you go to AA meetings." Referring to the self in the second person is a tip off that the ego state being referred to has been divested of ego cathexis and is now experienced as an object. The relapsing alcoholic's shifts of ego cathexis from sober ego state to drinking ego state and back are largely unconscious and out of his control. AMST and ACT can help the client, whether alcoholic or other diagnoses, by bringing the affects, sensations, and cognitions assembled with the disordered ego state to awareness, teaching new skills to manage these affects, and resolving those affects and experiences that are trauma coded.

The Development of the Self

The child's self develops over time beginning with representations of primary caretakers that are internalized and then become the patterns that structure the child's developing self. Many investigators contributed to the theory that children internalize a caregiver's representation. Bowlby (1969) spoke of internal working models. Piaget (Piaget & Inhelder, 1969) described the formation of schemas that are self-constructed mental structures. At birth the neonate has few schemas. Over the developmental time span schemas form, broaden, and differentiate through the processes of assimiliation and accommodation. Piaget's schema construct was largely cognitive. Mahler (Mahler, Pine, & Bergman, 1975) incorporated these concepts into a developmental view that emphasized the child's early symbiotic fusion with the primary caregiver and the subsequent separation and individuation of the child's evolving self out of the symbiosis. Kohut (Kohut & Wolf, 1978), a founder of self psychology, recognized that psychopathology, specifically the psychopathology of narcissistic personality disorder (NPD), originated in a "weakened or defective self that lies in the centre of the disorder" (p. 414). Although he did not mention affects specifically, he alluded to them when he explained that the weakened or defective self was characterized by extremely labile self-esteem and an extreme sensitivity to failures, disappointments, and slights. NPD arose because of failures of the caregivers to provide a sufficient source of mirroring that was both accepting and confirming. Furthermore, caregivers failed to furnish a source of idealized strength with which the child could merge. These failures set in motion the development of psychopathology, because the child does not have adequate images to internalize and rely on to structure the self.

According to Kohut, the responsive and empathic caregivers—he referred to them as *selfobjects*—are internalized as images and form the nuclei for the crystallization of the child's personality. The child develops its own autonomous self, because inevitably the caregivers fail in minor ways to meet the child's needs for mirroring and idealizing, and the child, relying initially on the selfobjects, learns to meet its own needs and in the process structures an autonomous self. Affective transactions between child and caregiver form the core of this process. Ideally, the selfobjects confirm the child's innate vigor, greatness, and perfection and provide an image of calmness, infallibility, and omnipotence. As we will learn in Chapter 2, the vigor Kohut referred to represents the affects of excitement and joy, and the quality of calmness in the selfobject represents the caregiver's ability to regulate its own affects. The quality of the adult self depended upon the quality of the relations between infant and caregivers in childhood according to Kohut's essentially developmental model. If the interaction was good enough, then the self of adulthood would have a firm and healthy structure. If the interaction was less than good enough, then varying degrees of damage resulted. The adult self has three dimensions according to Kohut: coherence, vitality, and functional harmony. On the dimension of coherence, the self can vary between cohesion and fragmentation. On the dimension of vitality, it can range between vigor and enfeeblement. On the dimension of functional harmony, it can locate between the poles of order and chaos.

This brief discourse on the self will structure the presentation of the affects that follows and will enable readers to better grasp the lessons of succeeding chapters that acquisition of affect regulation and structuring of the self are conjoint processes which cannot be separated. When the infant–caregiver dyad functions well enough, the infant acquires adequate affect regulation skills, and concurrently, an adaptive, positively functioning self is thereby structured. When the dyad does not function well enough, the infant does not acquire adequate affect regulation skills, and as a result a more or less maladaptive, more or less negatively functioning self organizes that is characterized by varying degrees of fragmentation, enfeeblement, and chaos. This understanding leads to the further awareness that AMST promotes structuring of the self as it transmits skills for affect regulation. Psychopathology is characterized by deficits of affect regulation which are equivalent to deficits of self structure, and as AMST teaches affect regulation, it concomitantly improves and enhances structuralization of the self, thereby contributing to resolution of the psychopathology.

THE PRIMARY AFFECTS

Theorists have attempted to compile a list of the basic affects and emotions (LeDoux, 1996). There are almost as many lists as there have been theorists. The minimum may be the two affective states of the newborn, distress and satiation, or it may be the four emotion response patterns of the electrically stimulated rat: panic, rage, expectancy, and fear. To the basic list of nine (interest–excitement, enjoyment–joy, surprise–startle, fear–terror, distress–anguish, anger–rage, dissmell, disgust, and shame), which has already been presented, some theorists have added more global action tendencies such as acceptance. Since our purpose is practical, rather than theoretical, the goal in this section is to transmit to the clinician the knowledge of affect she will need to assess her client, plan interventions, and properly use the AMST. Therefore, this chapter's presentation will stress the affects that clients present. Dissmell will not be discussed because it so rarely appears in therapy. Yearning, an affect not mentioned by any theorists, will be added, because of its prevalence in therapy.

Interest–Excitement

Interest–excitement is one of the appetitive, or positive affects. From infancy on, interest motivates all learning. It is the foundation of personal growth and creativity. Interest impels the change process, and it appears to be especially important to the change process of therapy. In the language of self-organization, interest provides the impetus for formation of new self-structure. Clinically, if there is insufficient interest–excitement to motivate a personality system controlled by fear, shame, or guilt, for example, change will be difficult. Interest must reach a sufficient threshold for the self to be able to mobilize healthy anger (assertiveness) to remove obstacles or barriers to change, including barriers in the self (inertia, laziness, unwillingness). In depression and in clients where there has been significant childhood deficit experience (e.g., neglect), the affect interest–excitement will not be well developed.

Interest is elicited by change of stimulation of the sense organs (Izard, 1991). Movement or animation activates interest, as do novelty and difference. Any stimulus that causes an optimal increase (i.e., within a certain range) in the rate and intensity of neural activity will trigger interest (Nathanson, 1992). Eliciting stimuli may include faces, lights, colored objects, drive states, images, visualizations, or memories. The function of interest is to amplify in the organism the increase in neural stimulation caused by the eliciting stimulus. At birth, the newborn's initial stimulus for interest may be mother's face.

Interest is expressed in the forehead portion of the face with the brows lifted or drawn together. The eyes track the object of interest, and the mouth is softly opened or the lips are pursed (Izard, 1991). Heart rate slows when interest is elicited, suggesting parasympathetic activation. Subjectively, the person experiencing interest reports feeling engaged, fascinated, and curious. Interest–excitement is a component of vitality, and the interested person wants to investigate, to learn, and to grow. He will endorse feeling alive and active. As Sylvan Tomkins wrote, "Interest is also a necessary condition for the physiological support of long-term effort. Excitement adds more than spice to life. Without zest, long-term effort and commitment cannot be sustained, either physiologically or psychologically" (cited in Demos, 1995, p. 72).

Izard (1991) created two scales for deconstructing affective experience. The Differential Emotions Scale (DES) assesses the degree to which other primary affects are assembled with the affect under study. The Dimensional Rating Scale (DRS) measures aspects of the subjective experience (pleasantness, self-assurance, impulsiveness, tension) of an emotion. In a sample of a normal population of college students, interest was accompanied on the DES by feelings of enjoyment and surprise. In this experimental situation, none of the aversive emotions emerged along with interest. On the DRS, these subjects endorsed pleasantness and self-assurance when interest was elicited, while the subjective experience of impulsiveness and tension were less strongly assembled with interest–excitement. Among the emotions tested in Izard's laboratory, only interest, enjoyment, and surprise were experienced as pleasant.

The function of interest is to promote selectivity of attention. Interest is the most prevalent affect in daily functioning. It motivates activity at all levels. One must be interested in one's teeth to floss them, interested in one's health to exercise, interested in people to get out of the house and socialize, interested in others in order to form friendships, interested in society in order to vote. We noted above that affects and perceptions interact, and interest provides a prime example because we only see or hear what is assembled with interest affect. Interest assembles with cognitions to form affective–cognitive orientations; that is, moods (Lewis, 2000). When interest is optimal, the mood is elevated, and the client experiences vitality, and when interest affect is suboptimal, the mood is depressed.

Interest is the first of the affects to be socialized, and the socialization process begins from the first days of life. Gaze transactions between maternal caregiver and infant stimulate interest–excitement. Over the early developmental periods, stimulation of interest contributes to formation of vigor, cohesion, and order as the child internalizes confirming, mirroring selfobjects and adequate self structure organizes itself. When caregivers fail to provide affective attunement, sensitivity, and responsiveness, impairments of self structure result conjointly with diminishment of vigor. AMST teaches clients to recognize interest affect, to tolerate it, and to regulate it. The protocol teaches the depressed client how to up-regulate it and teaches the manic client how to down-regulate it. Once a client can manage interest affect, he can manipulate it, importing it into activities he would like to have more "energy" to pursue.

Interest is the basis for successful social life, because interest attracts people. The individual with optimal levels of interest–excitement has friends, belongs to a social circle; the person with suboptimal interest–excitement does not have friends, is a loner, an outsider. Successful long-term sexual and marriage relationships depend upon maintenance of interest–excitement. Optimal interest is a necessary component of "good enough" parenting. A parent must be interested in his or her child for that child to thrive. In the parent–child dyadic relationship, interest guides the infant's looking, listening, vocalizing, and motor activity, and it promotes intersensory and sensorimotor coordination and skill building.

Interest may be a fundamentally important component of the therapeutic encounter, because the therapist demonstrates interest in the client, and as we have noted, through the affective social process the client's interest in himself is elicited, and the client becomes interested in his own well-being and improving his functioning. Tomkins (1962) sums up the importance of interest–excitement as follows, "There is no human competence which can be achieved in the absence of a sustaining interest" (p. 343).

Enjoyment–Joy

Clinicians often ask their clients, "How are you feeling today?" and clients may respond, "Oh, I'm feeling good." Enjoyment affect may be a component of the emotion experience a client labels *good*. But the client's response may be undiscriminated. She may be feeling good because her level of emotional pain has diminished, or she may be feeling good because she's feeling happy, an emotion that lies on the continuum of the second of the appetitive affects, enjoyment–joy. Clinicians know that depressed clients rarely enjoy life and realize how significant the absence of joy is to many psychopathological presentations.

In infants, enjoyment is elicited by the human face and by a high-pitched human voice, and from early childhood on, it is activated by a sense of accomplishment or goal achievement. Nathanson (1992) explains that a decrease in stimulus density and intensity of neural firing constitutes the eliciting stimulus for enjoyment–joy. We feel happy when we have finished the term paper, because the rate of neural firing we sustained while writing now decreases as we hit the print command. The affect enjoyment–joy amplifies this decrease in neural activity. The level of enjoyment we experience is directly related to the intensity and duration of the prior stimulus which has been relieved.

Izard (1991) noted that empirical research has demonstrated that there are individual differences in ability to experience enjoyment. In a sample of children, some began laughing as early as 12 weeks, while one did not laugh until 12 months. As we will explore, there are significant clinical consequences stemming from the distribution of thresholds for enjoyment across populations. These data suggested to Izard that "thresholds for emotions, including the emotion of joy, [are] to some extent determined by our genetic makeup" (p. 141).

Characteristically, enjoyment expression manifests in the corners of the mouth, which are pulled up in a smile, in wrinkles at the corners of the eye, and a raising of the cheeks that results in a narrowing of the eye fissure. Laughter denotes more intense enjoyment. Smiling appears in infancy, and from onset at 4 or 5 weeks to 4 or 5 months, infants will smile at any human face that nods from about 2 feet away.

The infant's smile and the affect of enjoyment–joy it expresses elicits behavior from mother, keeping her engaged. Enjoyment apparently promotes the attachment bond. In the dyadic relationship of attachment, the infant leads by smiling at mother, eliciting mother's smile response and empathic experience of enjoyment. The infant's smile also elicits play behavior from the parents. Joy, which is also known as contentment, is the affect that welcomes. In infancy, it communicates, "You are my mother." Later in life it says, "You are a member of my tribe." It is the opposite of contempt, which segregates. Enjoyment promotes personification; it is the emotion of appreciation and identification as opposed to objectification. A joyful person grants existence to the other, while a joyless person does not experience others as having existence, and consequently others feel objectified in the presence of a joyless person.

Joy apparently stimulates the sympathetic branch of the autonomic nervous system, because heart rate increases when enjoyment is elicited. Subjectively adults experience enjoyment as pleasant, desirable, positive, and rewarding. It is associated with comfort and well-being. Enjoyment is assembled into more complex affective–cognitive structures and orientations, contributing to vitality, authenticity, confidence, competency, and mastery.

AMST helps the client recognize the qualia of joy, the physiological signals that tell him he's feeling happy, elated, or joyous. Skill VII teaches clients how to up-regulate the positive affect of joy by employing the image of a gauge. Clients raised in environments that did not stimulate joy affect often have difficulty experiencing this affect and as a consequence they lack an important internal reward system. Through cognizing joy affect with AMST, clients bring joy to conscious awareness where it can be manipulated for personal benefit. Clients learn how to reward themselves for accomplishment, thus improving current functioning and increasing the probability of further increasing positive functioning in the future.

Yearning

My clinical work, and especially my work with eating disordered clients, has taught me there is a powerful affect motivating people to seek the kinds of merger experiences characteristic of love, sexuality, spirituality, religion, and child rearing. I call this affect *yearning*. We yearn for a return to the state of merger that was our primordial condition in the womb for the first 9 months of life. I believe that yearning affect motivates the neonate's attraction to mother and mother's caregiving behaviors for her child. In childhood it motivates the proximity seeking that characterizes the attachment bond. During postadolescence it motivates the search for a partner and establishment of a sexual pair bond. It appears to impel the merger experiences of lovemaking and sexual intercourse. Yearning may be the gravitational force that holds together the parts of the social system within which the self forms. Yearning that is not requited may have a place in psychopathology as well. It may be that yearning for merger is displaced into eating in the binge phase of bulimia and of binge eating disorder.

Theorists influenced by Tomkins would disagree that yearning affect exists, but clinical impressions appear to support its existence. According to Nathanson (1992), interest affect attracts the infant to mother, an attraction that is rewarded and reinforced by the joy affect that results when interest is requited by mother's attention. However, clients exposed to AMST consistently report a unique affect associated with particular sensations that motivates attraction to mother. These client reports are especially prevalent among the eating disorders. Often, in ego state work with a trauma coded scene from my patient's childhood—once we have cleared away the overlayers of sadness and anger—we have unmasked a deep longing for attachment to the primary mothering figure. When we reach it, this putative affect identifies itself by unique and distinct sensations and body locations. One client described a "rising sensation" in her upper chest and throat that was entirely different from the sensations assembled with either interest or joy affect for her. Reports from other clinicians support the idea of a yearning affect.

Several clinicians I have communicated with have affirmed the existence of an affect that motivates a search for merger. One clinician described recognizing the "longing that sits beneath the defensive structures of my clients. The longing to be held, known, loved etc. . . . I do believe both yearning and longing reference the same deeply primitive essence" (Schlesinger, personal communication, February, 2002). Another clinician nicely separated the emotion of sadness that she termed "the ache for the departed person" from "the drive that sends one to search for the loved one" (Gladu, personal communication, February 2002) that I want to call yearning. What I seek to do is discriminate yearning from sadness. Yearning, or longing, is the affect with a vector directed toward mother and her nurturance and nourishing quality. Sadness is the affect the infant, child, adolescent, and adult feels when the yearning is frustrated, thwarted, neglected, or punished.

Identifying yearning affect seems important to me. An infant's Bill of Rights would seem to include a provision that his or her innate longing to be held, known, and loved ought to be satisfied. Sadness and anger are the appropriate, normative affective responses when yearning to be loved is not requited. In my work with the eating disordered client mentioned previously, it was a powerful therapeutic moment when she realized how very much she yearned for connection to her mother. She then understood her sadness and anger as derivative from her unrequited yearning. Before that moment, she had been stuck on the sadness and the anger. She connected with her authenticity and vitality when she cognized her yearning.

Yearning may have evolved from a nursing reflex. In affect theory, the affects are believed to have evolved from simpler, more primitive reflexes. Nursing, a paleomammalian behavior (MacLean, 1990), involves the infant's reflexive turning to the breast, an action that is believed to be triggered by a pheromone produced by mother's nipple (Hudson, 1986). Yearning can be seen as evolving from this reflex. If this is so, then yearning would be the prototypical appetitive affect of infancy. While most affects are identified by a facial expression, yearning, because it is so archaic and primitive, may be identified by a whole body expression, the act of turning toward the object of one's yearning.

If it exists, yearning may be a component of the complex emotion experience of love. Nathanson (1992) wrote that "all love is based on the experience of positive affect, of interest–excitement and enjoyment–joy" (p. 240). Undoubtedly these play a significant part, but before interest can come into play, the self must be impelled to search for an object of love, and enjoyment can only arise after the object has been found. The hypothesis for a yearning affect appears to be supported by client reports, clinicians' observations, evolutionary considerations, and its explanatory power.

Surprise–Startle

Suprise is the affect that clears the mind to prepare the organism for dealing with a new event. In the facial signature of surprise–startle—Izard (1991) called this affect "surprise–astonishment"—the brows are lifted, wrinkling the forehead, the eyes are large and rounded, and the mouth opens in an oval shape. P. J. Lang (personal communication, January 9, 2002) distinguished between the "startle reflex, founded on a clearly understood neural circuit" and surprise–startle, "an affective experience . . . a theoretical construct for which the defining operations vary." Surprise is elicited by a sudden, unexpected event, one that sharply increases stimulus density. According to both Nathanson (1992) and Izard (1991), surprise functions to prepare the mind for a new, sudden event, and it does this by clearing the nervous system of current activity that would interfere with coping. Izard wrote, "it is as though ordinary thought processes are momentarily stopped" (p. 177). In normal populations (Izard, 1991), surprise is usually associated with pleasantness and self-assurance on the DRS. In Chapter 5, I will propose that surprise–startle affect may be elicited by tactile alternatin bilateral stimulation (TABS) and may well be responsible for increasing the effectiveness and efficiency of AMST skills acquisition.

Startle has been described as a neutral affect (Nathanson, 1992), but it appears to the contrary to be implicated in PTSD, DID, and other psychopathologies. I suggest that surprise–startle is anything but neutral. Inasmuch as the thresholds for each of the affects may be genetically determined, it is possible to have a low threshold for surprise–startle, and this could well be a predisposing factor in the emergence of a distressed self-organization. In traumatized populations, where surprise has been trauma coded (Schwartz et al., 1995a), the experience of surprise is exaggerated and can be extremely unpleasant (Bowie, Silverman, Kalick, & Edbril, 1990; Herman, 1992).

Carlson (1997) discusses the exaggerated startle response of traumatized persons in the context of reexperiencing in the form of physiological arousal. She suggests that the hypervigilance seen in PTSD represents reexperiencing startle affect in both the cognitive and affective modes. Furthermore, as we will discuss in Chapter 4, the mind-blanking aspect of surprise may be the basis for the phenomenon of dissociation. Clinical impressions suggest that dissociation arising from trauma coding of startle affect is sometimes the cause of clients' cognitive disjunctions like "spacing out" or "blanking out" and may also explain why clients sometimes dissociate affects out of awareness ("numbing out"). AMST can teach the client to recognize startle affect through its associated physiological sensations. The protocol can teach the client to tolerate startle and to reduce the arousal associated with it. When the client with startle associated cognitive impairments can manage startle affect, cognitive functioning may often improve.

Fear–Terror

Fear is the affect that responds to perceptions of danger by motivating survival behaviors. It could be said that we humans have survived evolution's vicissitudes because we are fearful. Fear is a biological system that detects danger and produces responses that maximize the chances of surviving the danger-fraught situation (LeDoux, 1996). The response set elicited by danger is similar in humans and other animals. Danger may trigger withdrawal or flight, behaviors designed to avoid the danger; the frightened animal may freeze, immobilizing itself to reduce a predator's pursuit response; it may attack defensively; it may submit and demonstrate appeasement behavior, especially in response to a dangerous animal of its own species.

Mammals have evolved behavioral means, motivated by fear, to signal danger to conspecifics; for example, a frightened beaver sounds an alarm by slapping its tail on the water. A frightened human signals his mates by means of facial expression as well as with vocal calls. In fear, the brows are lifted and pulled together, producing wrinkles across the center of the forehead (Izard, 1991). Eyes expressing fear are opened wide, often showing the whites, and the corners of the mouth are pulled back with the mouth slightly open. The caregiver employs the signature facial expression of fear affect to inform children and other adults of imminent danger.

A range of natural triggers elicits fear. Pain and pain anticipation trigger the fear system, as do being alone, the rapid approach of another human or other animal, strange situations, and heights. When triggered, fear produces a familiar cassette of mental and physiological responses. Fear stimulates the sympathetic branch of the autonomic nervous system, with an increase in heart rate, increase in blood pressure, and increase in energy supply all directed toward promoting either effective flight or effective fight responses. Fear focuses attention, producing the subjective experience of tunnel vision in more extreme states of fear arousal, and the focusing effect of fear is reflected in a reduction in the range of perceptions, cognitions, choices, and actions available.

In addition to the natural and external triggers of fear mentioned above, fear can be elicited by a range of intrapsychic stimuli. Patients regularly report fearing the experience of unresolved, trauma coded experiences and the affects assembled with them. Fear itself can induce still more fear in a downward spiral as the sensory feedback from fear's expressive behavior engenders more fear. Cognitions, whether appraisals of the possibility of harm or structures in memory, can induce fear. Clients may learn to fear emotions. For example, some clients may fear anger emotion, often because in childhood displays of anger were punished so severely by parents that the child learned to fear the experience of anger. Clients may also fear shame affect or fear disgust affect, and often the criteria defining a psychopathology may be understood as the fear-driven cognitive and behavioral defenses against the experience of these affects.

Humans have genetically determined thresholds for fear affect, and some people are more liable to experience fear than others in threatening situations. Persons with a low threshold for fear will be more likely to develop anxiety-related behavioral traits and psychopathologies. Serotonin plays a key role in the amygdala in determining a fear response. A recent fMRI study demonstrated that subjects with decreased serotonin transporter function showed heightened amygdalar activity when looking at fear expressing faces (Hariri et al., 2002). The authors measured activity in the amygdala during an affective task requiring subjects to match angry or fearful faces. Subjects were grouped according to genotype for the serotonin transporter gene. Subjects with one or two copies of the dominant *s* allele of the serotonin transporter gene showed significantly greater activity in the amygdala when they viewed fear expressing faces. Persons with the *s* allele have decreased serotonin reuptake and therefore have higher levels of synaptic serotonin, which is associated with increased anxiety and fearfulness. The Hariri and colleagues study demonstrated a link between serotonin uptake function and the response of the amygdala, which is known to be involved in fear response processing. Subjects with two copies of the *l* allele of the serotonin transporter gene showed significantly less amygdalar activity when viewing fear expressing faces, apparently because their more active serotonin uptake system reduces synaptic serotonin. This study showed that humans have different genetically based thresholds for fear affect, a factor that will influence the course of development of the self. An infant genetically disposed to fear by virtue of having the *s* allele of the serotonin transporter gene will be more likely to experience fear at the sudden approach of a large adult, in strange situations, or when threatened.

Fear affect can be classically conditioned. Recognizing the centrality of fear and its potential value for modeling, LeDoux (1996) set out to study the fear system through the use of fear conditioning. In fear conditioning, a conditioned stimulus (CS; e.g., a tone) is paired with an unconditioned stimulus (US; e.g., shock). The US produces the fear response. Eventually, CS elicits the fear response, which is termed the conditioned response (CR). Fear conditioning is rapid, sometimes establishing itself in one trial, and it persists. While fear conditioning can extinguish, it can spontaneously reappear under stress or trauma. Classical conditioning of fear provides a model for how the other affect systems may also be conditioned.

Humans and higher vertebrates have two pathways that mediate the fear response, one proceeding directly from the organ of perception to the emotion response systems and one that courses through the neocortex. Fear conditioning occurs in insects, mollusks, and many phyla of vertebrates, and it can occur in humans without conscious awareness of the CS or the relationship between CS and US. LeDoux argued that consciousness of "fear" does not necessarily mediate the organism's connection between CS and CR. Employing rats fear-conditioned to an auditory CS as experimental animals and lesioning brain regions to trace pathways, LeDoux and other researchers demonstrated a pair of circuits controlling the fear response (LeDoux, 1996). The two pathways diverge from the auditory thalamus, the structure receiving the signal from the ear. In the so-called low road, the signal travels from the auditory thalamus to the lateral nucleus of the amygdala, to the central nucleus of the amygdala, and from there to the emotion response systems. The emotion response systems of the brainstem and the autonomic nervous system produce the components of conditioned fear: behavioral freezing, analgesia, cortisol release, reflex potentiation, and the cassette of autonomic responses. The low road does not involve the neocortical regions of the brain. LeDoux wrote: "emotional learning can be mediated by pathways that bypass the neocortex" (p. 161).

The second pathway, which LeDoux termed the *high road* of emotion learning, does involve the neocortex. In this pathway, a different set of fibers leaves the auditory thalamus and connects it to cells in the auditory cortex. From here other fibers connect the cortical region to the lateral nucleus of the amygdala. Having two pathways for the fear response apparently confers evolutionary advantage, since the low road system has persisted over evolutionary time and across many vertebrate species. The low road, also known as the thalamo-amygdala pathway, is faster, because it involves only one link, while the cortico-amygdala path, or high road, which has several links, is nearly twice as slow. The low road pathway comprises broadly tuned neurons leaving the auditory thalamus, while the high road makes use of more finely tuned neurons. AMST is hypothesized to promote adaptive affect regulation by creating a new high road pathway through the neocortex. Writing about the neocortical pathway, LeDoux observed, "the cortex's job is to prevent the inappropriate response" (p. 165). In this regard, AMST apparently builds new pathways that prevent the client's maladpative, inappropriate, affect-driven, low road response.

The memory formation system of the hippocampus contributes to fear conditioning. The hippocampus, a limbic structure with robust connections to the amygdala, is responsible for creating a representation of the context within which fear is conditioned by the presentation of CS and US. For example, rats respond with fear to the cage in which shock and tone have been paired, just as a child will respond with fear to a room in which he has previously been spanked. Fear conditioning apparently contributes to the anxiety disorders. Contextual fear conditioning is but one function of the hippocampus. Hippocampal memory formation and retrieval plays a role in emotion dysregulation in psychopathology. AMST skills rely on retrieval of information from both the declarative and the implicit, or emotion, memory systems.

Fear conditioning is a well-researched phenomenon that provides a framework we can use to understand how other affects besides fear may come to be dysregulated. Here, I introduce the hypothesis that other affects can be similarly conditioned, and probably by a system working along the same principles that are now known to be operative in fear conditioning. Anger conditioning, shame conditioning, disgust conditioning, startle conditioning, yearning conditioning, interest conditioning, and joy conditioning may all be conceptualized as employing the same two thalamo-amygdala and cortico-amygdala pathways as fear conditioning. The hippocampus may well provide the same contextual conditioning for the other basic emotions as it does for fear, so that, for example, a child shamed for his performance in a specific classroom may subsequently feel shame in any classroom. Just as AMST builds new pathways that prevent the client's maladaptive fear response, so too can AMST build new pathways to prevent the shame-based client's maladaptive shame response. The conduct disordered client treated with AMST may build new pathways to interdict his inappropriate anger response. The bulimic client may learn new skills to prevent her disgust-driven purge behavioral response.

Anger

Anger is elicited by aversive stimulation, especially pain. One of our themes is that emotions evolved out of more primitive reflexes. The phylogeny of affect may be recapitulated in its ontogeny, an hypothesis supported by research on anger from Izard's laboratory (1991). He described a study in which infants were observed over the course of a diphtheria-pertussis (DPT) inoculation series in which injections were given at 2, 4, 6, and 18 months. He wrote that throughout early infancy "the infants' automatic instinct like response to this painful medical procedure was a physical distress or pain expression accompanied by loud crying" (p. 245). By 18 months, videotapes showed that 100% of the toddlers had also developed an anger response. A majority (72%) did show the pain response, but it was fleeting in comparison to the anger, "as though mad at the physical insult over which they had no control"(p. 246). Izard scored the anger response from the index facial expression in which the brows are drawn inward and downward, producing a bulge above the nose. The facial expression of anger also includes a narrowing and hardening of the eyes. In the most primitive anger expression, the mouth is open and the teeth are bared. When socialized, anger expression manifests in compression of the lips and clenching the jaw.

In addition to physical pain, anger can be elicited by restraint, whether physical or psychological. Blocking goal-directed action will elicit anger, as will being misled or unjustly hurt by others. Nathanson (1992) wrote that anger is elicited by steady state levels of stimulus density that are higher than those that elicit distress–anguish. A common example is the different emotion responses elicited by a neighbor's loud radio. In the range from 60 to 80 decibels, the stimulus density may be sufficient to elicit distress assembled with the verbal behavior, "That sure is loud. I wish he'd have some consideration and turn it down." As the stimulus density increases above 80 decibels, the affect anger surfaces, and one may be motivated by it to either ask him to turn it down or to call the police and have them make him do so.

Each person's experience of anger is unique. Experimental subjects report anger is accompanied by sensations of heat in the face and tension in muscles (Izard, 1991). Clinically, as we will learn, each client will describe his or her unique personal sensation (qualia) and body location for his or her anger. On the DRS, anger is accompanied by increases in tension, impulsiveness, and self-assurance. Anger is not experienced as pleasant by experimental subjects. Often, in experimental samples, anger copresents with disgust and contempt, in what Izard referred to as the "hostility triad" (Izard, 1991, p. 229). On the DES profile, fear is attenuated when anger is elicited, and Izard suggests that anger may inhibit fear. Anger may also diminish shame, a potent stimulus for anger (Izard, Ackerman et al., 2000). Acting recursively, shame elicits and amplifies anger, while the elicited and amplified anger may diminish the shame experience. The affect oriented clinician will explore associations among affects that may be part of the client's unique anger experience.

Anger's function is to prepare one for action. The type of action motivated by anger will depend upon the individual's cognitive appraisals of the situation and his socialization. The type of action will depend as well upon the behaviors of the other when the anger arises interpersonally. For example, appeasement will often prevent anger-motivated behavior, while counterthreat will usually provoke it. In healthy anger expression the genuine emotion is expressed, but controlled so as not to close off communication. Destructive anger expression seeks to win at all costs, rather than communicate.

AMST helps the client raise anger to conscious awareness, which is a first step in developing more adaptive skills for managing anger. The protocol can help the conduct disordered client recognize anger and the shame against which the anger defends. For some bulimic clients, bingeing provides a means for vicariously managing anger, and AMST can help this client by cognizing anger, an important step in the process of resolving it. Learning skills to manage anger builds self structure and expands consciousness.

Distress–Anguish

Distress is the affect we feel when we are overwhelmed by too much work or too much responsibility, or when we are separated from a loved one as happens in divorce or death. Tompkins identified distress–anguish as one of the fundamental affects. Izard prefers the term *sadness*. I prefer to think of sadness as an intermediate affective state lying on the continuum between distress and anguish. These are the affects of "too much." Nathanson (1992) noted that a constant, higher than optimal level of stimulation will provoke the appearance of the index response for extreme distress: crying or sobbing. The eliciting stimulus can be perceptual, as when a baby cries because the bottle is too hot, or the bath too cold, or the diaper too wet. Too much of a drive state, (e.g., hunger), can elicit distress. Sadness can be triggered by too much separation as well. Izard (1991) wrote, "Separation, whether physical or psychological, remains throughout life one of the basic and most common causes of sadness" (p. 185). Distress is a fundamental affective component of attachment. The objective of attachment is proximity to the attachment figure. Attachment is an adaptive, organized behavioral system. Distress is expressed in the infant's cry when separation has exceeded a threshold. As Feeney and Noller (1996) wrote, "Infants perceive separation (actual or threatened) from their attachment figure as a threat to their well-being and try to remain within the protective range of that figure" (p. 3). The distress call is meant to serve the function of reestablishing connection with the attachment figure. Later in life, sadness communicates distress to the self as well as to others. The trembling chin and tears of sadness tell the self and the community, "I am troubled. I need help."

Summarizing empirical research on sadness, Stearns (1993) noted that sadness is also a response to a goal lost or not attained. Thus sadness is elicited by events that have already happened. Fear, on the contrary, anticipates events yet to come. Appraisals of agency accompany sadness and distinguish it from guilt and anger. In sadness, according to Stearns, the self is not responsible for the eliciting event, nor is anybody else. Guilt occurs when the self is appraised as the responsible agent, and anger is the emotion that develops when another is believed responsible. Resignation is the response to events believed to be inevitable, while sadness connotes that events might have been otherwise.

The expression of distress involves the eyebrows, which are pulled together and up, the corners of the mouth which are pulled down, and the chin which is pulled upwards and trembles (Izard, 1991). As the activation of sadness increases (Lang, 1995), crying and sobbing ensue. In my clinical experience, an early, subtle, often fleeting sign of sadness is a flush in the skin of the face particularly over the cheekbones and around the eyes accompanied by a "glistening wetness" in the eyes. Subjectively, sadness is experienced as a heaviness in mind and body (Izard, 1991).

Sadness can be assembled with other emotions, especially with fear in the individual who has been punished for expression of distress. Many patients were told in childhood, "I'll give you something to cry about!" and thereby came to fear their sadness. AMST can help these clients by teasing apart the assembly of fear with sadness. When intense distress affect was denied expression it can be trauma coded and continue to influence behavior even though it is buried in the unconscious. A client's husband had never been allowed to express the anguish he felt over traumatic childhood events, and in adulthood he projected this unresolved sadness onto his wife by constantly asking her why she looked so sad. His unresolved sadness formed the basis of a projective identification, because she came to therapy to deal with sadness she felt and but that appeared to be unjustified by any cause.

Disgust

Disgust is a powerful affect that is often unrecognized yet is implicated in motivating many human behaviors. The primitive reflex from which the affect disgust may have evolved is the eliminative reflex that rids the mouth of a noxious substance. Disgust can be elicited by a drop of a bitter substance placed on the tongue or by the taste of spoiled food. Izard (1991) noted that the brainstem mediates the disgust response, and that functional cerebral hemispheres are not necessary to its elicitation. In its ontogeny, disgust extends to people, places, ideas, and things, as cognitive appraisals, learning, and memories accumulate. Like all affects, disgust is modular and can be assembled with internal images, even to the representation of the self. The client who verbalizes "I hate myself" is in part motivated by disgust affect, since hatred is a secondary affect compounded from anger and disgust. In my work with eating disorders (Omaha, 2000), I have argued that disgust can be sequestered in a part of the self (e.g., body fat), as a way of managing this powerful, primitive, and potentially overwhelming affect. Apparently the purge phase of bulimia provides the bulimic with a vicarious means for managing disgust affect. AMST can help the bulimic, the binge eater, and the client motivated by self-hatred by providing skills for affect management that are positive alternatives to the dysfunctional behaviors of their disorders.

The index facial expression of disgust brings the brows together and down with a wrinkled nose; the upper lip is pulled up, the lower lip down; the tongue is pushed forward. Subjectively, the qualia of disgust is experienced as revulsion, an extreme form of rejection or avoidance. When fully activated (Lang, 1995), disgust manifests in unique, specific physiological components, increased salivation, nausea, and vomiting. Haidt, McCauley, and Rozin (1994) have created a disgust scale that attempts to measure disgust sensitivity.

Neural mechanisms for disgust affect appear to reside in the insula, a deep and substantial portion of the cerebral cortex that is anatomically distinct from the amygdala. Researchers recorded event-related potentials in subjects shown faces expressing fear, disgust, happiness, surprise, or a neutral expression (Krolak-Salmon et al., 2003). Only electrodes placed in the ventral anterior part of the insula responded significantly to the faces expressing disgust. When the electrodes that had recorded disgust in the insula were used to deliver electrical stimulation to the insula, subjects reported an "unpleasant sensation in the throat spreading up to the mouth, lips, and nose. It was not painful but described as 'difficult to stand' " (p. 449). Stimulation of the insula appeared to elicit the qualia of disgust. These data have important consequences for socialization of affect and for the formation of self in children. The authors wrote that their results "suggest that this insular area plays a role in detection of disgust in congeners and feeling disgust oneself" (p. 451). Throughout the book I develop the theme that when parents socialize a child with broadcast disgust affect, that affect assembles with the child's self-representation where it becomes the basis for development of a distressed self. I believe that disgust affect assembled with the self-representation results in low self-esteem, feelings of unworthiness, and self-loathing. The data cited here demonstrate how a disgust face can be recognized and how "[m]echanisms used to perceive disgust in others thus would be linked to those involved in experiencing that emotion oneself, suggesting that observing might be a way to learn our emotional reactions" (p. 451). Because disgust socialization often occurs at an early age, the mechanism is still buried in the unconscious of the client, and AMST can help this client to cognize disgust affect and then resolve it through affect centered therapy.

Disgust is a powerful affect linked to cultural taboos and perhaps even to the defense of denial. Rozin, Haidt, and McCauley (2000) reviewed the literature on disgust. They noted Tomkins's claim that of all the emotions disgust has the most robust linkage to the hunger drive and that it functions to oppose incorporation. These authors examined the cultural evolution of disgust, arguing that a sense of oral incorporation, a sense of offensiveness, and contamination potency are necessary for disgust to occur. Disgust may motivate bigotry and xenophobia. This concept of contamination potency may have clinical relevance. For example, it can help us understand denial, the unconscious, self-deceptive defense system that prohibits recognition and acceptance of one's actual behaviors. The spousal abuser who denies hitting his wife may be motivated by disgust, the revulsion he would feel if he had to admit, that is *incorporate* into his self-concept, his battering behaviors.

Disgust may also motivate cognitive defenses against death. The odor of decay, which is the odor of death, is a powerful elicitor of disgust. Rozin and colleagues (2000) argued that "disgust can be understood as a defense against a universal fear of death . . . anything that reminds us that we are animals elicits disgust" (p. 642). This is a powerful observation. It suggests that those human inventions that attempt to transcend the plane of human existence, inventions as disparate as the machine, the corporation, and religion, may be motivated by the affect disgust.

Shame

Lewis (1993) grouped shame, embarrassment, guilt, and pride together, calling them *evaluative* emotions, because they require the development of cognitive abilities in order to be elicited. We will examine pride in Chapter 11, and for now merely note that it is intimately related to shame. Unlike the primary or basic emotions (joy, sadness, fear, anger, disgust), the evaluative emotions have less unique facial expression, and bodily action is as important to recognizing them as are facial expressions. Shame is often recognized by a forward bending of the neck and a hunkering of the shoulders. Casting down the eyes or averting the gaze may be the signature facial expressions of shame. Two more points of distinction: the evaluative emotions appear relatively later in life than the primary emotions; and they do not have specific elicitors, again unlike the primary affects. Exactly what does elicit shame is a subject of debate in the shame literature (Lewis, 1993b; Nathanson, 1992). One camp believes cognitive processes elicit shame; another insists affect itself is the elicitor.

Shame appears at the point in development when the infant is able to discriminate between familiar and strange faces. Each affect has its own ontogeny, and the affects begin as reflexes or reflexlike responses. As the developmental time line progresses and experiences accumulate, the individual's own emotion expression emerges. From the perspective of conjointly developing affect regulation and self structure, it is noteworthy that the development of shame has been traced to an infant's response to a stranger's face as if it were a familiar face. Apparently the infant must have developed the capacity to form complex representational constructs and then to compare them before shame can be experienced.

Development of self-recognition is apparently a precondition for the emergence of shame. Theoreticians who favor shame elicitation by cognitive processes point to the importance of the development of self-recognition as a necessary condition for the appearance of shame. Izard (1991) described Lewis's observations of children's responses to seeing themselves in a mirror. The experiments suggest that self-recognition appears at 15 to 18 months and by 21 to 24 months a majority (88%) of toddlers recognize themselves. At 22 months, 11 out of 44 toddler participants showed shame at seeing themselves with rouge applied to their noses. Interestingly, one of the criteria for shame was smiling followed by gaze aversion, the infant's way of signaling mother that the infant has had enough arousal (Schore, 1994).

Building on his empirical findings regarding self-recognition, Lewis (1993b) created a model for shame elicitation that necessitates a notion of self, a self-concept that appears to be essentially cognitive. In the course of forming the self-concept, the infant introjects a set of standards, rules, and goals (SRGs). The process of SRG introjection begins early in life. He wrote, "by the age of 1 year, children are beginning to learn the appropriate action patterns reflecting the SRGs of the culture" (p. 567). These SRGs are culturally determined. "By the second year of life," he continued, citing the work of Heckhausen and of Kagan, "children show some understanding about appropriate and inappropriate behavior" (p. 567).

Lewis (1993b) presented a cognitive–attributional model for how the self-conscious emotions might be elicited. In the model, once the SRGs are introjected, an evaluation process occurs in which the self's actions are compared to the self-concept. The evaluative process must be internal, meaning that the self must take responsibility for its actions rather than blaming others (external evaluation). The model requires some definition of what constitutes success or failure, and it requires a discrimination between globality and specificity in the self-concept. In global evaluations, the entire self-concept is judged negatively when there is mismatch between action and self-concept. In specific attributions, the evaluation focuses on particular actions the self has committed rather than on the total self-concept. Global attributions correspond to what Bradshaw (1988) called toxic shame, while specific attributions are akin to his concept of healthy shame.

Nathanson (1992) argued that it was emotion that elicited shame, not cognition. He wrote: "shame requires the presence of other affects" (p. 136). He believed that shame (shame-humiliation in Tomkins's lexicon) acts to limit affects when at their height, just as disgust limits the hunger drive. Specifically, Nathanson insisted that shame limits the positive affects interest–excitement and enjoyment–joy, and that we experience shame only when the affect interest–excitement or the affect enjoyment–joy is interrupted. He suggested that shame amplifies an impediment to interest or to enjoyment and shame's action is to impede the experience of further positive emotion. For Nathanson, shame functions as a sort of internal puritan or a biological blue law, because shame limits excitement or joy in situations where "compelling reasons for that positive affect remain" (p. 139). In his conception, shame's action is particularly draconian because the more intense the levels of enjoyment experienced, the more will shame interfere with joy's action of amplifying a decrease in stimulus density.

Must shame be elicited either by an impediment to interest, as Nathanson insists, or by a mismatch between behavior and self-concept as Lewis argues? As with all dialectics, the answer lies in a new synthesis, and Braun's behavior, affect, sensation, and knowledge (BASK) model provides the basis for one (Braun, 1988a). Braun discussed how perception of one's identity depends on the match or mismatch between one's self-concept and one's behavior. In the BASK terminology, our self-concept comprises Behavior, Affect, Sensation, and Knowledge, and comfort entails a match between these elements of the self-concept and the same elements in behavior. Braun illustrated his discussion by asking the reader to first experience a match by speaking aloud his or her own name. To experience a mismatch, the reader is asked to speak aloud, "I am John F. Kennedy." An error signal arises when the self-image does not match the image of action. I suggest that the error signal that arises when self-image and behavior don't match *is* the affect shame. The purpose of shame is to alert us to the discordance between self-concept and self's behavior. One can see this would confer survival advantage, as it provides for correction.

We can unify the cognitive (Lewis) and affective (Nathanson) theories by assuming that the interest affect is operative when there is a match between one's self-concept on the one hand and one's conscious awareness of one's behavior on the other. The interest affect may operate below the level of conscious awareness. When a mismatch occurs, when behavior suddenly no longer accords with the self-concept, interest affect is impeded, and shame results, with the effect of raising the mismatch to conscious awareness where we can do something about it.

When shame is triggered, it is a powerful, potentially overwhelming emotion. The qualia of shame are a wish to die, to disappear, or to hide, and a feeling of smallness. Patients often report feeling the shoulders hunch or draw in and the head duck. Heightened self-consciousness, self-awareness, self-attention, and increased awareness of inadequacy are further qualia of shame. Shame is highly aversive and painful, and it disrupts current behavior, confuses thought, and impedes speech. Lewis (1993b) appears to favor a fundamental affect that could be called *self-consciousness* as the basis of shame, embarrassment, guilt, and shyness. In self-consciousness one feels utterly exposed to the examination of others and one is conscious of being thus examined.

As the personality emerges, shame functions to strengthen the self because it stimulates self-evaluation. This is what Bradshaw (1988) meant by healthy shame. We are forced by healthy shame to be more objectively self-aware and to see discrepancies between self-concept and behavior. Through confronting shame, one builds autonomy and integrity.

Shame apparently functions in evolution to ensure social cohesion. It increases awareness of self in relation to others. The communicative function of emotion enables shame to be felt empathically, with one person broadcasting and another resonating (Nathanson, 1992). Communicating shame promotes social cohesion because it forces us to look at our own behaviors when the result of those behaviors is to produce shame in another.

This chapter has surveyed the human emotionscape and shown that affects motivate behavior, contribute to our consciousness of self, and structure that unique and particular self that we call *me* or *I*. Affects and emotions signal others in our social milieu regarding our own system's status from moment to moment, and they unite the group into a coherently functioning unit. As humans evolved from reptilian and protomammalian progenitors, the affect system evolved conjointly, and our affective capacity undoubtedly contributed to our survival as a species. Our cognitive functions evolved out of the limbic system as the neomammalian brain evolved, and as a result affect influences many forebrain functions like perception, cognition, and decision making. The physiological changes assembled with each affect tell us what we are feeling and as a collateral benefit they provide us with a sense of conscious awareness. The self experiences itself through affects and sensations. The self forms over the developmental time span in the context of a succession of dyads and social milieus within which the self acquires the skills of affect regulation. In a very real sense, the self system is a collection of experience-dependent ego states that regulate affects. The organism also accumulates records of experiences in memory, and these images assemble with affects, and as the affects are modified by experience they evolve into emotions. Just as molecules are constructed from elements, the more complex emotions will always be compounded from the elemental affects I have presented here. The affects remain the basic building blocks, and just as one must know the chemistry of carbon in order to understand the biology of a complex carbonaceous molecule like DNA, so too must one know the physiology of affects in order to comprehend the psychology and psychopathology of emotions and selves. Our review of the fundamental affects has demonstrated that interest motivates exploration, fear alerts us to danger, anger motivates overcoming obstacles to accomplishment, and joy rewards attainment. Yearning moves us to stay close to others of our species, and anguish tells us when we have gone too far away. Disgust separates us into social groups, and shame tells us when we have transgressed the norms of our own group. Surprise clears the mind, allowing us to transition from one affective state to another. With this background, we proceed to examine how the self organizes itself across the developmental stages as it acquires the skills of affect regulation.

Chapter 2

Development of a Healthy Self Structure

The ontogeny of human affect and emotion beginning at birth is intertwined with processes of attachment, neurobiological growth and development, and organization and structuralization of the self. As Schore (1994) noted, neurobiology, neurochemistry, embryology, psychology, ethology, evolutionary biology, and current psychoanalytic theory have all examined infant development. Bowlby created an ethological model (e.g., Cassidy, 1999) focused on the infant–caregiver dyad that conceptualized the infant's emotions as signals mediating the attachment to a caregiver (Magai, 1999). Development of the affect system itself has been presented as an independent subject of study (e.g., Lewis, 1993a). Mahler (Mahler et al., 1975) instituted the psychoanalytic study of infant development. LeDoux (1996) and MacLean (1990, 1993) have offered an evolutionary approach. Schore (1994) has presented an integrated socioaffective model that incorporates neurobiological changes accompanying affect development in the context of the evolving infant–caregiver dyadic relationship. Two principles characterize development: unity and the emergence of complexity (Sroufe, 1996). Unity means that human emotional ontogeny is so integrated into all other aspects of human development "that studying emotional growth requires studying the whole of development" (Sroufe, 1996, p. 39).

This chapter presents an overview of development from infancy through adolescence. This presentation has two goals. The first is to provide sufficient information so the reader will understand the skills presented in Part II of this book and the foundation of those skills in the neuroscience and psychology of emotion development. The second goal is to describe normal affect development in enough detail to provide a foundation for the discussion of affect and emotion dysregulation and its emergence in Chapter 4. Since affect development, neurobiological development, and the emergence of the self are coextensive, contemporaneous processes (Damasio, 1999; Nathanson, 1992; Schore, 1994), the chapter presents the emergence of affect regulation in the context of the acquisition of self-structure. This approach is critically important to a fundamental proposition underlying the AMST: When we teach affect regulation skills to our clients we are effectively re-mediating deficits in self structure. I have developed this chapter from material presented in Cassidy (1999), Marvin and Britner (1999), Schore (1994), Sroufe (1996), and Weinfield, Sroufe, Egeland, and Carlson (1999).

The infant–caregiver dyad is the structural unit within which the infant's developmental process manifests itself. The infant's growth and development cannot be separated from the dyad. While the dyadic unit develops, changing from period to period, it is also a constant across developmental time from birth through adolescence, and the end of adolescence is often marked by the young adult's participation in a new dyad (Allen & Land, 1999). The infant's physical, behavioral, emotional, cognitive, and neurobiological growth all occur within and are contingent upon the optimal functioning of the dyadic unit. Affective development occurs in the context of the dyad. The affective transactions central to emotion ontogeny occur within the dyad, and, as we will learn, because these transactions induce neurobiological growth, maturation of the brain depends on dyadic functioning. Sroufe (1996) accorded the dyad a place of prominence in development: "the vital role of the developing caregiving relationship in influencing thresholds for threat and the balance between excitation and inhibition, lays a foundation for understanding individual differences in emotional expression and the regulation of emotion" (p. 51). The dyad of infancy and childhood is internalized, becoming the basis for relations between the self and others and for relations between the self and the self system across the life span. As Schore (1994) wrote, there is "no dichotomy between the organism and the environmental context in which it develops" (p. 63).

BIRTH TO 5–6 MONTHS

The newborn exists in a state of mental and physiological nonorganization. Mahler called this state *normal autism* (Horner, 1984; Mahler et al., 1975). The state of normal autism illustrates the absence of a self structure. During the first 6 months, the symbiosis forms. For the infant, symbiosis is characterized by a blended or merged internal representation in which the infant's image of the caregiver is largely undiscriminated from the infant's nascent representation of self. The infant's representation of self has not yet separated out from its image of the caregiver. The infant's internal representation of the caregiver, a visual pattern assembled with primitive affects and physiological signals, develops over this period and constitutes the structural foundation for subsequent stages in emergence of self. AMST accords this period prime importance, because the fundamental building blocks of self are set here. Taking an affect focused history, the clinician asks the client, "Were you nursed?" because the client's response gives important information about this early developmental stage. I have divided the first six months into two periods to accentuate important events occurring in each.

The First Three Months of Life

During the first three months of life, the neonate's physiological state is the pre-eminent determiner of behavior. Distress during this period is most often caused by interoceptve stimulation. The newborn's responses to physiological distress are global and diffuse. Because coordination of responses to stimulation have not yet appeared, the newborn is at the mercy of the stimulus. Internal and external events induce a physiological state, the preemotional reaction, and this state is under the control of stimulus qualities, such as loudness or brightness; the stimulus content is unimportant. Sroufe (1996) presented a view that specific affects unfold from precursors observable in the neonate. These precursors are more re-flexive and cannot be called true emotions, because emotions, as Sroufe defined them, are assembled with meaning. Sroufe argued for three systems of preemotional reactions that are observable in the neonate.

The three preemotional systems are the pleasure system, the fear system, and the anger system. The newborn's reflexive smile signifies the preemotion reaction of the pleasure system. Sroufe argued that this smile expressed the central nervous system's immaturity, because any stimulation that elicits sufficient arousal will elicit the smile. Between 6 and 12 months the affect of joy develops out of the preemotional reaction of the pleasure system. The preemotional reaction characteristic of the fear system appears when the newborn's attention is captured by an object. Blocking the free flow of attention interrupts the infant's flow of behavior and activates the fear system. Unbroken attention ensues, and arousal escalates, culminating in distress and crying. The neonate's anger system, Sroufe's third system, can be activated by blocking a physical behavior; for example, restraining the newborn's head. A global, diffuse flailing response, the preemotional reaction of the anger system, will ensue that is the prototype for later frustration reactions and anger affect. During the first three months of life, the primordia of joy affect, fear affect, and anger affect can be observed in, respectively, the pleasure system, the fear system, and the anger system.

The infant–caregiver dyad operates to assure the infant's survival during this period. Marvin and Britner (1999) termed this period *preattachment*. The neonate's signals and motoric behaviors elicit the caregiver's interest affect and arouse her caregiving behavioral system. Mother's behavioral caregiving system, which is fully operational, illustrates many principles of the operation of a behavioral system, principles that we will see again as the infant's attachment system comes on-line. Mother's caregiving behaviors constitute a complex behavioral *system*. The caregiving behavioral system, like all behavioral systems, produces a predictable outcome, in this case achievement of the set goal of infant care. The caregiver chooses from a repertoire of behaviors such as nursing, bathing, holding, diaper changing, burping, those behaviors that bring the set goal closer. The behavioral system implies the existence of what Bowlby (1969) termed *internal working models* (IWMs), and what Piaget (Piaget & Imhelder, 1969) called *schemes*. For the caregiver, these IWMs constitute internal representations of the self, of the infant, of the environment, of her own behaviors, and of behavioral plans. Mother constructs and maintains representations of herself as caregiver of her infant and of her caregiving regimen. Mother's caregiving behavior constitutes her contribution to the behavioral dyad at this time, and it overshadows the infant's contributions.

For the infant, the predictable outcome of the caregiver's behavior is physical contact, nutrition, proximity, and warmth. In these early months, infant has not yet assembled a coherent image of the caregiver, does not "know" the other exists, and does not distinguish self from other. Visual cues are the most important exteroceptive stimuli at this time. At birth, the infant tracks, orients visually, and shows responsiveness to contour and pattern. By 4 weeks, the infant has developed a preference for human faces. The neonate is also responsive to auditory cues, in particular the human voice. The early stages of development of self structure can be seen in the emergence of infant's preference for human faces. Almost from birth, neonates prefer rounded shapes, and by 4 weeks sufficient neural structure has developed so the infant discriminates faces from other rounded shapes.

Infant's and caregiver's behavioral and physiological systems are closely coupled during these early months of life. Close coupling is a principle of general systems theory, and between the adult system and the infant system it provides for the infant's vitally essential internal and external needs. The infant could not survive physically on its own. Close coupling begins with mother's provision for her infant's nutritional and environmental needs (protection from predators and other dangers), and it expands to include mother's provision for her child's affect regulation needs as development proceeds. The caregiver's ability to sustain close coupling at this early stage will depend upon her own developmental history and her ability to tolerate the demands, frustrations, and stresses entailed. How well the caregiver provides for the infant's nutritional and environmental needs is a harbinger of how well she will withstand the stresses of the close coupling entailed in providing for the infant's emerging affective needs.

Within the context of the infant–caregiver dyad, the caregiver's behavior is goal-corrected. She selects from many available behavioral options those behaviors that bring the set goal of her infant's comfort closer. During these first months of the infant's life, the caregiver holds the responsibility for terminating one link in a behavioral chain and initiating the next link. As the infant develops, he acquires more responsibility for initiating and terminating chain links himself. The set goal of the attachment system is proximity, and during the first months that constitute the preattachment phase, the caregiver holds responsibility for maintaining physical closeness to her infant. The caregiver's attachment behaviors are goal-corrected for the objective of maintaining physical proximity.

Within the infant–caregiver behavioral dyad, the infant signals his needs with cries and his comfort with either the absence of crying or by smiling. Early in his life, he produces these behaviors in a relatively reflexive or automatic fashion in response to internal state changes that elicit global reactions. His behavior has a prominently physiological context, and his first adaptive task is to develop regularity in physiological cycles. Later, in the period these internal state changes generate more precise and coordinated reactions (Sroufe, 1996). The caregiver can either facilitate the development of regularity in physiological cycles or impede its development. The primordia of secure attachment are established when caregiver and infant are able to collaborate in launching physiological regularity, which presages the subsequent development of affective regularity. When the infant's physiological and environmental needs are inconsistently met, the early conditions exist for later development of insecure attachment.

The caregiver's face and her gaze transactions with the infant are critical to maturation of the infant's brain. During the months following her birth, the neonate's brain grows rapidly (Schore, 1994). Continuing until 18 to 24 months, the processes of cell division, axonal and dendritic elaboration, myelination, and synaptic synthesis result in an increase in brain weight to 1,000 gm at 12 months from the birth weight of 400 gm. The overall gain in weight reflects the differential growth of specific regions of the brain at unique times. Throughout this period, different regions of the brain mature according to precise schedules. Specific, highly critical external stimuli are essential during each of these developmental windows to promote optimal development. Each of these developmental windows opens and closes according to its own unique time lines. During the first months of life, the critical stimuli are provided by mother's face and develop in the context of the sustained, mutual gaze transactions between mother and infant. Schore (1994) called these time- and task-delimited developmental environments "ontological niches," that is to say a window of developmental opportunity defined by the developmental requirements of the period. In the first three months, the ontological niche entails gaze transactions between caregiver and newborn that are apparently essential to imprinting mother's face in the infant's brain. During this time, the infant's visual system is fixed and focused at 10 inches, and significantly, mothers have been shown to hold their infants 10 inches away from their own faces. Imprinting the caregiver's face begins the structuralization process that eventuates in formation of self. The face that is imprinted at this time is the face that will be the most important broadcaster of affect to the child during subsequent developmental stages.

As Sroufe (1996) noted, the infant at 6 months does not distinguish objects from one another, nor form concepts of the relationship between objects. Memory capacity has not formed, so that the idea of past, present, and future does not yet exist. Means and ends are not separated. Behavioral plans do not exist. Anticipation of outcome does not exist. Objects attract the infant's attention because of their novelty. What is novel is reached for and usually inserted in the infant's mouth. All of this begins to change during the ensuing three months.

Development of the Symbiosis: The Second Three Months of Life

Development is a cumulative process. A fundamental principle of development states that the outcomes of development at one stage influence the path of development in subsequent stages (Lewis, 2000). The gaze transactions between infant and caregiver during the first months of life contribute to establishment of the developmental stage that Mahler called symbiosis (Mahler et al., 1975). These gaze transactions facilitate experiences of merger between infant and caregiver, and empathic exchanges occur in this context that are required for the development of positive affect that occurs in subsequent stages. Merger in the dyad elicits release of the infant's endogenous opioids, thus inducing pleasure and rewarding the infant. The gaze transactions between infant and caregiver lay the foundation for emergence of functional behaviors in subsequent developmental stages. As the infant successfully transits each stage, the probability of successfully negotiating the subsequent stage increases.

Gaze transactions promote regulation of arousal. In the gaze transactions that contribute to development of the symbiosis, the infant gazes at her caregiver, and this induces the caregiver to gaze in return. The caregiver's face, particularly her eyes, are a forceful stimulus in the infant's world, and the infant focuses on the pupils of the caregiver's eyes. As she gazes at her child, the mother's pupils dilate, transmitting interest affect to the infant and inducing the infant's pupils to dilate; mother's dilated pupils apparently activate the infant's hypothalamic sympathetic centers, and this induces the infant's pupillary dilation. In this way, mother's gaze regulates the infant's arousal. Gaze transactions powerfully illustrate how the dyad functions as the developmental unit. When regulation of arousal eventuates through optimal gaze transactions, neural pathways are laid down that determine future adaptive arousal regulation. The pathways that lead to positive functioning in toddlerhood, childhood, preschool, and later have their inception in infancy.

The infant's gaze aversion signals the caregiver that he is overstimulated. In gaze transactions, infant averts his gaze to signal the caregiver when stimulation is exceeding optimal levels and becoming stressful. Gaze aversion is one of the earliest manifestations of the infant's taking control of transactions in the dyad. The attuned caregiver will respond to these gaze aversion bids to decrease stimulation and supply soothing. When the dyad is misattuned, the caregiver fails to respond to the gaze aversion bid, the infant becomes stressed, and distress affect (crying) is elicited. When the caregiver is attuned to the infant's gaze aversion signals, the infant learns that his needs will be met, and the basis of a secure attachment is established that will have effects across the life span. Infants whose signals are ignored or dismissed will thereby be launched on a developmental pathway in which an insecure attachment is more probable. Negative outcomes are more likely when an insecure attachment path is enjoined.

Formation of an inner representation of the attachment figure commences at the onset of the second three months of life. Beginning at this time, the infant orients and directs signaling toward one or more discriminated figures (Marvin & Britner, 1999). Up to this juncture, the infant had responded equally to most human figures. Hand–eye coordination has developed, and this part of the sensorimotor system serves the infant as he is now able to reach for the breast or grasp mother's clothing. Responding specifically to a discriminated figure begins a pattern that will culminate in the first appearance of attachment behavior at 7 to 8 months. Attachment is a behavioral system that develops gradually over several months. In the developmental dyad, the infant's attachment system and mother's caregiving system complement each other much like yin and yang. Over developmental time, the image of the attachment figure that is beginning to form beginning at 3 months will evolve, becoming the basis for the eventual emergence of self and the initial locus of control of impulses and regulation of affects.

Affect expression begins to develop out of the preemotional reactions in the second quarter of life's first year. At 4 months, infants begin to develop the capacity to amplify affects, and they begin to be able to increase enjoyment affect. Measurements of heart rate as an indication of interest affect show that beginning at 2 months infants are experiencing more intense levels of this affect. During this second quarter of the first year, the preemotional reactions develop into precursor emotions (Sroufe, 1996). The precursor emotions are psychophysiological processes that show the beginnings of specificity and coordination. Furthermore, the infant will become actively involved in producing stimulation. At 3 months, the pleasure system has advanced from producing smiles in response to internal states or any stimulus that produces sufficient arousal, to smiling at a toy, a specific stimulus. This transition indicates how the requirement for content is developing. The infant will even move a mobile to produce smiling and cooing. From the age of 2 months the infant has been acquiring the ability to regulate her own arousal state through gaze aversion.

Mutuality is a signature characteristic of the optimally functioning infant–caregiver dyad. The infant's smile and laughter, expressions of enjoyment–joy affect, illustrate the mutuality of the dyadic relationship. Izard (1991) wrote, "the smile is an innate expression, preprogrammed in the human infant to elicit and assure a strong bond with the mother . . ." (p. 158). Laughter appears first in response to tactile and auditory cues, and as it develops, visual and social stimuli come to elicit it. The infant's laughter teaches her that her expressive activity influences the behavior of others. In laughter situations, the infant often initiates the behavior sequence between herself and her mother that results in laughter. The presence of mutuality in the dyad determines the development of neural pathways in the infant that eventuate in a responsive, engaged child. This child expects mutual interaction and will act to produce it. Dyads characterized by suboptimal mutual responsiveness initiate developmental pathways that may be more likely to produce withdrawal or anxious avoidance in the child.

The fear system and the anger system begin to emerge during the second quarter of year one. As with the pleasure system, a content requirement is emerging. In the first three months, *any* object that captured the infant's attention would stimulate arousal culminating in distress. During the second three months of life, the stimuli for fear must have some significance in order to elicit fear. For example, during the second quarter of year 1, a stranger's face may elicit fear. Although the infant is attracted to human faces in general, when a specific face cannot be assimilated, precursor fear is elicited. Sroufe (1996) believed that precursor fear denoted the appearance of wariness, a distress reaction to the unavoidable or unassimilable. Like precursor fear, precursor anger unfolds in the second quarter of the first year. When a well-established motor pattern is interrupted, screaming may be elicited, perhaps by giving the infant a toy he cannot pull into himself. Precursor anger is not yet anger emotion because the required intentionality is not yet present. Pleasure, fear, and anger system transactions all illustrate how affective expressions "mark, pace, or complete" (Sroufe, 1996, p. 47) both social and nonsocial encounters, emphasizing the sensoriaffective, as opposed to sensorimotor quality of this stage of development.

5–6 TO 9–10 MONTHS

Beginning in this time frame and extending to the child's second birthday, the stage that Mahler (Mahler et al., 1975) termed *separation-individuation* begins. Separation-individuation has three subphases: hatching, practicing, and rapprochement. The hatching subphase extends from the age of 5 or 6 months to 9 or 10 months.

Mother or other primary caregiver increasingly becomes the baby's central focus during hatching as the attachment system emerges. Orienting toward and signaling a discriminated caregiver figure increases during the months of the hatching subphase. The infant restricts several behaviors to mother: termination of crying, crying at separation, smiling, vocalization, climbing and exploring, and the greeting response. Moreover, in the dyad, the infant begins to take more responsibility for initiating behavioral exchanges. Several new behaviors appear during this period. A careful examination of these behaviors reveals how they are recruited in the service of the attachment system. The appearance of locomotion in the form of crawling occurs during this time, and the infant can begin to control her proximity to mother, can begin to explore as well as get into significant danger.

At 6 months the infant shows differential following of mother when she leaves the room. At 7 months he approaches mother differentially, especially in a reunion or when he's distressed, and he will bury his face only in mom's lap. Also at 7 months, the exploratory behavioral system comes on line. With the appearance of exploration, a new aspect of the infant–caregiver dyad emerges as the caregiver begins to function as a secure base for the infant's first exploratory forays. As the exploratory system continues to develop, the caregiver's function as a safe haven appears, a place the infant can fly to when he is disturbed in the course of exploration. This function comes on line later at $8\frac{1}{2}$ months.

Developmental events during hatching highlight the importance for optimal maturation of having available a sensitively attuned, responsive caregiver. The attachment system appears to require the presence of at least one caregiver who is primarily preoccupied with the child. This is the individual who functions as a secure base and safe haven, and it is this individual's inner representation in the baby's mind that serves as the "seed crystal" for crystallization of the infant's self (Kohut & Wolf, 1978). When an attuned, responsive caregiver who is primarily preoccupied with the child is available, a secure attachment bond forms, and the child is more likely to enjoin a developmental pathway with a positive outcome. When a primary caregiver is unavailable, or is distracted, insensitive, or unresponsive for whatever reason, formation of a secure attachment appears less probable, and pathways of insecure attachment leading to less favorable outcomes appear more likely. Economic forces sometimes disrupt the infant–caregiver dyad, and the infant may have multiple, distracted caregivers; for example, in the day care setting. Mothers forced to work fulltime and to place their children in child care may be distracted and stressed when they are present. These factors may explain a recent study (Child-care, 2001) showing that the more time preschoolers spend in child care, the more likely their kindergarten teachers are to report aggression and defiance.

Cognitive Developments

The infant's cognitive development during hatching consists of the formation of IWMs of important figures and the assembly of chains of behavior directed toward achievement of a goal. The initiation of IWM formation is inferred from the behaviors of discriminating the primary caregiver from other figures. Between 6 and 9 months, the infant develops the ability to form intentions, to create an image of a set goal. Person permanence appears, which means that the infant holds an image of the caregiver (i.e., attachment figure), maintaining it even when the figure is physically absent. The set goal, proximity to the caregiver, for example, is an objective, and earlier chain-linked behaviors become organized in the service of attainment of the goal. For example, an early chain of linked behaviors is related to nursing. In this chain, which appears around 3 months, the sight of the breast activates the infant's mouth to open and for the infant to bring her hands to her mouth. By the 6th month, this chain has developed, and infant will signal his need to nurse, attract mother, and grasp her clothing as he roots for the breast.

The infant's expanding communication skills also indicate cognitive development. In the earlier stages, communication took the form of bids for attention in which infant and caregiver took turns in primitive, prelinguistic exchanges. By the hatching period, communication is used to regulate the behavior of others. While still nonverbal, the infant may request or reject objects and bid for or dismiss another's attention.

Affective Developments

During the hatching phase the affects continue their development out of the primordial pleasure, fear, and anger systems, and the first true emotions appear. The appearance of IWMs and intention formation during the third quarter of the first year marks the onset of the experience of true emotion. The infant's maturing capability to perceive and form internal representations allows for affects to assemble with images in ways unique to the infant. Subjective evaluation plays an increasing role in determining behavior. Interest affect, for example, assembles with an image of the caregiver, and the infant displays interest in her face, discriminating it from other faces toward which the infant may not show interest. When interest affect assembles with specific representations to motivate discriminated behaviors, interest emotion may be said to have appeared.

Physiology no longer occupies a place of primacy in determining behavior. For example, at the end of the 6th month, hunger no longer provokes the same arousal as it did at the end of the 1st month. Responses continue to become more coordinated and specific; for example, the 8-month-old infant will move to block an attempt to wipe her nose, where the neonate complained with her entire body. Situational context becomes important because the infant is able to form representations and remember past experiences. The third-quarter infant organizes emotion displays with respect to environment, preceding events, and the caregiver's availability.

In the third-quarter infant we see the beginnings of emotion's guiding influence on behavior and the integrating effect of emotion on the infant's personality. Earlier in life, events were separated and episodic. By the third quarter of the first year, events are unified and contextualized by the emerging self structure. Emotion-driven chains of behavior appear. Emotion will be seen to recruit from a variety of behaviors (grasping, reaching, crawling), ones that serve a set goal (proximity to the attachment figure). For example, yearning affect will have assembled with *this* infant's image and experience of *that* caregiver to form yearning emotion that motivates him to signal his needs to his own mother in a unique, highly personalized manner. Emotion comes to serve other behavior systems besides attachment; for example, exploration, wariness, and sociability. As emotions develop out of precursors, they are less expressive of pure arousal and reflect greater and greater assembly with meaning. The initial appearance of emotion during the third quarter prefigures the eventual emergence of mature emotion, "a subjective reaction to a salient event, characterized by physiological, experiential, and overt behavioral change" (Sroufe, 1996, p. 15).

9–10 TO 12–13 MONTHS

During the separation–individuation subphase called practicing that extends from about 9 to about 18 months, the infant acquires the ability to up-regulate positive affect and to attenuate negative affect, and as these skills are gained, the basic foundation of the self is laid down. These critical developmental events build on the groundwork established in the preceding symbiosis phase and hatching subphase. The critical events of the practicing subphase take place across all developmental dimensions: attachment, neurobiology, affect regulation, emergence of self structure. The practicing subphase is divided into early and late periods. A cluster of critical events occurs in early practicing, the period from 9 or 10 months to 12 or 13 months. Mother's principle contribution during early practicing is to amplify her child's interest affect and enjoyment affect experiences. These visual–affective communication transactions motivate the full realization of the attachment behavior system. In addition, activation of the infant's interest and enjoyment affects induces neurobiological developments resulting in maturation of a corticolimbic circuit that provides for vitality across the life span. Failures during this period can result in difficulties with vitality and can set the child on a pathway where depression and social withdrawal are more probable outcomes. AMST can help clients whose current psychopathology has its origins in deficits during this phase. Clinicians must understand the origins of affective impairments in the motivational system driven by interest affect and in the reward system driven by joy affect so they can use the AMST interventions to best help the depressed, withdrawn, or vitality-impaired client.

Amplification of Positive Affect

In early practicing, the infant–caregiver dyad functions to provide elicitation and amplification of the child's positive affect. When this vital function is provided, a key regulatory system for positive affect is induced in the child's brain. At the onset of early practicing, the infant is beginning to crawl, and the exploration behavioral system is appearing. The infant will make brief sorties away from mother's secure base. He will move toward the toy box and play for a brief period. Researchers have noted that the child becomes enervated after a play period, his initial excitement having abated. He appears glum, his attention is unfocused, and his hedonic tone is negative. He turns to mother, crawling to her, and reunion ensues. In the reunion event, an exchange of energy occurs. Mahler called this exchange "refueling." Mother attends to her junior toddler's expressive face, assessing his affective status. In a gaze transaction lasting just over 1 second, the infant reads mother's face and responds to her affect-regulating behaviors. Mother's face manifests interest and enjoyment, and her interest and enjoyment induce arousal of these affects in her child. The attuned mother's function in the dyad is to transfer optimal levels of interest affect and enjoyment affect arousal to her child (Schore, 1994). The infant's ability to experience high levels of activation of interest affect and enjoyment affect depend upon the successful completion of the symbiosis stage tasks of imprinting, gaze transaction, and merger. Mother's arousal of more intense levels of positive affect in her child build the attachment, induce essential neurobiological changes in the infant, continue the process of emotion development, and contribute to the emerging self structure.

Attachment

Attachment is a behavioral system that keeps infant and mother in close proximity and thereby improves the infant's chances for survival. Development of attachment is motivated by affective state. Cassidy (1999) wrote that attachment results from "a biologically based desire for proximity" (p. 4), a desire that I hypothesize is motivated by the affect of yearning. The attachment system arose through natural selection, and its biological function is protection from predators. In the environments in which humans and our evolutionary progenitors evolved, infants who wandered away from their mothers were subject to predation. MacLean (1990) observed that Komodo dragons eat their young if they find them, and he stated that infant caretaking is one of the behaviors that evolved as humans evolved from reptilian predecessors. Attachment is conceived of as a behavioral system that ensures a predictable outcome: increased proximity of the child to the attachment figure. Attachment behaviors operate to ensure attainment of the predictable outcome. The child's signaling behaviors such as smiling and vocalizing alert the caregiver to the child's desire for proximity, activating mother's caregiving behavioral system, and bringing her to the infant. The aversive stimulus of crying, a manifestation of distress affect, also functions to bring the caregiver to the infant with the goal of terminating the aversive behavior. In the child of 9 months, the locomotive behavioral system is appearing, and this provides the neotoddler with active behaviors to create proximity to the maternal caregiver, beginning with crawling and progressing to cruising and eventually upright locomotion. Almost all children become attached, whether the parents meet the child's physiological needs or not, and empirical evidence demonstrates that "infants become attached even to abusive mothers" (Cassidy, 1999, p. 5).

The affects yearning and joy function to establish the attachment, and interest affect and distress affect cooperate to maintain the optimal proximity between infant and caregiver. The affective vectors point from child to caregiver and caregiver to child in the developmental dyad. I have posited a yearning affect that operates in the infant and the caregiver to keep them in close proximity to each other. When the optimal proximity is attained, motivated by yearning, the affect felt is enjoyment, and its expression is the smile. When either dyad partner experiences too much separation, the affect felt is distress, expressed as crying in the infant, and that motivates the behavior of searching in the mother. Attachment and exploration are competing behavioral systems. The infant's interest affect motivates exploration, which manifests as moving away from the secure base afforded by the caregiver. The control systems approach adopted by attachment theorists says that increased separation resulting from exploration behavior activates the infant's attachment behavior and suppresses exploration behavior with the result that the infant returns to the safe haven, mother. A wariness system based on fear affect also impacts both the attachment system and the exploration system. The infant appraises the environment for adversity and caregiver proximity. If the environment is adverse, attachment is activated, and exploration is diminished. If the caregiver is too separated, exploration is attenuated. If the environment is benign and the caregiver is available, then exploration is activated, and investigation ensues. The infant explores, becomes emotionally depleted, and returns to mother for refueling. The refueling process has important consequences for the infant's neurobiological development. Maternal sensitivity is the central quality of the caregiver that determines the security of the attachment. Empirical research has demonstrated that maternal sensitivity during the first year of life predicted attachment security (Weinfield et al., 1999). This result held even when infant temperament was irritable. In fact, maternal sensitivity ameliorated the presence of infant irritability.

Neurobiological Development

The caregiver's stimulation of the junior toddler's interest affect and enjoyment affect in the reunion situation induces biochemical events in the child's brain resulting in the maturation of a neural circuit critical to vitality across the remainder of life (Schore, 1994). The central thesis of Schore's work was that "the early social environment, mediated by the primary caregiver, directly influences the evolution of structures in the brain that are responsible for the future socioemotional development of the child" (p. 62). During the early practicing subphase of separation-individuation, the structure that develops is the ventral tegmental circuit, a pathway that connects the orbitofrontal cortex (OFC) to subcortical limbic structures (Figure 2.1).

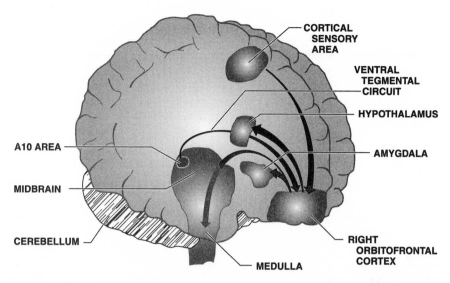

Figure 2.1. The ventral tegmental circuit of the OFC. A schematic representation of the activating circuit at the highest level of control of human affect and emotion responding. The brain's right hemisphere is shown. The right orbitofrontal cortex (OFC) is located in the frontal cortex of the right hemisphere. Directional arrows indicate neural inputs to the OFC and neural outputs from it to areas of the brain (hypothalamus, amygdala, medulla) controlling affective responding (heart rate, respiration rate, etc.). The ventral tegmental circuit is composed of dopaminergic neurons originating in the midbrain's A10 area that innervate the OFC. Optimal development of this circuit is experience-dependent. The ventral tegmental circuit mediates positive affects and emotions.

The OFC is the brain's highest control center for affective regulation and it is located on the ventral and medial surfaces of the frontal lobe and is enlarged in the right hemisphere. Affect regulation is lateralized, meaning that the right hemisphere and right OFC process affect in most people regardless of whether they are right- or left-handed. The OFC is a mesocortical, not neocortical, forebrain structure, and it is intimately connected to subcortical limbic areas. All sensory areas of the posterior cortex provide inputs to the OFC, including visual, somesthetic, auditory, and olfactory regions. Connecting to the hypothalamus, autonomic areas, and neuromodulator systems in the brainstem, the OFC functions as a central processing unit for emotional and motivational processes. Through single synapse connections to the hypothalamus, the OFC exerts a control function over the autonomic nervous system. Two circuits that mature during the practicing subphase supply information to the OFC and receive signals from it. One of these, the ventral tegmental circuit, consists of ascending dopaminergic fibers and descending cholinergic fibers. The ventral circuit matures during the early practicing phase, and its maturation depends upon arousal of positive emotion; that is, the interest and enjoyment affects, provided by mother to her junior toddler. The other circuit, the lateral tegmental circuit, matures a few months later and will be described in the next section.

The ventral tegmental circuit arises in dopaminergic neurons of the midbrain. These neurons send axons forward and upward, and as the axons grow rostrally, they send off collateral branches to many forebrain areas. In response to mother's arousal of her junior toddler's positive affect in reunion encounters over the approximately three months of early practicing, the dopaminergic axons sprout new synaptic terminals in the OFC and synthesize new dopamine receptors. This biochemical synthetic activity is experience dependent, which means that stimulation by the physical and social environment is required for its success. Optimal social and environmental stimulation results in the maturation of the ventral tegmental circuit linking the midbrain to forebrain regions. In addition to axonal growth, maturation is accompanied by growth of blood vessels, glial cells, and resident neurons of the OFC. Maturation of the OFC expresses itself in behaviors of hyperarousal, hyperactivity, activation of exploration, and arousal of interest affect to the level of excitement affect and of enjoyment to the level of joy. The OFC elicits arousal of the emotion response system by means of cholinergic fibers that exit the OFC and innervate the amygdala, the hypothalamus, and the medulla. These descending, cholinergic fibers project back down the neuraxis, relaying signals from the OFC through the amygdala and medulla to the eventual sites of action (Nathanson, 1992), the places where affect can be recognized as feeling. These sites of action are the heart, gut, pupils, sweat glands, blood vessels, muscles of the face and body, and hairs, that is, the places where the qualia of an emotion are generated.

The primary maternal caregiver's role has evolved, and she is now responsible for her child's affective socialization. The neurophysiological developments or early practicing depend upon this fundamental change in the ontogenetic niche taking place. Mother's role has shifted as her infant achieves locomotion, first through crawling and then by walking. In the previous niche, mother was primarily a caregiver. In the new niche she has become the agent of her junior toddler's emotional socialization. In the early practicing phase, her socialization function consists in optimal activation of the infant's positive affects. In parallel with developments in emotion socialization, brain pathways, and attachment, important changes are occurring in the infant's object relations and IWMs.

Object Relations and IWMs

Cognitive development flourishes in the early practicing period, as the child begins to develop goal-corrected behavior and as his images of the caregiver coalesce and become the basis for his nascent ability to regulate his own affects. In goal-corrected behavior (Marvin & Britner, 1999), the infant selects from a repertoire those behaviors that bring him closer to his set goal, reconfiguring his behavior plan according to feedback from the effects of the behavior. Goal-corrected behavior differs significantly from the chain-linked behavior patterns representative of the first months of life. Chain-linked sequences coordinate simple behaviors, and the termination of one link activates the next link. For example, the cry of a hungry 1-month-old infant predictably activates mother's caregiving behavior; she picks up the infant and presents the breast, which terminates the crying, and activates rooting behavior. Rooting terminates, and grasping the nipple with the lips ensues, followed by sucking, then swallowing. In goal-corrected behavior, the neotoddler may crawl toward mother, and, if mother were to move away, he might stop and cry in order to bring her to him. When she realizes his need and turns toward him, he may cease crying and hold up his arms indicating his intention to be picked up. The appearance of goal-corrected behavior indicates that the junior toddler is able to create behavioral plans and to organize them hierarchically. The emergence of goal-corrected behavior and behavioral plans implies that the junior toddler creates separate working models of self and of caregiver. These IWMs form out of established sequences of interactions that have already occurred in the past and that are assembled with affects. The infant is preverbal at this stage, displaying signals and nonverbal utterances. The junior toddler's IWMs are primitive, because at this stage she thinks about the caregiver only in terms of the caregiver's behaviors and then only in short sequences of behaviors.

During the last quarter of the first year, object relations first appear. The term *object relations* refers to the structural and dynamic relationships between the self-representation and the representation of the other, the object (Horner, 1984). Visual information about the caregiver, her face, and her behaviors requires representational memory and involves the OFC coordinating with the anterior temporal cortex, a member of the ventral tegmental limbic circuit. Object relations represent the self in interaction with the attachment figure. These representations are "abstractions of the infant's autonomic physiological–affective responses to the visual perception of the emotionally expressive face of the attachment object" (Schore, 1994, p. 178). The ability to generate such an internal, visual representation appears at 10 months and not before, and by 12 months, tactual stimuli are being assembled with the visual image.

By the close of the first year, solely in the context of the dyad, the infant has developed representations of self and other that unite image, affect, and sensation. The appearance of these representations, which are held in memory, reflects neurophysiological development and maturation. The infant employs these wholly preverbal representations to create plans and intentions. These internal representations constitute the foundation of the attachment, and they lay the structure for the emerging self with effects across the life span. The infant uses IWMs of self and other to regulate emotion. As Schore (1994) wrote, the IWM "can be accessed for regulatory purposes, even in the mother's absence" (p. 186).

By the close of the first year, individual differences in attachment behavior can be observed, with some infants already exhibiting secure attachment and others showing characteristics of insecure attachment. The term *secure attachment* describes the infant's perception in the dyad that the caregiver will provide comfort and protection should the need arise (Weinfield et al., 1999). The infant's physiology reflects the security of attachment, and securely attached infants are less prone to stress as measured by cortisol level. The child's cortisol levels reflect mother's social regulation of her infant's affect (Gunnar & Donzella, 2002), and by the end of the first year, the high cortisol reactivity of the newborn diminishes and "it becomes difficult to provoke increases in cortisol to many stressors" (p. 215) where there has been a history of responsive and sensitive caregiving.

The securely attached infant has developed IWMs in the dyadic experience that are constituted of experiences of yearning being requited, emotional and physiological needs being met, a caregiver being available as secure base and safe haven, interest and joy being activated, and of soothing following mismatch and stress. According to Cassidy (1999), the securely attached 1-year-old toddler has developed a "mental representation of the attachment figure as available and responsive when needed" (p. 7).

When the infant–caregiver dyad functions optimally, the experiential, neurophysiological, affective, and cognitive developments of early practicing establish the basis for an adaptive, well-organized self structure characterized by cohesion, vigor, and order. Because this child's needs have been consistently met, she will have naturally formed a complex inner image of safety and security that is the functional equivalent of the safe place image developed in AMST skill II (see Chapter 7). Her positive affect will have been optimally aroused with the result that she will naturally be aware of the qualia of interest affect and joy affect. Her attuned caregiver will have responded sensitively to her gaze avert responses, and as a result she will have developed internal resources for affect tolerance that correspond to the grounding resource taught by AMST (see pp. 288–291). She will have formed IWMs that she can use to amplify her positive affects herself. These IWMs are functionally equivalent to the AMST skill VII (regulation) gauge resource representation for amplifying positive affect.

12–13 TO 16–18 MONTHS

During the senior toddler phase, the emerging self structure further expands as the child acquires the skills to down-regulate a range of affects. With the onset of the late practicing phase of separation-individuation at about 12 months of age, the child becomes a senior toddler. This phase extends to about 18 months. For the first time, the junior toddler's exuberant, unrestricted exploration meets limitations. The potential for danger to the child appears in the environments in which humans evolved and in the contemporary environment, and the caregivers begin to restrict the toddler in order to protect him. Speech, one of the autonomous functions, appears, expanding the toddler's communication ability. IWMs develop further during late practicing as the toddler acquires knowledge about the caregiver's unique perceptions and goals and realization that these may be different from the toddler's. Finally, a process of neurobiological maturation takes place that will have profound effects across the life span: development of the capacity to down-regulate, inhibit, or attenuate emotion processes. This process of neurobiological maturation, occurring in the socioaffective context of the dyad, is called *emotion socialization*.

Socialization of Emotion

The term *emotion socialization* describes the process by which people come to feel as they do as a result of their relationships with others (Saarni, 1993). Emotions are socialized from birth. We have learned how the primitive emotion reactions of the neonate became emotion precursors and then true emotions in the socioaffective crucible of the infant–caregiver dyad. Schore (1994) has taught us how the infant's OFC and ventral tegmental circuit mature as a result of socio-affective induction supplied through mother's stimulation of infant's positive affect. The interchange within the dyad illustrates a principle that as the child's emotions are developing *in* the dyad, others, most importantly mother, are communicating emotions *to* the child. Often, these broadcast emotions emerge as a result of the caregiver's cognitive process of evaluating the child's emotional behavior (Saarni, 1993). This evaluative process is to a great extent culturally determined, and the emotion structure of which emotion to feel and how to express it under what circumstances and to whom will vary across cultures. The present presentation will not concern itself with these multicultural issues, because our aim is to describe the process of socialization in enough detail for the clinician to be able to use her own multicultural sensitivities to apply the skills of Part II to her own client population. In the socialization process, children are exposed to emotion-eliciting situations. They learn about the emotions involved. As a result, the child's self structure expands as the child incorporates the emotion-knowledge into his own emotionscape, the emotional map of "when to feel, what to feel, how to express feelings, and whom to express them to" (Saarni, 1993, p. 436).

Significant changes in the ontological niche mark the beginning of the first quarter of the toddler's second year. Conflict appears in the dyad for the first time. The toddler's omnipotence and grandiosity conflict with mother's reality-based plans. Where previously, the maternal caregiver had been uniformly supportive, even permissive, she now imposes restrictions on the toddler. Mother begins to use the word *no* for the first time when the toddler is about 15 months old. On the surface and to the adult participants, it may appear that the toddler's behaviors are what is being regulated; however, beneath the surface a far more profound affective regulatory process transpires. The emotion transactions within the dyad promote the infant's development of affect attenuation skills. Sufficiency or deficiency in these processes during this critical six-month period determines the nature of the developmental pathway the senior toddler will embark upon with consequences for the remainder of his life's journey.

In the process of emotion socialization, operating primarily in the social context of the child–caregiver dyad, the child learns to regulate her affects through internalization of images and experiences. These regulatory images—mother's disapproving face, for example—assemble with the affect being regulated, and in the process the affect becomes an emotion, an autobiographical construct belonging uniquely to this particular child. Emotion socialization is an affective process, not a cognitive process. What the child internalizes is the image of mother's disapproving face, tone of voice, and body language, not the verbal content of her disapproving words. Just as the caregiver socialized affect amplification during early practicing with her interested, joy-filled facial expressions, so too does she socialize affect attenuation in late practicing with optimal facial displays of disapproval. What is different in late practicing is that emotions are brought into play that have not previously been operative in the toddler's life. The first of these, in its most benign form, is maternal disapproval.

Disapproval lies in the domain of disgust (Izard, 1991) and is a milder form of that more primitive and exceedingly powerful emotion. In Izard's study, about 18% of 130 college students endorsed "dislike, disapproval of actions of other" as an antecedent feeling for the emotion disgust. Disapproval also resides in the domain of another powerful affect, contempt, according to Izard's data. Nine percent of the college students endorsed a feeling of "disapproval, disturbed by actions of others" as an antecedent of contempt. Not all theorists accord contempt a place among the pantheon of primary affects, and in Plutchik's theory of derived emotions (discussed in LeDoux, 1996) contempt is a primary dyad composed of anger and disgust.

Disapproval is the principal affective instrument the caregiver employs in socialization of her toddler's affect. A fundamental issue to which we return repeatedly concerns the caregiver's crucial affective role in the dyad during this phase. The caregiver must supply optimal levels of disapproval, and she must be able to tolerate her own emotions elicited by her toddler's frustration. These roles are demanding and difficult. The emotion of disgust that is the affective foundation for disapproval is extremely powerful and if used without restraint has the potential to damage the toddler. The caregiver must negotiate a narrow range of optimal disapproval expression in supplying supportive frustration experiences to her toddler. If she slips out of the optimal range of disapproval affect in the direction of expressing disgust affect toward her toddler, the effect can be a humiliation experience with lasting consequences. However, if she abdicates her caregiving responsibility and opts to slip out of the range of optimal disapproval in the direction of permissiveness, she risks another kind of damage, because the experience of the caregiver's disapproval is absolutely essential to development of the toddler's shame affect and with it emotion socialization and the ability to attenuate high levels of affective arousal.

Emotion Transactions in the Dyad of the Late Practicing Period

The late practicing period is characterized by the first appearance of disapproval–shame transactions between caregiver and child. Both the toddler's and mother's intentions become increasingly discordant as late practicing begins. Gates are installed blocking the toddler's crawlway. Cupboard doors that appear so inviting are now closed with child-proof fasteners just at the point when the toddler could finally reach them. Pots, toys, glass, CDs, pictures, shiny appliances, electrical outlets, and everything else attractive to the toddler because parents use them, are plugged or moved up out of reach. Mother tires of baby's game of "drop the carrot sticks on the floor and watch mom pick them up." The toddler, who has developed an expectation that his own positive states will be enhanced by mother as they have been for several months, experiences misattunement. Mother's face no longer always expresses excitement affect and joy affect. In its place is something new, disapproval. Disapproval affect, displayed on the caregiver's face and in the quality and volume of her voice, signal misattunement. This misattunement means that mother's and child's intentions are no longer always aligned. Because it partakes of disgust affect, caregiver's disapproval face betokens rejection. Caregiver's pupils, which have been dilated throughout early practicing are now constricted. Her brow, which had been smooth with eyebrows drawn up, has furrowed, narrowing the eyes. The mouth hardens with corners drawn down, where previously they had been drawn up. The effect of misattunement, signaled by disapproval, is to induce shame in the toddler.

Shame, when elicited optimally, is a primary socializing emotion, and the benign evocation of shame is essential to emotion socialization. Emotion socialization translates into impulse control and behavior delay. Shame affect appears between 12 and 18 months. Shame is an attenuator of other affects, and it is elicited when there is an impediment to expression of interest affect or joy affect (Nathanson,1992). Toddler's interest affect is interrupted by the discordant disapproval affect displayed on the caregiver's face, and shame is elicited. The toddler's autonomic system shifts from sympathetic arousal or dominance to parasympathetic arousal or dominance. Empirical research supports that shame is assembled with parasympathetic arousal. When shame is elicited by disapproval in the dyadic transaction, the infant's system shifts from hyperarousal to hypoarousal. The appearance of shame has a unique physical and physiological signature. Facial and cervical muscle tone decreases, and the toddler's head slumps and his smile fades. The eyes are cast down. The index physiological response of shame, the blush, may appear because parasympathetic activity suppresses sympathetically induced vasoconstriction.

In the healthy disapproval–shame transaction, mother's disapproval elicits optimal, that is, healthy, shame in her toddler. From an evolutionary perspective, facially displayed affective behavioral control of the toddler has considerable survival value. This system allows mother to control her toddler's potentially dangerous behavior from a distance. The disapproval–shame transaction immediately terminates the toddler's exploratory behavior, as the interest affect motivating that behavior is attenuated. For her part, mother must be capable of tolerating her own emotions as she creates optimal frustration for her child in the disapproval–shame transaction. The transaction has important, interrelated consequences in three other areas besides immediate behavioral control: The toddler's developing representation of the maternal caregiver is altered; neurobiological maturation is affected; and the toddler's capacity for emotion regulation is changed. These consequences contribute to the further development of the child's emerging self.

As mother supplies optimal frustration during the ontogenetic niche of the late practicing period, the senior toddler's image of her undergoes significant alteration. Her actions, which are inhibitory and prohibiting, are assembled by the toddler with his evolving image of the caregiver. This evolving representation of mother constitutes the maternal introject, and this introject begins to function within the toddler's self to regulate his behavior through his own shame that is organized with the image and the memories of the transactions. This inhibitory mechanism develops by 18 months and depends upon what Schore (1994) called "signal shame"(p. 210). This signaling mechanism, working internally, warns the toddler that based on past experiential transactions with the caregiver his continued behavior in the present circumstance will evoke painful levels of shame affect.

The appearance of shame affect in the disapproval transactions with mother during the late practicing period induces the final maturation of the OFC. Disapproval–shame transactions cause a deactivation of the dopaminergic, excitatory ventral tegmental circuit and activation of the noradrenergic lateral tegmental circuit. The lateral circuit is parasympathetic and inhibitory. Activation of the lateral tegmental circuit induces the noradrenergic fibers of the circuit, originating in the medulla, to sprout along their rostral course into the OFC. Further maturation is accomplished as prefrontal, cholinergic axons of the OFC, growing caudally, project backward down the neuraxis onto subcortical areas. Maturation of the lateral tegmental circuit is completed when fibers reciprocally innervate the OFC and nuclei in the medulla. Figure 2.2 illustrates the lateral tegmental circuit.

Completion of lateral tegmental circuit maturation at about 18 months, lays the groundwork for lifelong, healthy emotion regulation. Maternal activation of positive affect during the early practicing period induces maturation of the ventral tegmental circuit and provides the emerging self with the capacity to experience and to autostimulate excitement affect and joy affect. Caregiver facilitated optimal disapproval–shame transactions promote maturation of the lateral

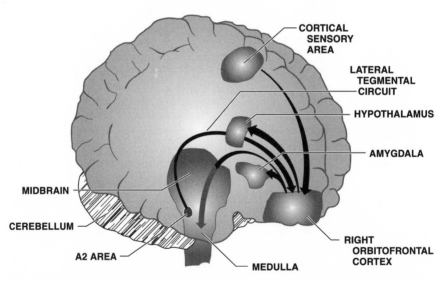

Figure 2.2.   The lateral tegmental circuit of the OFC. A schematic representation of the inhibiting circuit at the highest level of control of human affect and emotion responding. The right orbitofrontal cortex (OFC) is located in the frontal cortex of the right hemisphere. Directional arrows indicate neural inputs to the OFC and neural outputs from it to areas of the brain (hypothalamus, amygdala, medulla) controlling affective responding (heart rate, respiration rate, etc.) The lateral tegmental circuit is comprised of noradrenergic neurons arising in the medulla's A2 area and is inhibitory. Optimal development of this circuit is experience-dependent. The lateral tegmental circuit attenuates affective arousal and down-regulates distressing levels of both positive and negative affects and emotions.

tegmental circuit and endow the emerging self with the ability to down-regulate overly activated excitement affect and to regulate stress. Because the senior toddler has acquired the necessary neurobiological developments—acquisitions that absolutely depend upon the optimal social environment—she now has adequate emotional equipment in order for her to handle developments in attachment and for social learning in the preschool years.

The optimal disapproval–shame transactions of late practicing constitute the functional equivalent of AMST skills for down-regulating negative emotion, which is skill VII's disposal resource. When caregiving is "good enough," the child internalizes images of the primary caregiver that are used throughout life to facilitate emotion regulation. When there are deficits in caregiving, the child may not acquire these regulatory images or may not learn to use them to regulate the full range of emotions. When this happens, emotion dysregulation results. AMST skill VII provides a client-generated image to remediate the ontological deficit.

Attachment

During the second year and for most of the third year of life the organization of the attachment remains unchanged, even as profound cognitive, affective, and neurobiological changes are occurring. Attachment behavior does not diminish in frequency or intensity, and the 2-year-old will stay as close to the caregiver as a 1-year-old, although he will make more exploratory forays away from her. The toddler will monitor mother's movements and her attention, and if mother is not attending, the toddler will initiate attachment behavior. The set goal of the 2-year-old's attachment behavior has changed over the course of the second year of life. The 2-year-old's attachment needs may be satisfied by attracting the caregiver's attention, whereas at 1 year her attachment goal was greater physical proximity to caregiver. Two-year-olds are as distressed by separation as 1-year-olds, but attentional contact may be sufficient to allay the older child's distress, and if it is not, he can move to establish contact.

PRESCHOOL PERIOD

During the preschool period, building upon foundations established in the first 18 months of life, children develop most of the communication skills required for social integration. From 2 to 3 years, children increasingly recognize, understand, and discuss the feelings of others. Based on her experience of learning that mother has her own goals and emotions, the child realizes that others, children and adults, have their own feelings and plans. The child's IWMs develop to reflect this knowledge. IWMs expand to include the implicit and explicit rules of social behavior. The child's IWMs become more elaborate, more accurate, and less egocentric. Event representations appear, replacing the more primitive image-plans of the last quarter of the first year of life. Networks of image plans develop and displace the linear chain representations. The child asks "Why, Mommy?" and her answers facilitate the emergence of structure in the child's brain and mind. The child begins to develop the substitution skills necessary to insert caregiver's plans and goals into his own links of plans. He learns to inhibit or delay his own plan in order to accommodate the caregiver's plans, and he uses the emotion regulation skills he's acquired to manage the frustration attendant upon controlling his impulses.

Neurobiological Development During the Second Year

During the second year, the child enters a period Mahler called the rapprochement subphase of separation-individuation (Mahler et al., 1975). For the first time, father becomes an emotional object. During this time, the child is learning to hold mother's representation ambivalently (Horner, 1984). The "good mother" is the image of mother assembled with positive affect; the "bad mother" is her image assembled with negative affect. *Ambivalence* means the child develops a unitary representation of mother that melds both her good and bad, rewarding and non-rewarding aspects in the one representation. Father facilitates his child's continuing individuation as he takes a role in modulation and stimulation of his child's arousal. These affective transactions with father influence the growth and maturation of the left hemisphere's dorsolateral prefrontal system, much as transactions with mother induced developments in the right hemisphere. The right hemispheric representational system is affective and configurational, and IWMs developed there are nonverbal, affectively charged, and imprinted through exchanges with mother. In contrast, IWMs in the left hemisphere are verbal and imprinted through exchanges with father.

The Goal-Corrected Partnership

From the third to the fifth year, the attachment system matures. From the second birthday on, attachment is increasingly organized toward physical orientation, eye contact, nonverbal expressions, affect, and conversations about the dyad. By age 4, the child is not disturbed by separation if she and mother have negotiated a shared plan for separation and reunion prior to the departure. Most children of this age are competently acquiring the ability to think and talk about the feelings, goals, and plans of others in conversation with them. Nonverbal expressions become more complex, and the child uses them to regulate interactions. Complexity is revealed in the coy expressions children may demonstrate by this age. The use of posed expressions of happiness, surprise, anger, fear, sadness, and disgust illustrates how children can employ affective expressions to regulate interactions.

The maturation of attachment behavior is illustrated by children's developing ability to modulate their own behaviors in relation to the goals and intentions of others. Young preschoolers acquire the ability to insert caregiver's plans into their own plans. Learning to incorporate the goals of others represents a change in the organization of attachment behavior. The young preschooler's set goal may still be the achievement of proximity, but she has learned to inhibit her attachment behaviors in the short term in order to achieve her longer term goal. During the late preschool period, a new stage in maturation of attachment is appearing, the goal-corrected partnership. By the fourth birthday, the child can discriminate her own and others' perspectives and can maintain both perspectives in awareness.

She can assess these perspectives for match or mismatch. This child can operate on her action plan and another's action plan internally and simultaneously, and he or she can construct a shared perspective that becomes the new set goal. The set goal of the four-year-old has changed. Whereas at three years the set goal was physical proximity, by the fourth birthday it has become a shared plan for proximity. The goal-corrected partnership represents the last major phase or stage in the ontogeny of attachment.

Development of the goal-corrected partnership depends on prior development of skills for affect and emotion regulation. Children cannot develop the goal-corrected partnership if they have not learned to recognize, tolerate, and regulate affects of anger, sadness, fear, and interest. To participate in a goal-corrected partnership the child must be able to manage anger that arises when a parent's plan interferes with his own plan. The child must be able to manage distress–sadness affect at being separated by "too much" time from his goal. He must be able to manage fear that the parent's plan will always take precedence. Very importantly, he must be able to manage his interest affect that will tend to distract him from focusing on achieving his goal in the context of the partnership. The skills of emotion regulation that children develop in an optimally functioning child–caregiver dyad are the same skills that AMST transmits in the client–therapist dyad. Adaptive emotion regulation skills are a precondition for development of the goal-corrected partnership, and children who acquire these skills in early life can successfully take part in a succession of goal-corrected partnerships across the life span. The teacher–student relationship is a goal-corrected partnership that requires the student to have optimal emotion regulation skills for a successful academic outcome. Life is comprised of many other goal-corrected partnerships that necessitate adaptive affect management: employee-employer, athlete-coach, and husband-wife. If the child exits the developmental dyad with deficiencies of emotion regulation, he or she will experience difficulties in all succeeding goal-corrected partnerships, and his difficulties will be in direct proportion to his deficiencies. AMST remediates deficiencies in emotion regulation in the reparative context of the client–therapist dyad, and as a result of this remediation the client will begin to accumulate success experiences in the other partnerships in which he participates.

Qualities of the Securely Attached Child

By the time she enters kindergarten, the securely attached child will have developed a personality characterized by qualities of mastery and confidence. The basic structure of the child's personality has been deposited by this juncture. The qualities that the securely attached child will bring to the rest of his life have already been developed. Secure attachment arises when an infant has been consistently able to rely on the caregiver to provide protection and comfort when the need has arisen (Weinfield et al., 1999). Because he has been able to rely on his caregiver, this child has developed mastery and confidence. Mastery arises because the securely attached child has a secure base from which to explore his environment and a safe haven to return to when exploration becomes stressful. The child's confidence develops from the caretaker's consistent availability and effective comfort. The child of secure attachment internalizes the consistency of the dyad in which she was raised. As Weinfield and associates (1999) wrote, "What infants expect is what has happened before" (p. 70). Empirical research supports the belief that the caregiver's responsiveness in infancy engenders secure attachment.

Secure attachment developed in the first years of life provides a protective function against subsequent adversity (Sroufe, Carlson, Levy, & Egeland, 1999). Studies reported by Sroufe and colleagues (1999) demonstrated that securely attached children are more likely to rebound to adaptive functioning after a period of maladaptation than insecurely attached children. The stress of entering the peer group in kindergarten, the stress of moving to a new city, the stress of divorce, the stress of entering adolescence, are all tolerated better by the securely attached child.

Securely attached children are more likely to demonstrate qualities of self-efficacy, self-esteem, self-confidence, and self-worth. This is because the self that develops when the caregiver is responsive is complementary to the responsive caregiver. Self-efficacy emerges as a behavior trait from a pattern of attachment in which the caregiver was reliably responsive to the infant's attachment behaviors. When the caregiver is reliably responsive, the child experiences himself as reliably effective in eliciting caregiver's response, and the child's quality of self-efficacy develops out of this complementarity. Self-efficacy—along with self-esteem, self-confidence, self-worth, and sociability—contributes to the character trait of autonomy. The securely attached child, who has been treated with consistent sensitivity, experiences the world as good and responsive. This child develops a quality of self called *deservingness*. Carried forward to new environments, this child greets the world and persons in it with the same expectation of goodness and responsiveness of which that self feels deserving. This individual will come to formulate a personal Bill of Rights based on the quality of deserving to be treated fairly and with goodness.

Yet another essential quality that emerges from secure attachment is independence. Sensitive caregivers, responding to their infant's bids and cues, teach the child she can effect change in the world in the direction of getting her needs met. Effective independence develops from effective dependence. Empirical research demonstrates that securely attached children upon entering kindergarten exhibit less dependence upon teacher and less attention seeking, than insecurely attached children. When the qualities of autonomy, deservingness, and independence assemble with interest affect and enjoyment affect, the higher order units of enthusiasm and persistence emerge. Empirical research demonstrates that securely attached children score high for self-confidence and show optimum levels of enthusiasm and persistence in tool use tasks.

Securely attached children are empathic and prosocial. Secure attachment results from affective attunement, and the securely attached child manifests empathy or "heightened affective coordination" (Weinfield et al., 1999, p. 78). Empathy is the mirror image of aggression, and empathic children are less prone to aggressive behaviors. The empathic self is connected with others. Empathy is the basis of prosociability, and videotapes of preschoolers at play support the conclusion that empathic children are also prosocial. As reported in Weinfield and colleagues (1999), securely attached children never victimized playmates in studies of preschool children, and empirical studies correlated teachers' rating of children as empathic with assessment ratings of secure attachment.

Social competence is also correlated positively with secure attachment. Social competence entails the ability to make use of the environment and to use personal resources to achieve positive outcomes. Social competence develops as a consequence of the prior establishment of a goal-corrected partnership. Weinfield and associates (1999) summarized studies in which teachers rated securely attached children as dramatically more competent than anxiously attached children. Socially competent children formed friendships of greater intimacy, were accepted better by groups, adhered better to group norms, maintained gender boundaries better, and showed better task coordination and leadership abilities than less securely attached children.

Somehow in the United States the belief has arisen that providing for an infant's needs will spoil the child, whereas just the opposite is true. Consistent nurturing establishes the basis for the emergence of an empathic child. Empirical research supports this conclusion.

Emotion in the Infant–Caregiver Dyad

In the dyadic relationship between maternal caregiver and infant or child, the affective status of the mother influences how she perceives her child. Youngstrom, Izard, and Ackerman (1999) studied 137 mother–child dyads, assessing the mothers' anxiety, depression, and negative emotion. Mothers were asked to rate their own child and a comparison child for positive behavior and emotion and for negative behavior and emotion after watching a short videotape of each child performing a frustrating task. A panel of objective raters assessed each child's performance for comparison with the maternal ratings. The authors demonstrated that maternal dysphoria biases a mother's ratings of both the comparison child and her own child. The more depressed a mother, the more anxious a mother, and the more a mother endorsed her own negative emotion, the less positive behavior she saw in the comparison child. Furthermore, mothers' dysphoria strongly correlated with their assessment of negative behavior and negative emotion in their own children, assessments that were discordant with the assessments of objective raters. Youngstrom and colleagues (1999) discussed their findings in terms of a transactional model for the mother–child dyad, stating, "if the caregiver perceives that the child has a problem, then that child has a problem, regardless of the objective veridicality of the adult's view" (p. 914).

Research demonstrates that children require emotionally expressive environments that do not overwhelm, and children need acceptance of their emotions in those environments. Children raised in such an environment learn to explore their own emotions, and they learn to associate emotional experience with cues and situations forming the basis of emotion situation knowledge (Garner, Jones, & Miner, 1994). Maternal emotion exerts a powerful influence on a child's emotional development. Maternal anger displays provoke dysregulation in the child, and as a result the child's understanding of emotion is compromised (Denham,

Zoller, & Couchoud, 1994; Garner, Jones, & Miner, 1994). Denham and associates (1994) also demonstrated that mothers who talk about their own emotions and who avoid negative responses and provide positive responses to their children's emotions have children who are more adept at understanding emotions.

Many children who later in life become psychotherapy clients were raised by caregivers struggling with anxiety, depression, and negative emotions. As clients, their current problems with affect dysregulation may be traced to their childhood experiences. AMST can help these clients identify, tolerate, and regulate affects and emotions they did not learn to regulate in childhood. Affect centered therapy (ACT) helps clients to reconfigure the intrusive, deficient, or otherwise damaged parental introjects that continue to adversely impact these clients' lives long after leaving their family of origin.

Entry into the Peer Group and Prosociality

Children who recognize emotions and who regulate them well are more likable and more prosocial in peer relations. A child's emotion regulation status has a profound effect on his or her early social experience. Children arrive at preschool age (ca. 42 months) with the rudiments of emotion regulation already established (Denham et al., 1994). The adaptiveness of a child's emotion regulation system has consequences for that child in areas of peer interpersonal relations, relations to adults, performance in school, and personal psychological functioning. Parents' emotional education and emotional socialization of their children is a crucial factor in the children's understanding of emotion. When children are raised in optimal emotional environments they experience an easier transition from home to peer group. Prosociality is an important early indicator of peer group functioning.

Affective knowledge is a determining factor in the earliest prosocial behavior display, which is the situation of an older, preschool age child caring for a younger, toddler-aged sibling. Mothers who express positive emotion have children who are more likely to care for their younger siblings (Garner, Jones, & Miner, 1994). Research has demonstrated that it is the preschooler's affective knowledge and not cognitive skills that predict sibling caregiving (Garner, Jones, & Palmer, 1994). A key factor in the preschooler's knowledge of emotion, Garner, Jones, and Palmer (1994) discovered, was the preschooler's ability to identify another's emotion that is discordant with the normative emotion expected in the situation. Preschoolers who could correctly identify what another was feeling from the other's facial cues, when that other's emotion was at odds with what individuals usually feel in that situation (e.g., feeling sad when receiving a present), were more likely to care for a distressed younger sibling.

Childhood Consequences of Emotion Regulation and Dysregulation

Empirical research shows that children who can appraise and process emotional information respond appropriately to others and have skills that promote their own emotion regulation (Cicchetti et al., 1995). Furthermore, the more emotion knowledge children have, the greater the empathy and prosocial behavior they show toward peers, and the greater their peer popularity (Schultz et al., 2001).

Empirical evidence demonstrates that problems with emotion regulation have both interpersonal and intrapersonal consequences from an early age. Schultz and colleagues (2001) examined verbal capacity, attentional control, and behavioral control in economically disadvantaged preschool boys and girls. Two years later, in first grade, these children were assessed for emotion expression knowledge, emotion situation knowledge, social problems, and social withdrawal. The authors demonstrated that greater verbal capacity predicted better understanding of emotions. Attentional control and behavioral control in 5-year-olds predicted better emotion knowledge in 7-year-olds. Significantly, children with impaired emotion knowledge had social problems. The authors wrote, "Children who accurately labeled emotional responses to events and facial expressions showed less withdrawal from peers" (p. 61).

The quality of the emotion knowledge transmitted to a child during early socialization in the family determines the quality of peer relations as early as preschool. Denham, McKinley, Couchoud, and Holt (1990) examined the predictors of preschoolers' likability, a peer status rating. These authors reported that children's responses to the emotional distress of others can range from friendliness, nurturance, and altruism to aggression and preoccupation with their own distress. Children who cannot respond with positive interventions are at risk for being disliked. Significantly, preschoolers are able to discern differences in a peer's reactions to other's emotions. Children use this discrimination to determine likability, and once determined, the assessment is stable, Denham and associates showed. Children who confuse emotions, who misinterpret happiness for sadness, happiness for anger, or sadness for anger or fear, are at risk for being disliked. The authors demonstrate that children who are prosocial, displaying understanding, sympathetic, and helpful behaviors are better liked by their peers.

In addition to being at risk for peer rejection, children with impaired emotion knowledge are also at academic, social, and behavioral risk (Izard, Fine, et al., 2001). These authors assessed verbal ability, temperament, and emotion knowledge in preschoolers, and then in the third grade they determined social skills, academic competence, and behavior problems. After controlling for gender, intelligence, and temperament, the authors conclude that "preschool emotion knowledge contributed significantly to prediction of all three global outcome measures" (p. 20). The better a child's emotion knowledge in preschool, the better were the child's social skills—assertion, cooperation, self-control—four years later. Similarly, children with higher scores on emotion knowledge showed less behavior problems—externalizing, hyperactivity, and internalizing. Finally, preschool emotion knowledge was strongly correlated with academic competence in third grade, and the authors' path analysis demonstrated that emotion knowledge appears to mediate the effects of verbal ability on academic competence.

Infants, toddlers, and preschoolers who learn emotion regulation in the developmental dyad become schoolchildren who are judged likable by peers and teachers, who perform well academically, who endorse good social skills, and who demonstrate prosocial behaviors. Children whose childhood emotion socialization was deficient have difficulty in peer relations, they have difficulty in school, and they are at risk for psychopathology in childhood. These effects persist into adulthood. When these children reach adulthood and become clients, they still do not possess emotion regulation skills and they continue to have interpersonal difficulties. AMST can begin the remediation process by teaching skills to recognize, tolerate, and regulate affects and emotions, skills that were not transmitted adequately during childhood. Repair of deficits in affect and emotion regulation is the essential first step in returning these clients to adaptive, effective, positive social functioning.

JUVENILE PERIOD

The maturing child assumes more responsibility for his own safety and for meeting his emotional needs during the juvenile period. During the interval from age 3 to the onset of adolescence, the child increasingly spends more time with peers, teachers, and adults outside the family than with the parental caregivers, and the relationships with attachment figures change in response. The juvenile child receives increasing levels of responsibility for maintaining protective proximity to the attachment figure. Because the juvenile is still vulnerable to dangers, he must know where the parent is, and the parent must know where the juvenile is and who is responsible for him. An effective goal-corrected partnership is essential to the tasks of protecting the juvenile child. The set goal for attachment behavior during the juvenile period is availability of the attachment figure, not physical proximity. A line of communication must exist; the attachment figure must be available if necessary; and the juvenile must know that the attachment figure will respond to a signal for help. Juveniles with secure attachments were rated as less dependent by camp counselors and teachers. Juvenile children who developed adaptive emotion regulation skills in early childhood are better able to tolerate the stresses of elementary school.

On the Brink of Adolescence

Depression, poor self-esteem, negative emotionality, and psychopathology are consequences that may appear around the onset of adolescence and that are attributable to failures of emotion and affect socialization originating in childhood. The child with deficits of affect and emotion socialization will already have experienced difficulties in peer relations, social withdrawal, and internalizing in the years between kindergarten and fifth and sixth grade. On the brink of adolescence, this child may manifest symptoms of depression. Blumberg and Izard (1985, 1986) studied the relationship of self-reported emotion experience to depression in 10- and 11-year-old children. The authors discovered that emotion experience is highly associated with depression, while cognitive self-attributions are negligible predictors of depression. For girls in this age group, depression was most associated with anger directed against the self, shame, sadness, fear, and shyness. Boys' depression was most highly associated with anger. Furthermore, for girls, depression was significantly associated with the absence of joy.

Deficits of emotion socialization occurring in the family of origin are apparently causally related to childhood and adolescent depression. A recent longitudinal study tracked the same children from birth through adolescence and provided answers to the crucial question of the sequelae of deficits of emotional support for the child occurring in the family of origin (Duggal, Carlson, Sroufe, & Egeland, 2001). The study examined 168 at-risk children and tracked them into adolescence. A common factor in both childhood and adolescent depression was the absence of emotional supportiveness in early care. The absence of emotion supportiveness apparently equates to the factors of coaching and contingency examined by Denham et al. (1994). The term *coaching* refers to mothers' spontaneous explanations of emotions to their children; the term *contingency* refers to mothers' positive responses to children's emotions and absence of negative responses. Denham and associates (1994) and Garner, Jones, and Miner (1994) showed that family emotion socialization practices predict emotion knowledge. Several studies have correlated emotion knowledge with peer ratings (Denham, McKinley et al., 1990), prosocial responses to peer and adult negative emotion (Denham & Couchoud, 1991), sibling caregiving (Garner, Jones, & Palmer, 1994), and with behavior problems and social behavior (Izard et al., 2001; Schultz et al., 2001). When caregivers failed to provide emotional supportiveness in childhood, children were at risk for both childhood and adolescent depression.

Another common factor associated with childhood and adolescent depression identified by Duggal and colleagues (2001) in their longitudinal study was maternal depression. Youngstrom and colleagues (1999) showed that dysphoric mothers were more liable to see negative behaviors and emotions in their children than objective raters. The Duggal and colleagues (2001) study suggested that depressed mothers may be less capable of providing the coaching and contingency behaviors necessary for "good enough" socialization of their children's emotion knowledge.

These studies taken together suggest that the client who presents currently with depressive features may well have begun life in a family context lacking in emotional supportiveness. Mother may have endorsed depression herself. As a child, this client's interest and joy affects may not have been optimally aroused. In the absence of emotion coaching and emotion contingency, this child did not develop the emotion knowledge that predicts positive sociality. As a result, upon entering the peer group in preschool, this child was less prosocial and was judged unlikable. Withdrawal and internalizing ensued, persisting across the grade school years, and perhaps manifesting in childhood depression. At age 10 to 11, the female child endorses self-directed anger, shame, sadness, fear, and joylessness while the male child endorses anger. Adolescent depression is one likely outcome for these children. The client with depressed features who endorses such a history can be helped by AMST. In the context of the client–therapist dyad, AMST provides the emotional supportiveness that was lacking in the child–caregiver dyad. The AMST therapist provides the emotion coaching the client did not receive in childhood, and the client learns to recognize, tolerate, and regulate affects and emotions she was not taught to manage in childhood. While therapy for depression is complex and involves several interventions from affect centered therapy, it must begin by remediating childhood deficits in emotion regulation using AMST.

ADOLESCENCE

The structure of the self reorganizes during adolescence, and adolescents often experience a state that is similar to depersonalization. With the onset of adolescence the brain enters a period of heightened plasticity as the organism prepares for socialization and reproduction (Freeman, 1995). Profound neurobiological alterations are instigated by the increased release of somatic and neural hormones. Spear (2000) wrote that when the adolescent brain is compared to the preadolescent brain, "there is a massive loss of synapses in neocortical brain regions during adolescence . . . leading to an ultimate loss of almost one-half of the average number of synapses per cortical neuron" (pp. 438–439). In addition to synapses, receptors for several neurotransmitter systems are pruned during adolescence. Synaptic pruning occurs primarily in excitatory systems, presumably resulting in a "major decline in the amount of excitatory stimulation reaching cortex" (Spear, 2000, p. 439). In a discussion of dissociation, Braun (1988a) wrote, "many adolescents experience a condition that is probably akin to depersonalization disorder as a normal event of adolescence" (p. 7). Changes in the attachment accompany and may well be expressions of these changes in the adolescent brain. A genetically determined reproductive script comes on line that has been selected by evolutionary forces over millennia and is designed to assure successful entry into adult society, reproduction, and child rearing. "The adolescent or young adult begins to search for a permanent, goal-corrected partnership with an age mate, usually of the opposite sex" (Marvin & Britner, 1999, p. 63).

Attachment to Self

During adolescence a profound reorganization of the self structure occurs in which it appears that attachment behaviors that were previously directed toward the caregiver now come to be directed toward the self. I propose that over the course of adolescence, the brain's reorganization manifests in a shift in which attachment to self supplants attachment to the caregiver. The concept of attachment to self provides a pattern for weaving together threads from attachment, ontogeny of affect regulation, and neurobiology into a tapestry that will convey how healthy self-organization emerges and how early attachment style manifests in adult relations between ego and self system. Allen and Land (1999) reported that across adolescence, attachment organization becomes a "property of the individual and not just a reflection of qualities of major ongoing attachment relationships" (p. 329). For the securely attached person, the ego and self will maintain intimate proximity. Cassidy (1999) wrote of centrality or penetration, meaning the extent to which one person penetrates another's life. For the securely attached individual the penetration will be complete, and ego and self will map fully onto one another. This will not be the case with insecurely attached postadolescents, as we will see when we look at disordered development. The insecurely attached postadolescent will always be driven by yearning affect to "get close to" himself, and at the same time close proximity of self to ego may be accompanied by avoidance or anxiousness.

The concept of attachment to self suggests that the adult has an inner representation or IWM of self and that the quality of his relationships to that self-representation derives from the quality of his relationships to his childhood attachment figures. I propose that the elements of the attachment bond and IWMs of self and other, undergoing reorganization during adolescence, unite in the construct of attachment to self whereby the system of attachment organization, which has operated *upon* the individual, now operates *within* the individual, that is, intrapsychically. The quality of attachment to self will manifest in patterns of interaction with self over time and will be most apparent when self is stressed. The particular stress situations that will uncover individual differences in attachment to self will be those work, education, or career, situations that do not primarily involve others. How well does a person work without supervision, motivate himself to study without deadlines, or self-start his career all indicate the quality of attachment to self. Attachment to self may parallel adult attachment as observed in love relationships, sexual pair bonds, and marriage; attachment to self may even be the foundation of individual differences in attachment style observed in these adult dyads. The individual with a secure attachment to self will be able to comfort and protect the self in situations of stress. The individual with an insecure attachment to self will not be able to self-soothe.

ADULTHOOD

A psychologically healthy adulthood is the outcome of a developmental pathway that originated in a psychologically healthy infancy. The well-organized self of adulthood is synonymous with optimal emotion regulation and bespeaks a secure attachment. The well-organized adult self, optimally managing stress and the affective challenges of adult life is the presumed goal of parents making a decision to have a child.

The well-organized adult self is able to recognize and name a range of his own core affects and emotions, both positive and negative, and he will show an ability to identify and empathically experience these feelings in others. This person will demonstrate the ability to tolerate these emotions in a range of intensities, which implies the ability to stay grounded and present while describing prior affective experiences or while experiencing affects in real time. When providing a report of life events, the well-organized self will discuss her own emotions and those of others and will state her emotional response to the emotional responses (or absence thereof) of others. The ability to present past experiences in a coherent and collaborative fashion is a significant and compelling aspect of adult security (Weinfield et al., 1999). Infant security apparently predicts this component of adult security.

When reporting life events, the well-organized, emotionally expressive self will be experienced as believable and true by the listener, whether a therapist or not. His presentation will be coherent, and his report of events and affects and emotions assembled with those events will be conveyed without distortion, contradiction, or derailment of discourse. Importantly, the speaker who is secure in her attachment to the self collaborates with the listener, clarifying meaning, and using active listening skills to ensure she is understood. The conversation is a sort of goal-corrected partnership in which the communication plans of the speaker are integrated with those of the listener; the speaker is able to set aside his own needs for emotional proximity and verbal proximity, to insert plans of the listener for proximity, and for both to reach a common goal or mutuality. Arietta Slade (1999) described this skill as "coherence."

The well-structured self is able to manage the disturbing events and stressful exigencies of life. To do so requires the ability to contain disturbing events and affects and to prevent or limit their intrusion. This person will be able, at the appropriate time, to retrieve past disturbing events from memory in order to process them, and will demonstrate the capacity to observe the self remembering disturbing events, rather than becoming immersed in the memory. Similarly, whether in ongoing relationships or in the therapeutic encounter, the well-structured person will be able to maintain the observing self even while experiencing a disturbing event in real time.

The optimally functioning adult will demonstrate flexibility, virtuosity, and self-awareness in the domain of affective experience. She will evince the ability to autogenously up-regulate positive emotion and down-regulate negative emotion. This has been called a self-reflective function. Self-soothing will be accomplished by making use of inner images of safety, soothing, validation, and affirmation. The optimally functioning adult will not use drugs, alcohol, food, sex, relationship, or work to vicariously regulate affects. The well-organized self will manifest vitality and will be able to energetically and persistently pursue goals she sets for herself.

The adaptive self will possess integrated qualities, associated with inner images or representations, that support the self in daily functioning across contexts varying in stress content. These qualities, which are image-associated affective–cognitive structures, include self-efficacy, self-worth, deservingness, pride, and autonomy. Affective experience will serve the organized, well-structured, adaptive self as a basis for making decisions that support the self. The fully realized self will form relationships, whether marriage, coupleships, or sexual pair bonds, with an equal, one who similarly endorses a secure attachment, optimal self-organization, and affective competence. As parents, these persons will provide their children with dyadic environments that perpetuate these qualities of self.

Chapter **3**

. . . .

Causes and Effects of Emotion Dysregulation

Building upon the foundation of normal development and healthy emotion regulation, this chapter will discuss the origins of problems with affect management. Over its course, the chapter will advance a tripartite model that proposes three fundamental, interacting factors that condition the course of emergence of the self and result in styles of emotion regulation, either adaptive or dysfunctional. This three-factor model provides a developmental context for understanding the etiology of both healthy adaptation and psychopathology. The model will justify and clarify the intent of each of the affect management skills training (AMST) elements. Employing the model structures our thinking about the origins of the adult client's problems, it will guide the approach to therapy, and it provides a model for what the therapeutic outcome might look like.

The tripartite model clusters the welter of causal factors that impact developmental outcomes into three groups: genetics, attachment, and childhood socioemotional history. These three factors interrelate synergistically over time to determine the nature of the evolving person from moment to moment across the developmental time span. The structure of the self at any moment in the child's life is an emergent phenomenon. At each moment, the child's adaptation is the product of prior development and current circumstances. The genetic element determines the structure of the brain, the physiological platform for affect, thought, behavior, and memory. Yet expression of the genetic potential is experience dependent, and the genetic factor strongly and mutually interacts with both the attachment factor and the childhood socioemotional history factor. Genetics sets the thresholds for each of the affects and also determines in part the capability of the system to process adverse experience to an adaptive resolution. Attachment separates out early experience, the time period from birth through 3 to 4 years, because events of this period have a profound influence on the organization of the self and its ability to cope with subsequent events. Empirical research (Sroufe et al., 1999) supports a special role for early experience. The child's experiences in developmental periods subsequent to the attachment phase affect outcomes, but "attachment remains significant after later variables are entered" (Sroufe et al., 1999, p. 6). Early experiences have special significance because they are preverbal and are therefore less readily modified by later experience. The third factor, childhood socioemotional history, refers to the cumulative record of events and affective impacts over the period from 3 or 4 years through adolescence. The term *socioemotional* stresses two facts: First, during this period the child has moved out of the restricted confines of the infant–caregiver dyad and into an ever widening social milieu. In this milieu, other persons can impact the child's development for both good and bad. Second, events of this time have cumulative emotional impacts. As one psychotherapist stated, "It matters how a kid feels day after day" (Tom Cloyd, personal communication, March 15, 2003). Childhood socioemotional history mutually interacts with the attachment factor, because patterns of affect management established in the first 3 to 4 years of life determine how adaptively a child tolerates challenges provided by his social environment subsequently.

The tripartite model (Figure 3.1) conceptualizes the interrelated, synergistic interaction of the three factors of genetics, attachment, and childhood socioemotional history. The interrelationship among social conditioning, affect expression and regulation, and neurophysiology must always be kept in mind. As we investigate emotion dysregulation we will learn how it is dependent in part on genetic competence, in part on the quality of the attachment, and in part on the nature of childhood experience, just as healthy affect regulation is dependent on the balance and quality of these same three factors. As Sroufe (1997) wrote, "the starting point for a developmental approach to psychopathology is always a consideration of normal development" (p. 258).

THE GENETIC FACTOR

Some people are apparently more emotionally sensitive than others, and these differences in sensitivity may be due in part to variability in thresholds for affects. For example, an infant or child with a low threshold for anger affect would be expected to become angry with less environmental provocation, and this fact could have developmental consequences. It is possible that the attention deficit hyperactivity disorder (ADHD) child has a genetically determined low threshold for interest affect resulting in heightened distractibility, again with developmental consequences. Recent findings in the field of molecular biology appear to demonstrate the genetic basis for differences in thresholds for fear affect, anger affect, and distress–anguish affect. The threshold for an affect refers to the degree of stimulation required to elicit an affective response. Thresholds for affects may be determined by the activity level of regulatory proteins coded in the genome, or by the amounts of such proteins synthesized. The DNA of the human genome carries the genetic code for around 30,000 genes. These genes are packaged into 22 pairs of chromosomes, one from each parent, plus either a pair of X chromosomes in females, or an X and a Y chromosome in males. Most of the 30,000 genes code

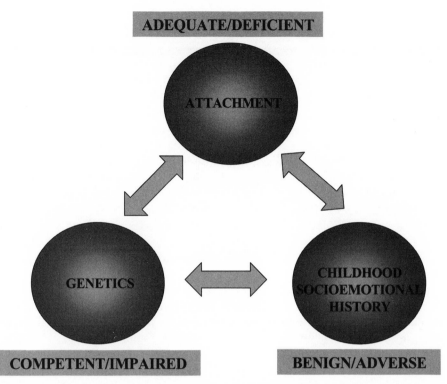

Figure 3.1.   The tripartite model. This figure diagrams the three classes of interacting causes for many Axis I and II disorders. The genetic component is the only within-child variable. It is a summative construct comprised of all the loci in the human genome, and it varies continuously between competent and impaired. The attachment component consolidates early experience through the first 3 to 4 years of life. It refers in particular to how well or poorly the infant–caregiver dyad functions. The foundations of emotion regulation are established within the context of the infant–caregiver dyad. Attachment varies continuously from adequate to deficient. The term *childhood socioemotional history* refers to the vicissitudes of life from about the beginning of year 5 through adolescence. This component is comprised of discrete experiences that vary from benign through adverse to traumatic.

for proteins, and some of these proteins are involved in neurophysiological processes. We will look at genes coding for regulatory proteins that appear to be involved in setting thresholds for fear, anger, and anguish.

Fear Affect Thresholds

The threshold for fear affect appears to be in part genetically determined. At the neurophysiological level, fear expression is a complex phenomenon involving the cooperation of many neurotransmitter systems. The serotonergic system is a prominent neurotransmitter system involved in fear expression. One protein, the serotonin transporter, exerts a functional "bottleneck" effect in serotonin-mediated neurotransmission (Lesch & Mössner, 1998). The serotonin transporter gene codes for a protein that scavenges serotonin from the synaptic space. The amount of transporter protein a person's neurons synthesize is genetically determined by a regulatory region of the gene. The regulatory region occurs in a more active form identified as *l*, and a less active form called *s*. People with two copies of the *l* regulatory allele make twice as much of the transporter protein, and therefore they have less serotonin accumulation in the synaptic space. People with the *s* allele, whether they are genetically *s/s* or *s/l* , make half as much of the transporter protein, because the *s* allele is dominant over the *l* form. Persons who are *s/s* or *s/l* have lower serotonin reuptake, because they have less of the transporter protein and therefore serotonin accumulates in the synaptic cleft. For some time researchers have known that the *s* allele is associated with increased anxiety and fearfulness and with significantly higher probability for affective illness (Lesch & Mössner, 1998).

The relationship between serotonin uptake and fear threshold was demonstrated in experiments in which subjects viewed fear-expressing faces while being scanned by fMRI to measure activity in the amygdala. Human subjects who had decreased amounts of serotonin transporter protein showed increased amygdalar activity when they looked at fear-expressing faces (Hariri et al., 2002). In the Hariri study, fMRI was used to measure real time amygdalar response in subjects required to select one of two faces, either angry or fearful, that matched a single target face expressing either anger or fear. This study is unique in that it associates serotonergic function with affect and with a specific brain structure. The results clearly demonstrated that subjects with the *s* allele showed heightened amygdalar activity when viewing fear-expressing faces. Hariri and associates (2002) concluded "the increased anxiety and fear associated with individuals possessing the *s* allele may reflect the hyperresponsiveness of their amygdala to relevant environmental stimuli" (p. 402). The study appears to demonstrate the existence of a lower threshold for fear in populations having the low activity *s* allele. Populations with the high activity *l* allele showed a higher threshold for fear.

Elevated levels of anxiety, susceptibility to fear conditioning, and predisposition to affective illness appear to be associated with carrying the low activity *s* allele (Hariri et al., 2002; Lesch & Mössner, 1998). The possibility that some individuals may have genetically determined lower thresholds for fear may have important implications for therapy focused on affects and for AMST. The serotonin transporter gene "influences a constellation of traits related to anxiety and depression" (Lesch & Mössner, 1998, p. 182). Allelic variation in serotonin transporter function appears to contribute 7 to 9% of the genetic variance for disorders of affect and temperament out of the 40 to 60% of total genetic-based variance. Lesch and Mössner (1998) calculated that 10 to 15 genes may contribute to anxiety disorders. Among other than anxiety disorders, the serotonin transporter is variably associated with psychopathology. Type 2 alcoholics—identified by impulsive–aggressive behavior and early onset—and alcoholics endorsing severe withdrawal were more likely to have the *s* form of the transporter gene. Lesch and Mössner (1998) suggested that low serotonin uptake function may confer susceptibility to severe alcohol dependence. Two more recent studies did not support the association between age of onset and decreased serotonin uptake function (Hill et al., 2002; Kranzler, Lappalainen, Nellissery, & Gelernter, 2002). Obsessive–compulsive disorder (OCD) patients were more likely to be homozygous for the *s* allele or homozygous for the *l* allele, whereas normal controls were more likely to be heterozygous (i.e., *l/s*). No association with variations of serotonin transporter uptake were found for panic disorder (Lesch & Mössner, 1998) or for anorexia (Sundaramurthy, Pieri, Gape, Markham, & Campbell, 2000), but binge eating obese women were significantly more likely to carry the reduced transporter phenotype than obese women who did not binge (Kuikka et al., 2001). The *s/s* genotype was associated with lower scores on three MMPI scales (psychopathic deviance, paranoia, and schizophrenia) in patients with affective disorders and with lower scores on the schizophrenia scale for normal controls (Golimbet et al., 2003). The authors suggest the lowered serotonin uptake associated with the *s/s* genotype may restrict expression of schizoid traits in normal and affectively disordered persons.

Additional candidate genes and chromosome fragments have been identified in mouse models of depression, anxiety, and stress susceptibility and in some cases these have been related to human psychopathology (Clement, Lepicard, & Chapouthier, 2001; Davidson, Putnam, & Larson, 2000; Koster et al., 1999; Schramm, McDonald, & Limbird, 2001; Sibille, Pavlides, Benke, & Toth, 2000).

Serotonin dysregulation may play a role in the genetically complex disorder of infantile autism (Lesch & Mössner, 1998). The profound disturbances of social interaction, the impaired communication, and the repetitive interests and behavior that characterize infantile autism appear from epidemiological studies to originate in genetic defects (Andres, 2002). While the long arm of chromosome 7 contains possible loci, no candidate gene has as yet been identified for autism.

Genetic factors such as the reduced serotonin uptake function will still always mutually interact with factors of attachment and childhood socioaffective history. The synergy among these factors swamps the contribution of genetics, and as Lesch and Mössner (1998) noted, the genetic contribution, while constant, only contributed 7 to 9% of variance. The greater importance of the quality of early experience is highlighted by results from the Minnesota Mother–Child Project, a long-term, longitudinal, prospective study (e.g., Sroufe et al., 1999). Research from the Minnesota Mother–Child Project demonstrated that more than 40 variables relating to the child had weak power to predict attention or activity problems in the sixth grade (Sroufe, 1997). The child variables may be more likely to be genetically determined. Child variables included: premature birth; less than optimal newborn neurological status; nurse reports of fussiness and other behaviors in the nursery; infant activity level; infant irritability; temperament as reported by parents. Weinfield and associates (1999) discussed the relationship between infant temperament and attachment, noting that infant temperament does not directly affect the security of attachment, a finding that is empirically supported. Downey and Coyne (1990), who reviewed twin and adoption studies, summarized the impact of genetic factors in their conclusion that "genetic factors can at best partially account for the problems of children with a depressed parent" (p. 50).

These data are important for affect oriented clinicians because they indicate the importance of teaching AMST skills to clients demonstrating a range of psychopathologies. The clinician cannot know whether a client's presenting problems have a purely genetic origin, an origin in deficit experience, or an origin in adverse or traumatic experience. What is most likely is that all three factors are variably involved. The data suggest that effects of many genetic impairments can be buffered by experience. AMST provides a powerful current intervention that can positively impact the effects of genetic impairments or deficit experience and can alter the trajectory of psychopathology toward adaptive functioning.

Anger Affect Thresholds

A genetic variation in serotonin synthesis is associated with anger expression and appears to influence the threshold for anger. The enzyme tryptophan hydroxylase (TPH) is the rate limiting biosynthetic step for serotonin. Individuals who carry a variant of the gene with a single nucleotide replacement in a coding region of the gene for TPH showed higher scores on assessments of state anger, trait anger, and angry temperament (Rujescu et al., 2002), and they scored higher for aggression, tendency to experience unprovoked anger, and to express anger outwardly (Manuck et al., 1999). The nucleotide replacement results in a less active form of the TPH enzyme, and so levels of serotonin are reduced. When subjects view angry facial expressions, the orbitofrontal cortex (OFC) and anterior cingulate cortex are activated (Davidson et al., 2000). The definitive experiment has not yet been done that relates genotype, viewing an angry face, and fMRI measured change in brain activity. Individuals with a genetically coded less active form of the TPH enzyme appear to have a lower threshold for anger.

These data relating genetically determined decreased activity of tryptophan hydroxylase to aggression have important therapeutic consequences. Completed suicide, especially completed suicide by violent means, is significantly associated with the less active form of TPH (Turecki et al., 2001). This same genetic variant was also associated significantly with manic–depressive illness (Bellivier et al., 1998). Individuals with the less active form of TPH may have had more difficulty managing anger from childhood on, because of having a genetically determined decreased threshold for anger. AMST may help clients genetically compromised for anger management by providing skills to recognize, tolerate, and regulate the affect.

Distress–Anguish Affect Thresholds

The threshold for distress–anguish may be regulated by a dopaminergic system. Distress–anguish is the affect elicited by a constant, higher than optimal level of stimulation. Distress–anguish affect can be elicited by higher than optimal perceptual stimulation, by excessive drive states, or by too great a separation from an attachment figure. Physical pain is an eliciting stimulus in the perceptual modality for distress–anguish affect. A recent experiment correlated central nervous system activation as measured by PET scans with elicitation of anguish affect and with genotype (Zubieta et al., 2003). Dopamine is degraded in the synapse by the enzyme catechol-O-methyltransferase (COMT). Humans have two variants of the COMT gene, COMT-H, which is highly active, and COMT-L, which is three- to fourfold less active. Because each parent contributes one copy, humans may be genetically H/H, H/L, or L/L. Because the genes are codominant—unlike the case with the serotonin transporter—three different phenotypes are possible. Persons who are genetically H/H, rapidly remove dopamine from the synapse; those who are L/L slowly remove dopamine; individuals who are H/L show intermediate rates of removal. When dopamine is rapidly removed, endogenous pain-killing endorphins are quickly released and pain is attenuated. When dopamine is slowly removed, endorphins are less rapidly released, and pain is not attenuated. In the experiment, anguish affect was elicited by injecting hypertonic saline into the jaw muscle. People who were genetically H/H—which apparently conferred a high threshold for anguish and for pain—were able to tolerate greater saline doses and reported low levels of pain. Their brains showed increased endorphinergic activity. Persons who were genetically L/L—which apparently confers a low threshold for anguish and pain—showed the lowest tolerance for saline dose and reported the highest sensory pain rating and more negative internal affective state. Subjects who were genetically H/L endorsed intermediate levels of negative affective state and tolerated intermediate doses of saline. The authors note that one quarter of the U.S. population carries the "stoic" (H/H) genotype, one quarter carries the "overly sensitive" (L/L) genotype, and one half is intermediate.

These data appear to have implications for understanding how genetics may be involved in psychopathology. A study of anorexic patients and their parents demonstrated that the high activity allele of the COMT gene is associated with susceptibility because individuals homozygous for the H allele have a twofold increased risk for developing anorexia (Frisch et al., 2001). This finding correlates well with the clinical observation that anorexics have a high threshold for anguish affect in that they can tolerate intense levels of hunger drive state during restriction of food intake. The observation also suggests that AMST can help the anorexic client by teaching her to become aware of distress affect, whether elicited by excessive hunger or by emotional stimuli.

Among alcoholics, the COMT gene polymorphism discriminates Type 1 alcoholics from Type 2 alcoholics, with Type 1 alcoholics apparently having a lower threshold for distress–anguish affect. Type 1 alcoholism is the late onset form of the disorder, and in a Finnish study, the frequency of the L allele of the COMT gene was significantly higher among Type 1 alcoholics than among the general population (Tiihonen et al., 1999). Type 1 alcoholics were 2.5 times more likely to carry the LL genotype than the HH genotype. Type 2 alcoholism is the early onset form, and in a sample of Type 2 alcoholics with severe antisocial behavior the COMT genotype was not associated with the development of the disorder (Hallikainen et al., 2000). These findings suggest that a dopamine-mediated lower threshold for anguish affect may have a role in late onset alcoholism, but not in early onset alcoholism. AMST may help in treatment of late onset alcoholism by assisting the client to cognize distress–anguish affect, to recognize the role of sadness in his disorder, and to help him develop new skills to regulate this affect.

Distress–sadness–anguish affect is a common finding in many psychopathologies. Data suggest that COMT gene polymorphisms may be associated with different thresholds for anguish affect and that these polymorphisms—and hence the putative variable affective thresholds—may be etiological factors in specific disorders. When data for the COMT gene are considered together with data for TPH and for the serotonin transporter, a picture emerges of the importance of genetic-based affective dysregulation in the etiology of some psychopathologies. These data further support the importance of teaching AMST affect management skills. Whether a client's problems with affect dysregulation arise from genetic vulnerability, deficit experience, or adverse experience, or—what is more likely—a combination of all three, the client can be helped by teaching the skills of affect and emotion regulation.

Accommodation and Psychological Self-Healing

The brain's ability to process early experiences of maltreatment to an adaptive resolution may be genetically determined. Accommodation is a component of the synthetic function of the CNS and refers to the brain's capability to change or adjust pre-existing structure to accommodate reality (Horner, 1984). Accommodation is the basis of learning. As we have proposed, Shapiro's putative adaptive information processing system (Shapiro, 1995, 2001, 2002) appears to be a construct formed during early socialization. Accommodation, the ability to change pre-existing neural structure to conform to reality, is an essential component of the socially constructed system for adaptive processing of adverse and traumatic experience. As conceived by ACT, adaptive resolution of adversity and trauma entails changing through accommodation the trauma coded neural networks established during early life to conform to the current reality of life in a wider social milieu. Some children may have a more robust, genetically determined capability to process adversity to an adaptive resolution through the process of accommodation.

Data from a study by Caspi and colleagues (2000) demonstrated that genetic variability in the neurotransmitter-metabolizing enzyme monoamine oxidase A (MAOA) may affect how capable children are in adapting to maltreatment. It appears that some maltreated children are genetically better able to accommodate to society's rules than others. The Caspi study examined maltreatment between the ages of 3 and 11 years and correlated it with MAOA genotype and four outcome measures: adolescent conduct disorder, convictions for violent crimes, personality disposition toward violence, and symptoms of antisocial personality disorder. The MAOA gene, like the serotonin transporter, has a regulatory genetic polymorphism that affects MAOA activity. MAOA degrades monamine neurotransmitters such as norepinepherine, serotonin, and dopamine. Previous studies cited by Caspi and colleagues had shown that when MAOA activity is high, aggression and antisocial behaviors are reduced, and when MAOA activity is decreased, aggression increases. In the present study, conducted on an unstratified sample of males, 8% of children experienced severe maltreatment, 28% experienced probable maltreatment, and 64% did not experience maltreatment. The cohort was assessed nine times between 3 and 21 years of age. Data show that for all outcome measures, the high MAOA genotype moderated the effect of childhood maltreatment. Maltreated males with low MAOA activity were 9.8 times more likely to be convicted of a violent crime, for example. Eight-five percent of low-MAOA maltreated males developed some form of antisocial behavior. Importantly, merely carrying the low-MAOA geno-type does not predispose to negative outcomes; maltreatment must be present for the low-MAOA genotype to express the antisocial behavior phenotype.

AMST may be able to help all victims of childhood maltreatment and espe-cially those victims with the low-MAOA genotype. MAOA is an important enzyme in control of neurotransmitters associated with affect regulation. Emo-tions are trauma coded in maltreated children and later are acted out through socially and personally dysfunctional behaviors (Carlson, 1997; Herman, 1992; Schwarz et al., 1995a, 1995b; Shapiro, 1995, 2001). Antisocial offenders are more likely to be genetically impaired in their ability to adaptively process emo-tions assembled with childhood maltreatment. Whereas a secure attachment has been shown to ameliorate the effects of childhood adverse experience (Weinfield et al., 1999), we may assume that the maltreated child is less likely to have received adequate emotion socialization in the context of positively functioning child–caregiver dyads. AMST has the potential to transmit skills for adaptive emotion regulation to adults who were maltreated as children and thereby to ameliorate the causal effects of past maltreatment on present behaviors.

ATTACHMENT

The tripartite model hypothesizes an interaction among genetics, attachment, and socioemotional history. Because of the developmental importance of the first four years of life, especially for affect regulation and neurophysiological maturation, the tripartite model accords early life experience, conceptualized as the attachment, a place among the three causal factors affecting outcomes. The term *attachment*, in the sense I am using it here, refers to "prior adaptation," and particularly to the developmental time frame from birth through the fourth year. Sroufe and associates (1999) used the phrase "early experience" (p. 2) for the same experience set that I am referring to as *attachment*. I set the boundary for attachment at 4 years of age because by this time the goal-corrected partnership will have been established in the securely attached child emerging from a healthy, adaptive dyad. Also at this time, the left hemisphere gains ascendancy over the right, providing another milestone for the end of the attachment phase.

The basic structure of the self is laid down during the attachment phase. How a child deals with current exigencies will depend upon the organizations of behavior and emotion—in sum, the organization of self—that the child brings forward from earlier phases of development. While attachment will influence subsequent adaptations in terms of self-concept and relationship-concept, it will not predict good or bad outcomes. Outcomes are predicted by the cumulative record in each component, genetics, attachment, and socioemotional history. As Weinfield and colleagues (1999) wrote, "it would be naive and incorrect to suggest that infant attachment is solely and directly responsible for adaptation during child-hood and adolescence" (p. 76). Affect oriented clinicians need to be aware of the relevance of experience during the attachment phase to current problems with functioning. AMST can help the client by remediating deficits that arose during the attachment period.

Deficit Experience

The quality of the attachment, which is determined by caregiver sensitivity and responsiveness to infant needs, can range from adequate to deficient. When the quality of the attachment is adequate, a secure attachment bond eventuates; when it is deficient, insecure attachment results. *Deficit experience* is the phrase I have chosen to refer to the omissions in areas of caregiver sensitivity, responsiveness, involvement, and emotion regulation transactions that lead to an insecure attachment. For the insecurely attached child, deficit experience means "things that should happen for every child and didn't for this child."

Many factors that are common in our society today can contribute to deficit experience. Demands of single parenting reduce the caregiver's opportunity to respond to her infant's emotional needs. An absent or emotionally uninvolved father, parental preoccupation with self, both parents employed, and many other vicissitudes have consequences for the mutual, attuned, dyadic relationship within which the child's affect regulation system and self-concept are meant to develop. Surrogate caregivers, (e.g., day care providers) no matter how well intentioned, have difficulty providing the primary preoccupation that characterizes the healthy dyad. These causal factors adversely impact the attachment and decrease the amount of time, attention, mirroring, and primary maternal preoccupation available to the infant and child. As a result, the child does not acquire a complete enough set of affect regulation skills, the self does not organize optimally, and problems arise in adolescence or adulthood. Before we examine the consequences for the attachment, I want to look at some examples of deficit experience in the attachment period.

Deficits Involving Positive Affect: Whatever the reason for its occurrence, failure to stimulate infant's positive affect during reunions across the early practicing period constitutes one form of deficit experience. Since development of the ventral tegmental circuit is experience dependent, it will fail to develop properly if the requisite arousal experience is not provided. Researchers have not yet defined the minimum "dose" of positive affect stimulation necessary to assure adequate development of the ventral tegmental circuit. Although the exact parameters are as yet unknown, we can nevertheless theorize that failure to stimulate infant positive affect will result in some degree of impairment of ventral tegmental circuit development with a resultant inability to feel high levels of interest–excitement affect and enjoyment–joy affect. As a result the child will manifest diminished vitality because adequate levels of interest affect are unavailable to motivate schoolwork, career, and self-improvement. This child will not evidence exploratory or prosocial behaviors because the sociability and exploration behavioral systems, which are apparently motivated by interest in others and interest in the world, will fail to develop adequately. Fear, shame, or anger may predominate. Separation and individuation will be incomplete, and the individual is positioned for depressive psychopathology made worse by the inability to feel the levels of interest affect and enjoyment affect necessary to escape from depression. As a result, a depressive personality structured by these deficits may emerge. By remediating deficiencies in positive affect arousal that originated in childhood deficit experience, AMST can help restore the client to more effective current functioning.

Deficits Involving Affect Attenuation: Another type of deficit experience is failure to provide optimal disapproval–shame experiences during the late practicing period. Development of the lateral tegmental circuit of the OFC is dependent upon these optimal disapproval-shame experiences. If the experiences are not provided, for whatever reason, the result will be inadequate development of the lateral tegmental circuit. When the lateral tegmental circuit does not develop adequately the child is less able to attenuate a range of affects including interest, anger, and sadness, and perhaps fear, and disgust. Failure of the lateral tegmental circuit to develop optimally may contribute to ADD/ADHD, to poor impulse control, to oppositional-defiant disorder, and other conduct disorders. Additionally, milestones in the separation–individuation process will not be attained and the child will not reach the stage of object constancy. Optimal internal working models (IWMs) will not form and will not be available for affect self-regulation. By teaching the client to down-regulate negative affects, AMST can remediate deficiencies that originated in childhood deficit experience and that contribute to current maladaptation.

Deficits in Qualities of Self: Deficiencies in attachment can contribute to current impairments in self-esteem. Qualities of self are dependent upon the quality of the caregiver's contributions to the infant–caregiver dyad. When the caregiver is sensitive to infant needs, a quality of deservingness emerges in the infant's self-structure. Caregiver insensitivity, harshness, neglect, and erratic behavior constitute forms of deficit experience. Insensitivity, harshness, and neglect promote a self structure based on unpredictability and unresponsiveness. A quality of "not deserving" emerges in the self structure. This quality assembles with shame affect and disgust affect. The qualities of self and expectations that are carried forward by the child treated with insensitivity are expectations of insensitive, unpredictable, or erratic treatment, and a self-experience of not deserving better or different. These qualities contribute to current psychopathology.

Another form of deficit experience is failure to nurture a goal-corrected partnership as the dyad matures into the preschool years. The child whose parents were unavailable or unable to promote development of goal-corrected partnerships will be at risk for social and emotional problems in school and across the subsequent life span. This person will have difficulty tolerating the frustration attendant on delaying needs gratification. It will be difficult for this person to negotiate with others and create a plan of action based on mutuality. This individual will have difficulty recognizing that others have their own desires, objectives, and emotional investments. Relationships, especially ones demanding intimacy, will be challenging for this person. In the reparative context of the client–therapist dyad, this individual can learn mutuality and interrelatedness as he acquires the AMST skills and proceeds in affect centered therapy (ACT).

Individual Differences: When there are deficit experiences during the attachment period, the security of the attachment is affected; patterns of secure versus insecure attachment are referred to as *individual differences*. The ontogeny of secure attachment has been presented. Empirical research supports the conclusion that poor caregiver responsiveness contributes to development of insecure attachment. There are three patterns of insecure attachment: avoidant, resistant, and disorganized–disoriented. Just as healthy development results in part from adequate attachment coupled with benign childhood experience, so dysfunctional development may begin with a deficient attachment and be compounded by adverse or traumatic childhood experience.

The securely attached infant's behavior is organized on the basis of consistent experiences of a caregiver providing comfort and protection when the need arises. When caregivers are not consistently available or have not produced effective soothing, then an insecure attachment develops (Weinfield et al., 1999). Quality of attachment is a bimodally distributed function clustering on secure attachment on the one hand and insecure on the other. Children almost always develop an attachment, even to an abusive parent. The quality of the attachment relationship manifests in individual differences in attachment, which may be either secure or insecure. Anxiety about the caregiver's availability or fear that the caregiver will be unresponsive or ineffective in attempts to respond results in insecure attachment. Empirical research has confirmed that caregiver insensitivity predicts subsequent insecure, anxious attachment (Weinfield et al., 1999). Anxiously attached infants' mothers were less sensitive and expressive during breast- or bottle feeding. A history of failure to respond or of erratic responding to the infant's needs leads to emergence of one or other of the two basic patterns of insecure attachment: in the resistant pattern, toddlers demonstrate attachment behavior when there is no stress in the environment; in the avoidant pattern, toddlers fail to produce attachment behaviors when there is stress. These two patterns may be "contextual distortions of patterns available to all infants" (Weinfield et al., 1999, p. 74), because when a maternal figure is lost, all infants demonstrate a predictable behavior sequence of protest, followed by despair, followed by detachment.

Child attachment is measured by the Strange Situation (Ainsworth, Blehar, Waters, & Wall, 1978; Solomon & George, 1999), a 22-minute behavioral assessment comprised of eight episodes in which the child's responses to a novel room, to a stranger's appearance, and to the parent's disappearance and reappearance are observed. As measured in the Strange Situation, attachment is not a trait construct, it is a relationship construct (Sroufe, 1997). The Strange Situation assessment can be administed as early as 12 months of age.

The tripartite model specifies interaction among the three factors, genetics, attachment, and childhood socioemotional experience. Interactions between the genetic factor, temperament, and maternal caregiving style, a component of attachment, has been demonstrated (Weinfield et al., 1999). When infants were irritable and mothers rigid and traditional, for example, the child was more likely to be anxiously attached.

Insecure Attachment, Resistant Type

Maximizing attachment behavior, even when environmental stress is low, is called insecure–resistant, or anxious-resistant attachment in children. In the first months of life, this infant will be fussy, noodgy, edgy, clingy, and whiny—the so-called dependent child. This child attempts to keep himself continually on mother's "radar screen" so that should real need arise, there is a chance she will be aware of him. However, when she does respond, this child pushes away, resisting her attempts to soothe. Hence the name *resistant* attachment.

In the Strange Situation (Ainsworth et al., 1978), the resistant child will be unable to use the caregiver as a secure base for exploration, instead seeking proximity with the caregiver in the novel room of the Strange Situation, an indication that the exploration system is attenuated. The resistant child will be wary of and unresponsive toward the stranger when she appears in the Strange Situation, indicating that the wariness system is activated. The separation event will significantly distress the resistant child. The child will seek contact with caregiver on reunion, but will not be comforted by that contact. This is the hallmark of resistant attachment: seeking contact with the caregiver, but resisting it with anger when it is achieved. Ambivalence between seeking caregiver contact and resisting it when it is attained characterizes the resistant attachment pattern. The resistant child produces distress signals more frequently than a secure child to assure the attention and proximity of a caregiver given to intermittent responsiveness. These basic patterns of anxiety and resistance persist into adulthood and can form the basis of current maladaptive functioning. The affect focused therapist can help the client first by teaching AMST so the client cognizes the affects involved and then by uncovering pivotal experiences and caregiver representations assembled with those experiences. Once uncovered these experiences can be reprocessed and the caregiver representations can be reconfigured.

Insecure Attachment, Avoidant Type

Anxious–avoidant, or insecure–avoidant, is the name given to the other prominent strategy of insecure attachment. The avoidant child will minimize demonstrations of attachment behavior in situations of distress in order to prevent the rejection he has come to expect. Avoidant attachment apparently results when parents act less often to terminate the infant's cries and hold the infant less frequently. The infant develops behavioral links in which its own behavior terminates its distress. In the Strange Situation, the avoidant child will explore toys in the novel room, but will avoid sharing them with the caregiver. Separation events are unlikely to produce distress. Response to the stranger will replicate the avoidant child's response to the caregiver. In the reunion event with the caregiver, the avoidant child will ignore her, turn away from her, or fail to maintain contact with her. Mothers of infants later classified as avoidant expressed aversion to physical contact when it was sought by the infant and expressed little emotion during interactions with infants. Empirical research demonstrates that avoidant infants' mothers were unresponsive to the infant's timing cues and appeared to dislike physical contact with their infants. When avoidant infants experience severe threat, they apparently maintain caregiver proximity by reducing distress signals to avoid alienating a caregiver prone to rejection (Sroufe et al., 1999). The affect oriented therapist will recognize patterns of childhood avoidance in the present client's behavior and will use AMST skills and ACT interventions to help this client.

Insecure Attachment, Disorganized–Disoriented Type

Under stress in the Strange Situation, the disorganized–disoriented child is apparently unable to maintain a coherent attachment pattern and demonstrates conflicted behaviors (Weinfield et al., 1999). Conflict may result in behavioral stilling. Contradictions may appear in the form of moving away from the caregiver while facing her or backing toward her.

Emotion and Attachment

Two primary emotions characterize the attachment-disordered child: fear and its close relative anxiety, and anger. Lack of responsiveness engenders anger in the infant, and Weinfield and colleagues (1999) noted, "anger seems to be a normative reaction to inaccessibility of caregivers" (p. 70). Ethological research in the home has revealed that anxiously attached infants were more overtly angry and noncompliant and cried more than securely attached infants. Furthermore, the mothers of these children were less sensitive in dyadic interactions, were more interfering in the child's behaviors, and were less accessible to their children's bids for proximity. Emotion expression patterns established during attachment may have repercussions across the life span.

Patterns of affect expression appear to be components of developmental pathways. These developmental pathways (Sroufe, 1997; Weinfield et al., 1999) are like branches of a tree in which each branch represents a personality structure that has been conditioned by previous history. Apparently the childhood context can set a child on an affective developmental pathway in which the traits of fear and anxiety that develop in an insecure–resistant attachment in infancy and childhood become the foundations for emergence of a fearful and anxious adult personality (Lewis, 2000).

The insecure–avoidant attachment entails a developmental pathway assembled with anger affect. An angry trait that develops in reaction to failure of caregivers to meet the infant's needs sets the basis for emergence of an angry juvenile, adolescent, and adult self structure. When anger in infancy becomes a part of the emerging self structure, it is carried forward into childhood, and the insecurely attached infant becomes an angry, aggressive child. Angry, aggressive patterns in the personality structure are also seen in the self that emerges from from a disorganized–disoriented attachment. Anger is the response of the infant to insensitive, rejecting parenting, or to parenting characterized by unavailability or neglect. The infant responds only to the actions of caregivers, not to their intentions, and it is not sufficient for the infant's needs that the caregiver "wanted to be there for the child."

Empirical research supports the concept of affective developmental pathways. Studies of preschoolers showed that children with anxious (insecure) attachment histories demonstrated more negative affect, more anger, and more aggression when compared to children with secure attachment (Weinfield et al., 1999). Empirical studies with elementary children support these findings. Empirical research further demonstrates intergenerational transmission of affective development, because a mother's anger in speaking of her own mother is significantly associated with her own infant's angry resistance (Hesse, 1999). Understanding how deficiencies in the child–caregiver dyad can manifest in affect dysregulation that influences current behavior is critical to an affect orientation to psychotherapy. AMST can help the adult whose anger today is related to deficits in childhood experience, first by assisting the client to recognize that anger, then to tolerate it, and then to regulate it. Once these goals have been accomplished, the client can use the anger to access archaic experiences that engendered it so they can be processed to an adaptive resolution.

Sequelae of Insecure Attachment: General Considerations

Individual differences in attachment security are carried forward and manifest as differences in affect regulation, as differences in behavior regulation scripts, and as differences in IWMs.

Research demonstrates that individual differences in attachment history affect how children construe the environment. Several different types of assessments have been employed to reach this conclusion. Children were asked to complete stories with separation themes; their reactions to cartoons depicting social conflict were observed; reactions to family pictures were measured; and memories for affective–cognitive stimuli were assessed (Sroufe et al., 1999). Children with insecure attachments were more likely to read hostile intent where there was ambiguity, were more likely to reject images of parents, and were less likely to fantasize successful resolution of conflict than securely attached children. Establishment of these propensities in childhood sets the basic structure of the self that persists into adulthood, and therefore adults with insecure childhood attachments are apparently more likely to read hostile intent into ambiguity, to reject images of parents, and to fail to fantasize successful resolution of conflict. These adult propensities may manifest in marriage, at work, in politics, or in social situations.

Research demonstrates that children with insecure attachment histories fail to form supportive, secure relationships (Sroufe et al., 1999). The avoidant child will approach social situations with a childhood self-concept of isolation, inability to achieve emotional closeness, and unworthiness of being cared for or cared about. This child's self-concept has set her on a developmental pathway leading to social maladaptation. Furthermore, research demonstrates that insecurely attached children have suppressed or defensively modified emotions like interest in others that would have facilitated affective communication.

Individual differences also manifest developmentally in the autonomy–dependency continuum, in the empathy–aggression continuum, and in the social competence–withdrawal continuum. Autonomy fails to develop or fails to develop fully when caregivers are unresponsive, erratic in responding, or neglectful of the infant's cues and bids. Children of such caregivers become insecurely attached, and they do not learn that they can effect change in the world in the direction of getting their needs met. Empirical research has demonstrated that juveniles as well as adolescents with insecure attachments of both the avoidant and resistant types were rated by teachers and camp counselors as more dependent than those with secure attachment histories (Weinfield et al., 1999). Self-confidence is an element of autonomy and has been equated in research with ego resilience, that is, the child's capability for flexible responses especially in frustrating situations. Empirical research also demonstrated that children with insecure attachment histories scored lower for ego resilience than securely attached children. Insecurely attached toddlers were less persistent in a tool task than securely attached toddlers, a result that held across Israeli, German, and American cultures (Weinfield et al., 1999). Insecurely attached children demonstrated lower competence, less vitality, lowered enthusiasm, and diminished persistence. Children who fail to develop autonomy in childhood carry the quality of impaired self-efficacy forward into adulthood. In adulthood, the person may identify with the quality and become dependent. Alternatively, the person may develop defensive structures that provide the illusion of autonomy.

Social competence appears to emerge out of the prior establishment of a goal-corrected partnership. The goal-corrected partnership develops in a secure dyad that teaches the infant that communication is contingent upon each partner's cues and responses. The insecurely attached infant, in contradistinction, learns from the caregiver's neglectful or insensitive responses that communication is a series of uncoordinated exchanges, and hence the child of an insecure dyad never learns the goal-corrected partnership skill. As a result this child experiences difficulties in the realm of social competence.

Two important sequelae of the toddler's (12–18 months) attachment status have been revealed from long-term longitudinal studies, some of which have been prospective: (1) with some caveats, the toddler's attachment style predicts that individual's attachment style 15 to 21 years later; and (2) mother's attachment style predicts her toddler's attachment style (Hesse, 1999). Understanding the import of these findings requires a brief description of adult attachment.

Whereas child attachment is measured by the Strange Situation (Ainsworth et al., 1978; Solomon & George, 1999), adult attachment is assessed by an 18-question interview (Adult Attachment Interview [AAI]; George, Kaplan, & Main, 1996; Hesse, 1999) regarding childhood experiences with parents and the current effects of those experiences on the self. The subject is required to produce memories and reflect upon them while maintaining coherence, consistency, and collaboration with the interviewer, a challenging process that surprises the unconscious (Hesse, 1999). Adult attachment is obtained by scoring the transcript of the entire interview. Four groupings emerge from the AAI interview: secure–autonomous, dismissing, preoccupied, and unresolved. Secure–autonomous interviewees produce coherent and collaborative narratives, even when reporting unfavorable events. Secure–autonomous speakers give answers with sufficient detail, yet they do not elaborate excessively, and they return the initiative to the interviewer. Significantly and consistently, secure–autonomous adults raise children who score as securely attached in the Strange Situation.

Adults are classified as *dismissing* on the AAI when their responses appear to minimize discussion of attachment-related experience. Parents are described in favorable or highly favorable terms, representations that would be called idealizing. Dismissing persons do not provide evidence to support the idealizations and may contradict them. There will be internal inconsistencies in the narrative, and answers may be brief or avoidant (e.g., "I don't remember"). The dismissing adult appears to want to provide a positive image of her childhood experiences and "to limit the influence of attachment relationships in thought, in feeling, or in daily life" (Hesse, 1999, p. 401). In large measure, dismissing adults endorsed an avoidant attachment in their own childhoods, and these persons will raise children who will themselves be classified as avoidant.

When adult interviewees produce lengthy narratives filled with apparently unresolved childhood memories assembled with anger affect, fear affect, or passivity, the individual is classified as "preoccupied." The preoccupied adult does not collaborate with the interviewer, and the content of the memories evoked by the interview so provokes the speaker that he cannot maintain a focus or contain his responses. Preoccupied adults appear to maximize attentional focus on childhood experiences with caregivers and consequently lose focus on the collaborative conversation. Empirical research demonstrates that a majority of preoccupied adults endorsed an insecure–resistant attachment pattern in toddlerhood. The children raised by preoccupied speakers are "typically judged resistant/ambivalent" (Hesse, 1999, p. 398.)

Speakers will be classified as *unresolved-disorganized* when they display lapses in monitoring their cognitive behavior during the AAI interview, particularly during discussions of loss or of abuse. The unresolved-disorganized adult will typically have endorsed a disorganized–disoriented attachment pattern when assessed as a toddler in longitudinal studies. Furthermore, the unresolved-disorganized attachment in the parent predicts disorganized–disoriented attachment in the child (Hesse, 1999).

Hesse (1999) emphasized the predictive correspondence between the parent's adult attachment pattern and that parent's infant's response in the Strange Situation. Both mother–infant and father–infant attachment patterns correspond to the parent's adult attachment, although toddlers may have different attachment patterns to each parent. Infants were assessed in the Strange Situation and their parents were assessed by AAI 5 years later. The match between secure, avoidant, and resistant attachment patterns for infants (n = 32) and their mothers' (n = 32) assessments for secure–autonomous, dismissing, and preoccupied attachment pattern was 75% with $p < .001$. The match for fathers and their infants was 69%, $p < .005$. Hesse writes, "the form in which an individual presents his or her life narrative (regardless of its content) predicts caregiving behavior in highly specific and systematic ways" (p. 398).

Adult attachment style obtained from AAI assessments *before* childbirth predicted infant attachment style at age 12 months in 96 dyads (Hesse, 1999).

Furthermore, a three-generation study of grandmothers, their adult daughters, and their children (grandchildren) demonstrated that the "grandmothers' adult attachment categories were significantly related to those of their grandchildren" (p. 407). A metanalysis of 14 studies involving 18 samples and 854 dyads conducted in six countries demonstrated that maternal attachment pattern was more strongly related to child attachment pattern (effect size: $d = 1.14$) than paternal attachment pattern ($d = 0.80$), while the match between adult dismissing and infant avoidant pattern was 1.02 and between adult preoccupied and infant resistant was 0.93.

Five longitudinal studies of attachment status demonstrate that infant attachment status is highly predictive of adult attachment style (Hesse, 1999). One study followed 50 lower- to middle-class adults (20–22 years) who were assessed in the Strange Situation at 12 months of age. Sixty-four percent of the adults maintained the same adult attachment style they had demonstrated in infancy, and for 72%, the secure versus insecure split of infancy was maintained in the coherent versus incoherent categorization in adulthood. When high risk groups are examined, however, the continuity of attachment status observed in these studies disappears (Weinfield, Sroufe, & Egeland, 2000).

Intergenerational transmission of disturbed attachment and negative affect were examined in a study of 49 severely disturbed young adults and adolescents (Diamond, & Doane, 1994). The parents were assessed for attachment to their own parents (grandparents of the subjects) using the 5-minute speech sample. Parental negative affect expression was scored from videotapes of interactions between the subjects and their parents. Criticism, intrusiveness, and guilting were indexed as negative affect expression. Disturbances in mother's attachment to her own mother significantly predicted negative affect expression toward the adolescent subjects. The authors suggest that a mother's emotional burdens arising from insecure attachment to her same-sex parent may motivate her negative affect displays toward her own children thus contributing to those children's disturbances.

Several mechanisms support the persistence of early adaptive style across developmental stages (Sroufe et al., 1999). Stable caregiving, whether responsive or not, promotes the emergence of increasing order in the personality structure, whether that order is represented by a secure attachment style or one of the forms of insecure attachment. When caregiving is stable, no matter what the quality of the caregiving, the push necessary to alter the personality system's trajectory is absent (Lewis, 2000). Continuity of attachment pattern is favored because continuity is a transactional process in which a self-regulating organism interacts with an environment. *Continuity* means that a child who forms a secure attachment will retain that style, while a child that forms an insecure attachment will persist in that style. Furthermore, the individual affects the environment in ways that assure continuity of prior adaption; that is, secure children who expect to be treated positively in social situations are treated positively, while avoidant children who expect to be rejected, experience rejection. Finally, patterns of attachment persist because they are based on preverbal experience that is less amenable to modification by subsequent experience.

Maternal insecure attachment is apparently a risk factor for infant and childhood clinical disorder. Hesse (1999) reported a study of 23 7- to 8-month-old infants hospitalized for failure to thrive in which only one of the mothers was judged secure–autonomous. In another study, none of the mothers of 20 severely sleep-disordered infants was assessed as secure–autonomous. A study of 20 children with behavior problems showed that 85% of the mothers (n = 17) were insecure. Among 20 children showing developmental delay and clinical problems, 100% of mothers endorsed an insecure attachment.

One of the sequelae of insecure attachment in childhood may be substance abuse later in life. It must be emphasized that individual differences in attachment in childhood do not cause downstream maladaptive behavior; "rather, they initiate pathways that are probabilistically related to certain later outcomes" (Weinfield et al., 1999, p. 75). A study examining quality of attachment to primary caretakers compared 62 adult substance abusers to 57 normal controls (Sicher, 1998). The substance abuse group reported parents who disciplined more harshly and threatened abandonment more frequently than controls. Parents of adult substance abusers reported their parents were less emotionally accessible and responsive in childhood. Recollecting their childhoods, these persons reported having fewer friends and less social support. The substance abuse group reported that during adolescence their parents were less encouraging of autonomy than controls and their parents provided less emotional support. As adults, the substance abusers reported difficulties in maintaining attachment in significant relationships, discomfort with intimacy, and fears of being abandoned.

Another study of 3,984 European adolescent participants examined the role of family structure on substance abuse in 14- to 15-year-olds (McArdle et al., 2002). The authors discovered that secure attachment to mothers was associated with reduced substance abuse. When attachment to mother was poor, and the adolescent could not confide in her, substance abuse was more prevalent. Comparison of binge drinking first year college students with nonbinge drinking controls demonstrated that the binge drinkers, both male (n = 55) and female (n = 55), were less securely attached to parents and were less capable of tolerating and regulating emotion (Camlibel, 2000). A follow-up study of persons who had completed an intensive outpatient rehabilitation program suggested that substance dependent patients were more likely to endorse an insecure style of adult attachment than a secure style (Frank, 2001). Security of adult attachment, in particular to sponsor and to the fellowship, predicted better drinking outcomes among members of AA than for members with an insecure attachment (Miller, 1996). Hofler and Kooyman (1996) have suggested that an infant's unmet needs, which will affect the quality of the early attachment, may play a role in the development of addiction and alcoholism in adulthood. In particular, they hypothesize that the addict has an attachment relationship of an avoidant type with the abused substance.

These general considerations of the developmental sequelae of insecure attachment demonstrate that a parent's attachment style is transmitted to children. A parent's own insecure attachment style can be a risk factor for the child's well-being. Furthermore, insecure attachment in childhood is a risk factor for adolescent and adult psychopathology. The affect oriented psychotherapist must be aware of the effect of childhood attachment style in determining the client's current functioning. AMST can help the adult child of insecure attachment by cognizing the affects that were insensitively responded to in childhood and that may now be dysregulated. In phase II of ACT, the clinician can help the client uncover the origins of these problematic emotions and then process them to an adaptive resolution.

Sequelae of Insecure Attachment, Resistant Style

Insecure–resistant attachment positions an infant on a developmental pathway with outcomes specific to the attachment pattern (Weinfield et al., 1999). Recall that the resistant infant, when distressed, has difficulty accepting caregiving when it is offered. Patterns of inconsistent caregiving or neglect are associated with resistant attachment, and the insecurely attached infant is hyperaroused and hypervigilant, never certain of the caregiver's availability. Insecure–resistant attachment is associated with diminished forcefulness, diminished confidence, and increased hesitance and anxiety when confronted with novelty. Resistant attachment also associates with passivity and withdrawal in empirical studies discussed by Weinfield and associates (1999). These infants are uncertain of their own effectiveness. In play pairs with avoidantly attached children, resistantly attached children were empirically demonstrated more likely to become victims. In videotaped free play situations, children with resistant attachment histories appeared to lack boundaries between another child's distress and their own; that is, when a resistant child witnessed another child becoming distressed, the resistant child became distressed.

A child's resistant attachment evokes specific behaviors from adults. When films of teacher interactions with children were rated for dimensions of teacher treatment, children with resistant attachment patterns were more likely to be controlled, to have their rule infractions tolerated, and to be nurtured, and less likely to be expected to comply (Sroufe et al., 1999). The authors wrote that this teacher treatment "may be seen as perpetuating the immaturity of those with resistant histories" (p. 7).

Insecure–resistant attachment entails emotion consequences. Children with resistant attachment histories are more likely to have problems with anxiety. This apparently arises because of the constant vigilance associated with the early attachment experience (Sroufe, 1997). Children with insecure–resistant attachments are known to be less capable of tolerating stress and frustration than securely attached children (Weinfield et al., 1999).

The insecure–resistant attachment is believed to be a gateway on a developmental path that can lead to psychopathology. Empirical research supports the belief that "a history of resistant attachment was found to be related specifically and uniquely to anxiety disorders" (Weinfield et al., 1999, p. 81). A longitudinal study from infancy to age 6 found that boys with histories of resistant attachment were more likely to demonstrate somatic complaints. Insecure–resistant children are at risk for developing depression due to their passivity and helplessness (Weinfield et al., 1999). An insecure attachment of the resistant type and a perception of a relative lack of maternal caring were uniquely associated with borderline features after gender, childhood adversity, Axis I disorder, and nonborderline Axis II symptoms were partialed out in a sample of almost 400 18-year-olds (Nickell, Waudby, & Trull, 2002).

The resistantly attached child will usually demonstrate a preoccupied adult attachment, and the AMST clinician must be aware that problems regulating fear affect characterize this individual. AMST can help this client by raising the distressing affects from childhood to conscious awareness where they can be worked on in succeeding stages of therapy.

Sequelae of Insecure Attachment, Avoidant Style

Insecure–avoidant attachment places a child on a developmental pathway with its own unique outcomes. Recall that under conditions of stress, the avoidant child fails to seek caregiver contact. In his previous experience with the caregiver, this infant has been chronically rebuffed. The caregiver has ignored or repulsed his attempts for physical contact. As a result, avoidant children demonstrate confidence in the face of novelty because they have developed the habit of exploration as a defense against insecurity in the relationship with the maternal caregiver.

Insecure–avoidant children have difficulties in social situations. Research demonstrates that insecure–avoidant children who expect peer rejection will often be rejected by peers (Sroufe et al., 1999), demonstrating that a child's expectations of the social environment will often produce the expected result. Empirical research reveals that avoidant attachment was associated in studies with the likelihood of victimizing playmates, and children rated by teachers as "mean" in preschool situations were always children with an avoidant attachment history.

Insecure–avoidant children demonstrate difficulties with emotion regulation. Aggressive, hostile behaviors both with parents and with peers are more likely to be evidenced by children with avoidant or with disorganized–disoriented attachment histories. Children with insecure–avoidant attachment histories demonstrate alienation, lack of empathy, and hostile anger, conditions believed to represent gateways to developmental pathways that lead toward conduct disorders (Weinfield et al., 1999), a belief supported by empirical research. Teacher ratings of third grade boys showed that an avoidant attachment history was associated with aggressivity.

The avoidantly attached child evokes specific behaviors from adults that are different from behaviors evoked by resistant attachment. Coding films of teacher–student interactions revealed that children with avoidant attachment histories were subject to teacher control, yet were not treated warmly by teachers, did not receive nurturance from teachers, and were the only group toward which teachers demonstrated anger (Sroufe et al., 1999). The authors noted that teacher responses perpetuated the avoidant students' expectations of rejection.

An avoidant attachment predicts the probability of psychopathology. In a long-term, longitudinal, prospective study, avoidant attachment assessed at 12 to 18 months was significantly correlated with the amount, duration, and seriousness of psychopathology at 17½ years in a sample of 170 individuals. Research confirmed that avoidant attachment predicts aggressiveness, bullying, and conduct disorders (Sroufe, 1997).

Children endorsing an avoidant attachment pattern are vulnerable to depression, but for different reasons than resistantly attached children. Insecure–avoidant children develop depression because of alienation and aloneness (Weinfield et al., 1999). A retrospective study demonstrated that alcoholics endorsed an avoidant attachment style (Frank, 2001). I hypothesize that a central causative element in depression occurring in adult children of avoidant attachments may relate to anger expression. The avoidant child is known to be an angry child. When the child's anger is punished, shamed, or otherwise denied expression by caregivers, it may turn inward and contribute to a developmental pathway toward adolescent and adult depression.

The client who endorses a dismissing adult attachment style was probably avoidantly attached in childhood. Clinicians who are aware of the client's attachment style will be better able to employ AMST skills to help the client. When a client demonstrates a dismissing adult attachment style, this is often accompanied by difficulties with anger emotion. AMST can help the avoidant-dismissing client cognize anger affect and then recognize how unresolved anger from childhood manifests as a personality trait and in current relationships.

Sequelae of Disoriented–Disorganized Attachment Style

When caregivers behave in confusing, alarming, or dissociated ways, the infant experiences fear of the attachment figure. The infant becomes confused when alarming parental behavior alternates with more supportive behavior. Faced with a paradox that the caregiver is both a source of alarm and a source of nurturance, the infant's emotion, cognitive, and behavioral systems disorganize and disintegrate.

Empirical research suggests that dissociative symptomatology in adolescent males and females may be predicted by a disoriented–disorganized attachment pattern in childhood. It is known that a parental unresolved–disorganized attachment pattern as assessed by the AAI predicts infant disorganized/disoriented behavior in the Strange Situation (Hesse, 1999). West, Adam, Spreng, and Rose (2001) studied 133 adolescents in psychiatric treatment. The sample was divided into one cohort (n = 69) endorsing an unresolved attachment and another cohort (n = 64) that was not unresolved. The authors found that an unresolved attachment correlated with dissociative symptomatology. Ogawa, Sroufe, Weinfield, Carlson, and Egeland (1997) showed that in a sample of 168 young adults from a longitudinal study of high risk children that both the avoidant and disorganized attachment significantly predicted dissociation. The association between a disorganized attachment history and dissociation held even after the effects of childhood trauma were partialed out (Weinfield et al., 1999).

CHILDHOOD SOCIOEMOTIONAL HISTORY

The third component of the tripartite model is childhood socioemotional history, which can range from benign in its positive aspect to adverse on the negative side. While attachment refers to "things that should happen for every child" during the first three to four years of life, the negative aspect of childhood experience refers to adverse and traumatic experiences, which are "things that should never happen to any child and did happen to this child." When the child's socioemotional history is characterized by adverse and traumatic experience, it indicates that powerful emotions were induced in the child. These powerful emotions threaten to overwhelm the child, and they are often unresolved, disappearing into the unconscious where they continue to exert effects on behavior over time. The term *childhood socio-emotional history* refers to the cumulative record of childhood experience whether benign, adverse, or traumatic.

Clinicians and researchers have known for some time that adversity in childhood was a risk factor for psychopathology. In the 1980s, the focus was more on sexual abuse trauma (e.g., Briere & Runtz, 1988) and its clinical sequelae. From the late 1990s onward, the literature speaks of adverse childhood experiences (Anda et al., 1999; Weinfield et al., 2000) that include a range of negative events as well as physical and sexual abuse. Anda and colleagues (1999) defined adverse childhood experiences as verbal abuse, physical abuse, sexual abuse, battered mother, household substance abuse, mental illness in the household, parental separation or divorce, and incarcerated household member(s). Verbal abuse was determined by answers to two questions that inquired how often did an adult "swear at you, insult you, or put you down?" or "threaten to hit you or throw something at you, but didn't do it?" (p. 1653). Weinfield and associates (2000) spoke of negative life events that include being born to a single mother, parental divorce, life-threatening illness of parent or child, serious parental drug or alcohol abuse, physical or sexual abuse of the child, and death of a parent or custodial attachment figure.

A 1997 study (Kessler, Davis, & Kendler) analyzed data from a large survey of U.S. households. The study demonstrated that loss events, parental psychopathology, assaultive traumas, natural disasters, and other adversities—the study examined 26 categories of adversity—where consistently associated with the onset of disorders of anxiety and mood, with addictive disorders, and with acting out disorders. The sequelae of childhood adversity persisted beyond childhood. Furthermore, adversity tended to cluster in children's lives, and the authors cautioned against thinking that a specific childhood adversity could predict a specific adult disorder. Much research, a small fraction of which will be summarized in succeeding pages, has focused on the outcomes from specific types of childhood adversity. Kessler and associates observation that adversity tends to cluster in children's lives must be kept in mind. Adversity rarely presents itself in a child's life as a lone bandit; it is more often a band of marauders laying siege to the youngster's world.

Two studies have recognized the cumulative nature of adversity. In a study of nicotine dependency, Anda and colleagues (1999) showed that greater cumulative prevalence of types of childhood adversity predicted earlier onset of nicotine use and greater chances of current use. Aguilar, Sroufe, Egeland, and Carlson (2000) demonstrated that cumulative risk in childhood predicts early onset/persistent adolescent antisocial behavior.

Born to a Single Mother

Being born to a single mother is a risk factor for subsequent maladaptation. In the Minnesota Mother–Child Project, 180 children were followed from birth through the sixth grade, and endogenous characteristics of the children such as activity level were measured as well as qualities of the parenting environment (Sroufe, 1997). The outcome variable was teacher reports of attention and activity problems on the Behavior Problem Checklist. Children who showed attention and activity problems in the sixth grade were more likely to have been born to single mothers. Other qualities of the parenting environment besides being born to a single mother contributed to eventual maladaptation. Measures of parental intrusiveness and overstimulation obtained at 6 months were predictive of attention and activity problems, and no endogenous child variable predicted parental intrusiveness. By age 3½, the children who were to become maladapted had changed, becoming distractible, an observational quality that modestly predicted ADHD behaviors later in elementary school. When contextual variables like parental intrusiveness and being born to a single mother were combined with preschool distractibility, 28% of variance in early elementary school attention problems could be predicted.

Parental Divorce

Parental divorce is an adverse childhood experience that can predispose to late onset alcoholism in adulthood. A large study in Britain investigated the association between alcohol consumption and parental divorce in childhood (Hope, Power, & Rodgers, 1998). The study assessed alcohol consumption at age 23 and again at age 33 in 4,606 men and 4,892 women. At age 23, only a weak, inconsistent association existed between the childhood experience of parental separation and alcohol consumption, but by age 33, the index adults reported higher levels of alcohol consumption, more problem drinking, and more heavy drinking than controls. Neither later divorce nor parental death increased alcohol consumption in those cohorts. Apparently, the sequelae of childhood experience of parental divorce can take more than two decades to manifest. Recall that late onset alcoholism was associated with the lower threshold for distress–sadness–anguish affect hypothesized to be caused by the low-activity form of dopamine inactivating COMT (Tiihonen et al., 1999). It is tempting to speculate that unresolved childhood sadness originating in the adverse experience of parental divorce manifests in late onset alcoholism. Certainly, the affect oriented therapist should be aware of this possibility.

Mental Illness in the Household

Parental mental illness is an adverse experience that can skew the childhood socioemotional history toward negativity and predispose to subsequent psychopathology. Downey and Coyne (1990) reviewed the literature regarding adjustment in children with a depressed parent. The authors emphasized that a contextual model stressing the interdependence of depressed persons and their social environment has supplanted traditional views that depression was an individual problem. Research has demonstrated that children of depressed parents have adjustment problems stemming from deficiencies in parenting behaviors, and these findings support a transmission model of maladjustment.

Early, uncontrolled studies on the effect of mental illness in the household compared children of depressed parents and children of schizophrenic parents (Downey & Coyne, 1990). When children of school age were assessed by a variety of measures for academic and social competence, the children of depressed parents showed similar impairments to children of schizophrenic parents in comparison with controls. This result holds for infants and preschool children as well. The specific parental diagnosis is less predictive of child impairment than are the chronicity and severity of the parental dysfunction. Marital discord plays a role in the adjustment problems of children with a depressed parent, but it is not a factor in explaining the adjustment problems of children with a schizophrenic parent. Longitudinal studies demonstrate that disturbances identified in childhood persist into adulthood. The late adolescent and young adult children of affectively disordered parents—rediagnosis of parents in the early studies showed that some depressed participants were actually bipolar—endorsed disturbance rates higher than normal controls and similar to adult children of schizophrenic parents. Affective disorders were prevalent among the adult children of affectively disordered parents, while personality disorders predominated among the adult children of schizophrenic parents.

Recent, controlled studies have examined children of affectively disordered parents in comparison to normal controls (Downey & Coyne, 1990). The infants and toddlers of depressed parents showed symptoms of depression and antisocial behavior that were apparent at age 2 and were still apparent 4 years later. In studies at school age discussed by Downey and Coyne (1990), children of depressed parents demonstrate higher levels of externalizing and internalizing symptoms than normal controls. These children are more likely to endorse clinical impairment on symptom checklists, receive more treatment for psychiatric disorders, demonstrate greater functional impairment and social and academic deficits, and assess for poorer physical health than controls. Affective disturbance predominated among children of depressed parents, with 25% showing considerable depressive symptomatology in comparison to normal controls, none of whom were depressed. Affective disorders of any type were three times more prevalent among children of unipolar-disordered parents when compared to normal children, and these children were six times more likely to show major depressive disorder. Children of bipolar-disordered parents endorsed cyclothymia and manic disorders. Prevalence of nonaffective disorders among children of depressed parents are inconsistent, but higher rates of ADHD, conduct disorder, and substance abuse disorder have been observed. Current research is examining the risk factors in the children and caregiving styles of the parents in an attempt to understand the etiology of the dysfunctions experienced by the children of depressed parents.

In their review, Downey and Coyne (1990) reported controlled studies of attachment showing that six of seven children of a bipolar parent were insecurely attached at 18 months. Studies with larger samples showed 79% of children of bipolar mothers and 47% of children of major depression mothers endorsed an insecure attachment. According to Downey and Coyne (1990), "insecure attachments were characterized primarily by avoidance or disorganized, disoriented behavior previously found in severely abused children" (p. 57). In a longitudinal study that uncovered an insecure attachment, all seven of the children of a bipolar parent demonstrated problems with empathy at 6 years as well as unusual behaviors in conflict situations.

The authors go on to review qualities of the caregiver's parenting behavior that might contribute to their children's maladaptation (Downey & Coyne, 1990). Observations of a depressed person's behaviors, when considered in light of Schore's theories of socioaffective development (1994), may provide insights. Depression reduces the caregiver's rate of behavior, speaking frequency, speaking intensity, gaze behavior, and response time. Affectively, depressed persons display hostility, irritability, sadness, and anxiousness. All of these qualities and behaviors may be expected to adversely impact the infant's socioaffective development. Depressed mothers may be unable to provide optimal gaze transactions that are essential to development of symbiosis during the second three months of life. During early practicing, the depressed maternal caregiver may be unable to provide the visual–affective communication transactions necessary to full neurophysiological development of the infant's ventral tegmental circuit and OFC. The maternal caregiver's helplessness and hostility may prevent her from being able to provide affective arousal to her child. Empirical research shows that depressed mothers have less positive attitudes toward parenting than controls, experience the demands of parenting negatively, and feel rejection and hostility toward their child. These qualities would prevent the depressed mother from optimally socializing her infant's affective development. These qualities would also negatively impact the development of the attachment bond; the children of depressed mothers would be expected to be insecurely attached. Furthermore, the infant's experience-conditioned maternal IWM would be a depressed representation unavailable to internally stimulate arousal of positive affect in the offspring of the depressed mother as he or she moved through the toddler, child, juvenile, and adolescent stages. Empirical research on depressed mothers supports this transmission hypothesis for how mother's depression could contribute to her offspring's affective disordering.

Depressed mothers were less spontaneous, vocal, or positive and more distant than controls in play with their 4-month-olds (Downey & Coyne, 1990). They expressed little positive affect, demonstrated lower rates of behavior, and responded less contingently and consistently. Downey and Coyne (1990) wrote, "depression impedes mothers' ability to imbue their speech with the affective signals thought to play an important role in the socialization of affect modulation" (p. 63). The hostility and rejection components of mother's depression may also impair her ability to provide optimal shame socialization necessary to socioaffective development of the child's lateral tegmental circuit during late practicing. Empirical research supports the conclusion that depressed mothers are more irritable toward their children and that maternal hostility increases under stress. Research summarized by Downey and Coyne (1990) suggested that depressed mothers' hostility apparently prevents them from developing a goal-corrected partnership with their children. These mothers resort to conflict resolution strategies that require less cognitive effort, instead enforcing obedience unilaterally and resorting to shouting or slapping. Indirect evidence from retrospective studies and direct evidence from longitudinal studies suggests that depressed mothers' negative, hostile parenting behaviors contribute to maladjustment in their children.

Other studies have examined the effect of parental mental illness on the prevalence of borderline pathology in the children and have examined the effect of parental borderline pathology. A study of 65 nonclinical participants revealed that parental mental illness and Axis I disorder were significant predictors of borderline features among participants (Trull, 2001). Rates of psychiatric disorders were found to be significantly higher in families of child and adolescent outpatients diagnosed for borderline personality disorder (Goldman, D'Angelo, & DeMaso, 1993). Rates of psychopathology in 44 index families were compared with rates in a psychiatric comparison group of 100 children and adolescents. Depressive psychopathology, antisocial disorders, and substance abuse disorders were more prevalent among families of borderline children. A study of 467 personality disordered inpatients showed that neglect by caretakers of both genders, inconsistent treatment by a female caretaker, and emotional denial by a male caretaker, in addition to sexual abuse, were significant predictors of borderline personality disorder (Zanarini et al., 1998).

Maternal borderline personality disorder increases the risk in her male and female early adolescent children for psychopathology, including impulse control disorders, when compared to children of mothers with other personality disorders (Weiss et al., 1996). Children of borderline mothers displayed a higher prevalence of ADHD (43 vs. 13%), a higher prevalence of borderline personality disorder (33 vs. 9%), and an elevated prevalence of disruptive behavior disorders (oppositional defiant disorder and conduct disorder) than controls. In addition, the children of borderline mothers endorsed significantly lower scores, in the nonfunctional range, on the Child Global Assessment schedule. Prevalence of abuse of all types were similar for index and control cohorts; 90% of children in each cohort had been abused. Among the children of borderlines, 33% endorsed sexual abuse and 62% physical abuse. Among the children of other personality disordered mothers, 22% had been sexually abused and 83% physically abused. When index and control groups were combined, trauma significantly predicted psychopathology.

Parental mental disorders contribute adverse experience to the childhood socioemotional history that can contribute to subsequent psychopathology. The affect oriented therapist should be aware when a client reports parental psychopathology that it may have determined the emergence of maladaptive functioning in the client. AMST can help the client who reports a history of parental mental illness, because affect dysregulation in adulthood is apparently predicted by having a parent with psychopathology. AMST can help the adult child of a mentally ill parent by teaching the emotion management skills that the parent was not able to teach. Having these skills will help the adult child of a mentally ill parent to manage emotions coded by trauma and adversity.

Impact of Emotional Abuse on Emotion Regulation in Offspring

Parental intrusiveness, emotional abuse, verbal abuse, and parental indifference are forms of adverse childhood experience that negatively impact child emotion regulation. In a study of a clinical sample of 265 patients with major depressive disorder, disordered functioning was most distinctly associated with paternal indifference and maternal overcontrol (Parker et al., 1999). Behavioral inhibition in children appears related to maternal criticism or emotional overinvolvement directed at the child (Hirshfeld et al., 1997). Behaviorally inhibited children are shy, quiet, and withdrawn in childhood. Although behaviorally restrained, they are physiologically aroused in novel situations. These children are at risk for anxiety disorders. The authors followed a cohort of children to age 11 years who were assessed as behaviorally inhibited at 21 months. Mothers' criticism and emotional overinvolvement were assessed in a 5-minute speech in which they discussed their relationship to the index child. The rate of maternal criticism was 48.8% in this sample and was associated with gender of the child; mothers tended to criticize their daughters. Behavioral inhibition was significantly associated with maternal criticism, and the criticized children showed more behavior disorders, more mood disorders, and more externalizing behavior. The authors suggest the possibility that the child's inhibited temperament may be a factor in eliciting maternal criticism. A corollary is that the mother's difficulties with emotion regulation and impulse and behavior control are uncovered in a dyad in which the child is temperamentally inhibited.

Dutton, van Ginkel, and Starzomski (1995) investigated the role of recollected childhood shaming and guilting experiences among 140 abusive men. Early experiences of shame were defined as public humiliation by parents, random punishment, or "parental treatment that affected the whole self" (p. 123). Guilt referred to parents' projection of responsibility for their own unhappiness onto the child. The authors assessed participants for borderline personality organization, anger response, abusiveness, and childhood trauma. Among these male batterers, both mother's (correlation = .33) and father's (correlation = .55) shaming were significantly correlated with borderline personality organization ($p < .001$). Parental shaming was significantly associated with the men's scores on the management of anger inventory and with their scores for both psychological and physical abuse. Recollected experiences of shame and guilt were highly correlated with verbal abuse and with physical abuse by both parents. Independent confirmations of the men's recollections were not obtained. The authors observed that "the data support the notion that global attacks on the self-concept . . . had significant effects on the maintenance of the self concept in adulthood" (p. 127).

The behaviors of parental intrusiveness, verbal abuse, and emotional abuse produce adverse affective consequences in the child. In healthy disapproval–shame transactions, mother's disapproval elicits optimal (healthy) shame in her toddler, resulting in functional socioaffective conditioning of the toddler's lateral tegmental circuit. In the dysfunctional disapproval–shame transactions characteristic of parental intrusiveness, verbal abuse, and emotional abuse, mother's disapproval moves into disgust and elicits toxic, overwhelming shame in her toddler. Display of too much disgust by a parent constitutes an adverse experience for the child that results in trauma coding of the lateral tegmental circuit. When shame or disgust is trauma coded, it is unresolved, held in a state-specific, excitatory form in which it is more likely to be elicited than other emotions in any situation. Affective transactions in which overwhelming disgust is directed at the toddler adversely impacts the youngster's nascent IWMs. On the one hand, mother's broadcast disgust assembles with the toddler's maternal introject, destroying its effectiveness for healthy behavioral self-regulation. This toxic level of disgust assembled with the maternal representation will prevent optimal separation-individuation, a portion of the self representation remains undifferentiated from the object representation, and an unresolved, disgust-based self- and object-representation persists. On the other hand, the caregiver's broadcast of overwhelming disgust assembles with the self-image, resulting in shame-based behaviors and reenactments. Either broadcast disgust or broadcast contempt can induce humiliation in the child, in which shame is assembled with anger affect. In humiliation, apparently both the parasympathetic and sympathetic branches of the autonomic nervous system are activated, and that activation results in trauma coding.

Verbal Abuse

A New York, community-based, longitudinal study investigated the prevalence of adolescent and early adult personality disorders among victims of childhood verbal abuse (J. B. Johnson et al., 2001). Investigators interviewed 793 mothers and their offspring at ages 5, 14, 16, and 22 years. Verbal abuse was defined as screaming at the child during the month prior to the interview, threatening the child with loss of love or abandonment, and threats of hitting. By these criteria, almost 10% of the youths in the sample had experienced verbal abuse. The study partialed out temperament, childhood physical and sexual abuse, physical punishment, neglect, and parental psychopathology. After statistically controlling the covariates, childhood verbal abuse was associated with increased risk for personality disordering in adolescence and early adulthood. Obsessive–compulsive disorder (OCD) was 14 times more likely, borderline personality disorder was 4.5 times more likely, and paranoid personality disorder was 3 times more likely. In addition to overt diagnoses, symptoms of personality disordering were also significantly elevated in the cohort that experienced verbal abuse in childhood.

Parental Substance Abuse

The extensive literature on the problems of children of alcoholic or drug addicted parents has been reviewed by J. L. Johnson and Leff (1999). Parental alcoholism places the children at risk for behavioral, neuropsychologic, psychologic, and cognitive impairments. Although the supporting research for the effects of parental drug abuse is not as extensive and rarely longitudinal, the data support a conclusion that, as with alcohol abuse, parental drug abuse places children at risk for later maladjustment.

A study of adult daughters of alcoholic fathers demonstrated that the daughters were less securely attached than a control group (Jaeger, Hahn, & Weinraub, 2000). The results of this study confirmed the observations made by Sicher (1998), reported above, that adult substance abusers endorsed a severely impaired attachment to their parents. Children with alcoholic fathers but nonproblem drinking mothers reported lower self-esteem and less secure attachment to father than children without an alcoholic father (Bice Brousard, 1998). Children can have different attachment styles to different caregivers (e.g., Sroufe, 1997). The index students reported their fathers' parenting style was inconsistent and unresponsive.

Paternal alcoholism affects how parents view their children at 12 months of child age. A study compared 115 families with alcoholic fathers to 101 control families (Das Eiden, & Leonard, 2000). Alcoholic fathers were more aggravated with their children than controls. Paternal depression mediated a father's alcoholic expression of aggravation toward his child. Apparently fathers' alcoholism affected mothers' ability to parent. The mothers with alcoholic husbands showed more aggravation with their children and less warmth, effects indirectly caused by their husbands' alcoholism. It appeared that the alcoholic husbands provoked depression in their wives, which in turn led them to a more aggravated mothering style than controls.

During free play, the alcoholic fathers scored higher in negative father–infant interactions than controls (Eiden, Chavez, & Leonard, 1999). Negative interactions were defined by decreased paternal sensitivity, diminished positive affect, reduced verbalizations, and increased negative affect. The infants were less responsive to alcoholic fathers. Fathers' alcoholism clustered with depression, antisocial behavior, and family aggression, three risk factors for subsequent child psychopathology.

Das Eiden, Leonard, and Morrisey (2001) also examined the effect of parental alcoholism on toddler compliance with parental directives at 18 and 24 months. Nonalcoholic controls (n = 96) were compared with father-only alcoholic families (n = 89), and with both parents alcoholic (n = 30). After a free play session, child compliance with parents during clean up was scored for committed compliance, passive noncompliance, overt resistance, and defiance. When compared to sons of nonalcoholic parents, the sons of alcoholic fathers scored higher for noncompliance. Interestingly, the daughters of alcoholic fathers showed an opposite pattern.

Mothers' alcohol or other drug use was associated with greater punitiveness toward their children in a study of 170 women who had current problems, past problems, or no problems with alcohol or other drugs (Miller, Smyth, & Mudar, 1999). Punitiveness was also predicted by a history of partner violence or parental violence.

Opiate-addicted mothers (n = 69) demonstrated less involvement in parenting their children than a control group matched for socioeconomic status (Suchman & Luthar, 2000). Opiate- or cocaine-addicted mothers, who also showed high rates of alcohol abuse and depression, raised children with high rates for any psychiatric disorder (60%), and who were assessed for major depression (24%), oppositional defiant disorder (20.5%), conduct disorder (13%), ADHD (10.5%), and substance abuse (7.5%) (Weissman et al., 1999).

Paternal depression comorbid with opiate addiction appeared to worsen the outcome for these patients' school-age and adolescent children (Nunes et al., 1998). When compared to sons of opiate addicts without major depression and to normal controls, the sons of addicts with depression showed greater prevalence of conduct disorders, social impairment, intellectual impairment, and diminishment of global functioning. Adolescent daughters of opiate addicts did not have greater prevalence of disorders, but were more poorly socially adjusted and showed diminished nonverbal intelligence. Male and female adolescent children of narcotic addicts (n = 285) reporting on their own behaviors prior to age 12, endorsed a negative view of the home environment (Nurco, Blatchley, Hanlon, & O'Grady, 1999). These adolescents reported severe and varied early deviance that was related to current drug and alcohol use, psychopathology, and association with deviant peers.

Childhood emotional abuse, verbal abuse, or parental drug abuse constitute forms of adverse childhood experience that negatively load the client's childhood socioemotional history factor. These adverse experiences predispose to current problems with affect regulation and to current psychopathology. The affect oriented therapist will employ AMST to help the client uncover and learn to manage unresolved emotions, coded by adversity that are involved in current maladaptations. Adult children of alcoholics have difficulty recognizing, tolerating, and regulating fear, anger, and shame among other affects. AMST can help this client with affect dysregulation resulting from deficits and adversities that are common in families where one or both parents abuse substances.

Traumatic Experience

Traumatic experience refers to the most extreme forms of adverse childhood experience: physical or sexual abuse. The history of our modern society is replete with traumatic abuse of children. Demause (1982) has written a history of infancy and childhood based on historical records and has shown that trauma—including infanticide, abandonment, beating, and sexual abuse—was widespread from antiquity through the 18th century in every European country. Unwanted babies were exposed and left to die. Babies who were not killed were often abandoned to wet nurses, as mothers, especially from the more wealthy classes, did not nurse their own children. Infants were restrained by yards of tightly wrapped cloth, a practice called swaddling, that rendered the child inert, passive, and withdrawn, but that served the caregivers' needs because swaddled infants could be ignored. Children were severely disciplined by beating with whips, canes, wooden and iron rods, and bundles of sticks. Demause wrote, "a very large percentage of the children born prior to the eighteenth century were what would today be termed 'battered children' " (p. 46). In addition to physical abuse, sexual abuse of both boys and girls was widespread. Rigorous obedience training continued into the 20 century.

Abuse is transmitted from one generation to the next. Miller (1998) has discussed the consequences of abusive childrearing practices. Describing the intergenerational transmission of abuse, Miller wrote, "one generation later, when the tormented children had themselves become parents, the former victims did the same with their children as had been done to them, with no feelings of guilt" (p. 578). While the fate of children born in Europe and America in modern times has undoubtedly improved, traumatic treatment of children persists. A 1998 study (Epstein et al.) sampled the United States adult female population and found that 9% of almost 3,000 respondents had been raped in childhood. Studying the prevalence of physical abuse, MacMillan and colleagues (1997) sampled

(N = 9953) the general population of Ontario, Canada, age 15 and older. Among males, 31.2% endorsed physical abuse, while among females the reported prevalence of physical abuse was 21.1%.

Chronic trauma in childhood prevents consolidation of the identity (Carlson, 1997; Herman, 1992; Ogawa et al., 1997). Splitting or fragmentation of the self may result, and overwhelming shame may assemble with the core, child self-concept, inhibiting further growth of this part. The sequelae of childhood trauma manifest in a range of severe psychopathologies. Kendall-Tackett, Williams, and Finkelhor (1993) reviewed 45 studies on the psychopathology of sexually abused children. Sexual abuse accounted for 15 to 45% of the variance in psychopathology between abused and nonabused children. Fears, PTSD, behavior and sexualized behavior problems, and poor self-esteem most frequently occurred. As Teicher (2000) wrote, "childhood trauma is not a passing psychological slight that one can choose to ignore" (p. 66).

Negative emotional states associated with severe trauma disable contextual learning. When this happens the emotion–cognition–action sequences lack goal orientation, and limbic activation with surfacing of limbic material is more likely to occur. The hippocampus mediates contextual learning, and it is not functional in early childhood. For this reason, trauma coded affective learning from childhood is associated with images and sounds and is independent of context. Trauma coded affective learning from childhood can surface and motivate behavior in adulthood (Jacobs & Nadel, 1985).

Eating disorders are associated with increased prevalence of traumatic experience. Negative life events in the histories of severely anorexic inpatients were studied (Horesh et al., 1995). Negative life events comprised separations, deaths, family disruptions, and being beaten or emotionally abused by mother or father. When compared to nonanorexic psychiatric inpatients and outpatient controls, the anorexics endorsed significantly higher prevalence of verbal and physical abuse from their parents than inpatient controls. Childhood histories were studied among bulimic individuals (Wonderlich, Ukestad, & Perzacki, 1994). In an interesting research design, bulimics were asked to compare themselves to siblings on measures of parental relationship quality. Participants were also rated by their therapists for personality disorders. When compared to normal controls, the bulimic participants rated their fathers as showing less affection and more control toward them than toward siblings. When bulimic participants reported that both mother and father showed less affection toward them than toward siblings, these bulimics were more likely to be assessed as having borderline personality disorder.

Traumatic experience is associated with borderline pathology in children. A study of 94 school-age children in day treatment examined the risk factors for borderline pathology (Guzder, Paris, Zelkowitz, & Feldman, 1999). Children with borderline pathology endorsed higher rates of physical abuse, sexual abuse, severe neglect, family breakdown, and parental criminality. Sexual abuse and parental criminality were the discriminating factors in a multivariate analysis. When childhood experiences of male borderline personality–disordered (BPD) patients were compared to nonborderline, personality-disordered controls, the experimentals reported a significantly higher prevalence of childhood sexual abuse (both greater frequency and severity), physical abuse (longer duration), separation and loss, and paternal control (Paris, Zweig-Frank, & Guzder, 1994a). In a parallel study, the same group examined the risk factors for borderline personality disorder in the childhoods of female patients, comparing them to nonborderline personality-disordered controls (Paris, Zweig-Frank, & Guzder, 1994b). The borderlines endorsed a greater frequency and severity of childhood sexual abuse. They also reported more physical abuse and lower maternal affection. Statistical analysis showed that only childhood sexual abuse discriminated borderline personality disorder from other personality disorders among these women.

A study of 41 patients diagnosed for borderline personality disorder examined the correlation between severity of sexual abuse and borderline symptoms (Silk, Lee, Hill, & Lohr, 1995). The duration of the retrospectively reported childhood abuse was the most significant predictor of pathology. Sexual abuse by a parent and type of sexual abuse were less significant predictors than duration. The authors note that the patients' expectation of malevolence and experience of the world as an empty place may result from the repetition of sexual abuse experiences in childhood. A study of 467 inpatients revealed that of the 358 with borderline personality disorder, 91% reported abuse and 92% reported neglect before age 18 (Zanarini et al., 1998). Borderlines were much more likely than other personality disorders to endorse emotional and physical abuse by a caretaker and sexual abuse by a noncaretaker. Among borderline patients, caretakers were more likely to withdraw emotionally, offer inconsistent care, parentify the children, deny children's thoughts and feelings, and fail to protect their offspring. Forty-two borderline inpatients were compared to controls with other personality disorders in a study of self-destructive behavior (Dubo, Zanarini, Lewis, & Williams, 1997). Patients with BPD were more likely to have self-mutilated or attempted suicide than controls, and these abusive behaviors were significantly associated with parental sexual abuse and emotional neglect. The authors stressed that sexual abuse must be considered in the context of emotional neglect in understanding the multifactorial etiology of borderline disorder. Fonagy (2000) proposed that early trauma inhibits the victim's capacity to form IWMs of the traumatizing caregiver and that some characteristics of BPD may derive from this inhibition.

Sexual and physical abuse in childhood are associated with subsequent affective disordering. Outpatients (n = 97) with early onset dysthymia were compared to outpatients with episodic major depression (n = 45) and to normal controls (n = 45) on interview and self-report measures of disturbance in the early childhood environment (Lizardi, Klein, Ouimette, Riso, Anderson, & Donaldson, 1995). The early onset dysthymic patients reported a significantly higher prevalence of physical and sexual abuse and significantly poorer parenting than the other cohorts.

Childhood physical and sexual abuse apparently predicts subsequent drug abuse (Marcenko, Kemp, & Larson, 2000). These authors assessed a sample of urban, low-income, African-American mothers, and discovered that their later drug abuse and its severity were correlated with sexual trauma. Furthermore, adult psychological distress was predicted by childhood sexual or physical abuse. Prevalence of suicidality and suicidal ideation among drug addicts is apparently directly related to reports of adverse experiences (Rossow & Lauritzen, 2001). Sexual assault, violent assault, parental bullying, parental alcohol abuse, and parental psychopathology all were associated with increased prevalence of attempted suicide, and the more areas of adverse experience endorsed, the greater the prevalence of suicidality.

Herman (1992) has made the point that ongoing childhood physical and sexual abuse is analogous to imprisonment in a concentration camp. Perhaps more forcefully than any other observer, Grossman (1996) described the effects of the impact of hate, and his description may help us understand the experience of a childhood victim of severe, chronic trauma. Describing the Nazi death camps, he wrote, "in the death camps it was starkly, horribly personal. Victims of this horror had to look the darkest, most loathsome depths of human hatred in the eye. There was no room for denial, and the only escape was more madness" (p. 79). Extraordinarily high prevalences of psychiatric disorders were uncovered among survivors of the death camps. A key factor in psychopathology among death camp survivors was the horror of the "inescapable fact that someone hates him and denies his humanity enough to kill him" (Grossman, 1996, p. 79). Consider for a moment the horror experienced by the child of an abusive parent. I propose that the child in the abusive situation experiences murder of the self, that looking at the face of his sexually or physically abusive parent he sees murderous hatred directed at him, and the result is assassination of the child's being.

ACT proposes that the unresolved, trauma coded affects experienced at the times of childhood traumas play a central role in current psychopathology: the more severe the trauma, the more severe the current psychopathology (Briere & Runtz, 1993). AMST can begin the process of recovery for the client who endorses a history of childhood trauma. Victims of trauma often have no relief from the relentless intrusions of trauma into current awareness. They often have no internal image of safety. Skill I (containment) can provide immediate relief from intrusion. Skill II (safe place) can establish an inner image of respite. Skills III to VII can help the client learn to regulate affects that have overwhelmed him or her since the times they were trauma coded by the abuse.

EFFECTS OF DEFICIT, ADVERSE, AND TRAUMATIC EXPERIENCE ON BRAIN DEVELOPMENT

Brain development and function and neuroendocrine function are adversely impacted by deficit and adverse childhood experience. Writing about the effects of early experience on brain development, Martin Teicher (2000) noted, "Our brains are sculpted by our early experiences. Maltreatment is a chisel that shapes a brain to contend with strife, but at the cost of deep, enduring wounds" (p. 67).

A rat model was devised to test the effects of chronic early life stress (Avishai-Eliner, Gilles, Eghbal-Ahmadi, Bar-El, & Baram, 2001). In tests of neuroendocrine responses to stress, neonatal (9-day-old) rats were stressed by limiting bedding material for 1 week in their cage. Profound changes in expression and activity of key regulators of the hypothalamic–pituitary–adrenal axis resulted from this stress. Research focused on corticotropin releasing hormone (CRH), a primary modulator of limbic function. Testing the effect of hormones on brain cells, investigators injected neonatal rats with a single dose of CRH and discovered that a year later these animals had 10 to 18% fewer hippocampal neurons and did poorer on tests of learning and memory than control animals (Brunson, Eghbal-Ahmadi, Bender, Chen, & Baram, 2001). Previous research pointed to glucocorticoids produced by the adrenals as the cause of hippocampal damage, but close inspection reveals that the damaged areas do not have glucocorticoid receptors. CRH may kill hippocampal cells by ramping up normal mechanisms of brain communication to excessive levels. Research on this rat model suggests that deprivation and stress in human children's early lives may similarly deplete the hippocampus and contribute to deficiencies in learning and memory.

Teicher (2000) has conducted studies of the neurophysiological effects of stress in animal models and compared the results to human outcomes. Childhood abuse is associated with a constellation of functional and anatomical abnormalities: limbic irritability; deficient left hemisphere development; deficient integration of left and right hemispheres; abnormal activity in the brain's middle strip that regulates emotional and attentional balance. Research with 253 psychiatric outpatients showed that patients who reported physical abuse scored 38% higher than nonabused patients on an assessment for limbic system dysfunction. Patients with only sexual abuse histories scored 49% higher, and patients who endorsed both physical and sexual abuse scored 113% higher on the assessment tool for limbic irregularity. Apparently the psychopathology and disorders of affect regulation that are predicted by childhood abuse are accompanied by functional and anatomical abnormalities in the limbic system responsible for affect expression and regulation.

Abuse, whether psychological, physical, or sexual is associated with abnormalities in left hemispheric brain function as revealed by EEG studies (Teicher, 2000). Psychological abuse was associated with abnormal EEG findings in 43% of cases overall, in 60% of physical abuse cases, and in 72% of cases of documented physical and sexual abuse. Left hemisphere deficits were six times more prevalent than right side deficits among persons reporting any abuse, and eight times more prevalent among psychologically abused individuals. When EEG coherence was studied to investigate the brain circuitry, Teicher and his colleagues discovered that abused patients had elevated levels of EEG coherence throughout the left hemisphere and particularly in the temporal lobe. These results indicate diminished development of neuronal signal processing interconnections in the left hemisphere. In other studies discussed by Teicher, MRI scans indicated that abused individuals had a 12% reduction in hippocampal size that was associated with diminished verbal memory scores. Individuals abused in childhood did not integrate hemispheres in thought. They used the left hemisphere when recalling neutral memories; the right hemisphere was activated in recall of disturbing memory. Furthermore, abuse was associated with deficiencies in development of parts of the corpus callosum, the connecting pathway between hemispheres. In boys, neglect produced the greatest reduction in size of the middle portion of the corpus callosum when compared to controls; in girls sexual abuse was powerfully associated with diminished size in this connecting region.

Trauma also appears to impair the ability of the cerebellar vermis to regulate electrical instability in the limbic system. Long believed to be only involved in motor coordination, Teicher and other neurophysiologists now think the cerebellum plays a role in regulating attention and emotion.

Neglect, in the form of diminished levels of attention, has a cascade effect on psychoneuroendocrine function. Teicher (2000) proposed a model based on maternal neglect in a rat model. Low rates of maternal attention, as are found in histories of insecurely attached infants for example, decreases thyroid hormone, which in turn attenuates serotonin receptor production in the hippocampus and affects glucocorticoid stress hormone receptor development. Feedback control of the stress hormone cortisol depends upon these glucocorticoid stress hormone receptors. Thus, the final outcome of maternal neglect is to ramp up the stress hormone response to adversity, which is exactly what is seen in the anxiously attached infant. Because the stress hormone response is elevated, the neglected infant experiences increased fear and adrenaline responses, and through a CRH mediated cascade this results in the inadequate development of the corpus callosum and abnormal development of the hippocampus and cerebellum we have discussed. Lack of maternal attention diminishes oxytocin production and enhances vasopressin synthesis. All of these neurobiological effects of neglect and abuse can be directly associated with psychopathology.

In his thoughtful review of a decade of neurophysiological research, Teicher (2000) hypothesized that a causal vector can be drawn from abuse and neglect through neurophysiological impairment to psychopathology. Reduced development of the left hemisphere may contribute to the depression seen as an outcome among insecurely attached children and among victims of adverse and traumatic childhood experience. Panic disorder and anxiety disorders may result from the increased limbic irritability that results from neglect. ADHD is reliably associated with reduced size of the cerebellar vermis, and vermis hypoplasia can result from neglect and abuse. These neurophysiological data suggest that neglect or abuse may be contributing factors to development of ADHD. BPD may result in part from the decreased integration of right and left hemispheres due to defects in corpus callosum development, a neurobiological correlate of the neglect and abuse that have been empirically correlated with development of this disorder.

Clinicians need to be aware that deficit experience and adverse or traumatic experience alter the structure of the brain. These alterations of brain structure may be lasting and may impose limitations on the extent of adaptive reorganization of the self that can be achieved through therapy. Within these limitations, AMST may prove to be a forceful intervention that can achieve positive outcomes within the neurophysiological limitations imposed by early deficit, adverse, and traumatic experience.

THE TRIPARTITE MODEL

The tripartite model is a heuristic that describes the influences contributing to the client's present functioning: genetics, attachment (early history), and childhood socioemotional history. The chapter has examined each of these individually and now closes with a description of their interactions. It is the interaction of these themes in a client's history that largely determines present behavior and adaptation. Many theoreticians, including Bowlby and Sroufe, have emphasized that current behavior reflects the interaction of genes, environment, and the history of adaptation to the present moment. As Sroufe wrote, "adaptation is always the joint product of current circumstances and early history" (Sroufe et al., 1999, p. 3). The significance of current behavior cannot be separated from the ontological context in which it occurs, and the influence of any present event on the system depends upon all factors, genetic, attachment, and cumulative childhood socioemotional experience.

The goal of psychotherapy is to facilitate the client in changing maladaptive behaviors. The developmental approach, conceptualized in the tripartite model, provides for change; it structures our therapeutic interventions. Change is possible across developmental time, although empirical research supports the belief that it becomes increasingly difficult as patterns establish. In clinical populations, the goal of therapy derived from affect management, trauma resolution, and attachment considerations is to facilitate the individual to reinstigate development from the point at which it stopped. The clinician helps the client to take an increasingly active role in adaptation, to become a change agent in his own life, to become an interpreter of his experience.

The tripartite model is meant to provide a portrait of the individual at the end of adolescence. Sroufe and associates (1999) referred to Bowlby's argument that while change is always possible, it becomes more difficult by adolescence if corruption of the developmental pathway continues unabated. As we have explained, the model proposes a special role for early experience because the effects of early experience are observable at least into early adulthood and are powerful predictors of outcomes in adolescence and early adulthood (Sroufe et al., 1999). Sroufe has repeatedly emphasized that deficit in early experience productive of insecure attachment, whether of an avoidant, resistant, or disorganized type, is not in and of itself psychopathological (Sroufe, 1997; Sroufe et al., 1999). However, attachment disordering appears to be a defective foundation upon which to build a personality, and subsequent adverse life experience may overwhelm the attachment disordered child with psychopathology eventuating.

Attachment and childhood socioemotional history interact. A securely attached child experiencing adversity will have a different outcome than an insecurely attached child experiencing the same adversity. Figure 3.2 illustrates the interaction, showing how a given event can be traumatic or not depending upon the degree of deficit experience the individual has suffered. Figure 3.2 is a heuristic that is meant to summarize several research threads; the figure is not derived from a specific experiment. In the figure, the trauma index is defined as the probability that an event will overwhelm the mind's capacity to process that event adaptively. The abscissa shows deficit experience increasing. For each form of abuse, sexual, physical, and verbal, the figure suggests that the healthier the attachment (less deficit experience), the lower the probability that the event will overwhelm the system. The validity of the figure is supported by empirical research. A met-analysis of 45 studies on sexual abuse discovered that about one third of victims

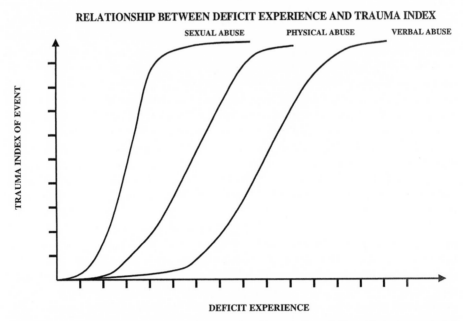

RELATIONSHIP BETWEEN DEFICIT EXPERIENCE AND TRAUMA INDEX

Figure 3.2.   This figure is a heuristic intended to diagram the relationship between deficit experience and a self system's trauma response to a single stressful event. The diagram demonstrates the protective function of a healthy attachment. *Deficit Experience* refers to failures during the attachment phase. Shown on the abscissa, the scale is arbitrary Deficit experience increases further from the origin. The *Trauma Index* is drawn from Shapiro's (1995) contention that events that traumatize a system are events that exceed the mind's capacity to process those events adaptively. Shown on the ordinate, the traumatic index increases further from the origin in arbitrary units. The three curves represent the probability that a single event of verbal, physical, or sexual abuse will traumatize the system. The diagram suggests that a secure attachment (low deficit experience) confers protection against trauma. The diagram summarizes empirical information suggesting that verbal abuse is less inherently traumatizing than physical abuse, and that sexual abuse is inherently the most traumatizing.

had no symptoms (Kendall-Tacket et al., 1993), a result that suggests that in some individuals genetic competence—for example, carrying the genotype for high levels of monoamine oxidase A (MAOA) expression—plus secure attachment combined to produce a personality sufficiently resilient to withstand the insult of sexual abuse. As Sroufe and associates (1999) noted, "the impact of current circumstances depends on the pattern of behavioral and emotional organization the child brings forward to that phase of development" (p. 2). Furthermore, research demonstrates that secure attachments facilitate a return to adaptive functioning following a period of maladaptation (Sroufe et al., 1999). The authors posited a "special role for early experience, as its effects appeared after a long passage of time and seemed to be as potent as later experience in predicting adolescent outcomes" (p. 8).

The complex interactions of attachment deficit and adverse experience have been studied. Weiss and colleagues (1996) assessed the separate contributions of trauma and maternal impairment to early adolescent functional impairment among offspring. Trauma alone accounted for 16% of variance, while maternal diagnosis explained 20% of variance. Adverse experience impacts the mother as well as her offspring. Golomb and associates (1994) stressed the interaction of the direct effect of stressful life events on a child as well as the impairment of mother's ability to parent caused by those same events. Their study compared 13 mothers of borderline adolescent daughters to a control group of 13 mothers of normal adolescent daughters. The family situation of the borderlines was extremely chaotic and characterized by multiple hardships, divorce, and concerns about finances. These events impacted the mothers who perceived their borderline daughters as need-gratifying objects, rather than as separate persons with unique, developing identities.

The interplay of temperament, a factor of the genetic component, attachment, and childhood experience has been investigated. Participant toddlers' behavioral inhibition, observable at 21 months, may have been in part genetically determined and may also have resulted from deficits in the attachment (Hirshfeld et al., 1997). Her child's behavioral inhibition appears to have elicited mother's criticism, an adverse factor in childhood experience. The interplay of the three factors produced a negative outcome, childhood psychopathology. A prospective, longitudinal study from birth to 16 years, examined the contributions of these three factors (Aguilar et al., 2000). The study assessed the contributions of (1) neuropsychological deficits and temperament difficulties; (2) early childhood experience; and (3) maltreatment history, to adolescent antisocial behavioral pathology. Their exhaustive data set supports two distinct pathways to adolescent antisocial behavior. These pathways can be distinguished in the early years. Early onset/persistent (EOP) antisocial behavior was predicted by psychosocial factors. The EOP subjects were more likely to be avoidantly attached at 12 and 18 months and to have had more impoverished caregiving and more depleted home environments throughout childhood and adolescence. Furthermore, EOP subjects experienced significant levels of maltreatment. However, the study did not provide any evidence that temperament or neuropsychological functioning predicted EOP. Children who later evidenced EOP did not demonstrate decreased verbal ability or language functioning *until after 64 months of age*. The authors argue that impoverished caregiving and maltreatment produce angry, avoidant behavior in the child and that behavior limits the external inputs necessary for normal development. The other form of antisocial behavior, adolescent onset (AO), was not associated with impoverished caregiving or home environments or with maltreatment. However, AO participants reported significantly higher levels of internalizing symptoms than normal participants. AO subjects scored higher than EOP subjects on measures of neuropsychological functioning. AO antisocial behavior has been called normative by some theoreticians, but Aguilar and colleagues (2000) emphasized that it is a psychopathological condition.

Research supporting the interaction of deficit experience and adverse experience proposed by the tripartite model also demonstrates that change is possible and identifies environmental characteristics that facilitate it. Weinfield and associates (2000) studied discontinuities in attachment stability over a 19-year period in a longitudinal, prospective study in a high-risk sample. The 57 young adult participants were part of the Minnesota Mother–Child Project. Their lives were characterized by low income and high risk for poor developmental outcomes, poor environmental stability, and instability in interpersonal relationships. This sample was characterized by a high proportion of negative life experiences; 91.2% of the participants had experienced at least one from the following list: born to a single mother, parental divorce, life-threatening illness of parent or child, serious parental drug or alcohol abuse, physical or sexual abuse, death of a parent of other attachment figure. In spite of the poor quality of their developmental environment, 59.6% of the sample demonstrated a secure attachment as measured by Strange Situation assessments at 12 and 18 months. At 19 years, however, when assessed with the AAI, insecure attachment was prevalent with 59.6% of participants endorsing an insecure-dismissing attachment style. A careful analysis of the data in Weinfield and associates (2000) illustrates how life experience and attachment interact.

Almost one third of the sample (29.8%; n = 17) endorsed an insecure attachment in childhood and remained insecurely attached at age 19. Significantly, 41% of these participants had been maltreated as they grew up. Maltreatment was defined as physical abuse, verbal abuse, neglect, or maternal psychological unavailability during childhood. In comparison, six participants who were insecure in early childhood transitioned to security at age 19, and *none* of these individuals reported maltreatment. Those individuals who transitioned to security reported better family functioning as assessed by observation of an interaction task than those individuals who started life insecure and remained so. Though the sample size is small, these data support ACT's proposal that movement toward positively adaptive functioning depends in part upon the quality of internal representations of developmentally important figures. When these representations are assembled with memories of maltreatment, change in a positive direction is less probable. The data suggest that maltreatment can thwart a system's capacity to accommodate, i.e., to change self structure to conform to present realities. Weinfield and colleagues (2000) wrote, "maltreatment seems to be relevant to the maintenance of insecurity from infancy to adulthood" (p. 701). The positive news is that change for the better is possible, that improvements in family functioning contribute to improved chances of transitioning from insecure to secure attachment across the early lifespan.

In the Weinfield and colleagues (2000) study, 57 participants, 38.6% (n = 22) moved from a secure attachment in toddlerhood to an insecure attachment in adulthood. Maternal depression was the the single factor that significantly predicted this transition from secure to insecure attachment. Mothers of insecurely attached infants also endorsed elevated levels of depression when compared to mothers of securely attached infants. Taken as a whole, these data support the hypothesis that maternal depression contributes to insecure attachment in child-hood and to transition from secure to insecure attachment across early life. Having established a solid foundation by describing the ontology of emotion dysregulation, we can proceed to a depiction of how emotion dysregulation manifests in the clinical and personality disorders.

Chapter 4

Emotion Dysregulation in Clinical and Personality Disorders

The objective of this chapter is to demonstrate for the clinician the primacy of emotion regulation in the clinical and personality disorders as they are presented in the *DSM-IV* and then to relate this knowledge to affect management skills training (AMST). The *DSM-IV* is a useful and widely used tool that coordinates a vast body of observations regarding psychopathology (APA, 1994). From the point of view of the present book, the *DSM-IV* integrates information about how deficit and adverse childhood experience manifest in childhood, adolescent, and adult psychopathology. *DSM-IV* observations focus on behavior for the most part and neglect affect. Here, I will examine the contribution of emotional dysregulation to several of the clinical and personality disorders. Clinicians can help clients diagnosed with any of these disorders by teaching the client to recognize, tolerate, and regulate the principal affects associated with the disorder using the AMST skills to be presented in Part II. Furthermore, since affect dysregulation arises from deficits in the attachment and results in inadequacies in the self-structure, learning affect regulation begins the process of remediation of deficiencies in the structure of the self.

PSYCHOPATHOLOGY AS DEVELOPMENT, NOT DISEASE

As valuable a resource as the *DSM-IV* is, its adherence to a strict medical or disease model opens it to criticism. The *DSM-IV* has become a tool that more often serves the needs of the insurer and the prescribing physician over the needs of patients, and the medical model forces a focus on treating a diagnosis rather than a person. This chapter adopts a developmental model for understanding the etiology and ontology of personality and clinical disorders in contradistinction to the medical or disease model that is the basis for the *DSM-IV*. Sroufe (1997) has described the distinctive features of the two models, and his discussion provides a basis for this chapter's comments.

Medical Model for Psychopathology

The medical model is based on the largely unexamined belief that psychopathological disorders are discrete phenomena with single causes that are located within the patient. The same conceptual frameworks applied to organic disease are applied to the theory, diagnosis, and treatment of psychological dysfunction. This approach has profound implications. The *DSM-IV*'s diagnostic classification of dysfunction reflects the medical model, in that problems are grouped into disorders, believed to be discrete, distinctive, and enduring states. In this sense the statements, "He has a heart murmur" and "He has ADHD" are epistemologically equivalent. The medical model sees the causes of organic disease, cancer for instance, as either intrinsic, originating in the dysregulation of a gene like MIC-1, or due to environmental pathogens, exposure to dioxin, for example, or to a combination of the two.

Application of the medical model to psychopathology is covert. Without acknowledgement or examination, the same conceptual model is applied to psychopathology that is applied to organic disease. The etiology of maladaptation is thought to reside within the child, juvenile, adolescent, or adult. According to the medical model, psychopathology represents a neurophysiologically abnormal functioning caused by genetic defect or environmental pathogen (e.g., lead poisoning). The medical model stresses medical treatment, which usually means pharmacotherapy. Symptoms are treated as if they were the pathology rather than expressions of the individual's adaptation in a particular environment. The medical model for psychopathology has never been empirically validated, yet it is assumed to be valid in every instance in which a diagnosis is assigned based on the *DSM-IV* classification. As Sroufe (1997) has observed, "the fact that the *DSM* system is being used cannot be taken as support for its validity" (p. 264). A developmental model for psychopathology differs in every respect from the medical model.

The medical model directs attention away from dysregulated affects and emotions. Where they are mentioned at all, affects and emotions are considered to *be* the pathology. For example, the *DSM-IV* states that the "essential feature of Dysthymic Disorder is a chronically depressed mood" (p. 345), a definition that asserts that the depressed mood is in and of itself pathological. The "depressed mood" floats about without anchor, seemingly unrelated to the client's attachment experience or to his childhood socioaffective history. The medical model makes no attempt to conceptualize the client's dysthymia as being this particular client's adaptation to the unique physical and socioaffective environment in which his self structure was formed.

The Developmental Model

The developmental model conceptualizes self structure or personality as emerging over the developmental time span through multiple transactions between the organism and the physical and social environment. The developmental model does not separate organism from context. Distressed adaptation is believed to develop according to the same principles as healthy adaptation. Behavioral disturbance and emotional dysregulation are hypothesized to develop through a succession of evolving adaptations. The unfolding of an adaptive, competent self, like the emergence of a maladapted, distressed self, occurs progressively and dynamically over time, with current personality determined by prior adaptations interacting with present exigencies. Emotion and affect dysregulation do not constitute the pathology, but rather are symptoms arising from failures in the attachment or produced by adversities in the early socioaffective environment. The developmental model entails a description of the qualities of environment and social milieu that are necessary to emergence of a healthy self structure. When the early environment and social milieu are "good enough," healthy adaptation and positive functioning will eventuate. Where there are failures during attachment or adversity in the childhood socioemotional history, psychopathology will eventuate in proportion to the failures and adversities. The developmentally oriented clinician will compare the distressed client's history to the "good enough" history to identify the failures and adversities. A developmental model holds the promise that failures can be remediated and adversities can be adaptively processed. The developmental model is a cornerstone of AMST and affect centered therapy (ACT), because AMST provides the skills that can remediate deficits of emotion regulation and ACT provides the tools to adaptively process the adversities and traumas.

Personalities follow developmental pathways as they emerge. Bowlby adapted Waddington's concept of developmental pathways (e.g., Sroufe 1997) to describe the ontogeny of personality. The self is now believed to organize itself as it develops along a pathway guided by principles of nonlinear dynamic systems theory (Lewis, 2000). Sroufe (1997) imaged developmental pathways as branches of a tree emerging from a trunk. The trunk represents the neonatal state of mental and psychological nonorganization that is the birth condition of almost all infants, a state that Mahler called *normal autism* (Horner, 1984). Some developmental pathways are continuously positive leading to healthy adaptation, that is, secure attachment, adaptive emotion regulation, impulse control. Some pathways begin positively and in response to life stressors veer off into maladaptation. Other pathways begin negatively and continue throughout adolescence, culminating in disorder. Discontinuities are possible along an individual's pathway (Weinfield et al., 2000) as empirical research demonstrates. In a discontinuity, an organism initially entrains a pathway in which a negative outcome is more probable and then shifts to a pathway with a favorable outcome.

Pathways to disorder are viewed as deviations over time that progressively increase the difficulty of negotiating the next developmental stage. For example, children with insecure attachments sometimes have problems effectively entering into peer groups in preschool and kindergarten. The insecure attachment represents a deviation in an early stage that makes it more difficult for the child to negotiate the subsequent stage of entering the peer group. The insecure attachment pattern of infancy is not in itself considered pathological, but rather is viewed as a branch in the developmental tree, which if followed increases the probability of pathology emerging at a later developmental time.

A specific developmental outcome can be reached by different pathways. Depression provides a good example. Two different attachment pathways lead to depression. As we have seen, the avoidant attachment pathway, if followed continuously, can lead to depression resulting from alienation. Another pathway to depression begins with the resistant form of insecure attachment. Depression results from the anxiety and helplessness that are concomitants of insecure–resistant attachment. There are multiple developmental pathways with the common outcome of addiction, or alcoholism, or eating disorders.

Embarking on a maladaptive pathway does not doom the infant to pathology. Research supports the conclusion that change is possible at many points (Weinfield et al., 2000). For example, some children identified as insecurely attached in the Strange Situation endorsed a secure–autonomous attachment as young adults. Recovery from substance abuse or eating disorder, smoking cessation, integration in dissociative identity disorder (DID), trauma processing in posttraumatic stress disorder (PTSD)—in short, the successful termination of therapy for any Axis I or II disorder—affirms our belief that maladaptation is not a permanent condition. At the same time, the longer a particular maladaptive self structure persists, the less likely is the possibility of transition to positive adaptation. Ongoing negative experiences and associated memories are integrated into the maladaptive personality organization leading to further negative experiences that produce a self-perpetuating cycle. Research on conduct disorders supports the belief that consistent pursuit of a path across developmental stages from early aggression and opposition through antisocial behavior will likely eventuate in criminality (Sroufe, 1997). AMST strongly asserts the principle that the trajectory of a maladaptive pathway can be changed. AMST provides remediation of the failures of affect regulation that contributed to entrainment of the particular maladaptive pathway. As the personality system acquires the adaptive affect and emotion regulation skills it lacked, it will reorganize itself in the direction of more positive functioning.

Self-Organizing Systems

A powerful approach to understanding how emotion development is organized derives from application of dynamic systems theory (Lewis & Granic, 2000). Dynamic systems theory complements the developmental model. In the language of dynamic systems theory, the personality is believed to self-organize, a process by which coherent, higher order structure arises from the interaction of many lower order components. In the field of developmental biology, the embryo is believed to self-organize. In psychology, the personality self-organizes over developmental time from lower order components. Some of the lower order components are the emotions, and others are cognitions. Attachment behavior is a higher order of behavior that organizes out of lower order components like nursing and gaze transactions. Internal working models (IWMs) are examples of higher order structures that self-organize or emerge during the first years of life. IWMs organize themselves from the lower order components of perceptions, affects, memories, and cognitions. Affective–cognitive structures also self-organize, and then these assemble with behaviors and affective–cognitive–behavioral structures emerge. Personality is an even higher order structure that emerges from interaction of these lower order components. The tripartite model suggests how these component elements interact to facilitate the emergence of an adaptive or a maladaptive personality. Whether adaptive or maladaptive, emotional development is characterized by intrinsic orderliness. Self-organization theory proposes that this intrinsic orderliness is "an emergent form, accruing from recurrent, self-perpetuating emotional processes in real time" (Lewis & Granic, 2000, p. 3).

Dynamic systems theorists apply the principles of self-organization across the spectrum of human behavior. For example, walking is conceptualized as a pattern of coordination that emerges from the recurring interactions of muscular and perceptual skills. Communication rituals emerge in the context of dyads (e.g., the infant–caregiver dyad) as actions, gestures, emotion expression, and speech are reciprocally and recursively coordinated. Later in life in the sexual pair bond, communication rituals emerge according to the same principles. Self-organization principles have been applied to emotions, emotional and personality development, personality formation, adult personality change, identity development, self-referential emotions, development of self, and consolidation of temperament (Lewis & Granic, 2000). "The interactions among the elements of complex systems are reciprocal, with constituents influencing each other simultaneously, and they recur over time, as systems continue to evolve or perpetuate their own stability" (Lewis & Granic, 2000, pp. 1–2).

Reviewing some of the fundamental principles of self-organizing systems (Lewis, 2000) will help us to understand the adaptive resilience of a healthy personality as well as the resistance to change of a distressed personality. Self-organizing systems become more ordered as time passes. The newborn's brain is relatively unstructured. From its first moments of life, the neonate is acquiring neurological, mental, affective, and behavioral structure. Bowlby's developmental pathways concept (e.g., Sroufe, 1997) was an early description of the acquisition of order by a self-organizing system. The pathway that begins with an adequate attachment experience productive of a secure attachment bond represents the accumulation of order; so does the pathway that begins with deficit experience leading to one of the forms of insecure attachment. Secure, insecure–resistant, insecure–avoidant, and insecure–disorganized–disoriented patterns of attachment all represent the accumulation of order in a personality organizing itself in a particular environment. Whether a personality's acquired order is adaptive or maladaptive, the order itself acts as an impediment to change. A highly organized, positively functioning personality will resist becoming disorganized and dysfunctional. A negatively functioning self, which is just as ordered, albeit maladaptively, will similarly resist reorganization to a more functional state.

In a self-organizing system, the structure acquired by the system arises spontaneously. No internal programming specifies that a child will become securely or insecurely attached; there are no hard-wired instructions that determine a priori that depression or a borderline personality organization will eventuate. Genetics may specify some of the components from which higher order structure builds, for example, high or low thresholds for specific affects, but the eventual personality structure depends on the social and environmental contexts with which those genetic components and a host of other components interact dynamically over time.

The neonate begins life with many degrees of freedom available to the self structure. Within limits set by his genetics, any personality structure is possible for every newborn. As his system self-organizes in response to current experience conditioned by prior adaptation, the child's self-structure loses degrees of freedom, becoming more determined and, more fully specified. Adolescence is a period during which degrees of freedom increase briefly as the brain undergoes reorganization (Spear, 2000). At the close of adolescence, however, the personality is largely fixed.

Self-organization theory explains that the personality is much more sensitive to disturbance occurring early in development, than to disturbance later in life. Childhood trauma (e.g., sexual abuse), severely disrupts a system that is less well-organized, and thus more sensitive to disturbance. The same sexual abuse trauma occurring in a well-organized, mature system is less likely to be disruptive. The adaptively organized self will resist trauma-induced disorganization, while the maladaptively organized self will incorporate current trauma into its worldview and thereby resist further disorganization.

Dynamic systems theory describes how over developmental time self-organizing systems become more complex. Developmental ontogeny across the period from birth to preschool illustrates this concept. The child at 3, acquiring the goal-corrected partnership, is more complex than the child at 1 year. Complexity arises in part as current experience is incorporated into prior structures, and those structures enlarge as they encompass more memories, expanded behavioral repertoires, and unfolding emotional palettes.

Both self-organization and developmental models stress that characteristics that emerge as the personality system organizes itself influence the course of subsequent self-organization. Abundant empirical research supports this fact. Insensitive, unresponsive parenting by a rigid caregiver who avoids physical contact with her child causes emergence of an avoidant attachment in the child, and this avoidant attachment influences interactions with toddler and preschool peers, which themselves condition further alienation and withdrawal. As Lewis (2000) wrote: "The products of a growth process constrain the conditions for further growth" (pp. 39–40), a process Lewis terms "cascading constraints" (p. 40).

Over developmental time, the fixed organization patterns that result from the process of self-organization are the personalities. When the structure is adaptive, a well-regulated or healthy personality structure is the result. When the structure is maladaptive, a clinical or personality disorder is the result.

A distressed personality with impaired functioning is nonetheless highly organized and as a consequence will require a greater force to shift it to a new trajectory. According to self-organization theory, a greater impetus is necessary to shift a system that is well ordered. Once a personality structure has acquired orderliness, whether adaptive or maladaptive, more force is necessary to disrupt that structure. This observation suggests why therapy is sometimes ineffective; for example, talk therapy with spousal abusers. The more orderly a system has become, the greater the probability that it will incorporate therapeutic interventions into the extant self-structure. The alcoholic personality is sometimes so highly organized that a legal problem such as a charge of driving while intoxicated or incarceration or divorce, is an insufficient impetus to initiate change.

Personality structure can be protective. Adaptive self-organization confers resilience that can palliate the effects of trauma. A secure attachment confers considerable ordering to a personality, and the disorganizing effects of child sexual abuse trauma can be ameliorated by preexisting secure attachment. Apparently, insecure attachment does not confer sufficient order to the self-structure to withstand the effects of child sexual abuse trauma, and such trauma may shift the self-structure of the victim toward a fragmented type of organization of the self.

The psychotherapeutic efficacy of AMST apparently results because it is a forceful enough intervention to shift a system's trajectory. Two components of AMST contribute to its capacity to impact a personality system forcefully. In part AMST is effective because it uses tactile alternating bilateral stimulation (TABS) to trigger surprise–startle affect. Startle affect is known to "blank the mind," and a consequence of using TABS in the AMST protocol is to disrupt the preexisting order in the system. The second part of AMST's effectiveness arises because it teaches the client to cognize affects and thereby intervenes in the defenses the client has previously used to manage the affects. These defenses represent considerable organization in the client's self structure. Experiencing affects in a functional and controllable form is in itself forceful and powerful enough to shift the personality system's trajectory. The challenge for the therapist is to be able to guide the process of personality system reorganization as it unfolds.

Tripartite Model

We revisit the tripartite model, this time in the context of a developmental paradigm, to demonstrate its predictive power. Figure 4.1 shows the three dimensions of the model, genetics, attachment, and childhood socioemotional history, displayed on the x, y, and z axes of a graph. This graph is meant as a heuristic to structure our thinking about how deficiencies in the attachment, adversity in childhood experience, and genetic impairments interact to predict severity of disordering. The graphic approach presented in Figure 4.1 is supported by Greenberg (1999) who has drawn a diagram for childhood psychopathology showing how risk factors of family adversity, insecure attachment, ineffective parenting, and child characteristics overlap, the areas of overlap representing increased probability of psychopathology. Figure 4.1 illustrates how increasing deficiencies in attachment couple with increasing adversity and greater genetic impairment to produce heightened severity of disordering, whether expressed in Axis I or II psychopathology. We cannot yet predict what specific clinical or personality disorders will result from which specific concatenation of attachment, genetic, or childhood experience factors. However, this heuristic will help us to structure our treatment plans and our approach to psychotherapy based upon information received during history taking.

The tripartite model as presented in Figure 4.1 conveys the importance and clinical relevance of AMST's interventions. The more severe a client's level of psychopathology, the more likely are there to be problems in all three dimensions.

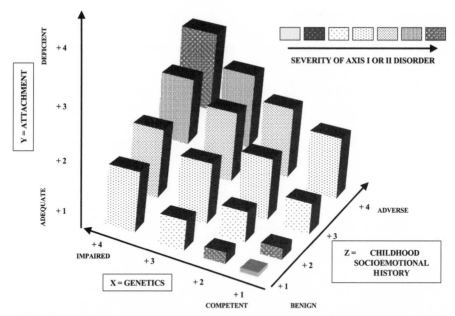

Figure 4.1. Genetics, deficit experience, and trauma or adverse experience interact to determine the severity of Axis I and II disorders. This figure is a heuristic. The abscissa shows the genetic component of the tripartite model increasing from competent to impaired. At the origin, a value of +1 indicates optimal thresholds for each affect and a optimally functioning system for adaptively processing adversity or trauma. The increments are arbitrary. The y-axis represents experience during the attachment phase, set here as the first four years of life. Again, increments are arbitrary and indicate increasing deficiency in caregiving. The z-axis indicates increasing adversity or trauma. At the origin, there is little adversity. The increments are arbitrary. A value of +4 suggests an accumulation of negative life experiences such as being raised by a single parent, and physical, psychological, emotional, and sexual abuse. As shown by the legend, more severe Axis I or II disordering is a function of more severe genetic impairments, more adverse childhood experience, and more deficient attachment.

A bulimic client who binges and purges several times per day every day of the week is more severely disordered than the bulimic client who acts out two or three times per week. AMST interventions can help both clients, but the more severely disordered client will need to spend more time learning the interventions and will probably need to develop more resources. The more severely disordered client will be more likely to endorse trauma that compounds deficit experience. Skill I (containment) will benefit both clients, but the clinician can expect to spend more time helping the more severely disordered client fill her visualized container with every disturbing thing in skill I. Both clients will be helped by skill II (safe place), but the more severely disordered client will need more practice using the skill in daily life. The more severely disordered client will also need more practice using skills III to VII to manage her affects and emotions in her daily life, and the clinician will need to write a treatment plan that makes allowance for this fact. Neither the clinician nor the client should develop false expectations about how rapidly or how easily the transition to positive functioning will be for the more severely disordered client. This is especially the case where personality disorders, particularly borderline features, complicate the presentation.

Attachment Strategies and Internal Working Models

Development of psychopathology is equivalent to the emergence of a maladaptive self structure. Attachment constitutes a primary influence on the development or emergence of adolescent and adult psychopathology, exerting its effect through the attachment strategies that self-organize over early developmental time. As we have seen, as the attachment bond develops, IWMs of self and caregivers organize. Attachment strategies are tactics for processing thoughts, feelings, and behaviors relating to the primary caregivers (Dozier, Stovall, & Albus, 1999). Attachment strategies are also called "attachment states of mind" (Dozier et al., 1999, p. 501). These strategies, originating in the vicissitudes of the infant–caregiver dyad, develop over time and have been empirically related to psychopathology. Dozier and colleagues (1999) wrote, "psychiatric disorders are nearly always associated with nonautonomous states of mind" (p. 515). Two forms of nonautonomous states of mind, dismissing and preoccupied, emerging from avoidant and resistant infant attachments respectively, are significantly associated with specific psychopathologies. Predisposition to externalizing disorders is associated with strategies that minimized attachment needs in childhood and limited access to self's emotion from childhood on through the life span. On the other hand, strategies that maximize attachment needs in childhood and defensively focus on self's needs and caregiver availability predispose to internalizing disorders in adulthood. The discussion of specific forms of psychopathology in succeeding sections will focus in part on the attachment states of mind, because these relate strongly to how affects are regulated in each disorder.

Observational Learning and Emotion Activation

Human beings acquire emotion-laden constructs in two ways, either by means of their own emotion experience or by observing and incorporating the broadcast emotion (Nathanson, 1992) of others. This book has so far focused primarily on intrapsychic emotion experience, the emotional consequences *within* the organism in response to deficit or adverse childhood experience and their effects on emotion regulation and dysregulation. Children also acquire emotion experience interpsychically, through the process of observational learning. For example, observational learning of fear occurs when a child observes in a parent's face fear of an object, event, or situation. The child immediately learns the same response (Izard, 1991).

LeDoux (1996) has described the phenomenon of observational learning of fear in monkeys. It was believed that monkeys are genetically programmed to fear snakes. Empirical research demonstrated that this belief is false, because monkeys raised without adult models do not fear snakes. Monkeys learn to fear snakes through observation, because if a monkey sees its mother react to a snake with fear, the young monkey will subsequently react with fear to snakes or snake shapes. The process by which affect displayed by one human evokes affect in another is called *primitive emotional contagion* (Wild, Erb, & Bartels, 2001), a rapid, largely automatic, mostly unconscious process. Wild and associates (2001) showed that viewing happy faces specifically evoked happiness in subject viewers, while viewing sad faces evoked sadness. Emotional contagion takes place within 500 milliseconds. It is stable and repeatable, and stronger expressions of emotion evoke stronger emotions in viewers.

Observational learning, or primitive emotional contagion, is centrally important to understanding the psychopathology of affects. The example of the infant monkey learning fear through observation provides an illustration. The infant monkey sees the image of the snake and forms a simple mental representation of it. Observing its mother's broadcast fear, the brain of the infant monkey assembles mother's fear with the mental representation of the snake and responds to the image with fear. Human children form self-representations, or IWMs. Emotions broadcast by a caregiver can assemble with these self-representations through the process of observational learning. If a child sees disgust in a parent's face broadcast toward the child himself, the child will learn to feel disgust at or toward himself. Just as observed fear in the parent assembles with the image of the snake, observed parental disgust directed at the self, assembles with the self-image. This child, unconsciously, learns "I am disgusting." Data from Krolak-Salmon and colleagues (2003) have demonstrated that viewing a face expressing disgust evokes electrical potentials in a region of the brain associated with facial processing, and these results support the belief that broadcast affect does indeed affect the resonator. Recent research has demonstrated the power of observational learning in human emotion dysregulation.

Abused children are more likely to perceive anger in faces than nonabused children. Pollak and Kistler (2002) investigated emotion identification and emotion discrimination in normal and abused children. Four emotions, happiness, anger, fear, and sadness, were studied. Using computer technology, blends of each emotion pair, using both male and female models, were created. Children were asked to discriminate between two emotion representations presented in pairs, then in a separate test they were asked to identify the presented emotion. As expected, all children had more difficulty making a discrimination when equal components of the two emotions were combined in a facial representation. Abused and nonabused children scored the same on the happy–fear and happy–sad continua. However, abused children differed from normal controls in their perceptual category boundaries when anger was a component of the continuum. For both the angry–fear and angry–sad continua, abused children demonstrated a broader perceptual categorization of anger, relative to fear and to sadness. On the emotion identification test, abused children overidentified anger relative to fear and to sadness. Apparently, the parents' broadcast anger altered the abused children's perceptual representation of emotion. Interestingly, the abused children did not differ from normal controls on discrimination or identification of fear, the emotion the child may have been expected to feel in the presence of an angry, abusive parent. It appears that parental broadcast anger assembled with the child's IWM of the parent, and this assembly served as the internal benchmark against which other representations were compared in order to arrive at an emotion appraisal.

The developmental model complements a therapy focused on affects because it helps us understand how events of both omission and commission occur across the early developmental time span and influence the emergence of a distressed personality characterized by affect dysregulation. This understanding then guides clinical application of AMST. During the attachment phase, failure to provide optimal arousal of the infant's interest–excitement and enjoyment–joy affects—an omission event—can entrain one of the developmental pathways leading to depression. Also, during the attachment phase, failures to provide optimal disapproval–shame experiences—another omission event—can entrain a developmental pathway leading to the inability to control impulses characteristic of ADHD and conduct disorders. Beginning in attachment and extending through adolescence, socializing a child with overly strong broadcast disgust affect or contempt affect—a commission event—appears to evoke this affect in the child where it assembles with the child's self-representation and becomes the basis for feelings of unworthiness and impaired self-esteem. When parents socialize children with overly strong broadcast anger affect, anger appears to assemble with the parental IWM, where it acts to engender fear in the child, adolescent, and adult, even in the absence of the parent. Lastly, when adverse or traumatic events—acts of commission—happen to a child, overwhelming affects are often engendered, in particular fear, anger, startle, disgust, and sadness. The developmental model teaches us that the personality emerges out of the dynamic, interrelated, mutual, transactional process between organism and social and physical environment. Each stage builds on the previous stages. Failure to provide adequate affective and emotional socialization in earlier stages will make it more difficult to tolerate adversity and trauma when it occurs.

AMST skills remediate the deficits in affect and emotion socialization. Where there is trauma or adversity, skill I (containment) helps the client safely sequester the disturbing events until he or she is capable of working on them. When the client was socialized with overly strong anger or disgust in childhood, AMST helps the client to recognize, tolerate, and down-regulate those affects that have persisted in a state-specific, excitatory form in which they have repeatedly surfaced and created current distress. AMST forms the foundation for ACT in which experiences of deficit, adversity, or trauma are recovered and processed to an adaptive resolution. From a developmental perspective, AMST and ACT facilitate the emergence of a more adaptive, more positively functioning self structure and with it a transition to a developmental pathway with a more positive outcome.

THE CLINICAL DISORDERS

This section will illustrate how developmental principles and affect orientation can be applied to understanding the clinical disorders. One purpose of the section is to demonstrate how deficit experience and adversity or trauma in the childhood socioemotional history contribute to the emergence of a distressed personality and psychopathology characterized by affect dysregulation. Another purpose is to indicate how AMST skills can remediate the deficiencies in affect regulation. The section will also highlight the differences in case conceptualization between the medical and developmental models.

Attention Deficit Hyperactivity Disorder (ADHD)

The case of Paul, a 13-year-old diagnosed with attention deficit hyperactivity disorder, presented by Barkley and Edwards (1998) has provided an opportunity to compare and contrast case conceptualizations based on a medical model and a developmental model. The case also demonstrates how differently an affect centered therapy, a behavioral therapy, and a medical therapy approach ADHD. ADHD is among the disorders usually first diagnosed in childhood or adolescence, and it has long been thought to be heritable. However, a recent genome wide scan of 126 sibling pairs found there is unlikely to be a major gene involved in ADHD susceptibility (Fisher et al., 2002). While these data appear to exclude the possibility that a mutation in a single gene causes ADHD, they do not exclude the possibility that a genetically determined lower threshold for excitement affect contributes to the development of ADHD.

Paul's presenting problem, which was also a problem for his teachers and parents, was his inability to finish assignments, his loss of homework, wandering about the classroom, inability to participate in academic activities, and avoidant behavior (Barkley & Edwards, 1998). He was fidgety and disorganized. His inattention, impulsivity, carelessness, distractibility, impatience, and hyperactivity were pathognomic for ADHD. Testing revealed Paul had an average IQ. His reading skills were above grade level. He tested negative for learning disabilities. He had excellent oral and written language skills and demonstrated curiosity.

Sifting through the authors' presentation, some features salient for a developmental approach stand out. Paul was the second of three children from his mother's second marriage. She had four children from a previous marriage living in the home when Paul was born. (Barkley and Edwards's failure to include a genogram, to enumerate the birth order and where Paul fits in it, or to note the ages of the siblings reveals much about the attentional focus of the medical model.) Paul's father, his mother, and every one of his siblings had learning or behavioral difficulties. Paul's mother was obese and depressed, and the family was characterized by manic-depression, alcohol abuse, antisocial behavior, and narcolepsy. The parents were characterized as "inconsistent" in their parenting style. In infancy Paul was "colicky," climbed out of his crib at 9 months, and could not be left unattended. He was hyperactive and impulsive "even as a toddler" (p. 217).

Paul presented a picture of emotional and behavioral contrasts. Edwards experienced Paul as "impressively personable, interactive, and attentive" (p. 218) at interview, and he was apparently prosocial, because "he is liked by all his classmates" and his teacher said he was "kind, sweet, and sincere" (p. 214). Yet, his disruptive behaviors caused his expulsion from five day-care providers. By the time he entered public school, teachers had developed the belief that Paul needed firm limits. He was routinely made to stand in the corner facing the wall at recess as punishment for talking out of turn. According to Paul's mother, in school he had gone from being eager to learn to inattentive, making excuses, and feeling inadequate. Paul began to throw up before school. He refused to board the school bus, and his mother had to drag him from her car into the school. Paul apparently had anger management problems and felt anger toward his mother (he threw a whole pizza at her at a family gathering). He had frequent temper outbursts, and he fought with boys at school. Edwards visited Paul's classroom and reported he had his head on his desk and appeared to be asleep.

Based on this information the medical model assigned Paul a diagnosis of ADHD and oppositional defiant disorder. Barkley and Edwards dismissed a developmental conceptualization of Paul's case, writing that the school officials and teachers "might easily and erroneously conclude that Paul's problems stemmed from his parents' problems" (p. 217). The authors categorized Paul's angry behavior as "impulsive." The clustering of attentional problems in Paul's family was taken as indicating that Paul had ADHD. Based on a cognitive–behavioral approach, Paul and his teachers were given several behavioral modification interventions, and his parents were referred to a parenting skills class. As indicated by a medical model, Paul was placed on Ritalin, which he resisted taking because he said he'd become identified as the class clown and also he did not like himself on medication.

I now present a developmental and affect-focused analysis of Paul's case to contrast it with the medical model. Combining developmental and affect-centered approaches results in a client-focused rather than diagnosis-focused case formulation. Furthermore, attention to developmental and affect dysregulation issues helps us understand and appreciate the forces and experiences that shaped Paul's life and determined his maladaptations. We can better appreciate the anguish he must have felt as revealed in his unwillingness to board the school bus and his vomiting before school. We can empathize with his emotional pain at repeatedly having to stand facing the wall. As clinicians we can respect and admire his qualities of courage, kindness, sweetness, and resiliency. Most importantly, we can consider ways to help him remediate the deficits that have produced his maladaptations. Here now is the approach a developmental, affect-centered clinician might take to Paul's case.

Paul's mother's depression coupled with the fact that she had five older children to care for indicates she may have had difficulty providing Paul with the attuned, responsive caregiving necessary to establishment of a secure attachment and to adaptive emotional socialization. Downey and Coyne (1990) reported that in three studies children of depressed parents showed significantly higher rates of ADHD and in three other studies showed significantly higher rates of conduct disorder. While Paul's attachment status was never assessed, the picture that emerged from the case report strongly indicated an insecure attachment of the resistant type. In a home where five older children competed for mother's attention, where mother was depressed, where there was alcohol abuse, narcolepsy, and antisocial behavior, the infant Paul may well have been anxious about the availability of his mother and her sensitivity and responsiveness to his needs. An insecure–resistant type of attachment bond may have formed in which Paul's "colicky," "hyperactive," "impulsive" behaviors in childhood had the effect of maintaining himself in her awareness.

Nathanson (1992) noted that the ADHD child appears to have difficulty focusing attention. Interest–excitement is the affect of sustained attentional focus. Paul's difficulties appeared to stem from problems with regulating interest affect. Although the most recent genome screening failed to locate a major gene conferring susceptibility to ADHD, it did not rule out the possibility that Paul either had a low threshold for interest affect that left him susceptible to any novel stimulus, or a high threshold that prevented him from paying attention to one stimulus for any length of time. The absence of a clear cut genetic basis for ADHD suggests that we must look to Paul's affective socialization experiences to understand the etiology and ontogeny of his condition.

The late practicing phase from 14 to 18 months of life is a crucial period during which the senior toddler acquires skills for attenuating activation of interest affect and the accompanying sympathetic arousal. Apparently Paul never acquired these skills. A clinician influenced by a developmental model would investigate whether Paul's caregivers provided the optimal disapproval experiences necessary for adaptive socialization of Paul's interest affect. Paul's mother's depression and the distraction of the older children may have prevented her from providing Paul with these experiences, or alternatively she may not have been able to tolerate her own emotional stress inherent in providing them. Provision of optimal disapproval experience, which necessitates eliciting optimal shame, induces maturation of the lateral tegmental circuit of the orbitofrontal cortex (OFC). The cholinergic fibers of the lateral tegmental circuit act to attenuate the sympathetic excitation accompanying arousal of interest affect. It would appear that Paul's lateral tegmental circuit failed to develop adequately because he did not receive optimal affective socialization experiences in late practicing period.

Paul's parents appeared to have used punitive socialization in raising him which further contributed to his maladaptation. Magai (1999) reported that ADHD children are subjected to greater numbers of affective interchanges in which anger is directed at the child. Empirical research demonstrates that mothers of ADHD children were more likely to punish the child for displays of fear or guilt. Maternal displays of anger, shaming, and guilting directed at a child are called *punitive affective socialization,* and it stands in stark contrast to the alternative: providing empathy, comfort, consolation, and help. As a result of their punitive socialization, ADHD children demonstrated a bias toward seeing more anger in ambiguous faces in a facial decoding task (Magai, 1999). Attachment theory predicted this bias toward seeing more anger, because ADHD children are exposed to more anger. Clinical theory, which was not supported, predicted a bias toward seeing more shame or fear in ambiguous faces, because ADHD children themselves experience more of these painful affects. ADHD children also saw significantly less fear in ambiguous faces than normals, and they discriminated less guilt. This result supports Tomkins's hypothesis that punitive socialization of an emotion, in this case fear and guilt, will result in a perceptual blindness to that emotion.

An affect oriented therapy based on a developmental model for psychopathology would conceptualize Paul's situation as follows. Paul apparently lacked the ability to recognize, tolerate, and regulate key emotions, particularly interest–excitement affect, anger affect, and fear affect. The deficiencies in Paul's affect regulation aptitude may be traceable to deficit experience. Paul's mother and father were apparently not able to provide the "good enough" caregiving necessary to formation of a secure attachment. His insecure–resistant attachment rendered him anxious about caregiver availability and prone to maximizing bids for attention. He apparently did not receive the optimal shame experiences necessary to help him regulate his interest–excitement affect and behaviors motivated by it. Parental punitive socialization employing anger, shame, and guilt in an attempt to control Paul's behaviors may have trauma coded these emotions for Paul. The finding that Paul vomited before school suggests that his parents may have also used disgust affect to manage Paul and that this emotion too was trauma coded. The deficiencies in affective socialization have left Paul with inadequate IWMs to rely on for affect regulation.

This case conceptualization is not mother-bashing, nor does it fault the parents. I distinguish between blaming and "noticing." The case formulation I have presented is an example of noticing the parents' involvement. Following Shapiro (1995), the formulation asks that we notice who is responsible for the child's upbringing. Clearly the parents are responsible. To blame the parents connotes justifying some current behavior on the basis of a judgment, as, for example, the alcoholic might blame his parents for his drinking problem. By "just noticing" the parents' contribution to Paul's affect dysregulation, we can then accurately assess the ontogeny of his problem with emotion regulation and employ interventions that remediate his deficiencies.

AMST would teach Paul to contain (skill I) any disturbing memories. Paul may well have disturbing memories of being dragged out of the car and into school by his mother, he may have been picked on by older siblings, he was made to stand in the corner at school. The protocol would help him form an image of a safe place (skill II), something he may well lack given the crowded, unresponsive, alcoholic environment of childhood. Skills III to VII would teach him to recognize, tolerate, and regulate affects that are troubling for him, including interest–excitement, fear, and anger. In the course of acquiring these skills, contextual learning would accrue that would remediate some of the deficiencies of Paul's infant–caregiver developmental dyad. The client–therapist dyad is in and of itself reparative, inasmuch as it provides the sensitive attunement, responsiveness, and affect orientation that Paul did not receive in childhood. Paul would be helped to visualize school scenarios in which he could adaptively apply his AMST skills, and he would be helped to solidify his successes and assemble them with feelings of pride. Affect centered therapy would help Paul identify, notice, and adaptively resolve his parents' contribution to his developmental trajectory. The ACT clinician would facilitate the emergence of a new, more positively functioning, more adaptive self structure to replace Paul's "class clown" personality.

Oppositional Defiant Disorder (ODD)

The essential feature of ODD is hostile behavior toward authority figures. Like ADHD, ODD is usually diagnosed in childhood or adolescence. Research implicates deficits in attachment, and 80% of clinic-referred children demonstrated an insecure attachment (Greenberg, 1999). The ODD client has difficulty regulating the affect anger-rage. The *DSM-IV* presents eight criteria for ODD, only one of which focuses explicitly on the affect anger, to wit "is often angry" (p. 94). However, the other seven criteria consist of behaviors ("argues with adults," "loses temper," "deliberately annoys") or attitudes ("spiteful or vindictive") that are motivated by anger.

A developmental approach conceptualizes the client's anger as a symptom of deficiencies occurring across the developmental time span. Anger is the normative response for infants whose caregivers were inaccessible (Weinfield et al., 1999). The anger and the ODD behaviors motivated by it are symptoms of a developmental disorder. The ODD child does not *have* ODD; the ODD child *has* deficiencies in attachment and perhaps adversity or trauma in his childhood socioemotional history that caused the emergence of a personality characterized by anger dysregulation, deliberately being annoying, arguing, and expressing hostility toward authority. A study of children admitted to an outpatient psychiatric clinic for disruptive behavior demonstrated that ODD was associated with a history of physical or sexual maltreatment (Ford et al., 2000). The abused child is more likely to perceive anger in another's face (Pollak & Kistler, 2002). If he was punitively socialized for fear and guilt, he will be less likely to perceive those affects in himself or others. AMST would teach containment of the disturbing experiences (skill I); provide a safe place (skill II); teach the client to recognize, tolerate, and regulate anger, fear, and optimal shame (skills III–VII). An affect oriented therapy would identify and process instances of abuse. Recall that the ODD client may be genetically impaired in his ability to adaptively process abuse due to deficiencies in mono amine oxidase A (MAOA; Caspi et al., 2002), and he may also have a genetically determined low threshold for anger affect. AMST may be of particular help to the child or adolescent with ODD.

Substance-Related Disorders

Substance abusing and substance dependent persons often endorse histories of deficit experience as well as adverse or traumatic experience. As we have seen, these developmental insults lead to affect dysregulation. The area of substance dependence and substance abuse disorders affords a clear distinction between the medical model and an affect-centered model for psychopathology. The *DSM-IV* identifies the essential feature of substance dependence as "a cluster of cognitive, behavioral, and physiological symptoms"(p. 181). There is no doubt that continued abuse of an addictive substance will produce physiological symptoms of tolerance or withdrawal, which are among the *DSM-IV* identifiers of dependence. Substance abuse, the *DSM-IV* specifies, is identified behaviorally; for example, failure to fulfill role obligations, using the substance in spite of the danger involved, and recurring legal problems. The medical model fails to relate substance abuse disorder to the large body of solid empirical evidence that demonstrates the prevalence of abuse in the histories of addicts and alcoholics (e.g., Amaro, Nieves, Johannes, & Cabeza, 1999; Cavaiola & Schiff, 1988; Dembo et al., 1989; Downs, Miller, & Gandoli, 1987; Fullilove et al., 1993; Grice, Brady, Dustan, & Malcom, 1995;

B. A. Miller, Downs, Gondoli, & Keil, 1987; Rounsaville, Weissman, Wilber, & Kleber, 1982; Swett, Cohen, Surrey, Compaine, & Chavez, 1991; Triffleman, Marmar, Delucchi, & Ronfeldt, 1995). The medical model ignores information available concerning the dysfunctional family situations of children who grow up to become substance abusers (reviewed in Kaufman, 1994; see also Anda et al., 1999). The medical model fails to consider the observation that 62% of substance abusers endorsed a preoccupied attachment (Fonagy et al., 1996). It ignores findings that alcoholics use alcohol to reduce negative affect and increase positive affect (Cooper, Frone, Russell, & Mudar, 1995). From the perspective of the medical model, chemical dependency is a chronic, fatal *disease* that one *has* (American Medical Association, 1973; Jellinek, 1960), which is either self-medicated (Khantzian, 1997; Khantzian, Halliday, & McAuliffe, 1990) or treated with a combination of drugs and therapy (Volpicelli, Pettinati, O'Brien, & McLellan, 2001), or a range of cognitive–behavioral therapies (Smyth, 1998a, 1998b).

Substance abusers use drugs, alcohol, or nicotine to regulate affects that were coded by trauma or adversity in childhood. I have investigated the role of emotion and how adverse child experience manifests in substance abuse (Omaha, 1998, 1999, 2001). I adapted the Gestalt "empty chair" communication technique (Levitsky & Perls, 1970) to the analytic task of uncovering the participant's cognitive, affective, sensate, and memorial associations to the substance of abuse. I have now incorporated this approach into a treatment for substance abuse. The participant or client is instructed to visualize his or her drug of choice in a factually empty chair. The interviewer elicits the client's image of the substance, what the substance is doing, what it thinks, and what it thinks about the client, what it feels, and what it feels toward the client. Next the interviewer elicits the same responses from the client regarding the drug: what is he thinking, what is he thinking about the drug, what is he feeling, and what is he feeling toward the drug. The client is asked to state the gender of the drug. The interviewer then reprises the information, explaining that the information describes the client's relationship to the drug, and then the client is asked to identify what other relationships are similar to his relationship to the drug. Integrating client histories with responses to these questions has uncovered startling information about the role the abused substance plays in addiction. Here are some of those findings.

Apparently, the abused substance, whether drugs, alcohol, or nicotine, functions to regulate the abuser's emotions. In this regard, it functions in two ways. First, the abused substance facilitates management of current emotions that would otherwise be overwhelming. Second, it furnishes a vicarious reexperiencing of unresolved emotions from childhood. Often these emotions are assembled with traumatic events that have not yet been processed to an adaptive resolution. Thus, in addition to emotion regulation, the abused substance also facilitates a reenactment in disguised form of unresolved childhood adverse or traumatic experience. Abused substances appear to group according to which emotions are regulated.

The case of participant Dennis demonstrates how alcohol facilitates management of anger (Omaha, 2001). Dennis, a 46-year-old Vietnam veteran, was severely physically abused by his alcoholic father. Placing vodka in the empty chair, he reported feelings of helplessness and rage. The alcohol's gender was masculine, and his relationship to alcohol was like his relationship to his father. For Dennis, alcohol appears to have facilitated management of anger arising both from his father's abuse and from his mother's failure to meet his childhood needs (Omaha, 2001). In avoidantly attached children, anger is a common finding, a normative response to deficits in the attachment in which the caregiver fails to meet the child's needs. As he looked at the alcohol in the empty chair, Dennis verbalized, "I'm on the verge of hate . . . anger, I guess."

Each of the drugs of abuse appears to facilitate management of a different affect or emotion. Based on my clinical experience, rage is the emotion vicariously expressed through methamphetamine abuse. The methamphetamine addict's rage is associated with either childhood physical or sexual abuse trauma coupled with failures of attachment. Cocaine abuse is associated with affects of shame and grandiosity arising from failures during practicing and rapprochement subphases of separation-individuation. Opiate addictions appear to arise from very early defects of attachment, and the opiates seem to facilitate management of yearning affect. James, an opiate addict who participated in the dissertation research, (Omaha, 2001) reported that when he placed time-release morphine in the empty chair it felt "loving and nurturing" toward him, and he felt "euphoric, supported, encouraged" as he looked at it. He identified morphine as having a female gender, and indicated his relationship to his mother was like the negative aspect of his relationship to morphine, "unavailable" and "abandoning." Marijuana abuse, as evidenced by marijuana-addicted research participants Paul and William, appears to facilitate reenactment of loss and abandonment experiences and to facilitate management of sadness affect (Omaha, 2001).

Empirical research supports the conclusions of my own work. Coffey and associates (2002) reviewed the literature in which the technique of cue reactivity was used to investigate emotion's role in substance abuse disorders. Participants with a history of drug dependence were presented with emotional, cognitive, or physical cues associated with their drug of choice, and then verbal, behavioral, or physiological reactions were measured. When negative emotion was induced in alcohol dependent individuals, craving increased. Another study of 133 cannabis users showed that the severity of depressive, anxious, and alexithymic symptoms increased progressively with the degree of involvement with cannabis (Troisi, Pasini, Saracco, & Spalletta, 1998).

A developmental and affect orientation toward substance abuse disorders engenders a therapy directed at teaching new ways of affect management and at resolving archaic trauma and adversity. AMST helps the substance abuser recognize, tolerate, and regulate affects he has previously managed with drugs, alcohol, or cigarettes. ACT helps him identify the traumas and adversities he has reenacted through his substance abuse, and then ACT helps him process these traumas and adversities to an adaptive resolution. ACT facilitates the emergence of a more positively functioning, more adaptive self structure.

Eating Disorders

Eating disorders are characterized by deficiencies in attachment and by experiences of adversity or trauma. Eating disorders primarily affect women (90% of diagnoses of eating disorders), and there is significant comorbidity with depression (75% of eating disordered women qualified for a depressed diagnosis as well). Dozier and colleagues (1999) summarized a number of studies regarding the childhood parenting experiences of females who became eating disordered. In retrospective studies, parents were described as providing a lower quality of care. Fathers were rejecting and emotionally unavailable, while mothers were overprotective, domineering, and perfectionistic. Neither parent supported the child's struggle for independence and often put their child in a double-bind in this area by appearing to support her independence while at the same time undermining it. The eating disordered daughters felt inadequate, rejected, and controlled. Studies show that sexual abuse, once believed to be a causative factor, is not strongly related to development of anorexia or bulimia.

Studies of attachment-related states of mind in eating disordered women are conflicting due to differences of exclusion criteria between studies. Dozier and associates (1999) attempted to resolve the conflict and suggested that the majority of pure eating disordered women qualify as dismissing. Reporting the work of Cole-Detke and Kobak, Dozier, and colleagues (1999) suggested that eating disordered women were unable to examine their psychological states due to their dismissing state of mind and that they therefore employed externally oriented eating behavior to divert their attention from attachment-related concerns.

I have employed the same Gestalt communication technique I used to investigate substance abusers' relationships to the abused substance to explore eating disordered clients' relationships to food (Omaha, 2000). I have learned that food, like drugs, alcohol, and nicotine, facilitates the three Rs: (1) regulation of current emotions that would otherwise overwhelm the client; (2) reenactment of unresolved childhood trauma or adversity; and (3) reexperiencing of unmetabolized emotions assembled with the trauma(s) at the time(s) of occurrence. Eating disordered clients apparently use food, whether rejecting it, bingeing on it, or purging it, as a means of regulating affects. My theoretical approach is congruent with Dozier and associates (1999), but shifts the analysis from the level of attachment-related states of mind to the level of affective processes. These are the basic emotions involved in the eating disorders and how each disorder represents a different, unique solution to the problem of managing these powerful emotions.

Anger: The eating disordered client shoulders a load of unresolved anger usually originating in childhood. The anger can result from an impaired attachment or from adverse or traumatic experience. Amy is a 30-year-old bulimic woman whose responses in the Gestalt exercise reveal the association between food, anger, and her relationship to her mother. Placing an imaginary 200-pound pile of ice cream in the empty chair, Amy visualized it inviting her, and desperately, relentlessly desiring her. Amy herself felt angry at the food and verbalized, "You're lying. The promises won't come true." She identified the food as having a female gender and associated her relationship to food to her relationship with her mother. For Amy, eating was an expression of unresolved anger she had carried from childhood. When she binged, she ate until she hurt physically, which she discovered in therapy was a reenactment of the abuse she had witnessed as a child.

The bingeing phase of bulimia is similar to bingeing in binge eating disorder (BED) in that it can be an anger management device. Carly, an overweight BED client, had significant impairments in her relationship to her female caregiver in childhood and was also sexually abused in early adolescence. She placed mounds of imaginary rich foods in the empty chair, identifying anger as the emotion she experienced as she looked at it, and associating her relationship to food to both her relationship to her childhood female caregiver and to the male relative who sexually abused her.

While the bulimic and BED client reenact, reexperience, and regulate anger through bingeing, the anorexic client regulates anger by *not* eating. An anorexic client, Elaine, who appeared to have had a childhood free of adversity, placed a small amount of imaginary dry cereal and a dry English muffin in the empty chair and identified "hate" as the emotion she felt for it. She associated her relationship to food to her relationship to her mother. She also came to realize that not eating kept her too weak to either feel or express her anger. She feared her anger and had been given no tools as a child to manage it.

Yearning: The affective picture in any disorder is complex, and simplistic case conceptualizations must be avoided. In addition to anger toward the food, eating disordered clients also often feel a deep yearning for it and for the unresolved, archaic relationship being reenacted through the food. As she looked at the imaginary food in the chair, Amy, the bulimic, said, "I want to be nurtured, to be taken care of, to feel good. I feel desperate to get it." Carly, the BED, expressed "longing" as she looked at the imaginary mound of food. The eating disordered client's yearning for attachment to the caregiver was often never requited in childhood, and so it remains unresolved in adolescence and adulthood where it fuels the disorder. Often it is buried under anger and sadness, the affective responses to failure to satisfy yearning for attachment. Once the client learns the AMST skills to recognize and regulate sadness and anger, she can cognize her deep seated yearning.

Disgust: The powerful and often unrecognized affect of disgust plays a central role in eating disorders. The three basic eating disorders—bulimia, anorexia, and BED—can be discriminated one from another by the strategy the client has developed for managing disgust. The eating disordered client carries a burden of unresolved disgust affect that may have been broadcast by a caregiver during punitive childhood socialization experiences or may have been trauma coded as it was felt by the child during adverse or traumatic experiences. The eating disorder provides a means for managing disgust that would otherwise overwhelm the patient.

The bulimic client regulates her unresolved, archaic disgust through vomiting. When Amy was asked to place imaginary vomit in the empty chair during therapy, she verbalized, "Now this is gross. This is disgusting. It doesn't get more disgusting than this." During therapy she came to realize that the vomit held her feelings of disgust regarding the abuse she had witnessed in childhood. Vomiting was a way to dissociate disgust affect out of awareness. As she verbalized, "The whole point is not to feel." Note how unresolved anger and unresolved disgust are interrelated in Amy's bulimia. In the binge phase of bulimia, food facilitates vicarious expression of unresolved, archaic anger; in the purge phase, vomiting facilitates vicarious expression of unresolved, archaic disgust. While the bulimic sequesters her disgust affect in her vomit and manages disgust by expelling it, in BED and anorexia a different solution to the disgust problem has emerged.

When I asked the BED client, Carly, to place her excess weight in the empty chair, she put 115 pounds of imaginary yellow, globular fat in it. In the course of therapy she realized that for years her body fat had been holding the disgust she had felt during her sexual victimization. For the BED client, food facilitates management of anger, and as she eats, she accumulates body fat which serves as a repository of disgust. Body fat serves the vital function of protecting the BED's psychological system. By holding the system's disgust, the fat prevents that disgust from assembling with the self-concept. The BED can say, "My fat is disgusting," and thus she can avoid saying, "I am disgusting." Disgust affect is extremely powerful, and clinicians must be careful to avoid eliciting it before the client has learned skills to manage it. If disgust affect is prematurely evoked and assembles with the client's self concept, decompensation and disorganization of the self-structure can result.

The anorexic client also uses body fat to manage disgust affect, but she does so by starving herself so that fat cannot accumulate and disgust is managed. However, since the disgust she is trying to manage is archaic disgust, it can never be removed by starving the self, which explains why anorexics believe they are fat, no matter how low their body weight. The client Elaine illustrates how the anorexic manages disgust affect. As she worked through the AMST protocol, she learned that sensations of "fullness" in her stomach were the physiological signals, the qualia, by which her body told her she was feeling disgust affect. With the skills in place to recognize, tolerate, and regulate disgust, Elaine could now place her body fat in the empty chair during the second phase of ACT. Elaine had adamantly refused to weigh herself, probably, I hypothesize, because she did not want to know how much disgust she was holding. I estimated that she weighed about 90 pounds and that her ideal body weight would have been about 115. She visualized 15 pounds of yellow, dimply, glistening fat flecked with blood. Looking at it, she verbalized feelings of disgust and hate, which is anger assembled with disgust. In therapy she realized that her parents had broadcast disgust at her in childhood when she had attempted to stop them from yelling at each other.

Clinician readers should note how a developmental and affect orientation traces the causes of eating disorders to deficits and adversities in the client's childhood history. The eating disorder is conceptualized as a self structure that emerged over the developmental time span in response to the vicissitudes of the client's life and affects and emotions assembled with them. The eating disorder is not something the client *has*, but rather it is a symptom of the self's struggle to deal with events and experiences in its history. Conceptualized in this way, therapy can address the problems of affect regulation and the deficits that engendered them. AMST can teach the client to recognize, tolerate, and regulate anger, disgust, and shame when these are causal factors. ACT can facilitate uncovering and resolving deficit experiences and experiences of trauma and adversity. In the context of a therapy that is developmentally and affectively oriented, the therapist can facilitate emergence of a new self structure that is more positively and adaptively functioning.

Depression

Depression is characterized by dysregulation of several affects including distress, interest, enjoyment, and shame or disgust. Anger dysregulation may also be a factor in some depressed states. The *DSM-IV* specifies "depressed mood" as the first criterion for major depressive episode, listing several affective identifiers: "feeling sad or empty," "appears tearful," "markedly diminished interest or pleasure," "feelings of worthlessness . . . or guilt." Tears are the visible expression of distress–anguish affect, and sadness is located on that affective dimension. "Diminished interest" indicates dysregulation of interest–excitement affect. "Diminished pleasure" indicates dysregulation of enjoyment–joy affect as does the criterion "emptiness," which may indicate presence of unconscious internal affective conflict that robs the individual of vitality. Elevated enjoyment affect characterizes vitality. While Tomkins did not identify guilt as a primary affect, Izard (1991) did, and Plutchik (1993) said it was a secondary dyad comprised of joy and fear. Interestingly, I can find no affective definition of either *worthlessness* or *emptiness* by any of the theorists whose work I have cited. *Worthlessness* appears to me to be an affective–cognitive structure in which the self-representation is assembled with disgust affect, shame affect, or both.

Affective markers for depression may be accompanied by behavioral and physiological indicators, including weight loss, sleeplessness or oversleeping, and fatigue, as well as cognitive and social impairments. The *DSM-IV* notes that the symptoms of depression themselves elicit further distress affect.

Terrence Real (1997) believed that depression is far more prevalent than the figures in the *DSM-IV* suggest (major depressive disorder 5–10%; dysthymic disorder, 2–5%, bipolar disorder, 0.5%). He suggested that clinicians focus only on the most severe forms of depression and fail to notice what he referred to as covert depression. He proposed that many males in Western society experience covert depression, but see it as a personal weakness which is therefore protected by male pride, a defense against shame. Covert depression is characterized by disconnection from emotions, a signpost of a dismissing attachment strategy. The covertly depressed male fears vulnerability and abandonment. He sublimates in work and uses alcohol to facilitate his yearnings for merger. Alcohol also vicariously facilitates his anger expression (Omaha, 1998, 2001). Agonized by fears of inadequacy he attempts to compensate by accumulating possessions. He may exercise compulsively to meet a socialized ego ideal. In the end, his covert depression robs him of his vitality and poisons intimacy in his relationships with his spouse and his children.

The great value of a developmental approach is that it helps us understand depression as a "cumulative and dynamic process" (Harkness & Tucker, 2000, pp. 186–187), in which a depressive self structure built upon early life experiences has organized itself over time. Where the medical model looks at symptom clusters in an attempt to discern whether the patient *has* major depressive disorder or dysthymia, an affect focused developmental model seeks to uncover the interplay of emotions and life experiences that have conditioned the emergence of the self-structure of the human being sitting before us in the counseling office. The developmental approach to depression presented by Harkness and Tucker (2000) supports the tripartite model in that it draws attention to the importance of deficit experience, particularly in regard to arousal—excitement affect and enjoyment affect—and to adverse and traumatic experience in the etiology of depression.

Empirical research demonstrated unique affect patterns characteristic of depression. Depressed 10- and 11-year-old children endorsed elevated levels of sadness, shame, anger, and disgust compared to nondepressed controls (Blumberg & Izard, 1985; Izard, 1991). Girls endorsed higher levels of self-directed hostility, fear, and shame than boys. Both depressed boys and girls demonstrated significantly diminished levels of interest affect and joy affect relative to controls. Lonigan, Carey, and Finch (1994) examined negative affect in a clinical sample of 233 children, average age 11.4 years, diagnosed for depression or anxiety. Results in Lonigan et al. supported Izard's findings. Depression assessed by the Children's Depression Inventory was associated with emotions of self-hatred, self-blame, badness, anhedonia, fear, sadness, disgust ("feels ugly"), hopelessness, feeling unloved, and loneliness. Carey, Carey, and Kelly (1997) studied the relative contribution of emotion, behavior, and cognition to depressive symptomatology in a sample of nonreferred adolescents. They discovered that emotional variables accounted for 67% of variance ($p < .0005$), while behavioral variables accounted for an additional 4% of variance ($p < .01$). The cognitive variable did not significantly contribute to an increase in variance accounted for. In this nonreferred sample, the most influential emotion variables were enjoyment (beta weight, $-.66$), shame (beta weight, .41), and guilt (beta weight, .29). The authors speculated that the self-hatred or self-directed hostility observed in other studies might be associated with the more severe depressive symptomatology seen in clinical samples.

Attachment related states of mind show different prevalences for different mood disorders. Overall, affective disorders are associated with a preoccupied state of mind. Research demonstrates that 69% of affectively disordered psychiatric inpatient adolescents endorsed a preoccupied attachment strategy (Dozier et al, 1999). Adult preoccupied states arise from childhood inability to control the availability of caregivers. This individual develops enduring object representations assembled with uncontrollability and a self-representation assembled with failure. The depressed adult child of unavailable parents carries an unresolved sadness, because parental unavailability is equivalent to chronic loss or death of a parent. Among the affective disorders, dysthymia was associated with preoccupied strategies, while major depression was significantly associated with autonomous states of mind. Dysthymia was more frequently associated with loss of a caregiver due to death or divorce, while major depression was less frequently associated with loss. The apparently paradoxical association of major depression with autonomous states of mind demonstrates how genetics, attachment, and trauma, the three factors of the tripartite model, interact. Coherence is the criterion for autonomy in the adult attachment interview (AAI). The possibility that an individual with major depression can maintain coherence suggested to Dozier and associates (1999) how major depression may differ from dysthymia, which is usually associated with a preoccupied strategy. Because major depression is more heritable than dysthymia, then less attachment disordering may be necessary to elicit the depression, and thus depression can occur in the presence of an autonomous state of mind. Alternatively, genetic vulnerability may combine with difficult life experiences to produce depression, even when an autonomous state of mind has emerged.

While sadness in the depressed adult may result from childhood parental unavailability, the significant joylessness associated with depression may be the outcome of childhood parental conflict or absence of emotional supportiveness. According to Izard (1991), "frequent bickering or open conflicts between parents can endanger the development of joy in the child" (p. 142). In a longitudinal study of 168 participants, Duggal and colleagues (2001) showed that childhood depression was predicted by cumulative effects of maternal depression, deficits in emotional supportiveness in early caregiving, abuse, and family stressors. By the time the children in the study had reached late adolescence, maternal depression and deficits in emotional supportiveness during early care specifically predicted adolescent depressive symptomatology. Whatever the cause, the joylessness associated with depression is in place at an early age. Seven-year-old children were screened for emotion knowledge (Schultz et al., 2001). The emotion situation knowledge assessment included the affect joy. Children with social problems or who were socially withdrawn were less able than average children to accurately name the joy affect experienced by a protagonist in a brief vignette. The joylessness associated with depression in the adult who had a deficit experience during childhood may be traceable to failures during early practicing (Schore, 1994). If the caregiver is unavailable, depressed herself, distracted, or otherwise stressed, she may not be available to provide the optimal affective stimulation necessary for activation of excitement and joy affect in the infant. As a result, the ventral tegmental circuit of the orbitofrontal cortex (OFC) may fail to develop fully, resulting in vulnerability to depression in the infant due to a lack of critical affective resources.

As a result of early childhood experience, the adult's enjoyment affect may be assembled with fear, shame, shyness, or guilt. For example, in certain highly controlled families, expressions of enjoyment affect may be punished, shamed, or the person may be made to feel guilty. These individuals will assemble fear with enjoyment and may feel ashamed at any stimuli that elicit it. This can be particularly true for persons who have been sexually abused at an early age. Enjoyment assembles with the sex drive and the affects shame and guilt.

As suggested by the developmental model, there appear to be several pathways to adolescent and adult depressive psychopathology. Two pathways are attachment related; in one, depression results from a resistant childhood attachment; alternatively, depression may emerge from avoidant attachment. Yet another pathway is related to childhood adversity or trauma. Here, depression is secondary to ongoing difficulties with managing anger, shame, or disgust (Carlson, 1997; Herman, 1992).

Depressive disorders are characterized by internalizing strategies that can include negative cognitions regarding the self. These negative self-attributions may encompass self-blame and self-deprecation that have arisen from messages of incompetence and unlovability transmitted by caregivers. Thus, the object representation will be unloving, and the self-representation will be assembled with unlovability. Often in my clinical experience with depressed clients, it appears that caregivers employed broadcast disgust affect to control and socialize the child. Thus a part of the self-representation—it may also be called an ego state—is assembled with disgust, which by the time this individual reaches the therapeutic encounter, has submerged into the unconscious. Intrapsychic conflict characterized by negative affective transactions results. The disgust-holding ego state conflicts with adaptive ego states holding the system's authenticity, with the result that the system's vitality is severely compromised and self-worth and self-efficacy are contaminated. The personality system feels anguish and confusion. This is because the system cannot comprehend the conflict since a component of the system, the disgust-holding ego state, is unavailable to consciousness. The result is the downward spiral of depression.

An affect and developmentally oriented therapy can help the depressed client. AMST teaches the client to recognize, tolerate, and manage the affects that are causally involved in his condition. Once the depressed client has cognized anger, for example, he can use the affect bridge technique (Watkins & Watkins, 1997) to uncover pivotal childhood experiences in which his anger was punitively socialized, and these experiences can be adaptively processed. AMST can help the depressed client identify excitement and joy affects and then enhance them. Working with visualized future templates, the client can learn to import excitement into situations (e.g., attending a movie or other social event). Building on the basis established by affect training, ACT helps the client uncover and bring forward child ego states that may have been assembled with disgust affect broadcast at the client in childhood by parents. As these archaic affects are adaptively resolved, the self reorganizes itself, and a new, more positively functioning self structure emerges.

Bipolar Disorder (BP)

In bipolar disorder, the client alternates between anguish in the depressed phase and intense excitement when manic. Bipolar disorder is apparently highly heritable, and a recent genomewide scan demonstrated significant linkage of BP with a site on chromosome 2 (Liu et al., 2003). Having a genetic marker reveals nothing about the function of the genes linked with BP. Nathanson (1992) suggested that the intense excitement displayed in the manic phase of bipolar disorder as well as in hypomanic and manic disorder may result from a genetic based defect in neurotransmitter function expressed as a low threshold for interest–excitement affect. BP significantly associates with a dismissing attachment-related state of mind in the AAI. Externalizing strategies and interpersonal hostility characterize the disorder. Summarizing the affects involved, bipolar disorder is associated with anger and interest–excitement dysregulation in the manic phase and dysregulation of distress–anguish affect in the depressed phase. BP illustrates a disorder in which the genetic component may be prominent, yet it remains the case that the organism with its genetic defect is still shaped by interaction with a physical and social environment. AMST, which teaches skills to regulate anger, excitement, and distress affects, may be able to ameliorate some of the difficulties the BP experiences. Eventually, empirical research will address the question of how AMST alone or in combination with pharmacotherapy can help improve the functioning of the BP client.

Anxiety Disorders

The anxiety disorders constitute a heterogeneous group of psychopathologies all characterized by difficulty regulating the affect fear–terror. LeDoux (1996) has written that "anxiety disorders reflect the operation of the fear system of the brain" (p. 230). Dozier and colleagues (1999) discriminated the anxiety disorders on the basis of the balance between predominance of fear and predominance of avoidance. When fear predominates, symptoms are internalizing and attachment needs are maximized. When avoidance predominates, externalizing symptoms prevail, and attachment needs are minimized. The genetic component is variable, appearing to be weak in generalized anxiety disorder and significant in OCD. Recent investigations have identified a specific gene variation that elicits heightened activity in the amygdala where the fear response originates (Hariri et al., 2002). The gene codes for the serotonin transporter protein whose function it is to remove serotonin from synapses. The gene naturally occurs in two variations, a short and a long form. Persons with the shorter variant of the gene produce less of the transporter protein. The shorter variant has been associated with anxiety. In addition to a genetic contribution, fear responses are conditioned, beginning in the context of the infant–caregiver dyad. LeDoux (1996) has noted that, "Fear conditioning contributes significantly to anxiety disorders" (p. 230).

Attachment theory traces adult anxiety disorders to childhood anxiety regarding the availability of the caregiver (Dozier et al., 1999). Children become anxious about caregiver availability in environments characterized by parental control through overprotection or through rejection. A developmental model for adult anxiety psychopathology suggests that the anxious self emerged in the context of one of four environments: The child worries about parental survival in the child's absence because there have been suicide threats or parental violence; the child worries about being rejected or abandoned, sometimes because of overt threats from parents, other times because of neglectful or abandoning behaviors; the child feels the need to companion the parent, especially where the child has been parentified; the parent has difficulty letting the child go and facilitating the child's autonomy, which may be particularly true if the parent's identity is structured by the parental role. In retrospective studies, anxiety disordered persons describe their parents as unloving and controlling. Research has demonstrated that a resistant attachment in infancy is significantly associated with anxiety disorders in late adolescence, even when temperament is partialed out. Resistant attachment in childhood associates with preoccupied states of mind in adulthood. We now examine some of the specific anxiety disorders.

Generalized Anxiety Disorder (GAD):   Fear predominates, expressed as anxiety about several life areas, and there is a minimal avoidant component. Rejection and role reversal in childhood consistently associate with generalized anxiety in empirical studies (Dozier et al., 1999). These studies have shown that persons with GAD endorse feelings of anger and vulnerability, both of which are consistent with preoccupied states of mind.

Panic Disorder: Fear is primary with terror often present. Avoidant behavior is minimal. Through limbic attachments to the autonomic nervous system fear's expressed in physical symptoms. Early loss of the caregiver or extremely inadequate caregiving are childhood adverse antecedents consistently associated with panic disorder.

Agoraphobia: The person associates fear with being in public, and the prominent avoidant component involves staying inside. Developmentally, agoraphobia is consistently associated with separation from mother or with parental divorce.

Phobic Disorders: Avoidance predominates, expressed as evasion of the feared stimulus. Fear becomes ascendant when the stimulus cannot be avoided.

Obsessive Compulsive Disorder (OCD):   Fear is a prominent feature, increasing as the compulsive behaviors are not practiced. OCD behaviors—the compulsions—developed as a means by controlling fear and constitute the avoidant moiety of OCD.

MacLean (1990) developed an explanation for some of the obsessive–compulsive symptoms that characterize OCD, based on his theory of the function of the R-complex, which is also known as the *striatal complex* and is a component of the reptilian brain. The function of this hind brain structure is to integrate the daily master routine and subroutines of the organism's life. MacLean (1990) discussed the compulsive, ritualistic behaviors seen in a case of Sydenham's chorea in which a girl of 13 had to count so many numbers before putting on clean underclothes that there was difficulty getting her dressed. She had to count to 100 after brushing her teeth. She would only enter the house by the back door and had to knock three times on the nearby window and again three times on the door itself before entering. MacLean suggested that this case illustrated how "morbid subroutines may drastically interfere with adherence to the daily master routine" (p. 221). In this case, the morbid subroutine is the counting and knocking behaviors; the master routines interfered with are dressing, entering the house, and grooming. MacLean hypothesized that inflammation in the striatal complex may be responsible for the appearance of these morbid subroutines in Sydenham's chorea. MacLean also discussed displacement behavior which he defined as "repetitious acts that seem inappropriate for a particular occasion" (p. 241). He observed that, "there are indications that displacement reactions are strongly conditioned by emotional factors" (p. 241). He noted that electrical stimulation of the limbic system propagates to parts of the R-complex where it may induce displacement behavior.

Based on MacLean's speculations, we may hypothesize that the repetitive behaviors that characterize OCD may be thought of as morbid subroutines that are elicited by emotional activity in the limbic system, an activity that spills over into the R-complex where it triggers the morbid subroutines. If these subroutines succeeded in diminishing the dystonicity of the emotional activity, then they would rapidly become conditioned responses. Since reenactment behaviors are also hypothesized to originate in the R-complex, building on MacLean we may hypothesize that the reenactments seen in sexual acting out and many other disorders, may originate in striatal complex activity that is triggered by discharges from the limbic system. As MacLean noted, "reenactment behavior, by definition, involves a precedent" (p. 241). In the case of sexual reenactments, the precedent may be provided by a prior, traumatic sexual experience.

Empirical research supports the effectiveness of AMST in alleviating symptoms of OCD (Waltner-Toews, 2002). While this was a small study, the results were very promising and suggest the need for further research. Clinical impressions support the conclusion that AMST can help the agoraphobic, panic disordered, or anxiety disordered client. In particular, AMST skill V (grounding) gives the client an image that facilitates staying grounded and present while feeling fear, and skill VII (regulation) uses the image of the disposal resource to decrease the neurophysiological arousal associated with fear. The author has personally used these two skills effectively to reduce his own fear associated with turbulence during airline flights.

Posttraumatic Stress Disorder (PTSD)

Fear is a significant affective component in PTSD and other disorders of extreme stress. Traumatic events happen suddenly, the victim feels the event is uncontrollable, and the event is valenced with negative affect, often fear, shame, or disgust (Carlson, 1997). Single or multiple events of many types can produce PTSD. Combat, physical abuse, sexual abuse, rape, traffic accidents, witnessing murder, catastrophic loss, and natural disasters are just a few of the types of traumatic events that may lead to PTSD.

Bowie and colleagues (1990) analyzed 1,000 incidents of rape. Their study concluded that two types of rape are found: blitz rape characterized by sudden, surprise attack by an unknown assailant using force or threat of force to control the victim. Blitz rape victims present a different affective picture from confidence rape victims. In confidence rape, the victim knows the assailant to some degree, and the assailant uses trust to gain control. Blitz rape victims show increased startle responses, anxiety, and depression. They fear the rapist may return, their sense of safety is shattered, and they feel dismay at having failed to protect themselves. The affective picture of the confidence rape victim is one of guilt and self-blame, and she will doubt her ability to discern who is trustworthy. Thus, blitz rape involves the affects surprise–startle, fear, and sadness, while confidence rape involves guilt.

AMST can be an important component of therapy for PTSD, because it teaches the client skills for compartmentalizing the trauma until the client is prepared to work on it (skill I, container). Skill II (safe place) transmits an inner image of safety and security that the client can employ to feel safe while doing trauma-processing work. Skills III to VII teach the client to control the intense emotions of fear, anger, helplessness, and disgust that may be associated with memories or images of the traumatic event. Learning the AMST skills prepares the client for trauma processing whether by EMDR or imaginal exposure, because AMST transmits qualities of mastery and competence to be able to tolerate and regulate the intense emotions that will surface when the traumatic material is removed from containment and addressed in therapy.

Dissociative Disorders

Dissociation means separation of a mode or modes of experience from the mainstream of consciousness. Braun (1988a) has proposed that behavior, affect, sensation, and cognitions can be dissociated. Dozier and colleagues (1999) discriminated identity dissociation seen in dissociative identity disorder (DID) and fugue, memory dissociation seen in dissociative amnesia, and consciousness dissociation as seen in depersonalization disorders. Braun (1988a) has proposed that in derealization sensation is dissociated and theorized that dissociation constitutes a continuum from normalcy—where hypnosis, ego states, and automatisms are the only manifestations of dissociation—to polyfragmented DID. Ogawa and associates (1997) disagreed, concluding from a longitudinal study in a nonclinical sample that psychopathological dissociation should be viewed as a separate taxon representing an extreme deviation from normal development.

Dissociation has been confused with fragmentation. I argue that separating the phenomenon of dissociation from the phenomenon of fragmentation provides the basis for a more satisfyingly orderly theoretical understanding. Dissociation has been identified with its most extreme pathological expression, as in DID, for example, which has obscured its prevalence. Dissociation is here defined as the separation of a mode or modes of experience from the normal stream of consciousness. Fragmentation is the formation of assemblages within the self-structure that are more or less autonomous and of which the personality system is more or less aware. Ego states (Watkins & Watkins, 1997) are produced by fragmentation and they are known in dynamic systems theory as "strong attractors" (Lewis, 2000). Once separated from fragmentation, the ubiquity of dissociation can better be appreciated, and its participation in many psychopathologies where it had not previously been recognized can be acknowledged. In particular, the dissociation of specific emotions out of awareness must be recognized as a component of several pathologies, in particular the ingestive disorders. These same considerations apply to the phenomenon of fragmentation in the self-structure. Theoretically, we should think of dissociation and fragmentation as discrete phenomena that merge in various unique combinations in the course of development of the specific psychopathologies.

Surprise–startle affect may play a significant role in development of dissociative psychopathology. Dozier and colleagues (1999) noted that threat produces hyperarousal of the sympathetic nervous system. When threat is chronic and combined with helplessness, freezing and trance replace hyperarousal. Freezing and trance are characteristics of dissociation. Sudden threat elicits startle affect, the effect of which is to clear out the neural apparatus in preparation for dealing with the threat (Izard, 1991; Nathanson, 1992). Carlson (1997) noted that for events to be traumatic, they must have the qualities of negative valence, suddenness, and uncontrollability. Where the trauma involves a perpetrator, negative valence is provided by the affects of fear, shame, disgust, and anguish elicited by the onset of the perpetrator's traumatizing behavior. In the abuse situation, where a caregiver is the perpetrator, the caregiver has suddenly transitioned from being the source of safety to being the source of threat. This sudden transition evokes startle affect, which clears the mind, and prepares it to cope with the new, sudden event and the consequences of that event. Current nervous system activity that would interfere with coping is suppressed, and the mind "goes blank" briefly. However, in the case of abuse by a caregiver, a situation of "fright without solution" (Dozier et al., 1999) obtains, the situation is uncontrollable, and the child is helpless. In this situation, the blank mind produced by startle affect is adaptive for the child victim of abuse. Emptying the mind renders the experience of abuse survivable. Emptying of the neural apparatus is the hallmark of dissociation. Thus, surprise–startle affect is the basis of the phenomenon of dissociation.

Prolonged, repeated trauma prevents the resolution of the surprise–startle affect elicited by trauma's sudden onset. In the nature of traumatic events (sexual, physical, ritual), there is a succession of new, sudden events as the trauma plays out over a period of time. This sequence of events elicits and reelicits startle affect, keeping the mind "empty." This explanation is supported by the empirical evidence that dissociation varies in severity in direct proportion to the severity and duration of the abuse (Briere & Runtz, 1993). Dozier and associates (1999) noted that when dissociation occurs frequently, neural networks are sensitized and compromised. Once a neural network is sensitized, less stimulus strength is required to evoke dissociation. Schwarz and colleagues (1995a) used the term *trauma coded* (p. 13) to refer to the controlling effects of trauma on the lives of survivors. We may speak of startle affect as being trauma coded. Traumatizing events that followed the experience assembled with startle affect, events characterized by negative valence and uncontrollability, and startle affect did not get resolved. It remained in a state-specific excitatory form where it was more likely to be elicited by any subsequent stimulus than other more adaptive affects.

Although dissociation may be adaptive during the period of abuse in childhood, it is maladaptive later in life. When trauma is prolonged over months or years, dissociation may become an adaptive defense. Dissociation engendered by trauma coding of surprise–startle affect allows the child victim to survive the abuse. However, later in life, the adult child of trauma will often dissociate many affects out of awareness. As a result, affects, such as fear, shame, anger, or disgust operate from the unconscious where they motivate maladaptive behaviors. AMST can help the adult client for whom surprise–startle affect was trauma coded in childhood, whatever the original eliciting stimulus, by teaching the client to recognize startle affect by its associated physical sensations, to tolerate it, and to down-regulate it. When the client learns to manage startle affect, he or she can then recognize and learn to manage other affects that were formerly dissociated out of awareness.

Disorganized–disoriented attachment may predict susceptibility to dissociation (Dozier et al., 1999). Attachment strategies break down for babies who have been abused or whose caregivers have an unresolved adult attachment style. When the caregiver is frightening or frightened, disorganized–disoriented attachment in the infant results, characterized by multiple, incompatible IWMs. For example, if the caregiver expresses fright toward the infant, the infant develops a self-representation as the perpetrator of the fright, and a caregiver representation of the victim emerges. When the caregiver is no longer frightened, the infant's self-representation becomes "rescuer" and the caregiver becomes the "rescued victim." Should the caregiver now provide care, the infant self becomes the "loved child" and the parental IWM becomes "competent caregiver." These multiple models cannot be integrated. Under stress in the Strange Situation, this infant experiences a dilemma because she cannot approach the caregiver for relief or avoid the caregiver for distraction.

In longitudinal studies, disorganized–disoriented infant attachment was associated with elevated symptoms of dissociation in elementary and high school and with greater self-report of dissociation symptoms at age 19 (Dozier et al., 1999). The tripartite model predicts interaction of attachment and childhood socioemotional history, and Dozier and associates (1999) have suggested that disorganized–disoriented attachment may increase vulnerability to the effects of abuse, leading to dissociative disorder, because up to 97% of those with dissociative disorder report an abuse history. These authors also suggested that the stress produced by the AAI situation may induce dissociation in the cognitive dimension in those individuals demonstrating the lapses of coherence taxonomic for unresolved adult attachment states of mind. Surprise–startle has been considered a neutral affect (e.g., Nathanson, 1992) having little clinical relevance, but as we can see from this discussion regarding the role played by startle affect in the psychopathology of dissociation, surprise–startle can hardly be considered neutral.

THE PERSONALITY DISORDERS

Personalities consist of the affective, cognitive, and behavioral structure that evolves over an individual's developmental time span. Dynamic systems theory conceives of personality as a state space (Lewis, 2000). In this framework, personality development means "change and stabilization in the state space of cognition-emotion interactions" (p. 54). Personality, or a sense of self, is an "orderliness" (p. 57) in this state space that has built itself up over time around the self's emotionally valenced goals. A healthy personality manifests adaptive orderliness and multidimensional approaches to goal attainment. Maturity characterizes the goals of the healthy personality and includes intimacy, self-realization, and self-efficacy. In a disordered personality, the orderliness is maladaptive, and the self structure has become organized around defenses or behavioral management scripts for dealing with specific affects. The disordered personality system has extremely limited approaches for resolving emotionally valenced goals, and the goals are immature, reflecting the unresolved objectives of childhood; for example, parental attention and responsiveness, meeting emotional needs, protection, nurturing, and attunement.

Borderline personality disorder illustrates well how a personality system can organize itself around a specific emotionally valenced goal.

Borderline Personality Disorder (BPD)

From an affect perspective the borderline personality is organized by the emotionally valenced goal of maintaining proximity. The emotional valences are yearning, fear and anger. The borderline client yearns for proximity. The BPD client fears loss of proximity, which the *DSM-IV* conceptualizes as "frantic efforts to avoid real or imagined abandonment" (p. 650), and the borderline client uses anger as a defense against loss of proximity. I use the word *proximity* because it is the basis of attachment. The goal of attachment behavior is maintenance of proximity. Borderline pathology demonstrates how a personality can organize itself around deficits in attachment. The term *proximity* can refer to physical or emotional closeness. Proximity can also pertain to intrapsychic "closeness," in which case it refers to the borderline client's felt closeness of the self-representation to representations of others. In the borderline personality organization, self-representations are unstable and underdeveloped. IWMs for others are also unstable and alternate between idealized and devalued states. The self fears abandonment by the idealized other, because the self's unstable self-representation depends on the idealized other for its structural integrity. When the borderline experiences abandonment, either intrapsychically or physically, the system complains intensely in an attempt to regain the other's attention. The adult borderline client's anger may represent a carrying forward into adulthood of the normative anger that all infants express when the caregiver is unavailable (Weinfield et al., 1999). Adult anger expression may also constitute a defense against shame affect associated with thoughts of being unworthy of the caregiver's attention. Shame affect and cognitions of unworthiness may be assembled with a covert child ego state. The borderline's anger affect is volatile and easily elicited by hints of rejection or abandonment.

In borderline pathology the personality disorder emerges from unique interactions between the attachment component and childhood socioemotional history component of the tripartite model. An insecure attachment of the resistant type is associated with later expressed borderline pathology. In adulthood, borderline pathology associates with a preoccupied attachment (75% prevalence, Dozier et al., 1999), in which attachment needs are maximized. It helps clinicians to understand the fact that while the prevalence of borderline pathology in the general population is only 1%, 15% of outpatients and 50% of outpatients with a personality disorder qualify for borderline diagnosis. These data suggest that people with a borderline diagnosis seek to meet their attachment needs in therapy. Borderline clients report early experiences of neglect and of long separation from mothers. Childhood abuse is a common finding (81% prevalence; Dozier et al., 1999); borderline clients report experiencing or witnessing physical or sexual abuse. They have experienced trauma without caregiver support, and often the caregiver has been frightened or frightening. Borderline clients form IWMs of caregivers as incompetent and inconsistently available and of themselves as inconsistently valued, and these representations cannot be integrated. Dozier and associates (1999) have written "the combination of maximizing strategies and the experience of unresolved abuse appears central to the borderline personality disorder" (p. 511). Not surprisingly, there is a 50% comorbidity of affective disorders and borderline disorder.

The chronic vigilance associated with anxious–ambivalent attachment becomes the basis for the borderline personality structure, because the self structure is organized around the anxious–ambivalent (insecure–resistant) attachment. This explains the centrality of fear affect to the borderline pathology. When there is trauma as well as insecure–resistant attachment, borderline personality disorder may result. Chronic vigilance carried forward, plus the cognition and behavior of maintaining tension to assure some caregiver awareness of the infant's presence (the infant now grown up into a child, adolescent, or adult) is the basis for "drama" and the necessity of creating drama seen in BPD, in cases with borderline features, or with many alcoholics and addicts.

AMST holds the promise of helping the borderline client, but clinicians are cautioned not to expect the same rapid results that may be observed with some clinical disorders. The developmental pathway leading to BPD is believed to diverge during the hatching subphase of separation-individuation (Horner, 1984), and by the time the borderline client reaches therapy, a well-structured, albeit maladaptive, self structure has emerged that will resist change. AMST's containment skill (skill I) can help the borderline client who has been sexually or physically victimized. Skill II (safe place) can provide a missing inner image of safety and security. Therapy should target visualizations of situations, past or future, in which the borderline feared abandonment. The client should be helped to employ the safe place skill in these visualizations. When the client reports successful use of safe place, these successes should be reinforced and then associated with joy affect and pride. AMST skills III to VII can help by teaching the BPD client to recognize fear of abandonment, anger—whether defensive, unresolved archaic, or a combination of the two—and shame. The client can learn to tolerate these affects at low intensities and to down-regulate them. Employing visualizations of situations in which these affects are evoked, the client can install the AMST skills and strengthen her successes when she reports them.

Antisocial Personality Disorder (APD)

Lack of empathy is a prominent feature in antisocial personality disorder. The medical model inherent in the *DSM-IV* emphasizes the APD's aberrant behaviors of law breaking, deceitfulness, impulsivity, fighting, and financial irresponsibility. From a developmental perspective, empathy results from the affective attunement of a competent infant–caregiver dyad from which a secure attachment eventuates. Empathy entails affective coordination between the self and others, and it is the mirror image of aggression. The APD client demonstrates a consistent disregard for the feelings of others (Dozier et al., 1999). Behavioral socialization builds upon optimal disapproval–shame transactions during the late practicing period, and evidently the APD failed to receive these experiences. Emotion knowledge forms the basis of empathy (Izard, 1991), and the APD appears not to recognize specific emotions in others. All three factors of the tripartite model manifest in APD: Heritability is moderate to high in APD, and more so among APD males than females, indicating a significant genetic component. Perhaps the APD client has genetically determined high thresholds for shame, the preeminent socializing affect. APD clients endorse deficits in attachment, and 89% of them have experienced prolonged separations. Mothers are described as unaffectionate and failing to provide supervision. Fathers of APD clients are often deviant. Physical abuse is common. The state of mind of APD clients toward attachment-related issues may be described as extremely dismissive, with disparagement or derogation of attachment figures or experiences (Dozier et al., 1999). Anger is the primary emotion experienced by the APD client, apparently in a repressed state. Childhood experiences of prolonged separation, combined with frightening, threats, produce an intense hate in which anger is assembled with disgust (disgust and anger are neighbors in Plutchik's emotional pie chart; LeDoux, 1996). The APD avoids emotion and emotion laden experience, perhaps even dissociating emotion out of awareness. His hatred (anger + disgust) exists in an excitatory, state-specific form—his hatred is trauma coded—in which it is more likely to be elicited than some other affect. He has dissociated it from awareness, (i.e., repressed it), and his hatred will be the most probable emotion to assemble with cognitions to form the affective–cognitive structures motivating his behaviors.

An affect-oriented approach to treating APD is subject to the same caveats as treatment of BPD; treatment will be protracted. A complicating factor with APD is that many APD clients are incarcerated or otherwise embedded in social situations where antisocial behavior is protective of the self. The APD client will have significant disturbing archaic material that can be contained (skill I). His childhood may have been deficient in the empathic, attuned caregiving necessary to developing internal images of safety and security, and skill II (safe place) can remediate this deficit. Skills III to VII can help him to recognize, tolerate, and down-regulate anger and disgust affects. ACT can help him uncover and resolve memories of deficit experience as well as of adversity and trauma. When integrated with a concurrent program emphasizing social rehabilitation, an affect focused psychotherapy holds the promise of helping the APD client. Where there is the risk of physical harm to a spouse, as, for example, when APD and domestic violence are copresenting, the clinician must adhere to standard guidelines of best practice. In these cases, AMST and ACT can supplement behavioral modification interventions enforced by threat of incarceration for any infraction.

Other Personality Disorders

From an affect-focused perspective, the other personality disorders can be discriminated by the dysregulated emotion central to each disorder. From a developmental and dynamic systems perspective, each personality disorder represents a type of personality structure that emerged over time and was conditioned by the emotionally valenced, unmet needs of infancy and childhood. Fear appears to be the central organizing affect in paranoid personality disorder, in which behaviors and cognitions are motivated by fear that others are plotting against the self. The schizoid and schizotypal personality is also fear-based, being organized around behaviors, thoughts, and perceptions motivated by fear, usually of close relationships. Fear of being out of control dominates in obsessive–compulsive personality disorder, in which the pathognomic obsessive behaviors decrease the client's fear of loss of control, becoming the organizing principle of the individual's self structure. Difficulties with shame and grandiosity define narcissistic personality disorder, and feelings of inadequacy plague the person with avoidant personality disorder. Neediness is the defining emotional characteristic of dependent personality disorder. AMST can help in each of these disorders by providing the tools to recognize, tolerate, and regulate the range of affects as well as the central affect at play.

SUMMARY

The first three chapters laid a developmental, epistemological, and psychoneurobiological basis for the present chapter in which some of the clinical and personality disorders have been reconfigured from an affect-focused point of view. I have demonstrated the primacy of emotion dysregulation in a range of psychopathologies. The human infant is fundamentally an affective organism. Early experience consists of affective transactions in the infant–caregiver dyad, and out of these transactions, the personality structure self-organizes. When those transactions are relatively benign, when the caregivers are supportive, attuned, sensitive, and responsive, then competent affect regulation and a healthy, adaptive self-structure ensue. When there is deficit experience, when caregivers are unsupportive, unavailable, distracted, insensitive, misattuned, and unresponsive, then affect dysregulation eventuates, increasing the probability of emergence of a maladaptive self-structure. When adverse or traumatic experience intrudes, especially when there is preexisting affect dysregulation, the affective load increases, and the likelihood of disorganized self structure of a more malignant type further increases.

ACT begins by remediating the client's deficits of affect regulation. This is justified by the developmental construct that emphasizes that the client's current problems originated with deficiencies in the attachment that resulted in affect and emotion dysregulation in childhood. The straightforward expedient of teaching affect management skills to clients presenting with clinical and personality disorders discussed above can ease their distress. The AMST can provide the client with the tools to manage overwhelming emotion that would otherwise derail treatment for trauma or adversity in ensuing stages of therapy. Conjointly, the experience of affective attunement, sensitivity, and responsiveness in the therapeutic client–therapist dyad can remediate the effects of deficits carried forward from the client's infant–caregiver dyad. As the therapist transmits the AMST skills in the context of the therapeutic dyad, the client reconfigures the internal self- and other representations and the relationships between them, and as a result the self structure begins to reorganize toward more positive, adaptive functioning. As has been emphasized, the self-organization of personality is largely conditioned by affective forces. Teaching the AMST skill set provides the self with the tools to manage these affective forces and thereby establish the organizational foundation for restructuring the self. Learning AMST skills builds mastery and confidence in the client that he or she can manage both positive and negative affects that were previously overwhelming. Establishing this basis is a prerequisite for the deeper therapeutic work to follow in the treatment plan.

Part II

AFFECT MANAGEMENT SKILLS TRAINING

Chapter **5**

AMST Foundations: Therapeutic Goals, Theoretical and Technical Frameworks

Chapter 5 builds on the models for healthy and maladaptive development presented in Part I. This chapter will orient the clinician to the hallmarks of affect dysregulation and insecure attachment related states of mind as they present in therapy. A brief overview of the entire affect management skills training (AMST) protocol will then be offered to contextualize the theoretical justification for why AMST benefits the client and how it does so. After discussing the practical value of AMST and the importance of the therapeutic dyad, the chapter will communicate the elements necessary for client preparation and to conduct an AMST intervention.

HALLMARKS OF AFFECT DYSREGULATION AND INSECURE ATTACHMENT

Affect and emotion regulation are central factors that determine how positively and how adaptively an individual functions. What makes a client a client is affect dysregulation. Whether the presenting problem is behavioral, work related, marriage related, substance related, or mood related, fundamentally it is a problem of maladaptive affect regulation. As the tripartite model suggests, today's child, adolescent, or adult client is a product of childhood deficit experience, adverse childhood socioemotional experience, and genetics. Emotion dysregulation results in part from childhood deficit experience associated with varying levels of attachment disordering. Children with insecure attachment histories have suppressed (avoidant) or defensively modified (resistant) emotion responses, and these modified emotion responses are not available to consciousness. As adults, their affect regulation is nonconscious or unconscious and must be raised to consciousness where it can be operated on consciously and subjected to change. Because affective signals are not cognized, adult children of insecure attachment will not know how to signal a need for support when they are distressed. They may become "stuck" in negative emotion leading to maladaptive functioning. Trapped in negative emotion, the person develops negative self-attributions that further the downward spiral. Moreover, the negative emotion trap stymies the individual's efforts to get support from social relationships.

Emotion dysregulation also arises from childhood adversity or trauma, often compounded by the effects of deficit experience. Adversity and trauma elicit levels of emotion that the system cannot process adaptively (Shapiro, 1995). These trauma coded or adversity coded emotions will be held in a state-specific, excitatory form where they are more likely to be elicited than other emotions. These archaic, trauma coded emotions are usually not appropriate in current interpersonal or social contexts and thus they interfere with adaptive functioning.

Recognizing Affect Dysregulation

Affect dysregulation occurs in a range of presentations. It will be helpful as a starting point to describe some of the clinical hallmarks of emotion dysregulation. Leeds (1997) has listed some of the characteristics of affect dysregulation the clinician may observe in the client in the initial phases of therapy for complex posttraumatic stress disorder (PTSD). The client may be flooded with affects, often fear or anguish, but these as well may include shame, disgust, anger, self-loathing, or unworthiness. Flooding will be an unmistakable indication of affect dysregulation, manifesting in tears, cowering behavior, or verbal distress. Flooding may occur in PTSD as well as in any of the personality disorders, substance abuse disorders, or other Axis I or II disorders.

Alternatively, the affect dysregulated client may shut down, tightly controlling all affective display. The clinician will need to carefully observe body language, eye contact, and verbal cues to recognize the nature of this client's dysregulation patterns. Some clients have developed a false self identity that is essentially devoid of affect and designed to please others in social situations. This identity functions to prevent the client from experiencing affects that seethe in the unconscious. The absence of appropriate affective display will suggest the presence of such a protective ego state.

Often, the affect dysregulated client is alexithymic and cannot name or describe the emotions and associated qualia she is feeling. The client may be dysthymic, reporting as well as appearing in session with persistent depressed mood and low self-esteem.

Behaviorally, affect dysregulated clients often avoid dealing with significant areas of concern; for example, an abusive marriage, work problems, substance abuse, or difficulties with children. Verbal reports of affect dysregulated clients may lack coherence, especially when concerning stressful interactions with family members. Emotional flooding or shutting down may be associated with such fragmented, incoherent accounts. These clients may be unable to coherently report the week's events.

Substance abuse problems, whether the abused substance is legal (e.g., alcohol, nicotine, prescription medications), or illegal (e.g., cocaine, heroin, marijuana), are presumed to indicate affect dysregulation. These clients employ the abused sub-stance to manage vicariously an affect that would otherwise overwhelm them. Eat-ing disorders, whether bulimia nervosa, anorexia nervosa, or binge eating disorder, also indicate problems with affect regulation. The eating disordered client appar-ently uses food to vicariously manage distressing affects. Process addictions, such as, gambling, sexual addictions, or Internet addictions, also indicate affect dysregu-lation. Self-injurious behavior (e.g., cutting or burning) signals that a client experi-ences overwhelming emotion she is unable to regulate in any other way.

In my clinical experience, the affect dysregulated client will resist self-attributions of worthiness, and the intensity of the resistance will directly correlate with the severity of the client's deficit or traumatic experience. Often, requests for a verbalization of self-worth can result in decompensation, and the clinician must be alert to this possibility.

All of these presenting behaviors should inform the clinician that the client is unable to regulate affect adaptively. As we have learned from the tripartite model, the client may lack the resources to regulate affects because the skills to do so were never transmitted (deficit experience), or the client may have experienced adversity that trauma coded emotions, or what is more likely, a combination of deficit and adverse experience.

Skills Necessary for Adaptive Emotion Regulation

Leeds (1997) called attention to skills that clients often do not possess. Lack of these skills contributes to the client's distress. Their absence also denotes the deficits of self structure that entail maladaptive functioning. These skills were not transmitted to the client in childhood, and they must be in place prior to trauma processing or deeper therapy. AMST transmits these skills to the client.

The client needs the perceptual skills to make and report accurate observations of the environment and the self that are free of self-criticism. It is important that the client be able to observe and report her own emotion states without becoming overwhelmed or stressed. The client needs to be able to trust his own emotions and perceptions as the basis for making decisions, setting limits, and coping with oth-ers. Clients also need affect modulation and self-soothing skills, according to Leeds, among which are grounding images and inner images of safety. Finally, clinicians must help the client develop autonomy, which amounts to a set of skills necessary to assure certain basic personal rights; for example, the right to be free of harm and threat, the right to set clear personal boundaries, and the ability to evaluate dis-crepancies between the other's behavior and what he or she has to say.

Recognizing Attachment Related States of Mind

During the initial interview with a client and while taking a history, the clinician should be attuned to the level of coherence and the extent of collaboration with the clinician that the client demonstrates. The ability to present past experiences in a coherent and collaborative fashion is a significant and compelling aspect of adult security (Hesse, 1999). Infant security apparently predicts this component of adult security. A coherent interview is believable and true to the listener. When coherently presented, events and affects intrinsic to early relationships are conveyed without distortion, contradiction, or derailment of discourse. The speaker collaborates with the interviewer, clarifying meaning and using active listening skills to assure he is understood. The interview is a sort of goal-corrected partnership in which the plans of the speaker are integrated with the communication plans of the listener; the speaker is able to integrate his own needs for emotional or verbal proximity with the listener's needs, and for both to reach a common goal or state of mutuality. Slade (1999) described this property as "coherence."

Furthermore, the clinician will want to note carefully the extent to which the client either excludes affect and restricts verbalizations regarding significant relationships from childhood (parents or other caregivers) or dwells obsessively on them. Affect avoidance indicates a dismissive attachment related state of mind and suggests the client may have problems regulating a number of affects, in particular anger. Obsessive focus on attachment related affects, stories, and memories suggests a preoccupied attachment status, and indicates the client may have difficulty regulating anxiety.

OVERVIEW OF AMST

AMST is a brief therapeutic intervention that immediately transmits affect regulation skills to the client. It can quickly assist the client to more adaptive functioning in both the short and long term, because it is designed to remediate deficits in affect regulation that are the basis of client psychopathology and maladaptation. In my own practice, I teach the AMST set to every client so as to establish a baseline of adaptive emotion functioning. Each clinician will integrate the AMST into his or her own established method of practice. AMST consists of seven fundamental and several ancillary procedures. Teaching the skills to a client is an active, collaborative process referred to as *installation*. Tactile alternating bilateral stimulation (TABS) facilitates each component of the installation process: eliciting sensations accompaninge affects, development of resources and regulatory images, development of cognitions and appraisals, and using images to increase or decrease levels of affective arousal. The protocol provides a means for assessing the success of client skills acquisition. The protocol is also designed to uncover missing resources or covert ego states that may impede successful installation of skills. When this is encountered, AMST provides interventions for developing missing resources—for example, the quality of trust is a resource that is often missing in adults who as children had deficit or adverse experiences—and for uncovering and renegotiating relationships with protective ego states whose helper function is no longer adaptive.

To facilitate a discussion of the theoretical and technical context for the AMST protocol, I will briefly sketch the seven basic skills here. Each of these skills will be presented in detail subsequently along with illustrative material. Chapter 11 presents advanced skills that augment the basic protocol. The AMST Flow Chart and Decision Tree, which may be found in Appendix B, presents the entire protocol in diagrammatic form.

Skill I: Containment

The containment skill transmits the ability to confine disturbing material by teaching the client to employ an "image of a container sufficient to hold every disturbing thing." This skill frees the client from intrusive thoughts and memories and assembled affects that would otherwise disrupt acquisition of subsequent skills. The skill conveys an immediate sense of relief, because with the disturbing material contained, the client no longer experiences fear, shame, disgust, or other affects relating to the material. A sense of mastery accompanies the feeling of relief, because the client now has choice about when to remove disturbing material for processing in therapy. The client can use this skill to containerize disturbing material that might arise between sessions, that might surface in response to daily events, or that might threaten to overwhelm the client during session.

Skill II: Safe Place

The safe place develops an internal image of safety and security in multiple perceptual modes (visual, auditory, olfactory, and tactile). Skill II expands an eight-step safe place exercise described by Shapiro (1995). The skill assembles the image of the safe place with a cognition ("I am safe"), an emotion ("I feel safe"), and the sensations that accompany the knowledge of safety and the feeling of safety. Clients will use this skill to self-soothe in stressful situations during daily life or during sessions when processing disturbing material.

The containment skill and safe place skill position the client to begin the next phase of AMST in which skills for regulating specific affects are transmitted. In preparation for skills III to VII, the client is helped to select a target affect that will be the focus of AMST. The first target affect is usually fear, and the client learns AMST skills for recognizing, tolerating, noticing, and regulating fear affect at a low level of intensity. Subsequently, clients learn to use the same skills for several other target affects such as anger, shame, sadness, joy, or excitement. The client is asked to describe a memory of a time when he felt the target affect at an agreed upon, manageable level of intensity. This memory constitutes the target scene. At this time, the client is taught the subjective units of disturbance (SUD) scale (Shapiro, 1995), which extends from zero, meaning benign or neutral, to 10, "the other end of the scale." SUD is a self-report rating scale clients will use to assess for themselves, and for the therapist the intensity, distress, or arousal level of emotion associated with a remembered event or a current experience. The client is asked to retrieve a memory of a time she felt the target affect at a level of 3 or 4. Target affect, target scene, and selection of SUD transmit mastery to the client, because she learns she can single out one emotion from many to focus on, and she can pick a level of intensity for that emotion. The remaining skills are modular in that they can be applied to any target affect, target scene, and SUD.

Skill III: Sensation–Affect Identification

The third skill assists the client in uncovering and naming the physical sensations (qualia) that tell the client he or she is experiencing the index emotion. For example, a client may report fluttering sensations in her stomach as she visualizes the target scene for the target affect fear. In this case, she will be asked to repeat the cognition, "The fluttering in my stomach tells me I am feeling fear."

In preparation for the fourth and fifth skills, the client is now helped to develop a grounding image, which is a representation of connection, usually to earth, that allows the client to stay grounded and present while experiencing the target affect. Common grounding images include a grounding cord, magnetic boots, grounding roots. The client is assisted to identify sensations that accompany the experience of being grounded and present.

Skill IV: Sensation as Signal

Skill IV links deployment of the grounding image to the sensations that identify the target affect. In this way the client's employment of the grounding image becomes sensation dependent rather than volition dependent.

Skill V: Grounded and Present

The fifth skill assembles the grounding image with the target scene and transmits the ability to remain grounded and present while experiencing the target affect. This is the skill that allows the client to tolerate moderately distressing levels of affect. This skill intervenes in behaviors that previously were acted out and allows the client to control his or her impulses.

Skill VI: Noticing

Erected on the foundation of previously established skills, skill VI builds awareness of thoughts, sensations, images, memories, and affects accompanying the target affect and the target scene. With the grounding image in place, clients can "just notice" the thoughts, memories, and affects assembled with the target scene. Previously, the client was unable to observe these assembled thoughts and memories, because they would trigger a cascade of emotion that would flood the client. This skill promotes development of the witnessing self, which is also known as "hypnotic duality."

Skill VII: Regulating

Skill VII teaches the client to down-regulate distressing affect using the disposal resource, an image conveying the idea of reduction of intensity. The disposal resource may be represented by a sink disposal unit, a garbage disposal, a black hole, or a bottomless pit. The client is taught to use the disposal resource to decrease the level of a negative affect. Skill VII also provides for up-regulation of positive affect using the image of the gauge resource.

With this brief summary of the basic AMST skills in place, we can look at how the protocol benefits the client by transmitting the ability to regulate affect at the same time as it builds the client's self structure.

IMPROVED AFFECT REGULATION
IS A THERAPEUTIC GOAL
. . . .

AMST furthers a key therapeutic goal of assisting the client to achieve a better organized, optimally affect regulating self. Skill I (containment) assists the client to compartmentalize disturbing archaic material that previously had free access and ability to influence current thinking and feeling. Watkins and Watkins (1997) described Federn's concept, enunciated in 1952, of the cycle between ego cathexis and object cathexis of an abusive introjected figure. The containment skill can break that cycle by allowing the client to encapsulate the disturbing memories of acts perpetrated by the abusive figure, thereby preventing them from influencing current functioning. When disturbing memories are placed in containment, they are no longer able to elicit distressing emotion, and the cause of the client's flooding is abated. Containment also facilitates the client's development of a capacity for goal-corrected partnerships. Many clients did not develop the goal-corrected partnership as a result of childhood deficit experience, and consequently, in relationships they are not able to set aside their own emotional needs temporarily in the service of a mutually shared objective. The container can function for the client in daily life—quite apart from its utility in therapy—as a "temporary storage," a means to put her concerns and thoughts "on hold" while pursuing a shared goal; for example, a relationship, a work on social situation or child raising.

Skill II (safe place) conveys to the client an inner image of safety and security, one of the resources Leeds (1997) has stated as being important to adaptive functioning. Shapiro (1995) introduced the idea of the safe place resource, and AMST expands on her conception by assembling the image of a safe place with cognition ("I am safe"), affect ("I feel safe"), and sensations that accompany the affect of safety. In AMST, the containment skill precedes the safe place skill, because clinically clients were unable to develop certainty about knowing or feeling safe until "every disturbing thing" had been contained.

AMST promotes the therapeutic goal of optimal affect regulation by teaching the client to recognize and name a range of both positive and negative core affects. Many clients confuse emotions, fail to discriminate one from another, or simply do not recognize or cannot name what emotion they are feeling. Drawing on affect theory, AMST improves the client's ability to discriminate affects one from another using the target affect modality. The client learns that he can focus on anger affect, for example, and distinguish it from shame affect, which previously may have been inextricably and unconsciously intertwined for him. Skill III (affect-sensation identification) teaches the client to recognize emotions by the physical sensations that accompany each one. The client learns that she experiences disgust differently from the way she feels shame.

The grounding resource transmits to the client the ability to tolerate a range of affects. Once the client has learned the skills to manage a target affect at a low intensity (SUD = 3), the client is asked to visualize a time he felt the same target affect at a higher intensity (e.g., SUD = 6), and then he is helped by the therapist to employ the same AMST set to manage this emotion at the increased potency. In this way the protocol teaches the client to regulate a range of intensities of emotions. With the grounding skill in place, the client can move in therapy to processing past adverse or traumatic experiences, because he now has the capacity to stay grounded and present while recalling prior affective experience or while experiencing distressing levels of affect in real time.

Once the client has acquired the AMST procedures, she will be better able to provide coherent reports of life events in terms of affective experience. After teaching the skills, the clinician will regularly return to them as she helps her client process the vicissitudes of his daily life. For example, the clinician may ask, "How did your meeting with your father go this week?" and as the client begins his report, she can remind him of his skills ("Put your grounding cord down") and help him to recognize his emotions ("What emotion is your jaw telling you you're experiencing?"). After several passes through the report, the client will be able to deliver a coherent verbal report with optimal affective content. Learning to provide a coherent report of life events contributes to creating "earned secure" attachment in clients who may have previously been dismissive or preoccupied.

Skill VI (noticing) creates an observing self that enables the client to witness the self either having or remembering disturbing events. Before development of the noticing skill, the client's emotions often had control of the client, and as quickly as the client experienced the distressing emotion, defensive behaviors such as acting out, drug use, eating, bingeing, binge-purge, or sexual or other process addiction were activated. With the skill set in place, the client has control over her emotions rather than being at their mercy, and she can observe herself experiencing them. This development represents a significant increase in structuralization of the self and contributes substantially to the client's optimal functioning.

Many clients are unable to regulate the intensity of experienced emotion. They do not possess the skills to increase their levels of comfortable affect or decrease their levels of distressing affect. They do not perceive themselves as having control over the strength of emotion experience and feel powerless to regulate it. The regulating skill (skill VII) teaches the client the ability to up-regulate positive emotion through the gauge resource and down-regulate negative emotion by means of the disposal resource. Clinicians can facilitate the client's optimal functioning by helping her to employ these affect regulation skills in the context of future templates (Shapiro, 1995). The future template is a prospective form of target scene. For example, the shy client who is considering accepting an offer of a dinner date might be asked, "As you visualize yourself accepting this date, what emotions come up for you?" The clinician can help the client employ AMST to down-regulate her shyness affect and to increase her experience of excitement affect.

AMST contributes to optimal client functioning by transmitting the ability to use affective experience as a basis for making decisions that promote safety. Many clients who have experienced childhood trauma or adversity are disconnected from the qualia of emotions and rely on cognitions as the basis for decision making. These clients are out of touch with the sensations and emotions that should be telling them when they are in danger. Their cognitions, which are themselves conditioned by their prior adverse or traumatic experience, often lead them into dangerous situations (trauma reenactment). By teaching the client to recognize emotions by their qualia, the client learns to use sensations and emotions as the basis for assessing whether a prospective experience is safe or dangerous. In this same regard, as the client learns to identify, tolerate, and regulate his own emotions, he develops the ability to identify and empathically experience feelings in others. This ability improves client functioning, especially in relationships and social situations.

Several other examples of how the protocol improves client functioning will be discussed in the chapters devoted to the specific skills. We turn our attention now to how AMST contributes to enlarging and amplifying the client's self structure.

INCREASED SELF-STRUCTURE
IS A THERAPEUTIC GOAL

The process of learning affect regulation through AMST in and of itself facilitates the emergence of a more adaptive personality structure in the client. According to the developmental model that informs the protocol, clients' disorders of self structure emerge in part because their childhood experience was characterized by deficits in the attachment that left them with inadequate or maladaptive emotion regulation skills. Deficits in emotion regulation indicate suboptimal self-structuring. In learning the skill set, the client is continually asked to combine memories or images with affects and then to assemble this combination with a cognition. For example, as the client completes skill VII and successfully down-regulates the target affect fear, the client is asked to repeat the words, "I am learning to decrease my fear." Then, after reviewing the client's work with the entire skill set, the whole AMST process is next made the subject of a metacognition when the client is asked to repeat the phrase, "I am learning to manage my fear." Once the client has acquired the complete skill set for several emotions, he is asked to verbalize a more encompassing metacognition, "I am learning to manage my emotions." Each recursion through the skill set with the addition of new cognitions and metacognitions contributes to building self structure, to elaborating the self. Furthermore, as new self structure is being created, the client's consciousness grows. This is embodied in even more comprehensive cognitions such as, "I am growing as a person." Psychologist Greg Mogenson (1989) explained building self structure as follows: "Psychologically speaking, what we see and declare one moment may be re-valued and re-visioned the next, as the subjective standpoint backing our perception becomes as well the object of reflection" (p. 5). AMST promotes the expansion of subjective standpoints in an iterative process as each new standpoint becomes the object of a new reflective observation.

AMST can remediate the deleterious effects of trauma and adversity on development of self-structure, just as it can remediate the effects of deficit experience. Where there is trauma or adversity in the history, the development of self-structure is often derailed or delayed. Teaching the client the skill set transmits to the client's self-system the assurance that the client possesses adequate skills to manage the powerful emotions assembled with the traumatic material, thus facilitating the system's ability to process that material. Furthermore, building a competent self structure with AMST creates a sufficiently adequate foundation—where previously one did not exist—within which the client can then incorporate the traumatic material as it is processed in therapy.

An example may be helpful. When the client was sexually abused in childhood, often the self structure does not develop coherently beyond the time in childhood when the trauma occurred. Instead, fragments emerge that are tasked with managing specific types of transactions with the environment. Sometimes a false self identity is created to handle transactions between self and the social environment, and as it elaborates over time, this self can appear mature and adequately functional. However, the core personality may be stuck in childhood thinking and may be incapable of assigning responsibility for the trauma or of processing guilt or shame assembled with it. Teaching AMST can build sufficient self-structure so that later, in processing the trauma, the client—both the child ego state and the adult client—can create appropriate verbalizations: for example, "He [the perpetrator] was responsible. He did it because he was a child molester. I thought he was a good man, but he was not, he hurt me." The false self identity can appear in many forms across populations; for example, placater, oppositional defiant self, businessperson, criminal, homemaker. The tip-off to the false self identity is always the degree to which, when it is the executive ego state, it is restricted in its connection to emotional experience.

The importance of installing the AMST skill set prior to attempting abreactive work deserves further emphasis. Paulsen (1995) distinguished crisis intervention, which is a stabilizing therapeutic intervention, from uncovering work, which is destabilizing. In this context, the protocol functions as crisis intervention in Paulsen's terms. The skill set creates the stability, which translates into adequate self structure, necessary for the client to proceed to and tolerate the destabilizing uncovering work. A fundamental principle of affect-focused psychotherapy states that clients lack and therefore must be provided with basic emotion regulation skills as a precondition for trauma processing. The traumatized system will protect itself, no matter how maladaptive that system's defenses may look to society, to outsiders, or to the therapist. Until the system is given alternative skills, it will resist change. Much of this resistance will be managed by the unconscious, which will recruit the verbal defenses (denial, justification, etc.) of the left brain to support itself. It is the therapist's role and ethical responsibility to provide the system with the missing skills. That is the job of therapy. The client's self system does not possess the requisite skills because through childhood deficit and adverse experience, the skills were not transmitted to the system.

A number of therapies (resource development and installation, Korn & Leeds, 2002; developmental needs meeting strategies, Schmidt, 2002; EMDR, Shapiro, 1995, 2001; imaginal nurturing, Steele, 2001) predicate themselves on a belief that the system has innate abilities to generate internal images of safety and security that can be mobilized in the service of emotion management. The empirically validated theory upon which AMST is founded questions whether this belief is valid across the range of psychopathologies and levels of severity.

Genetic evidence suggests that in fact all clients do not have equal innate abilities to regulate fear affect (Hariri et al., 2002), distress affect (Zubieta et al., 2003), or anger affect (Rujescu et al., 2002). In addition, all clients may not have equal innate abilities to adaptively process trauma (Caspi et al., 2002). Furthermore, since the expression of genetically determined potentials depends upon the quality of the infant–caregiver dyad during attachment (Schore, 1994), children of deficit experience and children of traumatic experience may often fail to develop the capacities required by some therapies to generate resources supportive of self. Empirical evidence supports the conclusion that, for example, the disorganized–disoriented child will be more likely to grow up to become a parent whose parenting style produces a disorganized–disoriented attachment in her own child (Weinfield et al., 1999). A parent's attachment related behavior toward his or her own child appears to measure the quality of that individual's capacity to produce resources for self-support and self-soothing.

Where EMDR has had its greatest successes is in just those cases where an adequate self-structure accompanied by adequate capacity for emotion regulation existed prior to the experience of trauma (e.g., single-incident, adult rape of a person with a well-organized self, or combat trauma where the individual was well structured prior to the traumatic events). EMDR's failures apparently occur where the system does not possess sufficient structure and emotion regulation capability to enable resolution of the adult onset trauma; or in the personality disorders where the self organized very early in development to manage experiences and emotions assembled with them relating to loss or acute trauma. AMST is configured to remediate early occurring deficits by supplying missing resources that the system does not possess at the onset of therapy.

HOW AMST WORKS

In this section we will examine the components of AMST in an attempt to convey what makes it such an effective, efficient, and powerful therapeutic intervention. It must be emphasized that AMST is a multimodal intervention that depends for its effectiveness on all of its components acting in concert.

AMST Interweaves Multiple Modes of Experiencing

Humans experience the world through the modalities of behavior, affect, sensation, cognition, image, and temporality. Braun (1988a, 1988b) conceptualized this concept in the behavior, affect, sensation, and knowledge model (BASK). Levine (cited in Rothschild, 2000) has developed the sensation, image, behavior, affect, and meaning (SIBAM) model to conceptualize the elements of experience. Both of these models were initially developed as tools for understanding dissociation. I will add two elements, *perception* and *memory*, to the models. The models can structure our thinking about how affect is integrated into a framework that includes other elements of overall experiencing. Learning and change is most effective when these elements are all addressed. The safe place skill (skill II) provides a good example. The client is facilitated in creating an image of a place where she knows she was safe. Sometimes clients are fortunate and can remember an actual place of certain safety; other times the client must be facilitated in creating an image de novo. The image, which may be retrieved in whole or part from memory, serves as an anchor with which perceptual elements are assembled as the client is asked to notice what she is seeing, hearing, smelling, and sensing through her skin as she holds the image of the safe place. Next, the cognitive element is assembled, as the clinician asks the client to verbalize "I am safe." A further cognitive element, an appraisal, is added when the clinician asks the client to assess how true the statement "I am safe" is on a 7-point scale. Next affect is assembled with the growing structure, as the clinician asks the client to verbalize "I feel safe." Again, an appraisal, a cognitive element, is elicited of how valid the statement "I feel safe" is. Finally, sensation is elicited and assembled with the package when the clinician asks the client to become aware of sensations she experiences in her body as she holds the image of the safe place, the perceptions, the knowledge of safety, and the feeling of safety. AMST is unique in that it employs tactile alternating bilateral stimulation (TABS) to accomplish an interweaving of these experiential elements. A subsequent section will offer an hypothesis about how TABS operates to facilitate assembly of these experiential elements into a coherent structure.

Visual Imagery and the AMST

Several of the protocol skills require the patient to produce visual images which are then used to manage affects. Clinicians may question whether material retrieved from memory or self-generated images has the same power as life experience. While by no means complete, research does support the belief that the pathways activated by AMST are the same pathways operating in daily life. It is important to understand that the connection between AMST emotion processing and "actual life" emotion processing is not spurious.

Izard, a pioneer in the empirical study of emotion experience has demonstrated that the emotions generated by recollection of an event are identical to emotions elicited by an actual event (Izard, 1991). Izard and his associates developed two scales: the Differential Emotions Scale (DES), which assesses 10 affects in all, requires the participant to visualize (recall) a situation or event in which a particular emotion was strongly experienced (Izard, 1991). In the DES, three affect-specific descriptors are given for each emotion and are rated for intensity on a 5-point Likert scale. For example, the three descriptors for interest–excitement affect are *attentive, concentrating,* and *alert.*" The instrument also reveals which affects are associated with the index affect. It demonstrates that when an individual visualizes a target emotion, a pattern of emotions emerges.

Izard and his coworkers also developed the Dimensional Rating Scale (DRS) for the affects (Izard, 1991). This scale measures participants' subjective experience of emotions using three dimensions of functioning: feeling, cognition, and behavior. Feeling reflects the sensations and bodily cues, such as heart rate, breathing, and muscle tension. Instructions to participants defined the behavior component of each emotion in terms of facial and postural expression. Cognitive appraisal of the emotion situation was assessed on the thought-level subscale. Each subscale was provided with a 3-point Likert response opportunity. From this study, Izard and coworkers selected four dimensions that represented most of the information provided: pleasantness, tension, impulsiveness, and self-assurance.

For our purposes, these studies are extremely valuable, because they demonstrate that when asked to visualize a situation in which the target emotion was felt, persons are able to do so. The fact that physiological markers associated with the target emotion when it is being experienced in real time are also elicited when persons are instructed to recall a situation in which they have experienced the target emotion, suggests that the visualization experience recreates an actual experience. This research gives the clinician confidence in working with AMST, because it demonstrates that the recalled emotions associated with the target scene are probably identical to the same emotions experienced in real life situations.

Evidence at the neurophysiological level also suggests that recalled emotion experience is identical to real-time emotion experience. Direct recordings from single cells in the temporal lobe (hippocampus, amygdala, entorhinal cortex) demonstrated that firing in these affect processing regions of the brain correlated with volitional visual imagery (Kreiman, Koch, & Fried, 2000a, 2000b). Furthermore, both incoming visual stimuli and recollected visual images appeared to be processed by the same pathways.

Cognizing Emotion

The AMST skill set develops the client's conscious awareness of his emotion experience. When a client becomes consciously aware of an emotion, he cognizes that emotion. The protocol helps the client to cognize emotion by directing her consciousness to the sensations accompanying affective experience. Many persons may know when they are feeling an intense level of an emotion, because the physiological response is overpowering. However, mild or moderate emotion often manifests in physiological responses that may be below the level of conscious awareness. AMST is designed in part to raise these less compelling signals to awareness.

Some clients may have been socialized out of awareness of their own affective experience. For example, a parent may have responded to a child's legitimate expression of anger with intense anger affect, punishing the child for anger expression, and thus inducing fear in the child. For this child, the felt experience of anger becomes assembled with fear affect, and anger may be dissociated out of awareness. As a result, this child, now become an adult, cannot mobilize healthy aggression (assertiveness) in the service of the self. Awareness of anger can also be socialized out of awareness by a parent's broadcast disgust affect. For this child, and for the adult he becomes, the experience of anger is assembled with disgust and dissociated out of awareness. Anger assembled with fear and anger assembled with disgust appear to be common findings in depression. Depression may result from the constant expenditure of energy over time to keep anger out of awareness. AMST can help these clients connect with the sensations and the affect of anger.

A Neurobiological Context

The science of neurobiology has advanced to the point where we may adduce a neurophysiological context for the AMST protocol which utilizes the same principles employed by the emotion system in healthy development to remediate the effects of maladaptive development. In healthy development, images and sensations formed over time are the means the system uses to regulate emotion. More specifically, over developmental time children assemble internal working models (IWMs) of mother and father, that is, images of the parents assembled with emotive and cognitive components, which the child and later the adult unconsciously employs for the purposes of emotion regulation. These emotion regulating IWMs are complex assemblies created over time through serial accretion of experience that consists of images, affects, sensations, and cognitions. These complex assemblies facilitate the same skills taught by AMST. When these skills are absent or are present in incomplete or damaged form, emotion dysregulation ensues. The skill set remediates a damaged or incomplete affect regulation system through a directed, planned, and programmed process that supplies images that were not provided to the system in early life.

AMST can ameliorate the innate vulnerability of the human mind to poor impulse control. The nature of the architecture of the human brain makes cognitive control of emotion-driven behavior intrinsically difficult. LeDoux (1996) noted that "conscious control over emotions is weak" (p. 19). The neuronal connections forward from the emotion systems to the cognitive systems are much more robust than linkages in the opposite direction, from neocortical regions backwards to limbic emotion generating and regulating areas. Two lines of evidence suggest how the protocol, by creating new associations of affect-sensation and cognition, can improve conscious control of emotion and emotion-driven behavior. The first line of evidence comes from LeDoux's work on auditory conditioning.

LeDoux (1996) has described how two pathways operate in auditory fear conditioning. The so-called low road pathway does not involve the brain's cortical regions. In the low road, acoustic signals received by the ear are transmitted to the auditory thalamus and from there proceed directly to the amygdala, which directly triggers the emotion response systems. The high road pathway involves the cortex. The high road runs from the ear to the auditory thalamus and then to the auditory cortex. Neurons connect the auditory cortex to the amygdala, which is connected to the emotion response systems. The low road pathway comprises broadly tuned neurons leaving the auditory thalamus, while the high road makes use of more finely tuned neurons. A conditioning experiment with laboratory rabbits illustrates the two systems. Rabbits were able to learn a conditioned response to one tone that had been paired with shock, discriminating it from a second tone that had not been shock associated. Researchers demonstrated that the auditory cortex (the high road) was required for this conditioning to occur, because if the auditory cortex was lesioned, the rabbits showed a fear response to both tones. LeDoux (1996) commented that, "the cortex's job is to prevent the inappropriate response rather than to produce the appropriate one" (p. 165). Activity in the auditory cortex, which was involved in the conditioned learning, can suppress amygdalar discharges and prevent it from triggering the emotion response systems. Our understanding of these pathways provides a paradigm that we can use as a basis for thinking about how AMST might work.

The client driven by fear affect may be thought of as using the low road, the direct pathway that circumvents cortical control. This client's fear responses may be triggered perceptually through sight or sound, or they may be triggered intrapsychically by a memory or by an IWM of a rageful parent, for example. Goleman (1995) called this emotional hijacking. Experience of the stimulus, whether arising internally or externally, triggers the thalamus, which then activates the amygdala and elicits the fear response. AMST can help the fear driven client by developing a new high road pathway that recruits the cortex to prevent the inappropriate response. The protocol accomplishes this by uniting images and sensation-affect structures with cognitions. In skill III (sensation-affect identification), the client learns to recognize the qualia accompanying a low level of fear. This is analogous to the experimental rabbit's learning to discriminate one tone that had been paired with shock from another that had not. Skills IV and V teach the client to mobilize a grounding image that allows her to tolerate the low level of fear, and these skills are hypothesized to increase cortical involvement, thereby building alternative pathways to the low road. Skill VI builds self structure that allows the client to "just notice" the process, and skill VII helps her to decrease her level of fear, which we may think of as damping down the amygdalar response. The client assembles the emotion control process with a metacognition when she verbalizes, "I am learning to control my fear," thereby increasing cortical involvement. This is how the AMST may be conceived to build new pathways in the brain that prevent maladaptive emotion responses. Building new pathways is equivalent to building awareness, and Freeman (2000) explained the neurophysiological basis of the curative effect of increased awareness as follows: "The crucial role that awareness plays . . . is to prevent precipitous action" (p. 232).

A second line of evidence for how AMST may work comes from research on the mind's multiple memory systems. LeDoux (1996) explained how two distinct systems operate in processing a given stimulus. One, the declarative, or explicit, memory system registers, stores, and retrieves cognitive memories of the stimulus. The other, the implicit memory system, which is also known as the emotion memory system, registers, stores, and retrieves memories of the emotional significance of a stimulus. The emotional significance of a stimulus entails sensation experience because the "systems that perform emotional appraisals are directly connected with systems involved in emotional responses" (p. 69).

AMST appears to involve both the declarative memory system and the implicit memory system. Declarative memories are those that can be brought to mind and described verbally. When the protocol asks the client for a target scene in the setup for skills III to VII, and she describes a time that she felt fear at a low level, the client's declarative memory system is engaged, and she produces a memory of an emotion. For example, client Helen was asked to, "Tell me a time you felt fear at level 3 or 4" and her explicit system produced facts about the fear inducing event, which she reported as, "I was going 50 in a 30 zone and a cop stopped me." Evoking the explicit memory apparently elicits the activity of the implicit, emotion memory system. A conscious memory can cause tension and arousal, because there are robust connections between the explicit memory system of the cortex and the emotion response activating circuits in the amygdala's central nucleus. As LeDoux (1996) wrote, "In order to have an aversive emotional memory, complete with the body experiences that come with an emotion, you have to activate an emotional memory system, for example, the implicit fear memory system involving the amygdala" (p. 201). Activation of the amygdala's central nucleus triggered Helen's emotion response system, and when I asked her to become aware of sensations accompanying the visualization, she immediately reported "trembling in my arms and legs."

The emotion memory system is also the arena in which classical conditioning occurs that does not depend upon awareness. Complicating matters of naming, the implicit, emotion memory system is also known as procedural memory because this is where certain skills, such as manual and mental tasks, are learned. AMST constitutes a set of mental tasks, the learning of which apparently requires participation of the implicit emotion memory system.

As the client progresses through the skills set, explicit and implicit memory meet in working memory, which consists in part of whatever material we are currently thinking about, but also has access to the contents of long-term memory. When the explicit and implicit emotion memory meet in working memory, an immediate conscious experience results; that is, a unified experience of the past memory together with present arousal. This becomes a new explicit memory. Apparently AMST operates by facilitating formation of a new explicit memory in which the old explicit memory and the emotion aroused are assembled with new visualizations, for example, grounding image and disposal resource, the experience of decreasing arousal, and with new cognitions (e.g., "I am learning to decrease my fear"). This new explicit memory is stored for the short term in the hippocampus, then transferred to long-term memory, which is held in the temporal lobe. Over time, long-term memories become consolidated, a process that takes place in the neocortex.

The regulation skill (skill VII) appears to be mediated by the orbitofrontal cortex (OFC) circuits described by Schore (1994). Recall that the OFC receives information from two circuits whose maturation is experience-dependent and occurs during the early and late practicing phases of development. The ventral tegmental circuit matures first and consists of dopaminergic input fibers and cholinergic output tracts that innervate effector sites where affects are recognized as feelings. The ventral tegmental circuit mediates the positive affects of excitement and joy. It is a component of the sympathetic branch of the autonomic nervous system and facilitates arousal. The lateral tegmental circuit, consisting of ascending noradrenergic fibers and descending cholinergic conduits down-regulates arousal states. The lateral circuit is parasympathetic and inhibitory. I propose that the AMST regulation skill (skill VII) recruits the ventral and lateral tegmental circuits, enhancing their functioning, and assisting the client to up-regulate positive emotion and down-regulate distressing emotion.

In the regulation skill (skill VII), the disposal resource serves to down-regulate distressing levels of affect. I hypothesize that the image of the disposal resource, for example a sink garbage disposal unit, promotes engagement of the lateral tegmental circuit. This circuit may not have developed fully if the client did not receive optimal disapproval–shame experiences in childhood. While it may not be optimally developed, the lateral tegmental circuit is believed to exist in a more or less rudimentary form if the client has any capacity at all to control impulses. Activation of the lateral tegmental circuit as promoted by the disposal resource activates the cholinergic tracts of the lateral tegmental circuit which act to inhibit arousal states associated with the target affect. The result is a decrease in levels of fear, disgust, sadness, shame or other target affects.

In an analogous manner, the gauge resource of skill VII (regulation) is hypothesized to engage the ventral tegmental circuit and to facilitate up-regulation of positive affect. The gauge resource enhances the functioning of the ventral circuit, which may not have developed fully because the client's positive affect states were not aroused sufficiently in childhood. Once recruited through the agency of the gauge resource, the dopaminergic, sympathetic tracts supplying the OFC stimulate firing of the efferent, cholinergic fibers. Branching out from sites in the amygdala, hypothalamus, and medulla, signals originating in the ventral tegmental circuit of the OFC, facilitated by the gauge resource, increase arousal in effector organs, (e.g., heart, lungs, smooth muscle). Increased heart rate, facial flushing, and increased breathing rate are some of the qualia often associated with increased positive affect states (excitement, joy, yearning). I hypothesize that this mechanism explains how the image of the gauge employed in the gauge resource of skill VII (regulation) promotes an enhancement or up-regulation of positive affects.

AMST and the Special Learning State

AMST can be included in the analysis Gilligan (2002) has made of the similarities and differences among direct hypnosis, Ericksonian hypnosis, and EMDR. AMST appears to employ the *special learning state* that is induced by EMDR, Ericksonian hypnosis, and direct hypnosis. All four are also similar in that they make use of this special learning state to help the client achieve a new integration of personality. There are significant differences among these modalities, however, as to how the state is induced and how the state is used in therapy.

Direct hypnosis differs from AMST, EMDR, and Ericksonian hypnosis in the means by which the special learning state is created and in the use made of it. Direct hypnosis induces a trance state through a standardized technique employing repetitive suggestions, deep relaxation, and concentration on the hypnotist's voice. The client is passive—eyes closed, immobile, and unspeaking. In this narrowed state of attention, the client is more open and susceptible to new ideas suggested by the operator. Power is invested in the authoritarian therapist, who controls the process of "rewiring" the client while he is in the special learning state. By these criteria, AMST is not hypnosis, and the special learning state employed by AMST is not a trance.

In Ericksonian hypnosis, a special psychological state is induced through a naturalistic procedure that employs the client's own behaviors and experiential states. Unlike direct hypnosis which creates trance from the operator's values, Ericksonian hypnosis creates trance from the client's values. In the state, the client's own potential for healing can be accessed and actualized.

EMDR is similar to Ericksonian hypnosis according to Gilligan (2002) because both focus on the client's resources. According to Gilligan, Shapiro's adaptive information processing system constitutes EMDR's special learning state, which is induced by the side to side eye movements. In the learning state induced by eye movements, the client's traumatic target memory is first desensitized and then incorporated into a new context. EMDR and Ericksonian hypnotherapy share a belief that the client's personality system will automatically attain a state of more positive functioning as the result of an innate capacity of the system to resolve the "ordered chaos" in the personality system that constitutes the symptom complex the client presents at the beginning of therapy. This approach could be characterized as *laissez faire* psychotherapy. In Gilligan's view, the EMDR therapist or Ericksonian hypnotherapist functions to create the necessary environment in which the client can surrender to the ordered chaos and allow the transformation to a new state to occur. The necessary environment provides for relaxation, direct access to core experiences, dual attention by which he means simultaneous attending to interior experience and outer environment, and trust that ordered chaos will eventuate in integration and the emergence of new personality structures.

AMST employs a special learning state that, like EMDR, is induced by alternating bilateral stimulation. AMST uses tactile alternating bilateral stimulation (TABS) rather than eye movements, and this appears to induce a less intense special learning state than that induced by eye movements, one in which a collaboration between clinician and client is facilitated. The collaborative position is central to AMST and sets it apart from EMDR and Ericksonian hypnotherapy. AMST's adoption of a collaborative approach is based on the development model which states that the client's self system was structured by interactions occurring within self-and-other dyads over the life span. The developmentally-earliest dyads involving maternal caregiver and infant have a more profound effect on structuring the self than later dyads, because the infant's system is unstructured at birth. The degrees of freedom available to the client for the spontaneous emergence of new personality structure are limited by the nature of preexisting structure. The nature of the transformation to a new personality state envisioned by EMDR is constrained by the quality of the ego states and introjects and the patterns of affective responding that the client brings to therapy. In AMST's collaborative model, the therapist functions within the therapeutic dyad to expand the nature and quality of the representations that contribute to the client's self structure. The therapist accomplishes this by: modeling ways of behaving and feeling that are not available to the client's self system; helping the client alter the functioning of ego states and introjects that would otherwise impede or limit the process of optimal transformation; and, where therapeutically indicated, helping the client develop and install more adaptively functioning representations than he or she possesses currently. Working collaboratively, the therapist and client expand the degrees of freedom available to the self system so that as it reorganizes the newly emerging personality optimizes qualities of authenticity, autonomy, and vitality.

Summarizing this section, considerable evidence at several levels indicates that AMST is an effective and efficient intervention for improving emotion regulation because the protocol changes brain structure. The images inherent in the protocol's skills promote neurobiological events. Neurons are recruited into new pathways as the mind is being retrained. Self-structure is being elaborated, and awareness grows. As Siegel explained to Wylie and Simon, "At the level of the brain, therapy changes the mind by changing neuronal connections" (Wylie & Simon, 2002, p. 34). Speaking to the same reporters, Cozolino put it this way, "[Neuroscience] teaches us about the importance of simultaneously activating dissociated networks in the brain—the fear circuits, and language circuits, for instance—in ways that enable clients to reorganize their neural networks. (Wylie & Simon, 2002, p. 35).

TACTILE ALTERNATING BILATERAL STIMULATION (TABS)

AMST employs TABS to increase the effectiveness and efficiency of transmission of the skills set. TABS stimulation is delivered through the hand-held probes of a battery powered device called a TheraTapper™, and it is experienced by the client as a gentle "buzzing" sensation in the palms. While it has not yet been subjected to a component analysis or empirically validated by research, I believe TABS is an essential constituent of the protocol. As noted earlier, AMST was initially conceived of within the environment of EMDR, and it has since become autonomous. EMDR employs side-to-side eye movements to alternately activate right and left hemispheres of the brain. EMDR achieves alternating hemispheric stimulation by eye movements, by alternating tones, or by alternating tactile stimulation (Shapiro, 1995, 2001). In my clinical experience and in the clinical experience of many psychotherapists, side-to-side eye movements are a powerful elicitor of repressed or suppressed material. Twelve to 14 saccades appears to be a threshold, and delivering more eye movements risks triggering the client. When I was creating AMST, I initially used eye movements for the installations, but I quickly discovered these were unsuitable for the protocol. The installations of AMST require fairly long sequences of alternating bilateral stimulation. Long sequences of eye movements defeated the goal of installing a skill, because unconscious material was elicited and interfered with the process. Use of tactile stimulation satisfies the requirement for long sequences of alternating bilateral stimulation, because tactile stimulation appears to be far less innately eliciting than eye movements. Therefore, instructions for the protocol prescribe the use of TABS.

EMDR and AMST propose different hypotheses for why alternating bilateral stimulation might work. I hypothesize that TABS improves the efficiency and effectiveness of AMST skills acquisition because of the affects elicited by TABS, a process I call *affect mediation*. Shapiro (2001) hypothesized that the eye movements of EMDR promote a "dual attention stimulation," which appears to be a cognitive construct. I hope research will one day uncover the true mechanisms which make AMST such a powerful intervention and EMDR such a forceful therapy. Until such time, however, I prefer to ground my theory in empirically validated research on emotion and its neurobiology that forms the basis for affect mediation.

The concept of affect mediation depends upon the proposal that TABS increases the effectiveness of the AMST protocol by eliciting the affect surprise–startle. Much research remains to be done to prove that TABS elicits suprise–startle affect and that eliciting startle affect increases skills acquisition. However, the following visualization will suggest how TABS might elicit startle affect and promote skills acquisition. See yourself for a moment sitting in a chair on the lawn on a cool summer evening. You are talking to a friend. Suddenly, you feel a mosquito land on the sensitive skin of the back of your hand. What affect does this event trigger? The answer is easy: surprise–startle affect. Startle is the affect triggered by a sudden increase in stimulus density, in this case the tactile sensations of the mosquito's landing. Notice in this visualization what happens next. Your conversation is quickly "put on hold" as you deal with the sudden intrusion. That is the function of startle affect; it clears the mind of current activity to prepare it to deal with the startling stimulus (Izard, 1991; Nathanson, 1992). After swatting the offending insect, you may notice in the visualization that you turned to your companion and asked, "Now, where were we?" The intrusion cleared your mind briefly. This sequence represents the action of startle affect.

My hypothesis is that TABS elicits startle affect at a low level below the threshold of conscious awareness. The tactile stimulus delivered by the TABS device is analogous to the mosquito's landing. The startle affect elicited by the TABS device has the effect of clearing the mind of ongoing activity, thus preparing it to deal with the AMST material that is paired with the startling stimulus. Lang (1995) has demonstrated that the startle reflex, from which startle affect apparently evolved, is extremely resistant to being extinguished, which would explain the robustness of the TABS effect over time. I hypothesize that TABS clears the mind of preconceptions and old patterns of responding, thus allowing new patterns to be formed. The new patterns that are acquired consist of the adaptive emotion-regulation skills and expanded self-structure taught by the AMST. It is the combination of TABS with the protocol that makes the skills acquisition so effective and efficient.

Other explanations of how TABS works are possible. Adherents to Tomkins's affect theory suggest that TABS may elicit interest–excitement affect. According to this hypothesis, the excitement affect elicited by TABS acts to decrease shame affect (Grindlinger, personal communication, August 16, 2002). Once shame is decreased, according to this theory, new learning can occur, since shame affect restricts learning. Alternatively, TABS could work by a neurophysiological method similar to the method Teicher (2000) proposed for EMDR. Since both TABS and EMDR involve alternating bilateral stimulation, Teicher's hypothesis for the involvement of the cerebellar vermis in the technique of EMDR could also explain why TABS renders AMST effective. Teicher writes, "we suspect that this technique [EMDR] works by fostering hemispheric integration and activating the cerebellar vermis (which also coordinates eye movements), which in turn soothes the patient's intense limbic response to the [traumatic] memories" (p. 65).

TECHNICAL FRAMEWORK: ELEMENTS OF AN AMST INTERVENTION

This section will present key technical components of the AMST intervention.

The Therapeutic Dyad and Directiveness of AMST

The therapeutic encounter constitutes a dyadic relationship of a particular sort. It is a curative or reparative relationship. Following the dictates of our developmental model, we understand that the client's childhood caregivers failed to facilitate development of an adequate attachment with the result that the child did not learn the skills of affect regulation. Or worse, the caregivers provided adverse or traumatic experiences. Those childhood failures conditioned the emergence of the client's distressed personality structure. Therapist and client form a dyad that recreates the infant–caregiver dyad in order to remediate failures remaining from that earlier dyad. In the context of the therapeutic dyad, the clinician functions at least in the early stages of therapy as a surrogate for the ideal parent that the client-as-child did not have. The clinician assists the client to remediate the emotion regulation deficits that were the sequelae of the client's particular childhood experience. Within the therapeutic dyad, the therapist functions to facilitate structuralization of the client's self, just as the caregiver does in a functional, healthy, "good enough" infant–caregiver dyad. Schore (1994) has said that the caregiver's right brain serves as a template for organization of the infant's right brain. By analogy, in early therapy with AMST, the clinician's right brain serves as a template for restructuring the client's right brain functions.

AMST, which constitutes the initial phase of affect centered therapy (ACT), is a directive therapy. The stance of the clinician is that of coach, one who knows more about emotions and their regulation than the client and whose job it is to teach the client. The therapist's duty is to facilitate a repair of deficits in the client's self structure. The need for directiveness in the therapeutic dyad, which may be uncomfortable for some clinicians, derives from the theoretical basis of a psychotherapy focused on affect. The therapist is encouraged to accept the theoretical basis of AMST that clients come to therapy because they have difficulty regulating their affects, and that they may unconsciously have formed fragments or significant amounts of their self structure around maladaptive affect management scripts. These scripts no longer work. The therapist's job is to recognize this state of affairs and to help the client to learn to recognize affects, to manage them, and eventually to build new structure. I believe the therapist has an ethical responsibility in the therapeutic dyad to accept the directive role and to provide the affect regulation skills the client failed to receive in childhood.

As a result of remediation of these basic deficits, the client attains a level of autonomy that is an essential prerequisite for person-centered, humanistic, family systems, or existential psychotherapy. The nature of the dyad can shift in the direction a goal-corrected partnership in which the client and clinician negotiate how the dyad will transit the path toward the client's more adaptive functioning. Until the client can adaptively manage his or her emotions, he or she cannot function optimally in the therapeutic dyad. The clinician has an ethical responsibility to work in beneficent ways with the client and to avoid maleficent ones. I argue that teaching the AMST protocol is ethically mandated because on the basis of the developmental model, to do so promotes beneficence and failure to do so may harm the client.

The Client History

Tables 5.1 and 5.2 present a useful client history. In the brief psychotherapy I practice, I often have the client complete this history and e-mail or fax it to me prior to our first visit. This history generates affective information that is useful to understanding the client's emotion regulation status and attachment related state of mind. I use the history to diagram the client's personality structure, affect regulation problems, and experience of trauma or adversity. The history and diagram prepare me for issues that will probably arise as we begin the AMST intervention.

Clients who are coming for problems with alcohol, drugs, or nicotine dependency receive additional questions that help me assess the severity of the ingestive disorder, which helps me estimate the probable extent of childhood deficit or childhood adverse or traumatic experience. These questions inquire about the drug of choice, route of administration, intensity of use, consequences, and chronicity. Similarly, for clients coming for treatment of an eating disorder, I inquire about the frequency of binge or binge and purge, consequences, chronicity, and the role of exercise.

ACT reads the client's history to assess the client's affect regulation status, attachment status, and level of childhood adversity or trauma. Reading through the

Table 5.1 Client History

Instructions. Please answer these questions giving me as much information as you want. Feel free to associate in as much material and whatever memories you come up with. If these questions make you uncomfortable, just stop and tell me that you have become uncomfortable.

1. Where are you in the birth order? What is your birth date? What are the sexes and birth dates of your siblings?
2. Tell me your earliest memory of your mother.
3. Tell me a pleasant memory of your mother.
4. Were you nursed?
5. Tell me a disturbing memory of your mother.
6. Tell me a time you were angry with your mother.
7. What did you do with your emotions regarding your mother?
8. Please give me five adjectives or phrases to describe your relationship with your mother during childhood, then tell me what memories or experiences led you to choose each one.
9. Tell me your earliest memory of your father.
10. Tell me a pleasant memory of your father.
11. Tell me a disturbing memory of your father.
12. Tell me a time you were angry with your father.
13. What did you do with your emotions regarding your father?
14. Please give me five adjectives or phrases to describe your relationship with your father during childhood, then tell me what memories or experiences led you to choose each one.
15. Tell me about the relationship between your father and your mother.
16. Was there alcoholism or addiction in your family?
17. Tell me about your siblings and how you related to them.
18. What was it like for you growing up in your family? What did you do?
19. Was there verbal abuse in your family? Was there physical abuse? Was there sexual abuse?
20. What was your family's relationship to religion and how did it affect you?

Table 5.2 Current Problems

1. What is (are) the personal problem(s) that is (are) bringing you to therapy?
2. Describe the problem(s) and your attempts to resolve it (them).
3. What is (are) the problem(s) in your relationship.
4. How do you manage the issue of money in your marriage?
5. How is power allocated and managed in your marriage? How are decisions made in the couple?
6. Do you have children? How old? If so, what is your relationship like with them?
7. How do you and your partner relate to each other sexually? What is the quality of your sex life? Are you satisfied with it?
8. How does intimacy manifest in your relationship? Give an example.
9. If the "miracle" were to happen and all your problems were resolved, what would your life and relationship look like?

client's responses, I will highlight the affects expressed and list these in a personality structure diagram that will be discussed below (see Figure 5.1 for an example). The client's affective responses to questions regarding parents reveal the nature of mother's and father's affective style in socializing their child. Did mother use anger affect or disgust affect to control her child's behavior and affective displays? And father? These questions also uncover the structure of both the maternal and paternal introjects and indicate the nature of "every disturbing thing" regarding mother and father that the client's unconscious may want to contain. Question 15 will uncover the client's internalized parental relational dynamic.

The structural coherence of client responses will indicate the client's attachment related state of mind with regard to parents. One client responded, "I'll have to get back to you on that," in answer to questions 8 and 14, indicating a dismissive style. Another client responding to question 8 e-mailed me an entire chapter from a novel she had written, indicating a preoccupied style. I look for emotions the client knows he feels and for those that he might be expected to feel, given his history, and does not verbalize. As I summarize the client's affective responses, I attempt to understand how well she manages these emotions. The questions (7 and 13) "What did you do with your emotions?" reveal much about the client's deficit experience and how it impacts her emotion management capability. One client reported "I ate!" Another client responded, "I went to my room and closed the door."

I look for indications of adverse or traumatic experience. Clients can usually report divorce, an adverse experience, if it occurred. Sometimes the client knows she was abused, though often she may not. If she does not, I look for clues such as intense addiction, for example with injection of a substance, or severe self-injury such as cutting, burning, or swallowing caustic substances.

Reading through the history again, I look for indications of ego states (Watkins & Watkins, 1997). If the client is ingestive disordered (eating disorder, addiction, alcoholism, nicotine dependency) or has a process addiction (sexual, gambling), I immediately hypothesize a symptom expressing ego state (SES). I created the SES concept in the course of my work with ingestive addictions in order to comprehend the self structure of the alcoholic, addict, smoker, or eating disordered client. The SES is a part-self tasked with regulating a specific assembly of emotions. For example, in bulimia, the binge ego state may regulate anger or yearning, and the purge ego state may manage disgust. While there are patterns among the ingestive disorders, the clinician must help the client to uncover his or her own emotion patterns being managed by the SES. As I look at the history, I ask if there are indications the client may have formed a false self identity, perhaps a teacher, professional, successful businessperson, or other that mediates the self's transactions with the world, protects the vulnerable core parts, and avoids the experience of affect. I look to see if the history suggests that there must be a wounded child ego state carrying the personality system's unworthiness that is hidden in the structure (Chu, 1998; Schwartz et al., 1995b; Watkins & Watkins, 1997). I look for indications of a dissociating ego state, a part that "numbs out" the client. Finally, I try to assess the client's level of authenticity, autonomy, and vitality.

The clinician must be aware of the possibility that the client's psychopathology may include a dissociative component. While the personal history may not uncover a dissociative disorder, it will provide enough hints to the astute clinician that she will want to use an assessment tool to inquire further whether dissociation is a primary feature of the client's self structure. An unresolved attachment-related state of mind, reflecting a disorganized–disoriented childhood attachment, increases the probability of a dissociative component. The clinician should administer a Dissociative Experiences scale assessment tool (Carlson, 1997). The dissociative disorders require special training, and no clinician should attempt to treat a dissociative client without supervision and prior special education.

The Personality Structure Diagram

A diagrammatic representation of the self structure may help the clinician conceptualize the client. Figure 5.1 presents a diagram I created for client Amy, a bulimic woman in her 30s. This type of diagram is unique to AMST. The diagram abstracts information from Amy's client history. Personally, I find that a diagram helps me to form a Gestalt of the client, and I may refer to the diagram before a session to refresh my mind. I create a diagram for every client, but if this is too confusing for the reader, it can be eliminated because it is not an essential component of AMST.

The diagram summarizes the socializing persons that were significant for the client and assembles them with affects, emotions, and behaviors they directed at the client. The figure also diagrams ego states or split off parts of the client's self structure and the emotions and behaviors these parts manage. In the diagram, mother's significant emotions and behaviors, which are "inviting, promising, lying, patronizing," are connected with her representation by a line. The maternal representation is shown partially fused with the central representation for the client, because the client appears to endorse a preoccupied attachment related state of mind, and she has also not completely individuated from mother. The client's report of a disturbing memory of her mother indicated trauma, and the arrow from mother directed at the client's self represents this trauma and suggests

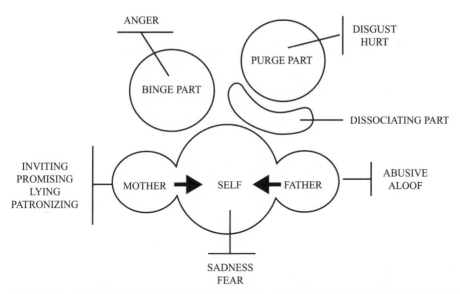

Figure 5.1.   The self-structure of Amy, a bulimic, is presented as abstracted from her history. Three ego states are shown, a binge part, a purge part, and a dissociating part. Trauma coded, unresolved, archaic motions managed by each part are indicated (e.g., the binge part appears to manage anger). The parents are shown as partly fused with the client's self, since she has not completely separated and individuated from them. Arrows indicate childhood trauma directed by the parents at the child. Behaviors of the parents directed at the child Amy are indicated. The key emotions felt by Amy currently—sadness and fear—are also indicated.

"traumatic bonding" (Chu, 1998, p. 106) that may contribute to Amy's failure to individuate and separate from her mother. The father's representation is assembled with his primary reported emotions and behaviors, "abusive, aloof." His representation is also shown partially fused with the client's self because she reported witnessing his abuse of a sibling that was very traumatic for her. Again, the trauma he inflicted on the client-as-child is represented by an arrow.

Because this client is a bulimic, I hypothesize that she has both a binge SES and a purge SES. These are diagrammed outside the circle of her self-representation, because these are unintegrated fragments of her total personality structure. Based on information in the history, I hypothesized that the binge part facilitated her managing anger affect and the purge part facilitated management of disgust. This client mentioned in the history that, "I hardly know what I am doing when I purge. It's like I'm not in my body," and from this I provisionally deduced a dissociating ego state, also diagrammed, tasked with preventing the system from integrating the purging behavior and disgust affect into the normal stream of consciousness. The dissociating ego state is drawn as a kidney shape to indicate that it prevents awareness of the affects managed by the purge ego state. Finally, the client's own current, real-time emotions are sadness and fear, and these are diagrammed as assembled with her self in the center of the figure.

206 PSYCHOTHERAPEUTIC INTERVENTIONS

Client Suitability for AMST

Regarding client suitability for AMST work, there are at present no indications that any client is a priori unsuitable for learning the skills. While all clients may be suitable for AMST, the more severe an individual client's disordering, the more carefully and slowly the clinician must proceed with the protocol. Experienced clinicians who work extensively with dissociative disorders regularly employ the protocol. Single case design studies support the usefulness of this affective intervention in treatment of OCD (Waltner-Toews, 2002), alcoholism, addictions, nicotine dependency, and eating disorders (Omaha, 1998, 1999, 2000). There are many Axis I and II disorders for which AMST has not yet been subjected to empirical test. It is my hope that publishing the protocol now will stimulate the empirical studies necessary to determining its usefulness in treating a range of disorders.

An AMST Treatment Plan

An AMST treatment plan can be written based on the history and any assessments that have been administered. For many Axis I disorders I allocate six 50-minute sessions to teach the skill set. The dissociative disorders will be an exception. As yet there is no information on application of the AMST to delirium, dementia, and schizophrenia and other psychoses. For Axis II disorders and for dissociative disorders, the clinician should plan for more than six sessions, adjusting the treatment plan to the client's progress. The treatment plan begins with client preparation, covered in the next section, and moves to skill I (containment) and skill II (safe place). I select the affects to be targeted in skills III to VII based upon the client's history. I usually begin with fear affect at SUD = 3 or 4 with the caveat that if the client is experiencing an affect currently in session, I will target that affect first. For example, a client may appear embarrassed and verbally endorse embarrassment emotion. If so, we will begin the AMST by targeting embarrassment. Flexibility is a useful personal resource for therapists using this protocol. I look for opportunities to target positive affect. Often, upon completion of skill I (containment), the client will report feeling relief, and if this occurs I will move immediately to skill III (sensation–affect identification) to teach the client to recognize the sensations that tell him he is feeling relief. As a general rule, I target the affects from more familiar to less familiar, or what is approximately the same, from less distressing to more distressing. A typical sequence might be, fear, anger, excitement, embarrassment, sadness, yearning, shame, and disgust. Appendix A consists of a worksheet the therapist can use to track his work with the client. Clinicians are encouraged to complete the entire AMST skill set, targeting a range of emotions with skills III to VII before proceeding to uncovering therapy.

Client Preparation

At the onset of our AMST work, I review with the client his goals for therapy and elicit an agreement on specific objectives. I derive the client's goals from question 9 under current problems in the client history. I carefully write down these goals using the client's language. The clinician will often need to return to these goals in the course of negotiating with ego states.

The first session continues with an explanation of the AMST process. I will often say to the client, "I want you to leave this first session with at least one valuable skill that will help you move closer to attaining your goals." I then introduce the skills as follows:

In our first sessions we will concentrate on teaching you skills necessary to recognize, tolerate, and regulate key emotions that many people feel. These skills are called affect management skills training, or AMST. The reason is that in my experience many people who come to therapy were not taught these skills in childhood. Often, many of the problems that bring people to therapy turn out to be the result of difficulties in regulating emotions, and once the client learns these skills life gets better right away. As you will quickly learn once we start, the AMST skills use images, emotions, and sensations to teach emotion regulation.

Shapiro (1995) has discussed the importance of forming a bond with the client. In my experience, teaching AMST provides an excellent means to accomplish this goal. As these initial sessions proceed, the client learns the clinician can be flexible, that the therapy is client-centered, and that the clinician is highly attuned to the client's emotion status, needs, and individual characteristics. The AMST process builds the client's feeling that he is respected and safe. The clinician endorses by his own behavior qualities of sensitivity and responsiveness, qualities that were often absent from the client's childhood attachment milieu. A therapeutic alliance builds during the skills transmission phase, and within this alliance, the client will develop a habit of honest communication. Trust accrues in the alliance, because as the client learns she can share her feelings as she learns the protocol, she develops the trust necessary to sharing her traumatic experiences later when therapy moves into a trauma resolution phase.

Introducing TABS

Next the client is introduced to TABS. Once I have told the client she will be learning emotion regulation skills, I explain that I use a little device that just gives a small tactile stimulus to each hand. I explain that this gentle tactile stimulation increases the effectiveness and efficiency of learning the AMST skills. At this point I show the device to the client and indicate the hand-held probes. I use language something like this:

The skills I will be teaching you can be transmitted more effectively and more efficiently by using a device that gives a small, tactile stimulus to each hand. It's just like a gentle buzzing sensation. It is not a shock. Something about it interrupts the old patterns that aren't working so well and allows new patterns to develop. I'd like to have you experience for yourself what it feels like.

At this point I will hand just one of the TheraTapper™ probes to the client and ask her to hold it. After telling the client, "Now, I'm going to turn on the Thera-Tapper for just one pulse so you can see how gentle it is," I will do so, turning the device off immediately. While almost all clients tolerate this well, the clinician must be aware that the dissociative identity disorder (DID) or dissociative disorder not otherwise specified (DDNOS) client could be startled into a dissociative state. Holding one probe and restricting the stimulus to one pulse will minimize the probability of this happening. Of course the best way to prevent an unexpected dissociation is to have screened and assessed the client adequately beforehand. Shapiro (1995) stressed the importance of client control of bilateral stimulation. The clinician should tell the client that if he needs to stop the TABS for whatever reason, all he needs to do is say "Stop" or hold up his hand. With this introduction and client preparation, the AMST work immediately begins.

Ideomotor Signaling

AMST employs ideomotor signaling to facilitate communication between the therapist and the client's unconscious. Ideomotor signaling is a technique for getting information from the client's unconscious by asking the client to raise an index finger when a skill has been completed. Ideomotor signaling bypasses the client's cognitive defenses. I will ascertain the client's handedness and then ask the client to signal with the nondominant index finger. This technique bypasses the client's cognitive appraisal mechanisms and engages the right brain. AMST uses ideomotor signaling to get status reports from the right brain. For example, in skill I (containment), when the client has been asked to, "Just form the intention that every disturbing thing will go into the container," the client will be asked to "raise your left index finger when as much has gone into the container as will go at this time." In this way the right brain can signal when a process has been completed. In skill VII (regulation), the clinician will instruct the client to signal with his index finger when the agreed upon percentage of negative affect has gone down the disposal mechanism.

Client Self-Report: The Rating Scales

AMST uses client self-report in the form of rating scales that allow clinician and client to monitor progress and to assess stress or discomfort. Shapiro (1995) has created two such rating scales that I have adapted for use in the protocol. Shapiro's 11-point Subjective Units of Disturbance (SUD) scale extends from zero, which is benign or neutral, to 10, the highest level of intensity. While Shapiro designed the SUD to measure a client's "anxiety" (p. 5), AMST uses this scale to assess the level of stress, discomfort, or arousal any target emotion causes the client. This tool is usually introduced when the target scene is elicited. After explaining the skill, the clinician may say, "Tell me a time when you felt fear at a low level, say a level 3, but not over a 4." This tool demonstrates to the client that she can fractionate stressful emotions, thereby transmitting a sense of mastery over emotions that previously threatened to overwhelm her. This tool can be applied to every emotion targeted by skills III to VII, from fear to shame to disgust. When a client has successfully learned to manage a stressful emotion at a low level, the clinician can assist her to select a somewhat more stressful level of the same emotion and help her to use the same skills to manage it.

The second of Shapiro's (1995) tools I adapted for the AMST is the Validity of Cognition (VoC) scale, a 7-point scale, from 1, "completely false," to 7, "completely true." Clients are encouraged not to think about their assessment, but rather to just let the unconscious respond. As Shapiro wrote: "the clinician should ask the client to report his 'gut level' response" (p. 59). The VoC scale enables clinician and client to track the client's progress toward AMST skill acquisition. This scale measures the emotional validity for the client of the positive affirmations, (i.e., the cognitions), that the clinician "installs" using TABS into the images of the skill set. The VoC scale forms the basis of the AMST's diagnostic value. The VoC interrogates the client's unconscious. If a client is unable to endorse a VoC of 7 where the protocol requests an assessment, that inability indicates that a resource may be missing or that an ego state is opposing the work.

The Positive Cognition (PC)

AMST employs the positive cognition to elicit thoughts and appraisals that are then assembled with images, affects, and sensations in each skill. Shapiro (1995) introduced the concept of the PC, which she intended to "set a direction for treatment, to stimulate the appropriate alternative neuro networks" (p. 59). AMST has adapted the PC as a means of recruiting the left brain's cognitive capability in order to assemble its cognitions with images, affects, and sensations in the course of building self structure. In the early stages of the protocol, PCs are usually process statements, such as, "I am learning to decrease my fear," rather than attainment statements, such as, "I can decrease my fear." The protocol uses TABS to increase the effectiveness and efficiency of assembly of PCs with visualizations, affects, sensations, and behaviors in each of the skills. Theory suggests that subthreshold startle affect elicited by TABS functions to clear the mind of established cognitions while a new, more adaptive cognition is installed. Fearful clients, for example, come to therapy believing that they cannot decrease their fear. This previously existing belief must be suspended while the more adaptive PC, "I am learning to decrease my fear," is put in place. TABS facilitates this installation. PCs are presented for every skill in the protocol. At the completion of skill I (containment), the clinician will develop the PC, "I am learning to contain every disturbing thing." When finished with installing skill II (safe place), the clinician will assemble the skill with the PC, "I am learning to create an inner image of safety and security for myself." The PC brings cognition into the growing assemblage of affect, sensation, and behavior, and its TABS-facilitated installation "rounds off" or completes each skill.

We have now established a sufficient foundation and can proceed to learn the individual AMST skills. Skill I (containment) is presented in chapter 6, skill II (safe place) in Chapter 7, and skill III (sensation–affect identification) in Chapter 8. Chapter 9 groups skills IV (sensation as signal), skill V (grounded and present), and skill VI (noticing). Skill VII (regulation) is presented in Chapter 10. Chapter 11 teaches advanced skills for enhancing self-concept, developing pride, modeling affect for the client, repairing attachment deficits, developing emotion knowledge, and creating a boundary against broadcast emotion. Chapter 12 introduces the clinician to techniques for integrating an affect orientation into therapy.

Chapter 6

Skill I: Containment

Figure 6.1 presents a diagrammatic representation of skill I (containment). The purpose of this skill is twofold: it is both therapeutic and diagnostic. Therapeutically, the skill is designed to prevent intrapsychic intrusion of the client's disturbing material and to provide control of the intrapsychic field for both the client and the clinician. By securing the intrapsychic field at the outset, the skill prevents the client's disturbing material from obstructing subsequent AMST steps. Skill I also provides the clinician and the client with a safety mechanism to use in case of therapeutic emergency, and the skill gives the client a tool to use should disturbing material surface between sessions. Developing the containment skill at the beginning of therapy facilitates control of trauma processing that will occur in subsequent phases of therapy.

Additionally, skill I alleviates some of the stress many clients feel at the outset of therapy. Whether she is aware of it or not, the new client feels stressed at the prospect of encountering her problem behaviors. Her self system may feel overwhelmed with emotions that may include shame at the thought of disclosing the problem. Unconsciously, she may fear that therapy will try to take away the behaviors—for example, eating disordered behaviors or addictive behaviors—that have allowed her to manage otherwise intolerable affects. She may fear facing those affects as well. Therapeutically, skill I provides the client with an immediately beneficial experience, because it facilitates separating off and encapsulating the thoughts and fears that are causing her stress. As noted in the previous chapter, in the first session, I often tell the new client, "I want you to leave here today with at least one skill that will provide you with some immediate benefit." Transmitting skill I fulfills this positive expectation. Clients often report experiencing a feeling of relief upon completion of the containment skill.

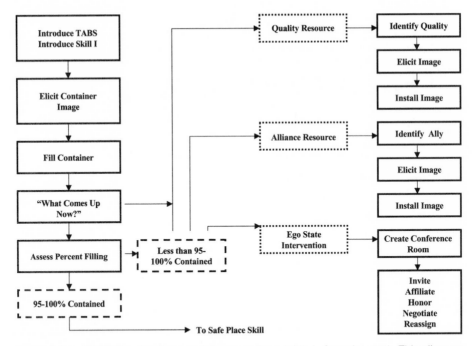

Figure 6.1. AMST Flow Diagram and Decision Tree (skill I, Containment). This diagram illustrates the succession of steps for creating an image of a container and then helping the client to visualize "every disturbing thing" moving in to the container. The diagram also shows interventions the clinician can use if filling is less than complete.

Diagnostically, skill I helps the clinician to uncover negative attitudes, missing resources, or covert ego states. Doubt is an example of a negative attitude the skill can uncover. Many clients have difficulty trusting themselves, and the skill can reveal this missing resource. Covert ego states operate to protect the system, but often their helper function impedes therapy. Skill I accomplishes its diagnostic goals through the self-report appraisals incorporated in the skill development process.

PROCEDURE FOR SKILL I (CONTAINMENT)

Immediately upon completion of the client preparation steps presented in Chapter 5, skill I is introduced as follows:

Sometimes people have unpleasant or disturbing memories that they may or may not be aware of. Before we begin our work, it is a good idea to get these into a container where they can't interfere with the rest of our work.

Once we have an image of a container, I'll help you fill it and then we'll seal it and put a valve on it that operates by your intention. That way you can add material or take something out to work on it without opening the lid or letting anything else out. We'll also put a sign on the container that says, "To be opened only when it serves my healing," so that you control when and if you want to take something out.

It's important for you to understand that you do not have to know what the disturbing material is. Your unconscious knows and that's sufficient. Please do not look at any individual disturbing thing. Do you have any questions before we get started?

The clinician attends to any questions the client may have following this introduction to skill I.

Obtaining a Container Image

Having explained the process, the clinician delivers the following instruction to obtain a container image.

Give me an image of a container sufficient to hold every disturbing thing.

Using her own notes or employing the tracking sheet provided in Appendix A, the clinician will write down all the details of the construction of the container the client describes. The essential quality of a suitable container is that it be circumscribed by solid walls. Clients have used images of steel boxes, wooden chests with steel bands, steel cylinders, a ship constructed of boiler plate. One client used a Sherman tank. Once the client has given an image, help the client to amplify the dimensions of the container and to note the material of which it is constructed. These should be carefully noted, and the clinician should repeat these details every time the container is employed. For example, it is far better for the clinician to say, "See your container, a 5-foot tall silvery steel cylinder like an oxygen tank," than it is to simply say, "Visualize your container."

The Status Report

The clinician next gives the client instruction for giving a status report at the termination of tactile stimulation. The clinician should say:

In a moment, I'll be turning the TheraTapper on and we'll fill the container. When it's as full as it can get at this time, I want you to indicate that by raising your left index finger. We'll complete the process and then I'll turn the TheraTapper off. When I do, I'll ask you to take a deep breath and let it out, and then I'll ask, "And what comes up now?" I'll ask this every time I turn the TheraTapper off. You may get a thought, a memory, an emotion, or a sensation, or nothing may come up. There are no shoulds or musts or oughts. Whatever happens is just fine. Whatever you get, I want you to report it to me without editing or censoring.

Shapiro (1995) has suggested that the instruction to take a deep breath and let it out gives the client an opportunity to "rest, reorient, and prepare to verbalize the new information plateau" (p. 143). She suggests the clinician inhale and exhale along with the client to increase bonding in the dyad and improve positive therapeutic effects.

Filling the Container

The clinician now moves immediately to helping the client to fill the container. I have described in Chapter 5 what tactile alternating bilateral stimulation (TABS) is and how I theorize it operates to increase the effectiveness and efficiency of skills acquisition. Filling the container represents the first time the clinician will employ TABS to facilitate a skill. In the instructions that follow, **TABS On** informs the clinician that he or she should turn on the TheraTapper™ or to begin tapping on the backs of the client's hands or on the client's knees a if a TheraTapper™ is not available. The instruction **TABS Off** tells the clinician to turn off the TheraTapper ™ or stop tapping on the client. These same instructional prompts are employed throughout the remaining chapters. The clinician begins facilitating the container filling operation with the following instructions:

TABS On *Visualize your container* [repeat client's description] *and notice that the top or lid is off right now. I'd like you to form the intention of having every disturbing thing move into the container. Good. Now, just watch it move into the container. Please do not look at the individual disturbing things. You may see a collective image like smoke or goo. I don't know what you're seeing, but whatever you are seeing is just fine. Good. Just watch it move in. Watch it move in. Let me know by raising your left index finger when as much has gone in as you think will go in at this time. Take all the time you need.* [Client raises finger.] *Now, put the lid on and seal it up. Weld it or glue it shut. Excellent. Now, become aware of the special valve with which you can take one thing out or put something in without letting anything else out. Attach the valve to the container. Good. And become aware of the sign that says, "To be opened only when it serves my healing." Good.* **TABS Off** *Deep breath. Let it out. And what comes up now?*

Every component of the containment skill is important and each component contributes to the effectiveness of this skill as well as the other skills in the protocol. AMST, like EMDR, is a "complex clinical intervention" (Shapiro, 1995, p. 26). All elements, including the images, intentions, the clinician's instructions, appraisals, affects, the verbalization ("And what comes up now?") at termination of installation, and the TABS are essential to the successful development of the skill. Refreshing the client's container image keeps the client's unconscious engaged. It is important to caution the client that he does not have to know or examine each disturbing thing and to provide his unconscious with an alternative, the "collective image like smoke or goo." The ideomotor finger signal gives the client control over the process so that she does not have to feel hurried.

The instructions for filling the container intentionally employ nonspecific language, specifiying the client should visualize "every disturbing thing" flowing into the container. The clinician should avoid triggering the client by mentioning any specific incident or memory. The client's unconscious is fully aware of what constitutes "every disturbing thing," and in my experience the client's unconscious is usually quite willing to cooperate with the clinician to fill the container. If clients ask for clarification, the clinician can explain that the container is intended to hold memories and images and related thoughts. Emotions are not intended to go into the container. When a traumatic memory is recalled, it is the memory that elicits the distressing emotions and sensations. With the memory in containment, the client is will be free of distress, since the elicitor of fear, disgust, or shame has been encapsulated by means of the containment image. Emotions are regulated by means of the disposal resource introduced in skill VII.

The image of the valve added to the client's container provides the client with control over the disturbing material contained. The clinician's instructions have informed the client that the valve provides the means by which he can take something out of the container to work on it. He has been told he can also use the valve to put material in. The image of the sign that says "To be opened only when it serves my healing" also gives control of processing to the client and thereby transmits a sense of mastery. The images of the valve and the sign are essential, and clinicians using the worksheet in Appendix A should check the appropriate boxes to confirm that these imagistic components were developed. It is also essential that the clinician carefully attend to the client's response to the question at the termination of filling the container, "And what comes up now?" Sometimes a positive affect will spontaneously emerge, and instructions follow below for dealing with that eventuality. Sometimes a disturbing thought or memory will surface, and the clinician can immediately make use of the valve to containerize it. Instructions for using the valve follow below. Sometimes the client will say "Nothing" and the clinician can affirm that the response is all right.

Readers will note in Figure 6.1 a solid arrow from the box "What comes up now?" that leads to the advanced interventions quality resource, alliance resource, and ego state intervention. This arrow has been included to prepare the clinician for the client who verbalizes a statement of doubt or distrust; for example, "I doubt that any container could hold all my disturbing stuff" when asked by the clinician at the termination of TABS, "Tell me, what comes up now?" These interventions will be described below in the sections that begin on page 217 with the title "Interventions When Filling is Incomplete."

Eliciting an Assessment

In the next step, the therapist elicits an assessment from the client, a self-reported appraisal by the client of progress in filling the container. The clinician's neutrality is an important component, and the clinician should be careful to keep his body language and tone of voice open, accepting, and clear of judgment. The following language is suggested:

Let's check on our progress. As you look at the container now, what percent of every disturbing thing is contained? Let your unconscious answer. Probably you're getting a number right now. Whatever you get is just fine. So, tell me, what is your unconscious telling you?

Some clients will be able to transfer every disturbing thing into the container in one attempt. These are clients with a relatively well-structured personality, minimal deficit experience, a reasonably secure attachment, and minimal trauma or adversity. If the client offers an appraisal like, "Well, it's all gone in," the clinician should attempt to elicit a more exact quantification by asking, "Can you put a number on that? Please give me a percentage." This number should be entered on the worksheet. If the client endorses a complete or nearly complete filling, then the clinician should proceed as follows:

TABS On *I'd like you to recall the process you've just completed. See how you came up with an image of a container, how you filled it by forming the intention that every disturbing thing would go in, and how 100%* [use the number the client has provided] *did go in. See how you sealed the container and installed the valve and the sign. Now, as you hold that image, please repeat after me, "I am learning to contain every disturbing thing." Good.* **TABS Off** *Deep breath. Let it out. And what comes up now?*

Again, note and attend to whatever the client verbalizes.

When Positive Affect Spontaneously Surfaces

Sometimes when clients succeed in getting disturbing material into the container, positive emotion surfaces which may be relief or freedom. The following example picks up at the close of filling the container. The client verbalizes the positive affect "relief," and the clinician proceeds as follows:

> Clinician: Attach the valve to the container. Good. And become aware of the sign that says, "To be opened only when it serves my healing." Good. **TABS Off** Deep breath. Let it out, and what comes up now?
> Client: It all went in, and I'm feeling like this enormous relief.
> Clinician: Let's work with that. **TABS On** Call up again the image of yourself successfully containing every disturbing thing, and hear yourself affirming that you are learning to contain every disturbing thing. Now, become aware of the emotion of relief that you expressed, and as you hold that awareness, just notice in your body where there are sensations that accompany that emotion, and let me know by raising your left index finger when you have recognized them. Good. [*Client raises index finger.*] **TABS Off**

Assist the client in naming the sensation (e.g., lightness), and the body location where he feels the the sensation (e.g., shoulders, or heart), and write these down in your notes or on your tracking sheet. Then proceed as indicated in the following example in which the client felt relief accompanied by sensations of lightness in his shoulders.

TABS On *As you see yourself containing every disturbing thing and hear yourself affirming it, you become aware of lightness in your shoulders that tells you you are feeling relief. Please repeat after me, "The lightness in my shoulders tells me I am feeling relief."* [Client repeats.] *Let that become completely true. Good.* **TABS Off**

When a Disturbing Thought or Memory Surfaces

Sometimes more disturbing material will arise after the client has signaled that filling is completed, as the following example illustrates. When this happens, the clinician should facilitate the client in using the valve image. This illustration picks up at the close of the filling process.

> **Clinician:** Attach the valve to the container. Good. And become aware of the sign that says, "To be opened only when it serves my healing." Good. **TABS Off** Deep breath. Let it out, and what comes up now?
>
> **Client:** Some more stuff. I didn't get it all in. There's more. There's more.
>
> **Clinician:** Let's get it into the container right away. We'll use the valve. **TABS On** See the big green compressed gas bottle that is your container. Good. Notice the valve. Now form the intention that the stuff that didn't get in is going to go in now. Good. Now open the valve. Nothing will come out. Just watch as the stuff that didn't go in starts to go in now. Just hold the intention that it will go in. Please don't look at any individual disturbing thing. Just watch it going in. Let me know with your finger signal when as much of the rest has gone in as will go in. Good. [*Client raises left index finger.*] Good. **TABS Off** Deep breath. Let it out, and what comes up now?
>
> **Client:** Whew! That worked. The rest went in.

INTERVENTIONS WHEN FILLING IS INCOMPLETE: QUALITY RESOURCE

Often clients will not be able to endorse complete containerization of every disturbing thing. Inability to contain all the disturbing material may indicate a deficiency in essential resources. One power of the AMST is that its self-report assessment function allows the clinician to uncover these deficiencies where they exist and provides appropriate interventions to employ in those cases. Some resources are qualities of the self (e.g., courage, persistence) that have been acquired by introjection of the desired quality observed in another. Other resources, such as the quality of meriting positive outcomes that I call "deservingness," develop as a concomitant of an adequate attachment. If the important caregivers in the client's childhood did not model a necessary quality, then it was not available to assemble with the internal working model (IWM), and the self will be deficient in that quality in adulthood. Alternatively, if the child was not responded to with sensitivity and attunement, then the quality of deserving attunement and sensitivity will not emerge and the adult self will be deficient in that quality. The clinician's responsibility is to employ the diagnostic component of AMST, to help the client identify the missing qualities, and to facilitate acquiring them.

AMST provides a structured set of interventions to guide the clinician in helping the client get most of the disturbing material into the container. When a client responds that less than, say, 95% of every disturbing thing has gone into the container, the clinician should turn to the flow chart for guidance in developing necessary resources. The AMST Flow Chart and Decision Tree (Appendix B) presents an overall view of the entire protocol and interventions. An intervention is a therapeutic maneuver inserted into the protocol that is designed to uncover and remediate the causes of a client's difficulty in completing a skill. Figure 6.1 lays out the sequence of interventions for the containment skill alone, directing the client to a series of interventions, the first of which is the quality resource. Developing the quality resource has three steps: identify quality, elicit image, and install image. These three steps are each boxed separately. Once the clinician has developed a quality resource, he will return to the containment skill and repeat the filling component, again eliciting a self-report at the completion of filling of how much has gone in. If there is still less than 95% of disturbing material in the container, the clinician will proceed to the alliance resource and follow the three boxed instructional steps indicated to the right of that resource in Figure 6.1. Returning to skill I, the clinician will facilitate transfer of more disturbing material to the container. If at least 95% has still not gone into the container, the clinician will proceed to the ego state intervention.

The first intervention, quality resource, raises the issue of what characteristic the client would need to have in order to be able to add more to the container. Korn and Leeds (2002) and Leeds (1997) have described a process of resource development and installation from which AMST resource development is in part derived. An installation consists of three steps. First the missing necessary quality is identified. Then an image embodying that quality is elicited. Third, the client is facilitated in internalizing the image, incorporating it along with its desirable qualities, emotions, sensations, or cognitions. With TABS facilitation, the client visualizes the image for the quality resource and then visualizes that image moving into his or her body bringing with it the desired qualities.

Identifying the Necessary Quality

The clinician formulates instructions for the client as follows:

Often, when all the disturbing material doesn't go into the container, it indicates that a client needs help in developing and strengthening some important quality that could help. Qualities are things like courage, trust, persistence, deserving-ness, powerfulness, and so forth. I wonder, what quality do you think you might need that would help you get some more of every disturbing thing into the container?

Sometimes clients will be able to name a missing quality, but more often they will at best be able to hint at the missing resource. In the latter case, the clinician will help the client formulate a quality, a process that will require creative collaboration between client and clinician.

Eliciting an Image

Once the desired quality has been identified and agreed upon, the clinician next assists the client in producing an image that embodies or constellates the desired quality. The clinician can instruct the client as follows:

Give me an image that embodies or constellates the quality of [name of quality]. *An image can be anything. It can be animal, vegetable, or mineral. It can be imaginary. If it's real, it can be, for example, any animal. It can be historical, someone who actually existed, or it can be biographical someone or some animal you have actually known. It can be a religious or spiritual image. It can be a cartoon character. It can be anything. I wonder if you're getting an image now that embodies the quality of* [name of quality]?

Within the context of the structure provided by the AMST's language, clients will often be able to verbalize an image. Of course, the more damaged the client, the more he or she may need the therapist to be directive. If the client has difficulty, the clinician can help the client to arrive at an image. If the client has difficulty with the verbal mode, the clinician may want to shift to a different mode, for example, drawing or play, making use of crayons and paper, the sand tray, or toys to assist the client in uncovering an image. Here is one of several areas in the AMST protocol where the clinician can mobilize his or her own creative therapeutic capabilities.

Installing the Image

Once an image has been agreed upon, the clinician facilitates development and installation of the image. The case of Gerald illustrates this procedure. Gerald, a middle-aged man, came seeking help for binge eating. He was in long-term recovery from alcohol and other drug use. He told me he was adopted and knew that he was held in a receiving home for several months before being taken by his adoptive parents. He described himself as fearful and procrastinating. He reported that his adoptive mother was a severe alcoholic and rageaholic and that he was terrified of her. He stated, "This has stuck with me my whole life." Following the protocol as presented, Gerald and I began our work with the containment skill. Gerald visualized his container as a large, graceful ceramic urn. It was 5 feet tall and 3 feet thick in the middle. He reported watching "blackness and bile" pour into the urn. When asked, he reported that 10% of every disturbing thing had gone into the container.

Following the protocol and guided by the Decision Tree (Appendix B), I inquired of Gerald what quality he would need to have in order to get more of every disturbing thing into the container, and he replied "discipline." He readily produced an image that embodied the quality of discipline, an image that he called "Military Man." This image had aspects of someone Gerald had actually known as a student. Military Man stood "ramrod straight, but was also a college professor, a jogger in addition to being military." The qualities of being a jogger and a professor seemed to soften the military image and make it more accessible. The clinician installed the quality resource, Military Man, as follows:

> **Clinician: TABS On** Bring up the image of the Military Man. Look at his face and notice how it manifests the quality of discipline. Look at his eyes and see how they convey that the quality of discipline is tempered by the intelligence and knowledge of the college professor. See how his hands, and his shoulders, and his neck embody the quality of discipline.

See how his ramrod straight posture embodies the quality of discipline. Now, step away from him just a little bit, and then just allow his image to merge with you. Maybe it will come in through your forehead or your chest, I don't know. Just let it come in. And as it does, it brings with it the quality of discipline. Allow that quality, carried by the image of Military Man, to spread out through your body, through your chest, your shoulders, your neck, your torso. Up into your head, your face, into your brain, into every cell of your brain. Bringing the quality of discipline. Good. **TABS Off**

The process of eliciting the image of Military Man and identifying the qualities he provides is called "developing an image." When TABS facilitation is employed to elaborate the image and then to assemble it with the quality of discipline, the process is called "installation of the image." In this case installation also entailed merger with the image, as with TABS facilitation the client was asked to blend, integrate, or amalgamate with the image by bringing it into his body and allowing the image to spread out through his body carrying the desired quality with it. Installation does not always entail merger, as we will see subsequently with other installed images.

Continuing the protocol, we now repeat the containment visualization, this time holding the Military Man visualization. Please note that the container was sealed after the initial filling and a valve was installed, and so it is necessary from now on to use the valve when adding material to the container. Here are the instructions for adding more material to the container while using the quality resource, again using Gerald as an example.

> **Clinician: TABS On** See your container, the graceful urn, and the valve. Form the intention that some more of every disturbing thing is going to flow into the container. Now bring up the image of Military Man and remind yourself of the quality of discipline that he embodies. Good. Now open the valve and just watch as some more material flows in. Hold the image of Military Man and the quality of discipline. Good. Just watch it flow, and let me know by raising your left index finger when as much has gone in as will go in. [*Index finger rises.*] Good. **TABS Off**

Continuing to follow the protocol, as the TABS is turned off, the client was asked, "What comes up now?" and he reported "Peace." I inquired of Gerald where in his body he was experiencing sensations that accompanied the feeling of peace, and he reported, "My face, back, and shoulders." He described the quality of the sensation as a relaxation.

Gerald's case highlights the importance of client self-reports in the AMST process. When the clinician elicits a self-report and the client verbalizes a positive affect, an opportunity is created to cognize that affect, to raise it to conscious awareness. That a positive affect would surface after the client has contained some or all of his disturbing material is not surprising, as Izard (1991) has explained that a sudden, complete reduction of fear activates joy, and Nathanson (1992) has written that joy is elicited by a decrease in stimulus density. In Gerald's case, the stimulus density that was decreased by the containment skill was his intrapsychic fear, apparently engendered by the maternal introject, his alcoholic, rageaholic adoptive mom who had, he reported, terrified him all his life.

Often clients will spontaneously verbalize a positive affect upon transferring all or part of every disturbing thing to the container. If not, the clinician can create an opportunity for positive affect to surface with the following instructions:

TABS On *Sometimes, when people get most of every disturbing thing into the container, they experience some new sensations. I'd like you to just notice your body, paying particular attention to any new sensations you are feeling, and let me know when you get them by raising your index finger on your left hand.* [Finger rises.] **TABS Off**

Continue the TABS for perhaps 20 seconds, and if the client has not raised her index finger, turn the TABS off. Let the client know that there are no "shoulds, oughts, or musts," that you and she were just investigating whether anything new had appeared, and that the client's experience was just fine. If the client does get a new sensation, ask where it is located in her body and ask her to name the sensation. Then ask the client if she can name the affect that her body is signaling her she is experiencing. She may immediately recognize "relief" or some variant of it. Relief is one manifestation of the affect joy that we experience when fear or other tension has been suddenly and completely decreased. If the client is not able to name the emotion, the clinician can help her identify it herself with the following instruction:

Imagine for a moment that we're doing a therapy group and that a client sitting over there [point to another chair] *has just put most of his disturbing material into a solid container. This client tells us he experiences a relaxation in his shoulders and his face. What emotion do you suppose his experience of relaxation in his shoulders and his face is telling him he is feeling?*

Sometimes asking the client to imagine what another person would feel will suffice to allow the client to name the affect. If he still cannot, then the clinician, accepting his role in the therapeutic dyad, can say, "It sounds to me like relaxation in your shoulders is signaling relief. What do you think?"

Whether arising spontaneously, as with Gerald, or elicited by the clinician, as soon as a positive affect surfaces, the clinician should immediately help the client cognize it. Having identified the sensations and the place in the body where they're being experienced, the clinician should proceed to develop a cognition that associates sensation, body location, and affect. Here are the instructions I gave to Gerald:

> Clinician: **TABS On** Recall our work a few minutes ago and how you developed an image of a container and then an image of Military Man and the quality of discipline he embodied. See how you were able to use those images to contain a lot of every disturbing thing. Become aware of your report that you felt peace and that you identified sensations of relaxation in your face, back, and shoulders that accompanied the feeling of peace. Please repeat after me, "The relaxation in my face, back,

and shoulders tells me I am feeling peace." Good. Let that become completely true. **TABS Off**

INTERVENTIONS WHEN FILLING IS INCOMPLETE: ALLIANCE RESOURCE

Continuing with client Gerald illustrates how following the AMST Flow Chart and Decision Tree facilitates movement to a second type of intervention, the alliance resource. Having taken a brief excursion to develop the positive affect of peace, I asked Gerald to return his attention to the container and to estimate for us what percentage of every disturbing thing was now contained. He replied, "Ninety percent." Readers should note that by developing the missing quality resource, embodied in Military Man, the client was able to increase the amount of disturbing material contained from 10 to 90%. In addition, once he now had a total of 90% of his disturbing material contained, the positive affect, peace, could emerge. Gerald's case emphasizes the importance of assessing the success of each intervention stage. Because Gerald still had significant amounts of uncontained material, I proceeded to the second intervention, the alliance resource (see Figure 6.1).

Identifying an Ally

The alliance resource asks the client the question, "Who could help get more of every disturbing thing into the container?" Clients often lack internal representations of important supportive figures, because their childhoods were characterized by an absence of such persons. The clinician should instruct the client that an ally can be anything that is supportive, helpful, and encouraging. It can be a real animal or person, an imaginary one, a mythical figure. Based on the client's response, an alliance resource is developed and installed. Again, Gerald's story exemplifies the process. When he stated that 90% of every disturbing thing was in the container, I suggested that it would be useful to see if we could get some more in, and then I asked Gerald, "Who could help get more of the disturbing material into the container?"

Gerald responded, "I don't know where this came from but the word *woman* just popped into my head."

At this point in therapy, the clinician should refrain from offering reflections or interpretations, no matter how seductive the impulse may be. Gerald's process would have been adversely impacted by the therapist's observations that the Military Man resource was a remediation of his absent, unavailable, and unprotective father's introject, and he would not have been helped by a suggestion that the woman ally was making up for the deficiencies of his alcoholic, rageful mother. The clinician's work is to lead the client to formulate these reflections for himself, and then only after a solid AMST foundation has been laid.

Eliciting an Image

With some guidance, Gerald identified some of the qualities that woman possessed. He said she was "warm and nurturing and she knows what I am feeling." We agree the latter quality is empathy and then proceeded as follows:

Clinician: **TABS On** As you hold the qualities of warmth and nurturing and
empathy, just allow an image of woman that embodies those qualities
to emerge from your deepest unconscious. There is nothing you need to
do. Just allow the image to come to you. Now, as the image begins to
appear, look carefully at the face of woman, look especially at her eyes
and her mouth, and see how her eyes and mouth embody the qualities
of warmth and nurturing and empathy. Look at her posture, how she
stands, and see how her body language conveys the qualities of warmth
and nurturing and empathy. Maybe you'd like to take her hand and just
feel how her hand embodies warmth, nurturing, and empathy. Good.
TABS Off

Installing the Image

At this juncture, the clinician needs to make a choice informed by her clinical experience and knowledge of the particular client as to whether to facilitate a merger
of the alliance resource with the client, as was done with the quality resource. If
the alliance resource is a nonhuman figure, I would facilitate a merger. However,
with a powerful female representation that evokes so many qualities of the healthy
mother this client never had, I chose not to facilitate a merger by, for example,
bringing the image of mother into the client through his forehead or chest. Of
course Gerald had formed a mental representation of the woman figure, but I
wanted to have this figure available "outside" the client for use in later situations
that I expect to arise (see the "Attachment Remediation, Safe Face Skill," Chapter 12). Without stopping the TABS, I move directly to using the alliance resource
to facilitate putting more disturbing material in the container.

Clinician: **TABS On** Now, bring up the image of the container. See the
valve, and form the intention that some more of every disturbing thing
is going to go into the container. Open the valve. Bring in the image of
woman and see her supporting you with empathy, warmly nurturing
you as some more material begins to flow in. Also, bring up the image
of Military Man and the quality of discipline he provides. Just watch as
more material flows in, and raise your left index finger when as much
has gone in as will go in at this time. [*Finger rises.*] **TABS Off**

The client is now asked to take a deep breath and let it out and is then asked,
"And what comes up now?' Gerald reported, "More peace. Woman helped me
get the last in." When I asked for an assessment of, "what percent of every disturbing thing is in the container now?" Gerald reported "100%." The reader
should note the direct correlation between progress toward full containment and
supplying the client's missing resources.

Readers should also note that 100% containment is not an absolute
requirement. If a client endorses 98 or 99%, I will ask, "Are you comfortable
with that? Does that feel all right to you?" and if the client says yes, we will
proceed to the next skill. The clinician should remember that once installed, a

skill such as containment is always available, and if necessary, therapy can return to it to containerize material that was left out at this juncture.

The Case of Charlene

Before proceeding, I want to offer the case of Charlene to illustrate another type of situation regarding filling the container. Charlene depicts a different type of missing quality and a demonstrates a unique image the client produced to embody the necessary quality. In her mid-30s, Charlene had come for help with binge eating, which had been refractory to therapy including EMDR therapy over several years. Summarizing her history, which included drug abuse and promiscuous sex, she wrote, "Looking at my story you'd think I had been sexually abused, but I really have no memory of it." In her previous therapy following standard EMDR procedures, she had experienced difficulty installing a safe place, stating, "There was no safe place where I could feel protected from my father." As I have stated, the AMST begins with containment for just this reason. Apparently her introjected father threatened her currently, as he must have at some time in the past. In her history, she disclosed that he had slapped her face in front of neighbors. According to Federn (1952; see Watkins & Watkins, 1997) when an introject is object-cathected, the self relates to it exactly as the self related to the actual person when the introject was first formed. In Charlene's case, her paternal introject elicits fear affect. Following the AMST protocol, I began my work with Charlene by asking her to create a container that would be sufficient to contain not only every disturbing thing, but specifically, "Dad and every memory and experience associated with him." I chose to emphasize "Dad," because the client had disclosed that there was no place she could feel safe from him, which apparently also meant that she could not be safe from him in her own mind.

Charlene responded, "I don't like to move him, because then I feel bad. [*Cries*] I feel like if I move him from where he wants to be then he'll be mad at me and I'll be mean to him." This statement strongly suggests a traumatic bonding between Charlene and her father (Chu, 1998). Chu wrote that "prolonged exposure to intermittent abuse predisposes persons to form powerful emotional bonds to abusers" (p. 106). It appears that Charlene is deficient in a quality that she would have to possess in order to enable her to separate herself from her introjected father. Following this therapeutic inference, I asked Charlene, "What quality would you need to have to move him, to tolerate moving him?"

Charlene responded, "I would need to have total indifference, to not be affected by anything I do in relation to him."

Mindful of the strength of traumatic bonding, and not wanting to overly stress my client, I opted to set a time limit on the duration of containment of her father. We were conducting an intensive therapy of 3 hours per day for 5 days, so I framed my request to her as follows: "For 5 days would you like to have total indifference for your father, so that would allow you to put him in the container? At the end of the 5 days you can make a decision about what you want to do with him then."

Charlene agreed. When asked for an image that embodied the quality of total indifference, Charlene described "The Thing," one of Marvel Comics' Fantastic

Four characters. "The Thing" is a physically very powerful figure who is made of rocks. Following the procedure already described, I facilitated the surfacing of the image of "The Thing" and her merger with the image bringing in total indifference to father for 5 days. Returning to the containment skill, Charlene was now able to place her father in a steel bank vault with 18-inch thick walls. As she completed the skill, Charlene laughed for the first time in session, and then stated, "This feels weird. This goes against who I am or what I feel like when I do something for me." The client's verbalizations suggest that acquisition of the missing quality and her ensuing success in containing an abusive paternal introject promoted the first stages of the emergence of her autonomy. Possessing the quality of total indifference, she could begin to recognize how different she felt when freed of the introject's influence. The work reported here for Charlene took place during the intensive therapy as noted above. Subsequent events in the therapy confirmed the supposition of traumatic bonding, because she recollected body memories and images that confirmed for her that her father had in fact molested her.

INTERVENTIONS WHEN FILLING IS INCOMPLETE: EGO STATE INTERVENTIONS

If a significant portion of the disturbing material is still not contained, this indicates that a covert ego state may be active and, in its protector function, is preventing the client from containing every disturbing thing.

The third intervention, ego state intervention (Figure 6.1), addresses the question: who is preventing every disturbing thing from going into the container? A fundamental principle of an ego state intervention is that ego states are recognized by their actions. One action of protector ego states may be to prevent disturbing material from being containerized. Although it may seem intuitively counterproductive that a helper ego state would prevent disturbing material from being contained, it is important for the clinician to accept the client's personality system as it presents itself. The clinician should avoid judgments and should seek to uncover with the client the organization and workings of the client's self system. However maladaptive that organization and functioning may seem to the clinician, it is important to realize that the organization and functioning emerged over developmental time to facilitate the client's ability to survive in the developmental environment. Only by accurately uncovering its operations can the clinician facilitate for the client the emergence of more adaptive functioning. The clinician's attunement to the client's difficulties in experiencing affects when they are called for or participating in the protocol are vital to recognizing the presence of covert ego states.

The Case of Irving

The case of Irving exemplifies the ego state intervention and provides an excellent framework for presenting the principles thereof. Irving was in his late 20s. He was enrolled in a very demanding college-level educational program, and he came seeking help with procrastination over schoolwork. He was the youngest of seven children, the only child of a mother and father who each brought three children to the marriage. The mother, who appears to have had significant borderline features, was extremely physically and verbally abusive. She hit her children with objects or threw objects at them, usually aiming for the head. Irving repeatedly witnessed abuse of his siblings.

Following the protocol, I asked Irving for an image of a container sufficient to hold every disturbing thing, and he visualized a "gallon Mason jar," and said, "The thickness doesn't matter, these are only thoughts." After the first attempt at transferring every disturbing thing to the container, Irving said, "I got an image of my mom beating my brothers" when he was asked "What comes up now?" Using the valve we had installed, we placed that image in the container and attempted to add more material. At the conclusion of the second attempt, Irving verbalized, "I saw my brother laughing as mother beats him [the brother]. Her existence became a joke at that time." Using the valve, this image was placed in the container. Explaining that I wanted to assess our progress, I asked the client what percent of every disturbing thing was in the container at this time, and he said 0.5%.

Structuring my intervention with the AMST Decision Tree, I asked Irving what quality he would need to enable him to get some more material into the container, and he stated "trust," spontaneously adding, "Because a son should be able to trust his mother." His image that embodied the quality of trust was a "group of young people supporting, as one person falls backwards into the arms of another." We developed and then installed this image exactly as described above. When asked, "What comes up now?" at termination of the installation and cessation of TABS, Irving produced the following feedback, "Doubt. Doubt in the lasting quality of any relationships based on the physical or social environment." Irving's words suggested that his self structure included an ego state that held the system's doubt. For conceptual purposes, this ego state was identified as "The One Who Holds the Doubt." Clearly, the existence of this ego state was related to the quality of trust he said he needed to be able to contain more material. Furthermore, his attachment was apparently contaminated by his inability to trust his mother not to beat him or his siblings, a fact he revealed when he said, "A son should be able to trust his mother." In this context, an ego state holding the system's doubt can be seen as protective, because if the ego state always doubts "any relationships based on the physical or social environment," then the system is protected against assault from a world that appears to it inherently untrustworthy.

Fundamentals of Ego State Intervention

The fundamentals of an AMST ego state intervention will be presented now, then we'll pick up Irving's story again to illustrate their application.

Identification: Identification is the first step in an AMST ego state intervention. Ego states are identified by their actions. Watkins and Watkins (1997) defined an ego state as "an organized system of behavior and experience whose elements are bound together by some common principle, and which is separated from other such states by a boundary that is more or less permeable" (p. 25). Sometimes, as with Irving, the ego state will make itself known by the system's answer to the question, "What comes up now?" Alternatively, when significant uncontained material remains after developing a quality resource and an alliance resource, the clinician will ask, "Is anyone preventing you from getting more material into the container?" Since ego states are semiautonomous helpers, they will usually either volunteer their existence or make themselves known when given the opportunity to do so. Identifying ego states by their actions or creating an opportunity for the ego state to "come forward" *if in fact it exists* provides the best protection against the therapist's creating a spurious artifact. Once identified, the next step is to elicit the ego state, or "bring it forward."

The Conference Room: Ego states are best encountered in a conference room visualization or "hallucinated room" (Watkins & Watkins, 1997, pp. 109–110). Creating a conference room is the second step in the intervention. Development of a conference room, which is a safe and secure place where parts of the self can emerge, can be facilitated with TABS or trance. AMST employs the special learning state that is created by the protocol and facilitated by TABS. As we have said, AMST does not itself employ trance or hypnosis. The conference room technique was originally developed by hypnotherapists, and it has been adapted to serve the needs of AMST for an ego state intervention. Clinicians trained in Ericksonian or formal hypnosis may elect to use a trance induction to facilitate the conference room visualization. Clinicians not trained in hypnosis can use TABS to facilitate the conference room visualization, asking the client to close his eyes as the clinician helps him develop the image. If elicited using TABS, the conference room visualization may be viewed as a deepening of the AMST special learning state that facilitates the emergence of part selves or ego states. If elicited using formal or Ericksonian trance, the conference room may be viewed as an example of how clinicians can interweave multiple therapeutic modalities into the AMST protocol. In any case, the clinician should use either TABS or trance to facilitate the conference room, but should probably not use them together. If TABS is used, stimulation should be provided continuously at a moderate to slow rate throughout the intervention.

The conference room is not necessarily the same visualization as a safe place, and I prefer to keep them separate unless the client insists otherwise. Whether trance induction is employed or the intervention is facilitated with TABS, the client is asked to visualize slowly stepping down three stairs, one at a time, that lead to a safe and secure room. At each stair, the clinician suggests, "As you step down onto the thick pile carpet covering the stair, your inward focus deepens twice as much." The clinician may accompany the client down the stairs or not, depending upon the client's desire. Once in the room, the client is asked to describe it, and the therapist will want to take notes about the furnishings, lighting, and windows for later use.

Inviting the Ego State In: After the client has described the room, the clinician proceeds to the third step of the intervention, inviting the ego state to enter the room, as follows:

I'd like to call your attention to the far end of the room. Notice a door there. It is almost completely open. There is a hallway beyond the door that disappears into the distance. I'd like you to form the intention that "The One Who Is Preventing the Container From Filling," if it exists, will come down the hallway and into the room, and I'd like you to tell me in a voice I can understand what you are seeing.

Ego states think concretely and literally, so it is important to name the ego state by its actions. In the case of Irving, we invited "The One Who Holds the Doubt" to come into the room. Later the ego state will be asked how it wants to be addressed. The ego state must be accepted on its own terms. Sometimes they want to stand in the hallway. Sometimes they initially present without a body, in which case the client will answer, "I didn't see anything" when asked to describe what she was seeing. In this case, I said, "I hear you saying you didn't see anything come into the room" and then asked, "I wonder did you get a sense that something came in that you may not be able to see?" Assuming that a figure has appeared, I next ask the client, "May I have permission to speak directly to the one who has come into the room." With permission granted, the fourth and fifth steps, affiliation and honoring, respectively, can be taken.

Affiliation: Affiliation, the fourth step, begins the process of building a relationship with the ego state, one in which it feels safe. Adapting Watkins and Watkins (1997), I ascertain that the ego state can speak to me. Sometimes they cannot, or do not feel safe doing so, in which case the clinician will need to develop ideomotor finger signals for "yes" and "no" and conduct the interview through that modality. I ask the ego state to validate that it is in fact the ego state we intended to "bring forward." I do this by asking, "Are you indeed 'The One Who Is Preventing the Container From Filling'?" I then ask the ego state for a name that it would like to be called. It is important to elicit a name that distinguishes the ego state from the client. I affiliate with the ego state by briefly introducing myself and then explaining, "[Name of client] has asked me for help in achieving some goals and in dealing with some life problems. I appreciate that you've come forward when asked, because it tells me our objectives are the same, to help [name of client].

Honoring: It is important to ascertain how the ego state conceives of its helper function and to honor it for all that it has done to help the client. Honoring constitutes the fifth step. I begin by recognizing the ego state's helper function and honoring its contribution by stating, "I know that you've been helping [name of client] for many years, and I appreciate that you have come forward when we asked you to, because it tells me you are here to help now." Having acknowledged the ego state's helper function, I move to learn how exactly it helps. I will ask the ego state to describe how it helps the client, by inquiring, "Tell me please [name of ego state], how you help [name of client]." I carefully note the ego state's responses.

Negotiation: The sixth step in the process is negotiation, which has several objectives. The first objective of the negotiation is to unblock the client's full and effective participation in the AMST process. The ego state will have been formed at an earlier developmental time when its actions were adaptive. It will not know that its actions are no longer adaptive. The clinician will use the client's stated objectives for therapy and the ego state's commitment to a helper function as levers to facilitate change. Another objective is to transfer responsibility for whatever is preventing more material from going into the container from the ego state to the client. For Irving this entailed having him state that he would take responsibility for recognizing, tolerating, and regulating the system's doubt.

Role Reassignment: The seventh step in the AMST ego state intervention is role reassignment. The objective is to enlist the aid of the ego state as a helper, sentinel, or bodyguard with a new function. It is important that the ego state not feel threatened with annihilation; proposing a new helper function obviates that threat. I review the negotiation with the client and ego state, having each one reaffirm its commitment to the new relationship. The client accepts responsibility for managing the behavior, attitude, or emotion that was preventing more material from going into the container, and the ego state agrees to cede responsibility to the client. The ego state agrees to a new helper function (e.g., as sentinel) and to signal the client when the problem behavior, attitude, or emotion is surfacing. The clinician helps the system arrange for a signal the ego state will use and elicits the client's agreement that he will pay attention to the signal.

With the completion of the ego state intervention, the clinician returns the client from the conference room to the counseling office. If the clinician has employed an Ericksonian or formal hypnotic trance to facilitate the conference room, she will want to use techniques appropriate to those modalities to terminate the trance. If TABS has been used to facilitate the conference room, the clinician may find that her client's special learning state has deepened considerably over the course of the conference room intervention. She should carefully observe her client and assess his level of inward focus. If necessary, she should reorient the client to the counseling office by counting backwards from three to one as indicated in the following example.

I see that your inward focus has deepened considerably, and so I'll be counting backwards from three to one to reorient you to the counseling office. Three. Please wiggle your toes in your shoes to reconnect with the floor of the office here. [Client wiggles toes.] *Good. Now, please wiggle your fingers and feel the arms of the chair.* [Client wiggles fingers.] *Good. Two. Deep breath, and connect with the air in the office here.* [Client breathes deeply.] *Good. Eyelids beginning to flutter. Coming back into the room.* [Client's eyelids flutter.] *Good. One. Completely back into the room. And a big stretch.* [Client and therapist both stretch.] *Good.*

As soon as the client is comfortably back, the clinician can proceed immediately to complete the containment skill.

The Case of Irving, Part 2

Returning to the case of Irving illustrates how an ego state intervention resolved his system's doubt. As you will recall, upon completion of an installation of a resource for the quality of trust, Irving expressed doubt in the lasting quality of any social relationship. I briefly explained the concept of an ego state and suggested that we might be meeting a part of his personality system that held the system's doubt. I described how this might serve to protect the personality system and obtained his agreement to pursue meeting this part.

Following the steps already presented, I used TABS to facilitate development of a conference room. Irving described a barren room with a bed, a night stand, and a lamp. With TABS continuing throughout the conference room phase, I called his attention to the door and hallway, I asked him to form the intention that "The One Who Holds the Doubt" would appear. A figure looking much like himself appeared and wanted to be called "What's the point." What's the Point had been with Irving for "too long to remember" and helped by "protecting against failure," which it accomplished by telling him that "life is pointless." What's the Point acknowledged that this tactic doesn't really protect against failure, but rather gives Irving a reason to explain failure when it inevitably occurs. The ego state expressed willingness to help Irving in a new way. Following my directions, Irving verbalized, "I take responsibility for trust" and What's the Point agreed to become a sentinel and alert Irving when he began to doubt. The two agreed on a signal—What's the Point would elbow Irving in the ribs to notify him—and Irving committed to noticing the signal and learning the AMST skills to manage his doubt. At this juncture, TABS was turned off, and Irving was brought back from the conference room to the counseling office. Irving's comments when asked, "What comes up now?" were benign, and so the work immediately returned to the quality resource installation.

Recall that Irving had produced an image for the quality trust of one person falling backwards into the arms of another as a supportive group of people watched. With TABS facilitation, I repeated the development and installation of this image, reminding Irving of his new ally, What's the Point, who will alert him if he begins to doubt. I reminded him of his own commitment to take responsibility for managing doubt. Having completed the quality resource intervention by installing the trust visualization, I returned, with TABS, to the containment skill, asking Irving to hold the intention that more material would go into his gallon Mason jar container and also asking him to hold the image of his trust resource and the image of his new ego state ally, What's the Point. Irving's container-filling process occurred in several segments. He would raise his finger, I would stop the TABS and ask for feedback, and he would verbalize some new "disturbing thing" that had surfaced, which we would then place in the container with TABS facilitation. The first disturbing memory that surfaced was "I failed the fourth grade," which was placed in the container with the reminder to use the trust quality resource and his ego state ally, What's the Point. The next memory was "Me being mean to other kids," which was also containerized. Then came a memory of "Me thinking I'd never be big and strong," and that too was placed in the container. At this point, a positive affective–cognitive verbalization appeared, which Irving expressed as "self-improvement."

As previously explained, when positive affect appears, especially early in the AMST process, and particularly with a client with such significant depressive features as Irving, the clinician should address the positive affect by eliciting the sensations that accompany it, the body location, and then developing an appropriate positive cognition (PC). Irving stated that he experienced "self-improvement" as sensations of physical stature that he felt throughout his body. With TABS facilitation, Irving was asked to notice the sensations of physical stature throughout his body and to repeat the positive cognition, "The sensations of physical stature throughout my body tell me I am feeling self-improvement." Readers should note the evolution of Irving's process during the course of this one-hour session. He visualized a container, but could not transfer much material to it, because he lacked the quality of trust, which he associated with his mother's untrustworthiness. As he developed an image for the missing quality, a protector ego state surfaced that had helped Irving's personality system by doubting social relationships. With the transformation of What's the Point to an ally, and with Irving's acceptance of responsibility for managing doubt himself, several disturbing memories could surface which he was able to contain. One of these was a negative self-concept that he would never be big and strong. With this disturbing self-reflective appraisal contained, a positive appraisal could now surface, "self-improvement," which notably was framed in terms of his stature.

As our first 1-hour session was drawing to a close, I asked Irving to assess what percent of every disturbing thing was now in containment, and he said 10%. The reader will note that development of the quality resource and the ego state intervention promoted a 20-fold increase from 0.5 to 10% in the amount of contained material. I asked my client to just be aware of What's the Point during the week until our next session. At the next session, Irving reported that What's the Point had elbowed him in the ribs several times during the week to inform him that he had begun doubting. Irving stated, "I have told What's the Point that I have to just plow through the schoolwork." He also stated he had used the trust visualization throughout the week, telling What's the Point, "I have to trust myself to do the schoolwork." At this point, I asked Irving to hold the image of himself using his trust visualization, working with What's the Point, trusting himself, and doing his schoolwork, and with TABS facilitation, I asked him to repeat this positive cognition, "I am learning to trust myself." We returned to the containment skill, and with TABS facilitation I asked Irving to form the intention that some more disturbing material would flow through the valve into the container. At the completion of the first attempt he verbalized receiving an "image of my sister who passed away." After placing this in the container, I asked for an assessment of what percent of every disturbing thing was now in the container, and Irving reported that 100% was is in the container.

ADDITIONAL CONSIDERATIONS
FOR CONTAINMENT SKILL

Clinicians teaching the containment skill to clients may at some point have a patient who doubts that the valve mechanism works. When the client says, "How do I know the valve works? How can I be sure stuff won't pour out if I open it?" the clinician can facilitate the client in practicing use of the valve. Ask the client to select a low-level disturbing thing that is now in the container. For one client this was a minor fender bender. Here is the instruction I gave the client:

TABS On *Visualize your container, which is a silvery steel tank, like an oxygen tank. See the valve and the sign. Realize that it will serve your healing to practice using the valve by taking out the image of the fender bender. Good. Now, form the intention that the fender bender will come out, but that nothing else will come out with it. Now open the valve, and watch as the fender bender incident comes out. Good. Let me know by raising your left index finger when the incident is out.* [Client's finger is raised] *Now, close the valve. Just take a moment to notice the fender bender incident. Good. Now form the intention that the fender bender will go back in the container. Open the valve. Watch as it goes in, and let me know by raising your left index finger when it has returned to the container.* [Finger rises] *Now, close the valve.* **TABS Off**

I asked the client if anything else escaped from the container when she took out the fender bender incident, and she answered, "No." I asked her then to hold the visualization of taking the fender bender out and putting it back in along with the realization that nothing else escaped and, with TABS facilitation, I had her repeat the following PC, "I am learning to trust my container."

Fearful clients may be helped by adding an alarm or a guardian image to the containment visualization. A client of a therapist who participates in my AMST discussion group on the Internet felt nervous that when containment was complete some disturbing material might ooze out or the valve might malfunction. The therapist facilitated installation of an alarm to alert the client in the rare event that would happen. One of my clients, whose container was a munitions bunker with 18-inch thick steel doors, placed a guard dog in front of the doors. The dog would bark if the disturbing material threatened to escape.

An important consideration for the clinician to recognize is that often the client's personality is organized by the disturbing things that have happened to him or her, and such clients become distressed when the self is separated from the disturbing material through the containment skill. One manifestation of this phenomenon occurs when the client places herself in the container with every disturbing thing. Although a rare occurrence, I have been contacted via e-mail by two different clinicians who reported the following experience with a client. In each case, the clinician had completed skill I (containment) and verified that 100% of every disturbing thing was contained; however, in each case the client did not report feeling relief, the expected outcome. Upon questioning, the clients disclosed that they had placed themselves in the container with every disturbing thing. If this happens, the clinician should repeat the containment skill, this time cautioning the client to visualize the container and to visualize himself outside the container, watching as it fills.

When a client's personality is organized by the adverse experiences of her life, the client will feel uncomfortable being separated from that material, because in the absence of the material she may feel disorganized. In these cases, follow the client's lead and do not force her to put more into the container than she is comfortable with. After the first round of container filling, some clients have stated, "I put the last in, but I'm not sure how comfortable I am with it in there." The clinician can offer this suggestion, "How about leaving it there for the duration of our session today. You will be learning some more skills that may make it easier to leave the things contained. At the end of the session, we can come back to the container, and you can decide then whether you want to leave it in or not. Will that work for you?" Other clients, after getting 60 or 70% into the container expressed comfort when asked "What comes up now?" Then, when filling continued and reached 80–90%, the client responded "I'm starting to feel nervous," when asked for feedback. In this case the clinician can ask, "What amount do you think you'd feel comfortable having in the container?" and can use TABS to facilitate removal of some of the disturbing material. With these types of clients, the clinician will want to return to skill I after creating a safe place and again after working through skills III–VII to see if the client has achieved sufficient stabilization to be able to contain more material. These cases illustrate the diagnostic function of the AMST. The clinician uncovers deficits in the organization and structure of the self that can be remediated in therapy.

The Case of Jennifer

The case of Jennifer illustrates how an ego state was uncovered whose function was to protect the self by preventing containment of 100% of disturbing material. At the time of our work together, Jennifer was in her late teens. She came seeking help for bulimarexia, which was defined by her behaviors of bingeing and purging, exercising compulsively, and restricting food. In our first session, following the protocol as described, Jennifer visualized a "tall, narrow, glass cylinder" for her container. With TABS facilitation, she visualized "every disturbing thing" flowing into the container. When asked to assess the completeness of filling, she reported seeing 100% moving into the cylinder, and then, "My head tells me I need to do the right thing, and my head empties the container by one half." It appeared clear to me that an ego state was making itself known through its action of emptying the container by one half, and at this point I elected to pursue an ego state intervention. The reader should note that while the AMST Decision Tree prescribes a quality resource and then an alliance resource before an ego state intervention, the ordering of the interventions is not absolute. Quality resource, alliance resource, and ego state intervention are skills, tools that the clinician can use as dictated by the flow of therapy. When an ego state like Jennifer's My Head surfaces, it should be addressed immediately. The appearance of an ego state like My Head is not accidental. Ego states are protectors and helpers, and the appearance of My Head indicated it felt safe enough to reveal its existence and to collaborate in the therapy. I immediately noticed its appearance, suggested that it had been helping by keeping some material out of containment, and asked Jennifer if she was willing to negotiate a new relationship with this part. She agreed.

The objective of the ego state intervention was to meet My Head and to negotiate a new helping relationship. Using trance, I assisted Jennifer in creating a conference room, and then asked her to invite My Head to enter the room. My Head, who looked much like the client, entered the room and stated, "I'm the one who wants Jennifer to do everything right." Apparently My Head manifested Jennifer's perfectionism. My Head acknowledged that it was responsible for removing half the disturbing material from the container. Thus it appears that My Head needed disturbing material to be uncontained in order to help Jennifer's personality system. My Head volunteered that it was the one who told Jennifer that she was ugly, stupid, and fat. Tailoring the negotiation to the fact that that we were just beginning therapy, I asked Jennifer to inform My Head that she wanted to learn new ways and that she wanted My Head to help. My Head agreed to help Jennifer as requested. Terminating the trance, we returned to the containment skill, and with TABS facilitation, Jennifer visualized every disturbing thing flowing into the cylinder. Asked for an assessment, she reported that 100% was now contained and staying in containment. She volunteered that she felt "comfortable all over."

USING CONTAINMENT IN SESSION
OR BETWEEN SESSIONS

The container is especially useful when disturbing material intrudes during a session. A technique I have employed when a client experiences a flashback during a session is designed to quickly extract the client from the disturbing scene. When the client reveals she is experiencing a flashback, I have the client immediately put the label "Flashback" on the scene and instruct her to just look at the label. Then I facilitate her putting the labeled scene into containment. I coach the client as follows:

TABS On *Label the scene with the word* flashback. *Condense the scene and just look at the label. You no longer need to look at the scene. Good. Now form the intention that the labeled scene is going in the container. Just see the label that stands for the scene. See the valve and open it. Now watch the letters go in. See the F go in. Now the L. The A, S, H, the B, the A, the C and the K. Good, now close the valve. Excellent. All in. Now repeat after me, "I am learning to contain my flashbacks." Let that become entirely true.* **TABS Off**

Once the client has acquired the containment skill and successfully transferred a significant portion of disturbing material to the container, the clinician should inform the client that he can use the skill between sessions should more disturbing material surface. The client can be taught to provide TABS by tapping on his knees or by means of the butterfly hug, in which the arms are crossed over the chest and the client taps alternately on each shoulder. The clinician can provide the following instructions, "If something disturbing should come up, just tap on your knees or shoulders, visualize your container, see the valve, form the intention that the disturbing thing will go into the container, open the valve, watch it go in, and then close the valve."

WORKING WITH DIFFICULT CASES

Clients with significant attachment disordering who also endorse trauma or adversity in their histories may have appreciable levels of fragmentation of self structure as well as severe affect dysregulation. These clients will qualify as difficult cases, no matter what the diagnosis. AMST's containment skill can help these clients, but care must be taken in its application. The clinician should be prepared to proceed slowly and should adapt the protocol to the special needs of the client. Application of skill I to the special case of borderline personality disorder (BPD) and to dissociative identity disorder (DID) will be presented. No clinician should attempt to work with these populations without special training and supervision. The International Society for The study of Dissociation has published guidelines for treatment of dissociative disorders.

Working with Children and Adolescents

Children present a special problem to the therapist because their cognitive and imagistic skills are not fully developed. Furthermore, depending upon their age, their internal working models are in the process of consolidating. In the child–therapist dyad, the therapist functions more as a surrogate for a primary caregiver. The therapist will use her supply of toys and figurines as well as drawing and modeling materials to teach the skills to her young client. Rather than focusing on containing every disturbing thing—a concept that will be much too abstract for the concrete mind of the child—the therapist will practice putting one bothersome thing in the container. Collaborating, the child and therapist may draw a picture of the container or construct one out of blocks. Children may not be able to work with the TheraTapper™ and one possible alternative is to ask the child to select a couple of figurines or toys that can be her helpers by tapping on her shoulders. Then, as the child is visualizing her one bothersome incident going into the container, the therapist can tap gently on the child's shoulders with the figurines. AMST therapy with children should have the quality of play.

Adolescents pose special problems for the affect-oriented therapist as well. In part, adolescents can be difficult because reconfiguration of neuron-to-neuron connections in the cortex occurring during this developmental phase can impair the adolescent's ability to think and to visualize. Adolescents can be difficult to work with because the oppositional defiant defense is employed as a protection against the identity fragmentation that is a common experience in this age group. Often, this client may be enmeshed in a family situation from which escape is impossible, and if the caregivers are unwilling to work as a family to help their adolescent child, this can compound the problems. The adolescent can be helped by working recursively, by using drawings to assist with visualization, and by avoiding insisting on appraisals that may trigger an oppositional response. After developing a container and filling it, the adolescent may respond "I don't know" when asked to assess what percent of every disturbing thing is in the container. The clinician should respond with acceptance, saying for example, "No problem," or "Okay, let's go on to the next skill." As the client learns the AMST and builds competence and as the therapeutic alliance grows, the clinician can return to Containment and get an assessment.

Working with Borderline Personality Disorder (BPD)

The borderline client will present the therapist with unique issues in developing the containment skill as the following case, summarized from the AMST discussion group, illustrates. A female client had been diagnosed BPD with comorbid alcoholism. She had several months of recovery, attended AA regularly, and expressed eagerness to learn the AMST skills. The client was able to contain 95% of every disturbing thing, and then stopped because she didn't feel safe. At this point the clinician made a therapeutic error, shifting to the safe place skill (skill II) instead of pursuing the direction prescribed by the AMST Decision Tree. The outcome is instructive because it reveals much about the material that had surfaced for the client in the containment skill. When asked, the client described a safe place in the arms of a man, a man that both client and therapist knew to be unreliable and who triggered the client's abandonment issues. The client's borderline rage was triggered by the therapist's suggestions that she identify some other safe place, apparently because the advice appeared to the client to be forcing her to separate from a figure who reenacted for her an unreliable, insecure attachment from childhood.

Shapiro (1995) has called attention to the "neuro networks" (p. 29) holding images, cognitions, sensations, and affects. Accessing a network is accompanied by evulsion of associated material, and the astute clinician can learn much about the client's self structure through noticing these associations. For this borderline client, something surfaced at the point when 95% of every disturbing thing was in the container, and the client began to feel unsafe. Containment of the remaining 5% threatened the client. The BPD client's next verbalization was associated with the disturbing material in a neural network, and the content of the verbalization demonstrated the core of the client's borderline pathology. The client associated the quality of safety with being held in the arms of a man she had previously identified as unreliable. In her neural network safety was assembled with the image of an unreliable male figure, with the affect anger elicited by the therapist's suggestion of separation, and with a cognition of deservingness that she verbalized as, "I deserve to be safe in the arms of a man." I hypothesize that in childhood, an important male figure was unreliable, and that this client-as-child formed an IWM of this unreliable male figure who provided what passed for safety in her young life. Her system's concept of deservingness assembled with this figure, and she came to believe that she deserved unreliable men who provided the illusion of safety. Apparently the last 5% of her disturbing material consisted in part of this image and all that was assembled with it in the neural network. She began to feel unsafe at the prospect of containing it, because her system's safety depended upon holding an IWM of an unreliable man. While the clinician's deviation from the AMST protocol provided valuable information, it also supports adherence to the protocol and helps us identify potential quality resources, alliance resources, and ego state interventions that might have been applied.

Adhering to the AMST protocol, the clinician ought to have asked, "What quality would you need to get the remaining 5% in containment?" From the foregoing discussion, we can suggest several qualities. One might be labeled *self-sufficiency*, meaning the ability to function without the organizing effect of an unreliable male introject. Of course the clinician would formulate this intervention in language appropriate for the client. Another quality might be tolerance for the anger she feels at the prospect of separation from this figure. Yet another quality might be "structuralization," meaning a "healthier organizing principle for my life than the image of an unreliable male figure." The clinician attuned to the deficits around which the borderline personality has organized will be able to conceive of alternative quality resources and will be able to guide the client with appropriate language to formulate an adaptive intervention.

If material remained uncontained after the quality resource, the clinician should inquire, "Who could help you get the remaining percent into containment?" (alliance resource). Here the clinician should be directive and suggest that the client identify qualities of an ideal paternal figure. Reliability, trustworthiness, and protection should be included among those qualities. With TABS, the clinician can facilitate for the client the emergence of an image from her unconscious that constellates the desired qualities.

Should material still remain uncontained, the clinician can proceed to an ego state intervention and ask, "Who is preventing the remaining percent from going in?" A core part self would be expected to surface who protects the system by telling her, for example, "All men are unreliable," "You can only be safe with unreliable men," "You need a man to provide safety, even if he's unreliable," or "You are so damaged that all you deserve is unreliable men." Following the ego state intervention presented above, this part can be negotiated into accepting a new job assignment.

Working with Dissociative Identity Disorder (DID)

AMST and in particular the containment skill can be valuable assets to assist the clinician in working with the DID. Several caveats must be emphasized before undertaking this topic. This section is meant *only* to suggest how the containment skill can be integrated into the stabilization phase (Paulsen, 1995) of therapy with DIDs, it is *not* meant to teach the treatment of this disorder. Treatment of DID requires extensive education, supervised practice, and long experience. No clinician should attempt to treat DID if such treatment is outside his or her area of expertise. The points presented below have been gleaned from exchanges with therapists experienced in treating DID that occurred on the on-line AMST discussion group regarding utilization of the AMST skills in helping the DID client.

Transmitting AMST skills to the DID client will be a protracted process. I have described the AMST as a brief therapy and noted that for many Axis I disorders the complete skill set can be transmitted in six, 1-hour sessions. This is not the case for the DID client. The stabilization phase of therapy (Paulsen, 1995) with the DID will be slow, and it will be slower if the client has been recently violated. The clinician must be aware of his or her own hope for a rapid reduction in symptoms and must be aware of the danger of setting the client up for failure through targeting unattainable goals. "The slower you go, the faster you'll get there" is a useful maxim. For many DIDs, just coming to therapy is the most they can manage, and what the client most needs is for the therapist to simply be present.

The value of the AMST for therapy with DIDs, or with any fragmented system whether the fragments are ego states or alters, is that the structured protocol promotes communication and cooperation among the fragments. Employment of the containment skill illustrates this point. The containment skill must be taught to each part, each alter as it appears, beginning with the part that is executive at the inception of therapy. The clinician will need to be patient and willing to return to skills that have already been transmitted to known parts when a new alter emerges. The containment skill can promote communication and cooperation as the clinician presents the possibility that parts can use the same containment image. If the parts have each demanded their own containers, the clinician may at some point suggest merging the disparate containers into one. Discussion among the parts promotes communication and cooperation. The discussion provides the clinician with the opportunity to inquire of an unwilling part what quality it would need to be able to combine containers. The clinician must be sensitive to setting impossible goals for the client and creating failure scenarios that could set the therapy back.

The container image provides a meeting place that begins the long process of restructuralizing the self system. As each part places the disturbing material it holds into the container, the parts get to notice one another, becoming aware of their separate existences within one body. Negotiating the use of the valve and the meaning of the sign "To be opened only when it serves my healing" involves the parts in a cognitive discourse over the question of who or what is meant by *my* and who or what determines what is healing. An example comes from my work with an alcoholic woman. I had helped her develop a containment image and installed the valve and sign, when suddenly and wholly unexpectedly an alter surfaced and informed me that my client had no idea what needed to be contained, insisting that it was the alter who could best decide. I asked the alter if she would be happy with one valve for herself and one for my client. The alter agreed, and we installed two valves, one labeled with the client's name and one with the alter's.

For the DID, containment implies more than confinement of disturbing memories, thoughts, and emotions. Often, DIDs need to contain their own bodies to prevent them from separating from consciousness. Physically, the DID may do this by walling herself in with pillows or surrounding herself with comforters. The DID may not have been provided with necessary body contact in infancy and hence may lack body experiences. Furthermore, for abused DIDs the body may be experienced as a dangerous place to be. The creative therapist may adapt the containment skill, uniting it with body-active components, to provide the client with images that allow her to hold herself together.

The special case of the hostile, destructive, or tissue-damaging alter must be addressed. Although a tempting expedient, placement of destructive alters in containment is therapeutically contraindicated. In childhood, many DIDs were often shut up in containers (e.g., closets, boxes, or basements). Often, in childhood, the DID formed IWMs of attachment figures who were hurtful, and these IWMs become abuser alters. The abuser alter will feel hated and rejected if placed in containment and will quickly lose trust in the therapist and may then impede therapy. Remember, the hostile alter is usually a protector, and the patient will feel more vulnerable if its defender is contained. A better way to proceed is to help the hostile alter put its overwhelming emotions and uncontrollable impulses to act out into containment. The pay off for the alter is that it gets to stay and "just notice" the therapy and learn for itself that the therapy is safe.

Work with DIDs will be recursive, moving between skills. For example, the therapist may develop a container for the "system manager," the alter that helps the system function in the world and the part that is usually executive at the onset of therapy. Some fraction of this part's disturbing material will be contained. Another part may then surface, and the clinician will develop a container for it and succeed in containerizing some of its material. The clinician may go on to skill II (safe place) with the system manager, and as this skill is being developed, another alter may surface. The clinician will need to help the newly surfaced part to form its own container, then return to the safe place with the "system manager." Working patiently and recursively like this over time, the clinician can develop a container and safe place for each part and succeed in getting most of each part's disturbing material contained.

SUMMARY

Skill I (containment) transmits a sense of mastery to the client at the outset of therapy by teaching him or her to containerize disturbing material until the client learns the skills and tools necessary for adaptive resolution of the material. Containment secures the intrapsychic field so the client can acquire the remaining skills without intrusion or interference from disturbing material. Clients often report immediate feelings of relief. The protocol teaches the clinician how to cognize and strengthen such feelings of relief when they surface. The protocol provides for self-reports that give the clinician information about the client's resources and ego states. When missing resources are uncovered—as evidenced by an inability to transfer every disturbing thing to containment—the protocol provides three interventions designed to remediate the deficiencies that have been uncovered: the quality resource, alliance resource, and ego state intervention. The chapter presented each intervention and gave case study illustrations of how they are applied. The reader will note how containment (skill I) builds structure in the client's self. The image of the container, the act of filling it and sealing it, adding the valve operated by intention, and placing a sign on it all build structure in the client's self system that was not previously present. At the beginning of therapy, the disturbing material could roam free in the client's mind, intruding on awareness, influencing dreams, and motivating maladaptive behavior. The structure built by transmitting skill I is assumed to have a neurophysiological basis. New pathways are constructed in the brain as the collective image of the disturbing material (e.g., smoke, oil, garbage) with its associated affects, emotions, memories, and thoughts is combined with the image of the container. Still greater structure is built when the client says, "I am learning to contain every disturbing thing." The skill I process illustrates how AMST assembles image, memory, affect and emotion, and cognition in a process facilitated by TABS. The positive outcome is demonstrated for both client and clinician when the client says, "Everything, 100%, is in the container. What a relief!"

Chapter 7

Skill II: Safe Place

Chapter 7 will teach the clinician how to develop for the client an internal image of safety or comfort and to assemble it with cognitions, affects, and sensations into a complete Gestalt. The process entails several steps. First the clinician facilitates emergence of an unrefined image, which is then developed into a rich construct through eliciting perceptual sensory associations to the image. This construct is next assembled with a knowledge-oriented cognition, "I am safe," and subsequently with an affect-oriented cognition, "I feel safe." The process is completed by helping the client to identify sensations accompanying the emotion of safety. Figure 7.1 diagrams the basic steps in this portion of the protocol. The entire process is referred to as an *installation*. Korn and Leeds (2002) and Leeds (1997) pioneered the concept of developing resources found to be deficient in many clients, calling the process *resource development and installation*.

Shapiro (1995) described an 8-step process for creating an "emotional oasis" (p. 122), or safe place, the client can use to recover emotional stability if disturbance arises or to help the hypervigilant client. Shapiro suggested the exercise be used with all clients. AMST amplifies Shapiro's exercise with instructions to help the client uncover important perceptual concomitants of the safe place visualization, thereby optimizing involvement of sensory cortical areas. As previously stated, the affect management skills training (AMST) protocol differs from EMDR, because AMST begins with the containment skill to confine disturbing material that has been clinically observed to contaminate the safe place if it is not first neutralized.

The safe place skill is the second of seven fundamental skills, all of which should be developed prior to the inception of uncovering therapy, trauma processing, or therapy directed toward resolving an Axis I or II disorder. In

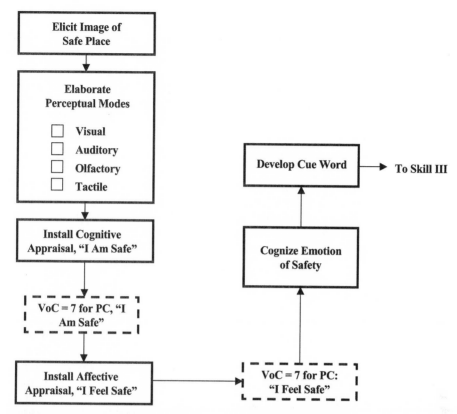

Figure 7.1.   Flow Diagram and Decision Tree (skill II, Safe Place). The straightforward development of a safe place is illustrated in this figure. In order to give a clear overview of the steps, interventions for dealing with complications have been omitted. Figures 7.2 and 7.3 illustrate interventions to be used when clients have difficulty with knowledge of safety or feeling safe.

particular, the safe place skill is theoretically justified by the fact that many clients whose childhoods were characterized by deficit, adverse, or traumatic experience do not have an internal image of safety and security. Children raised with "good enough" parenting form a complex affective–cognitive structure, assembled from multiple experiences occurring over the years, in which it was safe to express emotions, safe to be vulnerable, safe to love, safe to be a child. This affective–cognitive structure will share components with the internal working model (IWM) for a sensitive, responsive, attuned parent. By contrast, most clients either will not have such a structure, or will have a structure that is either incomplete or damaged in essential respects, rendering it unavailable to the client to a greater or lesser degree as an important internal, stabilizing asset. Providing the asset in the early phases of therapy contributes to expansion of the client's self structure and facilitates adaptive functioning both in therapy and in daily life.

PROCEDURE FOR SKILL II (SAFE PLACE)

The clinician's first task is to explain to the client the need for and value of an inner image of safety and security. Here are instructions the clinician can use:

Often, when people who come for therapy were children, they lived in situations in which they never had the experience of safety, never felt safe, so as adults they don't have an inner image of safety and security they carry with them and rely on during stressful times. At this point in our work, I want to help you develop an image of safety for yourself. You'll be able to use this in session to help you feel safe doing therapy, and you'll be able to use it in situations outside the counseling office when you want to produce a feeling of safety in stressful situations. You see, safety, the knowledge and feeling of safety, is something we carry within us. It does not depend upon the external situation. With an inner image of safety, it really doesn't matter what is happening around you, because you carry your image of safety inside.

Eliciting an Image

The clinician's next task is to help the client to produce an appropriate image. Here is a suggestion for applicable language:

What we're going to do now is develop an image of a safe place. Sometimes people have an experience or memory from adulthood of a time and a place where they actually knew they were safe and felt safe. If you have such a place I'd like you to share it with me. Ideally, this place should not depend for its safety on the presence of some person. The best kinds of places are often in nature. This should be a place where nothing bad happened. Now, if you've never had the experience of being someplace where you knew you were safe, that's okay, because we can construct such a place out of your imagination. So, having said all that, I wonder what is coming up for you now?

Should the client succeed in verbalizing a suitable image, (e.g., a beach or a woodland setting), the clinician should carefully record the image and then double check the suitability of the client's selection, as illustrated in this example: "You've said that you remember knowing you were safe on a beach. I just want to make certain that nothing bad ever happened on that or on any beach." If the client discloses that something bad did happen on a beach, but not the one she is visualizing, I suggest finding a new image, because the bad things that happened will contaminate the safe place through the mind's capacity to form associations between neural networks.

If the client is unable to produce an image of a remembered place, then ask the client to imagine a place of complete safety. The clinician may give instructions like these:

I'd like you to just let your mind relax. There is nothing you need to do. Just notice. And now, form the intention that an image of a safe place will emerge from your unconscious. Good. Let it surface, and let me know what you are seeing.

If the client still has difficulty, the clinician can repeat the instructions, this time facilitating the emergence of the image with TABS. When a client creates a safe place from imagination, its structure will give the therapist a view into the client's unconscious. The imagery may be rich or impoverished. The imagined safe place may be a magical sanctuary populated by mythical figures like unicorns, fairies, and elves, or it may be more barren.

Whether elicited from memory or imagination, the image produced at this junction is usually devoid of much detail. For example, the client may say, "It's at the ocean with a long curving sandy beach." Or, "I'm remembering a place in the woods by a stream." The clinician's next task is to help the client enrich the image by eliciting more perceptual information.

Strengthening Perceptual Modalities

This section will teach the clinician how to help the client summon up and strengthen perceptual information in four modalities, sight, sound, smell, and touch, associated with the image. Summoning up and strengthening perceptual information is termed *developing* the image. Note that TABS is used to facilitate the client's process of retrieving perceptual information. The subthreshold startle affect elicited by the gentle tactile stimulus is believed to facilitate the retrieval process by clearing the mind of extraneous "noise" and focusing the attention on the task at hand. The following instructions are useful:

What we're going to do now is enrich this image by having you just notice what you can see, hear, smell, and touch as you're in your safe place. Let's start with what you can see. I'll be turning on the TheraTapper in a moment and asking you to just look around at the safe place and notice what you can see. **TABS On** *See yourself in* [clinician repeats the client's words for the safe place]. *Just look around and notice what else you can see. Good. Good.* [Allow 10 to 12 seconds to elapse.] **TABS Off** *Deep breath. Let it out, and tell me, what did you see?*

Again, the clinician should carefully note what the client reports seeing, because this information is essential to refreshing the client's image throughout the process of installation. After developing the visual perceptual mode, the clinician should proceed to the auditory mode, then the olfactory, and finally the tactile sensory mode.

The Case of Tina

Here is an example of the process of developing the safe place image for Tina, a woman in her mid-40s who came for help in reducing the harm she was doing herself by smoking cigarettes. Note that the clinician elicits sensory information in four perceptual modalities: visual, auditory, olfactory, and tactile. This report also illustrates the operation of the therapeutic dyad and demonstrates the process of retrieval of a pleasant image from memory from a childhood that was largely chaotic and traumatic.

Clinician: I wonder if you could think back to a time when you knew you were safe.

Tina: It's been a long time.

Clinician: I believe that. Did you ever have a safe place, growing up?

Tina: Yeah. My safe house. My safe barn. Where the horses were. After I finished my chores, I went up there for years. I went up there and got to know the horses.

Clinician: Just to check, did anything bad ever happen in that barn or any other barn?

Tina: No.

Clinician: Good. Let's work with that. I'm going to turn on the TheraTapper in a moment, and I'd like you to just notice what you can see as you're in your safe barn. **TABS On.** See yourself in the barn now, your safe barn where the horses are. You've finished your chores, and you've gone up there to get to know the horses. I'd like you to look around now and just notice what you can see. Good. [*Allow 10 seconds to elapse.*] **TABS Off** Deep breath. Let it out, and tell me, what did you see?

Tina: I see chickens. The horses. A donkey. They were my friends.

Clinician: Excellent. This time, just notice what you can hear. **TABS On** See yourself in the barn, your safe barn. You've finished your chores and gone up there. There are chickens, the horses, a donkey. Your friends. Now, I'd like you to just notice what you can hear. Good. [*Allow 10 seconds to elapse.*] **TABS Off** Deep breath. Let it out, and tell me, what did you hear?

Tina: I heard the horses, snorting, moving around. The chickens clucking. There's a rooster that crows from time to time.

Clinician: Good. This time, I'd like you to notice what you can smell. **TABS On** See yourself in the barn, your safe barn. There are chickens clucking and a rooster that crows from time to time. The horses, your friends, are snorting and moving around. There's a donkey there too. This time, just notice any smells associated with the scene. Good. [*Allow 10 seconds to elapse.*] **TABS Off.** Deep breath. Let it out, and what did you smell?

Tina: Horse manure. The straw and grain. Barn smells.

Clinician: Wonderful. Now, this time, I'd like you to just notice what you experience through the sensation of touch. **TABS On** See yourself in your safe barn with your friends, the horses, the chickens, and the donkey. You can hear the chickens clucking and the rooster crows occasionally. You can smell the horse manure and hear the horses snorting and moving. This time, I'd like you to just notice anything you feel through the sense of touch. Good. [*Allow 10 seconds to elapse.*] **TABS Off** Deep breath. Let it out, and tell me, what did you feel through touch?

Tina: I felt the straw underneath me where I'm sitting. The rough boards against my back.

Readers will note the amount of repetition of descriptive detail as the clinician helps the client develop a strong image assembled with numerous perceptual observations. Each iteration strengthens the image and elaborates it as new sensory modalities are assembled with it. The next step is to create an association between this strong, vibrant image of a safe place and a cognitive appraisal of knowledge of safety.

Developing a Knowledge-Oriented Cognition

The clinician's next task is to install the knowledge-based cognition, "I am safe." This cognition embodies an appraisal of safety that involves an assessment of danger elements in the visualization as well as a judgment by the client of his intrinsic safety status. After installing the positive cognition "I am safe," the clinician will determine the validity of the client's cognition using the Validity of Cognition (VoC) scale. This element of the safe place skill has important diagnostic value as well as therapeutic worth. The client has stated that the image he has selected, whether retrieved from memory or created by the imagination, is factually safe. Thus, if the client is unable to endorse a certain validity for the cognition, "I am safe," it suggests that elements in the client's personality structure are responsible for the absence of safety. These elements may be missing qualities, or they may be introjects or ego states. After teaching the basic components of the skill, the chapter will go back over the material and teach the therapist how to uncover these elements when they exist and how to remediate them.

This step of the protocol enlarges the neurobiological structure already established by adding a cognitive element. The reader will realize how AMST has built a kernel of structure to this point through development of the safe place visualization and its consciously elaborated visual, auditory, olfactory, and tactile elements. Based on what is known of neurobiology, we may conjecture that we have primarily activated declarative memory and involved the sensory cortex, all right-side temporal lobe structures. The next step of the safe place skill enlarges this structure and involves the left hemisphere as a cognitive appraisal is invoked. The generalized instructions are:

We're going to assemble your image of a safe place with a knowledge-based statement now. I'll be recalling your safe place image and then asking you to repeat after me, "I am safe." This is different from feeling safe, and we'll get to the emotion of safety in a moment. First though, it is important for you to know with certainty you are in fact safe. **TABS On** *Bring up your image of your safe place again.* [Clinician repeats the name and all perceptual details of the client's safe place visualization.] *Now, as you hold this rich image, please repeat after me, "I am safe."* [Client repeats the phrase.] *Good. Let that become as true as it can be. Good. Good.* **TABS Off** *Deep breath. Let it out, and what comes up now?*

The content of the client's answer to the question "What comes up now?" determines what step the clinician takes next. In a moment we'll see Tina's positive, imagistic response. When the client produces a positive report, image, or memory, the clinician will want to strengthen the installation with another brief sequence of

TABS. Were negative memories, images, or thoughts to surface, I suggest placing them in containment. This will be illustrated later in the chapter.

Eliciting an Appraisal

Once the installation of the cognition "I am safe" is complete, the clinician solicits an appraisal from the client. At this juncture, the clinician introduces the VoC scale and then asks for an appraisal as follows:

From time to time we'll want to assess our progress with the work we are doing. This is one of those times, and so I want to introduce a rating scale now. This scale measures how true a statement is. The scale goes from 1, which signifies a statement is false, to 7 which indicates it is true. So, as you hold the image of your safe place [clinician will repeat enough detail so the image is optimally refreshed], *tell me, on a scale from 1 to 7, where 1 is false and 7 is true, how true is the statement "I am safe."*

Later in the chapter we will examine interventions the clinician can apply if the client's statement is less than completely valid.

The Case of Tina, Part 2

For the moment, we return to Tina and the completion of this stage of her safe place skill as she endorses complete validity for her knowledge-oriented cognition.

Clinician: TABS On Bring up the image of your safe barn again. See the horses, your friends, and hear them snorting and moving around. Smell the horse manure and straw and grain. See the chickens, and hear the rooster crowing. See the donkey. Feel the straw under you and the boards you are leaning against. Good. Now, as you hold this rich image, please repeat after me, "I am safe."

Tina: I am safe.

Clinician: Good. Let that become as true as it can be. Excellent. **TABS Off** Deep breath. Let it out, and what comes up now?

Tina: I saw a flower opening.

Clinician: TABS On Just go with that. Good. [*Let 5 seconds elapse.*] **TABS Off** Deep breath. Let it out. And what comes up now?

Tina: Some other flower, but a different kind.

Clinician: TABS On Just go with that. Good. [*Let 5 seconds elapse.*] **TABS Off** I'd like to check our progress now. To do that I'll give you a rating scale that measures how true something is. The scale goes from 1, which indicates that something is completely false, to 7, which indicates that it is completely true. So, as you hold the image of your safe barn, how true is the statement "I am safe" on a scale from 1 to 7, where 1 is false and 7 is true?

Tina: It's a 7.

Note the clinician's decision to affirm Tina's system's apparently positive and adaptive process when she verbalized an image of "a flower opening." The clinician knows that Tina is an artist, and he learns here the strength of her preferred mode of experiencing through the medium of images. Tina's positive neural networks produce imagistic associational material relating to the safe place image, and the clinician strengthens these associations by instructing the client to "just go with that" and adding another sequence of TABS. Our narrative will now address the topic of developing an affect-oriented cognition regarding the safe place.

Developing an Affect-Oriented Cognition

Once the client and clinician have developed a valid positive cognition for knowledge of safety and assembled it with the safe place visualization, the clinician should assist the client in developing a positive cognition regarding the feeling or emotion of safety. While safety is not a primary affect, it is a valid emotional construct that will be meaningful for many persons. The clinician can deliver instructions modeled on the following:

I want to turn our attention now to the emotion or feeling of safety. In our society people often do not discriminate between knowing they are safe and feeling safe, but these really are two different things. **TABS On** *Bring up the image of your safe place.* [Clinician repeats the name and all perceptual details of the client's safe place visualization.] *Recall that you know with complete certainty that you are safe in this place. Now, as you hold this rich image and the knowledge you are safe, please repeat after me, "I feel safe."* [Client repeats the phrase.] *Good. Let that become as true as it can. Good. Good.* **TABS Off** *Deep breath. Let it out, and what comes up now?*

After dealing with the content of the client's response to the question "What comes up now?" the clinician should request an assessment from the client regarding the validity of the positive cognition, "I feel safe." This can be presented as follows:

As you hold the image of your safe place [the clinician can repeat enough detail to refresh the image], *a place where you know with certainty that you are safe, on a scale from 1 to 7 where 1 is false and 7 is true, how true is the statement, "I feel safe"?*

Our narrative will provide instructions about interventions to employ if the appraisal is less than certain, but for now we will assume the client asserts the statement "I feel safe" is completely true and the clinicians proceeds to helping the client cognize the emotion of safety with its associated qualia.

Cognizing Safety Affect

Once the client has endorsed certainty, or near certainty, for the positive cognition "I feel safe," the clinician should proceed to help the client recognize the emotion of safety by the physical sensations he experiences that are associated with the emotion. The following instructions can be verbalized to the client:

I want to turn our attention now to helping you identify the sensations you feel in your body that accompany the feeling of safety. Our bodies tell us what emotions we are experiencing through these sensations, and we can improve our functioning by becoming aware of how our bodies communicate with us. **TABS On** *Bring up again the image of your safe place* [the clinician can repeat enough detail to optimally refresh the image]. *Recall that you know with certainty that you are safe and that you also know with certainty that you feel safe. Now, as you hold the image of the safe place and the knowledge you are safe and the feeling of safety, just notice where in your body there are sensations accompanying the image, the knowledge, and the feeling. Take all the time you need, and just signal me by raising your left index finger when you have become aware of the sensations. Good. Good.* [Client raises index finger]. **TABS Off** *Deep breath. Let it out, and tell me, what sensations came up for you?*

The clinician should help the client to verbalize the quality of the sensation; such as lightness, relaxation, peacefulness, and also the location in the body where the client is experiencing the sensations. Using the worksheet from Appendix A or her own notes, the clinician should record the name of the emotion, "safety," and the quality and location of the associated sensations. The clinician should then install a positive cognition that assembles safety emotion, sensations, and body location using the following language:

TABS On *Recall again the image of your safe place* [clinician can use the name and one or two details to refresh the image]. *Recall that you know with certainty that you are safe and with certainty that you feel safe. Now, become aware of the* [name of sensation] *that you feel in your* [body location] *and repeat after me, "The* [name of sensation] *in my* [body location] *tells me I am feeling safe."* [Client repeats verbalization.] *Let that become as true as it can become. Good. Good.* **TABS Off** *Deep breath. Let it out. And what comes up now?*

After attending to whatever verbalizations the client offers, the clinician should obtain a VoC for the appraisal by asking, "On a scale from 1 to 7 where 1 is false and 7 is true, how true is the statement 'The [name of sensation] in my [body location] tells me I am feeling safe.' "

The Case of Betty

The case of Betty illustrates how to apply these skills to help a client cognize the emotion of safety. Betty is a middle-aged woman who has come for help with binge eating. Her safe place was a pond that looked like an art nouveau painting. Following the protocol she amplified her visual perceptions. The pond was surrounded by pillars. A golden light infused the scene, pouring down through the trees beyond the pillars and the pond. In the auditory elicitation, she heard birds singing. In the olfactory segment, she could smell the oak trees and the musty, earthy smell emanating from beneath the trees. She could feel the sun, dappled by the trees, on her skin. The ambient temperature was warm, and she could feel the pond's cool water. Betty was able to endorse certainty for the knowledge-oriented cognition, "I am safe," and for the affect-oriented cognition, "I feel safe." I then proceeded as follows:

Clinician: TABS On Recall the image of the pond in nature. See the pillars and the golden light. Smell the oak trees and the odor of musty earth. Feel the sun, dappled by the trees, on your skin. By this pond, you know with certainty that you are safe and with certainty that you feel safe. Now, as you hold this image, I'd like you to just become aware of sensations in your body that accompany this visualization. Take all the time you need, and let me know by raising your left index finger when you get them. Good. Good. [*Betty raises her index finger.*] TABS Off Deep breath. Let it out, and tell me, what did you get?

Betty: I felt a grounded feeling. All over. And my chest is open.

Clinician: TABS On Bring up the image of your pond in nature where you know you are safe and you feel safe. Become aware of the grounded feeling all over and the openness in your chest. Now, please repeat after me. "The grounded feeling all over and the openness in my chest tell me I am feeling safe."

Betty: The grounded feeling all over and the openness in my chest tell me I am feeling safe."

Clinician: Good. Let that become as true as it can be. TABS Off Deep breath. Let it out. And what comes up now?

Betty: That feels true.

Clinician: So, on a scale from 1 to 7, how true is it?

Betty: It's a 7.

INTERVENTIONS WHEN KNOWLEDGE AND FEELING OF SAFETY ARE LESS THAN CERTAIN

The interventions presented in this section can be applied in the case of a client who has difficulty reaching complete validity for the knowledge-oriented cognition, "I am safe," or for the affect-oriented cognition, "I feel safe." The AMST Flow Chart and Decision Tree shown in Figure 7.2 will guide the clinician in applying the interventions where the client is unable to endorse certain validity for the knowledge-based cognition, "I am safe." As shown in Figure 7.2, the therapist will begin by assessing for missing qualities, then developing a quality resource. If validity is still less than certain after developing a quality resource, the clinician can assist the client to develop a helpful alliance resource. If validity still does not attain certainty, or near certainty, the clinician can seek to uncover a covert ego state, if one exists, that may be blocking achievement of complete validity. Once the client has endorsed certainty, or near certainty, for both the knowledge-oriented cognition and the affect-oriented cognition, the clinician should return to the protocol and facilitate the client's cognizing the emotion of safety. Figure 7.3

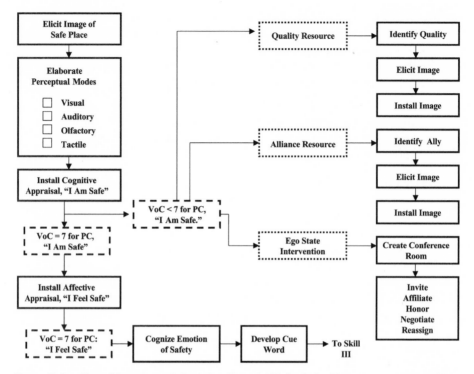

Figure 7.2. Flow Diagram and Decision Tree (skill II, Safe Place Interventions When Knowledge of Safety is Uncertain). This figure shows the decision point and interventions to be employed when the client is unable to endorse complete certainty for knowledge of safety in the visualized safe place.

reprises these same skills for the client who is unable to endorse certainty for the affect-oriented positive cognition (PC). "I feel safe."

The Case of Gerald

For the purposes of illustrating these interventions, the narrative will focus on the knowledge-oriented cognition, "I am safe." After assembling the image of the safe place with the knowledge-based cognition, the clinician should inquire, "As you hold the image of your safe place and the knowledge that you are safe, on a scale from 1 to 7, where 1 is false and 7 is true, how true is the statement, 'I am safe'?" When the client's response is less than 7, the clinician should inquire, "What quality would you need to have in order to increase your certainty that you are safe in your safe place visualization?" This constitutes the quality resource. The case of Gerald, the middle-aged man seeking help for binge eating, illustrates all three interventions that can be applied when validity is less than certain: quality resource, alliance resource, and ego state intervention. Recall that Gerald was adopted, that his mother was a rageaholic and an alcoholic, that he had been in recovery himself for many years, and that he described himself as fearful.

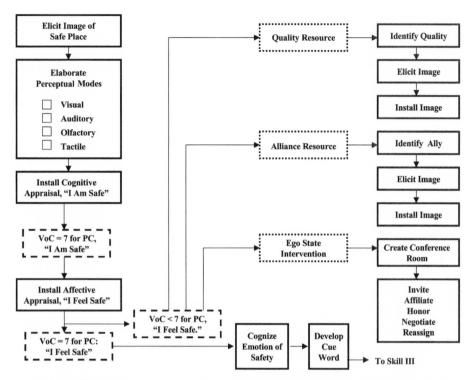

Figure 7.3. Flow Diagram and Decision tree (skill II, Safe Place Interventions When Feeling of Safety is Uncertain). This figures shows the decision point and interventions to be employed when the client is unable to endorse complete certainty for feeling safe in the visualized safe place.

When asked for an image of a place where he had experienced safety in his adult life, Gerald provided this initial description: "It's a beach along a creek near here. There's a swimming hole with granite boulders, and there's a rocky cliff you have to climb down to reach it." Following the protocol as presented, we developed more visual perceptual components, and Gerald added "his dogs, a view down the river, trees, cliffs across the river, and the sun, bright overhead" to his image. In the auditory mode, he was able to hear "the sound of water gurgling." When asked for smells, he reported "pine trees, a musty leafy smell, dry oak, and fresh air." He was able to feel "sand and rocks" in the tactile mode. Having developed the safe place image and explained the idea of knowing one is safe, the session proceeded toward installation of the knowledge-oriented cognition as follows.

> **Clinician: TABS On** See yourself at the swimming hole with the granite boulders. See the trees and smell the pines and oaks. See the view down the river and your dogs with you. See the rocky cliff and the sun. Feel the rocks and stones. Good. Now, as you hold this image, please repeat after me, "I am safe."
>
> **Gerald:** I am safe.

Clinician: Good. Let that become as true as it can be. **TABS Off.** Deep
breath. Let it out, and what comes up now?

Gerald: Stuff comes in and says "You're not safe."

Clinician: Just to check our progress, I want to give you a rating scale at this
time. This scale measures how true a statement is. The scale goes from
1, which is completely false, to 7 which is completely true. So, as you
hold the image of the swimming hole with the dogs and the cliff and the
trees, on a scale from 1 to 7, how true is the statement, "I am safe"?

Gerald: It's a 3.

The Quality Resource: The protocol has uncovered a deficit in Gerald's self-
structure: he apparently has difficulty knowing he is safe even in a situation that he
has appraised as factually safe. Recall that Gerald was adopted and that he spent
several months alone in a receiving nursery and that his mother was a severe alcoholic and rageaholic. We may surmise that deficits in his early infant–caregiver
environment resulted in deficiencies in his capability to know he is safe, even
when the environment is in fact safe. Following the protocol as shown in Figure
7.2, the clinician elicits Gerald's assessment of his missing quality and an image
that embodies that quality.

Clinician: Thank you. It's very helpful to know where we are. So, tell me,
what quality would you need to have to be able to increase the validity
of the statement "I am safe"?

Gerald: I think being more present in the visualization somehow.

Clinician: Can you give me an image that embodies being more present in
the visualization?

Gerald: Maybe if I could feel the sun on me more strongly.

Clinician: **TABS On** See yourself beside the river in the canyon. Feel the
sun on your skin. As you feel the sun on your skin, you realize that it
embodies the quality of being more present in the visualization. Just let
the sun warm your skin, penetrating it, and bringing with it the quality
of being more present. As it warms your muscles and bones and circu-
lates in your blood, the warm sun carries the quality of being more
present throughout your body, into every cell, into your brain, into your
mind, helping you to be more present in the visualization.

The clinician now reiterated the safe place visualization with TABS facilitation
and asked the client to repeat the knowledge-oriented cognition, "I am safe,"
while holding the feeling of the warmth of the sun and the quality of being more
present in the visualization that it afforded. Per the protocol, after turning off the
TheraTapper, the clinician asked the client, "Deep breath. Let it out, and what
comes up now?" The following exchange occurred:

Gerald: I feel a little calmer. I'm more willing to go there to the creek.

Clinician: Just to check our progress, as you look at the swimming hole
now, how true is the statement, "I am safe"?

Gerald: It's a 4. I had the thought that bad dudes could show up.

Clinician: Let's put the bad dudes in your container. **TABS On**. See your container, a graceful urn about 5 feet tall. See the valve in the side. Form the intention that the bad dudes are going to go into the container through the valve. Open the valve. Now, just watch them go in. Watch them go in. Let me know when they're all in by raising your left index finger. Good. [*Gerald raises his index finger.*] Close the valve. **TABS Off** Deep breath. Let it out, and what comes up now?

Gerald: That smoked 'em right up!

This segment of Gerald's session illustrates how the clinician needs to be flexible in using the protocol. The image of the bad dudes seemed to pull together into a cluster the misfortune that had appeared throughout Gerald's life, for example, in the many adverse experiences of being the adoptive child of an alcoholic, rageful mother. When this material surfaced, it immediately appeared to the clinician to fall into the category of "disturbing things," and he made a decision to place it in the container. After doing so, the clinician repeated the safe place visualization, refreshing the image of the swimming hole, and reminding Gerald of the sun bringing the quality of being present in the image, and also recalling the fact that the bad dudes were now in the container. Upon repeating the safe place installation, Gerald now stated that the validity of the statement, "I am safe," was a 5. The clinician proceeded to the next intervention, the alliance resource, as indicated by the AMST flow chart and decision tree, Figure 7.2.

The Alliance Resource: The alliance resource is designed to elicit an image of a helpful, supportive figure. In a healthy developmental environment, a child is surrounded by relatives and others who manifest qualities of competence, mastery, courage, self-reliance, and so forth. The child internalizes images of these persons that are assembled with the qualities they manifest, and across his lifetime the child, adolescent, and adult relies on these IWMS and their associated qualities for support in times of distress. This process is more or less conscious. Clients whose attachment period and socioemotional history lacks such role models will not have the supportive internal representations. Continuing with Gerald's session, we learn how the protocol assists the client to develop an ally and how the clinician helped the client to elaborate the ally's important qualities.

Clinician: I wonder who could help you become more certain that you are safe?

Gerald: What came up for me was Kain from the TV series *Kung Fu*.

Clinician: Fine. Let's install that. **TABS On** See the figure Kain from *Kung Fu*. See the rigorous training he experienced as a youth and how he endured the pain of being branded with the dragon. See his awesome martial arts skills. Realize that he has come to be an ally to help you develop more certainty that you are safe. Now, as you hold his image, allow that image to merge with you. It may come in through your forehead or your chest, I don't know, but the image of Kain comes in to help you achieve more certainty that you are safe. It moves out through your body, carrying the helper function to every cell in your body, to your brain, to every cell in your brain, bringing the knowledge that you have a powerful protector and ally. Good. **TABS Off** Deep breath. Let it out, and what comes up now?

Gerald: Nothing can hurt me.

Once again, with TABS facilitation, the clinician recalled Gerald's swimming hole and refreshed the perceptual components of the image. Reminding him of the quality resource, the sun warming his skin that allowed him to be more present in the scene, reminding him that the bad dudes were contained, and reminding him of Kain, his ally, the clinician asked Gerald to repeat the knowledge-oriented cognition, "I am safe." Gerald did so, and after turning off the TABS, he endorsed a VoC of 6 for the positive cognition, "I am safe," adding, "A boulder could drop out of the sky."

By now, I was seriously considering the possibility that Gerald had a covert ego state that protected him by preventing him from ever knowing with certainty that he was safe. Gerald had reached a plateau for the knowledge-oriented cognition, "I am safe." I decided to shift away from this cognition for a moment and to probe the emotion of safety by asking for an affect-oriented cognition. As will be seen, my client's response when asked for an appraisal of the validity of the statement "I feel safe" supported my belief that we were observing the action of a covert ego state. Explaining to Gerald that I wanted to shift our focus to the emotion of safety, I repeated the perceptual elements of his safe place with TABS facilitation, and this time asked him to repeat the positive cognition, "I *feel* safe." After turning off the TABS, Gerald responded to the question "And what comes up now" with the following verbalization, "I'm feeling turmoil . . . resistance . . . confusion, and tightness in my face. Anxiety." His VoC for the positive cognition, "I feel safe," was a 6. Based on what we had observed in session, I felt comfortable suggesting that perhaps we were seeing the action of a protector ego state that resisted allowing Gerald to know he was safe and to feel safe. Given Gerald's adverse childhood experience with a mother who terrified him, it is reasonable that his system would resist accepting the knowledge and feeling of safety. With Gerald's agreement, we proceeded to an ego state intervention.

Ego State Intervention: The fundamental principles of an ego state intervention were presented in Chapter 6 and will not be repeated here. With continuous TABS facilitation, Gerald developed a conference room, which he described as a sunken living room with couches on three sides and a coffee table in the middle. A thick, white carpet covered the floor. The room's ceiling was high. Greenery outside the room was visible through the large windows.

With the clinician's guidance, Gerald invited The One Who Resists Knowing and Feeling Safe to come into the conference room. The client reported feeling "fear, a hollowness in the pit of my stomach" that accompanied The One's entrance into the conference room. After obtaining Gerald's permission to speak to The One, I introduced myself, and learned that The One could talk and that he preferred to be called Surfer Dude. Gerald described Surfer Dude as having "spiky bleached hair and wearing surfer pants."

Surfer Dude explained that he had "always been around" for Gerald, and that his job was "to make Gerald afraid," because "by always being afraid, Gerald is protected from hurt." "Anybody could hurt Gerald," Surfer Dude explained. Gerald informed me that Surfer Dude was afraid of the clinician and that he also feared that "Kain was going to kick his ass." Gerald also volunteered, "The word 'Mom' comes up."

Following the principles for an AMST ego state intervention, the clinician mediated a negotiation between Surfer Dude and Gerald. In the bargain, Surfer Dude agreed to allow Gerald to learn how to manage his fear in future sessions. After thanking Surfer Dude for protecting him over the years, Gerald stated forcefully that he would take responsibility for his own safety from now on. Surfer Dude agreed to permit this, and he agreed to accept a new job description in which he would warn Gerald when he felt unsafe so that he could use his new skill (i.e., his safe place visualization), to create a feeling of safety for himself. A signal was agreed upon, and Gerald committed to paying attention to it. With this work completed, Gerald was gently brought back from the conference room visualization to the therapy office.

With TABS facilitation, Gerald recalled the image of his swimming hole, the granite boulders, the view downstream, the dogs, trees, the smell of the fresh air, the sound of gurgling water, and the feeling of rocks and sand. After instructing him to hold the quality resource, "warmth of the sun," the alliance resource, "Kain," and the image of Surfer Dude who will allow Gerald to take responsibility for his own safety, Gerald was asked to repeat the knowledge-oriented cognition, "I am safe." The client now endorsed a VoC of 7 for this cognition. Again with TABS facilitation, Gerald was asked to recall the image, "a place where you now know with complete certainty that you *are* safe," and this time to repeat the affect-oriented cognition, "I *feel* safe." The VoC for this cognition had also reached certainty. Continuing with the protocol, Gerald was asked to notice sensations accompanying the visualized safe place and the cognition, "I feel safe." He identified these sensations as "a relaxation in the pit of my stomach." He was asked to hold the image of the safe place, the emotion of safety, and the relaxation in the pit of his stomach, and with TABS facilitation he verbalized, "The relaxation in the pit of my stomach tells me I am feeling safe." This phase of Gerald's work was concluded when the image, the knowledge of safety, the emotion of safety, and the qualia of safety, as well as the quality resource, alliance resource, and the protector ego state, Surfer Dude, were assembled with a cue phrase, "swimming hole."

When a client is unable to endorse certain validity for the affect-oriented cognition "I feel safe," the protocol specifies the same three interventions that are specified for the knowledge-oriented cognition. Figure 7.3 diagrams the protocol for developing a quality resource, an alliance resource, and for executing an ego state intervention when the client's VoC for the affect-based cognition is less than certain. In this case the clinician inquires, "What quality would you need to have to feel safe?" and then elicits and installs an image for that quality. If the VoC has still not attained a level 7, the clinician asks, "Who could help you feel safe?" Finally, if the client still cannot attain certain validity for the PC "I feel safe," the clinician asks, "Is there anyone preventing you from feeling safe?" and then undertakes an ego state intervention.

DEVELOPING METACOGNITIONS

A metacognition is a contemplative statement, one in which the client is asked to make the therapeutic process itself an object of reflection. In particular, the clinician facilitates the client's reflection on the safe place skill. When eliciting a metacognition, the clinician assists the client in summarizing the work up to the moment and then asks the client to revalue and revision that work—using the language of Mogenson (1989)—by making it the object of a reflective statement (i.e., the metacognition). The metacognition builds self structure, because the subjective standpoint embodied in, for example, the knowledge-oriented positive cognition, "I am safe," becomes as well the object of the reflective metacognition, "I am learning to know that I can be safe." The client's self-concept expands through developing and installing metacognitions.

Metacognitions can be developed and installed at each stage of the safe place skill process. I have not diagrammed the development of metacognitions in Figures 7.1, 7.2, or 7.3, because to do so would complicate the presentation of the basic protocol. Also, the clinician will want to make her own judgment about when to install a metacognition, tailoring its application to the needs of the particular client. All clients should be taught the complete AMST protocol. Some clients will "get" the skill set faster than others and will quickly form their own metacognitions as the treatment effects generalize through the client's self system. Other clients will need more help, and the clinician can help this type of client by developing explicit metacognitions. In general, the more deficit experience in the client's history, the more the client will be helped by developing metacognitions. Clinicians can be sensitive to the client's guidance. When the clinician has pushed the development of metacognitions too far, the client will tell her, "I think I've got the idea now that I am learning to create images for myself."

Both the knowledge-oriented cognition and the affect-oriented cognition can be the basis of a metacognition. After successful development and installation of the valid cognition, "I feel safe," the clinician can install a metacognition such as, "I am learning that I can feel completely safe." Readers will note that metacognitions are framed as process statements, for example, "I am learning that I can feel safe," rather than as expressions of state (e.g., "I can feel safe"). The process statement is an expression of fact, in that the client is indeed learning that he can feel safe. The process statement is face valid. However, before an expression of state can become face valid, the client will need to amass experience over time using the skill to his benefit. As he gains experience, and as he acquires more of the AMST protocol, he also enlarges his self-structure to the point where his system is capable of making a face valid expression of state. The astute clinician can probe the client by inquiring if he is comfortable with an expression of state, such as, "I am capable of creating safety for myself." The clinician and client can mark the client's progress toward self-actualization as he acquires this ability.

Here are the instructions for a metacognition that were provided to Betty after developing a safe place visualization and assembling the knowledge of safety and the feeling of safety with it. Recall that Betty's safe place was a pond in nature that looked like an art nouveau painting, with pillars and trees.

Clinician: TABS On Bring up your image of the pond in nature with pillars
around it and trees beyond them. See the golden light, the trees, and
birds. Hear the birds singing, and smell the oak trees and the musty,
earthy smell from under the trees. Feel the sun dappling your skin, feel
the warmth of the air, and feel the cool water of the pond. Recall that in
this place you know with complete certainty that you are safe. Recall
also that you feel completely safe in this place and that you have identified sensations of openness in your chest and feeling grounded all over
that tell you you are feeling safe. Now, as you hold this rich image and
the cognitions of knowing you are safe and feeling safe, please repeat
after me, "I am learning to create an inner image of safety." [*Client
repeats the metacognition.*] Good. Let that become completely true.
TABS Off Deep breath. Let it out, and what comes up now?

Several reflective statements can be delivered in succession that will promote
metacognizing all aspects of the safe place skill. After developing the knowledge-
oriented cognition, "I am safe," the clinician may facilitate the metacognition, "I
am learning to know that I am safe." After installing the affect-oriented cognition, "I feel safe," the clinician can develop the metacognition, "I am learning
that I can feel safe with certainty." After helping the client recognize the sensations accompanying the emotion of safety, the clinician can help him develop the
metacognition, "I am learning to recognize how my body tells me I am feeling
safe." These stages themselves can be made the object of a further metacognition
such as, "I am learning to create an internal image of safety and security." And finally, a second order metacognition, "I am learning to create safety for myself,"
can be developed that encompasses the entire safe place skill at the same time as
it affirms the client's personal growth and change. This statement solidifies her
new learning for the client. Because of deficits or adversity in her childhood experience, she may never have developed an inner image of safety and security. Acquisition of the safe place skill adds to the sense of mastery she began to form
with skill I (containment), when she learned she could confine disturbing intrapsychic material. Her sense of ownership of her mental and emotional condition increases, and she becomes more of a self-aware agent in her life process. She
learns that she, not others, is responsible for and has the power to determine who
she is, how she thinks, and what she feels.

APPROACHING SELF-WORTH ATTRIBUTIONS

The self-worth attribution is a second order metacognition that is assembled with
an appraisal of worthiness and a complex emotional experience of worthiness.
When appropriate, the self-worth attribution is developed subsequent to installation of metacognitions. Like metacognitions, self-worth attributions have not been
included in the figures, because the clinician should adapt their installation to the
particular client's needs in the moment. An example of a self-worth attribution,
formulated as an expression of state, would be, "I am worthy of feeling safe." A
process formulation of the safe attribution would be, "I am learning to feel worthy

of feeling safe." Attributions of self-worth, when required too early in therapy can stress the client, and the clinician should be aware of this fact and should understand what it means for the client who has difficulty with repeating this phrase.

The more severely distressed the client, the less comfortable will the client be in making a self-attribution of worthiness. The clinician should avoid creating stress for the client by seeming to demand such an attribution. For this reason, as the therapist learns about the client's level of tolerance for feeling worthy, he should begin with very permissive and open-ended language. Here is an example:

As you hold the image of the safe place and the certain knowledge that you are safe and the complete conviction that you feel safe, along with the knowledge that you are learning to create an inner image of safety and security for yourself, I wonder how it would feel for you to affirm a statement like this, "I am learning to feel worthy of feeling safe"?

If the client states that he feels comfortable with the statement, then the clinician can go forward using TABS to install the self-worth attribution. The clinician can then ask for an appraisal of the validity of the attribution using the VoC scale. If the client expresses reluctance to affirm his self-worth, the clinician should not force the issue. The clinician may ask:

I'd just like to get a sense of how disturbing it feels when I suggest you say, "I am learning to feel worthy of feeling safe." On a scale from zero to 10, where zero is not disturbing at all and 10 is the other end of the scale, how disturbing is it when I suggest you say, "I am learning to feel worthy of feeling safe"?

If the client reports a disturbance level of 4 or above, the clinician should state, "Thank you. Let's just let that go for now." If the client reports a disturbance level of 4 or below, the clinician may suggest a less distressing, more permissive, more process-oriented form of the self-worth attribution. Here's one example.

As you hold the image of the safe place and the knowledge you are safe and the feeling of safety, would it feel comfortable to repeat this statement, "I am beginning to see that I could at some point learn to feel worthy of feeling safe"?

If the client agrees to this statement, the clinician, using TABS, can proceed to install the metacognitive statement, assembling it with the image of the safe place and the knowledge of safety and emotion and sensations of feeling safe.

Requesting a self-worth attribution without demanding it is a way of interrogating the client's personality system and demonstrates again the therapeutic and diagnostic functions of the AMST. If a client is not unduly stressed by making the suggested self-worth attribution, then the clinician opts for the therapeutic course and installs the statement of self-worth. If the client communicates distress at the suggested verbalization, then the diagnostic function is actuated. The clinician uncovers important information about the structure of the client's personality, information she will store away that will guide the later stages of the affect focused therapy. What might client distress at being asked for a self-worth attribution reveal about the structure of the personality?

Distress at being asked for a self-worth attribution may indicate the presence of a child ego state that holds the system's unworthiness, a situation often observed in persons whose childhoods were characterized by deficit, adversity, or abuse. The purpose of this child ego state is to facilitate the system's functioning by holding the system's unworthiness. With the unworthiness sequestered in the child ego state, the system can function, albeit at less than optimal levels. Of course, the unworthiness is never completely contained and will leak out and contaminate the system. When a client is unable to endorse a self-attribution of worthiness, the clinician should note the fact, because it will guide interventions later in the therapy. In later stages of therapy, with a solid foundation established by the AMST, employing techniques of affect centered therapy (ACT), the adverse or traumatic experiences that engendered unworthiness in childhood can be uncovered and resolved. Then, employing the conference room ego state intervention to encounter the child ego state, the clinician can help the client redeem the child part's innocence, purity, and innate perfection.

Chapter 11 presents several additional skills for enhancing the client's self-concept that the clinician can consider employing at this stage if the client seems able to tolerate them. As with the self-worth attribution, if the client appears stressed by the prospect of verbalizing an attribution of self-efficacy, for example, the clinician should postpone it until the client has developed sufficient skills.

CREATING A CUE WORD

Once the client has endorsed certainty, or near certainty, for the knowledge of safety and the feeling of safety, and after any necessary resources have been installed or interventions accomplished, the entire image, all the perceptions, the knowledge and affect cognitions, and the sensations accompanying the affect are assembled with a cue word that the client can use to evoke the affective–cognitive–imagistic construct for safety. Here is language the clinician can use to guide the client:

You've done really well creating a beautiful image for your safe place. What I'd like to do now is ask you for a cue word or maybe a phrase of not more than three words that you can use to bring up the image of the safe place, the knowledge you are safe and the feelings and sensations of safety. Then you can use the cue word to create a feeling of safety for yourself any time you might want to. So, tell me, what word would you like to use?

Using his own notes or the work sheet in Appendix A, the clinician should write down the cue word. Then he should immediately assemble the safe place construct with the cue word using TABS to facilitate the assembly. The client Betty offered "golden" as her cue word. Here are the instructions that were given to assemble her safe place image with the cue word:

> **Clinician: TABS On** Bring up the image of your pond in nature. See the pillars and the oak trees beyond. Notice the golden light, like a Maxfield

Parrish painting. Hear the birds and smell the oak trees and the musty, earthy scent. Feel the dappled sun on your skin, and feel the cool water of the pond. Recall that you know with complete certainty that you are safe in this place. Recall too that you know with complete certainty that you feel safe here and that your body tells you you are safe through sensations of openness in your chest and a grounded feeling all over. As you hold the image and all the perceptions, as you hold the knowledge of safety and the feeling of safety, please say your cue word Golden, out loud, letting the entire image and all its associations assemble with the word. [*Client repeats the word Golden.*] Good. Good. **TABS Off** Deep breath. Let it out, and what comes up now?

After attending to whatever the client verbalizes, the clinician can move immediately to teach the client how to use the safe place visualization to facilitate a more adaptive management of a forthcoming, potentially stressful situation.

THE FUTURE TEMPLATE

Shapiro (1995) described the future template as a device that enabled the client to make "new choices in the future" (p. 206). This is accomplished with TABS facilitation by assembling the safe place visualization with an expected future situation involving significant people or situations. Here is language the clinician can use:

I'd like to teach you now how to use your new skill, the safe place visualization, and your cue word, to create a more positive experience for you in some situation you expect to encounter in the next day or two. We're looking for a situation where dealing with a person or events would be improved if you felt safer within yourself. Let's stay away from situations where objectively it would be unsafe, where there was a real external danger. So, I wonder, what situation do you expect to come up in the next day or two where you could handle it better if you felt safer within yourself?

Clients have produced a wide range of such events over the years. Taking a test, talking to the boss, attending a board meeting, calling mom, and giving an oral report are a few examples among many. Should the client suggest a situation that is inherently dangerous, one where the client may be at risk based on objective criteria or prior performance (e.g., meeting with a partner who has been physically or emotionally abusive in the past), the clinician should insist that a different future template be selected. Betty suggested that she would like to feel safer when she called her son later on in the same day as our therapy session. She explained that he was experiencing his own difficulties dealing with a new job and new living situation and that she could stay out of trying to rescue him if she felt more safe and secure herself. Here are the instructions utilized for her application of the safe place visualization to her future template:

Clinician: **TABS On** See yourself preparing to call your son this evening. You become aware that you feel a little nervous because you want to rescue him from his difficulties with his new job and new apartment, and you know that he needs to find out for himself how to manage these situations. As you become aware of these thoughts and feelings, I'd like you to use your cue word. Say it out loud now. [*Betty says Golden.*] And as you say it, allow the image of your pond in nature to surface. Good. Let the knowledge that you are safe come up, and the feeling of safety accompanied by sensations of openness in your chest. Good. Now, as you hold the image and thoughts and feelings, see yourself dialing and then talking to your son, all the while holding a comfortable image and feeling of safety. Good. Now, please repeat after me, "I am learning to use my safe place visualization to create a feeling of safety for myself." [*Betty repeats the positive cognition.*] Good. **TABS Off** Deep breath. Let it out, and what comes up now?

Betty reported that when she used the safe place visualization she was able to see herself letting her son bring up his problems with his new roommates who were apparently drinking more than he was comfortable with. She saw herself asking him, "What comes up for you when that happens?" and listening to him rather than giving advice. She realized that she felt like a more supportive mom when she was able to affirm him and avoid giving advice and that this caused her to feel much better about herself. Based on her disclosures, the clinician proceeded to develop a metacognition as follows:

Clinician: **TABS On** See yourself using your cue word and calling up your safe place before you telephoned your son. Become aware again of how you felt safe and were able to act from that feeling of safety and allow your son to be independent. See yourself supporting him, rather than giving advice. Realize how much better you felt about yourself. Now, please repeat after me, "I am learning that when I use my safe place I can be the mother I want to be and let my son be independent." [*Betty repeats the metacognition.*] And again, repeat after me, "I am learning that when I use my safe place, I feel better about myself." [*Betty repeats the metacognition.*] Good. Let those thoughts become completely true. Good. **TABS Off** Deep breath. Let it out, and what comes up now?

WORKING WITH DIFFICULT CASES

Difficult cases result when there is contribution to client disordering in all three dimensions of the tripartite model. The client may have genetic impairments in thresholds for affects or may be genetically less competent to process trauma adaptively. There may also be severe deficit experience compounded by adversity and trauma. In these cases, affect dysregulation will be severe to extreme and the self organization may be fragmented. The result will be a challenging case for the clinician. The DID client exemplifies the challenging case, and the considerations that pertain to providing skills to the DID client apply as well to the border line, narassistic, or other personality disordered client.

Working with Dissociative Identity Disorder (DID)

With the caveats in mind that were presented in Chapter 6 regarding working with dissociative disorders, here are some useful considerations for applying the safe place skill with this population. Clients with DID may react strongly to the use of words like *safety* and *security*. One explanation is that they may never have felt either safe or secure, so that these words may have no meaning for them. Another explanation is that they may have only been safe in situations of abuse and deprivation. For these reasons, in working with these clients the clinician may want to substitute the words *comfort* and *ease* for the words *safety* and *security*. Also, the clinician may elect to refer to skill II as the *comfort place skill* in working with these clients.

The clinician should consider working recursively between containment skill and safe place skill with alters as they appear. AMST will most likely begin with the system manager, the construct that supervises the system's interactions with the outside world. As this part develops a container and safe place, a new alter may surface, and the clinician will address its needs for its own container and safe place. The concept of certainty regarding knowledge of safety and feeling of safety is an ideal that may not be attainable for the DID system until significant amounts of work have been accomplished. The clinician should avoid creating unachievable goals for the alters. If an alter is able to endorse, say, a VoC of 3 for a statement "I feel safe," the clinician may ask, "Are you comfortable with that?" and should accept the alter's affirmative response as being the best the system can do at that moment.

The safe place visualization can be used to promote communication and cooperation among alters. The clinician can invite alters to notice the process as the alter being worked with creates a safe place. If alters have created their own safe places, the therapist can invite them to consider merging safe places. Eventually, a group of alters can be offered the opportunity to collaborate in creating a safe place suitable to them all. In this way, the safe place skill promotes structuralization of the fragmented system.

SUMMARY

The safe place skill provides the client with a fully elaborated internal image of safety and security. The protocol specifies how the clinician can help the client evoke four perceptual modes of experience as a means of more fully anchoring the image. Clinical experience has demonstrated that skill I (containment) must precede development of the safe place. When clients endorse containment of 95% or more of every disturbing thing in the containment skill, then they are able to achieve certain validity for the PCs "I am safe" and "I feel safe" in the safe place skill. My clinical experience has proved time and again that if disturbing material was not contained, it surfaced and intruded on the safe place in the form of negative images, affects, or cognitions. For this reason, the AMST protocol is designed with skill I preceding skill II.

Development of the safe place in skill II illustrates the principles upon which AMST is based. An imaginal kernel is elicited and then it is elaborated on by adding perceptions to it. This elaborated imaginal kernel is then assembled with cognitions, first a knowledge-oriented cognition, then an affect-oriented cognition. Appraisals are assembled with the cognitions and the imaginal core in the form of the client self-reports of validity. Next, this structure is assembled with the emotion *safety* and the sensations accompanying it. The entire structure is tied together with yet another cognition tying sensation, to emotion, to image, to appraisal. One could conceptualize the process of developing skill I as being like the process of putting a Russian doll set together. The first tiny doll is the imaginal kernel. The next dolls holding the first are the perceptions. The smaller set is placed in a larger and then in a still larger doll. Finally, the assemblage is placed inside the largest doll of all, the metacognitions, when the client is facilitated in verbalizing, "I am learning to create an internal image of safety and security for myself."

The chapter has demonstrated how the protocol can be applied to clients presenting with problems with eating and with procrastination. These skills have been applied to a range of psychopathology. Suggestions have been offered for how to use the skills with difficult cases. Interventions have been presented to help clients who are missing vital resources, who lack internal representations of supportive persons, or who have covert ego states whose archaic helper function is currently maladaptive. Although it is admittedly a limited sample, these interventions have been sufficient to resolve all clinical difficulties that have arisen to date.

Chapter **8**

. . . .

Skill III: Sensation–Affect Identification

The goal of Chapter 8 is to transmit to the clinician the skills necessary to help the client recognize an affect by its associated physical sensation. Affect management skills training (AMST) refers to this skill as *sensation–affect identification* or skill III. Teaching skill III begins by designating a target affect and then selecting a remembered event, the target scene, in which the client believes he experienced the designated emotion at a predetermined, manageable level. Figure 8.1 diagrams the skill III procedure.

PROCEDURE FOR SKILL III
(SENSATION–AFFECT IDENTIFICATION)

. . . .

To this point in the protocol, the clinician has helped the client to free himself from intrusive thoughts, memories, and ego states and emotions assembled with them through developing skill I (containment), and she has assisted the client in creating a safe place (skill II) assembled with knowledge, feeling, and sensations of safety. With this solid foundation established, AMST now moves to teaching the client to recognize, tolerate, and regulate a selected emotion at a designated level of intensity. The techniques of emotion recognition, tolerance, and regulation are transmitted by skills III to VII and constitute the direct lessons of the protocol regarding affect management. There are several indirect lessons being transmitted at the same time as the overt techniques.

The indirect lessons are an important component of the AMST process. As she perfects the protocol's techniques, the client learns she can choose an emotion to focus on and experience. This indirect lesson promotes a shift in the client's understanding of emotion causation. Many clients believe the environment, events, or people cause emotion and that they themselves are powerless over what they feel and when they feel it. Beginning with the setup for skill III, the

264

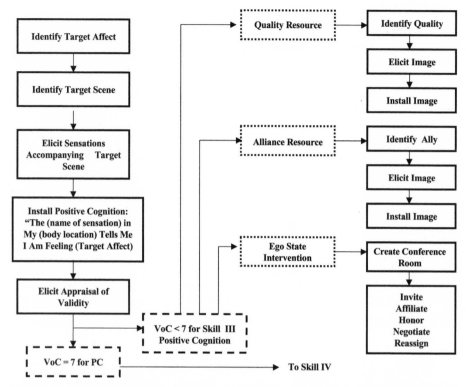

Figure 8.1. Flow Diagram and Decision Tree (skill III, Sensation–Affect Identification). This figure demonstrates the flow of steps in helping the client to identify an affect by the physical sensations associated with it. The figure also shows the decision point and interventions to be employed if the client is unable to endorse certainty for the skill III positive cognition.

client starts to view herself as an active agent in the interplay between self and surroundings. The setup for skill III also demonstrates to the client that she can select a level of intensity for the emotion she chooses to experience. Until this point, if she considered the emotion of fear, for example, she usually experienced the intense fear associated with prior, unresolved adverse or traumatic experiences. When asked by the AMST clinician for a time she felt fear at a low level, she learns indirectly that she doesn't have to "go there" to the trauma coded fear. Indirectly, the client develops familiarity with her emotions. She learns she can investigate her emotions, learn about them, and understand them, thereby demystifying the world of affect. She learns that she can know herself, and as she does, she begins to develop a sense of mastery.

Target Affect, SUD, and Target Scene

The setup for skills III to VII entails identification of the target affect and target scene. The target affect is the emotion that will be the focus for the skill set. Once agreed upon, the clinician will guide the client through skills III to VII as applied to the target affect. Having learned the skills with the first target affect, the clinician will suggest a second affect as the focus and will guide the client through the skills a second time, applying them to the new index affect. The first pass through the skills will require more time, because the client is learning a novel technique set. Most clients quickly acquire the set, and subsequent passes through the skills that focus on a different affect or emotion require less time.

The target scene is a recalled memory of an event or an incident in which the index emotion was experienced at an agreed upon low level of intensity. The level of intensity is determined using the Subjective Units of Disturbance scale (SUD). The SUD scale allows the client to set the level of intensity at which he will experience the target affect. Scenes recalled from memory will be assembled with different levels of intensity for the target affect. Guiding the client, the clinician will suggest that he provide a scene in which the index emotion was experienced at a low level, usually not over a 3 or a 4. TABS is not employed in the process of recalling a target scene.

The following instructions are useful for introducing the target affect, target scene, and SUD scale. Notice how these instructions are structured to present the concept of limitation of affect intensity level prior to suggesting an emotion target. In the context of the therapeutic dyad, this structure creates safety for the client.

Now that you've constructed a container and developed a safe place, you have established a solid foundation for the next stage of our work. What I want to do now is teach you some skills to help you recognize emotions, learn to tolerate them, and then regulate them. Many people who come to therapy were never taught these skills in childhood, and not having the skills contributes to problems later in life. Learning these skills will help you attain the goals you've set for yourself in therapy.

We'll start by setting a comfortable level for the emotion we decide to work on, a level that won't be overwhelming. Then we'll pick an emotion. After that, I'll be asking you to recall a time you felt that emotion at the low level we've agreed on. I want to give you a rating scale now so we can make certain to get a comfortable level. The scale goes from zero, which is neutral or benign, to 10 which is the other end of the scale. Please don't go there. Good. We're going to start at a low level, say a 3 and not over a 4. I'm going to suggest that we begin by focusing on the emotion of fear, because it's a basic emotion that many people feel. I wonder, can you tell me a time that you felt fear at a low level, a 3 or a 4?

Using his session notes or the worksheet in Appendix A, the clinician should record the target affect and information the client provides relating to the target scene. This information will be essential for refreshing the image and reeliciting the target affect throughout the process of teaching skills III to VII. The clinician should redirect the client if he provides a target scene that carries significant "loading" with important people, (e.g., parents or partners), or with events that may elicit traumatic material from associated neural networks. For example, a client offered a target scene as follows: "Yeah, I was afraid this morning when my mom called and started yelling at me about Thanksgiving plans."

The clinician responded, "You're on the right track, and this morning probably was a low level of fear. However, you've got a lifetime of history with your mother, and some of that might involve higher levels of fear. Please don't go there. Good. I don't want to trigger those. So, can you recall a memory of a time you felt fear at a low level that didn't involve one of your parents?"

Once the client has produced a memory of a suitable target scene, the clinician should ascertain a few factual details of the scene and record them. The following example from a client we've already met, Betty, illustrates the process of developing a target scene for the index affect fear at a low level. After an introduction as presented above, the clinician proceeds as follows:

Clinician: With that introduction, I wonder if you can recall a time, perhaps a recent time, when you felt a low level of fear, say a level 3 or 4?

Betty: Sure. A couple of weeks ago I got stopped by a cop and got a ticket.

Clinician: And where would you put that on a scale from zero to 10?

Betty: Oh, it wasn't that bad. My teenagers were with me in the back seat, and we were laughing about it while it was happening. Maybe a 2.

Clinician: Can you give me a little more detail?

Betty: Sure. My car was in the shop, and a friend lent me his car, and he forgot to tell me the registration tags were expired. It wasn't like I was speeding or anything, and we all had our seat belts on. It was more annoying, really. But, it was a motorcycle cop, and when the lights went on, I felt afraid.

Having developed a suitable target scene, the clinician immediately guides the client toward uncovering the physical sensations accompanying the scene. These sensations are the qualia of the target affect.

Identifying the Physical Sensations

As we have learned, recalling the target image from memory will elicit the index emotion, and the client will be experiencing it much as he did at the time the event actually occurred. The clinician now proceeds directly to skill III, which assists the client in identifying the physical sensations that arise as he holds the target image. Skill III is facilitated with TABS, and the clinician again uses the ideomotor finger signal that allows the client some control of the process and avoids unduly pressuring him. The general instructions for skill III are as follows:

TABS On *As you focus on the target scene* [repeat description of scene] *and realize that you are feeling* [name of target affect], *you become aware of sensations that are coming up for you. Just notice what those sensations are and where in your body you are feeling them, and let me know when you become aware of them by raising your left index finger. Good.* [Client raises index finger.] **TABS Off** *Deep breath. Let it out, and tell me, what did you feel?*

The clinician should record the sensation and body location in his case notes or on the worksheet. Every client is different, and each client will produce his or her own unique phraseology when naming the felt sensation. For the index affect fear, the client's descriptive words for the felt sensations usually convey the idea of tension: *tightness, tingling,* and *pressure* are typical examples. If the client has difficulty naming the sensation, the clinician can gently guide her to do so. The name of the sensation is important, and it should not be skipped over, because using this word will suggest the sensation and can be used both to reelicit the sensation at a later time and to discriminate the associated affect, in this case fear, from other affects. If the client has had difficulty naming the sensations, the clinician can always repeat the TABS-facilitated instructions to help the client become aware of the felt quality of the sensations and to arrive at a name for them. As soon as the sensations and body location have been identified, the clinician proceeds to install a cognition that assembles affect, sensation, and body location. Our narrative will describe the process of installing the skill III cognition and a case example will follow that illustrates both components, eliciting the sensations and installing the cognition.

Installing the Cognition

The skill III cognition expands a neural network that initially consisted of the target image retrieved from memory and the index emotion assembled with it. Expansion of the network began by eliciting the associated sensations and promoting awareness of them. The installed cognition acts to further expand the neural network by assembling the target image, index emotion, and associated sensations into a larger unitary structure. The following general instructions are suggested as a pattern for installing the cognition:

TABS On *See yourself in the target scene* [repeat descriptive elements of the scene]. *Become aware that you are feeling the same* [name of target emotion] *that you felt then. Notice again the sensations in your body that accompany the scene and the emotion. Good. Now, please repeat after me, "The* [name of sensation, e.g., tingling] *in my* [name of body location, e.g., hands] *tells me I am feeling* [name of target affect, e.g., fear]*." Good. Let that become as true as it can be.* **TABS Off** *Deep breath. Let it out, and what comes up now?*

As soon as the cognition has been installed, the clinician should elicit a client self-report, the Validity of Cognition scale (VoC), regarding the validity of the cognition.

Eliciting an Appraisal

The previously introduced VoC scale should be used to verify for both clinician and client that the client has acquired the skill. If the client endorses with certainty that his reported sensations tell him he is feeling the index emotion, then the clinician can proceed to develop a metacognition (see below) and then move on to the next skill in the AMST set. When the client is unable to endorse complete validity, then the clinician should turn to the AMST Flow Chart and

Decision Tree (Figure 8.1) and seek a quality resource or alliance resource or accomplish an ego state intervention to address the problems preventing the VoC from going to 7. An ego state intervention is presented later in the chapter. Here are generalized instructions the clinician can use as a pattern for eliciting an appraisal:

As you see yourself in the target scene [repeat descriptive elements of the scene], *on a scale from 1 to 7, where 1 is completely false and 7 is completely true, how true is the statement, "The* [name of sensation, e.g. tingling] *in my* [name of body location, e.g., hands] *tells me I am feeling* [name of target affect, e.g., fear]. *"*

The Case of Betty

Returning to the case of Betty, here is a presentation of the elicitation of her sensations associated with a low level of fear affect, installation of the skill III cognition, and generation of a self-report.

> Clinician: **TABS On** See yourself in the borrowed car a couple of weeks ago in a scene in which you felt a low level of fear. You have your teenagers in the back seat. You don't know it, but the tags on the car have expired. You're driving safely, and you all have your seat belts on. You look in the rearview mirror and realize a motorcycle cop is right behind you. He turns on his red lights and signals you to pull over. As you see yourself in this scene and realize you are feeling a low level of fear right now, I'd like you to just become aware of sensations in your body that accompany the scene. Take all the time you need, and let me know by raising your left index finger when you have become aware of the sensations. Good. Good. [*Client's finger raises.*] **TABS Off** Deep breath. Let it out, and what sensations did you get?
>
> Betty: Well, it was in my solar plexus. Hmmm. What to call it? It felt like, I don't know, a quickening. Does that make sense?
>
> Clinician: Certainly. What I hear you saying is that you feel a quickening sensation in your solar plexus that accompanies the experience of fear. So, that is how your body tells you you're feeling fear. Now, let's install that knowledge. **TABS On** See yourself in the borrowed car with expired tags. The cop has turned on his red lights and is pulling you over. You become aware of a quickening in your solar plexus that accompanies the level 2 fear you experience in this situation. Good. Now, please repeat after me, "The quickening in my solar plexus tells me I am feeling fear."
>
> Betty: The quickening in my solar plexus tells me I am feeling fear.
>
> Clinician: Let that become as true as it can. Good. **TABS Off** Deep breath. Let it out, and what comes up now?
>
> Betty: Not much. My friend felt bad and got the car registered. I paid my fine and that was it.
>
> Clinician: So, tell me, as you hold the image of the motorcycle cop stopping you, on a scale from 1 to 7 where 1 is false and 7 is true, how true is the

statement, "The quickening in my solar plexus tells me I am feeling fear"?

Betty: Oh, it's a 7.

The Betty case presentation illustrates the process of cognizing an emotion, a process that entails identification of sensations accompanying the emotion and then development of a cognition that assembles the affect, sensation, and body location into a unitary construct. Clients come with varying degrees of ability to cognize affects, some impoverished, others better developed. *Cognizing* is a formal verbal construction that means recognizing the affect by its sensations and raising that recognition to conscious awareness. Cognizing an affect builds self structure, and the action of cognizing the affect changes the client's relationship to the index affect. As Izard (1991) explained it, "Experiencing anger tends to elicit anger-related ('angry') thought and actions, and cognizing or reflecting on one's anger tends to alter the anger experience" (p. 74). Cognizing an emotion sets yet another stone in the foundation that contributes directly and immediately to improvement in client functioning.

Skill III (sensation-affect identification) builds connections between the cognitive processing and emotion appraisal-response systems. LeDoux (1996) showed that while the emotion appraisal and emotion response systems are tightly coupled, the cognitive processing systems are not tightly linked to the emotion response systems. When asked to "Give me an image of a time you felt a low level of fear," the client's declarative (explicit) memory system is activated. As the client verbally reports the incident and the clinician elicits more detail, the implicit (emotion) memory system is activated, producing emotion arousal, and physical sensations (qualia) accompanying the emotion are triggered. The sensory cortex is entrained when the clinician instructs the client to "become aware of sensations in your body accompanying the image." Neurobiologically, this instruction begins construction of a corticothalamic, high road circuit (LeDoux, 1996, p. 161) that will function as an alternative to the low road circuit and provide the client with more adaptive emotion response behaviors. Instructing the client to become aware of sensations directs the cognitive system to pay attention to, i.e., become aware of, what is occurring in the emotion system. Emotion awareness is elevated to the level of language, presumably involving the left hemisphere, when the client is asked to cognize the index emotion by repeating, "These [name of sensations] in my [body location] tell me I am feeling [name of emotion]." In this manner, skill III forges more robust interconnections between cognition- and emotion-processing systems.

RANGE OF CLIENT SENSATIONS FOR FEAR AFFECT

The range of sensations and body locations accompanying fear affect is as varied as the clients. One client reported pressure in the chest, upset in the stomach, and cold in the hands. Another felt a deep fluttery sensation in the middle of the chest, close to the heart. Fear was accompanied by tightness in shoulders, legs, and buttocks for one eating disordered client, while another eating disordered client felt fear as tightness in the whole body, jaw, shoulders, all the muscles. Yet another eating disordered client described burning and tension in the neck and shoulders when visualizing the target scene for fear. Still another eating disordered client felt stiffness in the hands, shoulders, and jaw that accompanied fear affect. A woman experienced sensations of gripping in her solar plexus accompanying the target scene for fear. A man reported tingling nauseous sensations in his stomach when he felt afraid. The list of sensations clients have reported is as long as the roster of clients. Through connecting with each client's qualia of emotion experience, the clinician engages the distinctiveness and specialness of each client. Through the exchange of verbal responses between therapist and patient that is inherent in the AMST protocol, the client experiences being "recognized and known" as one client expressed it. This emotion engagement with the client provides an indirect and very valuable benefit to the therapist as well, because the client becomes a person, rather than a diagnosis.

ORGANIZING THE AMST PHASE OF THERAPY

Having developed a target affect and target scene and successfully completed skill III (sensation-affect identification), the clinician should proceed to skills IV through VII, focusing on the same index emotion. These skills are presented in Chapters 9 and 10. The clinician should teach the client the entire skill set with the target affect at a low level before addressing the same affect at a more intense level. After completing the skill set targeting, for example, fear affect at first a low level and then a more intense level, the clinician should shift the focus to another affect. The ordering of affects and the affects targeted depends upon the treatment plan and is derived from the history taken prior to initiating therapy. I usually sketch out a plan for affect targets and ordering, but avoid a slavish adherence to the plan. The AMST clinician should allow for spontaneity and permit the client's process to guide the work. Having said that, it is important to cover all the key affects in the AMST phase of therapy. Here is a listing of key affects and an order in which they may be addressed:

Fear (SUD 3), Fear (SUD 6), anger (SUD <5), sadness, yearning, excitement, happiness, startle, shame, disgust.

This is a suggested listing, but the clinician should be spontaneous and should be sensitive to the client's affective process. While there are only a limited number of affects hard-wired into the system, there are hundreds of emotions a client may experience. When a client displays an emotion or verbalizes awareness of it, the attuned clinician should take a brief break in the progression of the protocol skills and help the client to cognize the emotion he or she is experiencing in the moment.

While I have suggested beginning AMST with fear affect, I want to offer an exception to that "rule." The exception arises if the client is feeling a strong emotion in the moment as we are beginning to do the AMST work. This is a case where the client's process should guide the work. If the client verbalizes an emotion or displays it, go with that emotion and teach the client the skills using as a target affect what the client is feeling in the moment. For a target scene, use the therapy office and the client's current affective experience. For example, as the clinician prepares the client for skills III to IV, he may notice that she appears sad, perhaps because her cheeks have momentarily reddened or her eyes are glistening. He should verify that the client is indeed feeling what he suspects by asking, "I wonder what you're feeling right now? I thought I saw your cheeks redden for a moment and it looks like your eyes are moist. What's coming up for you?" The client may respond, as clients have, "Oh, it just feels really sad that here I am 26 years old, and I'm having to learn about feelings because nobody taught me when I was a kid." The clinician should adapt to the situation as it presents itself with language something like this:

TABS On *Let's focus on what you were feeling just a moment ago. See yourself here in the therapy office. Your eyes have moistened and your cheeks reddened. You tell me that it feels sad that you are 26 and no one taught you about your emotions when you were a kid. As you hold that scene, become aware of sensations in your body that accompany it. Good. Take all the time you need, and just let me know by raising your left index finger when you've got them. Good.* [Client raises her index finger.] **TABS Off** *Deep breath. Let it out, and tell me what did you get?*

Having taught the client the AMST skill set (skills III–VII) targeting the sadness she is feeling in the moment, he can then go back to target fear or other affects.

ELICITING SPECIFIC AFFECTS AND EMOTIONS

This section addresses other specific affects besides fear affect that the clinician can target.

Interest–Excitement

Interest–excitement is one of the vitality affects. The clinician can elicit this powerful and important emotion directly by asking the client to visualize a time when he believed he had experienced excitement, and then proceeding with skill III as already presented. Often, the opportunity to uncover the sensations assembled with excitement affect will present itself spontaneously in the course of the AMST work. The clinician should be mindful of these opportunities when they occur and should take advantage of them. The case of Fred provides an excellent example of how AMST training provided a spontaneous opportunity to apply skill III to both excitement affect and joy affect.

Fred is a middle-aged man who came for problems with alcohol, eating, and depression. After developing a container (skill I) and safe place (skill II), AMST turned to fear affect, and the client learned skills III to VII using as a target scene a motor vehicle accident a few years earlier. After successfully teaching the skills, the client was asked for a time in the near future when he expected he might feel fear, and he quickly offered the date he had arranged for the following evening. When asked to identify the most disturbing elements of the situation, Fred responded, "If her face was closed, like if she looked away when I was talking to her." He assigned a SUD of 7 to the distress he felt as he visualized the scene. Using his newly acquired skills, Fred was able to decrease his fear by 98%, a level he set himself, at which point he verbalized, "I am feeling a tingling. I suddenly discover I like being me." When asked by the clinician what emotion he believed was replacing the fear, Fred stated, "Joyous anticipation." The word *anticipation* indicates excitement affect, while *joyous* suggests enjoyment–joy affect. Focusing again on the forthcoming date, Fred was able to identify sensations of "trembling" in his chest that accompanied the anticipation component, and the skill III positive cognition, "The trembling in my chest tells me I am feeling excitement," was installed according to the protocol. Returning to the visualized date and focusing on the joyous component, the client recognized a "glow" in his upper arms and face, and the positive cognition, "The glow in my upper arms and face tells me I'm feeling joy," was installed. Readers should note how the vitality affects excitement and joy were obscured by fear affect and how, once the client had learned the entire skill set and was able to down-regulate fear, he could then experience his authentic vitality. Readers will also note how AMST helped the client to discriminate excitement from fear and how each of these affects has a unique physiological signature.

Anger

After the client has acquired the AMST skill set using fear as the target affect, the next emotion the clinician may suggest is anger. The client is now knowledgeable about the process and has of course learned the skills. The clinician may say:

Now that you've learned the AMST process for fear, let's turn our attention to another emotion that people often feel, anger. Tell me a time when you recall feeling anger at a moderate level, say not over a 4 or 5.

Having developed a target scene for the index affect anger, the clinician proceeds according to the protocol as already presented. With TABS facilitation, the client is assisted to uncover the sensations that accompany anger, then to install the skill III positive cognition. The following examples illustrate how some clients have experienced anger.

The middle-aged man with drinking and overeating problems, Fred, recalled a time his girl friend had invalidated him after he had expressed his feelings to her. The incident had occurred in a car, and he saw himself banging the steering wheel with his hand. As he held this scene while receiving TABS stimulation, he became aware of sensations of blood rushing to his face, spinning and exploding in his head, and cold alternating with hot all over his body. The skill III positive cognition was installed for these sensations and body locations, and a VoC of 7 confirmed that the cognition was completely true. The clinician continued with the AMST process, applying skills IV to VII to the target affect anger using the same visualization.

Another client, Carly, is in her 40s and came for help with binge eating. When asked for a time she recalled feeling anger at level 4 or 5, she recollected her daughter's being irresponsible and ruining a CD and then refusing to express remorse about it. Holding this visualization, she became aware of sensations of heavy, strong pounding in her heart and heat in the top of her head, which she associated with being hot headed.

Heat is often associated with anger targeted in the protocol as the example of Elaine demonstrates. This client is in her early 20s and she came for help with anorexia. In her target scene, she recalled her parents yelling at her regarding her planning process to get her car gassed. She felt her parents were controlling her and would not listen to her, and she assigned the scene a SUD of 7. With TABS facilitation she identified sensations she described as "clenched" and "hot" everywhere in her body. Awareness of her anger was a novel experience for this anorexic, because her parents had forbidden her expression of anger throughout childhood and adolescence. As a result she had accumulated a heavy load of unresolved anger. She came to realize that one function her anorexia served was to keep her too weak to feel or express anger.

Healthy Aggression

Unresolved, archaic anger can have the effect of blocking the client's ability to use anger in a healthy manner. Often clients carry a burden of unresolved anger. The anger is unresolved because its expression was denied by caregivers at some past time when the anger was initially experienced. Unresolved anger is held in a state-specific, excitatory form in which it is more likely to be elicited than other emotions, but in clients who were denied expression of legitimate anger this unresolved anger is suppressed and seethes in the unconscious. In this form, unresolved archaic anger can block expression of healthy aggression that serves the self. Healthy aggression is useful anger that a person can employ to overcome obstacles to achievement of a desired goal. The case of Betty illustrates how when a client learns to recognize and then manage anger, awareness of healthy aggression then becomes possible.

Recall that Betty is a middle-aged woman who came for help with binge eating. Her case has appeared a few times already. She chose a driving incident for her target scene in which she believed she had experienced anger. In the scene, a car cut her off as she was exiting the freeway on her way home one night a couple of weeks earlier. She recalled honking at the driver and rated the SUD a strong 3. Following the protocol, she was able to identify sensations of intensity in her shoulders and a bearing down in her stomach that were the qualia of anger. Adhering to the protocol, she applied skill III, using the positive cognition "the intensity in my shoulders and the bearing down in my stomach tell me I am feeling anger," and then she continued with skills IV through VII. Using skill VII, she decreased her anger by 95%. At this point we discussed the driving situation from an objective point of view, which she could now do because she had decreased her anger. She was able to see that the thoughtless, self-absorbed driver who had cut in front of her posed a danger to her safety. She recognized that much of the anger she felt in the car that night was old anger that related to other thoughtless, self-absorbed people who had endangered her at earlier times in her life. When she could ground herself (skill V), notice the old associations (skill VI), and decrease her anger (skill VII), the rude driver of her visualization suddenly became impersonal. She realized he was little more than a pothole on the road, a danger to be sure, but something to be avoided. I asked her to visualize how she would drive were an unexpected danger to appear suddenly, and she said, "Well, I'd slow down and put some distance between my car and the danger." We returned to the target scene which no longer elicited anger and in which she could now recognize the thoughtless driver as a danger. I asked her to notice any new sensations. With TABS facilitation, Betty now felt a sensation of power in her solar plexus. The positive cognition "power in my solar plexus tells me I am feeling healthy aggression" was installed using TABS. Betty was then able to see that in the scene with the rude driver she could use her healthy aggression to motivate more adaptive behavior.

Clinician readers will note how the binge eater Betty held some anger in her stomach that she experienced as a bearing down. Readers will also note that as this woman connected with her healthy aggression she experienced it as power, which has a self-affirming, positive connotation, and that it replaced bearing down, which seems oppressive. Furthermore, the body locus shifted from her stomach to her solar plexus. Once she was aware of it, Betty was able to mobilize healthy aggression in the service of her therapeutic goals as our work together progressed, and she has used it to serve her recovery goals, mobilizing it to motivate her exercise program and to regularly attend a 12-step group.

Sadness

Following fear and anger, the AMST usually targets sadness affect. The experience of Fred, a client we've encountered before, demonstrates two important points regarding the development of a target scene and installation of the skill III positive cognition. When asked for a time when he believed he felt sad, Fred provided an incident from childhood that involved his mother. From his history and our work together to that point, I felt certain this scene would engage a large neural network freighted with intense, unresolved emotion. As a consequence I made a decision to ask the client for a different target scene. Fred's initial target visualization involved an incident from childhood in which his mother rejected him and he felt he didn't belong. I recorded his report and let him know that we would return to this scene later in therapy, but that for the moment I felt it was too emotionally charged. He agreed and gave an alternate scene in which he learned that a pet had died. Visualizing this target scene, he was able to recognize welling up in his eyes, trembling in his chin, tightness in his throat, and pressing in his chest as the qualia of sadness. Installing the skill III positive cognition was broken up into phrases, because there were so many sensations accompanying the scene.

> **Clinician: TABS On** As you hold the image of learning that your dog has died, please repeat after me, "The welling up in my eyes."
> **Fred:** The welling up in my eyes.
> **Clinician:** "Trembling in my chin."
> **Fred:** Trembling in my chin.
> **Clinician:** "Tightness in my throat."
> **Fred:** Tightness in my throat.

Clinician: "And pressing in my chest."

Fred: And pressing in my chest.

Clinician: "Tell me I am feeling sadness."

Fred: Tell me I am feeling sadness.

Clinician: Good. Let that become completely true. Good. **TABS Off** Deep breath. Let it out, and what comes up now?

Many clients report experiencing qualia of sadness that are similar to Fred's experience. Peter is a 40-year-old man who came for help with alcoholism. When asked for a scene in which he thought he might have felt sad, he spontaneously verbalized, "At some level I'm almost always sad," and then related an incident from his 20s when he and a girl friend separated. He identified sensations of tightness in his throat, tears in his eyes, heaviness all over, and hollowness in his chest as the qualia of sadness.

Sadness is often associated with unrequited yearning affect, as the experience of Betty demonstrates. Recall that Betty, a middle-aged woman, had come for help with binge eating. In our work together, I had asked for an image of a time she believed she felt yearning, and Betty recalled an image from childhood when she had been left by her parents in the care of her paternal grandfather. She wanted to be cared for by her mother, who did not "get it" that she wanted mother's attention. As she held this scene, Betty began to feel sadness, which she experienced as tearing in her eyes and sobbing in her throat. The clinician shifted to the more urgent affect, sadness, and developed and installed the skill III positive cognition "tearing in my eyes and sobbing in my throat tell me I am feeling sadness." Installation was facilitated by TABS. The clinician continued with skills IV to VII, which the client had already learned, and the client was able to decrease her sadness to a manageable level. At that point, Betty was able to identify the qualia of yearning affect, as illustrated in the following section.

Yearning

Recall that I have proposed that yearning affect motivates us toward merger with a desired object. Betty expressed this as she visualized the target scene where she was left with her paternal grandfather, when she directed these words to her mother, "I want to be cared for. Come get me." She sought merger with her mother. When she was able to regulate sadness using the AMST skill set, she could recognize sensations that she described as rising in her chest and throat. With TABS facilitation, the positive cognition "the rising in my chest and throat tells me I am feeling yearning" was installed. Upon completion of the installation, Betty reported she was starting to get flooded by the strength of her unrequited yearning for connection with her mother. She realized that this powerful affect had been hidden beneath two affects. One was sadness that her yearning had rarely been satisfied, and the other was anger directed at her mother for her failures to meet the child Betty's needs for empathic nurturing.

Like Betty, Fred, the 50-year-old man who sought help for problems with alcohol and overeating, used a target scene for yearning that he had also identified with sadness. This was the scene referred to above in which his mother had rejected him and he felt he didn't belong. I felt this visualization was appropriate for the target affect yearning because it involved a desired object of merger and also because the client had by this point learned to manage his sadness and anger affects using the entire AMST process, and I felt that he would be able to tolerate the emotion. Still, the power of his yearning affect was considerable, as this excerpt demonstrates. As Fred visualized the target scene in which his mother rejected him and he felt he didn't belong, he initially reported feeling sensations of "numbness all over, disorientation, and a spinning sort of a feeling in my arms and legs and hands and feet." The sensations of numbness and disorientation indicate mild dissociation. Based on our previous skill III work, the spinning sensations indicate anger. The clinician helped Fred to use the skills he had already learned to ground himself (skill V), notice what was happening (skill VI), and reduce the emotions (skill VII), and thereby intervene the dissociation. Then the client was able to identify a sensation of pressure that he felt in his chest as he yearned for connection with his mother. The skill III positive cognition "the sensations of pressure in my chest tell me I am feeling yearning" was installed. This work represented an enormous step for Fred because he was able to recognize for the first time how much he had desired connection with his mother that she was incapable of providing and furthermore how that unrequited desire had driven his drinking, his eating, and his relationship choices.

Embarrassment–Shame

Shame is the emotion felt when a person is exposed. Embarrassment is a less intense degree of shame affect. The case of Amy illustrates the element of exposure in a target scene for the index affect shame. Amy, whom we've met before, is a woman in her 30s who had come for help with chronic bulimia. For her shame affect target scene she recalled a time that she had binged on food that was being saved for a special occasion. Her transgression was discovered, and she was confronted about it. She rated the disturbance level for the scene as 7 as she recalled it. With TABS facilitation she identified sensations of stiffness in her forehead and pain in her stomach associated with the target scene. Following the protocol, the positive cognition for skill III, "the pain in my stomach and stiffness in my forehead tell me I'm feeling shame" was installed with TABS facilitation.

Embarrassment or shame are affects that clients sometimes feel in session. The case of Jennifer demonstrates how clinicians can use a client's presenting affect as a target scene. Remember that Jennifer is a young woman in her 20s who came for help with bulimia. Near the beginning of our work together, after she had developed a container and safe place, she began a session with a report of having binged and then purged the previous evening. She reported that she felt embarrassed telling me about what she perceived as a failure. She agreed to my suggestion to use the current experience of reporting her binge and purge to me as a target for embarrassment, and she assigned a disturbance level of 5 to the experience. Holding the visualization with TABS facilitation, she identified shrugging in her shoulders, "casting down" her eyes, and fidgeting in her hands and legs as sensations telling her she was feeling embarrassment. A skill III positive cognition based on these sensations was installed.

Jennifer felt exposed in session as she revealed that she had acted out bulimically the previous evening. The qualia of shame that she and other clients often report appear to reflect efforts to minimize the exposure experience. Jennifer reported shrugging her shoulders, while Fred identified hunkering and cringing of his shoulders. Peter, the alcoholic in his 40s, visualized a target scene in which his partner found his stash of empty beer cans, and he reported feeling small, apparently an exposure-reducing sensation. Like Jennifer, Fred reported that he lowered his eyes as he visualized the shame affect target scene. Betty, the binge eater, reported shame sensations more like those reported by Amy. Betty identified "scrunching" in her forehead, which appears similar to the stiffness that Amy recognized in her forehead in the shame affect target scene. Amy and Betty, who are both eating disordered, were also alike in that for each of them a component of the qualia of shame was located in the stomach. Amy stated she felt "pain" in her stomach, while Betty identified "sinking" in hers.

Disgust

Disgust affect is extremely powerful. Like other affects, it appears to occur in a range of intensities. Disgust affect is incorporated into affective–cognitive structures that motivate a broad sweep of behaviors from bigotry at the more extreme end to choices of friends, food, and voting behaviors at the less extreme end. The power and ubiquity of disgust affect are often underappreciated by therapists, and many people are unaware of their disgust affect or the place that parental broadcast disgust played in their early lives. For these reasons disgust affect should be targeted last, after the client has developed a firm command of the AMST process.

Recall that disgust affect apparently evolved from the emetic reflex that is activated by swallowing rotten food or taking it into the mouth. Thus, in parallel with the emetic reflex, disgust affect involves the mouth, tongue, salivary glands, esophagus, and stomach.

Unresolved disgust affect often plays a central role in the eating disorders, as the case of Betty illustrates. When asked to recall a scene of a time in which she believed she felt disgust, Betty initially described her purging behaviors from her teenage years. Since the clinician's treatment plan did not call for working on the client's eating disorder until she had acquired the AMST skills for the full range of emotion, he encouraged her to find something from her adult life, something more recent that did not involve food. She then recalled watching her mother screaming at her own dog. As she recalled the scene, she vocalized a classic nonverbal expression of disgust: "Eeeuw!" Following the protocol, the clinician asked Betty to hold the image of her mother yelling at her own dog and with TABS facilitation suggested she notice sensations accompanying the visualization. The client became aware of "clenching" in her stomach, "rising" in her esophagus, and "retraction" of her tongue. The clinician then installed the skill III positive cognition, "Clenching in my stomach, rising in my esophagus, and retraction of my tongue tell me I am feeling disgust." Betty's process working with disgust affect reveals how two, seemingly disparate experiences—Betty's bulimic acting out in adolescence and her experience watching her mother yelling at the dog—separated in time by perhaps 35 years, are apparently components of a single neural network assembled with and unified by disgust affect.

The experience of Elaine further illustrates how the qualia of disgust affect are experienced in the digestive tract. This woman in her 20s came for help with bulimarexia, which is characterized by restriction of food intake as well as by purging. For a target scene eliciting disgust affect, Elaine selected her "binge" the morning of our session. In the binge she consumed foods containing grains as well as a piece of fruit. She estimated the total intake amounted to about 300 calories. The scene was very disturbing to her, and she rated it a SUD of 10. When she brought up the image with TABS facilitation, she became aware of "fullness in my stomach" that accompanied the visualization. Following the protocol, a skill III positive cognition "the fullness in my stomach tells me I am feeling disgust" was installed.

Elicitation of disgust affect is not restricted to food, however, even in an eating disordered client, as the case of Carly demonstrates. Recall that Carly is the woman in her 40s who had come seeking help with binge overeating. When asked for a target scene that elicits disgust affect, she mentioned a work situation in which an administrator rewarded a poorly qualified coworker who curried favor with the administrator. With TABS accompaniment, Carly identified sensations of "nausea in my stomach" as the qualia of disgust affect. Again with TABS facilitation, the skill III positive cognition, "The nausea in my stomach tells me I'm feeling disgust" was installed. Focusing on a target scene from adolescence in which he was ridiculed by a coach, Fred, the middle-aged male seeking help for drinking and overeating, experienced the qualia of disgust as "churning in my stomach." Both Carly and Fred experienced disgust affect in situations that had nothing to do with food.

Contempt is an affect closely related to disgust. Izard (1991) has grouped contempt with anger and disgust in the "hostility triad" (p. 229) of affects. The case of Peter shows how stomach-related qualia of disgust were associated with contempt affect for this man. Peter is the man in his 40s who came for help with drinking. His father had often broadcast contempt at his young son, and in therapy Peter verbalized the negative cognition, "I am contemptible," about himself. He identified sensations of sickness in his stomach as the qualia of his contempt affect.

Startle

Surprise–startle is one of the hard-wired affects. For clients with posttraumatic stress disorder (PTSD) and other patients with trauma histories startle affect may well be trauma coded. These clients may benefit from developing awareness of startle affect and its associated sensations as well as from cognizing the affect. Clinicians experienced in treatment of PTSD and dissociative disorders can consider targeting startle affect and eliciting a target scene in which the patient felt the affect at a low level. Skills III to VII can then be applied to assist the client in managing the trauma coded startle response.

When startle affect is trauma coded in childhood, it is the affect most likely to be elicited subsequently in many situations because it is the affect held in an excitatory form. Startle has the effect of blanking the mind. When trauma coded startle affect is elicited later in life, it blanks the mind and makes it difficult for the adult to marshal resources to deal with current situations. A male client recalled that in his childhood his father would terrorize the client's mother by suddenly swerving the family car toward a cliff. These experiences apparently trauma coded startle affect in the young boy who witnessed them from the car's back seat. In adulthood, this client experienced difficulty speaking in public situations, particularly ones in which he was unexpectedly asked to talk, because he would "blank out." The clinician taught him the AMST process to help him recognize startle affect. For this client the qualia of startle consisted of jerking his head. Once he had cognized startle, the client learned skills III to VII to tolerate and decrease it. Having learned to manage startle, the client could apply his skills to visualized situations in which he was unexpectedly asked to speak and could connect with authentic excitement that the opportunity afforded him to share his ideas in his field of expertise. He reports successfully using his affect management skills in real life speaking situations.

Other Emotions

The fundamental hard-wired affects can assemble with each other, with cognitions, with appraisals, with memories, and with images to produce a myriad of emotions, each one of which may be expected to have a unique set of sensations that identify it. Some of the more common examples are presented here.

The emotion relief has already been mentioned as one that often arises early in the AMST phase of therapy when clients succeed in getting "every disturbing thing" into containment. The middle-aged man with a drinking problem, Fred, visualized a container that looked like a treasure chest and then transferred every disturbing thing to it. When asked, "and what comes up now?" he responded, "A profound sense of relief." The clinician immediately attended to this emotion. With TABS facilitation, he inquired, "As you hold your awareness of the sense of relief you are feeling, just notice where in your body there are sensations that accompany the emotion of relief." Fred quickly became aware of "buzzing in my head" and "tingling in my hands, legs, chest, and stomach." With TABS facilitation, a skill III positive cognition was installed that assembled the emotion, qualia, and cognition into a unitary construct. The alcoholic man in his 40s, Peter, also experienced relief as he transferred disturbing material into containment. He expressed the qualia of relief as "a weight's been taken off my chest."

Transferring disturbing material to containment often results in the appearance of positive affect, but clients do not always use the word *relief* to express what they are feeling. The anorexic, Elaine, volunteered that she felt relaxed in her hands after placing 60% of every disturbing thing in her container, a big garbage dumpster. When queried about what emotion the feeling of relaxation indicated, she stated it was calmness. Following the client's lead, the skill III positive cognition "the relaxed sensation in my hands tells me I'm feeling calmness" was installed with TABS facilitation. Another client experienced sensations that she identified as trust after successfully completing the containment skill. Carly, the woman who binged, reported feeling "clean breath" in her lungs and throat after getting her disturbing material into containment. For her these sensations indicated the complex construct trust.

Other emotions that often surface during the AMST phase of therapy include hope, which usually manifests in the heart or the chest, worthiness, and pride. The emotion safety has already been discussed in connection with the safe place skill in Chapter 7.

DEVELOPING METACOGNITIONS

The clinician can develop a metacognition linking the skill III positive cognition into a larger construct. After the skill III cognition linking affect and sensation has been installed, it can be assembled into a superordinate, self-referential construct, the metacognition. The metacognition is an *I* statement. The metacognition incorporates the index affect, the associated sensations, awareness of those sensations, the skill III cognition, plus the skill III appraisal into the *I* statement; for example, "I am learning to recognize how my body tells me I am feeling [name of emotion]." In the early stages of AMST, the metacognition should be a process statement, rather than an expression of state.

The following example from Betty's work with anger affect illustrates how the clinician creates the assemblage by reviewing the target scene, target affect, associated sensations, the cognition, and the appraisal and then develops the metacognition:

> Clinician: **TABS On** Recall the scene driving home the other night and a driver cuts in front of you at the freeway exit. See yourself honking. Become aware of intensity in your shoulders and bearing down in your stomach, the sensations that tell you you are feeling anger. Recall that you now know with complete certainty that these are the sensations of anger. Now please repeat after me, "I am learning to recognize how my body tells me I am feeling anger."
>
> Betty: I am learning to recognize how my body tells me I am feeling anger.
>
> Clinician: Good. Let that become completely true. **TABS Off** Deep breath. Let it out, and what comes up now?

SKILL III IS MODULAR

Use skill III whenever a new emotion surfaces. When joy or pride or self-worth surfaces later in the therapy, the clinician should take time to apply skill III to these emotions, identifying a body location and sensation and then creating a cognition that assembles them into a unitary construct.

INTERVENTIONS FOR DIFFICULT SITUATIONS

Sometimes clients have difficulty recognizing the sensations accompanying the index emotion in the target scene. This may manifest as difficulty achieving certainty for the skill III positive cognition. When the client is unable to endorse a VoC of 7 or close to it for the skill III positive cognition, the clinician should follow the protocol as presented in Figure 8.1. When the client reports a VoC of less than 7 for the PC, "The [name of sensations] in my (body location) tell me I am feeling [target affect]," the clinician should first inquire, "What quality would you need to have to increase your certainty?" As described in Chapters 6 and 7, the clinician should help the client develop a quality resource. If a validity of 7 has still not been obtained, the clinician should ask, "Is there anyone who could help you increase your certainty?" and move to develop the alliance resource. Finally, if certainty still has not been achieved, the clinician should inquire, "Is there anyone preventing you from knowing for certain that the sensations you experience are telling you you're feeling the target emotion?" In this case, the clinician should pursue an ego state intervention. The installation of a quality resource, an alliance resource, and the ego state intervention, have been described in detail previously, so these protocols will not be repeated here. Instead, I want to describe a situation that often occurs in which an ego state spontaneously reveals itself.

Recognizing Ego States When They Reveal Themselves

Sometimes covert helper or protector ego states will spontaneously make themselves known to the clinician. Often, an ego state functions to help or protect the self system by preventing the system from experiencing the sensations accompanying an affect or emotion. This action can be very adaptive in childhood or adolescence, because it prevents the system from experiencing emotions that would overwhelm it and that the system is prevented from discharging or has no skills to resolve adaptively. While this protective action was adaptive in childhood, it is maladaptive in later life and may contribute to the client's presenting problem. The attuned clinician will notice the spontaneous appearance of an ego state and will work with it for the client's benefit. When an ego state chooses to reveal itself in therapy it means it feels safe enough to do so, which indicates that the therapist has created an environment of safety and security in the therapeutic dyad. Having previously taught the client skill II (safe place) also seems to promote a feeling of safety for the helper ego state that makes it easier for it to disclose its existence.

A sensation-regulating ego state may make itself known in response to the clinician's query "and what comes up now?" during development of skill III. In answer to this question, a sensation-regulating ego state may surface in the form of a spontaneous verbalization that either directly or indirectly reveals its existence. In the direct form, the sensation-regulating ego state discloses itself through an *I* statement that is actually the voice of the ego state. For example, a client who was an exercise bulimic was asked to visualize a scene in which she experienced the emotion guilt, and with TABS facilitation she was encouraged to notice the sensations accompanying the scene. She reported, "As soon as I start to feel the feelings, I tell myself I have to exercise to deal with it." The ego state is the *I* that is speaking in the phrase "I tell myself."

In the indirect manner, the sensation-regulating ego state may reveal itself by preventing the client from experiencing the target scene. The client may say, "I can see the scene, but I can't get in it." The client may state, "I feel numb," or "Something is numbing me out." The covert sensation-regulating ego state is indirectly revealing itself by its action of preventing the client from entering the scene or numbing the client out as she visualizes the scene. Whether indirect or direct, the clinician's job is to be sensitive and attuned to the content of the client's verbalization and to pursue that content by getting to know the ego state that is asking for acknowledgement.

Affect regulating ego states emerge over developmental time to protect the personality system by separating the self from emotion experience. One means for accomplishing this is to separate the person from the physiological sensations through which the organism experiences affects and emotions. People who were not taught emotion management skills in childhood are often uncomfortable feeling emotion later in life. Similarly, individuals who were punished for emotion expression in childhood learned to fear emotion experience or to feel disgust at emotion experience. Also, people with trauma histories often dissociate emotions out of awareness, because the experience of trauma coded emotion feels overwhelming. Since emotion experience entails awareness of the physical sensations, the qualia, accompanying an emotion, the protector ego state often functions by numbing the individual. For these persons, the body is not safe, because the body is the locus of sensations that accompany emotion.

Numbing out is a form of dissociation in which the element of sensation is separated away from the ongoing flow of consciousness. Persons can dissociate sensations from awareness and yet have a low score on an assessment tool such as the Dissociative Experiences Scale (DES). I believe that dissociation is a much more common phenomenon than is usually recognized. Dissociation is thought of as pathognomic for dissociative identity disorder (DID) and dissociative disorder not otherwise specified (DDNOS). Consequently, when a client scores low on the DES, clinicians dismiss a dissociative disorder diagnosis and fail to recognize dissociative phenomena. Through its valuable diagnostic function, the AMST uncovers the dissociative phenomenon early in therapy, in the stabilization phase, and remediates it *before* it arises suddenly and unexpectedly later in therapy during trauma processing or uncovering work.

Therapists should consider an ego state intervention when a client is unable to experience sensations in the target scene. When a client reports numbing out or is unable to feel during development of skill III, this probably indicates the action of a covert ego state whose protector function is to separate the client from physical sensations and emotions. Recall the principle that ego states are recognized by their actions. The fundamentals of an ego state intervention were provided in Chapter 6. Application of these fundamentals is summarized here for the case in which sensation or emotion is dissociated during development of skill III. When a client reports numbing out or being unable to feel sensations, the clinician can describe the concept of a covert ego state and how it protects the client by "separating you from your feelings" or "separating you from the physical sensations that accompany emotions." Get agreement from the client that experiencing emotions or associated sensations would help him attain his therapy goals. Obtain agreement to meet the part, which is provisionally referred to as The One Who Separates You From Experiencing Sensations. Suggest a conference room as a way to meet the part, if it exists. Using trance or TABS to facilitate the conference room, the part is brought forward, and the clinician affiliates with it. The clinician should ascertain that the part that has come forward is indeed the One Who Separates. The part's helper function over the client's lifetime should be uncovered. Following principles of an ego state intervention, the clinician should facilitate a negotiation of a new relationship between the protector part and the self. In the new relationship, the protector part becomes a sentinel or body guard whose job now is to alert the client to when she is starting to "separate" so she can take responsibility for remaining integrated and use the skills she is learning. The final component is to arrange for a signal and get the client's agreement to notice it. Two cases illustrate how an ego state intervention was applied when clients dissociated the sensations associated with emotion.

The Case of Jennifer

The first case features Jennifer, the young bulimarexic woman we have met before. Having completed skills I and II, we progressed to work with fear affect. Jennifer produced a target scene of a minor fender bender that had occurred a year previously. Jennifer was not at fault, and no one was hurt. She assigned a SUD of 5 to the visualization of the accident. With TABS facilitation, the clinician asked her to hold the visualization and become aware of sensations in her body accompanying it. When asked, "What sensations came up for you?" she reported, "I can see myself, but I can't be in it." She was able to report minute details of the accident as well as thoughts that rushed through her mind, including fearing telling her father about the accident. However, she claimed to have no awareness of sensations, saying, "I'm stuck in my head." In an ego state intervention facilitated by trance, The One Who Separates Jennifer From Her Sensations was invited to come into the conference room. The client described a "big thing . . . it's fat . . . and taller than me" that came into the room. This ego state was unable to speak, so the clinician communicated with it through the medium of finger signals and by means of Jennifer's impression of what The One, as it agreed to be called, was thinking. Very importantly, the clinician ascertained from The One that Jennifer was capable of experiencing physical sensations accompanying her emotions. This fact assured the clinician that Jennifer did not have a physical impairment preventing her experience of sensations. The One agreed to help Jennifer by allowing her to experience her sensations. Returning to the target scene of the accident, the client was now able to identify sensations of "tingling" throughout her body and a "rush" to her head. With TABS facilitation, a skill III positive cognition, "Tingling throughout my body and rushing to my head tell me I'm feeling fear," was installed. Jennifer's case illustrates how an ego state intervention can reorganize the structure of the self system and lead to adaptive functioning, in this case providing the client with the capacity to experience the qualia associated with the emotion of fear.

The Case of Carly

The second case involves Carly, the woman in her 40s who sought help for binge-ing. Her target scene for fear affect at SUD 3 was camping alone in a California wilderness area. She identified deep fluttering sensations in the middle of her chest as the qualia of fear. Skills III to VII were developed, and the client reported successfully reducing her fear. At our next session, she reported that although she could manage her fear in session, she had gotten "really, really anxious" at home that morning and had "not been in my body" at that time. Using trance to facilitate an ego state intervention, The One Who Takes Carly Out of Her Body was invited into the conference room. An old woman with gray hair appeared, hunched over, looking a little like a witch and a little like a crow. This ego state asked to be called "Crow." Crow stated she had been helping Carly "always" and that she took Carly out of her body "so she won't feel so much and so that she will be able to get things done." Crow agreed to signal Carly with a "caw" to let her know if she was leaving her body, and Carly agreed to send down her grounding roots in response to the signal. The case of Carly illustrates how the ego state Crow revealed itself indirectly through her statement that she was not in her body. The clinician inferred from this statement that some agency, to wit an ego state, had taken her out of her body and made a therapeutic decision to seek to meet the ego state. The intervention promotes the client's well-being by cognizing her dissociative proclivity and by converting the fear-regulating, dissociating ego state into an ally that will signal the client to use her grounding resource to intervene the dissociative process.

SUMMARY

In Chapter 8 clinicians have learned skills to help clients identify sensations by which affects may be recognized. These skills are important because many clients who are victims of deficit experience and adversity or trauma are unable to name, to feel, or to regulate core affects and emotions. Failures of emotion knowledge and inability to regulate affects and emotions contribute to psychopathology. Transmitting AMST to clients promotes resolution of presenting psychopathology, because affect dysregulation is a central component of maladaptation. As clients acquire the ability to manage affects, as they develop the resources that enable affect management, and as they uncover covert ego states that may be operating in their self systems, they create more adaptively organized self structure. The chapter has taught how to identify the target affect, how to set limits on the intensity of affect by using the SUD rating scale, and how to elicit a target scene. Clinicians will use the target scene as the basis for teaching the grounding, noticing, and regulating skills that are conveyed in subsequent chapters.

C h a p t e r **9**

Skill IV: Sensation as Signal Skill V: Grounded and Present Skill VI: Noticing

Chapter 9 teaches three closely related skills erected on the foundation established by target affect, target scene, and skill III (sensation-affect identification). Skill IV (sensation as signal) links the affect-identifying sensations to deployment of a grounding image, a visualization of a connection between the client and the earth. This image allows the client to remain grounded and present while experiencing the index emotion, an ability that is installed with skill V (grounded and present). Skill VI (noticing self) establishes another layer of self structure as it teaches the client to "just notice" the emotions, sensations, thoughts, and impulses to action that accompany the target visualization. The purpose of these skills is to intervene in both fast processing in the limbic system and activation of the autonomic nervous system. Skill IV is diagramed in Figure 9.1; Figure 9.2 shows Skill V; Skill VI is presented in Figure 9.3.

The term *fast processing* refers to LeDoux's low road, the direct pathway from the perceptual receptor through the thalamus to the amygdala (LeDoux, 1996). The thalamic pathway is fast because it is direct. Skills IV through VI continue the process of building a high road that includes the perceptual cortex, creating an alternative to the low road. The purpose of this high road is to prevent the undesired physiological responses associated with the emotion. LeDoux has explained that the cortical pathway functions to prevent inappropriate responses. Installing a high road that involves the cortex intervenes in the physiological component of an affective response. Firing in the amygdala's central nucleus triggers the body's emotion responses across physiological systems (LeDoux, 1996). Building the high road through teaching AMST helps the client intervene in what was previously an automatic emotion response by which fear became terror, or anger built to rage levels. The grounding visualization provides an imagistic

286

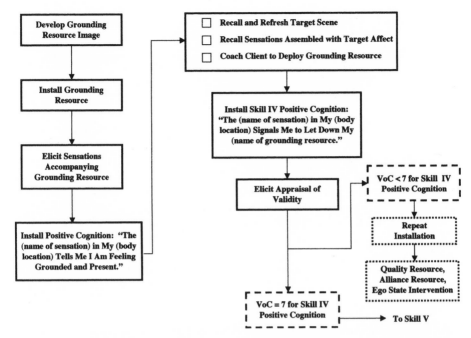

Figure 9.1.   Flow Diagram and Decision Tree (skill IV, Sensation as Signal). This figure presents the development and installation of the grounding resource and then shows how deployment of the resource is linked to sensations accompanying the target affect.

means by which the client can stay in the present moment for long enough to ac-tivate the cortical components accessed by the skill set.

Skills IV through VI create an alternative to acting out. For many clients, act-ing out is the means employed to manage difficult emotions. Often, for smokers, the surfacing of subthreshold levels of fear affect triggers the physiological fear response, which the smoker apparently manages with nicotine. Some alcoholics apparently manage anger affect through drinking while others may manage sad-ness. Each addict appears to manage a specific emotion with the drug of choice, and eating disordered persons use food, whether bingeing on food, purging food, or avoiding food, to regulate emotions that are unique for each individual. Build-ing a high road involving cortical input by installing the AMST process gives the client a means to tolerate the difficult emotion and provides tools for managing it through alternative behaviors to acting out. These skills may be useful for per-sonality disorders as well as for Axis I disorders. The borderline can use these skills to prevent physiological fear responses from developing when abandon-ment is triggered. The conduct disordered person can use them to intervene in the development of physiological anger responses when authority figures are encountered.

Finally, by grounding the client in the present, these skills prevent the retrieval and reexperiencing of archaic, unresolved emotion assembled with a particular affect-coded neural network. Because the visualizations presented in this chapter allow the client to interdict the low road sequence of fast processing they give the client control over impulses to act out and provide choices for alternative behaviors.

The following language can be used to explain how persons trapped in fast processing will often act out through maladaptive, compulsive behaviors:

Now that you have identified how your body tells you that you are feeling fear at a low level, our next task is to develop an image that will allow you to stay grounded and present while you feel this emotion. By learning to stay grounded and present, you learn to tolerate the emotion. Our eventual goal is to decrease distressing emotions, but before we can do that it is first necessary to learn to recognize the emotion and then tolerate it. The skill I am going to teach you now helps you stay grounded and present while you are experiencing an emotion. People often act out when they feel a disturbing emotion. That's because there is a direct neural pathway from the perception that triggers, for example, fear to the fear response. What we are doing here is building new pathways that will help you avoid acting out. The first step in building the new pathway is to develop a grounding image.

DEVELOPING THE GROUNDING RESOURCE

The grounding resource consists simply of an image of a connection between the self and the earth. Having explained the utility of the visualization, the clinician will ask the client to provide her own image of a connection. TABS is not used to evoke the image. The clinician will want to use language that gives the client permission to develop his own unique grounding visualization while at the same time suggesting by examples what the necessary qualities of the image are. The essential quality of the image is that it allows the client to stay grounded and present. AMST clinicians should use permissive words like *allow* and should avoid using words like *hold*, which carry the suggestion of trapping or imprisoning and can trigger unresolved, adverse, archaic material for the client who was, for example, locked in a closet or otherwise "held" or restrained in childhood. The clinician should also avoid using the image of being attached to "mother" earth, as the word *mother* may trigger negative material for clients with harsh and punitive, distancing and unresponsive, or abandoning maternal figures.

Grounding resource images are as individualistic as are clients. One image a clinician may offer as an example is the grounding cord, a cord of light like a fiber optic cable attaching to the tip of the spine and extending down to the center of the earth where it attaches. This visualization may not be appropriate for clients who cannot tolerate the image of anything attaching to the spine because this elicits traumatic material. Several clients have visualized magnetic boots that use earth's magnetic force field to allow the client to stay grounded and present. Clients have used grounding roots that sprout down into the earth from the soles of the feet. An image of a rock or boulder that the client holds onto has often surfaced. One client simply visualized herself sitting on the bare earth, and another saw himself on hands and knees, his connection to earth established through his fingertips and the palms of his hands. With children, adolescents, and clients who have difficulty visualizing, it may be helpful to draw a picture of the grounding resource.

The client will learn the grounding resource in therapy to be able to tolerate affect and emotion elicited by recalling a target scene in which the target affect was experienced. The client recollects the target scene *in session*, and recollection of the image elicits the target affect and associated sensations, again, in the moment, in the session. When the client visualizes deployment of a grounding image, he is doing this *in session* as he holds the target image. What he will be learning to tolerate is the affect produced by the emotion memory system that is triggered by recalling the incident from explicit memory. Acquiring the grounding resource is the necessary preliminary to skill IV in which mobilization of the grounding image is linked to sensations identifying the index affect and to skill V in which he affirms with a positive cognition that he can stay grounded and present while he experiences the index affect. Skill VI will teach him to notice this affect and skill VII will teach him to regulate it. I want to emphasize that he is recognizing, tolerating, and regulating an affect elicited from the emotion memory by recalling the target scene. The client can use the grounding visualization to stay grounded and present in his chair in the counseling office as he recalls the target scene and experiences the target affect. He may also return to the visualized target scene and replay it visualizing himself deploying the grounding resource in that recalled scene. By learning these skills with a recalled scene he prepares himself to deploy the grounding resource in real life situations outside the counseling or therapy office. The goal of this work is for the client to use his resources in current situations, in real life and real time, to change his behavior in the moment. What the client cannot do is travel backward in time and change how he felt and responded in the past. What he can do is change how he feels today when he recalls a past event. Clients may be confused on this point. Therapy can help a client accept how he actually felt and responded at the time of an event. AMST can help the client change how he feels today when he recalls the event and it can help the client feel and respond differently in the future to events that are similar to past distressing events.

Eliciting Sensations of Being Grounded

Once the client has imaged a grounding resource, his next task is to uncover the sensations that tell him he is grounded and present. Whatever image the client, guided by the clinician, arrives at, the clinician now proceeds to help the client identify sensations that accompany the grounding visualization. TABS is employed to uncover these sensations. It is vital to successful implementation of the grounding skill that the client experience sensations (qualia) that coincide with the visualization. For the grounding cord, clients have reported sensations of weight or tension as they visualize being grounded and present. One client who used a boulder as his grounding resource reported an experience of lucidity in his mind associated with pressing himself against the boulder. Skill III is employed to assist the client in raising the sensations of grounding to awareness and then cognizing them. With TABS facilitation, the client identifies the sensations accompanying the visualization, and then develops a positive cognition linking the grounding image, the sensations of being grounded and present, and the body location where those sensations are felt.

Once the clinician and client have agreed upon a visualization for the grounding resource, the following is language that can be used to develop and install the image. In this example, I have used the image of a grounding cord. The language should be adapted to suit the client's particular visualization. The clinician should record the nature of the client's grounding visualization either in his own notes or on the worksheet presented in Appendix A.

> Clinician: Now that you have gotten a grounding image, let's develop it and identify the sensations that accompany it. **TABS On** See your cord of light, like a fiber optic cable, attaching to the tip of your spine. You can tug on it to make certain it is firmly connected. Now, just let the cord go down, straight down, through the chair, through the floor, the dirt, rock, down to the center of the earth. See it attaching there. Tug on it to make certain it is well connected. Good. Now, I'd like you to just notice the sensations in your body that accompany this visualization of being grounded and present. Take all the time you need. When you get them, let me know by raising your left index finger. Good. [*Client raises index finger.*] **TABS Off** Deep breath. Let it out, and tell me, what did you get?
>
> Client: It's like an energy flowing down my back.
>
> Clinician: Good. Let's install that. **TABS On** See your cord of light attaching from the tip of your spine to the center of the earth. Good. Nice and bright and firmly attached. Now, become aware of the energy flowing down your back. Good. And repeat after me, "The energy flowing down my back tells me I am grounded and present."
>
> Client: The energy flowing down my back tells me I am grounded and present.
>
> Clinician: Good. Let that become as true as it can be. **TABS Off** Deep breath. Let it out, and what comes up now?

The importance of helping the client experience the qualia associated with being grounded is illustrated by the case of Jennifer, the bulimic woman in her early 20s. Her target scene for fear affect was a minor fender bender. She visualized a grounding cord for her grounding image, but reported experiencing "nothing really" until, with TABS facilitation, she "pictured the cord . . . and felt a physical tension between myself and the earth." Once she experienced the sensations accompanying the grounding visualization, she was able to stay grounded and present while visualizing the target scene and feeling the fear assembled with it.

Eliciting an Appraisal

The clinician should elicit a self-report from the client regarding the validity of the positive cognition (PC), "The [name of sensations] in my [body location] tell me I am grounded and present." For the example given above, the clinician can ask, "As you hold the image of your grounding cord, on a scale from 1 to 7 where 1 is false and 7 is true, how true is the statement, "The energy flowing down my back tells me I am grounded and present"? This statement should attain complete validity before proceeding to the next skill. If a client is unable to endorse certain validity, then I would first repeat the installation, slowly and carefully emphasizing all aspects of the image. If the client is still unable to endorse certain validity, then I would proceed as described previously for cases where the Validity of Cognition (VoC) is less than 7. Begin by developing a quality resource. If that doesn't bring the VoC to 7, ask the client if he has ever known a person who was grounded, or if he has an image of an animal or other ally that embodied the quality of being grounded and present. This should be developed as an alliance resource. Finally, if these installations are unable to produce certain validity, the clinician should effect an ego state intervention. Some clients, for example "flighty" individuals, may have an ego state that protects by preventing the client from being grounded. If this is the case, the ego state should be uncovered and converted to helping in a new way. Clinicians can follow instructions given previously for this intervention.

PROCEDURE FOR SKILL IV (SENSATION AS SIGNAL)

Having established the grounding resource visualization, the AMST protocol now returns to the target scene, and installs skill IV (sensation as signal) that cues deployment of the grounding image by the client's physical sensations for the target affect. The purpose of sensation as signal (skill IV) is to make deployment of the grounding visualization automatic. The low road through the thalamus and amygdala that triggers emotion responding has an advantage in that it is automatic; cognitive processing is apparently not involved in this pathway. By linking deployment of the grounding mechanism to physical sensations, AMST attempts to increase the competitiveness of the high road cortical path. By getting the high road into action as quickly as possible, the client minimizes triggering of physiological responding to the emotion stimulus. Linking deployment of the grounding visualization to the qualia of the index affect decreases the number of neuronal connections between experiencing the qualia and manifesting the grounding image. Decreasing the number of neuronal connections decreases the response time. Importantly, this mechanism is also designed to bypass the client's appraisal and self-will mechanisms. Involving the client's conscious decision-making apparatus in deployment of the grounding visualization will increase the number of neuronal connections, thus increasing the response time and decreasing the effectiveness of the visualization. If the client has to think "Should I use my grounding skill?" or "Is this emotion strong enough to warrant using the skill?" the physiological component of emotion responding will engage and defeat attempts to intervene it.

To install skill IV, the clinician instructs the client to revisualize the target scene. He refreshes the client's memory of the target scene to restimulate the qualia of the target affect. He reminds her of the sensations and their body location that tell her she is feeling the index emotion, and then he suggests that she allow these sensations to signal her to bring up her grounding visualization. The clinician should recapitulate the grounding mechanism for the client and remind her of the sensations that tell her she is grounded and present. Installation of skill IV (sensation as signal) is accomplished by having the client repeat the positive cognition, "The (name of sensation) that I feel in my (body location) signals me to use my (name of grounding visualization)."

The Case of Betty

The case of subject Betty clearly demonstrates development of the grounding resource visualization and installation of skill IV. Recall that Betty's target scene was a recent time she had been stopped by a motorcycle cop for having expired registration tags on a borrowed car. She experienced a "quickening in my solar plexus" as the qualia of fear. The ensuing excerpts illustrate this subject's process.

> Clinician: Now that you have identified how your body tells you that you are feeling fear at a low level, our next task is to develop an image that will allow you to stay grounded and present while you feel this emotion. In order to decrease a distressing emotion, it is first necessary to learn to recognize the emotion and then tolerate it. The skill I am going to teach you now helps you stay grounded and present while you are experiencing an emotion. People often act out when they feel a disturbing emotion. What we are doing here is building new pathways that will help you avoid acting out through bingeing.
>
> The first step in learning this skill is to develop an image for grounding. The grounding image helps you stay in the present moment while you are feeling the emotion. It helps you slow down the process of emotion responding so you can use the emotion regulation skills you will learn shortly. When we get away from the present by going to the past or the future, that is when we can act out. The grounding image creates a connection between you and the earth. What I'd like you to do now is just let an image come up for you that creates that connection between you and the earth. Some people have used a grounding cord. Others have used magnetic boots or grounding roots. Whatever comes up for you is just fine. I wonder what you are getting now?
>
> Betty: I'm seeing more of a grounding energy. Like a light energy coming down from the sky and up from the earth.
>
> Clinician: Good. What I'd like you to do now is focus on that image of light energy coming up from the earth and down from the sky, an image for being grounded and present, and let's identify some body sensations that accompany the image. **TABS On** See the light energy coming down from the sky and up from the earth. Notice how the light energy allows you to stay grounded and present. Just notice where there are sensations in your body that accompany the feeling of being grounded and present that the image transmits. Let me know by raising your left index finger when you get the sensations. Good. Good. [*Betty raises her left index finger.*] Excellent. **TABS Off** Deep breath. Let it out, and tell me, what did you get?
>
> Betty: It feels like an openness in my chest.
>
> Clinician: Good. Let's install that. **TABS On** As you focus on the image of light coming up from the earth and down from the sky, please

repeat after me, "The openness in my chest tells me I am grounded and present."

Betty: The openness in my chest tells me I am grounded and present.

Clinician: Good. Now let's make the grounding image work for you. Recall again the image of being stopped by the motorcycle cop. Become aware of the sensations of quickening in your solar plexus that tell you that you are feeling fear at level 2. Now, let those sensations signal you to bring up your image of light coming up from the earth and down from the sky. See the light coming up from the earth. See it coming down from the sky. Please repeat after me, "The quickening in my solar plexus signals me to bring up my grounding image."

Betty: The quickening in my solar plexus signals me to bring up my grounding image.

Clinician: Let that become as true as it can be. Now, as you see the light energy coming up from the earth and down from the sky, remind yourself of the sensation of openness in your chest telling you that you are grounded and present. Good. Feel that openness now. Good. **TABS Off** Deep breath. Let it out, and what comes up now?

Eliciting an Appraisal

The clinician can elicit an appraisal at this point by asking the client, "As you hold the image of the target scene and feel the sensations accompanying it, on a scale from 1 to 7, how true is the statement 'The [name of sensations] in my [body location] signal me to let down my [name of grounding image]?" The experience of Elaine demonstrates the importance of the appraisal process. Elaine, the young bulimic woman, experienced a slight difficulty mastering the AMST protocol the first time through. This is sometimes the case and seems to correlate with the degree of childhood deficit experience. Elaine's VoC for skill IV (sensation as signal) was 5 on the first pass through the skill set targeting fear affect. The clinician made a decision to teach the entire skill set, then to return to skill IV. Once the client had appreciated the overall skill set and its ability to help her reduce her fear, she was able to increase the validity for each skill in the pathway upon repetition. The VoC for skill IV increased to 7 the second time through the protocol.

PROCEDURE FOR SKILL V (GROUNDED AND PRESENT)

Skill V (Figure 9.2) builds on the foundation established by the previous skills: target affect, target scene, grounding visualization, skill III (sensation-affect identification), and skill IV (sensation as signal). In skill V, the client holds the target image in which she felt the index emotion; she experiences the qualia of the index emotion and allows them to signal her to use her grounding visualization; and she allows herself to experience the qualia of being grounded and present while she experiences the index affect. The clinician guides the client in assembling these components and then cements them by asking her to repeat the skill V positive cognition, "I can stay grounded and present while I feel (target affect)."

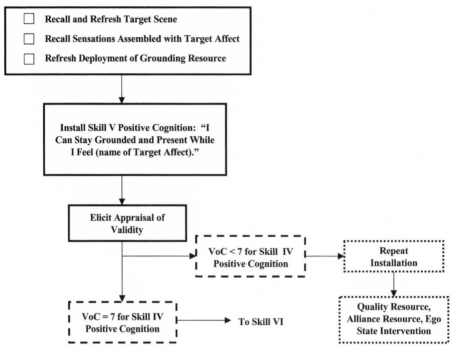

Figure 9.2.   Flow Diagram and Decision Tree (skill V, Grounded and Present). This figure shows the flow of steps involved in helping the client to stay grounded and present while experiencing the target affect.

Repetition is an important element in the AMST protocol. The clinician should remember that she is helping the client to construct new neural networks and that repetition facilitates the process. TABS accompanies the recapitulation of the previous work, apparently facilitating effective and efficient skills acquisition by clearing the mind of old, competing scripts. Returning to the target scene and refreshing the image using the client's language has the effect of retrieving once again the neural network from descriptive memory. When she reminds her client of the sensations that accompany the index emotion in the target scene, the clinician helps him reactivate the emotion memory, the index emotion, and the qualia of that emotion. The clinician should recapitulate skill IV, in which the sensations accompanying the index emotion signal the client to use his grounding visualization. She should remind her client of the sensations he feels that tell him he is grounded and present. The clinician can instruct the client, "Realize that as you hold the grounding visualization while you see yourself in the target scene that you are indeed grounded and present." She then installs the skill V positive cognition by having the client repeat the words, "I can stay grounded and present while I'm feeling (name of target affect)." What follows is general language for developing and installing skill V for any target affect, written for a client using a grounding cord image for the grounding resource.

TABS On *See yourself in the scene where you felt* [name of target affect]. *In this scene* [describe target scene using client's language and images]. *Become aware of* [name sensations] *in your* [body location] *that tell you you are feeling* [name of affect]. *These sensations signal you to let down your grounding cord. See it going down. Good. Feel the sensation of the gentle tension with the earth that lets you know you are grounded and present. Now you become aware that you can stay stay grounded and present while you feel* [name of target affect]. *Please repeat after me, "I can stay grounded and present while I'm feeling* [name of target affect]." [Client repeats verbalization.] *Good.* **TABS Off** *Deep breath. Let it out, and what comes up now?*

Eliciting an Appraisal

After attending to whatever comes up for the client, if anything, the clinician should solicit a self-appraisal for the success of the process. The following language can be useful:

Let's check our progress. As you hold the image of the target scene and as you visualize your grounding image, on a scale of 1 to 7 where 1 is false and 7 is true, how true is the statement, "I can stay grounded and present while I feel [name of target emotion]"?

The clinician should record the client's response in his session notes or using the worksheet. The AMST Flow Chart and Decision Tree provides the clinician with choices of interventions—quality resource, alliance resource, ego state intervention—should the client have difficulty achieving a VoC of at least 6.5. The clinician should continue strengthening the installation until the client achieves a VoC of at least a 6.5. The case of Elaine, the young bulimic woman, illustrates how a quality resource and an alliance resource can strengthen the skill V installation.

Elaine initially reported a VoC of 6 for the positive cognition, "I can stay grounded and present while I am feeling fear." In a second repetition, focusing on the same target scene, she was able to increase the validity to 7 by bringing in Angel, an image that embodied the quality of "comfort" and that had been developed earlier as part of the containment skill. She also brought up the image of her primary therapist, an alliance resource. As she achieved certainty that she could stay grounded and present while feeling fear, she volunteered that she felt "powerful," a quality she had not previously ascribed to herself. The clinician strengthened this association and developed a metacognition as follows:

Clinician: **TABS On** Visualize the skills you have learned so far: containment, safe place, and your grounding cord. Realize that you have contained every disturbing thing, and you have created a place of safety where you know with certainty you are safe and with certainty that you feel safe. Now you have learned how to identify and tolerate the emotion of fear. You have used your Angel resource and the image of your therapist to achieve certainty that you can stay grounded and present while you feel fear. Recognize that when you achieved that ability,

you experienced feeling powerful. I'd like you to repeat after me, "As I
am learning the skills to manage my emotions, I feel powerful."

Elaine: As I am learning the skills to manage my emotions, I feel powerful.

Clinician: Good. **TABS Off** Deep breath. Let it out, and what comes up
now?

Elaine: That feels right.

The benefit that the grounding resource visualization can bring to a client is illustrated by the following case selected from the AMST Internet discussion list. The
therapist involved had taken a weekend AMST workshop in which I advised participants to "use the skills you are learning here first thing on Monday morning
when you return to your office." Her first client on Monday was a woman who
was expecting difficulty getting through a meeting with her ex-husband. These
meetings usually produced intense sadness for this client and she would often "fall
apart and cry." The therapist transmitted AMST skills for affect recognition and
tolerance. Together, the therapist and the client decided to use the upcoming situation with the husband for a target scene. Next, the therapist taught the client to recognize her sensations of tension, which were identified as telling the client that she
felt she was falling apart. The client then learned to use those sensations to signal
her to put down her grounding resource, a grounding cord. The client identified
pulling sensations that told her she was grounded and present. Returning to the
next therapy session, the client reported that, "As soon as I felt myself getting tense,
I could feel my grounding cord pulling me down into the ground, and I got through
the meeting without crying for the first time since we divorced." The client reported
feeling "very pleased" with her success. Readers will note from the client's report
that her sensations signaled her to let down her grounding cord. This is the desired
result of AMST skill IV. The client's appraisal and decision-making processes are
bypassed, and the grounding cord is deployed automatically. Readers will also note
that the therapist accepted the client's emotion experience, which she labeled as
falling apart, as the basis for AMST work and did not try to redefine it in terms of
affect theory. AMST teaches us to honor and work with the client's experience. A
strict adherence to affect theory definitions introjected into the therapy would have
derailed the client's process and distanced her from the therapist. The client knows
what she is feeling, and if she chooses to call it "falling apart," her needs will not be
served by interrogating her about whether she's feeling anger, sadness, or fear.
AMST skills can be applied no matter what name the client gives to her emotion.

The Case of Carly

Clients often need to "tune" the grounding resource visualization they have selected. The clinician should be sensitive to the client's self-assessments regarding
the validity of the skill V positive cognition, "I can stay grounded and present
while feeling (name of target emotion)." A VoC of less that a 7 can indicate that
the client is having difficulty with the grounding visualization, as the case of
Carly illustrates. Readers may recall Carly, a woman in her 40s who came for
help with binge eating. In her target scene for fear affect, she was camping alone

in the mountains. She assigned a SUD of 2 to 3 to the scene, and she identified "fluttering in the middle of my chest" as the qualia of fear. In discussion with the clinician about the grounding image, she expressed resistance to attaching anything to the tip of her spine, but agreed that the grounding cord could attach to the small of her back. The following excerpt shows the development and installation of skills IV and V and illustrates the necessity for the clinician to adapt the grounding imagery to the client's needs.

> Clinician: **TABS On** See yourself camping alone in the wilderness. You become aware of sensations of fluttering in the middle of your chest that tell you you are feeling fear. Let these sensations signal you to let down your grounding cord. See it attaching to the small of your back. Tug on it to make certain it's well attached. Let it go down through the floor, through the ground, down to the center of the earth. Attaching there. Tug on it to make certain it's attached. Now just feel the gentle pull of the earth that tells you you are grounded and present. Please repeat after me, "The fluttering in the center of my chest signals me to let down my grounding cord."
>
> Carly: The fluttering in the center of my chest signals me to let down my grounding cord.
>
> Clinician: Now, become aware that you can stay grounded and present while you feel fear. Again, recall the gentle pull of the earth that lets you know you're grounded. Hold the image of your grounding cord. See yourself in your camp in the mountains. Repeat after me, "I can stay grounded and present while I feel fear."
>
> Carly: I can stay grounded and present while I feel fear.
>
> Clinician: Good. **TABS Off** Deep breath. Let it out. And tell me, on a scale from 1 to 7, where 1 is false and 7 is true, as you hold the image of camping alone in the mountains, how true is the statement "I can stay grounded and present while I feel fear"?
>
> Carly: It's a 5.
>
> Clinician: What quality would you need to have to increase the validity of the statement?
>
> Carly: I just need more time, I think. More time to let the grounding cord down.
>
> *[Repeat the skills IV and V installations with TABS]*
>
> Clinician: **TABS Off** Deep breath. Let it out, and what comes up now?
>
> Carly: I think the grounding cord isn't hooking on right.
>
> Clinician: Fine. Can you come up with a grounding visualization that works better for you?
>
> Carly: What I'm getting is an image of roots coming out of my feet.

This new grounding image was developed, and the installation of skills IV and V was repeated, and this time the client reported that she felt "totally different" and "unique" sensations accompanying letting down her grounding roots. She endorsed a VoC of 7 for the positive cognition, "I can stay grounded and present while I feel fear."

PROCEDURE FOR SKILL VI (NOTICING)

The noticing skill (skill VI) builds on the previously developed skills. Figure 9.3 diagrams this skill. Noticing refers to the ability to observe the self from a detached point of view as the self is experiencing an emotion with its associated sensations, images, thoughts, and impulses to behavior. The noticing skill has elements in common with the concept of "hypnotic duality" (Nadon, D'Eon, McConkey, Laurence, & Perry, 1988; Spanos, de Groot, Tiller, Weekes, & Bertrand, 1985) in which age-regressed hypnotized subjects report feeling like both adult and child as they watch themselves during the regression. The capability developed in the noticing skill has also been called the "observing self" and the "witnessing self." Jeff Doorn, a therapist who has worked extensively with clients with dissociative disorder (DID) suggested that I call this skill *noticing* to distinguish it from the dissociated state in which DID alters "just watch" what is happening to the self. The noticing skill functions in the normal stream of consciousness, and it should not be thought of as a dissociated state. Treatment-savvy clients may inquire if the skill will make them dissociative or DID, and the clinician should be prepared to normalize the noticing skill.

Wolinsky (1991) termed the process *witnessing* that is promoted in the noticing skill. He writes that "The moment you step outside of your problem to observe it, you create a larger context for it" (p. 61). Witnessing is a unified

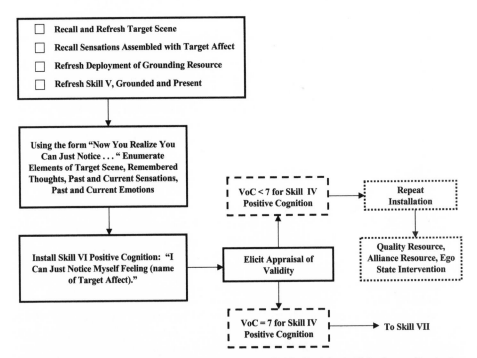

Figure 9.3. Flow Diagram and Decision Tree (skill VI, Noticing). This figure illustrates steps in development of the self-reflective skill called *noticing*.

experience according to Wolinsky and does not involve a splitting off of a region of the mind. He explains that in witnessing, "emphasis is placed on the awareness of the self or being behind the ongoing activity" (p. 62). The noticing skill promotes detachment, a capability that counteracts the enmeshment experienced by many adult children whose parents were self-absorbed (Brown, 2001). Many individuals appear not to be able to notice the self as the self thinks, senses, perceives, feels emotion, and acts. It may be that the quality of self-absorbtion is equivalent to the absence of the ability to notice the self. It appears that an individual lacking the ability to "just notice" the self must first acquire the capacity to stay grounded and present before the skill can be acquired. The noticing skill contributes significantly to structuring the self.

Clients often need encouragement at this point in the protocol. As you are coaching the client through the noticing skill it is beneficial to incorporate language that encourages the client and assures him that the pay-off—the freedom to decrease the uncomfortable affect—is coming shortly, that the client just needs to persevere and learn one more skill and then he will have the reward. Encouragement is useful, because clients sometimes feel mild discomfort at being asked to hold a disturbing emotion, even though it is a mild level of distress, for the period required to transmit skills III to VII. This mild distress usually peaks during the noticing self skill, because the client is being asked to maintain the grounding resource visualization while experiencing the low level of disturbing emotion and then "just notice" thoughts, feelings, images, memories, impulses, and behaviors assembled with the target scene. Letting the client know that the promised relief is close at hand can help the client stick with the process.

Development and installation of skill VI (noticing) begins by recapitulating with the client—with TABS facilitation—the target visualization and skills III through V. After the clinician coaches the client through skill V, reminding him "Using your grounding image, you realize you can stay grounded and present while you feel [name of index emotion]," the clinician instructs the client to "just notice" the sensations, images, memories, impulses, emotions, and cognitions that are occurring as he visualizes the target scene. The clinician's notes are a valuable resource for reminding the client of details assembled with the target scene. The following general language provides a template for skill VI. A specific example from work with client Betty is then presented.

TABS On *See yourself in the* [describe target scene]. *Become aware of* [name sensations] *in your* [body location] *that tell you that you are feeling* [name of affect]. *These sensations signal you to use your* [name of grounding image]. *See yourself using it. Good. Feel the* [name of sensation and body location] *that lets you know you are grounded and present. You realize that you can stay grounded and present while you feel* [name of target affect]. *Now you realize further that you can just notice yourself feeling* [name of target affect]. *You can just notice the* [enumerate cognitions, affects, sensations, memories, etc.] *Good. Now, please repeat after me, "I can just notice myself feeling* [name of target affect]. *"* [Client repeats positive cognition.] *Good.* **TABS Off** *Deep breath. Let it out, and what comes up now?*

After attending to whatever has come up for the client, the clinician can solicit a self-appraisal for the validity of the positive cognition by asking, "As you hold the image of the target scene, on a scale from 1 to 7 where 1 is false and 7 is true, how true is the statement, "I can just notice myself feeling [name of target affect]?" The client's VoC for the skill VI positive cognition should be recorded in the clinician's notes or on the worksheet.

Recall Betty, who came for help with binge eating. In her target scene for fear affect, she was stopped by a motorcycle cop for expired registration tags. These excerpts illustrate the repetition of previous skills and development and installation of skill VI.

> Clinician: This next skill develops your ability to observe yourself and what you are thinking and feeling and doing. It builds on the grounding skill, because when you are grounded and present, when you are not in the future or the past, then you can know what you're feeling right now. This is the last skill before the pay-off which is coming up next where you will learn to decrease the feeling of fear.
>
> **TABS On** What I'd like you to do is recall the time when the motorcycle cop stopped you. As you see the lights come on, you become aware of a quickening in your solar plexus that tells you you are feeling fear. The quickening in your solar plexus signals you to visualize the light energy coming up from the earth and down from the sky. You become aware of the openness in your chest that tells you you're grounded and present. You realize you can stay grounded and present while you feel fear. Now, what I'd like you to do is just notice what's happening in the visualization. Just notice the motorcycle cop. Just notice your teenagers in the back seat and the joke you made that got you all to laugh. Just notice the police officer telling you the registration tags are expired. Just notice the quickening in your solar plexus. Just notice it. Keep your grounding light flowing. Good. Just notice yourself feeling fear. Now, please repeat after me, "I can just notice myself feeling fear."
>
> Betty: I can just notice myself feeling fear.
> Clinician: Good. Just let that become as true as it can be. Good. **TABS Off** Deep breath. Let it out, and what comes up now?

After attending to whatever has come up for the client, the clinician should elicit a self-appraisal for the validity of the skill VI positive cognition as follows:

> Clinician: As you look at the scene where the motorcycle cop stopped you, how true is the statement, "I can just notice myself feeling fear"?
> Betty: It's a 7.

The noticing skill promotes structuralization of the self, as has already been mentioned. The following report, gleaned from the AMST discussion group archives, illustrates how this change of self structure can manifest, and how profound and rapid it can be. The therapist describes teaching the AMST to a client and how at the completion of skill VI (noticing), the client spoke spontaneously:

Client: Something important just happened! I'm a new person. I can't explain it. I used to see the world from this one position and now I see it from another. I don't need my mother anymore. I don't need her to take care of me and protect me. Even though she never did. I just kept setting myself up for a fall. But now I don't need to do that.

The therapist reports that the client's feeling of being a new person has persisted and that the client is using this healthier behavior in her primary relationship.

STRENGTHENING SUCCESSES

A good question to ask clients at the beginning of a session is, "What has been different this week?" It is the sort of question that will often elicit a report of a successful emotion regulation experience, such as the woman who used her grounding cord and got through a meeting with her ex-husband without falling apart and crying. When asked, "Tell me, were you aware of using the skills you learned last week?" clients often report "No," and the clinician should avoid expressing disappointment. Often, the client's employment of these skills occurs outside the boundaries of conscious awareness. The result, however, speaks for itself: the client got through the meeting with her recently divorced husband for the first time without crying. This is a success that needs to be strengthened. The clinician can use language like the following to strengthen such a success:

Clinician: Let's take a moment to strengthen the success you've had using your skills. **TABS On** See yourself about to meet your ex-husband. Recall how you became aware of feeling tense, a sensation that let you know you were feeling like falling apart. Notice that the tenseness automatically signaled your grounding cord to go down. Become aware that you felt the grounding cord pulling you gently to the ground. Realize that with your grounding cord down, you did not cry and fall apart as you have in the past. Recall how pleased with yourself you felt. If it feels right, I'd like you to repeat after me, "I am learning to manage my falling apart."

Client: I am learning to manage my falling apart.

Clinician: Good. Let that resonate. Let it become completely true. Now, here's another one. If it feels right, repeat after me, "When I use my skills to manage my falling apart, I function competently."

Client: When I use my skills to manage my falling apart, I function competently.

Clinician: And one more. "When I use my skills and function competently, I feel very pleased with myself."

Client: When I use my skills and function competently, I feel very pleased with myself.

Clinician: Let that resonate. Let it become completely true. Good. **TABS Off** Deep breath. Let it out, and what comes up now?

Client: That's all true. It *is* true.

Chapter 10 teaches skills the clinician can use to help the client increase her feeling of being pleased with herself, and the clinician would use those skills in the above situation. Also, depending upon the client's status regarding self-worth attributions, the clinician might have included an additional positive cognition, "I am worthy of successfully managing my tenseness." Chapter 10 provides the promised pay-off—for both the client and the clinician reader—the skills to regulate emotion, both to down-regulate distressing emotion and up-regulate positive emotion. Once the seventh, and final, skill of the AMST set has been presented, examples will be given in which a client is coached through the entire protocol focusing on one target affect, so the reader can appreciate the smoothness with which the protocol flows in an actual session. Several additional skills for strengthening the self concept will be presented in Chapter 11.

SUMMARY

Clinicians will notice how the skills presented in this chapter demonstrate AMST's promise to integrate image, memory, affect, sensation, and cognition. The setup for skill IV (sensation as signal) entailed eliciting an image for a grounding resource. AMST teaches the client to use this image to tolerate an affect or emotion—staying grounded and present while experiencing an affect or emotion is functionally equivalent to tolerating the affect or emotion—that has been evoked from emotion memory by recalling the target scene. Skill III has already taught the client how to recognize the emotion by its qualia, the physiological signals generated by the body that identify an emotion. Skill IV (sensation as signal) integrates sensation and affect with image by constructing a direct pathway in which the felt sensation associated with the affect triggers deployment of the grounding resource image. Skill V assembles a cognition with the image of the grounding resource, the affect, the sensation, the remembered scene, and the wholly intrapsychic behavior of staying grounded and present while experiencing an affect or emotion. Skill VI builds an observing capability into the self system, teaching the client to become aware of the sensations, affects, images, memories, and thoughts. Furthermore, the skill widens the neural network linked to the grounding resource image as the clinician recalls from her notes all the material the client had produced from memory relating to the target scene.

Clinicians who have struggled with clients who lacked insight and who were flooded with emotion will feel delighted to see these clients develop the skills to reflect on their affective experience as they learn to manage that experience. Readers may by now recognize how these skills build client self structure as the skills are installed. Sometimes the noticing skill seems to produce a quantum leap as the client acquires the ability to step outside his problem and the affects and emotions assembled with it and observe it and thereby build a larger context for it. That larger context *is* the growing self.

Chapter 10

Skill VII: Regulation

Chapter 10 teaches the seventh and last of the fundamental AMST skills, affect regulation. Affect regulation is the pay-off, the client's reward for staying with the process. Skill VII (regulation) remediates a developmental stage that for many clients was not completed in childhood when affect regulation should have been transmitted in the context of the mother–child and father–child dyads. *Regulation* means both down-regulation of distressing emotion and up-regulation of comfortable emotion. The objective of Chapter 10 is to teach clinicians visualizations that facilitate emotion regulation. As with containment, safe place, and grounding, skill VII (regulation) uses imagery to achieve the desired outcome. Down-regulation is accomplished by means of a client-generated image for a disposal apparatus, while the image of a gauge is employed to up-regulate positive emotion. Figure 10.1 illustrates the regulation skill for decreasing emotion activation.

PROCEDURE FOR SKILL VII (REGULATION): DOWN-REGULATION OF DISTURBING AFFECT

Our description of skill VII begins with the affective down-regulating portion of the skill. Down-regulation is introduced first because usually clinicians will begin the protocol with a negative affect, often fear, and the objective in work with the client will be to reduce the level of physiological arousal elicited by fear. Subsequently the narrative will describe the up-regulating imagery and the means by which it is employed.

The Disposal Resource

Development and installation of skill VII begins by helping the client create a disposal resource. The disposal resource is an imaginal asset that facilitates the

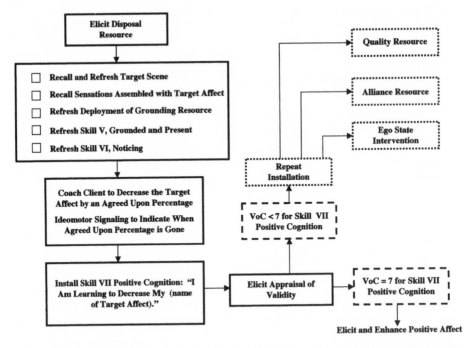

Figure 10.1. Flow Diagram and Decision tree (skill VII, Regulation—Down-Regulating Distressing Emotion). Steps in developing a disposal resource and then employing it to down-regulate a distressing emotion are presented in this figure. The figure also shows decision points for utilizing resources or an intervention.

client's ability to decrease distressing affects and emotions. The traditional psychology of affects separates the affects and emotions into two classes, positive and negative. These specious categories ignore the fact that so-called negative emotions, fear, anger, shame, disgust, and sadness, have beneficial functions at low intensities. Furthermore, the so-called positive emotions, excitement and enjoyment, can cause distress at elevated intensities. For these reasons the present work describes an emotion as either distressing or comfortable, although at times it will be convenient to use the established categories, positive and negative. The case of anger illustrates the perspective of AMST and how skill VII (regulation) views it. Anger, a so-called negative emotion, can be the cause of distress when it has been trauma coded or when it occurs at intensities that cause social problems. Anger can also cause problems when it is repressed and is thereby either unavailable or when it motivates behavior from the unconscious position. When distressing levels of anger are down-regulated using skill VII, clients often connect with a comfortable or favorable form of anger, healthy aggression, which is also known as assertiveness, that can be used in service of the self. The objective of the disposal resource is to decrease distressing levels of fear, anger, or any emotion to intensities that are comfortable for the client so that the emotion can then be used by the client to achieve favorable outcomes in personal endeavors or social situations.

A Neurophysiological Hypothesis

A neurophysiological basis may be hypothesized for the disposal resource. Having such a hypothesis may help the clinician conceptualize the resource and its utilization. As yet there is no empirical evidence supporting this hypothesis, although the proposal is certainly consonant with what is known about the neurophysiology of emotion regulation as it develops in childhood. The conjecture provides a convenient explanation for the effectiveness of the disposal resource, and it explains for the clinician what might be happening in the brain as the client acquires the skill. Deployment of the image of the affect down-regulating disposal resource image in skill VII is hypothesized to activate the parasympathetic fibers of the lateral tegmental circuit of the OFC. These noradrenergic fibers are inhibitory. Their activation apparently attenuates physiological arousal associated with the index affect. For the client, this translates into a decrease in sensations accompanying the target affect in the target scene.

One objective in presenting AMST at this time is to stimulate empirical research on its effectiveness. Future research investigating the basis of the AMST's effectiveness could use assessment tools such as the Aggression Questionnaire (Buss & Perry, 1992) or the Endler Multidimensional Anxiety Scales (Endler, Edwards, & Vitell, 1991) to validate empirically that clients' anger decreases via objective measure. Furthermore, fMRI and other neurophysiological imaging techniques could be employed to determine empirically if indeed the disposal resource does activate the inhibitory lateral tegmental circuits of the orbito-frontal cortex (OFC). What is known for certain is that clients endorse an attenuation of the index affect. Client reports of effectiveness constitute the bottom line for evaluating the utility and value of the AMST skill set.

Introducing Skill VII

Here is sample language the clinician can use to introduce skill VII to the client.

We've reached the pay-off now. You've done great work, and now you get the reward. You get to decrease the level of your [name of emotion]. *This is the seventh skill, which is called regulation. We'll begin by learning to decrease the level of the negative emotion* [name of emotion]. *Later you'll learn how to increase positive emotions using this skill.*

Creating Positive Expectations

As the clinician introduces skill VII, he will create positive expectations in the client by explaining that skill VII is the pay-off, the reward for the hard work the client has done so far. Clinicians next invite the client to join in the positive expectation by asking her to choose what percent of the target affect she would like to dispose of. Here is language the clinician can use to help the client select an appropriate percentage decrease for the index negative emotion.

In a moment we'll be creating an image to facilitate decreasing your level of [name of target affect], but before we do, I'd like to set a target, a goal for how much of your [name of target affect] you'd like to dispose of. Tell me, what percentage of your [name of target affect] would you like to get rid of?

Clients often express a desire to dispose of "all" of the distressing emotion. For very practical reasons supported by theory and clinical impressions, the clinician should discourage the client from trying to dispose of 100% of the index emotion. When a personality system has been defined by a distressing emotion over time, disposing of 100% of that emotion can destabilize the system. This is especially true when the system has limited positive affects available to replace it. The client defined for many years by her fearfulness will not recognize herself and may be quite uncomfortable in the sudden absence of her familiar anchor of fright. Good therapy in combination with successes in life experience over time will be required to facilitate the emergence of a new self structure anchored by courage or fortitude. In the meantime, the client should be advised to retain some of the negative emotion.

Clinically and theoretically, it is inadvisable to dispose of 100% of a distressing emotion, because the so-called negative emotions all have a protective function. Fear warns us of impending danger, and anger assists us in overcoming obstacles. Disposal of all of an emotion would take away important affective defenses, and the personality system would oppose doing so. It is the excess emotion that is removed through the disposal resource, the part that renders a useful emotion distressing. The clinician should counsel the client to retain 1 to 5% of the distressing emotion, briefly explaining the necessity and utility of doing so. The clinician should record the agreed upon number in her notes or on the worksheet.

Creating a Disposal Resource

Once the clinician has introduced skill VII and set a target goal, the next task is to help the client develop an image of a suitable disposal mechanism. The essential components of the ideal attenuation visualization are separation, bottomlessness, and certainty. The client-generated image should manifest a capability for taking away the designated amount of the client's negative emotion, usually by removing it to a great distance from which it cannot come back. "Separation" also means that once removed, the emotion is gone for good. It is not waiting nearby to return in a moment of inattention. The disposal resource should be of such a nature that it can be used over and over again without ever filling up. That is the component of bottomlessness. The desired image will embody a certainty that the removed emotion is gone, either because it has been ground up, as is the case with the sink disposal, or hauled away, as with the garbage chute. Some visualizations that have worked for clients are a bottomless pit, a black hole in space, a grotto, a sink disposal, or a garbage chute.

The illustration that follows provides language the clinician can use to introduce the disposal resource and to help the client develop an image for it. Note that eliciting an image of a disposal mechanism does not employ TABS.

The seventh skill is like some of the other skills in that it employs an image for its effectiveness. In this case, we'll need an image that allows you to dispose of the emotion, a mechanism for draining off the excess emotion. Some people have used a sink disposal, others have used a garbage chute like those in some apartment buildings. People have used bottomless pits and black holes in space. I wonder what image for a disposal mechanism is coming up for you?

The clinician should write down the client's disposal mechanism in his case notes or on the worksheet provided in Appendix A.

Using the Disposal Resource

After an image for a disposal mechanism has been elicited, the clinician and client will immediately use it to begin decreasing the level of affective arousal associated with the index affect. Use of the skill VII disposal resource is facilitated by TABS. Employing the disposal resource begins by recapitulating the target scene, recalling for the client the sensations associated with the target affect, and repeating skills III through VI. The purpose of this repetition is twofold. First, it serves to reelicit the index emotion. Second, each repetition contributes to more firmly structuring the new neural networks being created in the client's brain. Each iteration of the skills set establishes the pathways more concretely, presumably through long term potentiation, the production of changes in synaptic strength that result from stimulation of a pathway (LeDoux, 1996). In addition, stimulation of a pathway over time may induce nerve ending growth factor resulting in the formation of new synapses.

Skill VII employs ideomotor signaling. The clinician will instruct the client, "Raise your left index finger when the [agreed upon percentage] of [name of target emotion] has gone down the disposal." This language incorporates a positive expectation inherent in use of the word *when*, which suggests to the client that he will naturally and comfortably attain the desired goal. When the client raises his index finger, the clinician has some assurance that the disposal process has worked for her client. Furthermore, raising his index finger enhances success for the client through a behavior manifestation, which further enlarges the neural network for managing the index affect.

As the clinician is talking the client through the process of decreasing the negative emotion, it is advisable to instruct the client to breathe deeply and to direct the breath to the "spaces that are being vacated as the [name of emotion] drains away." This intervention enhances the physical experience of decreasing the negative affect. It also brings a positive, palpable element into the equation. Breath equates with life force, and as the client moves the breath or life force into the places that are emptying, he fills those spaces with positive energy.

Installation of a positive cognition solidifies skill VII through involving cognitive appraisal processes. An appropriate installation is: "I am learning to decrease my level of [name of target emotion]." Language the clinician can use to develop and employ the disposal resource follows. In this illustration, the target affect is anger, and the client has opted for a garbage chute as her disposal resource. This language demonstrates as well how the clinician can handle the client's desire to rid herself of all of the index emotion. Notice also how the clinician directs the client to breathe into the places where the anger is leaving.

> **Clinician:** Before we get started, tell me, what percentage of your anger would you like to dispose of?
>
> **Client:** Well, all of it.
>
> **Clinician:** Many people do want to get rid of it all, but actually some anger is helpful. Even fear, which seems all negative, is useful, because it alerts us to danger. Healthy anger helps us overcome obstacles. So, it's not a good idea to get rid of it completely. Just the excess. How about 99%?
>
> **Client:** Okay.
>
> **Clinician:** TABS On See yourself in the scene where the teacher gave you a B, and you thought you deserved an A. You become aware of tightness in your jaw that tells you you are feeling anger. The sensations signal you to use your grounding cord. Recall the tension in your lower spine that tells you you're grounded. Remind yourself that you can stay grounded and present while you are feeling anger. Now you can just notice yourself feeling anger. Notice the thoughts of how hard you worked and how important an A is to you. Notice how you thought about throwing your books on the floor. As you realize you can just notice your anger, you realize you now have the freedom to dispose of some of it. Bring up your visualization of the garbage chute. Get a black plastic bag. Now put 99% of the anger in the bag. Put in the same percentage of the associated sensations. Put in the same percentage of any associated thoughts, memories, or impulses into the bag. As you fill the bag, breathe into the place in your jaw where you feel anger. Let me know with your finger signal when all 99% is in the bag. [*Client raises index finger.*] Good. Tie it off. Now, raise the lid on the garbage chute and drop the bag in. Hear it falling. Falling. Good. All gone. Drop the lid. And repeat after me, "I am learning to decrease my anger.
>
> **Client:** I am learning to decrease my anger.
>
> **Clinician:** Good. Just let that resonate and become as true as it can. **TABS Off** Deep breath. Let it out, and what comes up now?

After addressing whatever has surfaced for the client, the clinician should obtain a self-assessment from the client by asking, "As you look at the target scene now, on a scale from 1 to 7, how true is the statement 'I am learning to decrease my [name of target emotion]'?" The client's report of a Validity of Cognition (VoC) for skill VII should be recorded on the worksheet or in the clinician's notes. The VoC should be at least a 6. If the client has difficulty endorsing a VoC of at least 6 for the skill VII positive cognition, the clinician should refer to the AMST Flow Chart and Decision Tree (Appendix B) and follow the suggested interventions.

The Case of Betty

The following case study illustrates skill VII for down-regulating the target affect fear. This case involves Betty, the woman whose target scene for fear affect involved being stopped by a motorcycle cop for expired registration tags. The following exchange between clinician and client illustrates how this woman developed and employed the disposal resource.

> **Clinician:** This is the pay-off, Betty. Now you get to decrease the fear. This skill is called *regulation*. Like some of the other skills, it uses an image to help you decrease the negative emotion. Once you learn it for the emotion of fear, you'll be able to use it for any emotion. What you'll need is an image for disposing of excess negative emotion. Some people have used a sink disposal, and others have visualized a garbage chute like in some apartment buildings. People have used bottomless pits and black holes in space. I wonder what is coming up for you?
>
> **Betty:** It's sort of a Peruvian image, like a tube, where the negative stuff goes down into the core of the earth.
>
> **Clinician:** Can we call it a disposal tube?
>
> **Betty:** Sure. That works.
>
> **Clinician:** Let's set a goal for how much fear you'd like to get rid of, bearing in mind that some fear is useful to keep us out of danger, so it's not a good idea to try and get rid of it all.
>
> **Betty:** Ninety-eight percent.
>
> **Clinician:** Excellent. **TABS On** Recall your target scene when the motorcycle cop stopped you a couple of weeks ago. See the lights in your rearview mirror. Become aware of the quickening in your solar plexus that tells you you're feeling fear. Those sensations signal you to use your grounding energy, and you see the light coming up from the earth and down from the sky. Feel the openness in your chest that tells you you're grounded and present. Remind yourself you can stay grounded and present while you feel fear. You can just notice yourself feeling fear. Good. Now, visualize your disposal tube, a Peruvian image of a tube that runs into the core of the earth. Form the intention that 98% of the fear will run down the tube. All you need to do is just hold the visualization of the tube and the intention. Watch as 98% of the quickening sensations in your solar plexus begin to run down the disposal tube. Watch it run down. Letting 98% of any associated thoughts run down. Just notice the fear running down. Breathe into your solar plexus where the fear is leaving. Let me know by raising your left index finger when all 98% has gone down. Good. [*Client raises her index finger.*] Good. Now, please repeat after me, "I am learning to decrease my fear."
>
> **Betty:** I am learning to decrease my fear.
>
> **Clinician:** Let that become as true as it can be. Good. **TABS Off** Deep breath. Let it out, and what comes up now?
>
> **Betty:** I remember that I had my daughter and a friend in the car, and I made a joke, and we all cracked up.
>
> **Clinician:** As you look at the target scene now, on a scale from 1 to 7, how true is the statement, "I am learning to decrease my fear"?
>
> **Betty:** It's a 7. It's true.

Clinician: Let's try another type of affirmation at this point, Betty, but only if it feels right for you. I'd like you to look over all the work we've done so far. You learned to use the container. You developed a safe place. You learned how to recognize how your body signals you that you're feeling fear. Then you learned tools to stay grounded and tolerate feeling fear. You learned to decrease your fear. As you hold all of this, I wonder if you'd be willing to affirm your process and yourself with this affirmation: "I am beginning to see that I am worthy of decreasing my fear."

Betty: Oh, wow. That is such a big one for me. I've been so fear-based all my life. I'll try.

Clinician: Good for you. **TABS On** Just recall all the work you've done up to now that has led to your successfully decreasing your fear. As you hold that visualization, please repeat after me, "I am beginning to see that I am worthy of decreasing my fear."

Betty: I am beginning to see that I am worthy of decreasing my fear.

Clinician: Let that resonate for you. Let it become as true as it can be. Good. **TABS Off** Deep breath. Let it out, and tell me, what comes up for you now?

Betty: Well it's a good thing you didn't ask me to say flat out that I'm worthy, 'cause I'm not there yet. But I am getting there, so it feels right. It feels pretty good too to say it. Really good.

Often the disposal process will take 5 to 10 seconds and sometimes more. During this time the clinician can repeat phrases referring to sensations associated with fear and thoughts and images associated with fear, reiterating the visualization of them going down the disposal mechanism. The clinician should also reiterate the instruction to breathe into the spaces being vacated by the fear.

Readers will note that the clinician developed a self-worth metacognition at the end of the installation. Accurately gauging his client, he tuned his formulation of the self-worth affirmation to the level of her progress. Chapter 11 will teach several additional self-concept strengthening interventions.

PROCEDURE FOR SKILL VII (REGULATION): UP-REGULATION OF COMFORTABLE AFFECT

Many people, only some of them clients, are unaware of the positive affects, interest–excitement and enjoyment–joy. Interest affect motivates much human activity: what books we read, movies we watch, sports we participate in, our regimens of health care, types of relationships, choice of career. For many, interest affect appears to register on the radar screen of awareness only at elevated levels, with the result that people do not appreciate its ubiquity. Also, many people do not understand that interest is an affect, and they do not discriminate it as a function of the self. This is most apparent in common language, as when, for example, a person states, "I am interested in sports." The construction *I am interested* reveals the degree to which interest affect is bound with self-concept into an

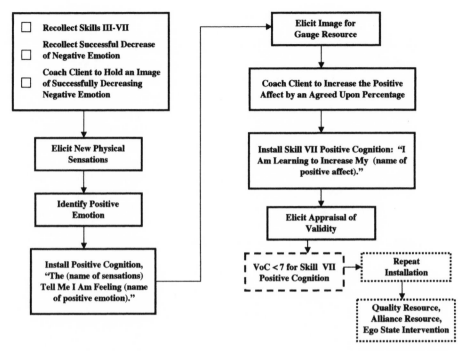

Figure 10.2. Flow Diagram and Decision Tree (skill VII, Regulation—Up-Regulating Positive Emotion). This figure presents the steps involved in up-regulation of a positive emotion.

unexamined, undifferentiated unit. The more insightful construction, *I feel interested*, suggests a person who discriminates between emotions and the self having them. When individuals are unaware of emotions, they are denied the freedom to consciously operate on them and the power to manipulate them for personal benefit. In addition, lack of awareness represents a contraction of the possible dimensions of what it means to be human. The AMST protocol is crafted to help clients recognize positive affect and then to increase it where appropriate using the gauge resource. Skill VII for recognizing and increasing positive affect is diagramed in Figure 10.2.

Recognizing Positive Affect

A principle of affect regulation states that what we would regulate, we must first recognize. Positive affect must be noticed before it can be increased. Once it has been raised to awareness, it can be manipulated. One of the clinically most readily available opportunities for working with positive affect often occurs after the client has decreased a distressing affect using the disposal resource. The client who has strained under an oppressive load of fear for years will often feel relief after he has disposed of the burden, however the client may well not notice the new sensations or recognize the affect they are signaling. The moment, and the opportunity afforded by it, will quickly pass unnoticed unless the clinician grasps the opportunity. After the client has disposed of the agreed upon percentage of the target distressing affect and after the skill VII positive cognition has been installed, the clinician can continue the TABS and proceed as illustrated using the following language:

TABS On *Often after a person has decreased a negative emotion as you have just done, he sometimes feels new sensations in the body. As you look back on the work you've just accomplished, how you've decreased your fear by 99%, I'd like you to take a moment and look around your body and see if any new sensations are coming up for you and let me know with our finger signal when you become aware of them. Good. Take as much time as you need. Just notice what your body is telling you.* [Client raises his index finger.] *Good.* **TABS Off** *Deep breath. Let it out, and tell me, what did you get?*

Clients have reported "I feel lighter," or "The tension's gone out of my neck." The range of possible responses is as varied as the clients, and some clients may not experience any new sensations. Assuming the client has identified a sensation, the clinician should ask, "What emotion do you suppose the sensation of lightness is telling you that you are feeling?" Sometimes clients will be able to name a positive emotion that corresponds to the sensations experienced. Other clients will need help. The clinician can interpret the client's sensation for him using normalizing and permissive language, such as: "Often when clients report a feeling of tension leaving the body, it is associated with the feeling of relief. How does that resonate for you?" Alternatively, the clinician can give the client a list of positive emotions and ask him or her to select one that seems right. Table 10.1 lists 37 positive emotions that people sometimes experience. Clients often feel freedom or relief after decreasing a negative emotion, but just as often they report feeling

Table 10.1 Positive Emotions

Beautiful	Fascinated	Pretty
Blissful	Free	Proud
Brave	Glad	Refreshed
Capable	Good	Relaxed
Cheerful	Gratified	Relieved
Contented	Happy	Righteous
Delighted	Inspired	Satisfied
Eager	Joyous	Sure
Ecstatic	Loving	Thankful
Energetic	Nice	Vivacious
Excited	Peaceful	Wonderful
Euphoric	Pleased	
Exhilarated	Powerful	

hope. The client's response is the best, because it will already be assembled with her own neural networks and will have ready meaning for her.

Cognizing Positive Affect

Once the client has named the positive emotion that her sensations identify she is experiencing, the clinician should apply skill III with TABS facilitation. Skill III will assemble the sensations the client has just experienced with the positive affect she has chosen and the positive cognition, "The [name of sensation] that I feel in [physical location of sensation] tell me I am feeling [name of positive emotion]." The following example repeats the instructions already given for noticing sensations associated with positive affect after decreasing fear using the grounding image. It then continues, demonstrating how the clinician helped the client to name the emotion, and then to develop a skill III positive cognition.

> Clinician: **TABS On** Often after a person has decreased a negative emotion as you have just done, she sometimes feels new sensations in the body. As you look back on the work you've just accomplished, how you've decreased your fear by 99%, I'd like you to take a moment and look around your body and see if any new sensations are coming up for you and let me know with our finger signal when you become aware of it. [*Client raises her index finger*] Good. **TABS Off** Deep breath. Let it out, and tell me, what did you get?
>
> Client: I felt a lightness. I just felt like unburdened.
>
> Clinician: Was there any particular place in your body that you felt the lightness?
>
> Client: Umm. My shoulders mostly, I suppose. Maybe some in my chest.
>
> Clinician: What emotion do you suppose the lightness in your shoulders and chest, the unburdened sensations, what emotion do you suppose they're telling you you're feeling?
>
> Client: I don't know. Help me a little.
>
> Clinician: Well, what do you suppose a person who had a burden lifted from her shoulders would feel?
>
> Client: If she didn't have to carry the load, she'd be relieved, I guess.
>
> Clinician: So it's relief. Does that feel right to you?
>
> Client: Sure.
>
> Clinician: Good. Let's develop that. **TABS On** I'd like you to recall the work you did with fear and how you visualized a garbage chute and got rid of 99% of it. See yourself raising your index finger to signal that all 99% really did go down the chute. Hear yourself saying "I am learning to decrease my fear" and as you say it, you become aware of the lightness in your shoulders. This lightness tells you that you're feeling relief. Now, please repeat after me, "The lightness in my shoulders tells me I am feeling relief."
>
> Client: The lightness in my shoulders tells me I am feeling relief.
>
> Clinician: Good. Let that become completely true. **TABS Off** Deep breath. Let it out, and what comes up now?

The Gauge Resource for Regulating Positive Affect

Once the client has cognized the positive affect, she can up-regulate it. The gauge resource is an image that facilitates the client in increasing positive emotion. It is useful to think in neurophysiological terms about how the gauge resource might work. I hypothesize that deployment of the gauge resource induces activation of the dopaminergic, excitatory ventral tegmental circuit of the OFC. Activation of the ventral tegmental OFC circuit leads to physiological arousal, which is reflected in increased intensity of the sensations associated with the index affect.

After naming the positive affect and employing skill III to cognize it, the clinician next creates a positive expectation that the affect *can* be increased by asking , "Would you like to increase the level of [name of positive affect]?" Most clients will answer in the affirmative, and the clinician can then enjoin the client in the positive expectation by asking, "How much of an increase would you like to have, bearing in mind that too much might be overwhelming?" As with negative affect, positive affect can be destabilizing to the client system unfamiliar with intense levels of excitement or joy. The prudent clinician will not be seduced by the depressed client's or the passive client's sudden desire to increase excitement "all the way!" or "as high as possible." The countertransferential impulse to give the client the excitement or joy he's never experienced can be damaging to the client. Inappropriately high levels of excitement affect will be experienced by the client as stressful, and a negative experience can set the therapy back. In the initial stages of working with positive affect, caution is advised, and the therapist should temper the client's enthusiasm. An increase of 10 points on a 100-point scale is usually safe. The clinician should be prepared to decrease the level of positive affect if the client shows signs of discomfort. He can do this by reversing the procedure given below for increasing affect with the gauge resource.

Developing and Using the Gauge Resource

The gauge resource can be used to increase any positive affect or emotion. The following discussion will focus on the comfortable emotion relief. After the client has cognized the emotion and attendant sensations and agreed to increase it by an appropriate amount, the clinician explains that as with the other skills, increasing an emotion is effected through the use of an image. The image for increasing an emotion is the gauge resource. The gauge can be a round gauge like a dial or a long gauge like a thermometer. The clinician should explain that an essential feature of the gauge is that it goes from zero to 100. In addition to steam gauges and thermometers, clients have produced automobile gas gauges and Caterpillar tractor fuel gauges. Development of the gauge resource does not require TABS facilitation, and the clinician can proceed as follows:

Increasing the level of an emotion is done with an image. In this case you'll use the image of a gauge. The gauge can be a round gauge like a steam gauge or a long one like a thermometer. Whatever the gauge you're seeing, its scale should go from zero to one hundred. Tell me then, what kind of a gauge are you seeing?

The clinician should record the client's gauge type in his notes or on the worksheet provided. The first use of the gauge is to measure the current level of the index positive emotion the client is feeling. This is accomplished by asking the client to form the intention that the gauge will measure the intensity of the index emotion. Here is a sample instruction:

Form the intention that the gauge will measure the level of relief you are feeling by measuring the intensity of the [name of sensations] *you are feeling in your* [name of body location]. *Now, as you look at the gauge, tell me, what is it reading?*

Again, the clinician should record the client's report of the gauge reading. He should then recall for the client that he expressed a desire to increase the index emotion, and he should remind the client of the client's set goal for the increase. Increasing an emotion is facilitated by TABS and accomplished by means of the clinician guiding the client to increase the intensity of the positive sensations and the affect they identify and then guiding the client to spread the sensations and affect out through the client's body, brain, and mind. As illustrated below, the client is instructed to hold the intention that the index affect will increase by the agreed upon amount. The client's part is to hold the intention, watch the gauge, and notice as the sensations and affect spread. The clinician intersperses his suggestions with numbers reflecting the increasing readings on the client's gauge. At the completion of the process when the gauge count reaches the target level, the clinician installs the positive cognition, "I am learning to increase my [name of positive emotion]." The clinician can also collect a self-report from the client.

The illustration that follows continues with the client who experienced the positive emotion relief as a lightness in her shoulders after she had decreased the negative affect fear. The clinician had helped the client to cognize relief and had installed a skill III positive cognition. Her gauge resource was a thermometer and registered 25 when she set it to measure relief. She set a target of a 10-point increase in the level of relief.

> **Clinician: TABS On** Just hold the visualization of the gauge and the intention that it will increase by 10 points from 25 where it is now. Just notice the lightness in your shoulders. Twenty-six. Notice as it increases in intensity. Twenty-seven. Let it begin to move from your shoulders down your back. Twenty-eight. Into your legs. Twenty-nine. Your lower legs. Thirty. Into your feet. Thirty-one. Feel the lightness move into your chest. Thirty-two. Into your abdomen. Thirty-three. Into your neck and up into your face, carrying with it the emotion of relief. Into your brain. Thirty-four. Into every cell. Into your mind. The lightness infuses your entire body with relief. Thirty-five. Good. Now, please repeat after me, "I am learning to increase my feeling of relief."
>
> **Client:** I am learning to increase my feeling of relief.
>
> **Clinician:** Good. Let that become as true as it can be. **TABS Off** Deep breath. Let it out, and what comes up now?
>
> **Client:** I feel more relieved, that's for sure.

Clinician: So, on a scale from 1 to 7, how true is the statement, "I am learning to increase my feeling of relief"?

Client: Well, I am. So it's a 7.

The gauge resource should be mobilized at any time that positive emotion arises for a client in session. When this occurs, the clinician should briefly repeat skill III followed by the gauge resource, increasing the positive affect by 5 to 10 points, and concluding with the self-efficacy affirmation. The therapist should also keep a running log of emotions, sensations, and body locations for the client either in his case notes or using the worksheet provided in Appendix A.

Should a client have difficulty increasing positive affect or be unable to endorse a VoC of 7, the clinician should return to the interventions previously described. The clinician should avoid expressing frustration with the client's difficulty. Furthermore, the clinician should maintain the attitude that the affect *can* be enhanced and that the client's difficulty presents an opportunity to uncover missing resources and thereby help the client even more. In the event of difficulty, the therapist should first repeat the skill, taking more time with the instructions. If the client is still unable to endorse validity, then the clinician should turn first to the quality resource and ask the client what quality she would need to be able to enhance the index positive affect. The second intervention is the alliance resource, should the client continue to have difficulty. Finally, the clinician should turn to the ego state intervention. It may be that a covert ego state is protecting the client by preventing arousal of positive affect. This may be the case if the client was punished in childhood for displays of excitement or enjoyment. These skills have been thoroughly described in previous chapters, so they will not be repeated here.

UNINTERRUPTED AMST SKILLS III–VII

Teaching and explaining the AMST protocol skill set for the purposes of this book has necessitated breaking up the set into components, and as a result, the fluidity of the process has not been adequately conveyed. The case presented in this section demonstrates the smooth, easy flowing quality of the dialogue between therapist and client. A clinician working according to traditional time scheduling should be able to teach skills III to VII the first time in a single 1-hour session unless significant resource installations or ego state interventions must be accomplished. Once the whole skill set has been transmitted, the clinician can select a new target affect and quickly move through the entire set, helping the client to reduce the level of the new index emotion. The following uninterrupted presentation of skills III to VII for the target affect shame illustrates how smoothly the protocol can be employed once the client has acquired it. Note that the clinician does not stop to check the validity of each step. It is sufficient to acquire a VoC for the overall positive cognition "I am learning to decrease my shame" at the completion of skill VII.

The following case demonstrates not only the power of AMST to help the client decrease shame, but also the emergence of a positive state that sometimes occurs when shame has been attenuated. This illustration involves Fred, the man in his early fifties who came for help with drinking and overeating. To orient the clinician-reader to scheduling, the work reported here took place in the fourth 1-hour session. A history was taken in the first session, and skill I (containment) was transmitted. Session 2 focused on safe place (skill II) and a future template for that skill. In session 3, the client acquired skills III to VII for the target affect fear, and then these were applied to a future template. In the present session, session 4, the AMST skill set was applied to target emotions anger and sadness during the first 40 minutes, and shame was the target affect for the last 20 minutes of the hour.

> **Clinician:** I'd like to turn our attention to another emotion now. This is the emotion people often feel when they are exposed. It is shame. Shame is an evaluative emotion. We experience it when there is a conflict between our behavior and our image of our self. With that introduction, I wonder if you can tell me a time that you think you felt shame?
>
> **Fred:** Sure. There was a time in junior high school once, when I stole a comic book and got caught at it. My parents made me return it, and I remember having to explain what I had done to the store owner. See I used to lie all the time. I always lied.
>
> **Clinician:** On a scale from zero to 10, how disturbing is this scene?
>
> **Fred:** A 6 or 7. It's a 7.
>
> **Clinician:** Okay. Let's first help you get the sensations that accompany shame. **TABS On** I'd like you to see yourself in the store. You've stolen a comic book and gotten caught, and now you are having to return it. You are explaining what you did to the store owner. As you hold this scene, just notice any sensations in your body that accompany the scene. Good. Take all the time you need, and let me know when you've got them by raising your left index finger. [*Fred raises his index finger.*] Good. **TABS Off** Tell me, what sensations did you feel and where did you feel them?
>
> **Fred:** There were a few. I felt flushed and hot. And . . .
>
> **Clinician:** You felt flushed and hot. Where in your body did you feel that?
>
> **Fred:** All over. I felt shaky all over too. I couldn't look at the store owner either. I kept looking at the floor.
>
> **Clinician:** So your eyes were lowered?
>
> **Fred:** Yes. And I was sort of hunkering with my shoulders. Almost cringing. That's it.
>
> **Clinician:** Got it. Now let's firm up the association of those sensations with shame. **TABS On** Recall the scene in the store when you had stolen a comic book and had to return it. As you see yourself explaining to the store owner, you become aware of feeling flushed and hot all over, shaky all over, your eyes are lowered, and you are hunkering your shoulders. Please repeat after me, "The hot and flushed feeling all over my body . . ."
>
> **Fred:** The hot and flushed feeling all over my body . . .

Clinician: ". . . the shakiness all over . . ."

Fred: . . . the shakiness all over . . ."

Clinician: ". . . my lowered eyes . . ."

Fred: . . . my lowered eyes . . .

Clinician: ". . . and the hunkering in my shoulders . . ."

Fred: . . . and the hunkering in my shoulders . . .

Clinician: "tell me I'm feeling shame."

Fred: . . . tell me I'm feeling shame.

Clinician: Now let those sensations signal you to let down your grounding cord. Please repeat after me, "The hot and flushed all over, the shakiness all over, my lowered eyes, and the hunkering in my shoulders signal me to let down my grounding cord."

Fred: The hot and flushed feeling all over, the shakiness all over, the . . . what?

Clinician: "My lowered eyes . . ."

Fred: "My lowered eyes, and the hunkering in my shoulders signal me to let down my grounding cord.

Clinician: Feel your grounding cord attached to the tip of your spine. Tug it to make certain it's firmly attached. Watch it going down to the center of the earth and attaching there. Now become aware of the calm centeredness that tells you that you are grounded and present. Good. Now repeat after me, "I can stay grounded and present while I feel shame."

Fred: I can stay grounded and present while I feel shame.

Clinician: Let that become completely true. Good. Now, just notice the hot and flushed sensations all over your body. Just notice them. Keep your grounding cord down. Good. Now, just notice the shakiness. Good. Just notice it. Hold the image of your grounding cord. Good. Just notice yourself explaining to the store owner what happened. Just notice. Good. Hold the grounding cord image. Just notice your lowered eyes and the hunkering in your shoulders. Good. Just notice the emotion of shame. Now, repeat after me, "I can just notice myself feeling shame."

Fred: I can just notice myself feeling shame.

Clinician: Good work. You're doing great. Now for the pay-off. Bring up the image of the sink disposal. Form the intention that 99% of the shame is going to go down the sink disposal. Turn on the switch. Hear the electric motor start up. Turn on the water faucet, and hear the water running. Now just watch as the shame begins to flow down the sink disposal. Hear the blades start to grind as the shame hits them. Good. Just hold the intention and watch and let me know by raising your left index finger when all 99% has gone down. Just watch as the flush and hot leaves your body. Good. Breathe into the places where the heat and flush is leaving. Just notice as the shakiness leaves. Just notice as the downcast look leaves. Good. Again, breathe into the places that the downcast look is leaving. Just notice as the hunkering in your shoulders runs down the drain. Washing it down. Washing it down. [*Fred raises his left index finger.*] Good. Now repeat after me, "I am learning to decrease my shame."

Fred: I am learning to decrease my shame.

Clinician: The word *manage* means recognize, tolerate, and regulate. You now have the skills to recognize, tolerate, and regulate your shame. Again, repeat after me, "I am learning to manage my shame."

Fred: I am learning to manage my shame.

Clinician: Let that become completely true. Good. **TABS Off** Deep breath. Let it out, and what comes up now?

Fred: I feel lighter. More clear, like a fog has been lifted. Hmmm. My thinking seems clearer, and something in my voice has changed. I've always felt like my voice wasn't fluent, and that seems to be gone.

Clinician: I wonder what quality those sensations are telling you that you're experiencing?

Fred: I don't know, but I feel more real.

Clinician: Let me take a chance here and see if this feels right to you. What I think I'm hearing when you say you feel more real is the quality of authenticity. What do you think?

Fred: That's it! That's it exactly! I feel more authentic.

Clinician: Let's strengthen that. **TABS On** As you hold the image of learning to manage your shame, repeat after me, "My clarity of thought and fluency of voice tell me I am feeling my authenticity."

Fred: My clarity of thought and fluency of voice tell me I am feeling my authenticity.

Clinician: Good. Let that become completely true. **TABS Off** Deep breath. Let it out, and what comes up now?

Fred: I'm seeing something really important. My lying all the time was me being inauthentic. Same with referring to myself in the second person, like you are always pointing out. That is my being unauthentic too. When I'm inauthentic, I can't speak fluently either. But I know that now. I don't have to be inauthentic anymore.

Clinician: Excellent. Before we go on, let's check our work. As you hold the image of explaining the stolen comic book to the store owner, on a scale from 1 to 7 how true is the statement, "I am learning to manage my shame"?

Fred: Oh, it's a 7. A solid 7.

Clinician: And as you look at the scene now, how disturbing is it on a scale from zero to 10?

Fred: Not at all. Maybe a 1. Maybe.

Clinician: I'd like to develop a different sort of affirmation now. I'd like you to recall all the work you've done learning to manage a range of emotions. You started by developing a container and learned to use it. Then you created a safe place and learned to create safety for yourself. You went on to learn skills to recognize, tolerate, and regulate fear, anger, sadness, and now shame. As you did this work you've had powerful insights into yourself. I wonder if, as you recall all this work would you be willing to affirm your accomplishment with this statement: I am worthy of managing my emotions.

Fred: Totally.

Clinician: Good. Let's do it. **TABS On** I'd like you to recall all the work you've done here in these four sessions. You've learned skills to recognize, tolerate, and regulate fear, anger, sadness, and shame. In an earlier session you learned to recognize and increase the feeling of relief. You've received some deep insights about yourself during this work. As you hold the image of all that you've accomplished, please repeat after me "I am worthy of learning to manage my emotions."

Fred: I am worthy of learning to manage my emotions.

Clinician: If it feels right, let's take it one step further. Will you repeat after me, "I am worthy of managing my emotions."

Fred: Yeah, I see the difference. Sure. I am worthy of managing my emotions.

Clinician: Okay. Let's go for one more. If this feels right, repeat, "I feel proud of my accomplishment."

Fred: I feel proud of my accomplishment. Yeah, That's the big one. I do feel proud of my accomplishment.

Four points about this illustration should be emphasized. First, the clinician did not ask the client for an experience of shame at a low level. By this juncture in the work, the client has applied the AMST skills to low levels of fear, to anger, and to sadness. He has developed a facility with the skills and may be expected to tolerate working on a higher level of shame. Second, the clinician-reader may have noticed how the clinician in the illustration repeatedly instructed the client to hold the image of his grounding cord while the client was "just noticing" the emotion of shame. Shame affect is very powerful, and it can quickly overcome the client's newly acquired skills. The clinician in the illustration was aware of his client's discomfort and reminded the client of his grounding skill to keep the client grounded and present. As the clinician becomes more and more adept at using the AMST protocol, he or she may well develop a seemingly uncanny ability to recognize clients' emotion states. This ability may reflect the unfolding of the clinician's right brain's communication with the client's right brain. Third, the reader will note how the clinician asked the client to "breathe into" the places being vacated by sensations draining away into the disposal resource. This simple expedient provides a means to "fill" the newly empty spaces with "something." Drawing air into the vacated spaces provides a sort of "pressure" to hasten the departure of remaining distressing affect. Air carries life force and vitality, and breathing into spaces being emptied draws these qualities into the client. Fourth, the example illustrates development of self-worth and pride metacognitions. Chapter 11 describes these self-concept strengthening interventions in greater detail.

MANAGEMENT OF VITALITY AFFECTS AND POSITIVE EMOTIONS

While tools for recognizing and increasing positive affect have been presented, the subject of positive affect requires more discussion, especially as it relates to vitality in depressed states on the one hand and to risk taking on the other.

Diminished vitality is a characteristic of depression, and the positive affects are the source of a person's vitality. When we experience excitement about daily events and take joy from our accomplishments, no matter how small, we are most alive, and life has color. The interested, excited person broadcasts this energy, and others resonate with it, and they feel better being in that person's presence. In the absence of joy and excitement, life is colorless, drab. Daily events become chores rather than opportunities for fulfillment. The apathetic person does not radiate positive energy, and people avoid this person. Soon the joyless, unexcited person begins avoiding social situations in which he or she expects to be avoided, and a downward spiral is initiated with depression and isolation often resulting. For the unexcited, joyless client, positive affect has usually become the source of difficulty for one of two reasons: either it was not stimulated in childhood, or it was punished. Positive affect becomes problematical for the risk-taking client often because it was inappropriately stimulated, sometimes through sexual abuse and sometimes through witnessing violence, and was thereby trauma coded.

Deficit experience in childhood can determine a developmental pathway toward adolescence and adulthood characterized by joylessness and absence of interest or excitement. Adult children of deficit experience often do not regularly experience the emotions listed in Table 10.1. One of the primary caregivers' core functions during the first four years of their child's life is to optimize positive affects for the child. When this function is not exercised for whatever reason, the child's positive affect response system apparently does not develop optimally, and as an adult this person has difficulty experiencing the vitality affects. Attenuated vitality affect appears to be a component of adolescent and adult depression.

Adverse childhood experience can set the child on a different pathway to the same outcome: problems with diminished enjoyment and interest appearing in adolescence and carrying over to adulthood. Children raised with adverse experiences often learn that the affect interest–excitement is dangerous, because its expression leads to physical punishment, or emotional punishment by means of broadcast anger, shame, or disgust. Alternatively, adverse experience can lead to disappointment of hopes assembled with interest affect. When a child's hopes are dashed, he or she gives up feeling excited about the future—which means giving up hope—because the sadness elicited by betrayal is more than the child can tolerate. The children of adversity quickly learn to suppress interest–excitement, and soon it is culled from awareness.

Joy affect can be unfamiliar to the adult for the same reasons as excitement affect. Joy may not have been stimulated in childhood, it may have been punished, or it may have been betrayed. Whatever the cause, elicitation of elevated levels of joy affect in the client who has no experience of it can be threatening. The clinician needs to be careful to avoid triggering a client's defenses by too quickly stimulating heightened levels of interest–excitement and joy in the client.

In the course of AMST, a client can "earn" vitality. The concept of "earned vitality" is drawn from the idea of earned security in attachment theory. The "earned secure" designation (Hesse, 1999) arises when a person reports childhood experiences that would ordinarily result in a pathway to an insecure attachment, yet the person demonstrates the ability to metacognitively monitor memories and language that is one characteristic of a secure attachment. Thus, the "earned secure" person has shifted to an unanticipated attachment trajectory. In dynamic systems language, a new self structure has emerged out of the interaction between prior adaptation and present circumstances. In much the same way, a person can "earn" his or her vitality. Through AMST an individual can acquire the skills to recognize sensations that signal the experience of interest affect and enjoyment affect. If the experience of these vitality affects threatens to overwhelm the client, the grounding visualization can be used to help the client stay grounded and present while experiencing these emotions. The noticing skill (VI) can be employed to develop a metacognitive awareness of the experience of vitality. Also, if ego states have emerged in the personality to protect the self from punishment for the experience of vitality, these ego states can be addressed through an ego state intervention. Finally, the gauge resource can be mobilized to increase the intensity of "felt" vitality.

WORKING WITH A DEPRESSED CLIENT

The clinician can use AMST to assist the client who has difficulty experiencing interest–excitement affect as a component of depression. The client's problems with interest affect will manifest as difficulties in making choices regarding major areas of life such as work, career, relationships, socializing, hobbies, education, or entertainment. A first step in helping this type of client will involve identifying and cognizing the problem affect, interest–excitement. The case presented next is not meant to illustrate a complete therapy for depression, but only to demonstrate how interest affect relates to other affects in the etiology of this man's depression and how the AMST functioned in his therapy.

The case of Robert illustrates the power that denied excitement affect can have. Robert is a man in his 40s who came for help with addictive behaviors. As our work together developed, it became apparent that he also experienced what Terrence Real (1997) called covert depression. In childhood, Robert's parents had socialized his healthy anger with fear, disgust, and shame affects, and as a result Robert's authentic anger terrified him. Because his anger had been punished and thereby trauma coded, his healthy aggression was unavailable to him to serve his needs. He lacked healthy aggression to motivate him to overcome obstacles in the pursuit of reasonable goals, and as a result he had lost many opportunities over the years. These losses engendered sadness affect. This was the understanding we had reached after working together for several months. As I was explaining how the downward spiral of unacknowledged anger, fear of anger, and sadness appeared to be robbing him of his vitality, Robert suddenly disclosed that he masturbated regularly, sometimes as often as twice per day. This surprise disclosure revealed a new affective component of Robert's depression, his displaced excitement affect. I asked Robert if he would be willing to forego masturbating for a week until our next session and to notice what new sensations, thoughts, and other experiences surfaced for him. He agreed. What follows is a recapitulation of the next session.

> **Clinician:** What I'd like you to do now is bring up an image of the past week, a week in which you didn't masturbate. As you recall the week,

I'd like you to notice what has been different for you, and tell me what's coming up.

Robert: I realize I did a lot more stretching every morning. Basic yoga. I went hiking several times.

Clinician: Let's see if we can uncover any associations that go along with those. **TABS On** As you see yourself stretching, doing yoga, and hiking, just notice your body, and see if there are any sensations that accompany the image of you hiking, and stretching, and doing yoga. Let me know by raising your left index finger when you get the sensations. Good. Good. [*Robert raises his index finger.*] **TABS Off** Deep breath. Let it out. Tell me, what did you get?

Robert: I felt more limber doing the yoga. I know that. I felt lighter walking. More energized.

Clinician: Any particular place in your body?

Robert: No. Pretty much all over.

Clinician: As you look at yourself doing yoga and hiking, what emotion do you suppose the sensations of limberness and lightness and being energized are telling you that you're feeling?

Robert: Well, when I realize that I felt those sensations because I didn't masturbate, I'd have to say they're telling me I'm feeling excited.

Clinician: Okay. Let's strengthen that. **TABS On** Recall this past week when you didn't masturbate. Notice how you did yoga and hiked more often. Become aware of the sensations of limberness, lightness, and being energized. Now, repeat after me, "The limberness, lightness, and being energized I feel throughout my body tell me I am feeling excitement."

Robert: The limberness, lightness, and being energized I feel throughout my body tell me I'm feeling excitement.

Clinician: Good. Let that become completely true. **TABS Off** Deep breath. Let it out, and what comes up now?

Robert: Not much. It feels right.

Once the client has cognized excitement, his experience of it can be elevated using skill VII's gauge resource. As the client learns to manipulate excitement affect, he can import it into future templates. For example, a depressed client may be having difficulty feeling interested enough in going to a movie to leave the house and drive to the theater. With TABS facilitation he can visualize himself importing the sensations accompanying excitement into the image of leaving his home and driving to the theater. He can up-regulate the level of excitement he feels about going to the movie by using his gauge resource. The positive cognition "I am learning to increase my excitement about going to the movies" can be installed. When he returns for his next therapy session, the clinician can solidify his success, assuming he had one, and then either elicit the client's joy affect or import it into the scene. This way of proceeding with therapy for depression assists the client to assemble interest–excitement with visualizations, cognitions, and drives to form new affective–cognitive structures and eventually to form new affective–cognitive–action patterns (thus altering behavior) and new affective–cognitive orientations (thus altering mood).

REENACTMENTS AND RISK TAKING

The so-called positive affect interest–excitement can be trauma coded. Trauma coding can happen because something highly arousing was done to a person in childhood that was assembled with excitement affect. Alternatively, trauma coding of excitement affect can occur because in childhood the person witnessed something highly arousing that was assembled with excitement affect. Excitement affect can be inappropriately stimulated through childhood sexual abuse. The personality system must find a way to manage the trauma coded excitement. For some adults who experienced childhood sexual abuse, reenactment emerges to manage this trauma coded excitement, and the individual engages in promiscuous sex. Alternatively, the personality systems of other adults who experienced childhood sexual abuse may displace the trauma coded excitement affect onto an acceptable object. Food can be such an object, and one of the many pathways to eating disorders is characterized by extremes of excitement generated by food and its consumption.

Excitement affect can also be inappropriately stimulated through witnessing violence. At the same time that family violence elicits fear and traumatizes, it can also stimulates excitement. Witnessing violence elicits excitement affect, as the national obsession with football and other contact sports attests. The child witnessing spousal abuse or other family violence will experience a complex of emotions that may include excitement as well as fear among others. Because of its association with violence witnessed at an immature developmental stage, the excitement will be trauma coded. The excitement affect experienced in witnessing family violence will usually be unacceptable to the child. As the personality develops, this trauma coded excitement affect may sublimate into high-risk activities like sky-diving, motorcycle racing, hang gliding, or other extreme sports. This is not to suggest that all persons who engage in extreme sports were witnesses to family violence, but rather to point out one developmental pathway and the trauma coded emotions associated with it that can sometimes result in high-risk behaviors. This affective analysis may help the clinician to create AMST treatment plans that target excitement affect for clients whose problems appear to arise from difficulties managing this critical affect.

SUMMARY

Chapter 10 culminates the presentation of the AMST protocol. Skill VII (regulation) teaches the client to down-regulate negative affect and emotion and to up-regulate positive affect and emotion using images generated by the client himself. Skill VII illustrates the cumulative process of AMST. Skill I (containment) allows the client to sequester disturbing material that would intrude on the process of skills acquisition were it not contained. With disturbing material contained, the client can learn AMST's skills and prepare himself to then deal with the contained material later in therapy. Skill II (safe place) establishes an inner image of safety and security that allows the client to move forward to recall times she felt distressing emotions and to be able to learn skills for managing them. Skill III begins by teaching the client to set limits on the level of arousal of negative emotion, and then it teaches the client to target a single affect and to elicit that affect by recalling a situation in which she felt it. The target affect and target scene then become the basis for learning skills III to VII. In the setup for skill IV, the client creates a grounding resource, a visualization he will eventually employ for a range of emotions. Skill IV links deployment of the grounding resource to sensations accompanying the index affect. Skill V affirms for the client that she can stay grounded and present while she experiences an emotion. Skill VI builds on the grounding skill by teaching the client how to notice thoughts, memories, other emotions, and impulses to behavior that are associated with the index affect or emotion and associated sensations. Finally, skill VII teaches the client images he can use to regulate the level of arousal for affects he wants to attenuate and for those he wants to enhance.

Through the skills acquisition process the client builds structure in the self or personality. The clinician will observe a steady increase in competence and mastery that accompanies the expansion of self structure. With that structure building process comes greater self-awareness as well as expansion of consciousness. Damasio (1999) emphasized that consciousness arises out of the sensations accompanying the experience of affects and emotions. Clinicians will watch the client's self-awareness and consciousness expand from session to session as she transmits the skills to the client. By the completion of phase 1 of affect centered therapy, when the client has developed AMST skills to manage a range of affects, both the clinician and client will feel confident that the uncovering and trauma-resolving work of phase 2 can be accomplished without undue danger to the client.

By the the time skills III to VII have been developed for a range of both positive and negative affects, the client and clinician will have collaborated in uncovering the organization of the client's personality structure. Missing resources will have been identified and supplied. Allies will have been developed. Where they exist, covert ego states will have been uncovered and their helper function transmuted to a form that is currently adaptive. The client will have become aware of his or her self structure at a level previously unknown. The process of raising the unconscious to consciousness will have been enjoined. As a result of acquiring the AMST skills the client will have become a more whole and complete, more positively functioning self. The result at this point in the therapy process will not look the same for every client, because some clients start out in a much more compromised state. Some clients experienced more deficit experience, some more trauma, others more genetic impairment. However, given each client's starting place, movement to more positive functioning, more adaptive functioning, and more competent self organization is always the more probable outcome.

Chapter 11

Advanced Skills

The objective of this chapter is to transmit several advanced skills to the clinician. These advanced skills are elaborations of the basic skills that have already been presented. As the clinician develops familiarity with the seven fundamental skills, he can select from the range of advanced skills to augment the basics as specific therapeutic situations arise. Like the expert skier who selects from his repertoire the appropriate skill to meet the immediate demands of the ski run, the skillful clinician adapts his approach to the needs of the client in the moment. While the skier may be attempting to optimize the elegance with which he carves the ski slope's face, the therapist seeks to maximize the benefit to his client, and if he can do so elegantly, so much the better. Optimally benefiting the client requires knowledge of a variety of tools. The advanced skills presented here all build on the solid foundation of basic techniques established in previous chapters.

ENHANCING THE SELF-CONCEPT

As used here, the idea of self-concept is amalgamated from two interrelating elements, self-efficacy and self-worth. Self-concept is a complex construction entailing an inner representation of the self assembled with memories, thoughts, sensations, emotions and affects. Reduced to its essentials, self-concept is a neural network constructed across the lifespan.

Self-Efficacy

Self-efficacy is an experience-based assessment that the self has the tools and skills to function adaptively and positively in the world. Self-efficacy says, "I can achieve my goals." It also says, "I can handle life's challenges." Adaptive functioning has several dimensions, and people will not necessarily function equally well or equally poorly across these dimensions. One can perform well or poorly in the social dimension, the dimension of relationships, or that of work and career. The challenges of the parenting dimension may be managed well or poorly. School is another dimension; so is daily activity; so is sex. Probably the most fundamental dimension of adaptive functioning is the emotional dimension, since harmonious functioning here promotes, although it does not ensure successful functioning in the other dimensions.

Self-efficacy in the adult develops out of childhood experiences of goal attainment in the context of the developmental dyad. The child who believes he is effective is a child whose parents responded to his needs. When parents do not respond to a child's needs, the child develops an internal representation of the self as ineffective. Many adults whose childhoods had deficit, adverse, or traumatic experiences have never developed a positive self-concept. These adults often do not hold a self-representation that is assembled with cognitions of effective functioning. Self-worth is the emotional component of the self-concept; self-efficacy is the evaluative component; self-worth and self-efficacy are interdependent. Thus, it is difficult for a child, adolescent, or adult to feel the self is worthy if the self has rarely if ever been effective.

In AMST, self-efficacy regarding management of the self is transmitted by means of the metacognitions that accompany each skill. The skill I metacognition, "I am learning to contain every disturbing thing," conveys acquisition of competence in managing the internal landscape, the field of one's thoughts, memories, images, and emotions. "I am learning to create safety for myself," the skill II metacognition, affirms the self's effectiveness in establishing the knowledge and feeling of safety in the internal environment. When the client practices using the safe place skill on a future template and then returns to therapy to report a success, the clinician installs a positive cognition affirming the success and thereby facilitates building self-efficacy for the client. When a client learns how to recognize sensations accompanying a target affect and affirms it with the skill III metacognition, "I am learning to recognize how my body tells me I am feeling (name of emotion)," the client expands his personal effectiveness. The self-concept grows. The ability to stay grounded and present while feeling strong emotion, the ability to "just notice" the self experiencing emotion, the ability to decrease distressing emotion, and increase favorable emotion all can be affirmed with metacognitions that contribute to building a sense of personal effectiveness. As a client's appraisal of his adaptive functioning improves, his feeling about himself improves as well, and the self-worth component of the self-concept is enhanced.

Self-Worth

The self-concept also comprises an emotion and affective appraisal that is the basis of self-worth. Fundamentally, self-worth appears to equate to a statement about how approachable one feels toward the self or the degree to which one accepts one's self. Lang (1995) pointed to an elementary emotional and behavioral dichotomy between approach on the one hand and avoidance or seeking to escape on the other, and he argues that the emotions inform us of which course of action to take. Viewed in this light, self-worth reflects an emotional response toward or about the self more than a belief about the self. Self-worth is summative. While there may be parts of the self or acts the self has committed that are unattractive, these are balanced against the favorable aspects and acts, and an overall emotive response is formed that constitutes self-worth. In common usage, people often say "I am worthy," when what they really mean is "I feel worthy about myself."

Self-worth can best be understood from a developmental perspective. Formation of self-worth begins with emergence of an IWM of the self (i.e., a self representation). It's anlage lie in late practicing and coincide with the appearance of shame affect and the emotion of guilt that require a self-representation. Over developmental time, memories, cognitions and appraisals, drives, emotions generated within the self, and emotions broadcast at the self assemble with the self-representation. Self-worth is largely determined by the emotions that are assembled with the self-representation. A self-representation that is assembled with excitement affect and joy affect will be approachable by the self system, in much the same way that we would approach another person who manifests excitement and enjoyment. In Lang's dichotomy, a self-representation assembled with excitement and joy will be accepted by the self system, and the self system will experience excitement and joy—or at least comfort—at being with that self-representation.

On the other hand, the ego or self system will avoid or seek to escape from a self-representation or a fragment (ego state or alter) thereof assembled with disgust affect or shame affect, or with emotions of guilt or contempt. This parallels the way in which humans tend to avoid others whose self-concept is shame- or disgust-based. Thus when the self-representation is assembled with any one or all of these distressing emotions, the personality system will manifest poor self-worth. Like self-esteem with which it is all but identical, self-worth appears to have two dimensions: stability and level (Kernis, Grannemann, & Barclay, 1989). Both stability and level may be understood as functions of coherence or fragmentation in the self system as well as the affects assembled with the unified self representation or its fragments. If the self-representation is coherent and assembled with positive emotion and generally positive memories and images, then self-worth will be high and stable. If the self-representation is coherent and assembled with negative emotion, self-worth will be poor and stable. Fragmentation of the self-representation appears in the form of ego states, or alters in the extreme case of dissociative identity disorder (DID). In the case of unstable self-worth, a covert ego state holds the system's disgust and a false self identity has emerged over the years to mediate between the self system and the world. Instability is revealed when events evoke the covert ego state and the system experiences the disgust or other negative affect held by that ego state. The false self identity maintains a simulation of high self-worth level that can rapidly crumble when challenged.

Attachment and Self-Worth

It appears that the same attachment behavior known to manifest in early childhood between caregiver and infant, later manifests in the relations between the ego, or self system, and the self, or self-representation. The attachment, whether between parent and child or between ego and self, can be secure or insecure. Secure attachment in childhood entrains a developmental pathway that usually results in a securely attached adult. One manifestation of a secure–autonomous adult attachment is a secure attachment to the self that will manifest in positive self-worth and well-founded self-efficacy. The self will be able to requite the system's yearning for merger with itself, and wholeness will eventuate.

An insecure adult attachment, in addition to its manifestation in interpersonal relations and in the test situation of the Adult Attachment Inventory (AAI), can also be expressed in the relations between the self and the self system. The style of the ego's relations to the self can be dismissing, preoccupied, or disorganized–disoriented, the same categories that characterize the style with which the adult self system relates to others. The self is unable to requite the system's yearning for merger with itself, and polarity or lack of coherence obtains. Apparently, any one of the insecure intrapersonal relationship styles can be associated with impaired self-worth. In relations between ego and self, the dismissive style will appear as lack of awareness of the needs of the self, an uninvolvement in the self and its care, and avoidance of relations between ego and self. A dismissive style in relations between self and self-system will manifest as poor insight, lack of intimacy, and wariness of introspection. Research may one day demonstrate that depression, especially covert depression, is associated with a dismissing adult attachment style in relations between the self and self system.

Insecure attachment can manifest as a preoccupied style in relations between self and self system. The self preoccupied with itself will be overly self-involved. Never certain that the self will meet the system's needs, this person will constantly refer to, and talk about the self, its involvements, experiences, and thoughts with the purpose of keeping the self's attention. Of course this has the outcome of focusing everyone else's attention on the self as well.

Emotion and Self-Worth

The relationship between emotion or affect and self-worth has been introduced, but it demands further examination. As has been noted, the self-representation can assemble with affects, and the particular dominant affect with which the self-representation is assembled will determine how the self system feels about itself. Because the affect system is modular, any affect can assemble with the self representation. Favorable outcomes result from assembly of positive affect with the self-representation. When enjoyment–joy affect is assembled with a self-representation, the ego will approach the self and the system will be happy. Self-esteem, a synonym for self-worth, is known to predict happiness (Averill & More, 1993). Epstein (1993) proposed that the need for self-esteem is one of four, equal, basic human predilections: the need to maximize pleasure and minimize pain; the need to assimilate data of reality into a stable, coherent conceptual system; the need for relatedness; and the need for self-esteem. The basic need for self-esteem leads to beliefs that develop over time about the degree to which the self is worthy (including competent and good) versus unworthy. Epstein's concept of self-esteem equates to self-worth. The notion of competence equates to the idea of self-efficacy, which we have discussed as a component of the self-concept.

The level and stability of self-worth determine the nature of the system's emotive or affective responses. When self-worth is high and stable, individuals do not experience the self as threatened in a variety of contexts and therefore are less likely to respond with anger. Individuals with high self-worth that is unstable, on the contrary, are more likely to respond with anger or rage to perceived threats to the self-concept as a defense against uncovering the part of the self-representation that is assembled with shame or disgust. Neurophysiologists distinguish defensive rage behavior from predatory attack behavior (Gregg & Siegel, 2001). Defensive rage is mediated by neural systems and transmitters that are distinct from the systems that mediate predatory attack, and the two forms of behavior are reciprocally inhibitory.

The degree of a person's self-esteem can be gauged from the extent to which a person is self-accepting versus self-rejecting, according to Epstein (1993). This echoes Lang's (1995) view of the fundamental dichotomy between approach and avoidance. The emotion system functions to tell a person what things should be approached and what should be avoided. Approach reflects self-acceptance, and avoidance equates with self-rejection. If the self-representation (or a part thereof) is assembled with negative affect, the system will reject that part and thereby the self to a greater or lesser degree. If the self-representation (or a part thereof) is assembled with positive emotion, the system will accept that part and thereby itself.

Self-worth will be seen to include appraisals (cognitions), emotions, and sensations assembled with the self-representation. Memories and images will also be assembled. From a neurophysiological perspective, the self-concept is a multidimensional neural network. It is therefore just as malleable, just as susceptible to change, as any other neural network or schema. It can be evoked by the word *I* or an image of the self or one of its parts. Gestalt does this regularly.

The emotions assembled with the self-representation can arise from within the self or can be broadcast at the self from without. As has been repeatedly emphasized, parents who socialize their children with broadcast anger, shame, or disgust affects risk causing these affects to become assembled with the child's self-representation. Children socialized with disgust affect develop a self-representation over time that is assembled with disgust. Because it is assembled with disgust affect, the system will reject this affective–imaginal structure, that is, the self-representation assembled with disgust affect. As a result the personality system will fragment. The child part of the personality system will be stuck in childhood and unable to develop and mature as the physical body matures. In order to function, a false self identity will emerge to meet the exigencies of daily life. This false self will be animated for the most part by fear affect, since its role is to protect the system against further emotional assault. One consequence of this fragmentation is that the developing system loses its authenticity. The child part "holds" the system's disgust, and because it does so, it also "holds" the system's unworthiness. As an adolescent or adult, this person will not feel worthy. In therapy this individual will react negatively when asked to verbalize attributions of self-worth. Fragmentation can take the form of ego state formation or alter formation. When the intensity of disgust or shame affects assembled with a part is too extreme, the ego state will become an alter. In the case of alter formation, a more or less impermeable boundary is created separating the alter and the affects bound with it from the rest of the self system. In this case, the false self identity conforms to the executive ego state or system manager ego state often found in DID.

Negative emotion evoked from within the child by abuse can also assemble with the self-representation. Sexual victimization of children and adolescents often results in affects of disgust or shame assembling with the self-representation, and again, this part then "holds" the system's unworthiness. The personality system cannot feel worthy if there is a part at the core that holds intense shame, disgust, and unworthiness. At the same time, this child or adolescent part or ego state also functions to support the personality system by virtue of holding the system's unworthiness and thereby separating it from the system. When a child part separates out intense negative affect, it prevents the intense negative affect from contaminating the system. The personality system is enabled to function as adaptively as possible because the ego state sequesters the unworthiness. If this unworthiness were to leak out, it would contaminate and overwhelm the system, and the system's functioning, however maladaptive, would be utterly compromised.

The clinician has been cautioned to avoid overly stressing a personality system that is unprepared to encounter its unworthiness, shame, and disgust. For distressed personalities, especially for victims of adverse childhood experience, the AMST skill set targeting the full range of emotions including shame and disgust must be installed before the client is ready to address unworthiness and worthiness. The DID and the victim of childhood sexual abuse will require even more extensive work. With these caveats in mind, the next section presents the the self-worth affirmation.

The Self-Worth Affirmation

A self-worth affirmation is a positive metacognition that validates the self system's positive regard for itself. It can be formulated in absolute terms regarding system state or trait in the form "I am worthy," or it can be developed in process terms as "I am learning to feel worthy." Clinicians can install self-worth affirmations at any therapeutically advisable point in the AMST flow chart. The self-worth affirmation can target the self directly, as above, or it can target the self's behaviors and accomplishments. The behaviors can include any part of the AMST protocol; for example, "I am worthy of just noticing myself feel fear," or "I am worthy of decreasing my fear." If these unreserved formulations appear too threatening to the client, a process statement is advised; for example, "I am learning to feel worthy of decreasing my fear." Self-worth affirmations can also target emotional responding. For example, the clinician may help the client develop the positive affirmation, "I am learning to feel worthy of feeling relief," or "I am learning to feel worthy of increasing my feelings of relief." After installing the self-worth affirmation the first time, whatever the target, the clinician should help the client locate where in her body she is feeling self-worth. As soon as she locates the sensations, the clinician should install skill III and then use the gauge resource to increase the feeling of self-worth by a therapeutically advisable amount. When a self-worth affirmation is subsequently employed, the clinician should remind the client of her sensations that accompanied the feeling of self-worth. The clinician should also ask the client for a self-assessment of the validity of the self-worth affirmation. Determining a Validity of Cognition (VoC) will ascertain the need for resource development or ego state intervention.

The following case material illustrates the process of working with an ego state that holds the client's unworthiness. The case demonstrates how unworthiness, that is, disturbance in the self-worth system, presented in therapy and how the advanced skills were interwoven by the clinician for the benefit of the client. This case also demonstrates how the AMST self-worth skill can be used to probe the client's self-system and gain important therapeutic information. The client here is Jennifer, one of the young women who sought help for bulimia. The clinician probed the client's self-worth status upon completion of the safe place skill II. Here is the exchange that occurred.

> Clinician: As you look at your safe place, a hill in the park, see the trees, the clouds. You feel the breeze on your skin and you can hear it rustling the green leaves of the trees. You see the force field surrounding the safe place, and you hold the image of the rock that brings you the quality of acceptance. As you hold this image, on a scale from 1 to 7 where 1 is false and 7 is true, how true is the statement, "I am safe"?
>
> Jennifer: It's a 7.
>
> Clinician: I'd like to see how this next statement resonates for you. If it feels right, please repeat it, if not, let me know what comes up for you. As you hold the image of your safe place and the knowledge you are safe, please repeat after me, "I am worthy of being safe."
>
> Jennifer: That doesn't work for me at all. I don't think I'm worthy of anything.
>
> Clinician: Okay. We'll let that go and come back to it in another session.

In a subsequent session, after the client had mastered the basic AMST protocol, the clinician again introduced the topic of self-worth.

> Clinician: In an earlier session you told me that you don't feel worthy of anything. I'd like to work with that feeling of unworthiness now that you have the skills to manage it. Is that okay with you?
>
> Jennifer: Sure.
>
> Clinician: I'd like you to tell me about a time when you think you might have felt unworthy.
>
> Jennifer: That would be right before I came here. I felt unworthy of everyone being so concerned about me. I remember sitting with my psych counselor at the health center and the dean of the college, and they were complimenting me on taking care of my grades. I thought, "There's nothing worth complimenting."
>
> Clinician: Good. Let's work with that. **TABS On** Please recall the scene from college where you were talking to the counselor and the dean and

they are complimenting you, and you just become aware of sensations in your body that accompanied the scene. Let me know by raising your index finger when you get the sensations. Good. Good. [*Jennifer raises her index finger.*] Good. **TABS Off** Deep breath. Let it out, and tell me, what did you get?

Jennifer: There's a tension in my shoulders. I see myself fidgeting while I'm talking to them, and I'm clenching my teeth and locking my jaw.

Clinician: Let's develop that association. **TABS On** Recall the image of yourself talking to your counselor and the dean and they are complimenting you. Now, please repeat after me, "The tension in my shoulders, fidgeting, clenching my teeth, and locking my jaw tell me I'm feeling unworthy."

Jennifer: The tension in my shoulders, fidgeting, clenching my teeth, and locking my jaw tell me I am feeling unworthy.

The clinician coached Jennifer through the remainder of the skill set focusing on her emotion of unworthiness. Jennifer was able to endorse that she was learning to decrease her emotion of unworthiness; however, the level of disturbance for the target scene had only decreased to a subjective unit of disturbance (SUD) 4 from the initial SUD 8.

At this point, the clinician inquired, "I wonder if there isn't a part that is helping you in some way we don't yet understand by holding onto the unworthiness?" Jennifer agreed this was possible and also agreed to meet The One Who Holds The Unworthiness. Using a trance, the clinician facilitated Jennifer's return to her conference room, and The One Who Holds the Unworthiness was invited to enter the room. Jennifer reported seeing a child, a small, unsmiling version of herself enter the room. The child stated that it wanted to be called "Me." Me said she did not know her age. She affirmed that she is the one holding unworthiness for the system. She acknowledged that it is a "big job." The clinician probed to determine the level of approach the system could tolerate by asking if Me was willing to climb up into Jennifer's lap, and Me declined to do so. Deciding that processing issues of childhood deficit and adversity would need to be completed before worthiness could be completely restored to the system, the clinician opted to negotiate for a sharing of responsibility for managing the system's unworthiness between Me and Jennifer. Me acknowledged awareness of the AMST protocol that Jennifer was learning, to use and she agreed to a 50/50 sharing of responsibility for managing unworthiness, although she volunteered that she believed Jennifer "is too weak to do her part." Returning from trance, Jennifer reported that the disturbance level of the target scene had decreased to SUD 2, and she commented spontaneously, "I think I can eat a healthy meal tonight."

DEVELOPING THE CLIENT'S PRIDE

Pride is a complex experiential phenomenon that involves affects, cognitions, and behaviors. Pride is an affective–cognitive structure. Enjoyment affect is a component of the experience of pride that requires accomplishment to be felt. Nathanson (1992) pointed out that the pride experience requires several cognitive components, intention, purpose, and goal direction, plus a behavioral component, accomplishment. Two affects are involved as well, interest–excitement and enjoyment–joy. When the self undertakes purposeful, goal-directed, intentional activity that is motivated by the interest–excitement affect, the activity is successful, and the goal is attained, enjoyment–joy results, because attainment releases the self from the neural stimulation of the activity. Enjoyment–joy affect then amplifies the decrease in neural firing. The AMST protocol itself provides opportunities for the clinician to elicit pride experiences for the client.

Completion of the skill set furnishes one such opportunity, since all of the elements necessary for the pride experience are present. Learning the skill set is a goal, and the client's purpose in being in session at the moment is to gain command of the skills. The client forms the intention of mastering the skills, a goal that is motivated by interest affect. Mastery of the skills, which is confirmed by a VoC of 7 for the positive cognition "I am learning to manage my (name of affect)," elicits enjoyment affect. The clinician can exploit this opportunity for the benefit of the client as the following exchange where shame was the target affect indicates.

> **Clinician:** As you repeated the statement, "I am learning to manage my shame," it looked to me as if you smiled, and I wanted to check that out.
>
> **Client:** Yeah, I did. Shame has been such a burden to me all my life, and it feels good to know I have some tools to deal with it.
>
> **Clinician:** The smile is the facial signature of the emotion of joy. Does that feel right to you?
>
> **Client:** Well, I feel happy, yes.
>
> **Clinician:** So let's strengthen that. **TABS On** Bring up the image of yourself completing the skill set for shame and repeating the affirmation, "I am learning to manage my shame." As you hold that image, become aware of your smile and any sensations you may be feeling. Now please repeat after me, "My smile tells me I am feeling joy."
>
> **Client:** My smile tells me I am feeling joy.
>
> **Clinician:** Let's try a couple more affirmations if they feel right to you. As you hold the smile and the emotion of joy, repeat after me, "I am learning to feel worthy of feeling joy."
>
> **Client:** I am learning to feel worthy of feeling joy. Actually, it's stronger than that. I *am* worthy of feeling joy.
>
> **Clinician:** I'd like you to hold that joy. I'd like you to recall that you set yourself the goal of learning to manage your emotions. That was your purpose in coming to therapy, or one of them anyway. You felt interested in accomplishing it, and now you have. You've learned to manage the range of emotions. Allow yourself to realize that you've accomplished your goal. When people set a goal and achieve it, they feel happy, and moreover, they often feel pride. If it feels right, I'd like you to repeat after me, "I feel proud of my accomplishment."
>
> **Client:** I feel proud of my accomplishment.
>
> **Clinician:** Good. Let that resonate. **TABS Off** Deep breath. Let it out. And tell me, as you hold the image of learning to manage your emotion, on a

scale from 1 to 7, how true is the statement, "I feel proud of my accomplishment"?

Client: That's true. I do feel proud. It's a 6.5. It's going to take some getting used to.

Another opportunity for developing pride presents itself when the client comes to session and reports a success in an area where she had set a goal for therapy. The experience of Elaine, the young anorexic woman, illustrates how the clinician helped develop his client's pride. By the beginning of the fourth 3-hour session of a 5-day intensive therapy, Elaine had mastered all the skills for a range of emotions. In the third session she had processed many of her issues related to food using Affect Centered Therapy that evolved out of an adaptation of EMDR for eating disorders (Omaha, 2000). Her mother's intrusiveness and her parents' verbal fighting were significant issues assembled with food for Elaine. At the beginning of the fourth session, the clinician inquired, "What's different today?" and the following process ensued.

Elaine: Well, I didn't binge. [*Elaine looks proud and broadcasts enjoyment.*]

Clinician: How do you feel telling me that you didn't binge?

Elaine: Happy. I feel happy. Also, I talked to my parents.

Clinician: How was that for you?

Elaine: They were supportive, which is a big change. They didn't say "Do you think it will last any longer than the last therapy?"

Clinician: Tell me what you ate yesterday.

Elaine: Some friends and I went to a restaurant downtown, and I had a chicken Caesar salad.

Clinician: How many calories do you suppose that was?

Elaine: I don't really know, and it's not that important. I used my skills. I kept my grounding cord down and just noticed my emotions. I was a little scared, so I put that down the disposal.

Clinician: Let's solidify your gains. **TABS On** I'd like you to recall all the work you've done here these past three days. See how you've learned the containment skill, and the safe place skill, and how you've learned the skills to recognize and tolerate and regulate several emotions. Recall how you've processed many of your issues regarding food, and how you've repaired your internal relations with your parents. I'd like you to notice that yesterday you used your skills to manage your emotions relating to food and to eating. Notice that you didn't binge, and you didn't restrict. Also notice that you were able to ask for and get your parents' support over the phone last night.

Now, as you hold these memories and thoughts and images, I'd like you to repeat after me, "I am learning to manage my emotions."

Elaine: I am learning to manage my emotions.

Clinician: "I am learning that when I manage my emotions I eat healthfully."

Elaine: I am learning that when I manage my emotions I eat healthfully.

Clinician: "I am learning that when I manage my emotions and eat healthfully, I feel happy."

Elaine: I am learning that when I manage my emotions and eat healthfully, I feel happy.

Clinician: "I feel worthy of managing my emotions and eating healthfully and feeling happy."

Elaine: I feel worthy of managing my emotions and eating healthfully and feeling happy. I do feel worthy. Wow. I really do!

Clinician: One more. I'd like you to look at this entire process of therapy we're doing. Become aware that you made a decision to get better, to deal with your anorexia. You set a goal. And you invested that goal with the emotion of interest. Your interest motivated you to call me and come here. Your interest kept you coming back, and now you are achieving the goal you set for yourself. As you hold that process, I'd like you to repeat after me, "I feel proud of my accomplishment."

Elaine: I feel proud of my accomplishment.

Clinician: Good. Let that resonate and become as true as it can. **TABS Off** Now, as you look at your work so far and your experience at the restaurant, how true is the statement, "I feel proud of my accomplishment"?

Elaine: Oh, it's a 7. For sure, it's a 7.

The clinician went on to help the client recognize sensations in her body accompanying the feeling of pride and then install the skill III positive cognition. The skill VII gauge resource was then employed to enhance her feeling of pride.

MODELING AFFECT FOR THE CLIENT

Sometimes clients need help experiencing an affect in therapy, and when that happens the therapist can rely on a valuable asset: the face. Therapists can coach a client to mimic an affect's facial expression or they can broadcast the desired affect using their own face. Most of the affects are expressed in unique facial expressions. Research has demonstrated that when a subject is asked to make the facial expression associated with an affect, the experience of the affect is elicited (Izard, 1991). Furthermore, witnessing the affect-specific facial expression can induce the index emotion. These facts about emotion expression provide the clinician with additional tools to help her client. Faced with a client having difficulty expressing happiness, the clinician can coach the client to mimic a smile. The following exchange illustrates the procedure.

Clinician: It looks like you're having difficulty enjoying your accomplishment.

Client: Happiness has never been my strong suit.

Clinician: Let's work on that. **TABS On** What I'd like you to do is recall all the work you've done in this session. You set yourself the goal of learning to manage your anger, and you've accomplished it. You came up with a target scene where you felt a low level of anger. You learned to recognize the sensations that go with anger. You made a grounding cord and learned to stay grounded and present while you felt anger and then just notice yourself feeling anger. Then you decreased it by 99%, and you confirmed you had done so because you gave it a 7 on the scale. As you hold the visualization of all the work you have done in session today, I'd like you to just let the corners of your mouth go up. That's it. A little more. Good. Let yourself smile. Let your teeth show. Excellent. Now, as you smile, just become aware of any other sensations you're feeling. Let me know by raising your index finger when you get them. Good. [*Client raises his index finger.*] What did you get?

Client: My face feels kind of warm.

Clinician: Good. Now repeat after me, "My smile and the warmth in my face tell me I'm feeling happy."

Client: My smile and the warmth in my face tell me I'm feeling happy.

Clinician: Now, go back and recall all the work you did in session today learning to manage your anger. Listen to yourself saying, "I am learning to manage my anger." As you do, bring in some warmth to your face. Let the corners of your mouth turn up. That's right. [*Client forms a smile.*] Good. Just a little more. Good. Now, please repeat after me, "I am learning to feel happy about my accomplishment."

Client: I am learning to feel happy about my accomplishment.

Clinician: Let that resonate. Good. **TABS Off** Deep breath. Let it out, and what comes up now?

Client: That was neat how you did that. Made me feel happy.

Clinician: I only facilitated your process. I can't make you feel any way. You made yourself feel happy, or allowed yourself to feel happy.

If the client continues to have difficulty experiencing enjoyment affect, the clinician can lead the client by broadcasting enjoyment at the client. By modeling the facial expression of enjoyment, the clinician can induce enjoyment in the client and then guide him to imitate it. The following vignette illustrates the process.

Clinician: Let's see if I can help you get in touch with your emotion of happiness. **TABS On** As I visualize all the work you have done in session today, I feel really happy. [*Clinician allows a broad smile to animate his face.*] Please look at my face. Notice my smile. Hear the lightness in my voice. See my eyes crinkle. As you look at me feeling happy, just let that resonate with you. Feel me broadcasting happiness at you. See if you can imitate it. Good. Let the corners of your mouth turn up. Just a little. Good. Now, as you recall all the work you've done today, let some lightness into your voice as you repeat after me, "I am learning to feel happy at my accomplishment."

Client: I am learning to feel happiness at my accomplishment. [*Client chuckles.*]

Clinician: Good. Just feel the happiness. **TABS Off** Deep breath. Let it out, and what comes up now?

Client: That's the damnedest thing. I really do feel happy. Thanks.

Were a client to continue to resist feeling enjoyment at accomplishing his goal, the clinician should pursue quality resource, alliance resource, and ego state interventions.

REPAIRING ATTACHMENT DEFICITS

In the infant–caregiver dyad, attachment provides the context for transmission of affect regulation skills from primary caregiver to child. Within this context, the healthy caregiver facilitates amplification of the child's positive or comfortable emotions and attenuates distressing emotion. The caregiver accomplishes many of these goals before the child fully acquires language, and so the mode of skills transmission is through behavior, touch, facial expression, and tonal modulation of the voice. The child is soothed through these modalities when feeling distressing emotion, and the parent's soothing function is internalized. Comfortable emotion is heightened through these same modalities, and again the parent's amplifying function is internalized. Through their actions the caregivers transmit the message that the child is safe when experiencing emotion, that the experience of emotion is normal, and that the caregiver's love will not be withdrawn or endangered by the child's emotion experience. In the healthy dyad, these are elaborated as the child acquires language, and they are extended across the developmental stages of separation-individuation, latency, and adolescence as the child matures, a process that in part necessitates directing strong emotion at the caregivers.

For childhoods characterized by deficit, adverse, or traumatic experience, the childhood family environment was not a safe place in which to experience emotion. In the deficit situation, the caregiver may not have facilitated affect modulation. The child on this developmental pathway may not have an internalized representation of a soothing caregiver. Parents may not have modeled emotional expressiveness, and boys were often expected to hold their emotions in like their fathers. Children of adversity may have been socialized by fear when they were sad by parents who said, "I'll give you something to cry about." The therapeutic dyad affords an opportunity for corrective action to repair deficits in the attachment. The therapist can supply the soothing tones and words and facial expressions, the normalization function, the function of unconditional acceptance, and where appropriate, the function of touch. Altogether these skills correct deficits in the attachment. Early in therapy, corrective action takes the form of an attachment intervention. Later, when the client has acquired the basic AMST protocol, corrective action consists in developing an internal image that can supply the soothing functions; this is called *attachment remediation*.

The Attachment Intervention

Early in AMST clients sometimes encounter strong emotion. At this stage of therapy the client has not yet acquired the entire skill set and therefore lacks the basis to accomplish a more elaborate, internalizing intervention. Strong emotion may surface during installation of skill I or skill II. For example, a client may suddenly experience sadness as he realizes how much control "every disturbing thing" has exercised over his life, or he may feel shame at having this reality exposed. It is important for the clinician to recognize and acknowledge such strong emotion occurring in session in that present moment. The clinician should take action to normalize emotion expression and to make it safe to do so *in the therapeutic situation.* The therapist must take responsibility for the therapy and the fact that the therapy at this moment has elicited strong emotion from the client. The clinician's actions will strengthen the therapeutic dyad. They will soothe the client, and they will begin the process of remediating the client's attachment deficits.

The attachment intervention provides the three critical elements of the attachment: physical connection, affective attunement, and secure emotional holding (Wesselmann, 2000). If it is ethically and clinically appropriate, the clinician can provide physical connection by tapping on the client's hands or shoulders. If it is not ethically or clinically appropriate for the therapist to touch the client, then the intervention can be facilitated with TABS. Affective attunement is provided by the therapist's language in which she affirms that she understands her client's emotion, because she has experienced that emotion herself. Secure emotional holding is transmitted by the clinician's expression of care for her client, a care that is unchanged when she learns that her client feels this strong emotion.

The following case material demonstrates an attachment intervention. The client here is Helen, a woman in her 20s who had come for help with bulimia. The client's father physically abused her in childhood. For Helen, intense sadness surfaced as she realized how unsafe she had felt for most of her life. The work reported here occurred during the second hour of the first 3-hour session in a 5-day intensive therapy. Helen had already successfully created and filled a container, and the therapy had progressed to skill II (safe place). Her safe place was a large playground area. She could hear birds and children playing in the distance. She felt the sun and a little breeze on her skin, and she smelled fresh cut grass. With TABS facilitation, Helen was asked to repeat the skill II positive cognition, "I am safe." She did so, and after the TABS was turned off, she winced and reported, "I don't feel safe, because there's no one there" when asked, "What comes up for you now?"

The therapist asked, "Who could help?" and the client responded, "My dog." With TABS facilitation, the dog, a yellow Labrador retriever, was brought into the safe place visualization. After the installation, the client offered, "I feel safer," but the VoC for the positive cognition "I am safe" was stuck at 6. The interchange then continued as follows.

Clinician: What prevents it from going to a 7?

Helen: My untrusting and never feeling this before. It's hard, because I don't trust anybody.

Clinician: It sounds like you might feel safer if you had the quality of trust. Can you give me an image that embodies that quality of trust?

Helen: What would help is a force field.

Clinician: Good. Let's install that. **TABS On** See the playground. Hear the kids in the distance and feel the breeze. See your dog. Now, visualize a force field, a large spherical field completely surrounding the playground. The force field is impenetrable. No one can get through it. The force field gives you the ability to trust. Good. **TABS Off** Deep breath. Let it out, and what comes up now?

Helen: Now I feel safe.

Clinician: On the scale from 1 to 7, how true is the statement "I feel safe"?

Helen: It's a 7.

Clinician: Are you getting any particular sensations in your body with that?

Helen: Yeah, my arms. They're relaxed.

Clinician: Let's strengthen that. **TABS On** Please repeat after me, "The relaxation in my arms tells me I am feeling safe."

Helen: The relaxation in my arms tells me I am feeling safe. [*Helen's face flushes slightly. Her eyes become moist, and the corners of her mouth turn down.*]

Clinician: **TABS Off** You look sad all of a sudden. Am I reading you right?

Helen: It *is* sad because I can only feel safe when I'm isolated from all contact with the world by the force field.

Clinician: Let's take a moment and do some work with this. What I'd like you to do is look at my face. Look carefully. I want you to notice the acceptance in my face. I'm going to turn the TheraTapper on, and just let the gentle pulses take the place of the hug that an ideal caring person might give you now. **TABS On** Good. Now just listen to my words.

I see that you are feeling sad. I see your eyes have gotten moist, and your face is slightly flushed, and the corners of your mouth have turned down. I hear you telling me it is sad for you that you can only feel safe when you're isolated from all contact with the world by a force field.

I believe I understand what you are feeling when you tell me you're feeling sad, because I have felt sadness myself.

As my client, I care for you. As your therapist, your well-being is important to me. I want you to know that my care for you is unchanged when you tell me you feel sad. As my client, my care for you is unconditional.

Just let that all resonate for a moment. Good. **TABS Off** Deep breath. Let it out, and what comes up now?

Helen: I *so* needed to hear that. My mom always said, "Get over it!" My dad would just threaten to hit me again. It was not okay to feel sad.

Four points in this therapeutic interchange deserve emphasis. First, the clinician's statement, "I have felt sadness myself," *must* be authentic. The clinician must display congruence. The most effective way for the clinician to do this is to allow an image or memory to surface of a time he or she did feel sad. The clinician should not lose affective control of the session, of course, but he must be believable. Second, the clinician must feel comfortable using his or her face to promote a therapeutic goal. It is vitally important that the therapist feel confident that he or she can broadcast acceptance and not disapproval or shame. Third, the reader will note that the clinician in this vignette adapted the standard AMST protocol to the flow of the therapy and the client's needs in the moment. Fourth, the reader will note that it was not until Helen experienced the physical sensations accompanying safety that sadness surfaced for her. Apparently experiencing the qualia of safety completed some neural circuit sufficiently to then trigger the emotion of sadness about never having felt safe before. This example illustrates the complexity of intrapsychic affective transactions.

Attachment Remediation: The Safe Face Skill

When strong emotion surfaces later in therapy, emotion that appears to need to be honored rather than down-regulated, and if the client has mastered the basic AMST protocol, the clinician can elect to develop an attachment remediating image. This is the safe face skill. Allan Schore volunteered the name *safe face* in a telephone conversation in 2001 when I described the attachment remediating intervention I had created. Adults who as children experienced deficit, adverse, or traumatic experience often lack an internal image of a warm, empathic, attuned, sensitive, responsive, and nurturing maternal figure. When this deficiency becomes apparent over the course of the clinical encounter, the clinician can introduce the idea of developing such an image for the client. The safe face visualization consists of an image and positive qualities assembled with it. The clinician then employs the visualization to provide the attachment experiences of acceptance and emotional attunement the client may never have had. The visualization creates a new object representation and imbues it with affirmative qualities. The client can use the safe face image at any time, and ideally it will become a resource helping the client to achieve "earned secure" attachment status.

Instructions for developing the safe face skill must assure the client that the skill is not meant to "get rid of" the client's real mother, but merely to provide the mothering figure that the client did not have in real life. The skill can be applied for developing an ideal father figure as well. Developing the skill begins by eliciting from the client a list of all the qualities the client would have wanted in an ideal mother or father. If the client omits qualities the clinician believes are significant, then the clinician should suggest that these qualities by added. Using TABS, the clinician facilitates the emergence of an image of a figure that embodies the listed qualities. Since this image is meant to remediate a relationship to an actual person, the author's clinical intuition has been not to facilitate a merger of client and image, in part because the therapeutic use of the image often involves having the client look closely at the eyes and mouth of the visualized safe face. Once installed, the clinician will facilitate the client's use of the image to provide physical connection, affective attunement, and secure emotional holding, the essential elements of attachment. Other potential uses of the image, including provision of affirmation, attunement, and support, are limited only by the needs of the client and the inventiveness of the therapist.

Case material from Carly illustrates the development and therapeutic use of the safe face visualization. Carly is a woman in her 40s who had trouble with overeating. This client's mother had abandoned her in childhood, and the client was raised by a female steprelative who was verbally and physically abusive. The client's birth mother posed as an aunt. In the course of our work together, the client verbalized the stress of trying to care for the needs of her own children and "wanting to run away, to be alone." This comment revealed a core deficit: the absence of an image of a mother sufficiently committed to the welfare of her child to endure the stress of child-rearing. The clinician felt the client imploring to be heard, to have her desire to run away understood. This desire appeared to cause the client emotional distress, since it so recreated her own abandonment. This was an ideal opportunity for the safe face intervention that was developed as the following interchange illustrates.

Clinician: I'm hearing you say that you feel like running away from your children, and that must be very painful for you given your own history with your mother who did run away. I get the sense that your desire to run away needs to be heard and understood in a way that only a truly empathetic person who'd worked through the same feelings could do. What I'd like to do is help you develop an image of a warm, empathic maternal figure who can really hear what you're going through. Does that make sense to you?

Carly: Oh, yes. Yes. That works for me.

Clinician: So then, what I'd like you to do is list for me the qualities that you'd like in an ideal mother. The mother you didn't have. We're not going to get rid of your actual mother. All we're doing is developing an image to give you what fate didn't provide. What qualities would your ideal mom have?

Carly: Well, she'd be accepting. She'd be demonstrative and loving. Understanding. She'd be wise. Centered, not scattered like the woman who raised me. She'd be honest. Something my real mom wasn't. I could trust her. She'd look at me and know what I was feeling, so she'd be empathic. She'd treat me with kindness, not yelling and raging. She'd have good boundaries and let me have them too. And she'd comfort me when I was feeling bad. That's about it.

Clinician: Wonderful. Now, in what follows, all you really need to do is just notice. Let your unconscious give you an image, and just watch as it emerges. **TABS On** What I'd like you to do is relax and just notice. Let an image emerge from your deepest unconscious as I repeat these qualities. Let an image begin to form of a woman who is accepting and who demonstrates her love. Just notice as the image begins to form of a female figure who is understanding and wise. Who is centered. Who is honest. The figure that is emerging is trustworthy and attuned. She is empathic. She is kind. She has healthy boundaries, and she comforts you. Good.

As this figure has emerged now, I'd like you to look closely at her face. Look at her eyes and see how they demonstrate love for you. See how her eyes manifest wisdom and trustworthiness. Look at her stance, how she carries herself, and see how her physical being embodies honesty. Take the hand she is offering you and see how it is a comforting hand, a kind hand. Look in her eyes and see the kindness and understanding. Feel how you know she has good boundaries and lets you have healthy boundaries too. Just be with her for a while now. Just getting comfortable with being together. Good. Good. **TABS Off** Deep breath. Let it out, and what comes up now?

Carly: My child part. [*She begins to cry gently.*] My child self is just feeling so good. These are all the things she tried to make happen with the woman who raised me, and they couldn't, and now they are happening for her.

Having installed the safe face, the clinician now returns to the issue that preceded and motivated the installation. Recall that for Carly this was her feeling of wanting to run from her own children. The therapeutic goals in utilizing the safe face visualization are the same as for the attachment intervention: physical connection, emotional attunement, and secure emotional holding.

> Clinician: Let's help you use this image of the ideal mother now. **TABS On** Recall that you said you felt anxious and stressed at not being able to meet the needs of all your children. Recall that you said you wanted to run away and be alone. As you recall those thoughts and feelings, bring up again the image of your ideal mother. Let her take your hands in hers. Feel the physical connection with her through your hands. Look into her eyes and become aware of her wisdom and empathy. Feel that she understands you. Let yourself be comforted by her. Listen to her as she says, "I'm hearing you say you feel stressed and anxious at not being able to meet your children's needs. I'm hearing you say that you want to run away and be alone. I believe that I can understand your anxiety and wanting to run away, because I've felt anxious with my children, and I wanted to run away myself." Listen to her comforting voice, her wise and understanding voice, as she says, "I want you to know that I love you and that my love is unconditional. I accept that you feel stressed by your children. Your stress does not affect my love. My love is unconditional. I love you when you tell me you want to run away. I accept that you have that thought, and your thought does not change my love for you." Good. Notice that you feel accepted just for who you are. You feel understood and comforted. Good. **TABS Off** Deep breath. Let it out, and what comes up now?
>
> Carly: That is so incredibly powerful. I felt so guilty for having those thoughts. I was never going to act on them, but just having them really hurt. Now I know I'm okay. It's all right to have a thought like that. It doesn't make me bad or wrong.

DEVELOPING EMOTION KNOWLEDGE

Often children of deficit experience, adversity, or trauma do not learn the skill of recognizing what emotion another is feeling. They may also not learn to identify what emotion a normal person might experience in a given situation. Another skill is the ability to identify an emotion that is not normative in a situation, an emotion that is discordant with what most people would feel. These are the skills of emotion knowledge. Children with underdeveloped emotion knowledge have difficulty in social situations in childhood and across the lifespan. The inability to recognize what emotion another is feeling contributes to marital difficulties, because often one partner assumes the other is feeling what he or she would feel, or the partner may project an emotion onto the other; in either case, the one partner does not recognize what the other is actually feeling. Furthermore, adults who experienced deficit, adversity, or trauma during childhood are hampered in working through their loss, misfortune, or trauma by underdeveloped emotion knowledge, because they often cannot name the emotions that were directed against them by a parent in childhood.

The clinician develops the client's emotion knowledge by teaching the ability to recognize what another is feeling by identifying facial and body cues and through awareness of what the client's sensations are telling him he is feeling as he looks at the visualized other. These skills are only meant to be used with clients who have already learned to recognize, tolerate, and regulate the index emotion themselves. The clinician uses his knowledge of facial and body cues of emotion expression and the normative emotions in index situations to create visualizations for such emotions as sadness, shyness, fear, anger, excitement, shame, or disgust. For example, for the index emotion sadness, the clinician might create the following vignette.

> Clinician: **TABS On** A man has just gotten a phone call telling him that his aunt has died of cancer. You are in the room with him. What do you see?
>
> Client: Hmmm. I don't know.
>
> Clinician: Look at his eyes. Tell me, what do you see?
>
> Client: They look a little moist and maybe a little red.
>
> Clinician: How about his cheeks? And what is his chin doing? And his mouth?
>
> Client: His cheeks were red, but it passed real quickly. His chin is like trembling maybe, but his mouth is set, like he's holding it in.
>
> Clinician: So, as you look at his moist and slightly red eyes, his cheeks that got red briefly, and his trembling chin and set mouth, what are you feeling in your body?
>
> Client: Tightness in my throat. Pressure in my chest.
>
> Clinician: And do you recall what emotion those sensations signaled?
>
> Client: Sadness. I had the same welling in my eyes and trembling chin too. So, he's feeling sad.
>
> Clinician: Good. Now repeat after me, "I am learning to use my own emotion awareness to recognize what another is feeling."
>
> Client: I am learning to use my own emotion awareness to recognize what another is feeling.
>
> Clinician: Good. **TABS Off** Deep breath. Let it out, and what comes up now?

The possibilities for utilizing this skill are nearly endless. The clinician can use this skill as a template for developing the client's awareness about what others are feeling in real life situations that the client brings to therapy. The skill is especially valuable for persons under relationship stress, where the clinician can ask the client to look carefully at the partner's face in the visualized distressing scene and notice what cues are there. The clinician can also ask the client to assume the partner's place in the visualized distressing scene and become aware of sensations and emotions the client would feel in the partner's role.

Many persons who come to therapy have developed defenses against awareness of another's felt emotion. For example, a boy raised in a family endorsing spousal abuse may have learned to create a barrier to resonating with distress–anguish affect felt by a woman or by any person. Individuals may use a dissociative defense, an emotional defense (e.g., shifting to anger), or a misdirecting defense (e.g., shifting attention to another stimulus). Helping the client develop emotion awareness gives the clinician the opportunity to confront these defenses and raise them to the client's attention.

THE BOUNDARY SKILL: A BARRIER AGAINST INTRUSIVENESS

Nathanson (1992) has emphasized that adults regularly broadcast emotions and that some other adults do not have filters or defenses against these broadcast emotions. A common example is broadcast lust, which is sex drive combined with excitement affect. Many female clients, especially those who experienced childhood sexual abuse, have difficulty managing the situation when a male broadcasts lust at them. One reason is that they lack a barrier, what Nathanson calls the "empathic wall" (p. 111), to deflect the broadcast emotion. The target individual for the broadcast emotion is called a *resonator*. As Nathanson explains, too permeable a barrier between resonator and broadcaster leaves the resonator vulnerable to being taken over by the affects of another. When this happens, the resonator's self-concept is damaged, and she loses a sense of a coherent, integral self.

The boundary skill facilitates the client's visualization of a barrier and links its deployment to cues produced by the broadcaster and sensations felt by the resonator. The clinician asks the client for an image of a barrier that would deflect uncomfortable or potentially dangerous emotion. With TABS facilitation, the image is developed as well as the client's sensations that tell her she is protected. Next, in an analogy to the target scene, the clinician elicits a memory of a time when someone broadcast the index emotion at the client. The sensations felt by the client and cues in the broadcaster are identified and then made the signals that tell the client to bring up her boundary visualization. The client is reminded of the sensations telling her she is protected, and then the positive cognition, "I am learning to protect myself from broadcast emotion," is installed with TABS facilitation. Future templates where the client expects to have a stressful emotion broadcast at her can be identified, and using the boundary skill can be facilitated in the situation. In subsequent sessions, the clinician can solicit a report on the client's success and then strengthen her successes where appropriate.

SUMMARY

In this chapter we have learned several skills that operate at a *meta* level to the level at which the seven fundamental skills function. Skills for enhancing self-concept invite the client to visualize the self-improved functioning and feel better about the self. These skills group into categories directed toward increasing self-efficacy and toward increasing self-worth. Skill VI (noticing) develops the client's self-reflective capability, and self-worth and self-efficacy enhancements rely on the self's ability to notice itself. The chapter has emphasized that self-efficacy affirmations (e.g., "I am learning to manage my fear") can be installed as soon as the client has acquired the skill. Self-worth affirmations, especially for the more severely compromised client, must be approached cautiously. Where there is a child part holding the system's disgust, shame, and unworthiness, the self system will be stressed by encountering issues of worthiness. The case of Jennifer illustrated how such a child part was uncovered. Chapter 12 will teach skills to uncover and resolve the trauma or adversity that engendered the disgust, shame, and unworthiness in the first place. The chapter will also teach the redemption intervention that can be applied to help the child part feel worthy once the trauma has been processed.

In addition to skills for enhancing the self-concept, this chapter has transmitted and illustrated skills to develop the client's pride. Skills were transmitted for helping the client get in touch with affects that were not adequately modeled in childhood. Other skills helped the client protect herself from broadcast emotions. Finally, the chapter taught two types of attachment interventions. One, tailored for early in therapy, makes therapeutic use of the clinician's broadcast affective attunement and acceptance. The second, which is meant to be employed later in the AMST process when a sufficient knowledge base has been developed, develops and installs an attachment figure—the safe face—that provides affective attunement and secure emotional holding. These skills illustrate once again how AMST consciously builds new, positively and adaptively functioning representations and assembles them with supportive affects and cognitions.

Phase II Skills: Uncovering and Resolving Causes of Affect Dysregulation

Two fundamental principles of Affect Centered Therapy (ACT) assert that affects are among the primary determinants of all human behavior and cognition and that the self is structured during and by the process of affective socialization. As we have stated, the problem of affect dysregulation and the dysfunctional organization of the self bring clients to the counseling office. Assembly of affects and emotions with current or archaic events makes these events distressing for the client. The Axis I disorders illustrate the principle that dysregulated affect creates problems that distress clients. In substance abuse disorder and the eating disorders, individuals employ a substance—alcohol, nicotine, drugs, food—to regulate otherwise overwhelming affect or emotion. In attention deficit hyperactivity disorder (ADHD), disorders of mood, and the anxiety disorders, dysregulated affect motivates hyperactive, depressed, or anxious behavior. The Axis II disorders appear to represent difficulties with affect regulation that appeared so early in the formation of personality that the self structure organized around dysfunctional affect management scripts. Affect driven developmental pathways were enjoined that conditioned the emergence of self structures grouping into the familiar personality disorder categories of borderline, narcissistic, dependent, antisocial, avoidant, paranoid, and obsessive compulsive. Affects and emotions appear to be primary motivators of both adaptive and maladaptive, positive and negative behaviors.

The third fundamental principle of ACT derives from the first and asserts that treating psychopathology entails uncovering and resolving the causes of affect dysregulation. As has been repeatedly emphasized, transmitting the AMST skill set to the client constitutes the essential first phase of psychotherapy. Once the client can recognize, tolerate, and regulate the range of emotions, then in the second phase of therapy, he can uncover and resolve the causes of emotion dysregulation. ACT assumes that once the client has mastered the skills of emotion regulation and has uncovered and resolved the early causes of affect dysregulation, a more positive and more adaptive self structure will emerge, facilitated in part by therapeutic interventions. The exact meaning of positive and adaptive social functioning depends upon the requirements, norms, and definitions imposed by the social context in which the therapeutic dyad is embedded. The gains of the two phases of therapy are solidified by identifying those recurring, crucial life situations in which a relapse to old behaviors is more likely and by importing the newly acquired affect regulation skills into visualizations of those scenarios.

The purpose of the present chapter is to demonstrate how principles of affect regulation developed in the previous chapters carry over into ACT. This chapter will illustrate how skills of affect recognition acquired in the AMST phase can be utilized by the client–therapist dyad in the second phase. These tools can be used in the second phase of psychotherapy to uncover and resolve the childhood causes of affect dysregulation. The tools can be used in a variety of contexts and with a range of psychopathologies. In no case is a complete therapy presented for any Axis I or II disorder. Rather, the presentation indicates how affect focused principles manifest in this therapy. This chapter does not teach ACT. Readers are advised to obtain supervised training in ACT before attempting to employ any of the clinical interventions presented in this chapter.

UNCOVERING THE ORIGINS OF DEFICIT, ADVERSITY, AND TRAUMA

Phase II of ACT depends absolutely upon the successful completion of phase I in which the client develops the skills to recognize, tolerate, and regulate the range of affects. Deficit experience and adverse or traumatic experience often copresent, and so clients may have difficulty managing emotions because they never learned to do so or because emotions were trauma coded in childhood and never subsequently resolved. Clients must learn to use AMST for both positive and negative emotions. Once the client has these skills in place, then and only then, can he or she uncover and resolve the origins of the deficits, adversities, or traumas. The first step in phase II involves uncovering the archaic experiences of deficit, adversity, or trauma. Once these are uncovered, then they can be resolved. Before the origins can be uncovered, however, the matter must be removed from containment.

Removing the Problem from Containment

Recall that at the beginning of phase I, the clinician helped the client place every disturbing thing into containment (skill I). Skill I is based on trust that the unconscious "knows" what is disturbing. The causes or origins of the client's pathology are among the disturbing things that were placed in the container in skill I. Recall that the skill I instructions included visualization of a sign attached to the container that said, "To be opened only when it serves my healing." The clinician must now assist the client in opening and removing from containment all the material that is related to the client's problem. How this is phrased will depend upon the client's presenting problem. Here is language the clinician can use when the presenting problem is the eating disorder bulimia.

> **Clinician:** You've completed the first phase of your work now. You have the skills to manage the whole range of emotions. You're now in a position to be able to work on finding and resolving the causes of the problem that brought you here, which is your bulimia. Are you willing to start on the next phase of your therapy?
>
> **Client:** Yeah. I'm feeling a little bit nervous, but I'm ready.
>
> **Clinician:** Remember your skills. If you get too nervous, you can use your grounding cord and sink disposal. Now before we start, you will need to take your bulimia and everything related to it out of containment. You can always put it back. But you won't be able to find the causes and resolve them if it's in containment, because it's confined. Recall the sign that says, "To be opened only when it serves my healing." Would it serve your healing to open the container valve now and take out just your bulimia and everything related to it?
>
> **Client:** Well, yes. I'm definitely using my grounding cord now. Okay.
>
> **Clinician:** Good. **TABS On** See your container. It's a large steel dumpster. The lid is welded shut. See the valve on the side and the sign that says, "To be opened only when it serves my healing." I'd like you to form the intention now that it will serve your healing to open the valve and take out your bulimia and everything related to it. Good. Now, form the intention that *only* your bulimia and everything related to it will come out. Good. And now open the valve. Hold the intention that only your bulimia will come out. Good. Just watch as it comes out. It may look like smoke or oil. I don't know. Please don't look at any specific thing. Good. And let me know with your finger signal when it's all out. Good. [*Client raises index finger.*] Good. Now close the valve. Good. **TABS Off** Deep breath. Let it out, and let's get started.

Clinicians should note the importance of the wording, *your bulimia and everything related to it*. This instruction ensures that the entire contents of the neural network that includes bulimia will be removed. The unconscious appears to be very literal, and so instructions must be explicit. Clinical experience indicates that failure to remove the presenting problem from containment will result in failure to find the causes of the problem; clients will be unable to experience emotions or sensations assembled with the problem. While the example given pertains to bulimia, the therapist must configure his instructions to suit the client's presenting problem without triggering the problem. It will be counterproductive to suggest to the borderline client who is unaccepting or unaware of her diagnosis that she "take her borderline personality disorder and everything related to it out of containment." The clinician might better suggest that she take her "difficulty with abandonment and everything related to it" out of containment.

Uncovering the Trauma, Adversity, or Deficit: Using an Image to Unlock a Neural Network

An image can be used to open the neural network containing unresolved emotions. In the case of the ingestive disorders, the clinician can employ a visualized image of the abused substance. A neural network is comprised of memories, cognitions, sensations, and behaviors assembled over developmental time beginning with the earliest experiences of deficit, adversity, or trauma. The ingestive disorders—alcoholism, addictions, nicotine dependency, and eating disorders—are particularly tractable for ACT because the abused substance, whatever it may be, provides an image that allows for access to the neural network. The present writer has described the process of unlocking the neural networks using visualized imagery for alcohol and drugs (Omaha, 1998), nicotine (Omaha, 1999), and food (Omaha, 2000). I originally called this model for addiction *chemotion*, because the abused chemical facilitated emotion regulation. At that time EMDR provided the treatment component, and ACT has evolved out of the fusion of chemotion and EMDR. I have also successfully employed the technique in the case of a process addiction, sexual compulsivity, and Internet pornography, and others have applied the principle to treatment of another process addiction, gambling. In another eating disorder application, the technique has been used to explore anorexic and binge eating clients' cognitive and affective relationships to body fat. The method adapts the Gestalt communication technique to uncover the cognitive and affective transactions at play in the relationship between the abuser and the abused substance. In the following illustration of the method, the transcript of Carly's session is presented. Recall that Carly is a woman in her 40s who sought help for binge eating. She had taken her problem out of containment, and the transcript picks up at that point. Notice that TABS is not used to facilitate this part of the work.

> Clinician: What I'd like you to do now is put all the food you would binge on in that empty chair there [*indicates empty chair facing Carly*] and tell me what you see.
>
> Carly: Oh, wow! All of it? Okay. I see chocolate croissants. Hundreds of them. Hundreds of pints of Ben & Jerry's "Wavy Gravy" ice cream. Trays and trays of baklava. German chocolate cake icing. Brownie mix and brownies. A ton. With lots of walnuts. Chai tea with gallons of half and half. Butter. Butter and sugar sandwiches on white bread. Linzertorts. Godiva chocolate. Bags of M & Ms. Potato chips. Gallons and gallons of milk. That's most of it.
>
> Clinician: As you look at the food in the chair, what is it doing?
>
> Carly: Just sitting there.
>
> Clinician: And what is it saying?
>
> Carly: "Eat me!" "Here I am." "I'm soooo good." "I'll make you feel better." "Come on!" "Don't worry, okay."
>
> Clinician: Excellent. And as you look at the food just sitting there, and it's saying these things, what is it thinking?
>
> Carly: "I'll get you. And I'll keep you, and I'll have my way with you."
>
> Clinician: And as it's thinking "I'll get you," what is it thinking about you?

Carly: "You are a stupid piece of shit!"

Clinician: And as it is thinking you are a stupid piece of shit, what is it feeling itself?

Carly: Oh, it feels haughty. Arrogant. It's self-centered. All-knowing.

Clinician: Tell me, what is the food feeling toward or for you?

Carly: Contempt. It feels contempt for me. Disdain. And repulsion. It feels repulsed by me.

Clinician: Let's shift our focus to you now. As you look at the food in the chair, and it's thinking and feeling these things, what are you thinking?

Carly: You're right. You got me. You tricked me good.

Clinician: And what are you thinking about the food?

Carly: There's too much of it. No wonder I'm fat.

Clinician: As you look at the food just sitting there and thinking and feeling these things, what are you feeling?

Carly: Sad. I feel overwhelmed. Scared, and also mildly repulsed.

Clinician: And what are you feeling for or toward the food?

Carly: I feel longing. Some regret. A lot of sadness.

Clinician: As you look at the food, what's its gender?

Carly: That's interesting. It's both. It's masculine and feminine.

Clinician: I want to review your responses now, and ask you to just notice that what your responses describe is a relationship to food. [*Clinician reviews the food's and Carly's thoughts and feelings.*] As you hold the image of your relationship to food, what I'd like you to do is just review all your relationships going back to your earliest relationships and tell me which ones are like your relationship to food.

Carly: Well, when you come at it this way, it's obvious. It's the same as my relationships with [*Carly names her abusive surrogate mother and the male relative who sexually abused her*].

In ACT for ingestive disorders, the abused substance is termed a *traumaphor*, because its abuse provides for reenactment of archaic traumas and reexperiencing of unresolved emotions assembled with those traumas. Clinicians will note how food reenacted Carly's surrogate mother's arrogance and how Carly felt overwhelmed by food and yet yearned ("longed") for the experience of connection or merger through the agency of the food. In subsequent therapy, Carly was able to uncover her own primary emotion assembled with food, which was anger. A dissociative part removed her anger from awareness. The above protocol, which is called traumaphor associations, began the process of uncovering the causes of Carly's binge eating, and she was subsequently able to resolve the unprocessed traumas from her relationship with her surrogate mother and with her abuser.

Uncovering the Trauma: Floatback or Affect Bridge

Another means for uncovering adversity or trauma employs the affect bridge (Watkins & Watkins, 1997) or "floatback" technique (Browning, 1999). Unresolved memories of trauma or adversity are assembled with unmetabolized emotions in neural networks. Shapiro (1995, 2001) has proposed that the unmetabolized emotions are held in the network in a state specific, excitatory form in which they are more likely to be elicited than other emotions. This property can be exploited by the therapist to trace the network back to the initial trauma. Once a client has cognized an emotion, she can use that awareness to return to a time when the index emotion was experienced. This process is called affect bridging or floating back. The affect bridge is only accessible after the index emotion has been cognized and AMST has been mastered. Prior to that, the client will not have developed the noticing skill (VI) and will be more likely to get stuck in acting out the emotion in the present than be able to use the emotion to trace the emotion back to the time of its trauma coding.

The following case study involving Helen illustrates how a client used a floatback on anger affect to access a pivotal scene from childhood. Recall that Helen, a woman in her 20s, came for help with bulimia. In the segment presented here, the therapy was focusing on her vomiting behavior and the vomit's function in her life. Helen verbalized that the vomit relieved her and in that regard it also comforted her. Something was set free in the act of vomiting, she stated. At the outset of TABS facilitated processing in which the image of vomit was the target, the following exchange occurred.

> **Clinician:** Good. Good. **TABS Off** Deep breath. Let it out, and what comes up now?
> **Helen:** I don't want to let the vomit go.
> **Clinician:** What do you need it for?
> **Helen:** It's my anger.
> **Clinician:** Let's go with that. **TABS On** What I'd like you to do is hold that anger you are aware of right now. Become aware of the sensations that accompany it. Good. Now as you hold the anger and the sensations, I'd like you to float back in time on that anger. Just let it carry you back to an earlier time, maybe the earliest time, that you felt the same anger and the same sensations. Floating back. Floating back. Let me know by raising your index finger when you get there. Good. Just floating back. [*Helen raises her index finger.*] Good. **TABS Off** Deep breath. Let it out, and tell me, what are you seeing?
> **Helen:** I'm just a little kid. Maybe 4 or 5. I don't know. Somewhere in there. My puppy made a mess, and my dad is yelling at me to clean it up. I don't know what to do. Nobody every taught me. Now he's like standing over me and screaming. I'm scared, but I'm also kind of mad, because I don't have any idea what I'm supposed to do. Then he slaps me. In the face. Hard.

As we processed this scene, Helen was able to identify several emotions that were bundled with this traumatic event. She felt hurt, afraid, betrayed, and helpless, as well as angry. She was angry at being hit, and that anger was compounded by the fact that she was hit for not doing something she had never been taught how to do. She was never allowed to express her anger. ACT hypothesizes that Helen's trauma coded anger eventually found expression through the vomiting component of her bulimia. Therapy focused on discharging the archaic anger and assignment of responsibility to her father for slapping her and to her mother for failing to protect her. Processing these events to an adaptive resolution contributed to Helen's recovery from bulimia. It is absolutely essential to understand that Helen was unable to identify anger affect at the outset of her therapy. The AMST protocol provided her with the tools to recognize anger, to tolerate it, and to regulate it. With these skills in place, *then and only then* could she engage the second phase of therapy in which she uncovered the affects that her bulimic behaviors regulated for her.

Affect bridging on disgust affect is illustrated by the following case material. The participant is Betty, the middle-aged client we have met before who came for help with overeating. Once she had developed the skills, Betty's therapy addressed the issue of food. Visualizing her binge food, Betty was able to recognize that she felt disgust directed at herself. She verbalized, "I did this to myself. . . . I feel such self-loathing. . . . How could I do this to myself?" The report picks up at this point.

Clinician: Would you like to discover where this disgust originated?
Betty: Yes.
Clinician: Good. The emotion of disgust is assembled with a whole neural pathway, and you can float back on the emotion to discover other memories that are assembled with the emotion. **TABS On** What I'd like you to do now is become aware of the sensations that signal you that you are feeling disgust. [*Clinician consults case notes.*] You identified clenching in your stomach, anxiety in your chest, rising in your esophagus, and scrunching in your face. Just become aware of those sensations now, and let them carry you back in time. Backward, backward to an earlier time when you felt those same sensations. Let me know with the finger signal when you're there. Good. Just letting the sensations take you back. Back. Good. [*Betty raises her index finger.*] Good. **TABS Off** Deep breath. Let it out, and tell me what are you seeing?
Betty: I'm getting an impression. It's really indistinct. This is from when I was maybe 2. I can see my mother's face all scrunched up. She's spitting words at me. Like venom.

Using ego state approaches facilitated with TABS, the therapy addressed mother's responsibility for the hatred—recall that hatred is composed of anger plus disgust—that she directed at the child Betty. Speaking the voice of her child part, Betty verbalized, "Mommy always told me I was difficult. That I was a pain. That I made her angry. She handled me rough." Facilitated by TABS, Betty was able to redeem her child part's lovability, purity, and innocence. Clinicians reading this case report will notice that as an adult the client reported a "scrunching" in her own face as one of the identifying sensations accompanying disgust affect and that as a two-year-old child she saw her mother's face "scrunched up." The mother's scrunched face broadcast disgust affect at her child, where it assembled with the child's self-representation, expressing itself toward Betty herself, across her life span, through the modality of her own facial scrunching.

At this juncture, suspecting that more traumatic material existed, the clinician asked the client to float forward toward the present on the emotion of disgust. In this part of the therapy, Betty connected with her anger and yearning affects that she had suppressed over the years.

> Clinician: I wonder if there aren't more times your mother treated you badly, and I'd like to find those and process them as well. **TABS On** Still holding the sensations in your esophagus, chest, and face, I'd like to start at age 2 and have you just slowly come back toward the present, looking for other times that you felt these same sensations and the emotion of disgust. Just floating slowly toward the present. Let me know with your finger signal when you get something. Good. [*Betty raises her index finger.*] Good. **TABS Off** Deep breath. Let it out, and tell me what you are seeing now.
>
> Betty: I'm being spanked. Hard. Now I'm about 5. I'm in the corner in the kitchen, and I'm in trouble for something I did. Mom's furious. I'm crying, and Mom's hitting a crying child. What I'm getting in touch with is how angry that child was, not just at how she was treated, but also at how no one came. No one saved her. No one protected her. [*Cries.*]

Using ego state techniques and TABS, Betty was facilitated in verbally expressing her anger at her mother. During this work she got in touch with her intense yearning for connection with her mother, a yearning that was rarely requited due to her mother's abusiveness. She also was able to verbalize her anger at her father for failing to save her, and she held him responsible for his failures. When asked to express her anger through action by hitting a pillow and thereby discharging the anger that was bound in her muscles, Betty's child part verbalized her fear that Betty would lose control as her mother had. Betty was able to assure the child part that she, the adult, now had the skills to manage her anger, and she committed to using those skills to promote assertiveness.

Affect Bridging to Uncover Deficit Experience

When a client's early life was characterized by deficit experience, the affect bridge can be used to find times the adult client felt the index emotion as a child and no one helped him or her to understand, tolerate, recognize, or regulate the emotion. The affect bridging principles are the same as have been illustrated for uncovering trauma and adversity. A middle-aged male client came for problems with depression. He had difficulty motivating himself to leave the house, and as a result his social relationships were impoverished. With help, he identified the qualia of excitement affect as a tingling in his face. The man's clinician facilitated a floatback on the client's excitement emotion. This client quickly accessed childhood scenes in which his parents gave their attention to his older siblings but not to him. "I was basically just parked," he disclosed. This client's interest–excitement affect was rarely aroused, and as a result of this childhood deficit experience, he had difficulty accessing interest affect to motivate current behavior. Therapy took the course of helping the client to recognize his parents' failures and to hold them responsible in a guided visualization. Subsequently he was helped to learn to increase his excitement affect using the gauge resource from skill VII (regulation) and then to import that affect into visualizations of himself going to the movies and arranging for a date. His successes were strengthened, and slowly his self-worth and pride were developed. As his self-concept grew, he took more chances and achieved more successes. Affect bridging helped this client identify times his excitement affect was not stimulated in childhood.

Uncovering Deficit, Trauma, or Adversity Using Sensations

As has been explained, the body uses physical sensations to signal the self system as to what emotion or affect is being experienced. Sometimes trauma coded sensations surface in therapy more readily than the emotions they signal. The affect-oriented clinician can exploit this situation for the client's benefit by employing a "sensation bridge," assisting the client to float back on the sensation to the time of the trauma or to access therapeutically useful material. The case of Peter illustrates the sensation bridge.

Peter is a man of about 40 who came for help with alcoholism. After he had acquired the AMST skills, his therapy turned toward uncovering and resolving the issues that had set his developmental path on a course toward alcoholism. The client had strongly resisted accepting that he was an alcoholic. For Peter, alcohol was the traumaphor that facilitated regulation of current affects that would otherwise have overwhelmed him, reexperiencing of unresolved childhood trauma, and reexperiencing of unprocessed emotions assembled with the old trauma. The second phase of ACT began the uncovering work by exploring Peter's relationship with the alcohol and the affective and cognitive associations involved in that relationship. The uncovering and resolving work continued with traumaphor focused processing, an ACT technique that developed out of an application of EMDR specifically designed for treating substance abuse and alcoholism (Omaha, 1998). ACT has emerged from this early work as my adaptions of EMDR (Shapiro, 2001, 2002) steadily led in the direction of a new psychotherapeutic orientation. In Peter's traumaphor focused processing, he held in mind the image of his traumaphor, alcohol, a negative belief about himself, and an emotion with its body location. First a set of TABS was applied in attempt to move him toward uncovering, and then two sets of the more intensely stimulating eye movements were provided. Neither form of alternating bilateral stimulation instigated any movement. Peter appeared to have a strong restrictor ego state that was opposing the therapy. However, an opening appeared at the completion of the third set of alternating bilateral stimulation when he was asked "What comes up now?" and he responded, "I'm getting a sinking feeling in my stomach." The therapist suggested a floatback on the sensation, and the following material was uncovered.

Clinician: You've told me you're feeling a sinking sensation in your stomach, and I wonder what emotion that tells you you're feeling.

Peter: That would be disgust.

Clinician: What I'd like you to do is just hold the sensation, just keep it in mind, and use it to float back to an earlier time that you experienced the same sensation. **TABS On** Good. Just hold the sensation of sinking in your stomach in awareness. Let that sensation carry you back to an earlier time that you felt the same sensations. Good. Let me know by raising your finger when you've gotten there. Good. [*Peter raises his finger.*] Good. **TABS Off** Deep breath. Let it out, and tell me, what did you get?

Peter: I'm thinking about a time in high school that I realized I had the potential to be a substance abuser. I had done a project on drugs for a psych class, and it got me to stop using drugs for a while. My teachers told me I was mature for my age. Then I started using drugs again, and I didn't hear that any more.

This scene was pivotal for Peter and his recovery, because he uncovered and disclosed for the first time a history of substance abuse. He realized how much disgust his substance abuse elicited in him, and he was able to understand that he also felt disgust about himself for his drinking. This work led directly to identifying times that his father broadcast disgust at him, and he was able to see that he had reenacted and reexperienced this dynamic through years of compulsive drinking. Peter's success in this phase of therapy depended entirely upon his previously having learned AMST. The protocol taught him how to recognize the qualia of disgust affect, and he was able to identify it subsequently in therapy when it surfaced in association with alcohol. The protocol also taught him how to tolerate and regulate this extremely powerful affect, and so his self system knew he had the ability to manage disgust, and the system could consider relinquishing the alcohol that had been the means by which he had managed disgust up to that time. Furthermore, as the therapy progressed, Peter's AMST expertise allowed him to identify the disgust on his father's face that was broadcast at him in childhood.

Uncovering Trauma or Adversity by Giving Sensations a Voice

Sensations can be used in another way besides floatback by giving them a voice. Sensations, especially sensations occurring in the throat, often indicate than an emotion has been trapped or stuck because its expression was denied at an earlier time. The following case material from Fred, the middle-aged man with alcohol and food problems, illustrates how "forbidden" emotions and words can become stuck in the throat and how ACT works with them. In this scenario, food was the traumaphor. The ACT technique described here initially developed out of an adaptation of EMDR (Shapiro, 2001, 2002) for treatment of eating disorders (Omaha, 2000). In this adaptation, Fred held the visualization of food and identified a negative belief about himself, as well as an emotion and a body sensation accompanying it. Holding these elements, processing was initiated with TABS. In the setup for this processing, Fred had identified a negative cognition, "I am flawed," assembled with the food. With TABS facilitation he associated this to his mother's telling him he would "never set the world on fire, but that he would get along." He also identified feeling "distress" and located that feeling in his throat. The following exchange occurred on the fifth set of TABS facilitated processing.

Clinician: TABS Off Deep breath. Let it out, and what comes up now?

Fred: Lots of emotion. Anger and betrayal, all in my throat.

Clinician: Let's let your throat express itself. **TABS On** You've mentioned your throat a couple of times. Your throat held distress. Now you're identifying anger and betrayal. Just let your throat express itself. We'll let the TheraTapper go continually. When you're ready, let your throat speak.

Fred: I feel like I'm being strangled. Like a global hysteria. It wants to say, "I am competent. I am unique. I am purposeful. I do matter. I am trustworthy."

Clinician: Yet you told me your mom said you'd never set the world on fire. Put her in the chair there [*indicates "empty chair"*]. What do you want to say to her?

Fred: Mom, I felt humiliated by you. I felt ignored by you. You ignored me, Mom. I felt unworthy. I so yearned for attention and nurturing. Mom, you never said "I love you" to me. I felt angry at never getting my needs met.

Clinicians will realize how Fred's conflicting emotions locked in his throat—his organ of speech—and caused distress. He identifies anger and betrayal. He felt betrayed by his mother's insensitivity as evidenced in her disparaging remark that he "would never set the world on fire." He felt angry about her betrayal, but as a child he probably felt fearful about expressing that anger and so repressed the emotion. The distress in his throat was caused by the conflict between fear and anger. Once his system could trust that he could manage these emotions— because he had learned the AMST skill set—he was free to uncover and verbalize his anger and betrayal. He could speak the unspeakable to his mother, and thereby free himself. He also was able to assert his worthiness to himself and to a visualized mother who had doubted it.

RESOLVING EXPERIENCES OF TRAUMA, ADVERSITY, OR DEFICIT

After the childhood scenes of deficit, adversity, or trauma have been uncovered, the next goal is to resolve those experiences. In treating rape and combat-related disorders with EMDR, Shapiro (1995, 2001) has stressed the importance of assigning responsibility. She speaks of assisting the client to recognize who was responsible, who was safe, and who had choices. While Shapiro is addressing her therapy to the sequelae of extremely traumatic events, the principle applies equally well to resolving the events of childhood that condition the emergence of maladaptive self structure or personality. Chu (1998) and Watkins and Watkins (1997) discussed the essential component of abreaction in treating posttraumatic stress disorder (PTSD) and other disorders of extreme stress. Following Herman (1992), Chu defined abreaction as "the reconstruction of a comprehensive verbal narrative of traumatic events" (1998, p. 86), to which Watkins and Watkins add the necessity of continuing "until the bound affect has been completely released, and understanding plus mastery is achieved" (1997, p. 119). Like Shapiro's principle of assigning responsibility, the principle of releasing bound affect through abreaction can also be applied to resolving childhood events that have resulted in the emergence of maladaptive personality structures. To summarize then, the essential components for resolving experiences of trauma, adversity, or deficit are: reconstructing a comprehensive narrative of the experience; releasing bound emotion; assigning responsibility; achieving understanding. Collectively these will be termed *abreaction interventions*.

ACT adopts a structured, guided approach to resolution of experiences of trauma, adversity, or deficit. The therapist guides the client's process, structuring the processing and resolution of the trauma coded scenes that have been uncovered. This structured process assures that the client identifies and expresses all the affects that were trauma coded and denied expression at the time of the trauma. The ACT process also assures that the unmet and unresolved emotional needs of child parts are addressed. In this way the child part can re-engage the developmental process that was derailed by the trauma. ACT's structured, guided approach to resolution of deficit, adversity, and trauma addresses the intrapsychic relations between and among ego states and introjects. In particular it attends to the cognitive and affective transactions between and among them.

ACT differs significantly from EMDR in the approach to resolution of trauma. EMDR focuses on the traumatic event itself, while ACT attends to the tramatic and adverse experiences in the context of the self system structure that has emerged as a result of the traumatic, adverse, or deficit experience. Moreover, while EMDR believes the traumatized self has sufficient innate resources to process unresolved trauma with minimal assistance, ACT strongly asserts that many clients lack the resources to adaptively process trauma and that the therapist's role in the therapeutic dyad is to provide guidance as a context within which the client is able to safely and effectively work through his own process.

EMDR (Shapiro, 1995, 2001) is based on the assumption that the self has sufficient innate resources to process a distressing event to an adaptive resolution. Shapiro hypothesized accelerated information processing and an innate self-healing mechanism to explain EMDR's efficacy. She wrote, "The intention of EMDR is to stimulate the dysfunctional material, activate the processing mechanism, and *allow information to flow along its natural course to adaptive resolution*" (Shapiro, 1995, p. 144; emphasis added). The EMDR therapist is instructed to avoid active listening or interpretations and to intervene only when the client gets stuck and begins to "loop" through a scene repeatedly. ACT assumes that the client lacks sufficient resources to process adverse or traumatic material adaptively without guidance. The therapist's responsibility in the context of the therapeutic dyad is to provide guidance and structure for the client's process of resolving the adverse or traumatic material. Clients were often failed in childhood by caregivers who defaulted on their responsibility of providing structure for the child's processing of emotionally charged experiences. As a result, these adults lack well-formed inner representations of caregivers to provide an emotionally supportive structure. The therapeutic dyad implies a contract in which one of the therapist's functions is to assist the client by providing structure for the client's processing of adverse or traumatic childhood events. ACT provides this structure through interventions that are formulated to suit the client's needs and are based on the client's self structure. These interventions include: abreaction intervention, ego state intervention, and conference room intervention. Employment of ego state and conference room interventions has already been introduced in the context of teaching AMST. Watkins and Watkins (1997) described both techniques. While a complete explication of the use of these interventions is beyond the scope of this book, attention is directed here to the affective components.

Abreaction Intervention

The essential elements of an abreactive intervention are: reconstructing a comprehensive narrative of the experience; releasing bound emotion; assigning responsibility; achieving cognitive meaning. Bilateral stimulation, whether provided by the eye movements of EMDR or by TABS, facilitates the abreactive process. When, with TABS facilitation, participant Betty uncovered the traumatic scene in which her mother beat her, she verbalized:

> Betty: I'm being spanked. Hard. Now I'm about 5. I'm in the corner in the kitchen, and I'm in trouble for something I did. Mom's furious. I'm crying, and Mom's hitting a crying child. What I'm getting in touch with is how angry that child was, not just at how she was treated, but also at how no one came. No one saved her. No one protected her. [*Cries.*]

This report constitutes the verbal narrative reconstruction of the traumatic event which is a component of abreaction according to Herman (1992) and Chu (1998). When Betty cries, she is releasing the emotion bound with the event (Watkins & Watkins, 1997), in this case her sadness that no one protected her or rescued her. She subsequently identified another bound emotion, anger, that she was able to release both verbally and through hitting a pillow. Part of her anger was directed at her father for failing to protect her from her mother's rage. She released this as well. Once the bound emotion was released, Betty could more accurately observe her mother and her mother and father's relationship. She said that her mother's own childhood abuse impacted her life and determined what kind of parenting she was capable of giving Betty. She understood her father's alcoholism and how he feared his wife and retreated into drinking to avoid her. As cognitive meaning emerged, Betty worked her way through this traumatic event. Emotion provides the key to this working through process. Apparently bound emotion keeps the events in emotion memory, and when the emotion is released, the events can finally be transferred to declarative memory (Siegel, 2002b), and trauma processing is completed.

Recognizing Broadcast Emotion

When a childhood experience coded by trauma or adversity has been uncovered, the therapist can often help the client recognize how the parent broadcast a powerful negative emotion at the child. This can happen when the client has cognized the emotion himself and can then recognize its display by the parent in the recollected childhood experience. In the following vignette, Peter, the alcoholic, uncovered a scene that was traumatic for him, recognized the broadcast emotion, and identified his own bound emotion. The vignette also illustrates how he reached an understanding, a central component of abreaction, by verbalizing the consequences of his father's actions. Peter uncovered this traumatic scene through an affect bridge on the emotion of contempt. In this scene he is eight-years-old. TABS is being provided continuously throughtout this scene.

Clinician: Tell me what you're seeing.

Peter: I'm walking into the living room. My dad is already there, and his paper isn't where it's supposed to be. I forgot to bring it in. He starts yelling at me. He's saying, "I work real hard. All you have to do is this one thing, and you didn't do it!" He's shouting. His voice is angry. I get teary and say I'm sorry, but underneath I am angry. I go and get the paper and bring it to him, and then I go to my room.

Clinician: Go back to the part of the scene where your father is yelling at you that he works really hard and all you have to do is bring the paper and you failed to do it. Look at his face. Look carefully. Tell me what emotion you see on his face. What is he feeling for you.

Peter: Disappointment. Contempt.

Clinician: And what is the 8-year-old you feeling?

Peter: Shame. He shamed me. He made me cry. And angry. But I couldn't show it.

Clinician: As you look at the scene, who's the adult, and who's the child?

Peter: Well, he's the adult. I'm the child.

Clinician: And who is responsible for raising the child?

Peter: He is.

Clinician: So then, who is responsible for making the child cry, for shaming the child, and for broadcasting contempt at the child?

Peter: He is.

Clinician: What I'd like you to do now is put him in the empty chair there [clinician indicates an empty office chair] and tell him that.

Peter: You didn't have to yell at me, Dad. I was only a little kid. You shamed me, Dad. I felt unworthy. Like you didn't love me. I hold you responsible for that. You were the adult, the parent. You and I could have gone out and gotten the paper together.

Clinician: Can you tell him what the consequences were for you, what happened to you when he directed all that disappointment and contempt at you?

Peter: Yeah. Dad, I never felt worthy. I hated myself. I always compared myself to other kids, and I felt lacking. If I was a disappointment to you, I must be disappointing. If you felt contempt for me, I must have been contemptible.

In this recollected scene, Peter's father broadcast contempt at his son. Contempt has significant features in common with its close relative disgust. The broadcast contempt assembled with Peter's self-representation. His self system reacted with shame to the child part at its core holding the contempt. Peter constructed a false self identity to mediate relations with the world and to defend this contempt and shame-filled core from being discovered by the world. This identity was a highly trained, very competent professional. Although Peter had removed his father's broadcast contempt from awareness, it continued to function from deep within his unconscious where it was assembled with his self-as-child representation. Peter and I verified this when he said, "I am contemptible" as he gazed at a visualized heap of thousands of empty beer cans in the traumaphor associations exercise.

Working with Parental Introjects

The case of Peter illustrates some of the key elements in resolving current distress that arose in the context of the child–caretaker dyad. The bound emotion must be abreacted. Often the primary bound emotion and the first to surface is sadness, expressed through tears. The adult child has carried enormous sadness over the years, because some part of the self system is aware of the loss he has suffered as a consequence of "things that didn't happen and should have" or "things that never should have happened and did." Anger is often next and is usually expressed verbally. Clients can be facilitated in releasing more bound anger through punching a pillow. Other emotions that may need to be unbound are fear, disgust, shame, and contempt.

Clinicians can assist their clients to develop the understanding required for a thorough abreactive intervention. It must by emphasized that the clinician does not supply that understanding, but rather supplies the structure and guidance the client may need to achieve it. Assignment of responsibility to the parent is one component of understanding. Verbalizing effects of parental actions on the child is another. A third entails verbalizing the consequences of the parent's actions for the child across developmental time. It is sometimes necessary for the clinician to be prepared to define for the client the difference between blaming the parent and holding the parent responsible for his or her part. Blaming is a way of justifying current behaviors in terms of past injuries. Holding responsible is a way of "just noticing" the parent's actions. As Alice Miller (1984) wrote:

> From this experience the parents as they once were emerge more and more clearly: they are not so strong as they then appeared, but neither are they so powerless as they are now that they are older; not so clever as they pretended to be, but also not so stupid as the patient experienced them in his emotional reliving of the past; not so bad as many of their actions indicated, but also not so good as the patient wanted to believe; and above all, not so truthful and trustworthy as they wanted their child to believe— and as the patient needed to think they were. (p. 206)

For reasons having to do with the countertransference, some therapists may resist helping the client hold his parents responsible for the quality of caregiving they dispensed. Miller (1984) suggested the therapist be "an advocate, whose concern is not to defend and protect the father, but to stand by the patient . . ." (p. 169).

Another key element in resolving parental introjects appears to be facilitating separation from the parental introject. A client who reenacts childhood scenarios of deficit, adversity, or trauma that were the responsibility of one or both parents often carries the image or representation of the parent in the mind in a form that is not separated from, not individuated from the self-representation. ACT believes it is important to assist the client to complete the separation–individuation process by moving the parent out of the client's head and placing the parent in an empty chair. If the parental introject is first met in a visualized scene, or if it appears in a conference room visualization, I encourage clients to place the parent in the empty chair and then to verbalize the statements of responsibility and consequences. Upon completion of the abreactive intervention, I encourage the client to verbalize a positive cognition of the form, "I've put you in the chair, and I will not allow you to come back inside me again." Once the client has metabolized the adverse or traumatic experiences and separated from the parent, then the possibility exists for developing an ambivalent image of the parent.

Resources for the Ego Function of Synthesis

Resolution of a parental introject carrying deficit, adversity, or trauma is completed when the client can form an ambivalent representation of the parent. Creating this ambivalent image requires the synthetic ego function. In a healthy childhood, the synthetic ego function develops during the third and fourth year of life. Synthesis provides for ambivalence, the hallmark denoting attainment of the developmental stage of object constancy. The child who has achieved object constancy is able to hold images of both the "good" mother and the "bad" mother, the rewarding and nonrewarding object relations unit, at the same time (i.e., ambivalently). The concrete, either–or, black or white thinking of childhood is replaced with flexibility (i.e., both–and thinking). Many children of deficit, adversity, or trauma fail to develop ambivalently held images of important caretakers. Consequently, as adults they remain stuck in black or white perceptions of not only parents, but also the self as well as significant others in relationships. This type of thinking produces stress in relationships, because the unmatured self acts toward others from an undeveloped foundation, often projecting either the "good" parent or the "bad" parent onto the pair-bond partner.

Once a client has processed the significant traumas, deficits, or adversities that have defined and conditioned the client's development, the clinician can assist her to produce an image that promotes an ambivalent perception of the parent. Bound emotion must be released before ambivalence can be attained. The ambivalence skill may not always be applicable. If a parent has sexually or physically abused a child, the "good" parent may be completely outweighed by the "bad" parent. Similarly, if a parent has provided unremittingly deficient or adverse caregiving, the client may not be able to recall any good images. When this situation arises in therapy, the clinician can interrogate the client about his or her wishes. Language like the following can give the client permission to decide what she wants to do regarding synthesizing an ambivalence image.

> Clinician: You've worked through a lot of material regarding your relationship to your father in therapy here, and I want to offer you an opportunity

now. What you do with it is up to you, and you don't need to make a decision now. I could help you create an image that embodies both parts of your father, the good parts and the bad. Then you'd be able to hold him ambivalently. He wouldn't be *either* bad, *or* good. Because of the way images work, he could be *both* bad *and* good. The image could be helpful, because many times you appear to deal with your boyfriend as either all bad or all good, and if you could hold your father ambivalently, probably you could extend that to your other relationships. What do you think?

Client: I see where you're going, but I'm just not ready to do that now. My father beat me, and he did bad things to me sexually. He was a sick man, and I'm not ready to forgive him. He wasn't that good either. Like maybe once or twice over my whole growing up period can I even remember him being nice. That's not enough. The work we've done here has allowed me to separate my boyfriend from my father. I'm not worried about that any more.

Clinician: I hear you saying you're not ready to develop an image for your father that would allow you to perceive him ambivalently, and that's fine. The choice is yours. If at some time in the future you did want to do that, please bring it up again.

In the counterexample that follows, Fred agrees to developing an image of ambivalence for his mother. Recall that Fred was a middle-aged man who had come for help with alcohol and eating. After he had completed working through the issues from childhood that pertained to his mother, the following exchange occurred.

Clinician: You've done such good work here. You were able to express the anger you had held for so many years that your mother did not meet your legitimate needs in childhood. You put her in the empty chair, and you assigned responsibility. I wonder if now you would be willing to develop an image that would allow you to hold both the bad parts and the good parts of her in one representation. In that way she wouldn't be either good or bad, but she could be both at once.

Fred: I'm willing to try.

Clinician: Excellent. What I'd like to do first is list your mother's positive and negative qualities.

Fred: Well, on the negative side she was dismissing. She distanced herself from me, and she could be verbally very abusive. She was inconsiderate. She was extremely self-centered. It was all about her. And she was insensitive.

   On the positive side, she was organized. She ran a business. She was a great hostess. Worldly. She was interested in the world. At the end of her life, she did develop some insight and actually expressed some remorse.

Clinician: Fine. In this part I'd like you to just be receptive and allow an image to form all on its own. **TABS On** Now what I'd like you to do is just let an image surface that allows you to hold the positive and negative qualities of your mother, an image that carries both the good and the not-so-good in one representation. The part that was a good hostess and was organized as well as the part that was self-absorbed and dismissing. Let the image come up, and let me know with the finger signal when you get it. [*Fred raises his index finger.*] Good. **TABS Off** Deep breath. Let it out, and tell me what did you get?

Fred: Tell me if this is right. I'm seeing this photo of her from college, some kind of social event. The college part conveys the organized side, the hostess side. But in the picture, she's aloof. She's separate, off to the side. It's all about her, and the others are just there to make her look good.

Clinician: That's an excellent image. Now we'll install it. **TABS On** Call up again the picture of your mom from college. Notice that in this one photo you can see both aspects of her. The good side that is worldly, organized, a fantastic hostess, and the not-so-good side that is self-centered and inconsiderate. See now how this photo, this picture, allows you to hold your mother ambivalently. You can see both sides of her in the one image, and now and forever more this is how she will appear to you. Both good and not-so-good united in the one image, positive and negative brought together in the one photo. Good. **TABS Off** Deep breath. Let it out, and what comes up now?

Fred: A feeling of peace. I feel a connectivity with her that I could never feel before.

Working with Ego States

Ego states often emerge in the self structure to handle distressing emotions or experiences. These fragments of the personality structure may develop more or less autonomous behavioral management scripts, cognitive management scripts, dissociative scripts, or they may find substances that facilitate affect management. The more severe the distress that must be managed, the more powerful the ego state becomes, and the more it dominates the behavior of the system. The obsessive–compulsive disorder (OCD) may be conceptualized as having an OCD ego state that is activated by distress and that engages in behaviors which when repeated decrease the distress. The alcoholic has an ego state that drinks, the cocaine addict has an ego state that uses, the nicotine addict has an ego state that smokes or chews. As a class, I call these *symptom-expressing ego states* (SEESs). The binge eater, has a binge SEES. The bulimic has both a binge SEES and a purge SEES. The anorexic has a restrictor SEES.

Once the client has uncovered and resolved the deficit, adversity, or trauma that set him on a developmental pathway toward the pathology that brought him to therapy, the original function of the SEES is no longer necessary. Affect centered therapy works with these ego states to develop a new function for them, that of sentinel or bodyguard. Using a conference room, the SEES will be brought forward. By this time, the client will be cognizant of the affective function the SEES has served. The therapist assists a negotiation with TABS facilitation between the client and the ego state. The client acknowledges the ego state for its help over the years and thanks it. The therapist determines that the ego state knows the client now has the skills and tools to manage the stressful affects. The client asserts that he will from now on manage those affects, and the ego state transfers that responsibility to the client. Then the client asks the ego state to take a new job description and become a sentinel or bodyguard and to alert the client to when he is feeling the index emotion. Ego states feel honored to be asked to take this responsibility, and they are usually tired and also pleased at the client's growth. A signal is arranged, and the client agrees to look for it and to use his skills when it is given.

Affect and emotion transactions are central to working with ego states. In phase I, AMST teaches the client to recognize, tolerate, and regulate key affects that the SEES has emerged over developmental time to manage. In phase II, the client uncovers the deficits, adversities, or traumas and their associated affects and emotions that the SEES was regulating. Phase II therapy focuses on adaptively resolving these experiences. With AMST in place, the client can now take responsibility for managing affects and emotions himself that the SEES previously managed. The SEES takes a new function as sentinel or bodyguard to alert the client's self system to when the problem affect or emotion has surfaced so the client can use his skills.

Redeeming the Child Part

ACT reaches its apogee when it redeems the damaged child part that has functioned from a covert position at the personality's core. As the client processes the adverse and traumatic experiences of her childhood to an adaptive resolution, it becomes possible to address the needs of her child part. As has been noted, the child part often bears the staggering responsibility of holding the system's unworthiness and unlovability. The system is able to function, however maladaptively, in large measure because the child part holds the system's unworthiness and thereby sequesters it. Before therapy, when this unworthiness was triggered, the system would often decompensate, indicating the extraordinary power of the unworthiness emotion construct. This must be stressed and cannot be overemphasized: The redemption intervention can only be undertaken after all the trauma and adversity has been processed adaptively and the adult self has taken responsibility for managing formerly unresolved emotions.

One purpose of the redemption intervention is to free the child part from affects like disgust, shame, anger, and contempt that were broadcast at the child. Another purpose of the intervention is to relieve the child part of emotions that were elicited by inappropriate verbal, physical, or sexual actions of an adult or caregiver. The redemption intervention also unburdens the child part of the onus of responsibility for the bad things that happened. Children often believe they caused the abuse or that they deserved it; often perpetrators or placaters blame the child. Sexually abused children whose only comfort comes from the abuser often at some point willingly go to the abuser, and the child part must be relieved of responsibility for this behavior too through the redemption intervention. In this intervention, which takes place in the conference room and is facilitated by

TABS, the child part is invited to come forward. The image of the child is strengthened. Then the therapist guides the client in redeeming the child part's lovability, worth, innocence, and purity. The adult self tells the child part, "It was not your fault." A correct attribution of responsibility is made for the emotions that were broadcast at the child and elicited within the child and for actions perpetrated on the child. The clinician should ask for permission to speak to the child and should then ask the child to repeat the affirmations and attributions it has heard.

RELAPSE PREVENTION

As the client transitions out of the second phase of ACT, a new self structure is emerging, one that is more adaptive and functions more positively in a variety of contexts. A goal of the end of the second phase of therapy is solidification of the new self structure. A useful tool for achieving the aim of personality consolidation is relapse prevention, which derives in part from the work of Marlatt (1985) and in part from Shapiro's instructions for client log keeping (1995). Shapiro's log is a "journal of the negative thoughts, situations, dreams, and memories" (p. 73). As used here, relapse prevention asks the client to identify future situations in which a relapse to old behaviors might occur. The clinician suggests the client describe at least five such situations. For each situation, the client is then asked to identify the trigger in the situation, to describe an image that surfaces, and to name a cognition, an emotion, and a sensation the client might have in the situation. In the language of EMDR, these identifying qualities are referred to as TICES. Next, the client is asked to name the recovery skills she has learned in her therapy. These skills include her affect regulation skills as well as her quality resources and alliance resources. Her ego state sentinels should also be named. The clinician can take this opportunity to develop other tools that would fall under the heading of case management. For example, the binge eating client would be encouraged to realize that calling her sponsor at Overeaters Anonymous is a recovery skill she can employ. The alcoholic should identify meeting attendance or using his phone list as a recovery skill. The anorexic should name her dietitian as a recovery resource.

Once the situation, the TICES components, and the recovery skills have been identified, the clinician employs TABS to facilitate the client in creating an adaptive future visualization in which she sees herself in the potential relapse situation, becomes aware of the TICES components, and visualizes herself using her recovery skills. The clinician develops a relapse prevention positive cognition and installs it with TABS facilitation such as, "I am learning to use my recovery skills to avoid a relapse to old behaviors." The relapse prevention skill can be used for addictions, alcoholism, smoking, eating disorders, as well as relapse to any Axis I or II behavior. When the client appears for the next session, the clinician should inquire, "What is different since our last session?" and if the client has successfully used her skills and avoided a relapse to old behaviors, this success should be strengthened with TABS facilitation. As the client recalls her successful recognition of the potential relapse situation and visualizes herself using her tools and succeeding, the clinician can install a positive cognition such as, "I can use my recovery skills to maintain my recovery." Another positive cognition would be, "I am worthy of using my recovery skills."

The clinician could complete the sequence by asking the client to repeat, "I feel proud of my accomplishment."

THE OPTIMAL FUTURE SELF-VISUALIZATION

Napier (1990) has created an excellent tool that can be developed at the close of phase II of ACT to furnish the client with goals and directions arising from a deep place within. In this visualization, which can be facilitated with continuous TABS, the clinician first asks the client to return to the safe place. The client is asked to develop a receptive state of mind and to "just allow an image of the self you are becoming to emerge from your deep unconscious." If, for example, the client's safe place is a beach, the clinician can say, "Just notice that way down the beach, a figure is appearing, walking slowly toward you. This is your optimal future self. There is nothing you need to do but allow this image to appear." Once the figure has appeared and is facing the client, the clinician can ask the client to notice how the gains the client has made in therapy are manifesting themselves in the optimal future self. "Notice how self-confidence and self-worth appear in the face and posture of your optimal future self," the therapist might say. A central element of the visualization entails asking the client to visualize herself stepping into the body of the optimal future self for a brief period of time. Once inside the body, the clinician can suggest the client notice how the optimal future self manages key emotions like fear, anger, shame, and disgust, as well as joy and excitement. For the eating disordered client, the clinician might say, "Notice how your optimal future self experiences her stomach and how she thinks about and relates to food." For clients who experienced less than optimal caregiving from parents, the therapist might suggest, "Notice how your optimal future self thinks about your mother and your father." The creative therapist will enjoy the opportunity afforded by this visualization to enumerate and solidify the gains the client has made in the therapy. The client then steps out of the body of the optimal future self and stands facing it, and the clinician next instructs, "If it feels right, then I'd like you to let an affirmation come up from your deepest self. If it feels right, I'd like you to say 'Yes!' to this self that you are becoming." Separation follows, and the clinician may say:

Now it's time to part. It's time for your optimal future self to return to the future. She begins to walk away, returning to the future from which she comes. Realize that with each day, you will come closer and closer to her, until one day you will know that you have become your optimal future self.

THE FUTURE OF AFFECT CENTERED THERAPY

Like the optimal future self, the future of ACT may be visualized. Some progress has already been made toward manifesting the principles of ACT. A coherent approach for treatment of eating disorders has been completed, as has a therapeutic protocol for alcoholism, addictions, and nicotine dependency. Preliminary

single case design studies appear to support the effectiveness of ACT for these disorders, but much more empirical research remains to be done. While the basic
principles will not change, their application will certainly develop as clinicians
learn to tailor them to the needs of the more severely traumatized clients.

The severest test of ACT will be the personality and dissociative disorders.
Can therapy based on remediating emotion dysregulation and adaptive resolution of adversity coded and trauma coded experience result in the emergence of a
more coherent, positively functioning self structure? How much facilitation in the
form of restructuralizing interventions will be required, and what form will these
interventions take? The basic shape of interventions designed to promote restruc-
turalization is already apparent in the ego state interventions of the AMST and of
phase II of ACT. Work in this area is only beginning and will require contributions from many skilled therapists already experienced in working with these
client populations, therapists who are open-minded and willing enough to learn
affect focused principles and restructure their own clinical approaches. If the
effort results in improved outcomes for these populations, then the challenge will
have been worth the work and emotional distress required to meet it.

Application of the principles of ACT to couples is a fascinating and virtually
untouched area. Uncovering, sorting through, and clarifying the affective transactions in the adult pair-bond should provide the clinician with satisfying challenges. In my own work, I have had the opportunity to teach the AMST skills set
individually to both members of a marital dyad, then to assist each member individually through a second phase of uncovering and adaptively resolving childhood trauma and adversity. The work culminated when the dyad came together
in the counseling office, and the partners began to work on their relationship issues
from a basis of self-aware emotion management skills held in common. The couple
recognized how affective transactions derived from childhood patterns had manifested in their marriage and prevented the intimacy they each desired.

The thrust of ACT is toward healing the children. For the adult who experienced a deficit, adverse, or traumatic childhood, this translates into remediating
the deficits, adaptively processing the adversity and trauma, and finally redeeming the inner child. This emerging school of psychotherapy must now develop
skills and tools to teach emotion regulation to the children who are still enmeshed
in compromised parent–child dyads and families. Additionally, age specific tools
must be developed for adolescents, a population that may be amenable to change
as a simple fact of the neurophysiological plasticity of adolescence. The challenge
here is made more difficult, of course, just because of that plasticity, because many
adolescents tend to defend against the nearly psychotic experience of adolescence
through oppositional–defiant behaviors. Working with children and working with
adolescents in most cases means working with families. If the affective transactions
occurring in an adult pair-bond are complicated, those taking place among parents and children in the context of the family are recomplicated again and again,
the more so as societal factors, divorce, remarriage, financial insecurity, alcohol,
drugs and a host of other vicissitudes of modern life impact the family unit.

A final challenge for ACT is to devise programs to deliver training in affect
recognition, tolerance, and regulation to nonclinical populations. Through coaching

centers and programs for schools and the workplace, delivery of these skills holds the promise of improving the lives of children today and even further improving the lives of children in generations to come. The structure of society is an emergent function conditioned by the same dynamic systems principles as the emergence of an individual's self structure. The positive changes we institute today multiply and remultiply across the generational time span until some optimal future time when there will be no children of deficit experience, no children of adverse experience, and no children of traumatic experience.

Appendices

Appendix A: AMST Worksheet

Patient name: _____

Skill I

Container: _____

_____

Install valve (check): [ ]   Install sign (check): [ ]

Percent contained: [ ]   Quality Resource: _____

Alliance Resource: _____

Ego State (Image, Age, Name, Function): _____

_____

Percent contained: [ ]

Skill II

Safe Place: _____

    Visual: _____

    Auditory: _____

    Olfactory: _____

    Tactile: _____

VoC ("I Am Safe"): [ ]   Quality Resource: _____

Alliance Resource: _____

Ego State (Image, Age, Name Function): _____

_____

VoC ("I Am Safe"): [ ]

VoC ("I Feel Safe"): [ ]   Quality Resource: _____

Alliance Resource: _____

Ego State (Image, Age, Name, Function): _____

_____

VoC ("I Feel Safe"): [ ]   Safety sensation _____
                          body location: _____

Patient name: _____

Skill III

Target Affect: _____

Target Scene: _____

_____

Sensation: _____

Body location: _____

    VoC ("The (name sensation) in My (body
    location) Tells Me I Am Feeling (Target Affect)"): ☐

Quality Resource: _____

Alliance Resource: _____

Ego State (Image, Age, Name, Function): _____

_____

    VoC ("The (name sensation) in My (body
    location) Tells Me I Am Feeling (Target Affect)"): ☐

Skill IV

Grounding Resource: _____

Grounding sensation: _____

Body location: _____

    VoC ("The (name sensation) in My (body location) Signals
    Me to Let Down My (name of grounding resource)"): ☐

Skill V

    VoC ("I Can Stay Grounded and Present
    While I'm Feeling (Target Affect).") ☐

Skill VI

    VoC ("I Can Just Notice Myself Feeling (Target Affect).") ☐

Skill VII

Disposal Resource: _____

    VoC ("I Am Learning to Decrease My (Target Affect).") ☐

Patient name: _____

Skill VII,
continued

Positive Affect: _____

Sensation: _____

Body location: _____

    VoC ("The (name sensation) in My (body
location) Tells Me I Am Feeling (positive affect)"):   [   ]

Guage Resource: _____

    VoC ("I Am Learning to Increase My (positive affect).") [   ]

- -

Target Affect: _____ Target Scene: _____

_____

Sensation: _____

Body location: _____

Skill III [ ] VoC ("The name sensation) in My (body
location) Tells Me I Am Feeling (Target Affect)"): [   ]

    Skill IV [ ]   Skill V [ ]   Skill VI [ ]

Skill VII [ ] VoC ("I Am Learning to Decrease/Increase My (Target Affect).")[   ]

- -

Target Affect: _____ Target Scene: _____

_____

Sensation: _____

Body location: _____

Skill III [ ] VoC ("The (name sensation) in My (body
location) Tells Me I Am Feeling (Target Affect)"): [   ]

    Skill IV [ ]   Skill V [ ]   Skill VI [ ]

Skill VII [ ] VoC ("I Am Learning to Decrease/Increase My (Target Affect).")[   ]

Patient name: _____

Target Affect: _____ Target Scene: _____

_____

Sensation: _____

Body location: _____

Skill III ☐ VoC ("The (name sensation) in my (body location) tell me I am feeling (Target Affect)"): ☐

Skill IV ☐   Skill V ☐   Skill VI ☐

Skill VII ☐ VoC ("I am learning to decrease/increase my (Target Affect)." ☐

- -

Target Affect: _____ Target Scene: _____

_____

Sensation: _____

Body location: _____

Skill III ☐ VoC ("The (name sensation) in my (body location) tell me I am feeling (Target Affect)"): ☐

Skill IV ☐   Skill V ☐   Skill VI ☐

Skill VII ☐ VoC ("I am learning to decrease/increase my (Target Affect)." ☐

- -

Target Affect: _____ Target Scene: _____

_____

Sensation: _____

Body location: _____

Skill III ☐ VoC ("The (name sensation) in my (body location) tell me I am feeling (Target Affect)"): ☐

Skill IV ☐   Skill V ☐   Skill VI ☐

Skill VII ☐ VoC ("I am learning to decrease/increase my (Target Affect)." ☐

Patient name: _____

Target Affect: _____ Target Scene: _____

Sensation: _____

Body location: _____

Skill III [ ] VoC ("The (name sensation) in My (body
location) Tells Me I Am Feeling (Target Affect)"): [   ]

Skill IV [ ]   Skill V [ ]   Skill VI [ ]

Skill VII [ ] VoC ("I Am Learning to Decrease/Increase My (Target Affect)." [   ]

- -

Target Affect: _____ Target Scene: _____

Sensation: _____

Body location: _____

Skill III [ ] VoC ("The (name sensation) in My (body
location) Tells Me I Am Feeling (Target Affect)"): [   ]

Skill IV [ ]   Skill V [ ]   Skill VI [ ]

Skill VII [ ] VoC ("I Am Learning to Decrease/Increase My (Target Affect)." [   ]

- -

Target Affect: _____ Target Scene: _____

Sensation: _____

Body location: _____

Skill III [ ] VoC ("The (name sensation) in My (body
location) Tells Me I Am Feeling (Target Affect)"): [   ]

Skill IV [ ]   Skill V [ ]   Skill VI [ ]

Skill VII [ ] VoC ("I Am Learning to Decrease/Increase My (Target Affect)." [   ]

Patient name: _____

Ego State (Image, Age, Name, Function): _____

_____

Ego State (Image, Age, Name, Function): _____

_____

Ego State (Image, Age, Name, Function): _____

_____

Ego State (Image, Age, Name, Function): _____

_____

Ego State (Image, Age, Name, Function): _____

_____

Ego State (Image, Age, Name, Function): _____

_____

- -

Safe Face (Qualities, Image): _____

_____

_____

_____

- -

Synthesis Image: _____

_____

- -

Optimal Future Self Visualization: _____

_____

_____

Appendix B

AMST Flow Diagram and Decision Tree

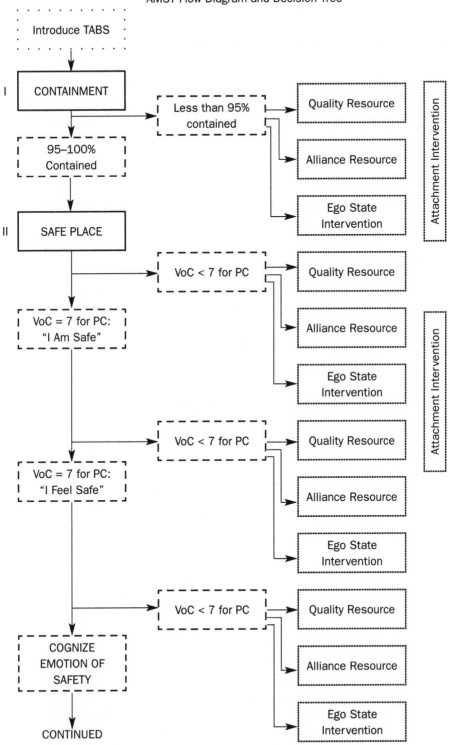

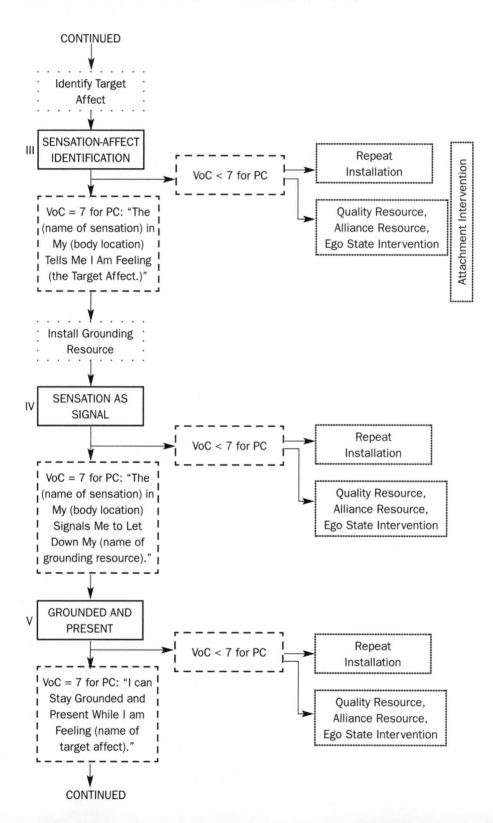

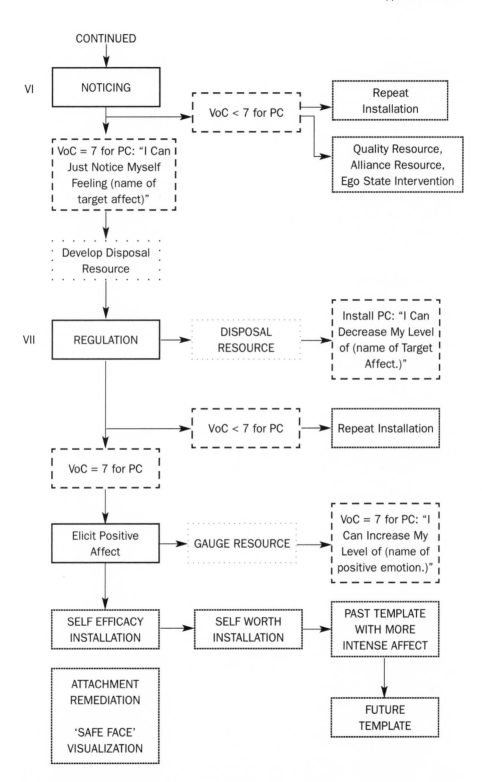

References

Aguilar, B., Sroufe, L. A., Egeland, B., & Carlson, E. (2000). Distinguishing the early-onset/persistent and adolescence-onset antisocial behavior types: From birth to 16 years. *Development and Psychopathology, 12,* 109–132.

Ainsworth, M. D. S., Blehar, M., Waters, E., & Wall, S. (1978). *Patterns of attachment: A psychological study of the strange situation.* Hillsdale, NJ: Erlbaum.

Allen, J. P., & Land, D. (1999). Attachment in adolescence. In J. Cassidy & P. R. Shaver (Eds.), *Handbook of attachment: Theory, research, and clinical applications* (pp. 319–335). New York: Guilford Press.

Amaro, J., Nieves, R., Johannes, S. W., & Cabeza, N. M. L. (1999). Substance abuse treatment: Critical issues and challenges in the treatment of Latina women. *Hispanic Journal of Behavioral Sciences, 21,* 266–282.

American Medical Association (1973). *Manual on alcoholism* (2nd ed). Chicago: Author.

American Psychiatric Association (1994). *Diagnostic and statistical manual of mental disorders* (4th ed.). Washington, DC: Author.

Anda, R. G., Croft, J. B., Felitti, V. J., Nordenberg, D., Giles, W. H., Williamson, D. F., & Giovino, G. A. (1999). Adverse childhood experiences and smoking during adolescence and adulthood. *Journal of the American Medical Association, 282,* 1652–1658.

Andres, C. (2002). Molecular genetics and animal models in autistic disorder. *Brain Research Bulletin, 57,* 109–119.

Averill, J. R. & More, T. A. (1993). Happiness. In M. Lewis & J. M. Haviland (Eds.), *Handbook of emotions* (pp. 617–629). New York: Guilford Press.

Avishai-Eliner, S., Gilles, E. E., Eghbal-Ahmadi, M., Bar-El, Y., & Baram, T. Z. (2001). Altered regulation of gene and protein expression of hypothalamic–pituitary–adrenal axis components in an immature rat model of chronic stress. *Journal of Neuroendocrinology, 13,* 799–807.

Barkley, R. A., & Edwards, G. (1998). Paul: An instructive case of attention deficit hyperactivity disorder. In R. P. Halgin & S. K. Whitbourne (Eds), *A casebook in abnormal psychology: From the files of experts* (pp. 212–234). New York: Oxford University Press.

Beck, A. T. (1976). *Cognitive therapy and emotional disorders*. New York: International Universities Press.

Bellivier, F., Leboyer, M., Courtet, P., Buresi, C., Beaufils, B., Samolyk, D., Allilaire, J. F., Feingold, J., Mallet, J., & Malafosse, A. (1998). Association between the tryptophan hydroxylase gene and manic-depressive illness. *Archives of General Psychiatry, 55*, 33–37.

Bice Brousard, D. (1998). Attachment to parents as mediator and/or moderator of psychyosocial functioning among young adults with alcoholic fathers. *Dissertation Abstracts International 59(4):* 1840-B.

Blanck, G., & Blanck, R. (1994). *Ego psychology: Theory and practice* (2nd ed.). New York: Columbia Univesity Press.

Blumberg, S. H., & Izard, C. E. (1985). Affective and cognitive characteristics of depression in 10- and 11-year-old children. *Journal of Personality and Social Psychology, 49*, 194–202.

Blumberg, S. H., & Izard, C. E. (1986). Discriminating patterns of emotions in 10- and 11-year-old children's anxiety and depression. *Journal of Personality and Social Psychology, 51*, 852–857.

Bowen, M. (1978). *Family therapy in clinical practice*. New York: Aronson.

Bowie, S. I., Silverman, D. C., Kalick, S. M., & Edbril, S. D. (1990). Blitz rape and confidence rape: Implications for clinical intervention. *American Journal of Psychotherapy, 44*, 180–188.

Bowlby, J. (1969). *Attachment and loss* (Vol. 1). New York: Basic Books.

Bradshaw, J. (1988). *Healing the shame that binds you*. Deerfield Beach, FL: Health Communications.

Braun, B. G. (1988a). The BASK model of dissociation. *Dissociation, 1:1*, 4–23.

Braun, B. G. (1988b). The BASK model of dissociation. Treatment. *Dissociation, 1:2*, 16–23.

Briere, J., & Runtz, M. (1988). Post sexual abuse trauma: Data and implications for clinical practice. *Journal of Interpersonal Violence, 2*, 367–379.

Briere, J., & Runtz, M. (1993). Childhood sexual abuse: Long-term sequelae and implications for psychological assessment. *Journal of Interpersonal Violence, 8*, 312–330.

Brown, N. (2001). *Children of the self-absorbed: A grownup's guide to getting over narcissistic parents*. Oakland, CA: New Harbinger.

Brown, S., & Gilman, S. (2003). EMDR Research Project. Retrieved August 12, 2003, from http://www.lifeforceservices.com/research.php

Browning, C. (1999, November). Floatback and float-forward: Techniques for linking past, future, and present. *EMDRIA Newsletter*, 12–34.

Browning, C., & Omaha, J. (2001, June) *Affect management skills training (AMST): Basic and advanced techniques*. Workshop presented at the meeting of the EMDR International Association, Austin, TX.

Brunson, K. L., Eghbal-Ahmadi, M., Bender, R., Chen, Y., & Baram, T. Z. (2001). Long-term, progressive hippocampal cell loss and dysfunction induced by early-life administration of corticotropin-releasing hormone reproduce the effects of early-life stress. *Proceedings of the National Academy of Sciences USA, 98*, 8856–8861.

Buss, A. H., & Perry, M. (1992). The aggression questionnaire. *Journal of Personality & Social Psychology, 63*, 452–459.

Calder, A. J., Lawrence, A. D., & Young, A. W. (2001). Neuropsychology of fear and loathing. *Nature Reviews, Neuroscience, 2*, 352–363.

Camlibel, A. R. (2000). Affectivity and attachment: A comparison of binge drinking and non-binge drinking first-year college students. *Dissertation Abstracts International 60(11):* 5757-B.

Carey, T. C., Carey, M. P., & Kelley, M. L. (1997). Differential emotions theory: Relative contribution of emotion, cognition, and behavior to the prediction of depressive symptomatology in non-referred adolescents. *Journal of Clinical Psychology, 53,* 25–34.

Carlson, E. B. (1997). *Trauma assessments: A clinician's guide.* New York: Guilford Press.

Caspi, Q., McClay, J., Moffitt, T. E., Mill, J., Martin, J., Craig, I. W., Taylor, A., & Poulton, R. (2002). Role of genotype in the cycle of violence in maltreated children. *Science, 297,* 851–854.

Cassidy, J. (1999). The nature of the child's ties. In J. Cassidy & P. R. Shaver (Eds.), *Handbook of attachment: Theory, research, and clinical applications* (pp. 3–20). New York: Guilford Press.

Cavaiola, A. A., & Schiff, M. (1988). Behavioral sequelae of physical and/or sexual abuse in adolescents. *Child Abuse & Neglect, 12,* 181–188.

Child-care researchers say their study was misrepresented. (2001, April 27). *San Francisco Chronicle,* p. A15.

Chorpita, B. F., Albano, A. M., & Barlow, D. H. (1998). The structure of negative emotions in a clinical sample of children and adolescents. *Journal of Abnormal Psychology, 107,* 74–85.

Chu, J. A. (1998). *Rebuilding shattered lives: The responsible treatment of complex posttraumatic and dissociative disorders.* New York: Wiley.

Cicchetti, D., Ackerman, B. P., & Izard, C. E. (1995). Emotions and emotion regulation in developmental psychopathology. *Development and Psychopathology, 7,* 1–10.

Clement, Y., Lepicard, E., & Chapouthier, G. (2001). An animal model for the study of the genetic bases of behaviour in men: The multiple marker strains (MMS). *European Psychiatry, 16,* 246–254.

Coffey, S. F., Saladin, M. E., Drobes, D. J., Brady, K. T., Dansky, B., & Kilpatrick, D. G. (2002). Trauma and substance cue reactivity in individuals with comorbid posttraumatic stress disorder and cocaine or alcohol dependence. *Drug and Alcohol Dependence, 65,* 115–127.

Cooper, M. L., Frone, M. R., Russell, M., & Mudar, P. (1995). Drinking to regulate positive and negative emotions: A motivational model of alcohol use. *Journal of Personality and Social Psychology, 69,* 990–1005.

Damasio, A. R. (1994). *Descartes' error: Emotion, reason, and the human brain.* New York: HarperCollins.

Damasio, A. (1999). *The feeling of what happens: Body and emotion in the making of consciousness.* New York: Harcourt.

Das Eiden, R., & Leonard, K. E. (2000). Paternal alcoholism, parental psychopathology, and aggravation with infants. *Journal of Substance Abuse, 11,* 17–29.

Das Eiden, R., Leonard, K. E., & Morrisey, S. (2001). Paternal alcoholism and toddler noncompliance. *Alcohol Clinical Experimental Research, 25,* 1621–1633.

Davidson, R. J., Putnam, K. M., & Larson, C. L. (2000). Dysfunction in the neural circuitry of emotion regulation—a possible prelude to violence. *Science, 289,* 591–594.

Demause, L. (1982). *Foundations of psychohistory.* New York: Creative Roots.

Dembo, R., Williams, L., La Voie, L., Berry, E., Getreu, A., Wish, E. D., Schmeidler, J., & Washburn, M. (1989). Physical abuse, sexual victimization, and illicit drug use: Replication of a structural analysis among a new sample of high-risk youths. *Violence and Victims, 4,* 121–138.

Demos, E. V. (Ed.). (1995). *Exploring affect: The selected writing of Silvan S. Tomkins.* Cambridge, U.K.: Cambridge University Press.

Denham, S. A., & Couchoud, E.A. (1991). Social-emotional predictors of preschoolers' responses to adult negative emotion. *Journal of Child Psychology and Psychiatry, 32,* 595–608.

Denham, S. A., McKinley, M., Couchoud, E. A., & Holt, R. (1990). Emotional and behavioral predictors of preschool peer ratings. *Child Development, 61,* 1145–1152.

Denham, S. A., Zoller, D., & Couchoud, E. A. (1994). Socialization of preschoolers' emotion understanding. *Developmental Psychology, 30,* 928–936.

Diamond, D., & Doane, J. A. (1994). Disturbed attachment and negative affective style: An intergenerational spiral. *British Journal Psychiatry, 164,* 770–781.

Downey, G., & Coyne, J. C. (1990). Children of depressed parents: An integrative review. *Psychological Review, 108,* 50–76.

Downs, W. R., Miller, B. A., & Gondoli, D. M. (1987). Childhood experiences of parental physical violence for alcoholic women as compared with a randomly selected household sample of women. *Violence and Victims, 2,* 225–240.

Dozier, M., Stovall, K. C., & Albus, K. E. (1999). Attachment and psychopathology in adulthood. In J. Cassidy & P. R. Shaver (Eds.), *Handbook of attachment: Theory, research, and clinical applications* (pp. 497–519). New York: Guilford Press.

Dubo, E. D., Zanarini, M. C., Lewis, R. E., & Williams, A. A. (1997). Childhood antecedents of self-destrictiveness in borderline personality disorder. *Canadian Journal of Psychiatry, 42,* 63–69.

Duggal, S., Carlson, E. A., Sroufe, L. A., & Egeland, B. (2001). Depressive symptomatology in childhood and adolescence. *Developmental Psychopathology, 13,* 143–164.

Dutton, D. G., van Ginkel, C., & Starzomski, A. (1995). The role of shame and guilt in the intergenerational transmission of abusiveness. *Violence and Victims, 10,* 121–131.

Eiden, R. D., Chavez, F., & Leonard, K. E. (1999). Parent-infant interactions among families with alcoholic fathers. *Developmental Psychopathology, 11,* 745–762.

Ellis, A., & Dryden, W. (1987). *The practice of rational-emotive therapy.* New York: Springer.

Endler, N. S., Edwards, J. M., & Vitelli, R. (1991). *Endler multidimensional anxiety scales (EMAS).* Los Angeles: Western Psychological Services.

Epstein, S. (1993). Emotion and self-theory. In M. Lewis & J. M. Haviland (Eds.), *Handbook of emotions* (pp 313–326). New York: Guilford Press.

Epstein, J. N., Saunders, B. E., Kilpatrick, D. G., & Resnick, H. S. (1998). PTSD as a mediator between childhood rape and alcohol use in adult women. *Child Abuse & Neglect, 22,* 223–234.

Federn, P. (1952). *Ego Psychology and the Psychoses.* New York: Basic.

Feeney, J. & Noller, P. (1996). *Adult attachment.* Thousand Oaks, CA: Sage.

Fisher, S. E., Francks, C., McCracken, J. T., McGough, J. J., Marlow, A. J., MacPhie, I. L., Newbury, D. V., Crawford, L. R., Palmer, C. G., Woodward, J. A., Del'Homme, M., Cantwell, D. P., Nelson, S. F., Monaco, A. P., & Smalley, S. L. (2002). A genomewide scan for loci involved in attention-deficit/hyperactivity disorder. *American Journal of Human Genetics, 70,* 1183–1196.

Fonagy, P. (2000). Attachment and borderline personality disorder. *Journal of the American Psychoanalytic Association, 48,* 1129–1146.

Fonagy, P., Leigh, T., Steele, M., Steele, H., Kennedy, R., Mattoon, G., Target, M., & Gerber, A. (1996). The relation of attachment status, psychiatric classification, and response to psychotherapy. *Journal of Consulting and Clinical Psychology, 64,* 22–31.

Ford, J. D., Racusin, R., Ellis, C. G., Daviss, W. B., Reiser, J., Fleischer, A., & Thomas, J. (2000). Child maltreatment, other trauma exposure, and posttraumatic symptomatology among children with oppositional defiant and attention deficit hyperactivity disorders. *Child Maltreatment, 5,* 205–217.

Forgas, J. P. (1995). Mood and judgment: The affect infusion model (AIM). *Psychological Bulletin, 117,* 39–66.

Fosha, D. (2000). *The transforming power of affect: A model for accelerated change.* New York: Basic books.

Frank, J. P. (2001). Adult attachment and its association with substance dependence treatment outcome. *Dissertation Abstracts International 62(5):* 2482-B.

Freeman, W. J. (1995). *Societies of brains: A study in the neuroscience of love and hate.* Hillsdale, NJ: Erlbaum.

Freeman, W. J. (2000). Emotion is essential to all intentional behaviors. In M. D. Lewis & I. Granic (Eds.), *Emotion, development, and self-organization: Dynamic systems approaches to emotional development* (pp. 209–235). Cambridge, U.K.: Cambridge University Press.

Freud, A. (1992). *The Harvard lectures.* Madison, CT: International Universities Press.

Fridja, N. H. (1993). Moods, emotion episodes, and emotions. In M. Lewis & J. M. Haviland (Eds.), *Handbook of emotions* (pp. 381–403). New York: Guilford Press.

Frisch, A., Lauger, N., Danziger, Y., Michaelovsky, E., Leor, S., Carel, C., Stein, D., Genig, S., Mimouni, M., Apter, A., & Weizman, A. (2001). Association of anorexia vervosa with the high activity allele of the COMT gene: A family-based study in Israeli patients. *Molecular Psychiatry, 6,* 243–245.

Fullilove, M. T., Fullilove, R. E., Smith, M., Winkler, K., Michael, C., Panzer, P. G., & Wallace, R. (1993). Violence, trauma, and post-traumatic stress disorder among women drug users. *Journal of Traumatic Stress, 6,* 533–543.

Garner, P. W., Jones, D. C., & Miner, J. L. (1994). Social competence among low-income preschoolers: Emotion, socialization practices and social cognitive correlates. *Child Development, 65,* 622–637.

Garner, P. W., Jones, D. C., & Palmer, D. J. (1994). Social cognitive correlates of preschool children's sibling caregiving behavior. *Developmental Psychology, 30,* 905–911.

George, C., Kaplan, N., & Main, M. (1996). *Adult attachment interview protocol* (3rd ed.). Unpublished manuscript, University of California, Berkeley.

Gilligan, S. (2002). EMDR and hypnosis. In F. Shapiro (Ed.), *EMDR as an integrative psychotherapy approach* (pp. 225–238). Washington, DC: American Psychological Association.

Goldman, G. D., & Milman, D. S. (1978). *Psychoanalytic psychotherapy.* Reading, MA: Addison-Wesley.

Goldman, S. J., D'Angelo, E. J., & DeMaso, D. R. (1993). Psychopathology in the families of children and adolescents with borderline personality disorder. *American Journal of Psychiatry, 150,* 1832–1835.

Goleman, D. (1995). *Emotional intelligence: Why it can matter more than IQ.* New York: Bantam.

Golimbet, V. E., Alfimova, M. V., Shcherbatich, T., Kaleda, V. G., Abramova, L. I., & Rogaev, E. I. (2003). Serotonin transporter gene polymorphism and schizoid personality traits in patients with psychosis and psychiatrically well subjects. *World Journal Biological Psychiatry, 4,* 25–29.

Golomb, A., Ludolph, P., Westen, D., Block, M. J., Maurer, P., & Wiss, F. C. (1994). Maternal empathy, family chaos, and the etiology of borderline personality disorder. *Journal of the American Psychoanalytic Association, 42,* 525–548.

Greenberg, L. S. (2001). *Emotion-focused therapy: Coaching clients to work through their feelings.* Washington, D.C.: American Psychological Association.

Greenberg, M. T. (1999). Attachment and psychopathology in childhood. In J. Cassidy & P. R. Shaver (Eds.), *Handbook of attachment: Theory, research, and clinical applications* (pp. 469–496). New York: Guilford Press.

Greene, J. D., Sommerville, R. B., Nystrom, L. E., Darley, J. M., & Cohen, J. D. (2001). An fMRI investigaton of emotional engagement in moral judgment. *Science, 293,* 2105–2108.

Gregg, T. R., & Siegel, A. (2001). Brain structures and neurotransmitters regulating aggression in cats: implications for human aggression. *Progress in Neuropsychopharmacology and Biological Psychiatry, 25,* 91–140.

Grice, D. E., Brady, K. T., Dustan, L. R., & Malcolm, R. (1995). Sexual and physical assault history and post-traumatic stress disorder in substance-dependent individuals. *American Journal of Addictions, 4,* 297–305.

Grossman, D. (1996). *On killing: The psychological cost of learning to kill in war and society.* New York: Little, Brown.

Gunnar, M. R., & Donzella, B. (2002). Social regulation of the cortisol levels in early human development. *Psychoneuroendocrinology, 27,* 199–220.

Guzder, J., Paris, J., Zelkowitz, P., & Feldman, R. (1999). Psychological risk factors for borderline pathology in school-age children. *Journal of the American Academy of Child and Adolescent Psychiatry, 38,* 206–212.

Haidt, J., McCauley, C. R., & Rozin, P. (1994). A scale to measure disgust sensitivity. *Personality and Individual Differences, 16,* 701–713.

Hallikainen, T., Lachman, H., Saito, T., Volavka, J., Kauhanen, J., Salonen, J. T., Ryynanen, O. P., Koulu, M., Karvonen, M. K., Pohjalainen, T., Syvalahti, E., Hietala, J., & Tiihonen, J. (2000). Lack of association between the functional variant of the catechol-o-methyltransferase (COMT) gene and early-onset alcoholism associated with severe antisocial behavior. *American Journal of Medical Genetics, 96,* 348–352.

Hariri, A. R., Mattay, V. S., Tessitore, A., Kolachana, B., Fera, F., Goldman, D., Egan, M. F., & Weinberger, D. R. (2002). Serotonin transporter genetic variation and the response of the human amygdala. *Science, 297,* 400–403.

Harkness, K. L., & Tucker, D. M. (2000). Motivation of neural plasticity: Neural mechanisms in the self-organization of depression. In M. D. Lewis & I. Granic (Eds.), *Emotion, development, and self-organization: Dynamic systems approaches to emotional development* (pp. 186–208). Cambridge, U.K.: Cambridge University Press.

Herman, J. L. (1992). *Trauma and recovery.* New York: Basic.

Hesse, E. (1999). The adult attachment interview: Historical and current perspectives. In J. Cassidy & P. R. Shaver (Eds.), *Handbook of attachment: Theory, research, and clinical applications* (pp. 395–433). New York: Guilford Press.

Hill, E. M., Stoltenberg, S. F., Bullard, K. H., Li, S., Zucker, R. A., & Burmeister, M. (2002). Antisocial alcoholism and serotonin-related polymorphisms: Association tests. *Psychiatric Genetics, 12,* 143–153.

Hirshfeld, D. R., Biederman, J., Brody, L., Faraone, S. V., & Rosenbaum, J. F. (1997). Associations between expressed emotion and child behavioral inhibition and psychopathology: A pilot study. *Journal of American Academy Child Adolescent Psychiatry, 36,* 205–213.

Hofler, D. Z., & Kooyman, M. (1996). Attachment transition, addiction, and therapeutic bonding: An integrative approach. *Journal of Substance Abuse Treatment, 13,* 511–519.

Hope, S., Power, C., & Rodgers, B. (1998). The relationship between parental separation in childhood and problem drinking in adulthood. *Addiction, 93,* 505–514.

Horesh, N., Apter, A., Lepkifker, E., Ratzoni, G., Weizmann, R., & Tyano, S. (1995). Life events and severe anorexia nervosa in adolescence. *Acta Psychiatrica Scandinavica, 91*, 5–9.

Horner, A. J. (1984). *Object relations and the developing ego in therapy.* New York: Aronson.

Hudson, R. (1986). Pheromonal release of suckling in rabbits does not depend on the vomeronasal organ. *Physiology & Behavior, 37*, 123–128.

Isen, A. M. (1993). Positive affect and decision making. In M. Lewis & J. M. Haviland (Eds.), *Handbook of emotions* (pp. 261–277). New York: Guilford Press.

Izard, C. E. (1991). *The psychology of emotions.* New York: Plenum.

Izard, C. E. (1993). Four systems for emotion activation: Cognitive and noncognitive processes. *Psychological Review, 100*, 68–90.

Izard, C. E., Ackerman, B. P., Schoff, K. M., & Fine, S. E. (2000). Self-organization of discrete emotions, emotion patterns, and emotion cognition relations. In M. D. Lewis & I. Granic (Eds.), *Emotion, development, and self-organization: Dynamic systems approaches to emotional development* (pp. 15–36). Cambridge, U.K.: Cambridge University Press.

Izard, C., Fine, S., Schultz, D., Mostow, A., Ackerman, B., & Youngstrom, E. (2001). Emotion knowledge as a predictor of social behavior and academic competence in children at risk. *Psychological Science, 12*, 18–23.

Jacobs, W. J., & Nadel, I. (1985). Stress-induced recovery of fears and phobias. *Psychological Review, 92(4)*, 512–531.

Jacobsen, E. (1964). *The self and the object world.* New York: International Universities Press.

Jaeger, E., Hahn, N. B., & Weinraub, M. (2000). Attachment in adult daughters of alcoholic fathers. *Addiction, 95*, 267–276.

Jellinek, E. M. (1960). *The disease concept of alcoholism.* New Haven, CT: College & University Press.

Johnson, J. B., Cohen, P., Smailes, E. M., Skodol, A. E., Brown, J., & Oldham, J. M. (2001). Childhood verbal abuse and risk for personality disorders during adolescence and early adulthood. *Comprehensive Psychiatry, 42*, 16–23.

Johnson, J. L., & Leff, M. (1999). Children of substance abusers: Overview of research findings. *Pediatrics, 103*, 1085–1099.

Johnson, S. M. (2002). *Emotional focused couple therapy with trauma survivors: Strengthening attachment bonds.* New York: Guilford Press.

Kaufman, E. (1994). *Psychotherapy of addicted persons.* New York: Guilford Press.

Kavanagh, D. J., Freese, S., Andrade, J., & May, J. (2001). Effects of visuospatial tasks on desensitization to emotive memories. *British Journal of Clinical Psychology, 40*, 267–280.

Kendall-Tackett, K. A., Williams, L. M., & Finkelhor, D. (1993). Impact of sexual abuse on children: A review and synthesis of recent empirical studies. *Psychological Bulletin, 113*, 164–180.

Kernis, M. H., Grannemann, B. D., & Barclay, L. C. (1989). Stability and level of self-esteem as predictors of anger arousal and hostility. *Journal of Personality & Social Psychology, 56*, 1013–1022.

Kessler, R. C., Davis, C. G., & Kendler, K. S. (1997). Childhood adversity and adult psychiatric disorder in the U.S. National Comorbidity Survey. *Psychological Medicine, 27*, 1101–1119.

Khantzian, E. J. (1997). The self-medication hypothesis of substance use disorders: A reconsideration and recent applications. *Harvard Review of Psychiatry, 4*, 231–244.

Khantzian, E. J., Halliday, K. S., & McAuliffe, W. E. (1990). *Addiction and the vulnerable self.* New York: Guilford Press.

Kohut, H., & Wolf, E. S. (1978). The disorders of the self and their treatment: An outline. *International Journal of Psycho-Analysis, 59,* 413–425.

Korn, D. L., & Leeds, A. M. (2002). Preliminary evidence of efficacy for EMDR resource development and installation in the stabilization phase of treatment of complex posttraumatic stress disorder. *Journal of Clinical Psychology, 58,* 1465–1487.

Koster, A., Montkowski, A., Schulz, S., Stube, E. M., Knaudt, K., Jenck, F., Moreau, J. L., Nothacker, J. P., Civelli, O., & Reinscheid, R. K. (1999). Targeted disruption of the orphanin FQ/nociceptin gene increases stress susceptibility and impairs stress adaptation in mice. *Proceedings of the National Academy of Science USA, 96,* 10444–10449.

Kranzler, H., Lappalainen, J., Nellissery, M., & Gelernter, J. (2002). Association study of alcoholism subtypes with a functional promoter polymorphism in the serotonin transporter protein gene. *Alcohol Clinical Experimental Research, 26,* 1330–1335.

Kreiman, G., Koch, C., & Fried, I. (2000a). Category-specific visual responses of single neurons in the human medial temporal lobe. *Nature Neuroscience, 3,* 946–953.

Kreiman, G., Koch, C., & Fried, I. (2000b). Imagery neurons in the human brain. *Nature, 408,* 357–361.

Krolak-Salmon, P., Henaff, M. A., Isnard, J., Tallon-Baudry, C., Guenot, M., Vighetto, A., Bertrand, O., & Mauguiere, F. (2003). An attention modulated response to disgust in human ventral anterior insula. *Annals of Neurology, 53,* 446–453.

Kuikka, J. T., Tammela, L., Karhunen, L., Rissanen, A., Bergstrom, K. A., Naukkarinen, H., Vanninen, E., Karhu, J., Lappalainen, R., Repo-Tiihonen, E., Tiihonen, J., Uusitupa, M. (2001). Reduced serotonin transporter binding in binge eating women. *Psychopharmacology, 155,* 310–314.

Lang, P. J. (1995). The emotion probe: Studies of emotion and attention. *American Psychologist, 50,* 372–385.

Lazarus, R. S. (1982). Thoughts on the relations between emotion and cognition. *American Psychologist, 37,* 1019–1024.

Lazarus, R. S., & Folkman, S. (1984). *Stress, appraisal, and coping.* New York: Springer.

LeDoux, J. (1996). *The emotional brain: The mysterious underpinnings of emotional life.* New York: Simon & Schuster.

Leeds, A. M. (1997, July 13). *In the eye of the beholder: Reflections on shame, dissociation, and transference in complex posttraumatic stress and attachment related disorders.* Paper presented at EMDR International Association Conference, San Francisco, CA.

Lesch, K-P., & Mössner, R. (1998). Genetically driven variation in serotonin uptake: Is there a link to affective spectrum, neurodevelopmental, and neurodegenerative disorders? *Biological Psychiatry, 44,* 179–192.

Levitsky, A., & Perls, F. S. (1970). The rules and games of Gestalt therapy. In J. Fagan & I. Shepherd (Eds.), *Gestalt therapy now* (pp. 140–149). New York: Harper & Row.

Lewis, M. (1993a). The emergence of human emotion. In M. Lewis & J. M. Haviland (Eds.), *Handbook of emotions* (pp. 223–235). New York: Guilford Press.

Lewis, M. (1993b). Self-conscious emotions: Embarrassment, pride, shame, and guilt. In M. Lewis & J. M. Haviland (Eds.), *Handbook of emotions* (pp. 563–573). New York: Guilford Press.

Lewis, M. D. (2000). Emotional self-organization at three time scales. In M. D. Lewis & I. Granic (Eds.), *Emotion, development, and self-organization: Dynamic systems approaches to emotional development* (pp. 37–69). Cambridge, U.K.: Cambridge University Press.

Lewis, M. D., & Granic, I. (2000). A new approach to the study of emotional development. In M. D. Lewis & I. Granic (Eds.), *Emotion, development, and self-organization:*

Dynamic systems approaches to emotional development (pp. 1–12). Cambridge, U.K.: Cambridge University Press.

Linehan, M. M. (1993). *Cognitive–behavioral treatment for borderline personality disorder.* New York: Guilford Press.

Liu, J., Juo, S. H., Dewan, A., Grunn, A., Tong, X., Brito, M., Park, N., Loth, J. E., Kanyas, K., Lerer, B., Endicott, J., Penchaszadeh, G., Knowles, J. A., Ott, J., Gilliam, T. C., & Baron, M. (2003). Evidence for a putative bipolar disorder locus on 2p13-16 and other potential loci on 4q31, 7q34, 8q13, 9q31, 10q21-24, 13q32, 14q21 and 17q11-12. *Molecular Psychiatry, 8,* 333–342.

Lizardi, H., Klein, D. N., Ouimette, P. C., Riso, L. P., Anderson, R. L., & Donaldson, S. K. (1995). Reports of the childhood home environment in early-onset dysthymia and episodic major depression. *Abnormal Psychology, 104,* 132–139.

Lohr, J. M., Tolin, D. F., & Kleinknecht, R. A. (1996). An intensive design investigation of eye movement desensitization and reprocessing of claustrophobia. *Journal of Anxiety Disorders, 10,* 73–88.

Lonigan, C. J., Carey, M. P., & Finch, A. J., Jr. (1994). Anxiety and depression in children and adolescents: Negative affectivity and the utility of self-reports. *Journal of Counseling and Clinical Psychology, 62,* 1000–1008.

MacLean, P. D. (1990). *The triune brain in evolution: Role in paleocerebral functions.* New York: Plenum.

MacLean, P. D. (1993). Cerebral evolution of emotion. In M. Lewis & J. M. Haviland (Eds.), *Handbook of emotions* (pp. 67–83). New York: Guilford Press.

MacMillan, H. L., Fleming, J. E., Trocme, N., Boyle, M. H., Wong, M., Racine, Y. A., Beardslee, W. R., & Offord, D. R. (1997). Prevalence of child physical and sexual abuse in the community. Results from the Ontario Health Supplement. *Journal of the American Medical Association, 278,* 131–135.

Magai, C. (1999). Affect, imagery, and attachment: Working models of interpersonal affect and the socialization of emotion. In J. Cassidy & P. R. Shaver (Eds.), *Handbook of attachment: Theory, research, and clinical applications* (pp. 787–802). New York: Guilford Press.

Mahler, M., Pine, F., & Bergman, A. (1975). *The psychological birth of the infant.* New York: Basic.

Manuck, S. B., Flory, J. D., Ferrell, R. E., Dent, K. M., Mann, J. J., & Muldoon, M. F. (1999). Aggression and anger-related traits associated with a polymorphism of the tryptophan hydroxylase gene. *Biological Psychiatry, 45,* 603–614.

Marcenko, M. O., Kemp, S. P., & Larson, N. C. (2000). Childhood experiences of abuse, later substance abuse, and parenting outcomes among low-income mothers. *American Journal of Orthopsychiatry, 70,* 316–326.

Marlatt, G. A. (1985). Relapse prevention: Theoretical rationale and overview of the model. In G. A. Marlatt, & J. R. Gordon (Eds.). *Relapse prevention: Maintenance strategies in the treatment of addictive disorders* (pp. 3–70). New York: Guilford Press.

Marvin, R. S., & Britner, P. A. (1999). Normative development: The ontogeny of attachment. In J. Cassidy & P. R. Shaver (Eds.), *Handbook of attachment: Theory, research, and clinical applications* (pp. 44–67). New York: Guilford Press.

Mascolo, M. F., Harkins, D., & Harakal, T. (2000). The dynamic construction of emotion: Varieties in anger. In M. D. Lewis, & I. Granic (Eds.), *Emotion, development, and self-organization: Dynamic systems approaches to emotional development* (pp. 125–152). Cambridge, U.K.: Cambridge University Press.

McArdle, P., Wiegersma, A., Gilvarry, E., Kolte, B., McCarthy, S., Fitzgerald, M., Brinkley, A., Blom, M., Stoeckel, I., Pierolini, A., Michels, I., Johnson, R., & Quensel, S.

(2002). European adolescent substance use: The roles of family structure, function, and gender. *Addiction, 97,* 329–336.

Miller, A. (1984). *Thou shalt not be aware: Society's betrayal of the child.* New York: New American Library.

Miller, A. (1998). The political consequences of child abuse. *Journal of Psychohistory, 26,* 573–585.

Miller, B. A., Downs, W. R., Gondoli, D. M., & Keil, A. (1987). The role of childhood sexual abuse in the development of alcoholism in women. *Violence and Victims, 2,* 157–172.

Miller, B. A., Smyth, N. J., & Mudar, P. J. (1999). Mothers' alcohol and other drug problems and their punitiveness toward their children. *Journal of Studies on Alcohol, 60,* 632–642.

Miller, G. A. (1996). Relationships between perceived adult attachment styles and alcohol use, psycholoigcal functioning, and life satisfaction in members of Alcoholics Anonymous. *Dissertation Abstracts International 56(12):* 7080-B.

Millon, T. (1998). Ann: My first case of borderline personality disorder. In R. P. Halgin, & S. K. Whitbourne (Eds.), *A casebook in abnormal psychology: From the files of experts* (pp. 9–22). New York: Oxford University Press.

Mogenson, G. (1989). *God is a trauma: Vicarious religion and soul-making.* Dallas, TX: Spring.

Montgomery, R. W., & Ayllon, T. (1994). Eye movement desensitization across subjects: Subjective and physiological measures of treatment efficacy. *Journal of Behavior Therapy and Experimental Psychiatry, 25,* 217–230.

Nadon, R., D'Eon, J., McConkey, K. M., Laurence, J-R., & Perry, C. (1988). Posthypnotic amnesia, the hidden observer effect, and duality during hypnotic age regression. *International Journal of Clinical and Experimental Hypnosis, 36,* 19–37.

Napier, N. (1990). *Recreating your self: Building self-esteem through imaging and self-hypnosis.* New York: Norton.

Nathanson, D. L. (1992). *Shame and pride: Affect, sex, and the birth of the self.* New York: Norton.

Nickell, A. D., Waudby, C. J., & Trull, T. J. (2002). Attachment, parental bonding, and borderline personality disorder features in young adults. *Journal of Personality Disorders, 16,* 148–159.

Nunes, E. V., Weissman, M. M., Goldstein, R. B., McAvay, G., Seracini, A. M., Verdeli, H., & Wickramaratne, P. J. (1998). Psychopathology in children of parents with opiate dependence and/or major depression. *Journal of the American Academy Child and Adolescent Psychiatry, 37,* 1142–1151.

Nurco, D. N., Blatchley, R. J., Hanlon, T. E., & O'Grady, K. E. (1999). Early deviance and related risk factors in children of narcotic addicts. *American Journal of Drug & Alcohol Abuse, 25,* 25–45.

Ogawa, J. R., Sroufe, L. A., Weinfield, N., Carlson, E. A., & Egeland, B. (1997). Development and the fragmented self: Longitudinal study of dissociative symptomatology in a nonclinical sample. *Development and Psychopathology, 9,* 855–879.

Omaha, J. (1998, July 11). *Chemotion and EMDR: An EMDR treatment protocol based upon a psychodynamic model for chemical dependency.* Paper presented at the meeting of the EMDR International Association, Baltimore, MD. Retrieved August 12, 2003, from http://www.johnomahaenterprises.com

Omaha, J. (1999, June 19). *Treating nicotine dependency: An application of the Chemotion/EMDR protocol.* Paper presented at the meeting of the EMDR International Association, Las Vegas, NV. Retrieved November 6, 2003, from http://www.johnomahaenterprises.com

Omaha, J. (2000, September 10). *Treatment of bulimia and binge eating disorder using the Chemotion/EMDR protocol.* Paper presented at the meeting of the EMDR International Association, Toronto, Ontario, Canada. Retrieved August 12, 2003, from http://www.johnomahaenterprises.com

Omaha, J. (2001). *The psychodynamic basis of chemical dependency.* Unpublished doctoral dissertation, International University of Professional Studies, Maui, HI.

Paris, J., Zweig-Frank, H., & Guzder, J. (1994a). Risk factors for borderline personality in male outpatients. *Journal of Nervous and Mental Disease, 182,* 375–380.

Paris, J., Zweig-Frank, H., & Guzder, J. (1994b). Psychological risk factors for borderline personality disorder in female patients. *Comprehensive Psychiatry, 35,* 301–305.

Parker, R., Roy, K., Wilhelm, K., Mitchell, P., Austin, M. P., Hadzi-Pavlovic, D. (1999). An exploration of links between early parenting experiences and personality disorder type and disordered personality functioning. *Journal of Personality Disorders, 13,* 361–374.

Paulsen, S. (1995). EMDR: Its cautious use in the dissociative disorders. *Dissociation, 8,* 32–41.

Perkins, B. R., & Rouanzoin, C. C. (2002). A critical evaluation of current views regarding eye movement desensitization and reprocessing (EMDR): Clarifying points of confusion. *Journal of Clinical Psychology, 58,* 77–97.

Piaget, J., & Inhelder, B. (1969). *The psychology of the child.* New York: Basic.

Plutchik, R. (1993). Emotions and their vicissitudes: Emotions and psychopathology. In M. Lewis, & J. M. Haviland-Jones (Eds.), *Handbook of emotions* (2nd ed., pp. 53–66). New York: Guilford Press.

Pollak, S. D., & Kistler, D. J. (2002). Early experience is associated with the development of categorical representations for facial expressions of emotion. *Proceedings of the National Academy Science, USA, 99,* 9072–9076.

Rapaport, D. (1953). On the psychoanalytic theory of affects. *International Journal of Psycho-Analysis, 34,* 177–198.

Real, T. (1997). *I don't want to talk about it.* New York: Fireside.

Rossow, I., & Lauritzen, G. (2001). Shattered childhood: A key issue in suicidal behavior among drug addicts? *Addiction, 96,* 227–240.

Rothschild, B. (2000). *The body remembers: The psychophysiology of trauma and trauma treatment.* New York: Norton.

Rounsaville, B. J., Weissman, M. M., Wilber, C. H., & Kleber, H. D. (1982). Pathways to opiate addiction: An evaluation of differing antecedents. *British Journal of Psychiatry, 141,* 437–446.

Rozin, P., Haidt, J., & McCauley, C. R. (2000). Disgust. In M. Lewis, & J. M. Haviland-Jones (Eds.), *Handbook of emotions* (2nd ed., pp. 637–653). New York: Guilford Press.

Rujescu, D., Giegling, I., Bondy, B., Gietl, A., Zill, P., & Moller, H. J. (2002). Association of anger-related traits with SNPs in the TPH gene. *Molecular Psychiatry, 7,* 1023–1029.

Saarni, C. (1993). Socialization of emotion. In M. Lewis, & J. M. Haviland (Eds.), *Handbook of emotions* (pp. 435– 445). New York: Guilford Press.

Schmidt, S. J. (2002). *Developmental needs meeting strategy for EMDR therapists.* San Antonio, TX: DNMS Institute.

Schore, A. N. (1994). *Affect regulation and the origin of the self: The neurobiology of emotional development.* Hillsdale, NJ: Erlbaum.

Schramm, N. L., McDonald, M. P., & Limbird, L. E. (2001). The alpha(2a)-adrenergic receptor plays a protective role in mouse behavioral models of depression and anxiety. *Journal of Neuroscience, 21,* 4875–4882.

Schultz, D., Izard, C. E., Ackerman, B. P., & Youngstrom, E. A. (2001). Emotion knowledge in economically disadvantaged children: Self-regulatory antecedents and relations to social difficulties and withdrawal. *Development and Psychopathology, 13,* 53–67.

Schwarz, M. F., Galperin, L. D., & Masters, W. H. (1995a). Sexual trauma within the context of traumatic and inescapable stress, neglect, and poisonous pedagogy. In M. Hunter (Ed.), *Adult survivors of sexual abuse: Treatment innovations* (pp. 1–17). Thousand Oaks, CA: Sage.

Schwarz, M. F., Galperin, L. D., & Masters, W. H. (1995b). Dissociation and treatment of compulsive reenactment of trauma. *Sexual compulsivity.* In M. Hunter (Ed.), *Adult survivors of sexual abuse: Treatment innovations* (pp. 42–55). Thousand Oaks, CA: Sage.

Shapiro, F. (1995). *Eye movement desensitization and reprocessing: Basic principles, protocols, and procedures.* New York: Guilford Press.

Shapiro, F. (2001). *Eye movement desensitization and reprocessing: basic principles, protocols, and procedures second edition.* New York: Guilford Press.

Shapiro, F. (2002). Introduction: Paradigms, processing, and personality development. In F. Shapiro (Ed.), *EMDR as an integrative psychotherapy approach* (pp. 3–26). Washington, DC: American Psychological Association.

Sibille, E., Pavlides, C., Benke, D., & Toth, M. (2000). Genetic inactivation of the Serotonin(1A) receptor in mice results in downregulation of major GABA(A) receptor alpha subunits, reduction of GABA(A) receptor binding, and benzodiazepine-resistant anxiety. *Journal of Neuroscience, 15,* 2758–2765.

Sicher, B. L. (1998). Relationship between security of attachment and substance abuse. *Dissertation Abstracts International 59(4):* 1868-B–1869-B

Siegel, D. J. (2002a). The developing mind and the resolution of trauma: Some ideas about information processing and an interpersonal neurobiology of psychotherapy. In F. Shapiro (Ed.), *EMDR as an integrative psychotherapy approach* (pp. 85–121). Washington, DC: American Psychological Association.

Siegel, D. J. (2002b). *The developing mind: How relationships and the brain interact to shape who we are.* New York: Guilford Press.

Silk, K. R., Lee, S., Hill, E. M., & Lohr, N. E. (1995). Borderline personality disorder symptoms and severity of sexual abuse. *American Journal of Psychiatry, 152,* 1059–1064.

Slade, A. (1999). Attachment theory and research: Implications for the theory and practice of individual psychotherapy with adults. In J. Cassidy & P. R. Shaver (Eds.), *Handbook of attachment: Theory, research, and clinical applications* (pp. 575–594). New York: Guilford Press.

Smyth, N. J. (1998a). Substance abuse. In J. S. Wodarski & B. A. Thayer (Eds.), *Handbook of empirical social work practice. Vol. 2: Social problems* (pp. 123–153). New York: Wiley.

Smyth, N. J. (1998b). Alcohol abuse. In J. S. Wodarski & B. A. Thayer (Eds.), *Handbook of empirical social work practice. Vol. 2: Social problems* (pp. 181–204). New York: Wiley.

Solomon, J., & George, C. (1999). The measurement of attachment security in infancy and childhood. In J. Cassidy & P. R. Shaver (Eds.), *Handbook of attachment: Theory, research, and clinical applications* (pp. 287–316). New York: Guilford Press.

Spanos, N. P., de Groot, H. P., Tiller, D. K., Weekes, J. R., & Bertrand, L. D. (1985). Trance logic duality and hidden observer responding in hypnotic imagination control, and simulating subjects: A social psychological analysis. *Journal of Abnormal Psychology, 94,* 611–623.

Spear, L. P. (2000). The adolescent brain and age-related behavioral manifestations. *Neuroscience and Biobehavioral Reviews, 24,* 417–463.

Spitz, R. A. (1965). *The first year of life.* New York: International Universities Press.

Sroufe, L. A. (1996). *Emotional development: The organization of emotional life in the early years.* Cambridge, U.K.: Cambridge University Press.

Sroufe, L. A. (1997). Psychopathology as an outcome of development. *Development and Psychopathology, 9,* 251–268.

Sroufe, L. A., Carlson, E. A., Levy, A. K., & Egeland, B. (1999). Implications of attachment theory for developmental psychopathology. *Development and Psychopathology, 11,* 1–13.

Stearns, C. Z. (1993). Sadness. In M. Lewis, & J. M. Haviland (Eds.), *Handbook of emotions* (pp. 547–561). New York: Guilford Press.

Steele, A. (2001, October). *Therapy from the right side of the brain: A role for EMDR with imaginal nurturing in the treatment of early neglect.* Paper presented at the meeting of the EMDR Association of Canada, Vancouver, British Columbia, Canada.

Stickgold, R. (2002). EMDR: A putative neurobiological mechanism of action. *Journal of Clinical Psychology, 58,* 61–75.

Suchman, N. E., & Luthar, S. S. (2000). Maternal addiction, child maladjustment and sociodemographic risks: Implications for parenting behaviors. *Addiction, 95,* 1417–1428.

Sundaramurthy, D., Pieri, L. F., Gape, J., Markham, A. F., Campbell, D. A. (2000). Analysis of the serotonin transporter gene linked polymorphism (5-HTTLPR) in anorexia nervosa. *American Journal Medical Genetics, 96,* 53–55.

Swett, C., Cohen, C., Surrey, J., Compaine, A., & Chavez, R. (1991). High rates of alcohol use and history of physical and sexual abuse among women outpatients. *American Journal of Drug and Alcohol Abuse, 17,* 49–60.

Teicher, M. H. (2000). Wounds that time won't heal: The neurobiology of child abuse. *Cerebrum, 2,* 50–67.

Tiihonen, J., Hallikainen, T., Lachman, H., Saito, T., Volavka, J., Kauhanen, J., Salonen, J. T., Ryynanen, O. P., Koulu, M., Karvonen, M. K., Pohjalainen, T., Syvalahti, E., & Hietala, J. (1999). Association between the functional variant of the catechol-O-methyltransferase (COMT) gene and type 1 alcoholism. *Molecular Psychiatry, 4,* 286–289.

Tomkins, S. S. (1962). *Affect/imagery/consciousness.* Vol 1: *The positive affects.* New York: Springer.

Tomkins, S. S. (1963). *Affect/imagery/consciousness.* Vol. 2: *The negative affects.* New York: Springer.

Triffleman, E. G., Marmar, C. R., Delucchi, K. L., & Ronfeldt, H. (1995). Childhood trauma and posttraumatic stress disorder in substance abuse inpatients. *Journal of Nervous & Mental Disease, 183,* 172–176.

Troisi, A., Pasini, A., Saracco, M., & Spalletta, G. (1998). Psychiatric symptoms in male cannabis users not using other illicit drugs. *Addiction, 93,* 487–492.

Trull, T. J. (2001). Relationships of borderline features to parental mental illness, childhood abuse, Axis I disorder, and current functioning. *Journal of Personality Disorders, 15,* 19–32.

Turecki, G., Zhu, Z., Tzenova, J., Lesage, A., Seguin, M., Tousignant, M., Chawky, N., Vanier, C., Lipp, O., Alda, M., Joober, R., Benkelfat, C., & Rouleau, G. A. (2001). TPH and suicidal behavior: a study in suicide competers. *Molecular Psychiatry, 6,* 98–102.

Volpicelli, J. R., Pettinati, H. M., O'Brien, C. P., & McLellan, A. T. (2001). *Combining medication and psychosocial treatments for addictions.* New York: Guilford Press.

Waltner-Toews, K. (2002). *A pilot study of AMST application to an OCD group.* Manuscript submitted for publication. Retrieved August 12, 2003, from http://www.johnomahaenterprises.com

Watkins, J. G., & Watkins, H. H. (1997). *Ego states: Theory and therapy.* New York: Norton.

Weinfield, N. S., Sroufe, L. A., Egeland, B., & Carlson, E. A. (1999). The nature of individual differences in infant–caregiver attachment. In J. Cassidy & P. R. Shaver (Eds.), *Handbook of attachment: Theory, research, and clinical applications* (pp. 68–88). New York: Guilford Press.

Weinfield, N. S., Sroufe, L. A., & Egeland, B. (2000). Attachment from infancy to early adulthood in a high-risk sample: Continuity, discontinuity, and their correlates. *Child Development, 71,* 695–702.

Weiss, M., Zelkowitz, P., Feldman, R. B., Vogel, J., Heyman, M., & Paris, J. (1996). Psychopathology in offspring of mothers with borderline personality disorder: A pilot study. *Canadian Journal of Psychiatry, 41,* 285–290.

Weissman, M. M., McAvay, G., Goldstein, R. B., Nunes, E. V., Verdeli, H., & Wickramaratne, P. J. (1999). Risk/protective factors among addicted mothers' offspring: a replication study. *American Journal of Drug Alcohol Abuse, 25,* 661–679.

Wesselmann, D. (2000, March) *Interventions for treating core attachment issues and related problems.* Workshop presented by Montclair Seminars, Iselin, NJ.

West, M., Adam, K., Spreng, S., & Rose, S. (2001). Attachment disorganization and dissociative symptoms in clinically treated adolescents. *Canadian Journal of Psychiatry, 46,* 26–30.

Wild, B., Erb, M., & Bartels, M. (2001). Are emotions contagious? Evoked emotions while viewing emotionally expressive faces: Quality, quantity, time course and gender differences. *Psychiatry Research, 102,* 109–124.

Wolinsky, S. (1991). *Trances people live: Healing approaches in quantum psychology.* Las Vegas, NV: Bramble.

Wonderlich, S., Ukestad, L., & Perzacki, R. (1994). Perceptions of nonshared childhood enviornment in bulimia nervosa. *Journal of the American Academy of Child and Adolescent Psychiatry, 33,* 740–747.

Wylie, M. S., & Simon, R. (2002, September/October). Discoveries from the black box. *Psychotherapy networker, 26,* 26–68.

Youngstrom, E., Izard, C., & Ackerman, B. (1999). Dysphoria-related bias in maternal ratings of children. *Journal of Consulting and Clinical Psychology, 67,* 905–916.

Zajonc, R. B. (1984). On the primacy of affect. *American Psychologist, 39,* 117–123.

Zanarini, M. C., Williams, A. A., Lewis, R. E., Reich, R. B., Vera, S. C., Marino, M. F., Levin, A., Yong, L., & Frankenburg, F. R. (1997). Reported pathological childhood experiences associated with the development of borderline personality disorder. *American Journal Psychiatry, 154,* 1101–1106.

Zubieta, J-K., Heitzeg, M. M., Smith, Y. P., Bueller, J. A., Xu, K., Xu, Y., Koeppe, R. A., Stohler, C. S., & Goldman, D. (2003). COMT val[150]met genotype affect μ-opiod neurotransmitter responses to a pain stressor. *Science, 299,* 1240–1243.

Index